Confronting Development

Confronting Development

*Assessing Mexico's Economic
and Social Policy Challenges*

Edited by
Kevin J. Middlebrook
and
Eduardo Zepeda

STANFORD UNIVERSITY PRESS

CENTER FOR U.S.-MEXICAN STUDIES
UNIVERSITY OF CALIFORNIA, SAN DIEGO

2003

Stanford University Press
Stanford, California

© 2003 by the Board of Trustees of the
Leland Stanford Junior University

Printed in the United States of America
on acid-free, archival-quality paper

Library of Congress Cataloging-in-Publication Data

Confronting development : assessing Mexico's economic and social policy
challenges / edited by Kevin J. Middlebrook and Eduardo Zepeda.
        p. cm.
    Includes bibliographical references and index.
    ISBN 0-8047-4589-7 (cloth) — ISBN 0-8047-4720-2 (paper)
    1. Mexico—Economic conditions—1994- 2. Mexico—Economic
policy—1994- 3. Mexico—Social policy. l. Middlebrook, Kevin J. ll.
Zepeda, Eduardo.
HC135.C663 2003
330.972—dc21

                              20002156074

Original Printing 2003

Last figure below indicates year of this printing:
00 09 08 07 06 05 04 03

Acknowledgments

This volume examines economic and social development policies in Mexico during the 1980s and 1990s. All but two of the contributors' essays were presented in draft form at an international conference hosted by the Center for U.S.–Mexican Studies in June 1999; the chapter by Keith Griffin and Amy Ickowitz and that by Lorenza Villa Lever and Roberto Rodríguez Gómez were added to the collection of essays in 2000 and 2001, respectively. All the papers were subsequently revised and updated.

The June 1999 conference was one of three such events organized to celebrate the twentieth anniversary of the founding of the Center for U.S.–Mexican Studies at the University of California, San Diego. Each of these conferences focused on a substantive area that has formed an important part of the Center's research agenda: Mexico–U.S. relations, economic and social policy issues in Mexico, and political change in Mexico. Financial support for these events came from the Center's core grant from the William and Flora Hewlett Foundation.

Collaborative books depend heavily upon the commitment and goodwill of the participating authors. Those qualities were especially important in bringing to conclusion a volume of this length and complexity. The contributors were exemplary in their dedication to this common effort.

Sandra del Castillo, the Center for U.S.–Mexican Studies' highly talented principal editor, had responsibility for the initial copyediting and typesetting. Her skills and professional dedication made vital contributions to this project. At Stanford University Press, Norris Pope provided enthusiastic support and invaluable guidance for the volume from its inception through its completion. Janet Gardiner superbly coordinated final production work.

Contents

Figures and Tables   xi
Acronyms   xix
Contributors   xxv

PART I
Introduction

CHAPTER 1
On the Political Economy of Mexican Development Policy   3
KEVIN J. MIDDLEBROOK AND EDUARDO ZEPEDA

PART II
Economic Policy and Finance

CHAPTER 2
Macroeconomic Challenges for Mexico's Development Strategy   55
ALEJANDRO NADAL

CHAPTER 3
Mexico's Financial System and Economic Development:
Current Crisis and Future Prospects   89
CELSO GARRIDO

CHAPTER 4
Foreign Investment in Mexico after Economic Reform   123
JORGE MÁTTAR, JUAN CARLOS MORENO-BRID, AND WILSON PERES

PART III
Trade, Export-Led Growth, and Industrial Policy

CHAPTER 5
Mexico's Trade Policy: Financial Crisis and Economic Recovery   163
GUSTAVO VEGA AND LUZ MARÍA DE LA MORA

CHAPTER 6
Mexico's Industrial Development: Climbing Ahead or Falling
Behind in the World Economy?   195
GARY GEREFFI

CHAPTER 7
Industrial Policy, Regional Trends, and Structural Change in
Mexico's Manufacturing Sector   241
ENRIQUE DUSSEL PETERS

PART IV
Social Policy and Rural Development

CHAPTER 8
Education and Development in Mexico: Middle and Higher
Education Policies in the 1990s   277
LORENZA VILLA LEVER AND ROBERTO RODRÍGUEZ GÓMEZ

CHAPTER 9
The Transformation of Social Policy in Mexico   320
ASA CRISTINA LAURELL

CHAPTER 10
The Agricultural Sector and Rural Development in Mexico:
Consequences of Economic Globalization   350
HUBERT C. DE GRAMMONT

PART V
Inequality, Employment and Wage Problems, and Poverty

CHAPTER 11
Welfare, Inequality, and Poverty in Mexico, 1970–2000   385
JULIO BOLTVINIK

CHAPTER 12
Income Distribution and Poverty Alleviation in Mexico:
A Comparative Analysis   447
DIANA ALARCÓN

CHAPTER 13
The Dialectics of Urban and Regional Disparities in Mexico   487
GUSTAVO GARZA

CHAPTER 14
Employment and Wages: Enduring the Costs of Liberalization
and Economic Reform   522
CARLOS SALAS AND EDUARDO ZEPEDA

PART VI
**Historical and Comparative Perspectives on Mexican
Development**

CHAPTER 15
Mexico's Development Challenges   561
VÍCTOR L. URQUIDI

CHAPTER 16
Confronting Human Development in Mexico   577
KEITH GRIFFIN AND AMY ICKOWITZ

CHAPTER 17
A Comparative Perspective on Mexico's Development
Challenges   596
CLARK W. REYNOLDS

Index   607

Figures and Tables

FIGURES

FIGURE 2.1
Mexico's Fiscal and Financial Charges, 1980–2000   65

FIGURE 3.1
Economic and Financial Cycles in Mexico, 1970–1999   103

FIGURE 4.1
Fixed Investment as a Proportion of Total Gross Domestic Product
and Manufacturing-Sector Product in Mexico, 1970–1994   138

FIGURE 4.2
Ratio of Investment to Total Output and Growth of
Manufacturing Product in Mexico, 1970–1996   139

FIGURE 4.3
Gross Fixed Capital Formation in Mexican Manufacturing,
1970–1994   139

FIGURE 6.1
Shifts in the Regional Structure of U.S. Apparel Imports,
1990–2000   223

FIGURE 7.1
Exports of Goods and Services as a Proportion of Mexico's Gross
Domestic Product, 1980–2000   251

FIGURE 7.2
Index of Mexico's Exports and Domestic Demand, 1988–2000   252

FIGURE 7.3
Gross Domestic Product Per Capita for Selected Mexican States,
1970–1996   268

FIGURE 11.1
Opportunities for Social Welfare in Mexico, 1981–2000   401

FIGURE 11.2
Three Versions of the Evolution of Poverty in Mexico, 1968–2000   404

FIGURE 11.3
Real Per Capita Public Social Expenditure in Mexico, 1970–2000   416

FIGURE 14.1
Informal-Sector Employment as a Proportion of Total
Employment in Mexico, 1987–1998   525

FIGURE 14.2
Type of Occupation by Age Group in Mexico, 1998   527

TABLES

TABLE 2.1
Mexico's Gross Domestic Product and External Accounts,
1981–2000   57

TABLE 2.2
Rate of Inflation and Monetary Base in Mexico, 1980–2000   60

TABLE 2.3
Rate of Inflation and Exchange Rate Valuation in Mexico,
1980–2000   61

TABLE 2.4
Mexico's Fiscal Policy, 1980–2000: Public and Primary
Economic Balances   64

TABLE 2.5
Tax and Non-Tax Revenues in Mexico, 1989–2000   66

TABLE 2.6
Mexico's Outstanding Public and Private External Debt,
1980–2000   68

TABLE 2.7
Interest Payments on Mexico's Outstanding Public and Private
External Debt, 1982–2000   70

TABLE 2.8
Calendar of Maturities for Mexico's External Debt, 1999–2003   71

TABLE 2.9
Mexico's Public External Debt Indicators, 1982–2000   72

TABLE 2.10
Mexico's Total Public Domestic Debt, 1988–2000   74

TABLE 2.11
Total New Commercial Bank Loans and Nonperforming Loans
in Mexico, 1994–1999   81

TABLE 2.12
Total Final Consumption Expenditures in Mexico by Class of
Goods and Services, 1989–1999   86

TABLE 3.1
Mexico's Privatized Banks, Listed by Territorial Coverage, 1990s   94

TABLE 3.2
Mexico's 500 Largest Corporations by Property Type, 1987,
1990, and 1996   96

TABLE 3.3
Evolution of the Mexican Federal Government's Corporate
Bailouts, 1970s–1990s   98

TABLE 3.4
Evolution of Mexico's Banking System and Stock Market
under Changing Financial System Regulations, 1980s–1990s   100

TABLE 3.5
Credit Expansion and Banking Crises in Selected Developing
Countries, 1970s–1990s   102

TABLE 3.6
Fiscal Costs of Mexico's Bank Rescue Programs, 1995–1998   116

TABLE 4.1
Growth in Gross Fixed Capital Formation, Gross Domestic
Product (GDP), and the Investment/GDP Ratio in Mexico,
1970–2000   127

TABLE 4.2
Net Inflows of Foreign Direct Investment to Latin America,
1991–2000   132

TABLE 4.3
Foreign Companies' Strategies in Latin America and the
Caribbean, by Sector   136

TABLE 4.4
Composition of Fixed Investment in Mexico's Manufacturing
Sector by Division, 1970–1994   144

TABLE 4.5
Mexico's Main Exports to the United States and Canada, 1985
and 1998   148

TABLE 4.6
Mexico's Share of U.S. and Canadian Import Markets, 1985 and
1998   149

TABLE 4.7
Technological Specialization Index for Latin America and
Southeast Asia, 1977–1995   150

TABLE 4.8
Capital Formation in Mexico and Growth of Manufacturing
Exports, 1980s–1990s   152

TABLE 4.9
Capital Formation and Manufacturing Growth in Mexico,
1980s–1990s   154

TABLE 5.1
Mexico's Total Trade, 1991–2000   167

TABLE 5.2
Regional Trade under the NAFTA, 1993–2000   174

TABLE 5.3
Mexico's Trade with Selected Latin American Partners, 1991–2000   184

TABLE 5.4
Mexico–European Union Trade, 1991–2000   187

TABLE 5.5
Foreign Direct Investment Flows to Mexico, 1994–2000   188

TABLE 6.1
Mexico's Top Ten Exports to the World, 1980–1999   206

TABLE 6.2
Industrial Upgrading Scorecard: Category Distribution of Canada's
and Mexico's Top Ten Exports to the United States, 1985–1999   208

TABLE 6.3
Mexico's Car Production, Domestic Market and Exports,
1994–2000   216

TABLE 6.4
U.S. Imports of Motor Vehicles and Parts from Canada and
Mexico, 1980–1999   218

TABLE 6.5
Mexico's Top Apparel Exports to the U.S. Market, 1990–2000   226

TABLE 6.6
Restructuring by Major Firms in the U.S. Apparel and Textile
Industry   230

TABLE 7.1
Business Establishments and Employment, by Firm Size, in
Mexico's Manufacturing Sector, 1988–1998   254

TABLE 7.2
Annual Growth Rate in Business Establishments and
Employment in Mexico's Manufacturing Sector, 1988–1998   255

TABLE 7.3
Aggregate Sales and Employment in Mexico's Export Sector,
1993–1999   256

TABLE 7.4
Export Sales and Employment as a Proportion of Mexico's
Total Export Activity, 1993–1999   257

TABLE 7.5
Evolution of Mexico's Manufacturing Sector, 1988–2000   258

TABLE 7.6
Typology of Mexico's Manufacturing Sector by Growth Rate
of Exports, 1988–1996   264

TABLE 8.1
Profile of Mexico's Middle Education System, 1990–2001 291

TABLE 8.2
Distribution of Mexico's Middle Education Enrollments by
Program Type, 1970–2001 293

TABLE 8.3
Private Middle Education in Mexico, 1998–1999 School Year 294

TABLE 8.4
Higher Education Enrollments in Mexico by Program Type,
1980–2000 303

TABLE 8.5
Academic Personnel in Mexico's Higher Education System by
Program Type, 1980–1999 303

TABLE 8.6
Enrollments in Mexico's Public and Private Higher Education
Systems, 1980–2000 304

TABLE 9.1
Selected Poverty Programs in Mexico, 1995–1999 340

TABLE 9.2
Selected Poverty Indicators for Mexico, 1994 and 1996 342

TABLE 10.1
Agricultural, Livestock, and Forestry Production Units in
Mexico by Size of Holdings, 1991 355

TABLE 10.2
Mexico's Agricultural and Livestock Imports, 1982–2000 358

TABLE 10.3
Mexico's Agricultural and Livestock Exports, 1982–2000 359

TABLE 10.4
Mexico's Trade Balance in Agricultural and Food Products,
1990–2000 360

TABLE 10.5
Destination of Mexico's Agricultural Production, 1991 362

TABLE 10.6
Credit and Overdue Loans in Mexican Agriculture, 1984–1997 364

TABLE 10.7
Agricultural and Livestock Credit in Mexico, 1978–1997 366

TABLE 10.8
People Employed in Mexico's Agricultural and Livestock Sector,
1991 and 1999 368

TABLE 10.9
Employment Patterns in Mexico's Agricultural and Livestock
Sector, 1991 and 1999   370

TABLE 10.10
Population Employed in Agriculture and Livestock Raising in
Mexico, 1960–1999   372

TABLE 10.11
Mexico's Employed Agricultural Population by Activity and
Size of Locality, 1970 and 1990   374

TABLE 11.1
Opportunity Set for Social Welfare in Mexico, 1981–2000   394

TABLE 11.2
Non-Egalitarian Opportunity Set for Social Welfare in Mexico,
1981–2000   398

TABLE 11.3
Household Income Distribution in Mexico, 1984–2000   403

TABLE 11.4
Equivalent Incidence of Educational, Living Space, and Housing
Services Poverties in Mexico, 1970–2000   408

TABLE 11.5
Equivalent Incidence of Health Care and Social Security
Poverties in Mexico, 1970–1999   412

TABLE 11.6
Incidence, Intensity, and Equivalent Incidence of Poverty in
Mexico, 1984–1998   419

TABLE 11.7
Mortality and Survival Proportions in Rural and Urban Mexico,
by Standard-of-Living Stratum, 1990   427

TABLE 11.8
Evolution of Mortality Rates by Age Group and Economic
Growth in Mexico, 1970–1999   430

TABLE 11.9
Overall Assessment of the Evolution of Well-Being in Mexico,
1970s–1990s   436

TABLE 12.1
Indicators of Human Development for Selected Latin American
Countries, 1999   449

TABLE 12.2
Economic Growth Rates in Mexico, 1970–2000   451

TABLE 12.3
Economic Indicators for Mexico, 1980–2000   452

TABLE 12.4
Total Income Per Capita in Mexico by Decile, 1989–1994   456

TABLE 12.5
Estimates of Extreme Poverty in Mexico, 1984–1994   457

TABLE 12.6
Estimates of Poverty in Costa Rica, 1971–1995   470

TABLE 12.7
Headcount Indices of Poverty in Costa Rica, 1981 and 1989   471

TABLE 12.8
Incidence of Poverty in Costa Rica by Socioeconomic Group,
1980–1992   472

TABLE 12.9
Estimates of Poverty in Chile, 1969–1996   474

TABLE 13.1
Mexico's Gross Domestic Product by Region and State,
1970–1999   490

TABLE 13.2
Characteristics of Mexico's Urbanization by Region and State,
1970–1995   496

TABLE 13.3
Distribution of Mexico's Urban Population by City Size,
1970–2000   502

TABLE 13.4
Mexico's Gross Domestic Product by Main Cities and Sectors,
1985 and 1993   508

TABLE 14.1
Structure of Employment in Mexico's Urban Areas, 1991–2000   526

TABLE 14.2
Distribution of Urban Employment in Mexico by Selected
Occupation and Age Group, 1991 and 1998   527

TABLE 14.3
Proportion of Wage-Earning, Self-Employed, and Unpaid
Workers among Mexico's Employed Urban Population, by
Economic Activity, 1991 and 1998   528

TABLE 14.4
Mean Hourly Income from Labor in Mexico, 1991 and 1998   530

TABLE 14.5
Proportion of Urban Wage Earners in Mexico Receiving
Different Kinds of Fringe Benefits, 1991 and 1998   531

TABLE 14.6
Structure of Urban Employment in Mexico by Industry and
Size of Economic Unit, 1996–2000   532

TABLE 14.7
Changes in the Number of Fixed Business Establishments and
Employees in Manufacturing, Commerce, and Services in
Mexico, 1988–1993   534

TABLE 14.8
Real Wage Trends in the Stable Labor Force in Sixteen Major
Mexican Cities, 1987–1998   546

TABLE 14.9
Hourly Wages in Mexico's Stable Labor Force by Educational
Level, 1987–1998   548

TABLE 14.10
Hourly Wages of the Stable Labor Force in Sixteen Major
Mexican Cities, 1987–1988 and 1993–1994   550

TABLE 14.11
Relative Wages by Region in Mexico, 1987–1988 and 1993–1994   552

TABLE 15.1
Average Annual Economic and Population Growth Rates in
Mexico, 1951–2000   562

TABLE 15.2
Mexico's Population and Gross Domestic Product, 1950–2000   564

TABLE 15.3
Mexico's Balance of Payments, 1990–2000   570

TABLE 16.1
Mexican Population Living in Extreme Poverty, 1984–1994   584

TABLE 16.2
Proportion of Mexico's Population Living in Extreme Poverty,
1984–1994   584

TABLE 16.3
Comparisons of Income and Human Poverty among Ten
Countries, 1990s   590

Acronyms

ADE	Programa de Apoyo Inmediato a Deudores / Immediate Support Program for Debtors
AFORE	Administrador de Fondos para el Retiro / Retirement Fund Administrator
ALADI	Asociación Latinoamericana de Integración / Latin American Integration Association
ANUIES	Asociación Nacional de Universidades e Instituciones de Enseñanza Superior / National Association of Universities and Institutions of Higher Education
BANCOMEXT	Banco Nacional de Comercio Exterior / National Foreign Trade Bank
BANRURAL	Banco Nacional de Crédito Rural / National Rural Credit Bank
BANXICO	Banco de México / Bank of Mexico
CAPUFE	Caminos y Puentes Federales / Federal Roads and Bridges
CBI	Caribbean Basin Initiative
CENEVAL	Centro Nacional de Evaluación de la Educación Superior / National Center for the Evaluation of Higher Education
CEPAL	Comisión Económica para América Latina y el Caribe / Economic Commission for Latin America and the Caribbean
CEPPEMS	Comisión Estatal de Planeación y Programación de la Educación Media Superior / State Commission for Planning and Programming of Higher Middle Education
CNBV	Comisión Nacional Bancaria y de Valores / National Banking and Securities Commission
CNIE	Comisión Nacional de Inversiones Extranjeras / National Foreign Investment Commission
COMPITE	Comité Nacional de Productividad e Innovación Tecnológica / National Committee for Productivity and Technological Innovation

CONACYT	Consejo Nacional de Ciencia y Tecnología / National Council of Science and Technology
CONAEMS	Comisión Nacional de Educación Media Superior / National Commission for Higher Middle Education
CONALEP	Colegio Nacional de Educación Profesional Técnica / National College of Professional-Technical Education
CONAPO	Consejo Nacional de Población / National Population Council
CONASUPO	Compañía Nacional de Subsistencias Populares / National Basic Foods Company
CONPES	Comisión Nacional para la Planeación de la Educación Superior / National Commission for Higher Educational Planning
CONPPEMS	Comisión Nacional Para la Planeación y Programación de la Educación Media Superior / National Commission for Planning and Programming of Higher Middle Education
CONSAR	Comisión Nacional del Sistema de Ahorro para el Retiro / National Commission on Retirement Savings
COPLAMAR	Coordinación General del Plan Nacional de Zonas Deprimidas y Grupos Marginados / General Coordination of the National Plan for Depressed Areas and Marginalized Groups
CRECE	Centros Regionales para la Competitividad Empresarial / Regional Centers for Business Competitiveness
CTM	Confederación de Trabajadores de México / Confederation of Mexican Workers
EAP	economically active population
ECLAC	Economic Commission for Latin America and the Caribbean
ENE	Encuesta Nacional de Empleo / National Employment Survey
ENEU	Encuesta Nacional de Empleo Urbano / National Urban Employment Survey
EU	European Union
EZLN	Ejército Zapatista de Liberación Nacional / Zapatista Army of National Liberation

FDI	foreign direct investment
FEMEVAL	Fondo de Apoyo al Mercado de Valores / Stock Market Support Fund
FICORCA	Fideicomiso para la Cubertura de Riesgos Cambiarios / Exchange-Rate Risk Hedge Fund
FIDELIQ	Fideicomiso Liquidador de Instituciones y Organizaciones Auxiliares de Crédito / Liquidation Fund for Credit Institutions and Supplementary Credit Organizations
FIMPES	Federación de Instituciones Mexicanas Particulares de Educación Superior / Federation of Mexican Private Institutions of Higher Education
FIRA	Fideicomiso Instituido en Relación con la Agricultura / Investment Fund for Agriculture
FOBAPROA	Fondo Bancario de Protección al Ahorro / Bank Savings Protection Fund
FOMES	Fondo para la Modernización Educativa / Fund for Educational Modernization
GATT	General Agreement on Tariffs and Trade
GDP	gross domestic product
GNP	gross national product
IADB	Inter-American Development Bank
IFPRI	International Food Policy Research Institute
ILO	International Labour Office
IMF	International Monetary Fund
IMSS	Instituto Mexicano del Seguro Social / Mexican Social Security Institute
INAH	Instituto Nacional de Antropología e Historia / National Institute of Anthropology and History
INBA	Instituto Nacional de Bellas Artes / National Institute of Fine Arts
INE	Instituto Nacional de Ecología / National Ecology Institute
INEGI	Instituto Nacional de Estadística, Geografía e Informática / National Institute for Statistics, Geography, and Informatics
IPAB	Instituto para la Protección del Ahorro Bancario / Bank Savings Protection Institute
IPMM	integrated poverty measurement method

IPN	Instituto Politécnico Nacional / National Polytechnic Institute
ISI	import-substitution industrialization
ISSSTE	Instituto de Seguridad y Servicios Sociales de los Trabajadores del Estado / Social Security Institute for State Workers
LICONSA	Leche Industrializada CONASUPO, S.A. / Industrialized Milk CONASUPO
MERCOSUR	Mercado Común del Sur / Common Market of the South
MFA	Multi-Fiber Arrangement
MIDPLAN	Ministerio de Planificación y Cooperación / Ministry of Planning and Cooperation (Chile)
NAFIN	Nacional Financiera / National Credit Bank
NAFTA	North American Free Trade Agreement
NBES	normative basket of essential satisfiers
NIEs	newly industrializing economies
OBM	original brand-name manufacturing
ODM	original design manufacturing
OECD	Organisation for Economic Co-operation and Development
OEM	original equipment manufacturing
OPEC	Organization of Petroleum Exporting Countries
PAN	Partido Acción Nacional / National Action Party
PDE	Programa de Desarrollo Educativo / Program of Educational Development
PEMEX	Petróleos Mexicanos / Mexican Petroleum Company
PFF	Programa de Fortalecimiento Financiero / Financial Strengthening Program
PITEX	Programa de Importaciones Temporales para Producir Artículos de Exportación / Program of Temporary Imports to Produce Export Goods
PME	Programa de Modernización Educativa / Program of Educational Modernization
PND	Plan Nacional de Desarrollo / National Development Plan
PNDU	Programa Nacional de Desarrollo Urbano / National Urban Development Program

PNR	Partido Nacional Revolucionario / Revolutionary National Party
PREALC	Programa Regional de Empleo para América Latina y el Caribe / Regional Employment Program for Latin America and the Caribbean
PRI	Partido Revolucionario Institucional / Institutional Revolutionary Party
PRM	Partido de la Revolución Mexicana / Party of the Mexican Revolution
PROCAPTE	Programa de Capitalización Temporal / Temporary Capitalization Program
PROGRESA	Programa de Educación, Salud y Alimentación / Program for Education, Health, and Nutrition
PROMEP	Programa de Mejoramiento del Profesorado / Program for the Improvement of the Professoriate
PRONASOL	Programa Nacional de Solidaridad / National Solidarity Program
PROPICE	Programa de Política Industrial y Comercio Exterior / Program for Industrial and Foreign Trade Policy
SAG	Secretaría de Agricultura y Ganadería / Ministry of Agriculture and Livestock
SAGAR	Secretaría de Agricultura, Ganadería y Desarrollo Rural / Ministry of Agriculture, Livestock, and Rural Development
SAHOP	Secretaría de Asentamientos Humanos y Obras Públicas / Ministry of Human Settlements and Public Works
SAM	Sistema Alimentario Mexicano / Mexican Food System
SAR	Sistema de Ahorro para el Retiro / Retirement Savings System
SARH	Secretaría de Agricultura y Recursos Hidráulicos / Ministry of Agriculture and Water Resources
SECOFI	Secretaría de Comercio y Fomento Industrial / Ministry of Commerce and Industrial Development
SEDESOL	Secretaría de Desarrollo Social / Ministry of Social Development
SEDUE	Secretaría de Desarrollo Urbano y Ecología / Ministry of Urban Development and Ecology

SEIT	Subsecretaría de Educación e Investigación Tecnológica / Undersecretariat of Education and Technological Research
SEP	Secretaría de Educación Pública / Ministry of Public Education
SESIC	Subsecretaría de Educación Superior e Investigación Científica / Undersecretariat of Higher Education and Scientific Research
SHCP	Secretaría de Hacienda y Crédito Público / Ministry of Finance and Public Credit
SIEFORE	Sociedad de Inversión Especializada de Fondos para el Retiro / Specialized Investment Retirement Fund
SITC	Standard International Trade Classification
SNI	Sistema Nacional de Investigadores / National System of Researchers
SPP	Secretaría de Programación y Presupuesto / Ministry of Programming and Budget
STPS	Secretaría del Trabajo y Previsión Social / Ministry of Labor and Social Welfare
SUPERA	Programa de Superación del Personal Académico / Program for the Improvement of Academic Personnel
TNC	transnational corporation
UAM	Universidad Autónoma Metropolitana / Metropolitan Autonomous University
UDI	unidad de inversión / investment unit
UNAM	Universidad Nacional Autónoma de México / National Autonomous University of Mexico
UNDP	United Nations Development Programme
UNESCO	United Nations Educational, Scientific, and Cultural Organization
UNIDO	United Nations Industrial Development Organization
UNT	Unión Nacional de Trabajadores / National Union of Workers
USGAAP	U.S. generally accepted accounting principles
WTO	World Trade Organization

Contributors

Diana Alarcón is a social development specialist at the Inter-American Development Bank in Washington, D.C. She has also held positions at the International Labour Office and the United Nations Development Programme. Her research focuses on income distribution, poverty, and the impact of economic restructuring on employment, with particular regard to Mexico. Dr. Alarcón, an economist, is author of *Changes in the Distribution of Income in Mexico and Trade Liberalization* (El Colegio de la Frontera Norte, 1994) and coauthor of *North American Economic Integration: Theory and Practice* (Edward Elgar, 1999). She has also published numerous articles and book chapters on social development issues, employment policy, and anti-poverty strategy.

Julio Boltvinik is Research Professor at the Center for Sociological Studies at El Colegio de México. Professor Boltvinik, an economist, has written extensively on poverty and basic needs, food policy, and social marginality in Mexico and Latin America. He is author or coauthor of *La asignación de recursos públicos a la agricultura en México, 1959-1976* (Economic Commission for Latin America and the Caribbean, 1979), *Necesidades esenciales y estructura productiva en México: lineamientos de programación para el proyecto nacional* (COPLAMAR, 1982), *La pobreza en América Latina y el Caribe* (Programa de las Naciones Unidas para el Desarrollo, 1990), *Social Progress Index: A Proposal* (United Nations Development Programme, 1992), and *Pobreza y distribución del ingreso en México* (Siglo Veintiuno, 1992), as well as numerous journal articles and book chapters.

Hubert C. de Grammont is Research Professor in the Department of Political Science and Sociology at the Universidad Nacional Autónoma de México (UNAM). His research focuses on rural issues in Mexico (especially the living and working conditions of agricultural day laborers and the organization of agricultural workers) and, most recently, questions of democracy and citizenship. Professor C. de Grammont is author of *El Barzón: clase media, ciudadanía y democracia* (Plaza y Valdés/ UNAM, 2001) and the editor or coeditor of *Globalización, deterioro ambiental y reorganización en el campo* (UNAM, 1995), *Agricultura de exportación en tiempos de globalización* (Juan Pablos, 1999), and *Empresas, reestructuración productiva y empleo en la agricultura mexicana* (Plaza y Valdés, 1999).

Luz María De la Mora is director of Mexico's Trade Office for South America and Mexico's representative to the Latin American Integration Association (ALADI). She previously served as economic counselor at the Trade Office in the Embassy of Mexico in Washington, D.C., and as a member of Mexico's NAFTA negotiation team. Dr. De la Mora's publications include articles on the political economy of trade reform in Latin America and the North American Free Trade Agreement.

Enrique Dussel Peters is Associate Professor at the Graduate School of Economics, Universidad Nacional Autónoma de México (UNAM). His research interests include economic development, industrial organization, and trade theory, as well as the evolution of industrial, trade, and regional patterns in Mexico and Latin America. He is the author of *Polarizing Mexico: The Impact of Liberalization Strategy* (Lynne Rienner, 2000), coauthor of *Pensar globalmente y actuar regionalmente: hacia un nuevo paradigma industrial para el Siglo XXI* (UNAM/Fundación Friedrich Ebert/Jus, 1997), and coeditor of *Dinámica regional y competitividad industrial* (UNAM/Fundación Friedrich Ebert/Jus, 1999).

Celso Garrido is Research Professor in the Department of Economics at the Universidad Autónoma Metropolitana–Azcapotzalco in Mexico City. He has published extensively on the financial sector, industrialization, and the role of entrepreneurs in Latin America. Professor Garrido is author of *Grandes empresas y grupos industriales latinoamericanos: expansión y desafíos en la era de la apertura y la globalización* (Siglo Veintiuno, 1998), editor of *Reforma financiera, crecimiento económico y globalización: México en la perspectiva international* (Universidad Autónoma Metropolitana–Azcapotzalco, 2000), and coauthor or coeditor of *Empresarios y estado en América Latina: crisis y transformación* (Centro de Investigación y Docencia Económicas, 1988), *Mercado de valores, crisis y nuevos circuitos financieros en México, 1970–1990* (Universidad Autónoma Metropolitana–Azcapotzalco, 1991), *Ahorro y sistema financiero en México: diagnóstico de la problemática actual* (Grijalbo, 1996), and *Emerging Markets: Past and Present Experiences, and Future Prospects* (Macmillan/St. Martin's Press, 2000).

Gustavo Garza is Research Professor at the Center for Demographic and Urban Development Studies at El Colegio de México. He has published widely on urbanization, urban planning, and demographic trends in Mexico. Professor Garza is author of *El proceso de industrialización en la Ciudad de México, 1821–1970* (El Colegio de México, 1985), coauthor of *Planeación urbana en grandes metrópolis: Detroit, Monterrey y*

Toronto (El Colegio de México, 2002), and editor of *Una década de planeación urbano-regional en México, 1978–1988* (El Colegio de México, 1992), *Atlas demográfico de México* (Consejo Nacional de Población, 1999), and *La Ciudad de México al fin del segundo milenio* (El Colegio de México, 2000). During 1999–2001 he was a member of the panel on urban population dynamics at the U.S. National Academy of Sciences.

Gary Gereffi is Professor of Sociology and Director of the Markets and Management Studies Program at Duke University. He is the author of *The Pharmaceutical Industry and Dependency in the Third World* (Princeton University Press, 1983) and coeditor of *Manufacturing Miracles: Paths of Industrialization in Latin America and East Asia* (Princeton University Press, 1990), *Commodity Chains and Global Capitalism* (Greenwood, 1994), and *Globalization and Regionalism: NAFTA and the New Geography of the North American Apparel Industry* (Temple University Press, 2002). Professor Gereffi's research focuses on regional integration, the competitive strategies of global firms, and industrial upgrading in East Asia and Latin America.

Keith Griffin is Distinguished Professor of Economics at the University of California, Riverside. He is the author of, among other works, *The Political Economy of Agrarian Change: An Essay on the Green Revolution* (Harvard University Press, 1974), *World Hunger and the World Economy* (Holmes and Meier, 1987), *Alternative Strategies for Economic Development* (St. Martin's Press, rev. ed., 1999), and *Studies in Development Strategy and Systemic Transformation* (St. Martin's Press, 2000). Professor Griffin's research interests center on issues of globalization, human development, and the economic transition in the ex-socialist countries.

Amy Ickowitz is a Ph.D. candidate in economics at the University of California, Riverside. Her research focuses primarily on sub-Saharan Africa, particularly communal tenure systems, shifting patterns of cultivation, and rural development. Her published work includes a study of the distribution of wealth and the pace of development.

Asa Cristina Laurell is Secretary of Health in Mexico's Federal District Government. She was previously Professor of Social Medicine at the Universidad Autónoma Metropolitana–Xochimilco in Mexico City. She has written extensively on social security and health policy issues in Mexico, including *El desgaste obrero en México: proceso de la producción y salud* (Era, 1983), *Estado y política social en el neoliberalismo* (Fundación

Friedrich Ebert, 1992), and *La reforma contra la salud y la seguridad social* (Fundación Friedrich Ebert/Era, 1997).

Jorge Máttar, an economist, is Coordinator of Research at the Economic Commission for Latin America and the Caribbean (ECLAC)–Mexico. He has been a lecturer and visiting researcher at several academic institutions, a consultant for the United Nations Industrial Development Organization, and director of sectoral studies at the Grupo Financiero Serfin. His main research interests lie in economic and industrial development policy and competitiveness. He is coauthor of *La economía cubana: reformas estructurales y desempeño en los noventa* (Fondo de Cultura Económica, 1997) and *Desarrollo económico y social en la República Dominicana: los últimos 20 años y perspectivas para el Siglo XXI* (Pontificia Universidad Católica Madre y Maestra, 2000).

Kevin J. Middlebrook is Lecturer in Politics at the Institute of Latin American Studies at the University of London. Between 1995 and 2001 he was director of the Center for U.S.–Mexican Studies at the University of California, San Diego. He is the author of *The Paradox of Revolution: Labor, the State, and Authoritarianism in Mexico* (Johns Hopkins University Press, 1995) and editor or coeditor of, among other works, *The United States and Latin America in the 1980s: Contending Perspectives on a Decade of Crisis* (University of Pittsburgh Press, 1986), *The Politics of Economic Restructuring: State-Society Relations and Regime Change in Mexico* (Center for U.S.–Mexican Studies, 1994), *Conservative Parties, the Right, and Democracy in Latin America* (Johns Hopkins University Press, 2000), and *Party Politics and the Struggle for Democracy in Mexico: National and State-Level Analyses of the Partido Acción Nacional* (Center for U.S.–Mexican Studies, 2001).

Juan Carlos Moreno-Brid, an economist, serves as Regional Adviser at the Economic Commission for Latin America and the Caribbean (ECLAC)–Mexico. He has held research positions at Harvard University's David Rockefeller Center for Latin American Studies, the University of Notre Dame's Kellogg Institute for International Studies, and the Universidad Nacional Autónoma de México. His publications include articles in the *Journal of Post-Keynesian Economics*, the *International Review of Applied Economics*, and Banca Nazionale del Lavoro's *Quarterly Review*, as well as various book chapters.

Alejandro Nadal is Research Professor at the Center for Economic Studies at El Colegio de México. He is also coordinator of El Colegio de

México's Science and Technology Program. Professor Nadal has published extensively on the economics of technological change, with an emphasis on technology and natural resource management and alternative strategies for Mexico's sustainable development. He is the author or coauthor of *El plan de emergencia de Laguna Verde* (El Colegio de México, 1989), *Esfuerzo y captura: tecnología y sobreexplotación de recursos marinos vivos* (El Colegio de México, 1996), and *The Environmental and Social Impacts of Economic Liberalization on Corn Production in Mexico* (Worldwide Fund for Nature/Oxfam, 2000).

Wilson Peres is Chief of the Industrial and Technological Development Unit of the United Nations Economic Commission for Latin America and the Caribbean (ECLAC) in Santiago, Chile. He is coauthor of *Growth, Employment, and Equity: The Impact of the Economic Reforms in Latin America and the Caribbean* (ECLAC/Brookings Institution Press, 2000) and editor of *Políticas de competitividad industrial: América Latina y el Caribe en los años noventa* (Siglo Veintiuno, 1997) and *Grandes empresas y grupos industriales latinoamericanos: expansión y desafíos en la era de la apertura y la globalización* (Siglo Veintiuno, 1998), as well as a special issue of *World Development* titled *The Microeconomics of the New Economic Model in Latin America* (September 2000).

Clark W. Reynolds is Emeritus Professor at the Food Research Institute, Stanford University. He was founding director of the U.S.–Mexico Project and the Americas Program at Stanford. His research has dealt primarily with international trade and development, macroeconomic policy, employment and migration, productivity growth, income distribution, and regional development policies for market completion. He is author of *The Mexican Economy: Twentieth-Century Structure and Growth* (Yale University Press, 1970) and coeditor of *U.S.–Mexico Relations: Labor Market Interdependence* (Stanford University Press, 1992). Dr. Reynolds is currently completing a book manuscript titled "The North American Economy: Challenge of Interdependence."

Roberto Rodríguez Gómez is Research Professor in the Department of Sociology at the Universidad Nacional Autónoma de México (UNAM), as well as a member of the Mexican Academy of Sciences. He is coauthor of *Universidad contemporánea: racionalidad política y vinculación social* (Miguel Ángel Porrúa, 1994) and coeditor of *Escenarios para la universidad contemporánea* (UNAM, 1995). Professor Rodríguez has also published many journal articles on the relationship among higher education, development, and politics in Latin America.

Carlos Salas is Research Professor in the Division of Postgraduate Studies at the Universidad Nacional Autónoma de México (UNAM). He has served as a consultant on labor market issues to the International Labour Office, the United Nations Development Programme, and Mexico's Ministry of Labor and Social Welfare, and he has published numerous journal articles and book chapters on the structure of employment and employment policy in Mexico and Latin America. Professor Salas is coeditor of *Cuestiones de integración y desarrollo* (Universidad Autónoma de Madrid/UNAM, 1996).

Víctor L. Urquidi is Research Professor Emeritus at El Colegio de México. He is the former president of El Colegio de México (1966–1985) and a past winner (1977) of Mexico's Premio Nacional de Ciencias Sociales. Dr. Urquidi is the author of *Free Trade and Economic Integration in Latin America* (University of California Press, 1962), *The Challenge of Development in Latin America* (Praeger, 1964), and *México en la globalización: informe de la Sección Mexicana del Club de Roma* (Fondo de Cultura Económica, 1996), as well as coauthor or coeditor of, among other works, *La explosión humana* (Fondo de Cultura Económica, 1974), *América Latina en la economía internacional* (Fondo de Cultura Económica, 1976), and *Crisis y crecimiento en América Latina: material para un diagnóstico* (Tesis, 1989). His research interests include Mexican development policy in the context of globalization and policies for environmental improvement and sustainable development.

Gustavo Vega-Cánovas is Research Professor at the Center for International Studies at El Colegio de México. He has held visiting appointments at Brown University, Duke University, the University of North Carolina at Chapel Hill, and Yale University. His research has focused primarily on U.S.–Mexican economic relations and, since 1989, on North American integration. He is coauthor of *The Politics of Free Trade in North America* (Centre for Trade Policy and Law, 1995) and coeditor of *Las prácticas desleales de comercio y la resolución de controversias en los procesos de integración en el continente americano: la experiencia de América del Norte y Chile* (Universidad Nacional Autónoma de México/Secretaría de Comercio y Fomento Industrial, 2001), as well as numerous journal articles and book chapters.

Lorenza Villa Lever is Research Professor at the Institute for Social Research at the Universidad Nacional Autónoma de México, and a member of that institution's political and social science faculty. She is the author of articles and book chapters on educational policy, vocational training, and social exclusion in Mexico, as well as editor of *Perspectivas de la investigación en educación* (Universidad de Guadalajara, 1991).

Eduardo Zepeda is Research Professor in the Department of Economics at the Universidad Autónoma Metropolitana–Azcapotzalco in Mexico City. He previously held research positions at El Colegio de la Frontera Norte and the Centro de Investigación Socioeconómica at the Universidad Autónoma de Coahuila. His research focuses on international economics and economic development. Dr. Zepeda is coauthor of *Liberalización comercial, equidad y desarrollo económico* (Fundación Friedrich Ebert, 1992), *Empleo y servicios en la frontera norte de México* (Fundación Friedrich Ebert, 1994), and *North American Integration: Theory and Practice* (Edward Elgar, 1999), as well as coeditor of *El sector servicios: desarrollo regional y empleo* (Universidad Autónoma de Coahuila/Fundación Friedrich Ebert, 1996) and *Reestructuración económica y empleo en México* (Universidad Autónoma de Coahuila/Fundación Friedrich Ebert, 1999).

Part I

Introduction

1

On the Political Economy of Mexican Development Policy

Kevin J. Middlebrook and Eduardo Zepeda

Since the 1980s Mexico has alternately served as a model of market-oriented economic restructuring and a cautionary example of the limitations associated with a market-led development strategy. It was a leader in the process of structural adjustment and economic reform that swept Latin America beginning in the 1980s. In response to the 1982 debt crisis and the apparent "exhaustion" of import-substitution industrialization, successive Mexican governments shifted away from state-led, essentially inward-oriented development policies. Embracing a new economic model, reformers liberalized trade, deregulated foreign direct investment and financial markets, and aggressively privatized state-owned enterprises. The pace and breadth of the reform process made Mexico a paradigmatic case of economic liberalization. Indeed, U.S. policy makers and multilateral financial institutions such as the International Monetary Fund and the World Bank hailed the Mexican experience as an exemplar of the so-called Washington Consensus that guided economic reform in Latin America and other developing countries during the late 1980s and the 1990s.[1]

Economic liberalization helped engineer important changes in Mexico. Accession to the General Agreement on Tariffs and Trade (GATT) in 1986 and implementation of the North American Free Trade Agreement (NAFTA) with Canada and the United States in 1994 increased Mexico's access to foreign markets, facilitated the importation

The authors gratefully acknowledge helpful comments on an early version of this chapter from Helga Baitenmann, Enrique Dussel Peters, Asa Cristina Laurell, and Víctor L. Urquidi.

[1] For an explication of the Washington Consensus, see Williamson 1990, 1997. For an analysis of economic reform in Latin America since the mid–1970s, see Morley, Machado, and Pettinato 1999.

of intermediate goods, and attracted substantial flows of foreign investment. By the year 2000, these changes (along with such factors as consistently low wages) permitted Mexico to emerge as Latin America's largest exporter of manufactured goods and the United States' second largest trading partner (after Canada). Manufactured exports (primarily destined for the U.S. market) became the principal source of foreign exchange earnings and one of the country's most dynamic areas of economic growth, modest as it has been.[2] The wholesale privatization of state-owned enterprises produced a substantial shift in the balance of power between the public and private sectors, while the relaxation of restrictions on foreign investment modified the weight and roles of national and foreign capital. As a consequence, export-oriented foreign firms, Mexican-owned conglomerates with access to international capital markets, and other national companies allied with transnational corporations have become the main engines of growth—a transformation that may lay the bases for long-term Mexican competitiveness in international markets, but which has also produced further economic segmentation as less successful firms and sectors have fallen behind.

Yet far-reaching reform and orthodox macroeconomic policies have neither delivered rates of growth equal to those achieved from the 1940s through the 1970s nor guaranteed economic stability. Indeed, trade and investment opening increased the Mexican economy's vulnerability to external shocks, and the volatility of short-term capital flows contributed to a devastating financial crisis in 1994–1995. In the late 1990s, the high interest rates required to attract and retain foreign capital, cover the costs of a weakened banking system, and reduce inflation also deprived major segments of the Mexican economy of the resources necessary to create jobs or adapt to more competitive markets. Equally seriously, the legacies of economic crisis and adjustment during the 1980s and 1990s included a substantial external and domestic debt burden, an enfeebled banking system, greater inequality in the distribution of income and wealth, and reduced state capacity to promote infrastructure investment or fund public welfare programs on a scale commensurate with Mexico's social needs.

Because of the importance of the Mexican experience in continuing debates about the options available to developing countries, and because many observers have questioned whether market-oriented economic restructuring in Mexico has indeed succeeded in laying the foundations for sustained growth and equitable socioeconomic development, the contributors to this volume undertake a comprehensive,

---

[2] The sharp depreciation of the peso in 1994–1995 was an important stimulus to Mexico's export boom.

interdisciplinary assessment of the principal economic and social policies Mexico adopted during the 1980s and 1990s. Substantial time has passed since Mexico initiated a broad process of economic reform. This is, then, an opportune moment at which to reflect upon the consequences of economic liberalization and the major development challenges facing Mexico.

The sixteen chapters in this book are grouped into four thematic sections and a final, overview section. The first four parts of the volume examine: (1) *macroeconomic and financial policies*, including the impact of the adjustment process on economic growth, inflation, external account balances, and Mexico's foreign and domestic debt burden; the origins and implications of the continuing crisis of the Mexican banking system; and foreign direct investment trends, the sectoral performance of capital formation in the Mexican economy, and implications for the future growth of export-competitive manufacturing activities; (2) *trade, export-led growth, and industrial policies*, with attention to the impact of trade liberalization and North American economic integration on macroeconomic performance, major actors and strategies behind the rapid expansion of Mexican manufactured exports in the 1990s, and the limitations of this export-led growth model as a basis for national development; (3) *major social policies and rural development issues*, focusing especially on efforts to improve middle and higher education, the consequences of policy changes affecting retirement pensions and health care, and major problems facing rural Mexico; and (4) *inequality, employment and wage problems, and poverty*, with particular attention to income distribution and poverty trends, the efficacy of targeted poverty-alleviation policies, urban and regional disparities, and the consequences of economic liberalization for employment and wage levels.

The fifth, overview section features short essays analyzing the Mexican development experience of the 1980s and 1990s in historical and comparative context. These pieces highlight the ways in which the country's economic and social policies during this period differed—in both their core characteristics and their results—from Mexico's earlier import-substitution model and from the experiences of other developing countries in Latin America and East Asia during the late twentieth century.

This introductory essay sets the stage for the contributions that follow by addressing four overarching questions. First, what were the main elements of economic liberalization in Mexico and the domestic and international circumstances in which it occurred? Second, what political factors accounted for the scope of economic opening, the speed with which it took place, and the absence of substantial, politically mobilized opposition to this major policy shift? Third, what have been the most important consequences (both positive and negative) of economic liberalization since the mid–1980s? And finally, what are the key development challenges (including those produced or exacerbated by the way in which economic liberalization occurred) confronting Mexico at the beginning of the twenty-first century?

ECONOMIC OPENING IN MEXICO

The principal catalyst for market-oriented economic reform in Mexico, as in Latin America more generally, was the debt crisis of the 1980s and its impact on the country's access to capital. From the early 1940s through the 1970s, Mexican decision makers had embraced import-substitution industrialization (ISI) as their main strategy for achieving economic growth. Pursuit of this strategy, whose goal was to supply national demand with domestically manufactured consumer durable goods and intermediate products rather than with foreign imports, led successive presidential administrations to adopt policies designed to promote local industry. These measures included higher tariff barriers, direct import controls, tighter government restrictions on foreign direct investment (FDI), tax concessions for manufacturing firms, and, at different times, exchange-rate policies that (under the economic regime then in place) encouraged the large-scale importation of machinery and equipment.

By the late 1950s, Mexican policy makers (unlike their counterparts in Argentina and Brazil) had realized their double goals of producing steady economic expansion and rising per capita income while at the same time controlling inflation. Manufacturing activities' share of gross domestic product (GDP) grew from 18.0 percent to 25.3 percent between 1940 and 1965. Substantial public investment in roads, electrical power generation, dams, and irrigation projects helped to commercialize agricultural production and facilitated the expansion of the domestic consumer market. Over the 1940–1965 period, Mexico's gross domestic product rose at an average annual rate of 6.3 percent in real terms, and per capita GDP increased by 117.2 percent.[3] There were good reasons, then, why domestic and foreign observers alike referred

---

[3] These data are drawn from Reynolds 1970: tables 1.1, 1.4, 2.1, 2.2. Víctor L. Urquidi (this volume, table 15.1) provides data disaggregated by decade on real GDP and GDP per capita growth rates for the 1951–1980 period. Over the 1941–1981 period, gross domestic product rose by an annual average of 6.5 percent in real terms; authors' calculation based upon data presented in INEGI 1985: vol. 1, table 9.1.

to the country's economic performance during these years as "the Mexican miracle."

Many analysts subsequently noted that, over the longer term, import substitution policies created problems that contributed to serious economic difficulties in the 1970s and 1980s.[4] These negative consequences included excessive dependence upon imports of intermediate and capital goods, overvalued exchange rates and chronic balance-of-payments problems, inefficient domestic industries producing high-cost consumer goods for a heavily protected national market, and a very limited capacity to export manufactured goods. Domestic producers encountered especially severe difficulties in consolidating the "vertical" stage of import-substitution industrialization, involving the more fully integrated manufacture of consumer durable goods, backward integration toward the production of more capital-intensive and technologically sophisticated intermediate products and capital goods, and diversified export promotion. Moreover, the industrial sector proved incapable of generating sufficient employment to meet the demands of a rapidly growing labor force. And despite Mexico's macroeconomic successes, income inequality generally worsened over time.[5]

In his overview assessment of the country's post–World War II development experience, Víctor L. Urquidi (this volume) argues that by the 1970s the constraints facing the Mexican economy were sufficiently serious that, had it not been for the sharp rise in international oil prices after 1973 and the discovery of substantial new petroleum reserves in Mexico in the mid–1970s, Mexican policy makers would have been forced to liberalize the economy at that time.[6] However, the oil bonanza permitted Mexico to engage in heavy—ultimately unsustainable—borrowing in international capital markets flush with Middle Eastern "petrodollar" deposits and sparked rapid economic growth,[7] thus permitting the government to expand public-sector expenditures and postpone necessary policy reforms. It was not until international oil prices fell in 1981–1982 and Mexico found itself unable either to service

---

[4] For evaluations of the import-substitution strategy in Latin America and its limitations, see Hirschman 1968 and Thorp 1992. See Cárdenas 1996 for a more detailed assessment of the Mexican experience.

[5] For a summary of these issues, see Middlebrook 1995: 213–16, and Evans and Gereffi 1982: 120–27.

[6] See Cook, Middlebrook, and Molinar Horcasitas 1994: 17–18 for a brief discussion of the political struggles surrounding economic policy debates in the early 1970s.

[7] Gross domestic product rose by an annual average of 8.4 percent per year in real terms between 1978 and 1981; authors' calculation based upon data presented in INEGI 1985: vol. 1, table 9.1.

its foreign debt (thereby detonating the Latin American debt crisis of the 1980s) or to secure the foreign exchange necessary to finance essential imports that alternative economic policies were seriously considered.

Beginning in the 1980s, the administrations of Miguel de la Madrid Hurtado (1982–1988) and Carlos Salinas de Gortari (1988–1994) implemented structural adjustment policies and an increasingly radical series of market reforms that included trade, exchange-rate, and industrial policy liberalization; deregulation of foreign investment flows and domestic commercial and financial activities; and the large-scale privatization of state-owned enterprises.[8] With accession to the GATT in 1986, Mexico's maximum tariff rate fell from 100 to 50 percent; by 1987 it was a comparatively low 20 percent, and almost all import licenses had been eliminated.[9] In 1984 the government also began lifting the extensive restrictions on foreign direct investment that had been enacted from the mid–1940s through the early 1970s.[10] Sector-specific industrial policies were abandoned in favor of sector-neutral policies. Tertiary activities, including road construction and telecommunications, were also deregulated and opened to private ownership. And perhaps most spectacularly, the De la Madrid and Salinas administrations undertook the massive privatization of public enterprises. The total number of state-owned firms, decentralized agencies, and investment trusts fell from 1,155 in 1982 to 232 in 1992. The wave of privatizations included some of Mexico's largest state-owned firms.[11]

At several critical points, the reform process was pushed forward by the Mexican government's pressing need to secure external financing. Policy makers had a strong incentive to adopt market reforms because multilateral and commercial bank creditors made at least part of the

---

[8] See Ros 1994: 68–72, Clavijo and Valdivieso 2000, Dussel Peters (this volume), and Urquidi (this volume) for overviews of the principal economic policies adopted during the post-1982 period of financial crisis and economic stagnation. For an "official" exposition of the reform project's rationale and anticipated consequences by a key participant, see Aspe Armella 1993.

[9] See Vega and De la Mora (this volume). Enrique Dussel Peters (this volume) reports that by the late 1990s average import tariffs had fallen to 11.8 percent.

[10] See Vega and De la Mora (this volume) for a summary of the changing rules concerning foreign direct investment in Mexico.

[11] Valdés Ugalde 1994: table 9.2; also table 9.3 and figure 9.1. The firms that were privatized included the two airline companies (Mexicana de Aviación and Aeroméxico), the two largest copper-mining companies (Compañía Minera de Cananea and Mexicana de Cobre), the country's largest telecommunications company (Teléfonos de México), and the commercial banks, which had been nationalized in 1982.

potentially available external funding conditional upon their doing so.[12] However, it was the additional shock of a further drop in international oil prices in 1985–1986, renewed recession, and the prospect of gaining access to substantial additional external financing under the terms of the Baker and Brady plans[13] that led to more rapid trade liberalization — and an acceleration of market-oriented reforms more generally — after 1985.[14]

On the basis of these policy transformations, Mexico was widely identified as a "model" country. As Gustavo Vega and Luz María de la Mora observe in their chapter in this volume, in the late 1980s and early 1990s foreign investment surged, the economy grew robustly, government policy makers gradually reduced inflation to single digits, and real wages in manufacturing began to recover after a decade of continuous decline. Despite growing current-account deficits, the International Monetary Fund, the World Bank, and private investors held Mexico up as an exemplary case of successful structural adjustment and economic reform.[15] It took the forced devaluation of the peso in December 1994 and the ensuing financial and economic crisis to prompt a reexamination of what economic liberalization and orthodox macroeconomic management had accomplished. Indeed, the political backlash produced by the devaluation, financial chaos, and the largest drop in gross domestic product since the Great Depression of the 1930s prompted a reconsideration of what Mexico's new economic model was *capable* of achieving in terms of promoting sustained economic growth, creating adequate employment, reducing poverty, and, more generally, laying the bases for equitable socioeconomic development.[16]

---

[12] Ros 1994: 83; see pp. 82–86 for his "political economy model of structural reform." See Williamson 1990 for a formulation of what were regarded as essential elements in the new market-oriented approach, and Teichman 2001: chap. 6 on the role of multilateral financial institutions in the Mexican reform process.

[13] These were the foreign-debt restructuring and relief plans coordinated by, respectively, U.S. Treasury secretaries James A. Baker III and Nicholas F. Brady.

[14] Related reform measures designed to maintain business confidence included the elimination of government budget deficits, more effective tax collection, and greater institutional autonomy for the Banco de México.

[15] Even in the early 1990s, however, some analysts questioned whether Mexico had consolidated the bases for sustained economic growth. See, for example, Ros 1994 and Dornbusch and Werner 1994.

[16] See, for example, Krugman 1995; Sachs, Tornell, and Velasco 1995; and Edwards 1997.

THE POLITICS OF ECONOMIC RESTRUCTURING

In outlining the domestic and international circumstances under which economic liberalization occurred in Mexico during the 1980s and early 1990s, the preceding discussion concentrated primarily on the timing and direction of policy change. However, students of comparative political economy have also drawn attention to the scope of economic opening and the rapidity with which broad market-oriented reforms were implemented in Mexico,[17] as well as to some of the inconsistencies and omissions in the reform agenda. This section briefly examines the political context of economic restructuring in Mexico.

Three interlinked political factors help explain the extent and speed of economic opening in Mexico.[18] First, the political regime that emerged following Mexico's 1910–1920 social revolution concentrated substantial authority in the federal executive, an arrangement that permitted the president to define national policy goals without major constraint. Acting on the conviction that a strong executive was required to implement the revolution's social agenda and ensure the political stability necessary for economic development, delegates to the 1916–1917 Constitutional Convention placed preeminent authority in the presidency and limited the powers of the legislative and judicial branches of government. The 1917 Constitution thus laid the legal foundation for postrevolutionary governments' relative decision-making autonomy, which was further reinforced by the gradual consolidation of a strong, interventionist state apparatus in the decades following the 1910–1920 revolution.[19]

---

[17] See, for example, Ros 1994: 67–68, and Máttar, Moreno-Brid, and Peres (this volume). Nonetheless, in the broader Latin American context, Stallings and Peres (2000: 49–50, 203) characterize Mexico as a "cautious reformer."

[18] This discussion draws in part upon Cook, Middlebrook, and Molinar Horcasitas 1994. For other analyses of the political dimensions of economic reform in Mexico, see Aitken, Craske, Jones, and Stansfield 1996; Serrano 1997; and Thacker 1999.

The January 1994 revolt led by the Zapatista Army of National Liberation (EZLN) quickly put to rest the view that Mexico's liberalizing reformers had engineered a far-reaching program of economic restructuring without provoking major political or social upheavals.

[19] Over time, the federal executive acquired special legal authority over the definition and implementation of economic policies. As late as 1982, for example, a series of constitutional reforms confirmed the state's guiding role in a mixed economy consisting of public, private, and social sectors—including exclusive state responsibility over communications, petroleum and basic petrochemicals, nuclear energy, electrical power generation, railroads, and banking. For details, see Valdés Ugalde 1994: 223–24.

In addition to the influence he derived from this division of constitutional authority, the president exercised important de facto powers in
Mexico's one-party-dominant system. The formation of an "official"
political party in 1929 marked a significant step in the institutionalization of postrevolutionary Mexican politics and further accelerated the
trend toward the centralization of political power. The Revolutionary
National Party (PNR) was organized principally to constrain factional
rivalries within the postrevolutionary political elite. The PNR and its
successors[20] provided a framework for mediating competing interests
and limiting conflict within a heterogeneous governing coalition that
included organized peasants and workers. The postrevolutionary elite's
control over the state apparatus gradually permitted the "official"
party to establish its electoral hegemony, and the party's assured electoral triumphs constituted an important basis for both political legitimacy and reliable legislative majorities.

Where the redefinition of economic policy in the 1980s and early
1990s was concerned, the president's largely unfettered capacity to
make substantial numbers of senior and mid-level administrative appointments during his term in office—thereby shaping both policy debates and elite mobility opportunities—was particularly important.
During the De la Madrid and Salinas administrations, a new generation
of "political technocrats" rose to power on the basis of their administrative experience and specialized training, which frequently included
postgraduate study in economics or related disciplines at leading U.S.
universities.[21] Salinas, for example, had earned a doctorate in political
economy at Harvard University in 1978, and, as he assumed increasingly important administrative positions in the economic policy-
making bureaucracy during the 1980s, he assembled around himself a
cohort of young economists and policy professionals committed to
opening the economy, redefining the established pattern of state/
private-sector interactions, and promoting export-oriented growth. This
shift in intra-elite mobility patterns generated tensions within the ruling
coalition as more traditional politicians, who had based their careers on
elective office and positions in the Institutional Revolutionary Party

[20] In 1938 the "official" party was reorganized as the Party of the Mexican Revolution (PRM) on the basis of labor, agrarian, military, and "popular" sectors. The
military sector was formally eliminated in 1943, and in 1946 the party was re-
named the Institutional Revolutionary Party (PRI).

[21] Camp (1985: 98) coined the term "political technocrat" to suggest that virtually
all high-level Mexican decision makers have political skills, even though some individuals' education, career experience, means of recruitment, and sources of influence emphasize professional training and technical expertise. See also Centeno
1994.

(PRI), were sometimes pushed aside in the competition for jobs, resources, and influence.[22] However, given the substantial powers of the Mexican state, the economic policy teams assembled by De la Madrid and Salinas were positioned to make significant policy changes as they sought to reorient Mexico's development strategy.

Second, despite the existence of legal opposition parties and periods during which opposition forces substantially improved their electoral performance by successfully mobilizing sociopolitical discontent, the continued overall strength of the PRI during the 1980s and 1990s insulated liberalizing reformers from electoral challenges. The unprecedented support garnered by a leftist opposition coalition in the 1988 presidential election indicated that the PRI could no longer take its dominance for granted,[23] and in 1989 the center-right National Action Party (PAN) broke the PRI's long-standing monopoly on state governorships by winning the Baja California gubernatorial election. Moreover, during the 1988–1991 period, the PRI no longer controlled the two-thirds majority in the federal Chamber of Deputies that permitted the government to reform the constitution at will. The Salinas administration was, therefore, compelled to forge legislative coalitions with the PAN in order to enact such measures as the reform of Article 27 (permitting the privatization of *ejido* lands).[24]

Viewed comparatively, however, the PRI's generally secure position during this period established the electoral and legislative conditions underpinning rapid, extensive economic reform. In fact, in the 1991 midterm elections the PRI recovered its two-thirds majority in the federal Chamber of Deputies, and opposition party electoral support declined significantly.[25] One of the reasons for the PRI's recovery was Salinas's success in persuading important segments of the Mexican

---

[22] Internal tensions within the PRI were, of course, aggravated by the 1982 debt crisis and prolonged economic stagnation, weakening public confidence in the government's capacity to manage the economy or address crises such as the 1985 Mexico City earthquakes, and the declining availability of patronage resources as international and domestic financial circumstances constrained government expenditures.

[23] The coalition's candidate, Cuauhtémoc Cárdenas, officially won 31.1 percent of the valid vote, and the PRI's share fell to a new low of 50.7 percent. For an analysis suggesting that Cárdenas may in fact have won more votes than the PRI's candidate (Carlos Salinas de Gortari), see Castañeda 1999: 527–38 ("Apéndice: 6 de julio de 1988").

[24] The ejido, a collective form of land ownership, was a principal vehicle for the distribution of land during Mexico's postrevolutionary agrarian reform.

[25] The PRI won 61.4 percent of the valid vote in the 1991 congressional elections; its nearest rival, the PAN, won only 17.7 percent. See Klesner 1994: table 7.1.

population that there were real benefits to be derived from trade liber-alization and other economic reforms, manifested most immediately by the expanded availability of lower-cost imported consumer goods and the effective control of inflation.[26]

The third political element explaining why it was possible to liber-alize economic policy so rapidly and extensively in the 1980s and early 1990s was the network of state-society alliances underpinning Mexico's distinctive form of authoritarian rule. In the decades after the 1910–1920 revolution, the new political elite constructed a durable alliance with mass social actors. The state's extensive intervention in socio-economic affairs provided government decision makers with the means to formulate development policies that responded to key peasant and labor demands, thus permitting them to forge strong political ties with leading mass organizations while simultaneously using their control over the means of coercion to repress challenges from more radical opponents.[27] At the same time, the hegemony of the "official" party helped cement mass actors' loyalty to the regime by providing the leaders of favored peasant and worker organizations with a channel of upward political mobility. These organizations' affiliation with the governing party symbolized their inclusion in the postrevolutionary ruling coalition.

Particularly where organized labor was concerned, the governing elite's effective control over mass demands constituted a principal po-litical foundation for economic crisis management. From the early 1950s onward, successive presidential administrations provided a broad range of legal, financial, and political subsidies to "official" labor

---

[26] Among the factors contributing to the PRI's electoral recovery in 1991 was the political success of the National Solidarity Program (PRONASOL), the hallmark anti-poverty initiative with which Salinas was personally identified.

Paradoxically, it was precisely because key Mexican publics accepted the Salinas recipe for national economic success that the 1994–1995 financial crisis had such a dramatic and sustained impact on the PRI's electoral performance. The PRI lost its majority in the federal Chamber of Deputies in 1997, and in 2000 the "offi-cial" party lost control of the presidency for the first time since its founding.

[27] For example, extensive land distribution in the 1930s and the creation of credit and marketing arrangements to subsidize small-scale agricultural production transformed peasant communities into a reliable source of electoral support for the "official" party. Similarly, urban and industrial workers benefited from such measures as enterprise profit-sharing and a broad range of publicly financed so-cial welfare programs, including subsidized access to basic commodities, health care, housing, and consumer credit. For the most part, these were benefits that peasant and worker organizations would have had difficulty winning on their own. Securing them depended principally upon their political alliance with state elites.

organizations such as the Confederation of Mexican Workers (CTM), the largest and most politically important national labor confederation and the PRI's labor sector. For their part, state-subsidized labor organizations gave crucial backing to the established regime in political and economic crises. For example, government-allied labor leaders' willingness—and their capacity—to contain rank-and-file demands and block worker mobilization allowed government policy makers to control inflation during periods of economic instability. The CTM's agreement to limit wage increases proved vital to the success of government economic stabilization programs following devaluation crises in 1954, in 1976–1977, and after 1982.[28] More generally, the combination of state legal and administrative controls on strikes and other labor activities, and the continued political discipline of the "official" organized labor movement, permitted government decision makers considerable freedom of maneuver in the 1980s and early 1990s as they redefined national development strategy.[29]

Just as core elements of Mexico's postrevolutionary authoritarian regime explain the rapidity of extensive economic liberalization in the 1980s and early 1990s, so too do political factors account for important inconsistencies or omissions in the reform agenda. Two examples illustrate this point.

The first example concerns the terms under which Mexican banks were reprivatized in 1991–1992 and the limited degree of financial-sector liberalization that occurred under the provisions of the NAFTA. Along with reform of Article 27 and negotiation of a free-trade agreement with Canada and the United States, the sale of publicly owned financial institutions to private investors was among the most important steps that Salinas took to gain political backing from the national private sector. The September 1982 bank nationalization had ruptured long-established understandings concerning the respective roles of the public and private sectors in Mexican economic development, and it had contributed directly to entrepreneurs' growing support for the opposition National Action Party. Faced with the increasing strains that structural adjustment and economic liberalization were producing among the PRI's traditional bases, Salinas was intent upon using mea-

---

[28] In his acute analysis of Mexico's post–1982 structural adjustment process, Ros (1994: 72–73, 77, 78–80) highlights the importance of the established pattern of state-labor relations and "the low degree of indexation in the wage/price system."

[29] Nevertheless, the "official" organized labor movement retained important political leverage in this unequal alliance. During the late 1980s and early 1990s, for example, the CTM successfully blocked both proposed reforms of the federal labor law and modifications in the structure of the PRI that would have diminished the internal party influence of sectoral organizations such as the CTM.

sures like the sale of publicly owned banks and investment houses to forge a new governing coalition in which financiers would consolidate their leadership. Given the importance of the bank privatization to Salinas's overall political strategy, it is little surprise that the insider sale of financial institutions occurred on terms favorable to Salinas's principal allies in the private sector.[30] These terms included, in exchange for a high initial purchase price, the government's assurance to bank purchasers that financial-sector liberalization would be delayed. Thus, despite demands from U.S. negotiators, the terms of the NAFTA restricted foreign equity participation in Mexican financial institutions for an extended period.[31]

The second example involves wage policy and state-labor-business relations in general. In marked contrast to the "state withdrawal" agenda that economic reformers pursued in other arenas, government officials during the 1980s and 1990s showed little interest in dismantling the complex array of legal and administrative controls regulating wage and contract negotiations, union formation, and strikes. Limiting wage increases in order to achieve macroeconomic stability and make workers' low compensation a basis of international comparative advantage was a key element in government economic strategy during this period. As part of its efforts to control wage increases and break the link between legal minimum wages and "market-determined" wages, the Salinas administration forcefully used its executive powers to hold minimum wages in line with restrictive macroeconomic targets. Because minimum wage trends influence adjustments in many labor contracts (Fairris, Popli, and Zepeda 2001), overall wage levels therefore remained depressed. Indeed, despite renewed economic growth, significant productivity gains that often led to wage hikes, and an increase in real average wages in manufacturing industries between 1989 and 1992, the inflation-adjusted hourly compensation of Mexican production workers in 1992 was only three-quarters of what it had been in 1979 (Middlebrook 1995: 297). More generally, at a time when cuts in

---

[30] The Salinas administration restricted participation in the auction of these publicly owned firms to a small number of large national corporations and favored investors. Sale of the banks generated some 83 percent of the total proceeds from the privatization of state-owned firms between 1989 and 1992. See Valdés Ugalde 1994: 237–39. For additional discussion of the government's management of the financial sector during this period, see Garrido (this volume).

[31] See Trigueros 1994 for a summary of the NAFTA's provisions concerning financial services. In late 1998, as a result of the 1994–1995 financial crisis and the growing insolvency of many banks, the Mexican government eliminated restrictions on foreign participation in bank ownership. A number of Mexico's most important banks were subsequently purchased by foreign financial interests.

public-sector employment and drastic shifts in major firms' industrial relations strategies undermined the mobilizational capacity and negotiating strength of labor unions, government policy decisively tilted the industrial restructuring process in favor of business interests.[32]

In concluding this discussion, it is useful to consider what impact the sequencing of economic liberalization and political opening had on the course and character of economic reform in Mexico in the 1980s and 1990s. As president, Salinas argued explicitly that economic liberalization should precede democratization.[33] He no doubt anticipated that economic opening would produce more rapid growth, permitting the PRI–led regime to bolster its performance-based legitimacy sufficiently to prolong its grip on power. In practice, there is little doubt that core characteristics of Mexican authoritarianism—the concentrated power of the federal executive, economic policy makers' general insulation from sociopolitical opposition, and long-established state controls over mass actors like organized labor—contributed substantially to the speed and relative ease with which far-reaching economic reforms were enacted from the mid–1980s through the early 1990s. Yet the fact that economic opening occurred while many of the authoritarian elements in Mexico's postrevolutionary regime remained intact also meant that popular groups had limited capacity to redress their accumulated socioeconomic needs or influence national policy debates so as to define a more inclusive economic strategy.

THE CONSEQUENCES OF ECONOMIC OPENING

Export Production and the Transformation of Mexico's Economic Profile

Economic liberalization and the transformations in economic and political power associated with it produced a number of important changes in Mexico's political economy. The most dramatic of these has been the shift since the late 1980s in the importance and content of Mexican exports. By the late 1990s, export activity was equivalent to

---

[32] For a paradigmatic example of the extent to which government officials were prepared to set aside their rhetorical commitment to the free play of market forces and employ state power to achieve the outcomes they desired in the strategically important area of labor affairs, see Middlebrook 1995: 283–85 on the Salinas administration's handling of worker-employer conflict at Volkswagen's large car and motor manufacturing complex in 1992.

[33] Specifically, Salinas maintained that simultaneous political and economic opening (as in the former Soviet Union) risked undermining market reforms; *New Perspectives Quarterly* 8:1 (Winter 1991): 8.

almost one-third of overall GDP and an important source of economic growth (Dussel Peters, this volume, table 7.1). Exports totaled US$166.4 billion in the year 2000, making Mexico one of the most important trading nations in the world.[34]

The bulk of these exports were manufactured goods.[35] Over the course of the 1980s and 1990s Mexico achieved a significant degree of industrial upgrading in its export profile. In 1980, Mexico's top ten exports consisted mainly of primary products (petroleum and natural gas, vegetables and fruit, nonferrous metals, coffee, and seafood), but by 1999 only two of the country's top ten export items were primary goods (petroleum, and vegetables and fruit). Transport equipment (especially automobiles and auto parts), electrical machinery and appliances, telecommunications equipment, office machines and automatic data-processing equipment, apparel, and power-generating machinery dominated the list.[36] Underlying these developments were improvements in productivity, the growing use of total-quality management systems, and a substantial increase in the number of exporting firms, which rose from 22,000 enterprises in 1994 to 34,000 in 1998.[37]

A significant shift in foreign direct investment since the 1980s has underpinned this transformation in Mexico's industrial focus. In their contribution to this volume, Jorge Máttar, Juan Carlos Moreno-Brid, and Wilson Peres demonstrate that overall trends in gross fixed investment followed a trajectory similar to that of the country's gross domestic product. Despite momento of rapid investment growth (during, for example, the period preceding implementation of the NAFTA, which coincided with the privatization of telecommunications and several other key economic activities), periodic economic crises and macroeconomic uncertainty constrained the investment process. As a result, real gross fixed investment in the year 2000 was only slightly higher

---

[34] Keith Griffin and Amy Ickowitz (this volume) caution that the volume of exports rose much more rapidly than their value, and that export earnings per capita rose by only 0.2 percent per year over the 1980–1996 period.

[35] Dussel Peters (this volume) reports that, in the year 2000, 87.3 percent of Mexico's exports were manufactured products. Even excluding the *maquiladora* (in-bond processing) sector, manufactures represented 73.1 percent of Mexico's exports in 1998; Stallings and Peres 2000: table 6.2.

[36] See Gereffi, this volume, table 6.1. In 1990, capital-intensive and high-technology products represented, respectively, 15.2 percent and 5.6 percent of Mexican exports; in 1998, these categories constituted, respectively, 23.4 percent (31.6 percent if one excludes maquiladora production) and 36.8 percent (19.9 percent if one excludes maquiladora production) of Mexico's total exports; see Stallings and Peres 2000: table 6.4.

[37] Gereffi (this volume). See also Hernández Laos 2000a.

than in 1981, and the investment/GDP ratio in 2000 (20.5 percent) was actually lower than in 1981 (26.5 percent) (Máttar, Moreno-Brid, and Peres, this volume, table 4.1). The shortfall in capital formation was particularly evident in such sectors as oil and natural gas, electrical power, highways and ports, and water and sanitation, where public investment was sharply cut in order to promote macroeconomic adjustment.[38]

Nevertheless, despite considerable unevenness across different sectors and the overall fragility of the capital formation process, since the mid–1980s there has been substantial investment to modernize plant and equipment in export-oriented manufacturing activities. Foreign investors responded positively to the liberalization of regulations governing foreign direct investment and to Mexico's increasing integration into the North American economic bloc. As a consequence, the proportion of FDI in gross fixed capital formation jumped from 3.2 percent in 1980–1985 to 14.8 percent in 1994–1998 (Máttar, Moreno-Brid, and Peres, this volume), and by the late 1990s Mexico was the second most important recipient (after Brazil) of foreign investment in Latin America.[39] In the early 1990s most new foreign investment had been devoted to communications and producer services (Zepeda and Félix 1995: 108–11), but by the end of the decade some three-fifths of the FDI flowing into Mexico went to manufacturing activities, including the rapidly growing *maquiladora* (in-bond processing) industry (Máttar, Moreno-Brid, and Peres, this volume).

The automobile, electronics, and textile and apparel industries represent leading examples of Mexico's success in securing investment in manufacturing activities with a strong export potential.[40] In the case of the automobile industry, the liberalization or elimination of production and export restrictions on vehicle manufacturing accelerated a process of industrial restructuring, promoting specialization in small and mid-size cars, light trucks, engines, and auto parts. At the same time, Mexico attracted large new inflows of foreign investment as the U.S. "Big Three" (DaimlerChrysler, Ford, and General Motors) and Volkswagen substantially expanded production for export and as other international

---

[38] In their comparative evaluation of the Mexican development experience, Griffin and Ickowitz (this volume) underscore the long-term negative consequences of the significant decline in federal government expenditures for capital formation.

[39] See Gereffi (this volume) and Máttar, Moreno-Brid, and Peres (this volume, table 4.2).

[40] See Máttar, Moreno-Brid, and Peres (this volume) for a more detailed discussion of FDI in different manufacturing activities and these activities' subsequent growth performance.

automobile firms, reacting to the NAFTA's strict rules of origin, established facilities in Mexico to produce for an expanded North American market.[41] There was, moreover, some indication that the expanded automobile production encouraged by the NAFTA had promoted joint ventures and production clusters that allow independent Mexican auto parts producers to gain expanded access to the capital and technology necessary to produce export-competitive products (Vega and De la Mora, this volume).

Similarly, the new opportunities for electronics exports (including color televisions, computers, and computer parts) under the NAFTA encouraged transnational companies to expand their production facilities in Mexico. As a result, cities such as Tijuana and Mexicali in Baja California and Guadalajara in the state of Jalisco became major nodes in the global electronics industry. Over time, foreign firms also transferred some of their research and development activities to Mexico. By the year 2000, the electronics sector accounted for almost one-third of Mexico's total trade.

Under the NAFTA integration process, Mexico also relied heavily upon inputs imported from the United States to become the leading supplier of textile and apparel products to the U.S. market.[42] As Gary Gereffi argues in his chapter in this volume, this development reflected an important process of industrial upgrading. Mexican producers' prior participation in assembly networks (using imported inputs to produce clothing) provided them with knowledge about the price, quality, and delivery standards used in international markets and experience in working with the other manufacturers, trading companies, and brokers forming part of the global apparel commodity chain. Over time, the most successful Mexican textile and apparel firms moved into full-package production, in which they undertake all operations from spinning and weaving through apparel production and finishing. A few Mexican firms have gone even further, taking initial steps toward the creation of their own brand-name products in selected apparel categories.

As important as the NAFTA has been in the transformation of Mexico's industrial profile and to comparatively rapid (though notably un-

---

[41] These latter companies included BMW and Honda. By the late 1990s the automobile industry had become Mexico's most important manufacturing activity. The principal vehicle and engine manufacturers employed more than 500,000 people (Gereffi, this volume).

[42] See Gereffi (this volume, table 6.6) for a detailed assessment of developments in the Mexican textile industry as leading U.S. firms relocated part of their global production to Mexico.

even) economic recovery after the devastating 1994–1995 financial crisis, it should be noted that the country's export successes were based in part upon what had been achieved through decades of import-substitution industrialization. Based on this prior industrialization process, Mexico entered the free-trade era with an experienced workforce and a substantial infrastructure for manufacturing production. As a result, some of the most dynamic economic activities under ISI became the principal sources of manufactured exports during the 1990s.[43]

Perhaps the best illustration of this point is the automobile industry (finished vehicles and auto parts), which had been a central policy focus of successive presidential administrations' efforts to "deepen" import substitution industrialization. In particular, a series of governmental decrees (issued in 1962, 1972, 1977, 1983, and 1989) sought to increase the local content of finished vehicles by, for example, encouraging transnational firms to make engines and transmissions in Mexico and lower the industry's perennial trade deficit (Gereffi, this volume). Building upon these earlier developments, the automobile industry became a star performer under the post–NAFTA free-trade regime. By the late 1990s it accounted for more than 11 percent of Mexico's manufacturing product, 22 percent of total manufactured exports, and some 20 percent of all exports. Vehicles and auto parts represented the largest single component of NAFTA trade (Vega and De la Mora, this volume).

Not all aspects of Mexico's move toward export-oriented production have been an unqualified success. Throughout the 1990s the maquiladora industry was the fastest growing part of the manufacturing sector. In 1999 it was responsible for 46.7 percent of Mexico's total exports (Dussel Peters, this volume, table 7.4), and by January 2001 there were 1.31 million people employed in 3,713 maquiladora plants.[44] As noted

---

[43] See Ros 1994: 96–97 and table 3.4, and Dussel Peters (this volume), table 7.6. The measurements of structural economic change performed by Máttar, Moreno-Brid, and Peres (this volume) show considerable continuity in the industrial branches that most increased their share of GDP in the 1970–1981 and 1984–1994 periods, further indicating the importance of Mexico's industrialization experience prior to trade liberalization.

[44] These data are from the Instituto Nacional de Estadística, Geografía e Informática's (INEGI) Web site (www.inegi.gob.mx). Both total employment and the number of maquiladora plants fell over the course of 2001 as a consequence of the economic slowdown in the United States.

In the year 2000, maquiladora workers represented approximately 30 percent of total manufacturing employment in fixed establishments (Salas and Zepeda, this volume).

Under the terms of the NAFTA, the special tariff exemptions (inputs, regardless of their origin, could be imported duty free so long as all production was ex-

above, there was some evidence that leading foreign firms in the industry were transferring more complex manufacturing operations and (in a few cases) research and design activities to their Mexican plants. Nevertheless, the industry remained very heavily dependent upon U.S. imports for assembly and re-export to the U.S. market; indeed, in 2001 domestically produced goods represented only 3.6 percent of the raw material inputs used in maquiladora production.[45] As a consequence, although the export of technologically sophisticated goods by maquiladoras demonstrated that Mexico had laid some of the groundwork for more profitable integration into the global economy (Máttar, Moreno-Brid, and Peres, this volume), the links between export-oriented manufacturing and other parts of the Mexican economy often remained weak.[46]

Among other consequences, Mexico's emergence as a major exporter of manufactures has altered the country's center of economic gravity. Export-oriented firms have gained new political leverage from their position as the principal engine of national economic growth. The result has been greater segmentation in the economy between export-oriented companies with access to foreign capital markets and ties to leading transnational enterprises, and smaller firms that remain focused on the domestic market and face significant credit and technological constraints.[47]

Similarly, the center-north and northern states that were the main sites of the rapidly growing maquiladora industry or were otherwise closely linked to the U.S. economy were among the most economically dynamic regions in Mexico during the 1990s. Gustavo Garza's detailed analysis (this volume) of disparities across states in the distribution of population and gross domestic product does not support the strong

---

ported) that initially fueled the maquiladora industry's growth ended on January 1, 2001. Since then, only Canadian- and U.S.-origin imports can be imported into Mexico free of duty. However, defensive lobbying by the industry won the extension of comparable benefits in some activities, especially electrical and electronic products. See Federal Reserve Bank of Dallas 2001: 4–5 for details.

[45] Domestic inputs as a proportion of total inputs averaged 2.2 percent over the 1991–2000 period; authors' calculation based upon data from the INEGI Web site (www.inegi.gob.mx).

[46] Moreover, Carlos Salas and Eduardo Zepeda (this volume) show that, with the important exception of large manufacturing firms in the late 1990s, the link between export performance and employment creation was also somewhat tenuous during the economic reform period. See Dussel Peters (this volume) for further discussion of this point.

[47] See Dussel Peters (this volume) and Máttar, Moreno-Brid, and Peres (this volume).

claims that some observers have made about the rapidly polarizing regional effects of economic liberalization in Mexico. His overall conclusion is that major changes in the distribution of population and economic wealth occur quite slowly, generally over a period of decades. For this reason, despite some decrease in regional disparities between 1970 and 1988 as economic crisis weakened the Mexico City metropolitan area's industrial base, at the end of the 1990s the traditionally dominant Center-East region[48] still accounted for 41.7 percent of national production, with the Federal District and the State of México alone concentrating over a third of Mexico's industrial production.

Nonetheless, Garza does observe that during the 1993-1999 period three states on the Mexico–U.S. border (Baja California, Chihuahua, and Coahuila) grew faster than the national average, perhaps suggesting that over the longer term the stimulus of North American economic integration and the concentration of export production in these areas will produce significant changes in the national distribution of population and wealth.[49] He concludes that Monterrey and the surrounding area (including the cities of Saltillo, Nuevo Laredo, Reynosa, and Matamoros) may become a particularly important pole of economic growth.

Institutional and Political Consequences of Economic Liberalization

Although this discussion so far has focused mainly on the economic consequences of market-oriented reforms, it is important to note that not all the transformations attributable to economic liberalization occurred in the economic sphere. There were important institutional and sociopolitical effects as well. For instance, the Salinas administration's efforts to control inflation, bolster foreign investor confidence (Maxfield 1997), and prevent its legacy of economic orthodoxy from being undermined by "populist" opponents (Boylan 2001) prompted a constitutional reform that increased the Banco de México's autonomy. Institu-

---

[48] This region comprises the Federal District and the states of Hidalgo, México, Morelos, Puebla, Querétaro, and Tlaxcala.

[49] Garza shows that the six northern border states' (Baja California, Chihuahua, Coahuila, Nuevo León, Sonora, and Tamaulipas) share of GDP decreased from 21.1 to 20.6 percent between 1970 and 1988 but then rose from 21.4 to 23.3 percent between 1993 and 1999. These states' share of both the national population and the urban population also remained essentially constant over the 1970–1995 period.

For a case study of the NAFTA's limited impact on Oaxaca, one of Mexico's lagging states, see Tamayo-Flores 2001.

tional changes of this kind were not always part of the original design for market-oriented reform, nor were they necessarily introduced voluntarily. It was, for example, strong pressure from foreign investors in the wake of the 1994–1995 peso crisis that compelled government officials to demonstrate greater transparency in the publication of official statistics concerning government financial reserves.

In political terms, it is certainly not accurate to conclude that economic opening inevitably promoted political democratization in Mexico. Economic liberalization had multiple, sometimes contradictory, and still poorly understood political consequences, some of which reinforced rather than undermined authoritarian rule. The main thrust of pro-democracy struggles during the 1990s — the effort by opposition parties to ensure transparent, fair elections — generally proceeded quite autonomously from developments in the economic realm. If anything, it was *resistance* to structural adjustment policies and the market-oriented reform project and the new model's *failures* that contributed to the unraveling of the postrevolutionary governing coalition and Mexico's durable authoritarian regime. In particular, the 1994–1995 financial crisis and its lingering effects on incomes, poverty levels, and public expectations concerning the PRI's performance in government contributed directly to the "official" party's accelerating electoral decline and its loss of control over the federal Chamber of Deputies and the Federal District government in 1997 and the presidency in the year 2000.

Nevertheless, one might also argue that economic liberalization, especially when viewed over the longer term, had a number of significant, often unintended sociopolitical effects that contributed to political opening. At the elite level, the De la Madrid and Salinas administrations' economic reforms created new lines of division within the ruling coalition, thereby strengthening the party-based political opposition. In the countryside, the Salinas administration officially suspended land distribution and largely eliminated a complex system of price supports and production credits, thus reducing the state's economic presence in a way that weakened the PRI's clientelist networks and perhaps undercut its traditional bases of rural electoral support.[50] Similarly, constrained state resources, industrial restructuring at the firm level, and the relentless political hostility of technocratic reformers undercut the position of the traditionally dominant CTM and encouraged the emergence of rival labor groups like the National Union of Workers (UNT).

---

[50] For a succinct overview of economic reforms in the Mexican countryside, see Pastor and Wise 1998: 63–70. Randall 1996 presents a more detailed assessment of the potential implications of the reform to Article 27.

Although the main outcome of this process was more an overall weakening of the labor movement than an upturn in independent worker organization, pro-government union leaders' declining control over patronage resources may well have undermined workers' support at the polls for PRI candidates.

More generally, reducing the state's role in economic affairs contributed to greater pluralism in state-society relations, and it implicitly questioned the legitimacy of the state's long-dominant position vis-à-vis organized social forces. Although it is important not to exaggerate the dimensions of this phenomenon, the resulting change in public expectations may have encouraged the emergence of a more densely textured, more autonomous civil society in which interest groups gradually mobilized to demand increased political representation and greater accountability on the part of governmental authorities.[51] However, this was a contradictory process because, over time, economic restructuring also undermined social structures and organizational networks that had sustained popular mobilizations in earlier periods.

Finally, Mexico's new economic strategy had important effects on the country's foreign relations. In the early 1990s Mexico negotiated a landmark free-trade agreement with Canada and the United States, and in 1994 it became a member of the Organisation for Economic Co-operation and Development (OECD) and the World Trade Organization (WTO). Through these initiatives, economic reformers sought to institutionalize market-oriented policies and bolster private investors' confidence that the country would not revert to the protectionist policies of the past. At the same time, they sought the long-term access to markets in industrialized countries that would permit Mexico to reap the full benefits of openness. Indeed, during the 1990s Mexico negotiated comprehensive (versus sector-by-sector) free-trade agreements with an increasingly diverse set of countries in Latin America, Europe, and elsewhere.[52]

---

[51] For an overall assessment of changes in civil society during the 1980s and 1990s, see Olvera 2001.

One part of this process has been the emergence (albeit with considerable unevenness and uncertain impact) of transnational civil society coalitions linking sociopolitical actors in Canada and the United States with those in Mexico. The original catalyst for this development was debate over a proposed North American free-trade agreement in the early 1990s. The most important such coalitions have focused on indigenous rights and citizenship issues, workers' rights, women's rights, and environmental defense. For a stimulating examination of these developments and their implications, see Brooks and Fox 2002.

[52] By the year 2000, Mexico had negotiated free-trade agreements with nine Latin American countries (Bolivia, Chile, Colombia, Costa Rica, El Salvador, Guate-

North American economic integration had a particularly marked impact upon Mexico's relations with the United States. During the administrations of Carlos Salinas de Gortari and Ernesto Zedillo Ponce de León (1994–2000), and especially under President Vicente Fox Quesada (2000–2006), Mexico moved away from its traditionally defensive posture vis-à-vis the United States. Foreign policy elites in both countries took steps toward defining a more equitable relationship appropriate to long-term economic and strategic partners. During the 1990s, for example, the Mexican and U.S. governments made further efforts to institutionalize the conduct of bilateral relations via mechanisms that bring together cabinet-level officials on a regular basis. There were still tensions in bilateral relations over drug trafficking and other sensitive matters (including the implementation of some NAFTA provisions). However, closer economic ties did slowly redefine expectations concerning the mutual importance of the relationship, permitting Mexican foreign policy leaders to introduce previously excluded topics such as immigration onto the bilateral negotiating agenda.

UNRESOLVED CHALLENGES OF MEXICAN DEVELOPMENT

Despite the positive transformations associated with economic liberalization, Mexico continues to face a number of serious development problems. This section draws upon contributors' essays to outline key challenges posed by sluggish growth and the continuing risk of macroeconomic instability; financial-sector weakness and uneven capital formation; inequality, wage stagnation, and poverty; and pressing educational and social welfare needs. Rather than provide a detailed summary of contributors' analyses, the goal here is to highlight points of overarching consensus on these topics.

Sluggish Growth and Risks of Macroeconomic Instability

The strongest single indictment of Mexico's new economic model is that it has not produced robust growth. There were short periods of relatively rapid economic expansion in 1989–1992 and 1996–2000.[53]

---

mala, Honduras, Nicaragua, Venezuela) and with the European Union, Iceland, Israel, Liechtenstein, Norway, and Switzerland. See Vega and De la Mora (this volume) for a discussion of Mexico's extensive network of bilateral investment agreements.

[53] Alejandro Nadal (this volume) cautions that these short periods of more rapid growth were accompanied by serious external imbalances, and that Mexico's current account did not achieve a surplus at any time during the 1990s.

However, in inflation-adjusted terms, gross domestic product rose at an average rate of just 2.7 percent per year over the two decades between 1981 and 2000. Even if one excludes the 1982–1988 period and the worst effects of the 1982 debt crisis, the average real annual growth rate between 1989 and 2000 was only 3.7 percent.[54] Real gross domestic product per capita rose by an average of merely 0.4 percent per year between 1981 and 2000 and only 1.3 percent per year during the 1991–2000 period. This record compares very unfavorably with the 6.4 percent average annual increase in real GDP and 3.3 percent increase in real GDP per capita that Mexico achieved during the 1951–1980 period (Urquidi, this volume, table 15.1).

The causes of Mexico's sluggish economic performance are complex, but as Alejandro Nadal observes in his essay in this volume, one important reason is that during the 1980s and 1990s successive governments made control of inflation their principal policy objective.[55] In their efforts to restore macroeconomic stability and thereby regain the confidence of foreign investors and international creditors, government officials adopted highly restrictive monetary and fiscal policies. Large national conglomerates engaged in export production were less severely affected by these policies because they received earnings in foreign currencies and could secure financing in international capital markets. But the combination of high domestic interest rates (necessary to attract the short-term capital flows required to cover the trade deficit that accompanied the shift to an export-oriented economy, as well as to control inflation), a scarcity of investment capital to facilitate economic adjustment at the firm level, and increased foreign competition resulting from trade liberalization, all had a devastating effect upon the midsize and small businesses that, in the aggregate, constitute a significant proportion of the domestic economy and a major source of employment growth (Urquidi, this volume). Severely depressed wages further reduced domestic demand,[56] while tight budgetary constraints prevented the public sector from leading the capital formation process as it had done during Mexico's import-substitution period. Although private capital flowed to faster-growing export activities, businesses focused

---

[54] Authors' calculations based upon data presented in Nadal (this volume), table 2.1. In conjunction with an economic downturn in the United States, GDP fell by 0.3 percent in 2001.

[55] See Nadal (this volume) for a discussion of the different policy instruments (including an overvalued exchange rate, which makes imports cheaper) that government economic decision makers employed in the struggle against inflation.

[56] Private consumption as a proportion of final demand fell from 62.0 percent in 1989 to 50.7 percent in 2000 (Nadal, this volume).

primarily on the stagnant domestic market (including most of the agricultural sector) were starved for investment.

Moreover, as Enrique Dussel Peters and several other contributors to this volume show, weak linkages between the manufactured-export sector and those economic activities focused primarily on the domestic market have prevented export expansion from generating rapid, sustained growth in the economy as a whole.[57] For example, Vega and De la Mora (this volume), while stressing the positive contributions that trade policy and a new export orientation have made to the Mexican economy, recognize that backward linkages with other activities need to be stronger if the domestic productive structure is eventually to become as dynamic as the export sector. In assessing the causes of these weak linkages, Vega and De la Mora, Dussel Peters, and other contributors note that rapid trade liberalization was not accompanied by sufficient governmental attention to tailored policies that might have permitted highly protected sectors to adapt more effectively to increased foreign competition.[58]

Economic stagnation has been a particularly persistent problem in the agricultural and livestock sector. The sector was lagging well before trade liberalization began in the mid–1980s, but this problem has been greatly exacerbated by intense import competition and a sharp fall-off in public-sector investment, production subsidies, price supports, and so forth. The NAFTA formally included an exceptional fifteen-year transition period for maize and beans, a provision designed to provide Mexican farmers more time in which to prepare to compete with more

[57] In his comparison of the Mexican and East Asian development experiences, Clark W. Reynolds (this volume) observes that, like Mexico, China also has an uneven pattern of economic development. One of the main differences between the Mexican and Chinese cases, however, is that the one-fifth of the Chinese population that has benefited significantly from economic opening and export-led growth constitutes a domestic market "large enough to promote economies of scale and to generate growth and capital accumulation even without the diffusion of development." Even so, Reynolds notes that in the late 1990s Chinese decision makers began to modify major policies in order to bolster backward regions and the domestic market.

[58] Vega and De la Mora primarily attribute this failing to a lack of adequate state administrative capacity to develop and implement such policies—especially insufficient state autonomy to guide national firms while at the same time avoiding "pressures from rent-seeking groups calling for privileges and protection." Dussel Peters, in turn, argues that key architects of Mexico's liberalization strategy were strongly opposed to anything other than sector-neutral policies. The limited industrial promotion initiatives undertaken during the 1990s were generally designed to be self-financing and involved small government budgetary commitments.

efficient, generally more highly capitalized grain producers in Canada and the United States. However, in practice the Mexican government reduced tariff and nontariff barriers to maize imports much more rapidly than the NAFTA provisions required, with very negative consequences for many small-scale and midsize agricultural producers. As a consequence of policies such as these, trade opening accentuated dualism in Mexican agriculture—providing growth and employment opportunities in a comparatively small number of export-oriented agribusinesses (several thousand firms exporting fruits, vegetables, and some livestock), while forcing many less efficient producers out of business and contributing to further stagnation of the rural economy.

These trends are important for two reasons. First, as both Hubert C. de Grammont and Clark W. Reynolds observe in their contributions to this volume, from the 1940s through the 1960s the agricultural and livestock sector provided both staple foods for the urban population and inputs for industry, thus making important contributions to Mexican economic development. With adequate investment and sufficient access to technology and marketing skills, it could potentially do so again—as a source of staple foods, raw materials for manufacturing, and foreign exchange earnings, and, especially, as a continuing source of economic livelihood for rural communities.[59] As Reynolds argues, the experiences of several East Asian countries indicate the important long-term returns to be derived from a productive agricultural sector and more equitable integration of backward rural areas into the national economy.

Second, the countryside remains important in aggregate economic terms. In 1995, the agricultural and livestock sector accounted for 6.4 percent of Mexico's GDP, and agroindustry (food products, beverages, and tobacco) represented another 31.3 percent, for a combined 37.7 percent of GDP. Similarly, in 1997 agriculture and livestock raising employed over nine million people, 24.1 percent of total national employment (C. de Grammont, this volume). Therefore, even though it may be

---

[59] See C. de Grammont (this volume) for an overview of the agricultural and livestock sector's growing problems during the 1970s and 1980s and government policies during the 1990s. For a discussion of changing production strategies in the Mexican countryside, see Rodríguez Gómez and Snyder 2000.

Migrant remittances are an important economic phenomenon, and at times they provide the main source of income for poor rural communities. Hubert C. de Grammont (this volume) notes that in some developing countries small credit and savings institutions have provided important sources of capitalization in rural areas. Institutions such as these might draw upon remittances to help meet the agricultural and livestock sector's financial needs. However, both federal and state governments and nongovernmental organizations would need to be actively involved in establishing such arrangements.

more stylish to focus on such topics as the increasing technological so-
phistication of Mexico's manufactured exports, the agricultural and
livestock sector remains too important in employment terms (especially
in the many smaller cities and towns that do not host major manufacturing facilities) to be ignored.[60]

Beyond the question of aggregate growth rates and the performance
of key sectors, there remains concern about the risk of renewed macroeconomic instability in Mexico. The potential sources of instability lie
not only in the economy's openness and its consequent vulnerability to
international financial shocks, but also in such areas as Mexico's heavy
dependence upon the U.S. market and the uncertainty of growth and
interest rate trends in the United States. Future difficulties might also
arise because of the very substantial cost of servicing the country's total
(domestic and foreign) public debt—including the huge burden that the
post-1995 bank rescue will continue to impose on domestic financial
balances—and because of a persistent trade deficit. The trade deficit is
an especially troubling problem because it is embedded in the pattern
of industrialization and export promotion that Mexico has adopted.[61]

Financial System Weakness and Capital Scarcity

There is widespread agreement among the contributors to this volume
that the weakness of Mexico's financial system constitutes a fundamental constraint on the country's future development prospects. A
shortage of capital for productive investments (versus short-term investments in the Mexican stock market) has been a near-constant problem ever since the debt crisis of the 1980s. Moreover, as Celso Garrido
demonstrates in his chapter in this book, this situation worsened significantly as a consequence of the country's 1994–1995 financial crisis.
The problematic terms of the post-1995 bank bailout—especially the
larger-than-anticipated amount of delinquent loans that resulted from
adopting more rigorous standards for the accounting of nonperforming
assets, and government policies that protected bank assets but deprived
banks of liquidity and the incentive to reinitiate lending to businesses
and individuals—had particularly important longer-term implications.

---

[60] In 1990 agriculture was the main source of employment for localities with fewer
than 10,000 inhabitants; it was the third most important economic activity in localities with from 10,000 to 49,999 inhabitants (C. de Grammont, this volume, table 10.11).

[61] Dussel Peters (this volume) argues that Mexico's persistent trade deficit represents a major threat to the liberalization model's macroeconomic viability.

Although the 1994–1995 crisis had significant nonfinancial costs,[62] the main point is that the post–1995 bank bailout saddled the economy with a huge fiscal burden.[63] Servicing a greatly expanded public-sector debt absorbs a substantial proportion of government revenues, an outcome with serious consequences for the public sector's capacity to undertake needed investment and address social needs. In the year 2000, for example, total interest payments on domestic debt surpassed expenditures on education and health care combined (Nadal, this volume). By raising the demand for public funds, the bank bailout also negatively affected private financing and slowed domestic economic recovery. This outcome, when combined with large external debt obligations even after the successful rescheduling of Mexico's foreign debt in 1989, meant that Mexico began the twenty-first century with a significant proportion of its financial resources devoted to servicing its domestic and external public-sector debt. Indeed, interest payments on total (domestic and foreign) public-sector debt in 2000 were equivalent to income tax revenues or receipts from oil and gas sales, and they were 1.8 times greater than investment in plant and equipment (Nadal, this volume).

This situation has direct consequences for Mexico's future growth prospects and the economy's capacity to generate more and better-paid jobs. As Carlos Salas and Eduardo Zepeda indicate in their chapter in this volume, one of Mexico's persistent development challenges has been to create more employment. By the late 1990s, the high population growth rates of past decades had produced a huge potential labor supply (people between the ages of 15 and 64).[64] The rapid expansion in the number of people holding low-productivity, low-paying jobs in the urban service sector in part reflected the incapacity of manufacturing industry and economic activities such as construction, commerce, and communications to absorb the available labor supply. Indeed, both employment in large manufacturing plants as a proportion of total manu-

---

[62] Celso Garrido (this volume) notes the nonfinancial costs (especially the degrading of financial firms' institutional capabilities) of Mexican banks' repeated bankruptcies and the cycle of nationalization, privatization, and de facto re-nationalization that they have experienced since 1982. Moreover, as a result of the 1994–1995 crisis, some of Mexico's largest industrial conglomerates lost their financial divisions and an important means of generating financing for their operations.

[63] In 2001, the liabilities of the Bank Savings Protection Institute (IPAB, the agency that inherited the promissory notes issued in exchange for banks' nonperforming loans) totaled US$74 billion.

[64] Women's increasing involvement in economic activities outside the home was an especially important factor in Mexico's sharply higher labor force participation rates (Salas and Zepeda, this volume).

facturing employment, and the proportion of wage earners in the total employed population, declined substantially during the 1990s.[65] As a consequence, Mexican workers lost both wage income and access to the important fringe benefits (health insurance, paid holidays, bonuses, and so forth) that wage-earning occupations—and especially jobs in large manufacturing firms—typically provide.[66]

The agricultural and livestock sector provides another telling example of the negative consequences of credit scarcity. Drastic cuts in federal government spending (including public investments, production subsidies, and price supports) during the 1980s led to severe financial distress in the countryside, and agricultural loan delinquencies increased sharply. In the period between 1987 and 1994—even before Mexico's 1994–1995 financial crisis—overdue loans jumped from 1.4 percent to 7.6 percent of sectoral GDP. By 1997, overdue loans represented 33.5 percent of all credits granted to agricultural and livestock producers. Even more important in terms of the sector's longer-term productive capacity, the land area planted with the support of bank financing fell dramatically from the late 1980s through the 1990s (C. de Grammont, this volume). A principal justification for the reform of Article 27 and the redefinition of land tenure arrangements was to give producers clear title to their land so that, on the basis of secure collateral, private commercial banks would have greater incentives to lend in rural areas. Yet with the exception of a comparatively small number of agro-export firms, private banks have not filled the financing gap created by the withdrawal of state development banks.

Inequality, Wage Stagnation, and Poverty

One of the most disappointing aspects of Mexico's development experience during the 1980s and 1990s was the failure of economic reform policies to improve the living standards of large portions of the population. Serious problems of poverty and inequality existed prior to this period, and it is not surprising that this situation worsened during the post–1982 period of deep recession and structural adjustment. Nevertheless, there is powerful evidence that the central characteristics of

---

[65] In their comparative assessment of the impact of economic reforms in Latin America and the Caribbean, Stallings and Peres (2000: chap. 5) found that market-oriented development strategies were not very successful at generating employment, especially in labor-intensive activities. However, they did note (pp. 196–97) that there was a relative increase in labor-intensive employment in Mexico following economic liberalization.

[66] See Salas and Zepeda (this volume) and De Oliveira and García 1997.

Mexico's new economic model—especially macroeconomic policies that depressed real wages and aggregate demand in order to control inflation, relatively modest employment creation in export-oriented sectors of the economy, and changes in government social welfare policies that reduced public-sector health care and social security benefits—seriously aggravated these problems.[67] Indeed, in his contribution to this volume, Julio Boltvinik concludes that "greater inequality is intrinsic to Mexico's new development model."

In the course of his detailed assessment of the evolution of inequality, poverty, and welfare in Mexico, Boltvinik (this volume) shows that income inequality grew considerably from the mid-1980s through the year 2000 (worsening systematically from 1984 to 1994, improving temporarily during the 1994–1996 period, and then worsening again through the year 2000).[68] Income distribution in Mexico had improved consistently between 1963 and 1984, but the Gini coefficient of total (monetary and non-monetary) income rose from 0.429 in 1984 to 0.481 in the year 2000 (Boltvinik, this volume, table 11.3).[69] What is most disturbing in this regard is that income concentration grew during periods of both economic stagnation (1984–1989) and growth (1989–1994 and 1996–2000).

Boltvinik distinguishes systematically between changes in income poverty and trends affecting what he labels "specific poverties" (that is, deprivation in specific needs). He argues that the overall social welfare of an individual or a household derives from multiple sources—current income, basic assets such as housing and consumer durable goods, an individual's or a household's borrowing capacity, access to publicly provided goods and services (including household services such as piped-in water, sewerage, and electricity; education; health care; and social security), free time, and knowledge—and that these factors may evolve independently of one another. Making these distinctions is important because Boltvinik's analysis demonstrates that there was, in fact, both an *increase* in income poverty and a *reduction* in specific poverties during the 1980s. During the 1990s, income poverty fluctu-

---

[67] See Székely 1998; Boltvinik and Hernández Laos 2000; and Cortés 2000.

[68] Boltvinik reports that inequality decreased in the 1994–1996 period because, while incomes generally fell as a result of the 1994–1995 economic crisis, the decline was greatest for the tenth (richest) decile. For further analyses of changes in income inequality, see Hernández Laos 2000b, De la Torre 2000, and Hernández Laos and Velázquez Roa 2002.

[69] In their evaluation of Mexico's recent development experience, Griffin and Ickowitz (this volume) note that, in the World Bank's 1999 assessment of income distribution in 96 countries, only 12 countries had a more unequal distribution of income than did Mexico.

ated, while educational, living space, and housing services poverties decreased at a rate that was slower than in the 1970s but faster than in the 1980s.[70] Over the entire 1981–2000 period, however, most opportunities for social welfare declined, leaving the majority of Mexicans less well off in the year 2000 than they had been two decades earlier.[71]

Boltvinik's findings underscore the central impact of government policy on poverty and welfare trends in Mexico. Wage policy has been particularly important in this regard. The same political and administrative controls that permitted government decision makers considerable flexibility in implementing economic stabilization measures and pursuing far-reaching economic reform hamstrung workers and their organizations in efforts to defend wages and fringe benefits, employment levels, working conditions, and so forth. Despite the fact that a larger number of workers were using improved technologies, were employed in internationally competitive firms, and had links to the global economy, Mexican workers generally lost economic ground from the mid–1980s through the 1990s. Salas and Zepeda (this volume) conclude that

> During the 1980s, average real wages decreased dramatically in a twofold process of reduced income per capita and a more concentrated distribution of income. Wages as a proportion of national income collapsed as the per capita net wage fell and the number of people in wage-earning positions decreased. The recovery of a growth trajectory in the early 1990s presented an opportunity to reverse these deteriorating trends, and real wage levels did improve. However, wage gains were not equal for all workers, and most of what was gained was lost again in the 1994–1995 crisis.

Beyond the obvious social welfare costs for those directly affected by these negative trends, wage stagnation for the majority of workers and

---

[70] Social security poverty was the principal exception to the overall pattern of declining specific poverties during the 1990s; it rose during the first half of the 1990s and was stagnant for the 1989–1999 period as a whole (Boltvinik, this volume). This pattern resulted from both a decline in Mexican Social Security Institute (IMSS) coverage and processes of industrial restructuring that deprived many workers of permanent employment status (and thus mandatory social security coverage). For analyses of these developments, see the chapters in this volume by Boltvinik and Asa Cristina Laurell.

[71] Total consumption per adult equivalent was essentially stagnant over the 1981–2000 period. Only educational levels improved somewhat.

growing informal-sector employment prevented the domestic market from becoming a factor in propelling economic growth.[72]

Yet at the same time that government wage policy contributed to significant increases in income poverty and inequality, Boltvinik argues that other government policies during the 1980s and 1990s prevented a potentially much worse deterioration in general social well-being and mortality rates among younger age groups. Boltvinik's data indicate that real public social expenditures per capita did not fall substantially during the 1980s, and that they grew gradually in the 1990s—albeit at a pace that was slower than in the 1970s.[73]

These conclusions regarding the joint impact of economic and social policies on welfare are strongly supported by Diana Alarcón's comparative assessment (this volume) of the Costa Rican and Chilean development experiences. Alarcón emphasizes that "macroeconomic policy affects not only the rate of economic growth, but also the distribution of the benefits of growth across economic sectors and social groups." Furthermore, she insists that the degree of coherence between macroeconomic and social policies is the key to promoting equitable development over the longer term. Macroeconomic policy determines the economic opportunities available to the poor; social policy plays a vital role in incorporating the poor into the growth process by increasing their access to productive assets and the productivity of those assets.

In her examination of the Costa Rican and Chilean cases, Alarcón shows that, even though the incidence of poverty increased sharply in both countries as a result of economic crisis and structural adjustment, poverty levels eventually fell substantially because broad-based processes of economic growth both generated new employment and benefited those sectors and population groups where poverty was concentrated. Governments in both countries promoted labor-intensive economic activities, increased the poor's access to productive assets, and invested in infrastructure and human capabilities that raised productivity levels in sectors relevant to the poor. As a result, they were rela-

---

[72] Salas and Zepeda (this volume) point out that data on average wage trends obscure sharp contrasts between different segments of the labor force, and they report evidence on increasing wage differentials in the late 1980s and early 1990s. These differences are an important part of the growing income inequality that has characterized Mexico since the 1980s.

[73] Boltvinik (this volume), figure 11.3. Boltvinik notes that the government achieved adjustment in education and health services by depressing the real wages of teachers, doctors, nurses, and other personnel, rather than by reducing the volume of employment and services.

For a different assessment of social spending patterns during the 1980s, see Lustig 1998: table 3.7.

tively successful in ensuring that gains from expanded export production were distributed throughout the economy.

In assessing the prospects for poverty reduction in Mexico, the analyses by Alarcón and by Keith Griffin and Amy Ickowitz (this volume) place special emphasis on developments affecting agriculture and the rural economy. Griffin and Ickowitz stress that poverty in Mexico is increasingly a rural phenomenon, noting that in 1994 some 79 percent of the poor lived in rural areas.[74] Achieving a sustained reduction in poverty and inequality will, therefore, require viable means of reducing segmentation in the agricultural and livestock sector (by stimulating nontraditional exports and ensuring that the benefits of export production are distributed more evenly throughout the rural economy) and generating productive employment in rural areas.[75] Here again, Alarcón's (this volume) comparative analysis of the Costa Rican and Chilean experiences shows that effective action against rural poverty was a crucial element in these countries' overall poverty reduction efforts. In Costa Rica, for example, there was a decline in the incidence of poverty during the 1980s mainly because of the economic gains made by producers of nontraditional agricultural products.

The severity and persistence of inequality and poverty in Mexico raise crucially important questions concerning the efficacy of government economic and social policies, including those specifically designed to eliminate extreme poverty. Among the contributors to this volume, Alarcón and Ana Cristina Laurell undertake overall assessments of Mexico's two most prominent poverty reduction schemes, the Salinas administration's National Solidarity Program (PRONASOL) and the Zedillo administration's Program for Education, Health, and Nutrition (PROGRESA). As both authors indicate, there has been much debate about how best to target appropriate beneficiaries, about whether partisan political interests were more important than objective needs in determining the distribution of PRONASOL and PROGRESA funds, and, more generally, about how effective and cost-efficient such targeted programs have been in reducing extreme poverty and regional disparities.[76] Their principal conclusions, however, are that targeted

---

[74] In a similar vein, Diana Alarcón (this volume) reports that 64.1 percent of Mexico's rural population was poor in 1997.

[75] Of course, the lack of well-paid employment opportunities in agriculture has other implications as well. Rural poverty is a principal stimulus for out-migration to urban areas in Mexico and to other countries, especially the United States.

[76] For discussions of the different assumptions underlying Mexico's "old" and "new" poverty agendas, see Boltvinik (this volume) and Laurell (this volume). For analyses of the impact of partisan political considerations on PRONASOL and PROGRESA, see, respectively, Molinar Horcasitas and Weldon 1994 and Rocha

poverty programs (and the comparatively modest resources they command) can at best have only a limited effect. The focus and social consequences of economic policies—especially their success in achieving sustained growth and the ways in which the urban and rural poor are integrated into growth sectors—are far more important in terms of their impact upon national levels of well-being and trends in poverty, income distribution, and regional inequality.

Educational and Social Welfare Challenges

Educational Policy

The quality of Mexico's national education system and its capacity to serve the needs of a heterogeneous population will be crucial determinants of the country's longer-term economic and social development. Although Mexico made considerable progress during the 1980s and 1990s in improving access to primary education,[77] secondary and higher education coverage remained much more limited. In 1997, for example, 56.6 percent of the 15- to 19-year-old population had a complete (six-year) primary education, and another 41.2 percent had an incomplete primary education. Of this same age group, 27.5 percent had completed an additional three years of middle school, and 2.5 percent had a higher (university) education (INEGI 2000: 34).[78] There is still much to be done, then, to lay the educational groundwork for Mexicans' more effective competition in the global economy and meaningful citizen participation in a democratic society.

In their assessment of middle (secondary) and higher education policies during the 1990s, Lorenza Villa Lever and Roberto Rodríguez Gómez (this volume) emphasize the importance of education in a "knowledge society," in which science and technology inform almost all areas of life and knowledge becomes the key force behind economic growth and social cohesion. They note, however, that both resource constraints and weak links between the educational and productive

---

Menocal 2001. See Graham 1994 for a comparative evaluation of so-called demand-based social programs.

[77] In their chapter in this volume, Lorenza Villa Lever and Roberto Rodríguez Gómez note that, although by the late 1990s Mexico had achieved nearly universal access to primary education, there were some states (Chiapas, Guerrero, and Oaxaca, all of which were comparatively poor and had substantial indigenous populations) where the primary education system reached less than 60 percent of the eligible population.

[78] Only 2.2 percent of the 15- to 19-year-old population had no education. In the mid–1990s, average schooling in Mexico was 7.9 years (Villa Lever and Rodríguez Gómez, this volume, citing Inter-American Development Bank sources).

systems limit education's impact on economic growth in Mexico. Reforms undertaken during the 1990s focused especially on improving institutional coordination in middle and higher education, making middle-school curricula more flexible, and broadening the educational coverage of university programs. One of the government's most important initiatives was to create a system of two-year technological universities located in midsize cities throughout Mexico. Private institutions came to play an increasingly important role, especially in higher education, and state governments gradually began to share with the federal government some responsibility for planning and financing secondary and university education. Yet overall constraints on government spending limited the resources available to expand and improve education systems. Middle schools still have poor retention capacity, and the quality and relevance of the educational experience are often inadequate. Upgrading teachers' skills remains a particularly serious challenge.

These issues are important not least because of the increasingly strong relationship between educational achievement and earnings in Mexico.[79] The essays in this volume by Salas and Zepeda and by Villa Lever and Rodríguez Gómez both note that, as the structure of economic activity in Mexico changed during the 1980s and 1990s, there were increasing returns to education. During this period, workers who had completed primary school (and even those who had finished junior high school) saw their inflation-adjusted earnings decline, while employees who had completed high school or had some university education made real gains. Labor market and technological shifts thus contributed to a pattern of wage dispersion that favored better-educated employees over those with lower educational levels. Given the obvious implications for longer-term trends in social stratification in Mexico, there is a strong imperative to improve access to, and the quality of, the national secondary and higher education systems.

Social Welfare Policies

Mexico's process of economic reform had major consequences for established social welfare programs. Under the pressures of fiscal adjustment and reduced government subsidies, declining real wages, and stagnating formal-sector employment, public welfare programs experienced significant financial shortfalls during the 1980s. As a result, the Mexican Social Security Institute (IMSS) and the Social Security Institute for State Workers (ISSSTE) — the decentralized state institutions

---

[79] Stallings and Peres (2000: 128, 135) identify similar trends in several Latin American countries.

that were the pillars of Mexico's public health and social welfare systems, together providing coverage for about 55 percent of the national population[80] — experienced a general shortage of resources and a deterioration in the availability and quality of the services they offered. Beyond these considerations, however, Laurell (this volume) argues that Mexico's neoliberal reformers sought to create a new social welfare order by "commodifying" services and benefits. The project envisioned a substantially reduced state role in the provision of social welfare and a correspondingly greater responsibility for individuals and families to fulfill social needs in the marketplace. In this arrangement, most public social welfare activity would be restricted to providing means-tested programs targeted to the extremely poor.

One of the most important social policy departures involved Mexico's pension system. The existing "pay-as-you-go" scheme, which was based on publicly administered common funds with guaranteed annuities, was replaced by individual retirement accounts managed by private financial intermediaries (Retirement Fund Administrators, AFOREs).[81] The reform's main goals were to expand the insured population and increase domestic savings. However, even though the 1995 Social Security Act guaranteed eligible retirees a minimum annuity equal to the minimum wage, the AFORE system reduces beneficiaries' financial security because the amount in the fund varies depending upon the individual's savings and the fund's investment performance. Laurell (this volume) indicates that, even under the most optimistic assumptions about financial market performance and the average time a worker might be employed over her or his lifetime, pension benefits are likely to be lower under the new scheme than the old one. Moreover, because the state must underwrite transition costs (in essence, the value of current annuity obligations, which are no longer covered by contributions from the presently employed) equivalent to as much as 1 to 1.5 percent of GDP per year over a period as long as six decades, Laurell argues that the instauration of the new fully funded private pension scheme "will effect the largest transfer of public funds to private financial groups ever experienced in Mexico."[82]

---

[80] Self-employed and informal-sector workers are excluded from IMSS and ISSSTE coverage.

[81] See Laurell (this volume) for details.

[82] Furthermore, Laurell maintains that in order to protect the value of future annuity payments, the government may need to continue subsidizing the private pension system by ensuring that the funds earn sufficient returns to offset the effects of inflation.

Health services have also been the focus of important reform initiatives. In an effort to introduce market criteria into health care provision, the Zedillo administration promoted changes permitting individuals to choose between public and private health insurance and services. Under the old social security health regime, individuals paid a fixed percentage of their income as a premium and received services according to need; under the new approach, all insured individuals pay the same premium and receive care from public or private managed-care organizations. In principle, all citizens are guaranteed a comprehensive health package. However, Laurell (this volume) expresses concern that the main result will be to make health care provision subject to managed-care providers' financial situation, thereby reducing the availability and quality of health care and intensifying inequalities in health status.

Laurell's overall emphasis is on the contributions to improved social justice in Mexico that were made historically by social security and health care programs providing universal coverage. This aspect of her argument finds support in Boltvinik's conclusion (this volume) that government social spending during periods of economic crisis in the 1980s and mid–1990s prevented an even worse deterioration in the population's well-being (and that reductions in public-sector social security coverage in the 1990s largely explained worsening poverty in this specific area). Similarly, Alarcón's comparative assessment (this volume) of economic and social policy in Chile and Costa Rica shows that long traditions of universal coverage in basic social services were very important elements in explaining the progress these countries made in reducing poverty during the 1990s. These conclusions reaffirm, then, the continuing value of an important element in Mexico's pre-liberalization social policy regime.

ADDRESSING MEXICO'S DEVELOPMENT CHALLENGES: INTERNATIONAL AND DOMESTIC CONSTRAINTS ON POLICY

In assessing the principal economic and social policies that Mexico adopted during the 1980s and 1990s, the contributors to this volume join an expanding effort to evaluate the consequences of economic liberalization in Latin America and the Caribbean.[83] This book is distinctive in that it analyzes in depth the recent development experience of a single Latin American country.[84] Mexico merits such detailed attention

---

[83] Two leading examples of this growing literature are Bulmer-Thomas 1996 and Stallings and Peres 2000.

[84] Although the contributions to this volume cover a wide range of topics, there are a number of important development issues that are not examined here. They include, among others, environmental issues (including air and water pollution,

because of its regional and international importance,[85] because its experience with market-oriented economic reform is longer than that of any other major Latin American country except Chile, and because, in line with the export-oriented industrialization strategy that is the new development orthodoxy in much of the world, it has succeeded in reorganizing its productive structure to make manufactured exports a major focus of economic activity. What links this volume's contributors to more broadly comparative assessments of the impact of economic reform is their general sense that economic liberalization in Mexico, as in Latin America more generally, has failed to produce anticipated gains in economic growth rates, employment levels and job quality, and overall opportunities for social welfare.

This concluding section briefly outlines the international and domestic factors that are likely to influence the formulation and implementation of economic and social policies over the medium term. The discussion specifically examines the impact of political democratization in this regard, and it considers the main lessons that Mexican decision makers should learn from the country's recent experience and — within probable international and domestic constraints — seek to apply to the definition of future development strategies.

The International and Domestic Context

Much has changed both internationally and domestically since Mexico undertook economic liberalization in the mid–1980s, yet some of the most important international constraints on economic and social policy choice remain firmly in place. In the aftermath of the 1982 debt crisis, the shortage of (and conditions attached to) external financing compelled Mexican policy makers to push forward with market-oriented reforms. Two decades later, Mexico hosted the United Nations' International Conference on Financing for Development (held in Monterrey in March 2002), a gathering of political leaders from fifty-one countries; the directors of the World Bank, the International Monetary Fund, the World Trade Organization, and major multilateral development agencies; and representatives of nongovernmental organizations and the private sector. In the official communiqué issued at the close of the Monterrey summit, industrialized countries committed themselves to providing developing nations with expanded financial assistance on

---

land and water use, preservation of natural resources and biodiversity, hazardous waste disposal, and so forth) and energy policy.

[85] Data collected by the International Monetary Fund indicate that in 2001 Mexico was the world's ninth largest economy, ranking ahead of Spain and Brazil; IMF 2001.

more favorable terms. This turn of events suggested considerable evolution in official international views concerning developing countries' economic needs and the financial constraints they face.

Nevertheless, there was no indication at the Monterrey forum that the U.S. government had retreated in any significant way from the core elements of the Washington Consensus concerning the economic policies that developing countries should embrace.[86] Nor has there been any substantial change in the bias that globalized private capital markets hold in favor of orthodox macroeconomic policies. The fact that Mexico's senior economic officials have remained firmly committed to macroeconomic orthodoxy in such matters as avoiding fiscal deficits reflects more than the ideological preferences of particular individuals; rather, this stance indicates the very real limits on policy choice defined by the international environment in which Mexican decision makers operate (affecting, among other things, the amount of foreign exchange reserves that the Mexican government must hold in order to protect the economy from crisis-induced financial volatility). Minimizing these external constraints and defining policies that promote sustained growth, domestic market expansion, and improved income distribution are among the most pressing challenges facing Mexico.

What have changed much more obviously since the mid–1980s are the national political circumstances surrounding the formulation and implementation of development policies. In July 2000, the country's slow, uneven process of political democratization brought the opposition National Action Party to national power, ending seventy-one years of uninterrupted control over the federal executive by the Institutional Revolutionary Party. The election of Vicente Fox as president did not in itself mark the consolidation of democracy in Mexico. Indeed, much remains to be done to eliminate the formal and informal political controls constructed during decades of postrevolutionary authoritarian rule, including legal and administrative restrictions on nonelectoral forms of mass participation. Building democracy in Mexico will also require more effective guarantees of the freedom of association, meaningful protection against arbitrary state action and equal treatment of all citizens under the law, and institutionalized procedures to ensure that citizens can through the rule of law hold elected and appointed officials accountable for their public actions.[87] Ensuring the political

---

[86] The Monterrey Consensus itself stressed "the need to pursue sound macroeconomic policies," including "prudent fiscal and monetary policies." United Nations General Assembly 2002: 3.

[87] Urquidi (this volume) argues that reforms to increase the accountability of public officials should include overturning Mexico's constitutional ban on reelection for

independence and integrity of judicial personnel and public security forces is a particularly high priority.

Democracy is an important value in and of itself, and Mexican citizens' struggles to achieve electoral transparency, overcome political centralism, and limit official impunity underscore their commitment to establishing democratic governance. What are particularly relevant to the present discussion, however, are the shifts in the policy-making process that are likely to occur as a consequence of democratization. At a minimum, the PAN's victory disrupted networks of concentrated economic and political power encrusted during seven decades of PRI rule. Given Fox's personal background in business and the strong private-sector presence in his cabinet, it is naïve to think that big business will lose its political influence. Yet party alternation in power at the national level, a more independent Congress, more critical attention from mass communications media, and closer public scrutiny of government actions may reduce or eliminate some forms of corruption and mismanagement and, more generally, introduce a greater degree of transparency and accountability in economic policy making. Especially in the wake of the national political scandal that erupted over the Zedillo administration's handling of the post–1995 bank bailout (which, in the absence of uniform criteria and sufficient legislative oversight or public scrutiny, produced deals highly favorable to financiers with close personal ties to senior government officials), it will henceforth be much more difficult for government officials to rescue major firms engaging in "morally hazardous" business practices. Democratization may thus help break the cycle of financial crises that has beleaguered Mexico since 1976.[88]

Equally important, there is some indication that—in part because of its democratic origins—the Fox administration may be more sensitive to the country's accumulated social needs than some previous governments. During the 1980s and 1990s the PAN was a strong supporter of economic liberalization, and there are multiple reasons (including the PAN's long-standing commitment to an expanded role for the private sector in national economic development, Fox's own business background and the importance of private-sector actors in his political coalition, and the international financial constraints outlined above) why the Fox administration is unlikely to depart significantly from macro-

---

members of Congress, governors, and mayors (with the possible establishment of term limits).

[88] See Garrido (this volume) for an analysis of Mexico's cyclical financial crises.

economic orthodoxy.[89] Nevertheless, early in his term Fox clearly signaled his recognition that future economic policies must generate more widely distributed benefits than they have in the past.

The Fox administration's national development plan for the 2001–2006 period was illustrative in this regard.[90] The document defined human and social development as the country's highest priority, and it proposed devoting substantial new resources to education (increasing expenditures from the equivalent of 5–6 percent to 8 percent of GDP, with the goals of improving the overall quality of instruction and raising the average educational level to a complete secondary education) and expanded health care coverage. Similarly, the plan highlighted proposals to promote integrated rural development, although it was ambiguous with regard to where the government would secure resources on the scale required to undertake serious public-sector initiatives to reduce rural poverty. The government also reaffirmed its commitment to providing micro-credits to small businesses and self-employed individuals, despite the controversy produced by its initial foray into this area. And in a parallel effort to redress regional inequalities, Fox launched the Puebla-Panama Project, an ambitious scheme to address problems of poverty and inequality in southern Mexico by channeling private and public investment from both national and international sources into priority areas (especially infrastructure projects) in the region stretching from the state of Puebla to the Central American nation of Panama.

Yet Mexico's new democratic order also imposes its own limits on economic policy making. Some of the Fox administration's early difficulties in securing congressional approval for specific initiatives may simply have been part of a necessary learning process in the wake of a historic change of regime. But other political constraints are likely to persist in the medium term. These include divided party control over the executive and legislative branches of the federal government, sharp partisan divisions within the Congress, and electoral and party rules that give party leaders substantial influence over individual legislators, thereby making it more difficult for a president to translate personal popularity into a working legislative majority.

The fate of the fiscal and tax reform initiative that the Fox administration proposed in 2001 is an important case in point. The proposal sought to resolve continuing problems with the Mexican financial sys-

---

[89] On the PAN's development and its principal ideological and programmatic orientations, see Loaeza 1999 and Middlebrook 2001. For a brief biographical profile of Fox, see Valencia García 2001: 242 n31.

[90] See Poder Ejecutivo Federal 2001.

tem by making transactions more transparent (by, for example, barring insider trading and regulating conflicts of interest and the use of privileged information in stock market transactions). It also proposed modifying the federal budgetary approval process in order to prevent executive-legislative deadlock from jeopardizing continued governmental operations at the end of each calendar year.

However, the most controversial elements in the legislative initiative concerned taxes. In an effort to increase the national savings rate and secure the tax bases for future social spending, education, and infrastructure development, the Fox administration proposed tax increases equivalent to approximately 2 percent of gross domestic product. In promoting the measure, the administration highlighted a number of its elements that would supposedly have benefited taxpayers (a reduction in the number of tax brackets, simplified payment and administrative procedures, steps to reduce tax evasion, the creation of investment tax credits for small firms, and an expanded home mortgage system). Yet the prospect of significant tax increases generated considerable opposition, much of it focusing on the proposal to extend the 15 percent value-added tax to most foods and medicines (categories of goods that had previously been exempted from the tax). Government officials argued that lower-income segments of the population would be protected by income tax exemptions up to 50,000 pesos per year, wage credits to compensate for higher value-added taxes, direct income transfers via targeted social programs, and the poor's free access to medications.

Despite their intensive lobbying of Congress, Fox administration officials were unable to overcome opposition from across the partisan spectrum to key provisions in the bill. In the end, although the financial transparency and budgetary approval provisions were passed, the Congress rejected the proposal to extend the value-added tax to most foods and medicines. The final tax increase produced additional revenues equivalent to only 1 percent of Mexico's GDP in 2001. And because of the controversy that accompanied the tax reform initiative, there was considerable doubt about whether the Fox administration could marshal political support for an early reconsideration of the matter.

The Fox administration's initial experience with fiscal and tax reform thus underscored the problems that any elected government might encounter in addressing difficult economic issues while navigating the political constraints established by a competitive, multiparty democracy. Tax reform and other measures that will provide additional public-sector development resources and increase domestic savings are, however, vitally important to Mexico's future. Federal government tax revenues as a proportion of GDP remain very low by international standards,[91] and the Mexican economy has suffered the consequences of more than two decades of reduced public investment in infrastructure (including roads, irrigation systems, and potable water and sanitation facilities) and other projects that might improve social access and promote the more equal distribution of market opportunities.[92] Similarly, a low rate of domestic savings has been a root cause of Mexico's sluggish and volatile economic performance. In order to attract the correspondingly greater amounts of foreign capital required, real domestic interest rates must remain high—which reduces investment options in productive activities, constrains capital formation, and slows growth.[93]

The Path Forward

The core challenge facing Mexican policy makers is to identify the options for promoting socially equitable, sustainable development that are viable for a smaller public sector facing very real international and domestic financial constraints. In addressing this challenge, they can draw upon lessons from other countries' development record and, especially, Mexico's own experience during the 1980s and 1990s.[94]

On topics such as industrial policy, for instance, there is an emerging consensus among international analysts in favor of a reasonable mix of across-the-board and sector- or activity-specific industrial promotion policies that, within the limits imposed by Mexico's commitments

---

[91] In 1998, public-sector tax revenues as a proportion of GDP totaled 13.9 percent in Mexico. This level was substantially lower than in Chile (18.4 percent), Brazil (19.0 percent), the United States (20.4 percent), Costa Rica (23.1 percent), Spain (28.1 percent), and a number of other OECD countries. See World Bank 2001: 300–301.

[92] The focus of this discussion is on political factors affecting development policy. Of course, the efficacy of government efforts to improve public services, reduce poverty, and lessen income and regional inequalities may have a significant effect on public attitudes toward government, the effective exercise of citizenship rights, and the overall character of democracy in Mexico.

[93] Domestic savings in the late 1990s represented approximately 20 percent of GDP. Ros 1994 and Nadal (this volume), among others, argue that it will be difficult for Mexico to increase domestic savings while pursuing policies that depress the domestic market and the population's real income.

Mexico's heavy dependence upon foreign capital has at least two other negative consequences. First, it necessarily makes the economy vulnerable to volatility in international capital markets. Second, a heavy inflow of foreign funds promotes an overvalued exchange rate, which biases investment decisions in favor of relatively capital-intensive projects, encourages the consumption of imports over domestically produced goods, and penalizes exports with a high domestic content.

[94] In the course of their specific analyses, the contributors to this volume point to useful lessons from Chile, China, and Costa Rica.

within the NAFTA and the WTO, would strengthen linkages between leading export activities and the rest of the economy.[95] Mexico's sluggish growth since the 1980s has been due in part to the fact that imports have increasingly substituted for domestically produced goods, thus weakening the supplier networks that would transmit the benefits of expanded export production to other economic activities. Even with limited financial resources, governmental agencies could do more to provide technical assistance to small and midsize firms seeking to restructure their operations in order to compete more effectively in domestic and international markets. This assistance might include help in product development, quality control, inventory management, marketing, and so forth. [96]

In formulating future economic and social development policies, national decision makers would do well to consider approaches that take constructive advantage of the transformations that have occurred in both the balance of power between the state and the private sector and in the character of Mexican federalism. A smaller and less interventionist state need not be inactive where development promotion is concerned. However, future government initiatives will need to acknowledge in practice the facts that foreign companies and large national firms have displaced the public sector as the principal engine of economic growth, and that in a highly competitive global economy, states have fewer points of direct leverage over the behavior of transnational firms than they did in the past.

One of the major challenges facing Mexican government officials, therefore, may be to identify innovative ways of promoting state/private-sector partnerships. For instance, to the extent that global commodity chains have become a principal vehicle for the international dissemination of technology, production techniques, and marketing skills (Gereffi, this volume), one valuable public-sector contribution would be to engage much more actively in efforts to help Mexican firms forge advantageous alliances with leading transnational firms in key export sectors.[97] This might be a productive way of increasing the odds that, in the game of globalized production and international

---

[95] See, for example, Katz 2000 and Dussel Peters (this volume).

[96] See Dussel Peters (this volume) for a brief survey of the industrial development policies Mexico adopted in the 1990s.

[97] For an examination of different Mexican firms' success at industrial upgrading in the textile and apparel industry, see Bair 2001. The success of some Mexican organic fruit and vegetable producers in forging transnational partnerships to finance and market their crops (Marsh and Runsten 2000) also provides a suggestive example of areas in which modest government support might significantly increase the market competitiveness of small and midsize Mexican firms.

subcontracting, Mexico will attract a larger share of high-skill, high-technology manufacturing activities and thus ensure that Mexican managers and workers participate in the benefits of globalized production.

In the same fashion, national policy makers must recognize that the federal government need not be exclusively responsible for devising or implementing development policies. In fact, the public sector may be able to play a more positive role in promoting equitable, sustainable development when federal and local (state and municipal) governments collaborate effectively in an increasingly vigorous federal system.[98] Local governments, for example, may be able to adopt various measures that enhance states' or cities' ability to attract investment, generate skilled jobs, and improve their overall economic competitiveness. These include steps to improve the efficiency of governmental institutions, strengthen local research and development capacity, raise the quality of local infrastructure and services, increase the educational level and technical training of the labor force, and so forth.[99]

There are, nevertheless, some development problems whose scale and complexity make federal government action the only practical option. This category includes phenomena that naturally exceed the jurisdictional spheres of individual state or municipal governments (for instance, the environmental degradation of large ecosystems) or that obviously affect the country as a whole. One highly relevant example is the problem of unequal growth among Mexico's different states and regions, an issue identified as being of high priority in the Fox administration's national development plan for the 2001–2006 period. During the 1990s the national government essentially "renounced its leadership in urban development planning in the belief that the market could control land use and build basic infrastructure" (Garza, this volume). A lack of financial and political support severely constrained the specific decentralization programs that were established, contributing to greater regional inequalities.

Whatever the specific form of public/private-sector or intergovernmental collaboration, the range of actors responsible for Mexico's fu-

---

[98] Since the 1980s there has been a significant degree of administrative decentralization in Mexico as states and municipalities have assumed expanded responsibility for education, health care, and other services. Federal government transfers to states and municipalities—the main source of income for subnational governments—rose from 1.9 percent of GDP in 1982 to 6.3 percent in 1988 and 7.2 percent in 2000; Poder Ejecutivo Federal 2001: 140.

[99] See Alba Vega 2001 for an illustrative discussion of the policies that the state government of Jalisco adopted in the late 1990s in order to promote the development of electronics manufacturing.

ture development policies will be broader than in the past. Given the magnitude of the country's problems, there is a very high premium on shaping innovative strategies that take maximum advantage of available opportunities in a policy-making environment characterized by significant international and domestic constraints. Pragmatic innovation in the formulation and implementation of public policies will increasingly be the watchword in addressing the multiple economic and social challenges that confront Mexico.

References

Aitken, Rob, Nikki Craske, Gareth A. Jones, and David E. Stansfield, eds. 1996. *Dismantling the Mexican State?* London: Macmillan.

Alba Vega, Carlos. 2001. "Economía, sociedad y políticas regionales frente al NAFTA: el caso de Jalisco." Paper presented at the conference "Producción de exportación, desarrollo económico y el futuro de la industria maquiladora en México," Center for U.S.–Mexican Studies, University of California, San Diego/Departamento de Economía, Universidad Autónoma Metropolitana–Azcapotzalco, Mexico City, June.

Aspe Armella, Pedro. 1993. *Economic Transformation the Mexican Way.* Cambridge, Mass.: MIT Press.

Bair, Jennifer. 2001. "The Maquiladora Industry and Development in Mexico: Lessons from the Textile and Apparel Industries." Paper presented at the conference "Producción de exportación, desarrollo económico y el futuro de la industria maquiladora en México," Center for U.S.–Mexican Studies, University of California, San Diego/Departamento de Economía, Universidad Autónoma Metropolitana–Azcapotzalco, Mexico City, June.

Boltvinik, Julio, and Enrique Hernández Laos. 2000. *Pobreza y distribución del ingreso en México.* Rev. ed. Mexico City: Siglo Veintiuno.

Boylan, Delia M. 2001. "Democratization and Institutional Change in Mexico: The Logic of Partial Insulation," *Comparative Political Studies* 34 (1): 3–29.

Brooks, David, and Jonathan Fox. 2002. *Cross-Border Dialogues: Mexico–U.S. Social Movement Networking.* La Jolla: Center for U.S.–Mexican Studies, University of California, San Diego.

Bulmer-Thomas, Victor, ed. 1996. *The New Economic Model in Latin America and Its Impact on Income Distribution and Poverty.* London: Macmillan.

Camp, Roderic A. 1985. "The Political Technocrat in Mexico and the Survival of the Political System," *Latin American Research Review* 20 (1): 97–118.

Cárdenas, Enrique. 1996. *La política económica en México, 1950–1994.* Mexico City: Fondo de Cultura Económica/El Colegio de México.

Castañeda, Jorge G. 1999. *La herencia: arqueología de la sucesión presidencial en México.* Mexico City: Alfaguara.

Centeno, Miguel Ángel. 1994. *Democracy within Reason: Technocratic Revolution in Mexico.* University Park: Pennsylvania State University Press.

Clavijo, Fernando, and Susana Valdivieso. 2000. "Reformas estructurales y política macroeconómica." In *Reformas económicas en México, 1982–1999*, edited by Fernando Clavijo. Mexico City: Fondo de Cultura Económica.

Cook, Maria Lorena, Kevin J. Middlebrook, and Juan Molinar Horcasitas. 1994. "The Politics of Economic Restructuring in Mexico: Actors, Sequencing, and Coalition Change." In *The Politics of Economic Restructuring: State-Society Relations and Regime Change in Mexico*, edited by Maria Lorena Cook, Kevin J. Middlebrook, and Juan Molinar Horcasitas. La Jolla: Center for U.S.-Mexican Studies, University of California, San Diego.

Cortés, Fernando. 2000. *La distribución del ingreso en México en épocas de estabilización y reforma económica*. Mexico City: Centro de Investigaciones y Estudios Superiores en Antropología Social.

De la Torre, Rodolfo. 2000. "La distribución factorial del ingreso." In *Reformas económicas en México, 1982–1999*, edited by Fernando Clavijo. Mexico City: Fondo de Cultura Económica.

De Oliveira, Orlandina, and Brígida García. 1997. "Socioeconomic Transformation and Labor Markets in Urban Mexico." In *Global Restructuring, Employment, and Social Inequality in Urban Latin America*, edited by Richard Tardanico and Rafael Menjívar Larín. Miami: North-South Center, University of Miami.

Dornbusch, Rudiger, and Alejandro Werner. 1994. "Mexico: Stabilization, Reform, and No Growth," *Brookings Papers on Economic Activity* 1: 253–315.

Edwards, Sebastian. 1997. "The Mexican Peso Crisis: How Much Did We Know? When Did We Know It?" NBER Working Paper No. 6334. Cambridge, Mass.: National Bureau of Economic Research (NBER).

Evans, Peter, and Gary Gereffi. 1982. "Foreign Investment and Dependent Development: Comparing Brazil and Mexico." In *Brazil and Mexico: Patterns in Late Development*, edited by Sylvia Ann Hewlett and Richard S. Weinert. Philadelphia, Penn.: Institute for the Study of Human Issues.

Fairris, David, Gurleen Popli, and Eduardo Zepeda. 2001. "Minimum Wages and the Wage Structure in Mexico." Paper presented at the international congress of the Latin American Studies Association, Washington, D.C., September.

Federal Reserve Bank of Dallas (El Paso Branch). 2001. "NAFTA, the U.S. Economy, and Maquiladoras," *Business Frontier* 1: 1–6.

Graham, Carol. 1994. *Safety Nets, Politics, and the Poor: Transitions to Market Economies*. Washington, D.C.: Brookings Institution.

Hernández Laos, Enrique. 2000a. *La competitividad industrial en México*. Mexico City: Universidad Autónoma Metropolitana/Plaza y Valdés.

———. 2000b. "Crecimiento económico, distribución del ingreso y pobreza en México," *Comercio Exterior* 50 (10): 863–73.

Hernández Laos, Enrique, and Jorge Velázquez Roa. 2002. *Globalización, desigualdad y pobreza: lecciones de la experiencia mexicana*. Mexico City: Universidad Autónoma Metropolitana/Plaza y Valdés.

Hirschman, Albert O. 1968. "The Political Economy of Import-Substituting Industrialization in Latin America," *Quarterly Journal of Economics* 82 (1): 1–32.

IMF (International Monetary Fund). 2001. *2001 IMF Economic Outlook.* Washington, D.C.: IMF.

INEGI (Instituto Nacional de Estadística, Geografía e Informática). 1985. *Estadísticas históricas de México.* 2 vols. Mexico City: Secretaría de Programación y Presupuesto.

————. 2000. *Los jóvenes en México.* Mexico City: INEGI.

Katz, Jorge. 2000. *Reformas estructurales, productividad y conducta tecnológica en América Latina.* Santiago, Chile: Comisión Económica para América Latina/ Fondo de Cultura Económica.

Klesner, Joseph L. 1994. "Realignment or Dealignment? Consequences of Economic Crisis and Restructuring for the Mexican Party System." In *The Politics of Economic Restructuring: State-Society Relations and Regime Change in Mexico,* edited by Maria Lorena Cook, Kevin J. Middlebrook, and Juan Molinar Horcasitas. La Jolla: Center for U.S.–Mexican Studies, University of California, San Diego.

Krugman, Paul. 1995. "Dutch Tulips and Emerging Markets," *Foreign Affairs* 74 (4): 28–44.

Loaeza, Soledad. 1999. *El Partido Acción Nacional: la larga marcha, 1939–1994; oposición leal y partido de protesta.* Mexico City: Fondo de Cultura Económica.

Lustig, Nora. 1998. *Mexico: The Remaking of an Economy.* Rev. ed. Washington, D.C.: Brookings Institution Press.

Marsh, Robin, and David Runsten. 2000. "The Organic Produce Niche Market: Can Mexican Smallholders be Stakeholders?" In *Strategies for Resource Management, Production, and Marketing in Rural Mexico,* edited by Guadalupe Rodríguez Gómez and Richard Snyder. La Jolla: Center for U.S.–Mexican Studies, University of California, San Diego.

Maxfield, Sylvia. 1997. *Gatekeepers of Growth: The International Political Economy of Central Banking in Developing Countries.* Princeton, N.J.: Princeton University Press.

Middlebrook, Kevin J. 1995. *The Paradox of Revolution: Labor, the State, and Authoritarianism in Mexico.* Baltimore, Md.: Johns Hopkins University Press.

————. 2001. "Party Politics and Democratization in Mexico: The Partido Acción Nacional in Comparative Perspective." In *Party Politics and the Struggle for Democracy in Mexico: National and State-Level Analyses of the Partido Acción Nacional,* edited by Kevin J. Middlebrook. La Jolla: Center for U.S.–Mexican Studies, University of California, San Diego.

Molinar Horcasitas, Juan, and Jeffrey Weldon. 1994. "Electoral Determinants and Consequences of National Solidarity." In *Transforming State-Society Relations in Mexico: The National Solidarity Strategy,* edited by Wayne A. Cornelius, Ann L. Craig, and Jonathan Fox. La Jolla: Center for U.S.–Mexican Studies, University of California, San Diego.

Morley, Samuel A., Roberto Machado, and Stefano Pettinato. 1999. "Indexes of Structural Reform in Latin America." Serie Reformas Económicas, no. 12 (LC/L.1166/I). Santiago, Chile: Comisión Económica para América Latina y el Caribe.

Olvera, Alberto J. 2001. *Sociedad civil, gobernabilidad democrática, espacios públicos y democratización: los contornos de un proyecto.* Cuadernos de la Sociedad

Civil No. 1. Xalapa: Instituto de Investigaciones Histórico-Sociales, Universidad Veracruzana.

Pastor, Manuel, Jr., and Carol Wise. 1998. "Mexican-Style Neoliberalism: State Policy and Distributional Stress." In *The Post–NAFTA Political Economy: Mexico and the Western Hemisphere*, edited by Carol Wise. University Park: Pennsylvania State University Press.

Poder Ejecutivo Federal. 2001. *Plan Nacional de Desarrollo, 2001–2006*. Mexico City: Presidencia de la República.

Randall, Laura, ed. 1996. *Reforming Mexico's Agrarian Reform*. Armonk, N.Y.: M.E. Sharpe.

Reynolds, Clark W. 1970. *The Mexican Economy: Twentieth Century Structure and Growth*. New Haven, Conn.: Yale University Press.

Rocha Menocal, Alina. 2001. "Do Old Habits Die Hard? A Statistical Exploration of the Politicisation of Progresa, Mexico's Latest Federal Poverty-Alleviation Program, under the Zedillo Administration," *Journal of Latin American Studies* 33 (3): 513–38.

Rodríguez Gómez, Guadalupe, and Richard Snyder, eds. 2000. *Strategies for Resource Management, Production, and Marketing in Rural Mexico*. La Jolla: Center for U.S.–Mexican Studies, University of California, San Diego.

Ros, Jaime. 1994. "Mexico in the 1990s: A New Economic Miracle? Some Notes on the Economic and Policy Legacy of the 1980s." In *The Politics of Economic Restructuring: State-Society Relations and Regime Change in Mexico*, edited by Maria Lorena Cook, Kevin J. Middlebrook, and Juan Molinar Horcasitas. La Jolla: Center for U.S.–Mexican Studies, University of California, San Diego.

Sachs, Jeffrey, Aaron Tornell, and Andrés Velasco. 1995. "The Collapse of the Mexican Peso: What Have We Learned?" Working Papers Series, no. 95-7. Cambridge, Mass.: Center for International Affairs, Harvard University.

Serrano, Mónica, ed. 1997. *Mexico: Assessing Neo-Liberal Reform*. London: Institute of Latin American Studies, University of London.

Stallings, Barbara, and Wilson Peres. 2000. *Growth, Employment, and Equity: The Impact of the Economic Reforms in Latin America and the Caribbean*. Washington, D.C.: Brookings Institution Press.

Székely, Miguel. 1998. *The Economics of Poverty, Inequality, and Wealth Accumulation in Mexico*. New York: St. Martin's.

Tamayo-Flores, Rafael. 2001. "Mexico in the Context of the North American Integration: Major Regional Trends and Performance of Backward Regions," *Journal of Latin American Studies* 33 (2): 377–407.

Teichman, Judith A. 2001. *The Politics of Freeing Markets in Latin America: Chile, Argentina, and Mexico*. Chapel Hill: University of North Carolina Press.

Thacker, Strom C. 1999. "NAFTA Coalitions and the Political Viability of Neoliberalism in Mexico," *Journal of Inter-American Studies and World Affairs* 41 (2): 57–89.

Thorp, Rosemary. 1992. "A Reappraisal of the Origins of Import-Substituting Industrialisation, 1930–1950," *Journal of Latin American Studies* 24 (Quincentenary Supplement): 181–95.

Trigueros, Ignacio. 1994. "The Mexican Financial System and NAFTA." In *Mexico and the North American Free Trade Agreement: Who Will Benefit?* edited by Victor Bulmer-Thomas, Nikki Craske, and Mónica Serrano. London: Macmillan.

United Nations General Assembly. 2002. "Monterrey Consensus: Outcome of the International Conference on Financing for Development." Document A/AC.257/L.13. New York: United Nations.

Valdés Ugalde, Francisco. 1994. "From Bank Nationalization to State Reform: Business and the New Mexican Order." In *The Politics of Economic Restructuring: State-Society Relations and Regime Change in Mexico*, edited by Maria Lorena Cook, Kevin J. Middlebrook, and Juan Molinar Horcasitas. La Jolla: Center for U.S.-Mexican Studies, University of California, San Diego.

Valencia García, Guadalupe. 2001. "The PAN in Guanajuato: Elections and Political Change in the 1990s." In *Party Politics and the Struggle for Democracy in Mexico: National and State-Level Analyses of the Partido Acción Nacional*, edited by Kevin J. Middlebrook. La Jolla: Center for U.S.-Mexican Studies, University of California, San Diego.

Williamson, John. 1990. *Latin American Adjustment: How Much Has Happened?* Washington, D.C.: Institute for International Economics.

———. 1997. "The Washington Consensus Revisited." In *Economic and Social Development into the XXI Century*, edited by Louis Emmerji. Baltimore, Md.: Johns Hopkins University Press.

World Bank. 2001. *World Development Report, 2000-2001*. Washington, D.C.: World Bank.

Zepeda, Eduardo, and Gustavo Félix. 1995. *El empleo y los servicios en la frontera norte*. Mexico City: Fundación Friedrich Ebert.

Part II

Economic Policy and Finance

2

Macroeconomic Challenges for Mexico's Development Strategy

Alejandro Nadal

INTRODUCTION

In 1987 Mexico adopted a new economic strategy based on the realiza-
tion that the import-substitution industrialization model (ISI) was exhausted in terms of its effectiveness. The new approach rested on three
premises. First, trade liberalization would allow Mexico's economy to
reap the benefits of its comparative advantages, opening the way to
sustained export-led growth. Second, restrictive monetary and fiscal
policies would restore stability to domestic macroeconomic aggregate
indicators, reestablishing investor confidence and eliminating the dead
weight of mistakes from Mexico's populist past. Third, market forces
would lead to a more efficient allocation of resources on the domestic
front and improve the population's living standards.

This chapter analyzes three key macroeconomic aspects of Mexico's
development strategy. The first section considers the relationship between stabilization policies, growth performance, and external accounts, taking note of the inability of the Mexican economy to grow
without incurring serious external imbalances. The analysis covers the
stabilization policies' impact on growth performance. The second section concentrates on Mexico's debt burden. There seems to be consensus that this aspect of Mexico's economy is not a problem. There are,
however, important warning signals, including the increasing importance of domestic debt—a theme closely related to the approach employed to rescue the banking sector in the wake of the country's 1994–
1995 financial crisis. The third section examines the protracted crisis of
the banking sector, as well as the drawbacks of the government's rescue

This essay is part of a larger research project on alternative development strategies
for Mexico, which has received financial support from the John D. and Catherine T.
MacArthur Foundation.

scheme. The conclusion considers the way in which these three themes are interconnected, and it explores some implications for a future research agenda on Mexico's development strategy.

STABILIZATION, GROWTH, AND EXTERNAL IMBALANCES

In the 1970s, after four decades of sustained economic growth averaging 6 percent per year, Mexico's import-substitution strategy seemed to have exhausted its potential to sustain economic expansion. During those years, public spending replaced private investment as the main source of economic dynamism, leading to huge fiscal deficits. Public indebtedness was artificially sustained by new petroleum discoveries at a time (1976) when oil prices were thought to be on the verge of a durable upward trend and huge financial surpluses generated by petroleum-exporting countries ("petrodollars") were seeking profitable placements. Irresponsible fiscal policy and external indebtedness proved to be an unsustainable combination. In August 1982, Mexico suspended principal payments on outstanding debt, contributing to an international debt crisis. This crisis marked the demise of ISI in Mexico.

During the 1980s the Mexican economy underwent a sweeping structural reform whose main objective was economic growth with healthy external accounts and stabilization on the domestic front.[1] However, despite the depth of the reform program, Mexico's economic performance fell short in terms of growth rates (Dornbusch and Werner 1994), employment generation (Salas and Rendón 1996), and the country's external accounts (Nadal 1996).

Since the early 1980s, growth rates of Mexico's gross domestic product (GDP) have been mediocre. Even limiting the focus to the 1988–2000 period—thereby excluding the negative effects of the 1982 debt crisis—the country's economic performance has been unsatisfactory. GDP growth has remained far below the level required to meet employment needs and improve living standards. The average annual

---

[1] After Mexico declared a unilateral moratorium on debt service in August 1982, a strong exchange-rate adjustment was followed by high inflation in 1983 and 1984. After 1983, the Mexican government tried to redress the excesses in public spending of the late 1970s and to regain private-sector confidence. Later, it engaged in trade liberalization and joined the General Agreement on Tariffs and Trade (GATT) in 1987, launched a huge privatization program, and proceeded to deregulate the economy. The government's strategy combined restrictive monetary and fiscal policies with price stabilization through heterodox "economic solidarity pacts" with business and organized labor, the goal being to curtail inflationary pressures. The 1987–1988 pacts sought to control wages in exchange for government commitments regarding exchange rates and inflation targets.

TABLE 2.1. Mexico's Gross Domestic Product (GDP) and External Accounts, 1981–2000 (percentages and billions of 1993 U.S. dollars)

Year	Annual Percent Change in GDP	Trade Balance	Trade Balance as Percentage of GDP	Current Account Balance	Current Account Balance as Percentage of GDP
1981	8.5	−5.2	−1.4	−21.8	−6.1
1982	−0.5	18.3	3.8	−15.3	−3.2
1983	−3.5	33.8	8.9	14.0	3.7
1984	3.4	26.6	7.0	8.4	2.2
1985	2.2	20.2	4.3	1.9	0.4
1986	−3.1	17.5	3.6	−4.8	−1.0
1987	1.7	28.8	5.8	13.9	2.8
1988	1.3	4.8	1.4	−4.4	−1.3
1989	4.1	0.7	0.2	−9.8	−2.6
1990	5.2	−1.3	−0.3	−10.8	−2.8
1991	4.2	−9.1	−2.3	−18.3	−4.6
1992	3.5	−17.6	−4.4	−27.0	−6.7
1993	1.9	−13.5	−3.3	−23.4	−5.8
1994	4.5	−21.5	−4.4	−34.6	−7.1
1995	−6.2	11.7	2.5	−2.6	−0.6
1996	5.1	8.5	2.0	−3.1	−0.7
1997	6.8	0.7	0.2	−8.5	−1.9
1998	4.8	−9.3	−1.9	−19.4	−3.8
1999	3.4	−5.0	−1.1	−13.4	−3.0
2000	6.9	−8.0	−1.6	−18.0	−3.3

Source: El Colegio de México, Science and Technology Program, Project on Mexico's Development Strategy, with data from Secretaría de Hacienda y Crédito Público.

growth rate for the 1988–2000 period was 3.5 percent (table 2.1), a rate best described as semi-stagnation. Worse, per capita GDP dropped, real wages plunged, and poverty increased dramatically over this period.

In the 1970s, the Mexican economy could only grow by generating substantial external imbalances. Since 1982, not only have spurts of positive GDP growth been short lived, but these episodes have remained stubbornly linked to serious imbalances in the country's external accounts. Mexico's current account did not achieve a surplus at any point during the entire decade of the 1990s, even under the severe conditions of the 1995 recession and the sharp temporary fall in imports. Although exports expanded vigorously, Mexico's new economic strategy has thus far been unable to achieve economic growth accompanied by external equilibrium.

There are many reasons for this situation, but the core explanation is closely related to a stabilization process that accords high priority to the struggle against inflation. This strategy, in turn, has relied heavily on a relatively restrictive stance on monetary and fiscal matters, as well as an overvalued exchange rate. This has led to high interest rates that have stifled growth and damaged Mexico's external position. The negative trend in the external trade balance has not been countered by the impressive expansion of Mexico's exports.[2]

The Mexican government has tackled its top domestic macroeconomic priority—controlling inflation—using a variety of fiscal and monetary policy instruments, along with strategies to reduce aggregate demand. Monetary policy has been kept passive, in line with attempts to adhere to a monetary approach to the balance of payments problem. Mexico's money base fell dramatically in real terms during the 1980s and 1990s from 145.4 billion pesos in 1980 to 50.2 billion pesos in 1998 (measured in 1993 pesos; see table 2.2). In 2000, the money base represented an insubstantial 4.0 percent of GDP, down from 6.4 percent in 1986. Of course, this drop may correlate positively with reductions in inflation (although the robustness of this policy outcome remains doubtful). In addition, restrictive monetary policy is also associated with sharp interest rate hikes and a powerful brake on growth.

Mexico's monetary policy has, in fact, brought high real interest rates. On average, the prime rate (government securities with a 28–day maturity) was 6.7 percent in real terms during the 1990s.[3] The downstream effects were highly significant given that commercial bank rates (approximately 40 percent) are much higher than the prime rate. In addition, it is important to note that these are *passive* rates; *active* rates (that is, rates actually charged to loan recipients) have been much higher. The margin between passive and active rates in Mexico's banking system is excessive by international standards, and this has led to extremely high interest rates for commercial credit. Very few productive investment projects can boast rates of return high enough to cover these financial charges. Thus the strategic objective of price stability has been attained, but with deleterious side effects on investment, production, and growth.

---

[2] It should be noted, however, that official statistics exaggerate Mexico's export success by including total *maquiladora* (in-bond processing) operations, not just the value added due to processing operations in Mexico. Making the appropriate correction, Mexico's exports in 2000 totaled US$104.7 billion, versus the US$166.4 billion reported in official statistics.

[3] The high inflation rates that result from exchange-rate adjustments have provoked episodes of negative real rates (in 1995, for example).

Other instruments used against inflation include suppressing aggregate demand and using the exchange rate as an anchor for the system of relative prices. The heterodox adjustment of 1987–1988 quashed the hyperinflation of preceding years. One of its key components was an "economic solidarity pact" among government, business, and organized labor that constrained wage demands. The ensuing impact on aggregate demand was instrumental in reining in inflation, but poverty levels have continued to expand ever since.

An overvaluation of the peso played a decisive role in keeping inflation under control by making imports cheaper (see table 2.3).[4] However, the financial crisis that exploded in December 1994 forced a drastic adjustment in the exchange rate, and inflation resumed its upward spiral. The gains in the struggle to control inflation during the early 1990s, which had been achieved at heavy social costs (especially in terms of real wage deterioration), vanished rapidly with the 1994–1995 devaluations.

Moreover, using the exchange rate as an instrument to counter inflation directly contradicts one of the basic tenets of the open-economy model. Trade is considered so beneficial under this model that efforts to restrict trade through tariffs or nontariff barriers are proscribed. The appropriate use of exchange rate adjustments is to correct a significant trade imbalance. Overreliance on the exchange rate to reduce inflation leads inexorably to a worsening of the trade balance, and it therefore runs counter to an essential component of the open-economy model.

Officially, the use of the exchange rate to anchor the price system has been replaced since 1995 by greater reliance on a monetary aggregate and a floating exchange rate. But relying on a monetary aggregate administered to restrict demand leads to higher interest rates, relieving pressure on the exchange rate and leading to its overvaluation. Thus an overvalued currency remains the cornerstone of Mexico's anti-inflation strategy and continues to dominate the country's macroeconomic landscape.

Exchange rate overvaluation is also linked to capital inflows, and this has continued to pose serious problems for the intersection of exchange rate and interest rate policies. For extended periods in the 1990s, foreign capital in the form of portfolio investments financed

---

[4] In table 2.3, an exchange rate index value greater than 1.0 means that pesos cost more in U.S. dollar terms, making imports cheaper and exports more expensive. Exchange rate valuation was calculated according to Banco de México methodology, which relies on purchasing power parity. The formula for the real exchange rate is: Real Exchange Rate = $(P^*/P) \times (E/E^*) \times 100$, where P^* and P are external and domestic prices, respectively; E is the exchange rate (pesos per dollar); and E^* is the exchange rate of a basket of currencies per dollar, which is provided by the Banco de México.

TABLE 2.2. Rate of Inflation and Monetary Base in Mexico, 1980–2000

	1980	1981	1982	1983	1984	1985	1986	1987	1988	1989
Inflation rate[1]	29.6	28.7	98.9	80.8	59.2	63.7	105.8	159.2	51.7	19.7
Monetary base[2]	145.4	167.2	198.7	164.5	160.4	121.3	65.9	55.9	44.0	44.3
Monetary base as percentage of gross domestic product	15.1	15.9	19.0	16.5	15.5	11.4	6.4	5.4	4.2	4.0

	1990	1991	1992	1993	1994	1995	1996	1997	1998	1999	2000
Inflation rate	29.9	18.8	11.9	8.0	7.1	52.0	27.7	15.7	18.6	12.3	9.0
Monetary base	46.3	48.7	48.4	47.2	52.5	44.7	43.4	47.4	50.2	61.9	61.9
Monetary base as percentage of gross domestic product	4.1	4.1	3.9	3.8	4.0	3.6	3.4	3.4	3.5	4.2	4.0

Source: El Colegio de México, Science and Technology Program, Project on Mexico's Development Strategy, with data from the Secretaría de Hacienda y Crédito Público and Banco de México.

[1] Percentage change on previous year.

[2] Monetary base balance at end of year (in billions of 1993 pesos).

TABLE 2.3. Rate of Inflation and Exchange Rate Valuation in Mexico, 1980–2000

Year	Rate of Inflation[1]	Exchange Rate Valuation Index
1980	29.6	1.2
1981	28.7	1.4
1982	98.9	1.0
1983	80.8	1.0
1984	59.2	1.2
1985	63.7	1.2
1986	105.8	0.8
1987	159.2	0.8
1988	51.7	0.9
1989	19.7	1.0
1990	29.9	1.0
1991	18.8	1.1
1992	11.9	1.1
1993	8.0	1.2
1994	7.1	1.1
1995	52.0	0.6
1996	27.7	0.9
1997	15.7	1.2
1998	18.6	1.3
1999	12.3	1.4
2000	9.0	1.4

Source: El Colegio de México, Science and Technology Program, Project on Mexico's Development Strategy, with data from Banco de México.

[1] Percentage change on previous year.

Mexico's current account deficit.[5] This financing could only be available as long as the Banco de México's commitment to a stable exchange rate

---

[5] These capital flows helped sustain imports. Artificially sustained imports may depress aggregate income because of their contractionary impact on the domestic market and economic activity level (Bhaduri 1998). This occurs through a perverse operation of the Kahn-Keynes multiplier, where the substitution of domestic goods by imported goods provides the initial impulse, but as the output of domestic goods decreases, so too do profits, wages, and employment. This leads to further declines in aggregate demand and output, with negative effects on the productive structure of the recipient country. Given the pace at which trade liberalization occurred and the importance of these capital flows, it is reasonable to conclude that the Mexican economy may have been suffering this effect in the 1990s. In this case, the contraction of the domestic market that resulted from restrictive anti-inflation policies was also aggravated by the gradual decline of the domestic productive apparatus.

remained credible. Thus, in addition to maintaining a semi-fixed exchange rate in order to quell inflation, exchange rate rigidity served to assure foreign capital holders.[6]

In summary, keeping inflation under control is key to attracting foreign investment to Mexico and to maintaining a competitive base with the country's main trading partners. However, a tight monetary stance has also reduced the flow of credit for productive activities and kept interest rates high. This, in turn, has had a very negative effect on the evolution of the non-performing loan portfolio and placed the entire banking system in jeopardy.

Fiscal policy is another macroeconomic instrument that Mexico has used successfully in the fight against inflation. Mexico's huge fiscal deficits of the 1980s have been reduced dramatically. However, this reduction was achieved through drastic cuts in public expenditures, and even with these reductions the federal budget has rarely achieved a surplus in its overall public balance. According to official statements, the goals of this restrictive fiscal policy are to free up resources for the private sector and to encourage a healthy economic environment. Such reasoning might make sense under other economic circumstances, but when national economic policy makers' top priority is to control inflation, fiscal discipline does not necessarily increase resources for the private sector. In fact, interest rates respond primarily to the money supply and foreign capital flows; they are only minimally influenced by fiscal austerity. Similarly, foreign capital requirements are largely determined by the size of the trade deficit and by external debt servicing requirements; they are affected only marginally by fiscal discipline. Thus, despite significant reductions in public spending—and important tax cuts in 1990–1991 and 1999—the private sector is far from being able to lead the growth process, and in this instance fiscal sacrifice has proved an ineffective tool for promoting investment.

The federal government's primary economic balance conveys information about revenues and expenditures net of debt service (see table 2.4, figure 2.1). Although it has limitations, this is usually considered a trustworthy indicator of fiscal policy because it displays an accurate picture of real revenues and expenditures. Mexico has generated a primary balance surplus not by raising tax revenues but by lowering expenditures. Indeed, tax revenues as a share of GDP dropped from 11.7 percent in 1989 to 10.8 percent in 1999. Budgetary appropriations

---

[6] However, capital inflows must be "sterilized" in order to keep the monetary base stable. Sterilization takes place through the issuing of government debt to absorb Mexican pesos. As capital inflows increase and sterilization continues, more debt is issued. These operations have serious implications for the evolution of domestic debt.

for programmable expenditures[7] tumbled from about 25 percent of GDP in the early 1980s to 16.7 percent in 2000, with serious impacts on social well-being. It is true that some expenditure items (in education, for example) were transferred from the federal government to the states in the context of decentralization efforts, but this resource transfer amounted to no more than 2 percent of GDP and does not explain the large drop in overall expenditures. Among other consequences, the government has been unable to strengthen the economy's capacity to adjust to increased international competition and assist those social groups that have suffered as a result of trade liberalization [8]

Instead, resources released by the adjustment in expenditures have gone to debt service. When debt service is taken into account, a systematic deficit appears in the federal budget. Thus the debt burden has continued to exert an ominous impact on fiscal policy even though interest rates dropped throughout most of the 1990s. If interest rates rise again, the negative impacts on Mexico's fiscal policy will reappear with renewed force, and they will be exacerbated by the liabilities inherent in the post–1995 rescue of the banking sector.

In this context, it is important to note that interest payments on total (domestic and foreign) public debt are comparable in amount to income tax revenues and to such non-tax revenues as income from sales of oil and gas. A detailed analysis of public spending reveals that interest payments on total public debt are the number one item in the expenditures column, exceeding all individual items in federal appropriations and expenditures. In real terms, interest payments exceeded investment in plant and equipment and public works by a factor of 1.8 in 2000.

This situation has detrimental effects on the health care, housing, education, and infrastructure needs of Mexico's growing population. Budget appropriations as a percentage of GDP have declined to their lowest levels in two decades. Moreover, debt service is forcing the government to postpone indefinitely some of the public-sector investments

---

[7] Programmable expenditures are defined as total expenditures excluding interest payments and revenue sharing with states and municipalities.

[8] The most dramatic example is the plight of corn farmers. In the late 1990s, these producers suffered severely as a result of about a 50 percent drop in producer prices, a 40 percent fall in income support mechanisms, and the disappearance of the most important market-regulating institutions, which threw the price formation process into disarray. The reason is that the imperatives of a balanced budget prevailed over considerations regarding investment and support for corn producers during market transition. In this sense, the government's restrictive fiscal stance endangered the goals of trade liberalization. For details, see Nadal 1999.

TABLE 2.4. Mexico's Fiscal Policy, 1980–2000: Public and Primary Economic Balances (millions of current pesos)[1]

	1980	1981	1982	1983	1984	1985	1986	1987	1988	1989
Public balance	-335.9	-866.2	-1,660.3	-1,540.6	-2,504.8	-4,535.2	-12,685.6	-31,000.0	-48,734.5	-28,455.0
Primary economic balance	-133.9	-489.8	-245.6	723.6	1,414.6	1,860.6	1,962.4	11,034.4	31,530.5	41,936.3

	1990	1991	1992	1993	1994	1995	1996	1997	1998	1999	2000
Public balance	-26,914.4	-12,981.9	4,930.3	8,242.8	-1,734.9	-200.7	282.9	-23,011.0	-47,918.6	-56,861.6	-52,502.0
Primary economic balance	75,194.1	77,403.1	90,539.4	43,989.5	36,199.7	84,655.2	108,700.6	105,063.0	63,314.1	113,740.8	149,340.5

Source: El Colegio de México, Science and Technology Program, Project on Mexico's Development Strategy, with data from the Secretaría de Hacienda y Crédito Público.

[1] The public balance includes income and budgetary expenditures, with interest payments. The primary economic balance includes income and budgetary expenditures, without interest payments.

FIGURE 2.1. Mexico's Fiscal and Financial Changes, 1980-2000

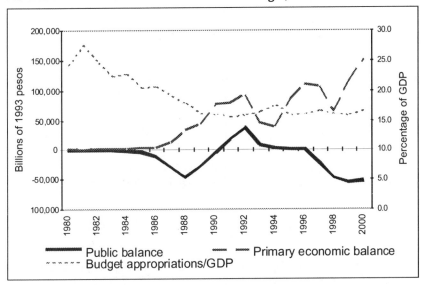

Source: Same as table 2.4.

that were considered essential to the ongoing restructuring of the Mexican economy as a result of trade liberalization.[9]

A closer look at the structure of fiscal revenues also reveals the effects of a self defeating macroeconomic strategy (see table 2.5). In essence, fiscal revenues stagnated, or at best increased only modestly in real terms (1993 pesos), over the 1990s. Total revenues in 2000 were 40.6 percent higher than in 1989, but this figure oscillates with fluctuations in petroleum prices. Tax revenues represent 11 percent of GDP, roughly the same proportion as in 1989. This evolution of tax revenues indicates that the strategy of controlling inflation through restrictive monetary and fiscal policies can backfire as the growth of tax revenues slows in direct response to a stagnant GDP.

---

[9] Commitments under the Uruguay Round of the GATT and the North American Free Trade Agreement (NAFTA) require a decisive effort to reorient productive resources efficiently. This effort requires income support systems and strong investments in hydro-infrastructure and technical assistance. However, agricultural producers have been left without the promised support mechanisms. This not only prevents comparative advantages from materializing, but it is also a bad omen for income distribution because agriculture absorbs almost a quarter of the employed labor force and remains a key sector despite its low contribution to GDP.

TABLE 2.5. Tax and Non-Tax Revenues in Mexico, 1989–2000 (millions of 1993 pesos)

Year	Total Revenues	Tax Revenues[1]	Income Tax Revenues	Value-Added Tax Revenues	Non-Tax Revenues
1989	184,337.1	128,359.2	54,410.9	34,862.2	55,977.9
1990	183,301.2	125,747.3	53,095.3	39,693.8	57,553.9
1991	218,580.9	127,230.5	53,895.1	38,195.1	91,350.3
1992	230,566.6	139,391.1	62,000.7	33,485.1	91,175.5
1993	193,769.5	143,155.2	64,951.1	35,232.6	50,614.3
1994	202,960.3	147,831.5	65,012.4	35,535.6	55,128.7
1995	187,241.0	113,827.8	47,189.7	34,611.8	73,413.2
1996	202,723.5	116,711.0	50,175.1	37,237.8	86,012.5
1997	221,165.1	135,903.3	58,732.0	42,491.0	85,261.7
1998	208,241.3	154,402.3	64,735.1	45,787.4	53,839.0
1999	222,244.5	170,841.2	70,324.7	49,858.7	50,314.0
2000	259,197.9	174,372.7	69,579.4	50,375.0	85,546.0

Source: El Colegio de México, Science and Technology Program, Project on Mexico's Development Strategy, with data from the Secretaría de Hacienda y Crédito Público.

[1] The "tax revenues" category includes revenues from special taxes, such as those on the sale of alcohol.

Income tax revenues in 2000 were only 7 percent greater than in 1994. Revenues from the value-added tax (VAT) expanded a bit more rapidly, but this was partly the result of a rise in the VAT from 10 to 15 percent in 1995. The evolution of income taxes and value-added taxes as shares in total tax revenues between 1989 and 1998 also demonstrates that the VAT is becoming more important. However, because the VAT bears directly on consumption, it remains a regressive tax.

The weight of non-tax revenues has remained comparable to what it was at the beginning of the 1989–2000 period (table 2.5). Fluctuations in non-tax revenues primarily reflect movements in the price of petroleum (petroleum exports are the primary source of non-tax revenues and account for more than 25 percent of total fiscal revenues).[10] The drop in international petroleum prices in 1998 exposed the dangers of an over-reliance on oil revenues, and in 2001 reductions in oil prices forced significant cuts in the federal budget. This perilous state of affairs will not change as long as macroeconomic priority hinges on restrictive monetary, credit, and fiscal policies.

THE DEBT BURDEN REVISITED

There is widespread confidence in official circles that Mexico has the capacity to service its external debt. This confidence rests on a number of considerations, including the debt's composition, size, maturity profile, and, more important, three basic indicators that traditionally appear in the literature on debt theory and in official analyses. However, these indicators—the ratios of total debt to GDP, debt growth rate to GDP growth rate, and export earnings to debt service payments—are misleading, and a more comprehensive analysis is required.[11]

A crucial event in the evolution of Mexico's external debt since 1980 was the government's renegotiation of the debt in 1989 (see table 2.6), after which the administration of President Carlos Salinas de Gortari (1988–1994) announced that the external debt problem had been resolved. Indeed, outstanding external public debt decreased by about 6

---

[10] The petroleum sector's fiscal importance is great due to revenues generated by special taxes on the sale of gasoline.

[11] The following discussion of foreign and domestic debt employs the conventional definition found in the literature on this topic, including the World Bank's *World Debt Tables*. A different approach, advocated by Atkeson and Ríos-Rull (1995), consists of taking *all* liabilities (that is, all international capital flows) into account. According to this probably more rigorous approach, the ratio of Mexico's total external debt to GDP is much more *unfavorable*. This should be kept in mind when analyzing the constraints on external borrowing that are addressed in the Atkeson/Ríos-Rull model.

TABLE 2.6. Mexico's Outstanding Public and Private External Debt,
1980–2000 (millions of U.S. dollars)

Year	Total	Public Sector	Non-Bank Private	Banking Sector	Banco de México
1980	54,425.8	33,812.8	16,900.0	3,713.0	0.0
1981	80,997.6	52,960.6	21,900.0	6,137.0	0.0
1982	87,368.2	59,730.0	19,107.0	8,531.0	0.2
1983	93,779.0	59,650.0	26,016.0	6,909.0	1,204.0
1984	96,650.9	69,377.9	18,500.0	6,340.0	2,433.0
1985	96,566.1	72,080.1	16,719.0	4,824.0	2,943.0
1986	100,990.9	75,350.9	16,061.0	5,551.0	4,028.0
1987	107,782.6	81,406.8	15,384.1	5,873.0	5,118.7
1988	100,087.6	81,003.2	8,015.3	6,283.0	4,786.1
1989	94,442.9	76,059.0	6,038.2	7,220.0	5,125.7
1990	106,743.2	77,770.3	9,039.6	13,425.0	6,508.3
1991	117,016.9	79,987.8	12,035.0	18,235.0	6,759.0
1992	116,501.1	75,755.2	15,840.5	18,948.0	5,957.4
1993	130,524.8	78,747.4	23,226.0	23,756.0	4,795.4
1994	139,817.6	85,435.8	25,427.6	25,094.0	3,860.2
1995	165,645.2	100,933.7	26,518.3	20,911.0	17,282.2
1996	157,155.1	98,284.5	26,411.8	19,180.0	13,278.8
1997	149,021.3	88,321.2	34,793.6	16,819.0	9,087.5
1998	160,257.4	92,294.5	43,762.0	15,821.0	8,379.9
1999	166,380.4	92,289.5	55,498.7	14,124.0	4,468.2
2000	160,761.6	90,160.3	54,094.5	13,040.0	3,466.8

Sources: El Colegio de México, Science and Technology Program, Project on Mexico's Development Strategy, with data from Poder Ejecutivo Federal, *Primer informe de gobierno: anexo* (2001), and Ciemex–Wefa.

percent from its 1988 level (from US$81.0 to $76.1 billion), and private debt dropped from US$8.0 to $6.0 billion.[12] Nevertheless, Mexico's total external debt rose steadily following the 1989 debt renegotiation, reaching US$165.6 billion in 1995.[13] The rescue package put together

---

[12] Mexico returned to international voluntary capital markets in 1989–1991, and outstanding external debt began to increase once again. As Cline (1995: 42) noted, this development can be interpreted in two ways—as a negative, if one feels that Mexico was still struggling with the debt problem of the early 1980s, or as a positive because Mexico was gaining access to new financial resources.

[13] The 1995 peak was due to the conversion of domestic debt (US$15 billion in Treasury securities issued in 1993–1994) into external debt as Mexico's economic authorities absorbed exchange-rate risks.

by the International Monetary Fund (IMF) and the U.S. Department of the Treasury in the aftermath of the 1994–1995 financial crisis was intended to address this new jump in Mexico's external debt. Yet Mexico has continued on its historic trajectory; in 2000 the country's total debt represented 26.1 percent of GDP.

One striking event in the evolution of Mexico's outstanding public external debt was the shrinking of the debt from US$100.9 billion to $88.3 billion between 1995 and 1997. This reduction was due basically to Mexico's success at refinancing the debt and to the fact that holders of Mexican Treasury bills (*tesobonos*), who were expected to remain within Mexican economic space, opted to leave despite the strong IMF–U.S. Treasury economic rescue package. Most of these bond holders chose to withdraw their funds from Mexico as soon as the tesobonos reached maturity.

Total interest payments exceeded US$116.9 billion during the 1980–1997 period. Average annual payments reached US$6.8 billion, although they fell to an average of $5.9 billion between 1990 and 1997 despite increases in debt principal (see table 2.7). The reduction is explained in part by the drop in interest rates after 1993 and in part by the impact of the 1989 debt renegotiation. If interest rates rise by 1 or 1.5 percentage points in the near future, debt service could increase by as much as US$500 million annually, depending on the total amount of outstanding debt.[14]

In 1997, Mexico placed US$7.2 billion worth of securities in international capital markets, allowing Mexican authorities to improve the maturity profiles of the country's debt. However, the cost of these refinancing operations may well have been high, notwithstanding government claims to the contrary, and this may explain why implicit interest rates increased by almost one percentage point between 1995 and 1997.

Since 1990, the non-bank private-sector's external debt has increased by a factor of three. Its share of total external debt went from 8.5 percent in 1990 to 18.2 percent in 1994 and to 33.6 percent in 2000. The traditional view within the Mexican government has been that private-sector debt is not a problem. However, this perception — which parallels

---

[14] The data in table 2.7 reveal that the private sector is probably paying higher interest rates on its outstanding debt than is the public sector. This is explained by the fact that a large proportion of public debt is with multilateral organizations, which charge lower rates than do commercial lenders. Also, public debt frequently has performed better than private debt in fetching lower rates in voluntary capital markets. On average, the interest rate on private external debt was 15 percent. The impact of these private-sector interest payments on Mexico's current account balance should not be disregarded.

TABLE 2.7. Interest Payments on Mexico's Outstanding Public and Private
External Debt, 1982–2000 (millions of U.S. dollars)

Year	Total Interest Payments	Interest on Public Debt	Interest on Private Debt	Implicit Rate of Interest	Total Outstanding Debt
1982	12,203.0	8,179.0	4,024.0	14.1	86,512.4
1983	10,102.9	6,488.3	3,614.6	10.4	96,685.2
1984	11,715.5	7,611.1	4,104.4	12.1	96,650.9
1985	10,155.9	7,601.0	2,554.9	10.5	96,566.1
1986	8,342.1	6,130.8	2,211.3	8.3	100,990.9
1987	8,096.7	5,700.3	2,396.4	7.5	107,782.6
1988	8,638.7	6,353.0	2,285.7	8.6	100,087.6
1989	9,277.6	6,929.1	2,348.5	9.8	94,442.9
1990	9,222.0	5,515.4	3,706.6	8.6	107,416.2
1991	9,215.2	5,794.4	3,420.8	7.8	117,743.8
1992	9,610.6	5,337.5	4,273.1	8.2	117,050.1
1993	10,934.4	4,803.9	6,130.5	8.4	129,978.8
1994	11,806.9	5,361.0	6,445.9	8.5	138,859.6
1995	13,575.4	6,574.3	7,001.1	8.2	165,464.2
1996	13,360.9	7,135.4	6,225.5	8.5	156,443.1
1997	12,436.2	6,489.2	5,947.0	8.3	149,027.3
1998	12,499.7	6,063.1	6,436.6	7.8	160,257.5
1999	13,018.0	6,881.7	6,136.3	7.8	166,380.4
2000	13,981.3	6,832.0	7,149.3	9.4	149,322.0

Source: El Colegio de México, Science and Technology Program, Project on Mexico's
Development Strategy, with data from Secretaría de Hacienda and Crédito Público
and Poder Ejecutivo Federal, *Primer informe de gobierno: anexo* (2001). Private interest
payments were calculated from Banco de México data.

the so-called consenting adults' view on current account deficits — may
be unjustified.[15] In a scenario of increasingly short-term maturities with
rapid and disorderly exchange rate adjustments, private corporations
may find themselves in difficulty, and in the past the Mexican government has had to offer support through several mechanisms.

The structure of Mexico's public external debt in terms of maturity
periods is not currently a serious problem: US$83 billion are long-term

---

[15] This "consenting adults" view (also called the Lawson view, for Nigel Lawson,
former British chancellor of the exchequer) starts from the premise that current
account deficits arising primarily from private-sector decisions, rather than from
fiscal imbalances, are of no consequence. The Mexican experience in 1994 should
put this idea to rest.

TABLE 2.8. Calendar of Maturities for Mexico's External Debt, 1999–2003 (millions of U.S. dollars)

	1999	2000	2001	2002	2003
Total external debt	20,453.7	18,192.0	10,235.2	12,197.3	7,196.3
Public sector	7,001.2	6,768.1	6,019.8	8,556.9	5,550.6
Market	1,543.2	3,940.9	2,695.0	4,997.8	2,911.8
Non-market	5,458.0	2,827.2	3,324.8	3,559.1	2,638.8
Private sector	10,247.1	8,510.3	4,163.2	3,614.3	1,645.7
Banco de México[1]	3,205.4	2,913.6	52.2	26.1	

Source: El Colegio de México, Science and Technology Program, Project on Mexico's Development Strategy, with data from Secretaría de Hacienda and Crédito Público and Banco de México.

[1] Liabilities with the International Monetary Fund.

maturities and $7 billion are in short-term instruments. Market-based instruments maturing through 2003 amount to slightly over US$16 billion (see table 2.8), and some of this amount may be rolled over or refinanced. In the case of debt associated with non-market instruments, the absolute amount maturing through 2003 is US$17.8 billion. Most of these obligations are with international financial organizations and can be rescheduled without difficulty.[16]

Despite these seemingly favorable patterns, it is important to assess Mexico's debt burden using more meaningful indicators. One traditional indicator, used in both academic research and official analyses, is the ratio of total debt to GDP.[17] The ratio appears to have remained healthy between 1988 and 2000, but this indicator fails to grasp the full impact of debt service.

Another typical indicator is the relative weight of debt service to total exports. In the Mexican case, the ratio of exports to interest payments maintained a healthy level throughout the period (see table 2.9). The second column in table 2.9 shows a rather favorable evolution, with total exports equaling more than twenty-four times the amount re-

---

[16] In contrast, a full 48 percent of the private sector's external debt is represented by short-term maturities. Once again, exchange-rate adjustments, especially if they are sudden or are accompanied by market overreactions, will have the capacity to disrupt seriously the private sector's ability to service its debt.

[17] See, for example, SHCP 1993; Cline 1995; Banco de México 1998; Poder Ejecutivo Federal 1998. It is also customary to compare growth rates of outstanding debt and GDP in order to unravel trends in the evolution of total debt. For the Mexican case, this comparison also gives an impression of a relatively limited debt burden.

TABLE 2.9. Mexico's Public External Debt Indicators, 1982–2000

Year	Export Earnings/ Interest Payments[1]	Trade Balance/ Interest Payments[1]	Current Account Balance/Interest Payments[1]
1982	2.6	0.9	−0.7
1983	3.4	2.2	0.9
1984	3.2	1.7	0.6
1985	2.8	1.1	0.1
1986	2.6	0.8	−0.2
1987	3.6	1.5	0.7
1988	3.0	0.4	−0.4
1989	3.0	0.0	−0.8
1990	3.8	−0.1	−1.0
1991	6.3	−1.1	−2.2
1992	6.4	−2.2	−3.4
1993	10.8	−2.8	−4.9
1994	11.4	−3.4	−5.5
1995	12.6	1.1	−0.2
1996	13.4	0.9	−0.2
1997	15.7	0.1	−1.1
1998	19.4	−1.3	−2.6
1999	19.8	−0.8	−2.1
2000	24.4	−1.2	−2.6

Source: El Colegio de México, Science and Technology Program, Project on Mexico's Development Strategy, with official data from Banco de México and Secretaría de Hacienda y Crédito Público.

[1] Interest payments on outstanding public debt.

quired for interest payments in the year 2000. From this perspective, it appears that servicing the debt has not been a serious problem for Mexico.

However, export earnings must also cover imports. Thus a more relevant comparison would be between the cost of debt service, on the one hand, and the foreign trade and the current account *balances,* on the other (see table 2.9, columns three and four, respectively). In this regard, the available data tell a much less favorable story. In the third column, a coefficient in the neighborhood of 1.0 indicates that currency earnings shown in the trade surplus are roughly equal to interest payments. A coefficient above (below) 1.0 indicates that the trade surplus exceeds (does not exceed) interest payments. A small positive value for this coefficient thus indicates a modest trade surplus, and negative numbers point to a trade deficit. This coefficient shows a negative sign beginning in 1990, and this trend continued until the 1994 crisis.

A key point to note here is that whereas the conventional indicator (total exports/interest payments) remained favorable throughout the 1990s, the more meaningful trade-balance-to-debt-service coefficient indicates that the Mexican economy is far from solving its debt burden problem.[18] When the trade balance has registered a surplus, as in 1995–1996, these resources have been channeled entirely to pay interest on outstanding public debt (table 2.9).[19] But when the external account has reversed direction, as in 1997, a downward trend reappears in this indicator. The levels of stress experienced in 1994 were readily apparent once again in 2000.

In the context of deregulated and interdependent financial markets, current account deficits are widely considered to be the new driving force behind indebtedness (Cline 1995), making the current account balance/interest payments coefficient the most meaningful indicator in table 2.9.[20] From 1988 until the 1995 crisis, the coefficient displayed a steadily worsening negative sign. Although the conventional indicator continued to mislead by sending positive signals, the negative threshold reached in 1993–1994 was approached again in 2000, underscoring the huge drain that the debt burden imposes on Mexico's financial resources.

Increments in 1999–2000 in the rate for thirty-year U.S. Treasury bonds drove interest rates up across the entire spectrum of short- to long-term lending instruments. This development had a number of negative effects on the Mexican economy. First, total interest payments on most of the country's external debt increased. Second, if rate increases dampen the dynamism of the U.S. economy (as finally occurred in 2000), there will be less demand for Mexican exports to the U.S. market, where Mexico is heavily concentrated.[21] Hence pressure on Mexico's cur-

---

[18] Official documents using conventional indicators (debt/GDP, debt/exports, and debt service/exports) are available on-line at www.presidencia.gob.mx.

[19] It is important to note that these are interest payments on the external *public* debt. If one includes interest on private debt, the indicators would show an even more pronounced negative trend.

[20] Ironically, Cline (1995) completely disregards the indicators considered here, relying exclusively on the debt/GDP ratio, the interest payments/total exports ratio, and the ratios between rates of growth in these variables.

[21] In light of the fact that more than 85 percent of Mexico's trade is with the United States, a slowdown in the U.S. economy reduces Mexican exports significantly.

Another way to assess the importance of Mexico's debt service burden is to compare interest payments with petroleum exports. During the 1990s, an average of 70 percent of oil revenues went to interest payments. This is particularly dis-

TABLE 2.10. Mexico's Total Public Domestic Debt, 1988–2000
(outstanding balance in millions of current pesos)

1988	1989	1990	1991	1992	1993	1994
108,947	137,601	165,417	159,107	133,478	134,769	178,960

	1995	1996	1997	1998	1999	2000
	155,360	192,162	273,656	378,256	506,389	596,389

Source: El Colegio de México, Science and Technology Program, Project on Mexico's Development Strategy, with data from Secretaría de Hacienda y Crédito Público.

rent account deficit will increase significantly. Third, an upward movement in U.S. rates would lead to increases in Mexico's domestic interest rates, thus raising the cost of servicing domestic debt. The drop in U.S. interest rates during 2001 had the opposite effect, but this occurred in the context of a recession in the United States that had other serious negative effects for the Mexican economy. The resulting economic slowdown in Mexico brought about a significant contraction in tax revenues, thus aggravating the cost of servicing public domestic debt. An objective assessment of Mexico's debt burden must include domestic as well as external debt because any distinction between the two blurs in the context of an open economy. In effect, efforts to assess the sustainability of Mexico's debt burden must look at *total* public debt (table 2.10).[22]

Table 2.10 shows that, in contrast with the performance of Mexico's external debt, public-sector net domestic debt increased dramatically between 1988 and 2000. Interest payments on domestic debt (1.5 percent of GDP) have already become a source of concern. By 2000, domestic public debt consolidated with the Banco de México had increased to a full 16.6 percent of GDP. This was the result of the Banco

---

turbing when one considers that there are indications of overexploitation of Mexico's oil resource base. Also, about one-third of total government fiscal revenues comes from petroleum exports. If oil prices drop and interest payments on the public external debt remain constant or increase, the impact on Mexico's public spending and investment will be severe.

[22] That the distinction between domestic and external debt tends to be fuzzy is best illustrated by events in 1994–1995, when a significant share of domestic debt was transformed into external debt. Foreign investors holding Mexican Treasury obligations (peso-denominated *tesobonos*) obtained a promise from Mexican authorities to absorb losses caused by exchange-rate fluctuations. This effectively transformed the tesobono obligations—essentially a short-term debt issuance—into external debt. The outstanding external debt rose by US$15 billion (see tables 2.6 and 2.7).

de México's adjustments in the monetary base to prevent the inflationary pressures that could have been generated by an increase in money supply resulting from inflows of international capital. Thus the need to "sterilize" capital inflows in order to control the money supply led to greater domestic debt. At the same time, this accumulation of international assets permitted a reduction in net external indebtedness. In practical terms, then, *domestic debt was substituted for external debt* (Banco de México 1998).

THE BANKING CRISIS AND ITS AFTERMATH

Another key factor in the expansion of Mexico's public domestic debt was the government's rescue of the banking sector between 1995 and 1998. The 1994–1995 economic crisis crippled the country's banking system, and the rescue program implemented by the administration of President Ernesto Zedillo (1994–2000) threatens to affect fiscal policy for decades. Moreover, there are indications that the rescue is not working as expected, and the banking system may be left without adequate deposit guarantees for some time. For these reasons, perhaps the greatest challenge for Mexico's economic policy makers in upcoming years will be to place the country's banking sector back on a secure footing.

Because of their ability to manage risk and their informational advantages regarding the microeconomic behavior of other agents, banks can bridge the gap between savings decisions and uncertainties concerning the maturity of investment projects. On the other hand, individual depositors' inability to calculate the degree of liquidity of their deposits has generated a demand for a social guarantee of their savings. The systemic crisis of Mexico's banking system between 1995 and 1997 underscored the need for this type of protection.

Mexico's banks were reprivatized between 1990 and 1993 in order to increase competition and efficiency in the sector.[23] At the same time, the government significantly reduced its regulatory control over banking in order to reduce costs, diversify banking services, cut margins between passive and active rates, enhance efficiency, and improve the conditions of bank clients. From a macroeconomic perspective, privatization was also expected to bring about increases in domestic savings because economic agents would perceive better opportunities, higher returns, and a wider scope of services. In addition, the deregulation of

---

[23] The privatization process was marred by noncompliance with the basic ground rules the government itself had established for this process.

the sector widened the scope of economic activities in which banks could participate.

Deregulation of the banking sector was not, however, accompanied by investment liberalization. In a surprise move, the North American Free Trade Agreement (NAFTA) failed to open fully banking, insurance, and other financial services to foreign investment. Annex VII of the trade agreement established ceilings for foreign investment in the form of maximum percentages that foreigners could control in each branch of financial services. For banking services, the ceiling was set at 15 percent, probably as a concession to the new owners of recently privatized banks. But in the context of the 1994–1995 financial crisis, this protection became a serious obstacle to efforts to rebuild capital reserves through foreign investment in the sector. Since then, the federal government has sought total liberalization of foreign investment in banking.

Unfortunately, privatization of the banking sector did not fulfill its ultimate objectives. Interest rates stayed high during the 1990-2000 period, the margin between passive and active rates was one of the highest in the world, and efficiency remained an elusive goal. Meanwhile, banks' nonperforming portfolio reached critical dimensions.[24] The crisis of 1994-1995 led to spectacular interest rate hikes and drops in real wages and incomes, producing a general payments crisis. Defaults on loans skyrocketed, and bad notes pushed most banks to the brink of bankruptcy. This situation led Mexican government authorities to implement a rescue scheme that would allow the banks to rebuild their capital and reserves positions, the argument being that this was essential to safeguard deposits.

The main instrument employed in the rescue scheme was the Bank Savings Protection Fund (FOBAPROA), a program established in 1990 to accept loan portfolio transfers from the banking system in exchange for a larger degree of capitalization.[25] Under the terms of the rescue, troubled banks transferred loan portfolios to FOBAPROA and received promissory notes in exchange. These promissory notes, although not negotiable, generated interest at the compound rate of 28-day Mexican Treasury securities plus a spread of 1.2 percentage points. Interest and principal were payable at maturity (ten years). Banks also transferred

---

[24] Even as the privatization process was under way, the size of banks' nonperforming portfolio grew. The volume of bad loans in the agricultural sector had begun to exceed reasonable levels as early as 1989.

[25] FOBAPROA, the special trust fund responsible for these operations, acquired flows from duly qualifying loans (which in principle had to meet certain minimum criteria) for an amount equivalent to twice the fresh capital contributed by stockholders.

restructured loans to investment units (indexed to the inflation rate) and received special Treasury securities in exchange.

Academic analysts and policy makers have identified the basic principles that should guide the restructuring of a banking system (Hausmann and Rojas-Suárez 1997). The first key point is that the parties that benefited through risktaking must bear the brunt of losses. This means that bank stockholders are the first to face possible capital losses. The second principle is that banks in difficulty must not be allowed either to extend high-risk loans or to capitalize interest earnings; such behavior would be an abuse of the public resources committed to the bank bailout. Yet FOBAPROA's operations contravened these key lessons learned in banking crises elsewhere in Latin America. In effect, it rescued Mexico's bankers from the discipline of the market. Not only did FOBAPROA not protect depositors, it released bankers from all responsibility.

Loans taken over by FOBAPROA were removed from a bank's balance sheet and transferred to its off-balance accounts. Thus the risks associated with nonperforming loan portfolios accrued to the trust fund, while the banks registered FOBAPROA securities received in this exchange on their balance sheet. These transfers changed the profile of the banks' balances, and in several cases this operation helped attract foreign investors to Mexico's banking sector. However, the government's use of FOBAPROA to purchase bad notes from banks and pay for them with promissory notes was itself an illegal operation.[26]

In December 1998 a new Bank Savings Protection Institute (IPAB) was created. The new agency inherited FOBAPROA's liabilities, and it was charged with the task of establishing a new system for protecting bank deposits by the year 2005.[27] IPAB provided the same guarantees as its predecessor to holders of FOBAPROA promissory notes, but these liabilities were not consolidated as public debt.

The IPAB has three sources of funding: sales of assets inherited from FOBAPROA, fees collected from all commercial banks, and federal

---

[26] FOBAPROA's operations violated several federal banking and securities laws. The fund's technical committee was not legally empowered to sign the promissory notes because they far exceeded the fund's assets, and the federal government was not allowed to sign as guarantor because express consent from Congress was required in order to issue new debt. Moreover, sitting on FOBAPROA's technical committee turned the federal government into both the prime issuer and the guarantor of these promissory notes, something expressly forbidden in Mexican law.

[27] Investment units (UDIs) are units of account indexed to the rate of consumer inflation and used to adjust financial and commercial operations to inflation. Their value is adjusted daily. In April 1995, the value of one UDI was one peso.

budget appropriations. However, given the staggering volume of its liabilities, it seems unlikely that IPAB will be able to meet its obligations without further support. In 2001, total IPAB liabilities exceeded US$74 billion (mostly in inherited FOBAPROA promissory notes, of which approximately 90 percent are due to mature in 2006 and 2007), and annual interest payments totaled approximately US$12 billion. By 2005, moreover, IPAB will have to usher in the new system of limited guarantees of deposits.

In order to meet IPAB's multiple obligations, Mexican government officials devised a strategy comprising two main avenues of action. First, IPAB is to pay the real component of interest due in order to keep liabilities constant. Second, IPAB will reschedule its liabilities in order to extend maturity periods and obtain better market conditions. According to government officials, paying the real component of debt service (that is, debt service at an inflation-adjusted rate of interest) will reduce total liabilities as a percentage of GDP. [28]

The Mexican Congress authorized 35 billion pesos from the 2000 federal budget to cover the first full year of IPAB's operations, and IPAB estimates that it will recover 20 billion pesos from the sale of assets and 6 billion from bank fees.[29] Of these total receipts of 61 billion pesos, 59 billion were allocated to pay real interest accruing on outstanding liabilities, and the remainder was set aside to build the reserves required by the social guarantee system due to start in 2005.[30] At the end of 2000, then, IPAB had covered part of the total interest due, but it still faced huge outstanding liabilities and had accumulated little toward the financial reserves it must build for the near future.

The second component of the government strategy for liabilities management includes rescheduling IPAB's old debt. The legal limit on

---

[28] It must be emphasized that, from the perspective of those holding FOBAPROA's promissory notes (later taken over by IPAB), interest payments should appropriately include the fraction that government authorities call the "inflationary" component. From the perspective of a strategy designed to rebuild banks' capital reserves, the inability to cover full interest payments also leaves much to be desired because new investments in the banking sector will not be forthcoming as long as full servicing of the old liabilities is not guaranteed. This is why the government is also attempting a debt rescheduling.

[29] IPAB's assets dropped from an estimated 552 billion pesos in early 1998 to 206 billion in 1999. Recovery of assets has been slow, and the total amount expected to be recovered will probably not exceed 30 billion pesos.

[30] Under IPAB regulations, banks' annual dues must equal at least 0.04 percent of the total liabilities of all commercial banks. Extraordinary dues may be levied, but given the unhealthy situation of most banks, this is unlikely to occur. In addition, IPAB rules prevent it from using more than 75 percent of the dues it receives to pay interest on debt obligations.

IPAB's capacity to issue new debt is 6 percent of all commercial banks' total liabilities for a period of three years. In the year 2000, commercial banks' overall liabilities totaled 1.197 trillion pesos (approximately US$124 billion),[31] meaning that IPAB cannot issue more than US$74 billion in new debt until 2003. If all goes well, IPAB will be able to reschedule approximately 10 percent of total liabilities. However, the basic maturities profile would remain unchanged, with approximately 600 billion pesos maturing between 2006 and 2007.[32]

In December 1999, in an action with far-reaching consequences, the Mexican Congress enacted a law that eliminated all limits on the IPAB's capacity to issue debt.[33] The new legislation instructed the Banco de México to serve as financial agent for the issuance of new IPAB debt, and it authorized the central bank (without instruction from the Ministry of Finance and Public Credit [SHCP]) to charge IPAB debt service costs against its normal SHCP account if and when IPAB lacks sufficient funds. The treatment granted to IPAB liabilities through the central bank's capacity to charge its SHCP account is reserved for public domestic debt. Thus the government's strategy was clear; not only will IPAB be able to reschedule the old FOBAPROA promissory notes, but these notes will be converted into public debt.

The strategy of covering the real component of interest due on IPAB's liabilities has been presented as a useful means of reducing the burden of IPAB-related debt as a percentage of gross domestic product. This is, however, an elusive objective because the inflationary component of interest payments continues to accumulate as part of assets in banks' balance sheets. In other words, this strategy divides total interest payments due on IPAB's liabilities into two parts: one is related to the real interest rate, the other to the inflationary component. Budget appropriations have only been requested to cover part of the real component: 35 billion pesos in 2000, 24 billion in 2001, and 28 billion in 2002. The rest of the real component has been covered by the recovery of assets and the fees that IPAB has collected from banks.

In March 2001 the federal government finally recognized that the inflationary component of total interest payments also had to be taken into account in order to have a more accurate measure of the total fiscal deficit. In 2001 this amounted to 42.9 billion pesos, equivalent to 0.7

---

[31] These data are from the National Banking and Securities Commission (CNBV).

[32] This amount corresponds to the bulk of promissory notes issued by FOBAPROA officials during the 1995–1997 period as the generalized crisis of payments unfolded.

[33] It is important to note that the draft revenue law the president submitted to Congress acknowledged the limit to IPAB's indebtedness.

percent of GDP. This sum has not effectively accrued to the banks, but it has been noted on their balance sheets and must be covered one day. The fact that the administration of President Vicente Fox Quesada (2000-2006) recognized the public sector's total financial requirements (equivalent to 3.5 percent of GDP) signalled its willingness to assume the obligations contracted by its predecessors. Yet covering the total fiscal cost of the banks' rescue package is ultimately incompatible with healthy public finances and adequate levels of programmable expenditures.

There are several difficulties with the new IPAB mechanism. First, there are serious doubts concerning the legal soundness of the entire operation. It is doubtful, for example, whether Congress has the constitutional authority to lift the limits imposed on the IPAB's capacity to issue debt. Mexico's revenue law has a one-year duration, so IPAB will need annual authorization to continue issuing debt beyond its legal limits. Moreover, the authorizing legislation may conflict with other pieces of federal legislation, most notably the statutes governing the Banco de México and the Ministry of Finance and Public Credit.[34]

Servicing IPAB's liabilities will continue to exert an untenable burden on Mexico's fiscal policy for years to come. The government needed US$7.8 billion in federal funds to service its domestic debt in 2000. Federal budget appropriations in 2000 for agriculture (US$2.3 billion), health (US$1.8 billion), and the environment (US$1.4 billion) were already dangerously low for a country with Mexico's needs. Only appropriations for education (US$8.2 billion) exceeded the interest on the domestic debt. But if one includes the US$3.5 billion authorized for interest payments on IPAB's liabilities, total interest payments on domestic debt did, in fact, surpass by a significant amount expenditures on education and health combined. And considering IPAB's new capacity to draw on federal resources, the domestic debt burden will rise significantly in coming years and may well become the primary item in the federal budget.

Perhaps the most distressing aspect of the bank rescue is that, despite its colossal cost, it does not appear to be working. Data from the National

---

[34] This is no minor issue. Legal certainty is a crucial component of adequate policy making, especially given Mexico's urgent need to attract foreign investment. The bank rescue was tainted from the start by a host of illegal actions taken within FOBAPROA, and this may continue to undermine the objective of increasing foreign investment in the banking sector, Citicorp's recent acquisition of Banamex (Mexico's largest bank) not withstanding. This takeover was perhaps more the result of an individual firm's strategic calculations than a display of sector-wide confidence in Mexican authorities' capacity to cover all required interest payments.

Table 2.11. Total New Commercial Bank Loans and Nonperforming Loans in Mexico, 1994–1999 (millions of 1993 pesos)

Year	Total New Loans	Nonperforming Loans
1994	569,278.7	47,773.1
1995	521,881.9	64,321.6
1996	457,676.4	52,136.9
1997	407,950.7	61,116.6
1998	411,452.3	53,435.7
1999	364,160.2	48,041.1

Source: El Colegio de México, Science and Technology Program, Project on Mexico's Development Strategy, with data from Comisión Nacional Bancaria y de Valores.

Banking and Securities Commission (CNBV) show that the nonperforming loan portfolio continues to expand. In real terms (1993 pesos), the total nonperforming portfolio for all commercial banks was 47.7 billion pesos in 1994; four years later, it had increased to 53.4 billion pesos. Although nonperforming loans have dropped from the extremely high levels of 1995 (table 2.11), they have declined as a direct result of the drastic reduction in new loans.[35] Banks may be inclined to take fewer risks, and most nonperforming loans are attributable to past mistakes or previous economic policies. Yet the fact remains that banks are not carrying out the task for which they exist, a conclusion confirmed by the additional fact that bank deposits stagnated in the late 1990s.

Recent initiatives to enact a new bankruptcy law that would enhance creditors' capacity to make effective their rights over loan guarantees and collateral have been heralded as the answer to the banking crisis. Although there is a clear need to update Mexico's antiquated legislation on corporate bankruptcy, this will not increase credit flows to productive investment projects or to consumption. The real limitation does not come from uncertain rights over guarantees but from a restrictive monetary policy that is expressly designed to impose a high cost for access to credit.

---

[35] A significant part of the relative decline in the size of the nonperforming loan portfolio was the consequence of a change in accounting practices. Transactions with FOBAPROA (now IPAB) do not appear under the "nonperforming loans" category on a bank's balance sheets, making it appear that nonperforming loans have been cut significantly. In fact, this reduction is artificial.

CONCLUSION

Mexico's economic policy makers claim to have succeeded not only in bringing the country out of the financial crisis of 1994-1995, but also to have given Mexico enough room for maneuver to have ensured a peaceful and uneventful transition to a new administration in December 2000. International reserves increased to a historical high of US$40 billion in December 2001. The trade deficit was within reasonable limits, and the current account was considered to be fully under control. But the rate of GDP growth, which reached 7 percent in 2000, fell to –0.3 percent in 2001.

Yet similar claims were made in 1991 and 1992. Inflation was in the single digits in early 1993. Reserves were at an all-time high, and modest GDP growth coexisted with a seemingly reasonable deficit in the external account. Officials described the trade deficit as symptomatic of an expanding economy eagerly renovating its stocks of capital goods. And the government proclaimed a primary fiscal surplus as a certain sign of successful fiscal policy.

But Mexico's economy in 1991 and 1992 was highly vulnerable. The growth rate was inadequate, and anti-inflation policy relied too heavily on an overvalued exchange rate and efforts to contain aggregate demand. The expanding trade deficit was strongly associated with increasing imports of intermediate and consumer goods. And the public balance (income and budgetary expenditures, with interest) showed a deficit, indicating that savings from cutbacks in badly needed public expenditures were simply being redirected to debt service. The combination of external vulnerability and economic stagnation on the domestic front led to economic crisis in 1994–1995.

Although cycles are a hallmark of evolving capitalist economies, there will probably not be another crisis like that of 1994–1995. The reason is that the Mexican economy is operating under very different conditions: the current account deficit appears to be quite manageable (3.1 percent of GDP in 2000, down from 8 percent in 1994), and the mountain of six-month Treasury securities has disappeared. However, some new negative factors have emerged as well. Perhaps the most prominent is the fact that the banking system has still not recovered sufficiently to perform its normal functions, and the cost of the bank rescue will have a profound impact on future fiscal policy. A second negative feature is that the productive system remains weak. The lack of strong backward linkages has been a serious problem since the 1980s, and it was worsened by the 1995 recession. Third, the social costs of the 1995 crisis have not been eradicated, and poverty has expanded precipitously. Prospects for reversing these negative trends are not bright.

If these negative trends are not reversed, the Mexican economy will continue to deteriorate severely on many fronts. Monetary, credit, and fiscal constraints will continue to degrade the foundations of the real economy, and they will also deepen the negative tendency that has characterized the evolution of several key macroeconomic aggregates. This is not surprising given that the economic policy package leading to the 1994–1995 crisis continues to provide the basic architecture for Mexico's economic strategy. Thus external vulnerability and domestic stagnation continue to weigh upon the country's development prospects.

Portfolio investments and private-sector external debt will continue to play an important role. Mexico's capital account showed a substantial inflow of funds in 1999 and 2000. Foreign direct investment (FDI) surpassed US$11 billion in 1999 and US$13 billion in 2000. Short-term portfolio investments reached US$3.8 billion in 1999, but the flow reversed (that is, capital moved out of Mexico) in 2000. The resulting current account deficit had to be covered through non-bank private sector debt of US$9.3 billion. Unless portfolio investments are substantial, one can anticipate that greater indebtedness will be required to finance the current account deficit, which will keep interest rates high. Even a small reversal of short-term capital flows could trigger volatile exchange-rate adjustments that would obliterate previous achievements in lowering the rate of inflation.

Mexico's continuing ability to attract capital flows depends upon maintaining high interest rates. Although it is true that nominal rates can be cut as inflation eases, *real* interest rates must remain high.[36] This keeps credit expensive and exerts a negative impact on banking sector operations. The high interest rates required to maintain current levels of capital inflows sacrifice all prospects of growth for productive sectors of the economy.

Capital inflows will also contribute to an overvalued exchange rate. Adjusting for differentials in Mexican and U.S. inflation rates, in late 2001 the peso was 30 percent above its real value. Exchange rate overvaluation plays two critical roles in Mexico's economic strategy—one in the struggle against inflation, and the other in providing assurances of stability to foreign capital that is placed in peso-denominated investment instruments. Thus, even though this rigidity places Mexico's exporters at a disadvantage, exchange rate adjustments will not soon be forthcoming. Instead, economic policy makers will rely, as in the recent past, on higher interest rates to keep foreign portfolio investment in

---

[36] Inflation-adjusted annual rates (28-day Treasury bonds) were 7.4 percent in 1999, 9.6 percent in 2000, and 7.6 percent in 2001 (January-October).

Mexico—even though this affects credit, production, and growth, as well as the health of the ailing banking sector. Firms' ability to generate sales and to expand will continue to be impaired. Their competitiveness in the face of increasing imports will continue to suffer. When one adds the cost of bailouts for banks and large businesses—and the associated negative impacts on the domestic economy and the federal budget—the short-term outlook is not rosy.

Does Mexico's new open economy need more time in order to deliver on its promise of sustained growth and balanced external accounts? The answer is "no." After more than fifteen years under a regime of structural reform and comprehensive deregulation, there should be clear signs that the new strategy is working. Instead, negative indicators continue to dominate the economic landscape, official rhetoric notwithstanding. And alarming signals persist in the real economy as well.

Does the new economy require deeper structural reforms? Again, the answer is "no." Most key structural reforms have already been accomplished. The policy debate over privatizing the energy sector ignores the fact that there are more than political obstacles to such a change; privatizing the energy sector would deprive the federal government of more than 30 percent of its fiscal revenues.

That the responses to these two questions are negative finds further support in the core contradictions inherent in the open-economy model implemented in Mexico. The main contradiction is that the policy package aiming at exchange-rate stability and inflation control also led to a weakened external sector, damaged prospects for increased domestic savings, perpetuated an unhealthy public debt situation (both foreign and domestic), undercut the domestic market's ability to expand, and generated an unhealthy fiscal environment. The self-defeating nature of this combination is the source of economic vulnerability and instability. The strategic objective of *growth with external stability* becomes increasingly remote under this strategy.

Ironically, greater external vulnerability may also result from the conditions imposed as part of the international financial rescue package made available to Mexico during the 1994–1995 crisis (Grabel 1999) and from the Financial Strengthening Program (PFF) launched in June 1999. The PFF, with total reserves of US$16.9 billion, was designed to help Mexico avoid another end-of-presidential-term financial crisis in 2000. PFF funding came from several sources: US$4.2 billion from a standby arrangement with the International Monetary Fund, to be repaid in 2003–2005; US$5.2 billion in World Bank loans to improve social conditions and reinforce macroeconomic stability; US$3.5 billion from the Inter-American Development Bank for institutional development and social programs; and US$4 billion in credit lines from the U.S. EXIM-BANK to finance imports. These resources allowed Mexico to preserve its overvalued exchange rate (not an unimportant consideration in an election year), but an overvalued peso will continue to weaken the external sector and drive up the need for capital inflows. In addition, the macroeconomic policy conditions accompanying approval of these resources involved severe restrictions on growth, monetary, and fiscal policies, exacerbating the contradictions noted above.

An additional and crucial contradiction relates to the evolution of domestic savings. Increasing domestic savings has long been a key policy objective of Mexico's macroeconomic strategy. However, domestic savings suffered a very important reduction between 1990 and 1994, falling from 20 to 14 percent of GDP. Mediocre GDP growth had to be fueled by external capital inflows. The severe contraction of the economy after the 1994–1995 crisis led to an apparent recovery of domestic savings (to 21 percent of GDP in 1997). However, this was achieved through a forced-savings process. By 1998 domestic savings were back to their 1990 level of 20 percent of GDP, demonstrating that the domestic market contraction resulting from recessive macroeconomic policies is incompatible with an increase in domestic savings. Indeed, not only is the objective of increasing domestic savings far from being fulfilled, it will actually become increasingly difficult to attain as time goes by.

The official explanation for the dramatic drop in domestic savings between 1990 and 1994 notes three factors (SHCP 1997): the overvalued exchange rate and rising imports of consumer goods; economic actors' optimistic expectations regarding future income, leading to greater consumption; and greater availability of credit for consumption. Thus the official explanation is that consumption levels have been too high, and the government's strategy to increase domestic savings focuses on the notion that these high levels of domestic consumption must be reduced. This view is flawed, however. It disregards the fact that Mexico's macroeconomic policy package—with its restrictive monetary policy, high interest rates, and falling real wages—has led directly to appalling stagnation in the domestic market. In 2000, private consumption accounted for 50.7 percent of total final demand, down from 62 percent in 1989.

Moreover, the recent evolution of final consumption expenditures by class of goods and services is discouraging (see table 2.12). The measures for basic consumption items such as food and drink were the same in 1997 as they had been in 1994 (barely recovering from the downturn in 1995), and by 1999 they had increased by only 10 percent over their 1994 level. Even more discouraging is the fact that total con-

TABLE 2.12. Total Final Consumption Expenditures in Mexico by Class of Goods and Services, 1989–1999 (millions of 1993 pesos)

Year	Total Consumption	Food and Drink	Clothing and Shoes	Housing and Energy	Furniture	Health Care	Transportation	Education
1989	770,646	217,619	44,576	95,665	70,660	36,729	100,413	23,898
1990	816,117	229,282	47,852	100,454	74,280	37,886	107,892	24,938
1991	852,864	236,124	49,400	106,093	78,939	38,707	113,313	25,786
1992	891,505	246,032	52,169	111,508	82,308	39,126	117,801	26,090
1993	907,069	252,527	50,050	116,937	82,152	39,973	114,522	27,290
1994	950,670	264,546	49,343	122,034	85,403	39,928	125,137	27,917
1995	872,156	251,408	38,543	126,231	74,462	39,539	102,441	26,881
1996	890,035	256,115	39,177	131,084	76,198	38,637	109,381	26,960
1997	946,609	266,782	41,562	135,492	84,686	40,891	121,247	28,261
1998	997,181	280,808	42,890	139,117	89,320	42,831	132,715	29,123
1999	1,037,775	293,776	42,942	144,309	92,479	43,495	138,767	29,856

Source: El Colegio de México, Science and Technology Program, Project on Mexico's Development Strategy, with data from the Secretaría de Hacienda y Crédito Público.

sumption increased by only 9 percent over the 1994–1999 period. Expenditures on basic items such as health care, education, clothing and shoes, and furniture remained depressed throughout the period prior to the crisis of 1994–1995. Clearly, the economic strategy in operation prior to the crisis was insufficient to ameliorate conditions in terms of domestic consumption. A strategy to reduce domestic consumption will not lead to greater savings; instead, it will lead to greater levels of poverty and deprivation.

In sum, the contradictions in Mexico's economic strategy are leading to a dead end. Its basic elements must be revised. Whether a different macroeconomic approach is possible in the context of globalization's deregulated and interdependent financial markets remains an open question. The obstacles to implementing an alternative strategy with an expansionary and egalitarian agenda may be great, but an objective assessment of these constraints is required to determine whether this is so. Researchers need to examine linkages between growth, income distribution, and external imbalances in the context of an open economy. More specifically, they must examine, first, how alternative monetary and fiscal policies can be rendered compatible with the objective of attaining a more competitive insertion into the global economy and, second, how external constraints can be minimized. In particular, the notion that egalitarian domestic market expansion always runs counter to international competitiveness must be put to the test. Dogmatic adherence to a policy agenda that views neoliberal macroeconomic strategy as a recipe to be implemented everywhere is clearly not advisable at this stage. This insistence on adopting the neoliberal economic strategy without questioning its performance is therefore the first obstacle that must give way in order to move ahead with a more meaningful research agenda on Mexico's economic and social development.

REFERENCES

Atkeson, Andrew, and José Víctor Ríos-Rull. 1995. "How Mexico Lost Its Foreign Exchange Reserves." NBER Working Paper Series, no. 5329. Cambridge, Mass.: National Bureau of Economic Research.

Banco de México. 1998. *The Mexican Economy 1998: Economic and Financial Developments in 1997, Policies for 1998*. Mexico City: Banco de México.

Bhaduri, Amit. 1998. "Implications of Globalization for Macroeconomic Theory and Policy in Developing Countries." In *Globalization and Progressive Economic Policy*, edited by Dean Baker, Gerald Epstein, and Robert Pollin. Cambridge: Cambridge University Press.

Cline, William R. 1995. *International Debt Reexamined*. Washington, D.C.: Institute for International Economics.

Dornbusch, Rudiger, and Alejandro Werner. 1994. *Mexico: Stabilization, Reform, and No Growth.* Brookings Papers on Economic Activity. Washington, D.C.: The Brookings Institution.

Grabel, Ilene. 1999. "Emerging Stock Markets and Third World Development." In *Foundations of International Economics: Post-Keynesian Perspectives,* edited by Johan Deprez and John T. Harvey. London: Routledge.

Hausmann, Ricardo, and Liliana Rojas-Suárez. 1997. *Las crisis bancarias en América Latina.* Mexico City: Fondo de Cultura Económica.

Nadal, Alejandro. 1996. "Balance of Payments Provisions in the GATT and NAFTA," *Journal of World Trade* 30 (4): 5-24.

———. 1999. "Maize in Mexico: Environmental Implications of the North American Free Trade Agreement." Report to the Commission for Environmental Cooperation. Montreal: Commission for Environmental Cooperation.

Poder Ejecutivo Federal. 1998. *Quinto informe de gobierno.* Mexico City: Presidencia de la República.

———. 2001. *Primer informe de gobierno.* Mexico City: Presidencia de la República.

Salas, Carlos, and Teresa Rendón. 1996. "Ajuste estructural y empleo: el caso de México," *Revista Latinoamericana del Trabajo* (2): 49-76.

SHCP (Secretaría de Hacienda y Crédito Público). 1993. *Deuda externa pública mexicana.* Mexico City: Fondo de Cultura Económica.

———. 1997. *Programa nacional de financiamiento del desarrollo 1997–2000.* Mexico City: SHCP.

3

Mexico's Financial System and Economic Development: Current Crisis and Future Prospects

Celso Garrido

INTRODUCTION

This chapter examines the recent evolution of and prospects for Mexico's financial system, taking as its perspective the functions that a financial system must fulfill in order to support sustained expansion of productive sectors and of a national economy as a whole. The context for the study is the exchange-rate and financial crisis that erupted in Mexico in December 1994. Since then, the Mexican financial system has been virtually paralyzed with regard to its ability to fulfill its development functions, creating major stumbling blocks for individuals and companies.

Analysts of Mexico's 1994–1995 financial crisis generally explain it in terms of conjunctural factors.[1] Some point to the crisis in international financial markets; others identify internal difficulties, such as economic policy errors or weak institutions, or even the crises of confidence often associated with transitions between presidential administrations in Mexico. Mexico's Ministry of Finance and Public Credit (SHCP) posits that the crisis was the result of inadequate domestic savings, which forced the country to rely excessively on potentially volatile short-term external savings (SHCP 1997).

However, little attention has been paid to the fact that the Mexican economy has moved through several cycles since 1976. Nor has much importance been accorded to the facts that Mexico's privately owned banking system has fallen into bankruptcy twice since 1982, that on both occasions it was saved by government bailouts whose fiscal and institutional costs had grave implications for the relationship between

---

[1] For an interpretation along these lines, see, for example, Calvo et al. 1996.

finances and production, or that on two occasions the availability of large extraordinary sources of income—petroleum revenues from 1977 to 1982, and easy access to international financial markets from 1990 to 1994—ended in financial breakdowns rather than sparking a cycle of investment.

These issues raise several questions. What is the relationship between the 1995 banking crisis and the economic and financial trends generated during this period, on the one hand, and the recurring financial dynamic of the last quarter-century, on the other? Likewise, given that the period between 1976 and 1994–1995 encapsulated such radically different institutional environments and conditions—from strong protectionism and state regulation and interventionism, on the one hand, to rapid trade liberalization, on the other—what are the constants that explain the recurring cyclical dynamic referred to above? And what significance do the aforementioned changes in institutional environment have for this cyclical financial dynamic and Mexico's continuing financial difficulties?

In this chapter it is assumed that the 1995 crisis and the resulting evolution of the relationship between finances and production can be explained by four factors. These elements generated long-term cycles in the domestic economy and its relationship to the international economy and financial system. The first of these factors is the financial-industrial group structure that prevails among large Mexican corporations. By coalescing in financial-industrial groups, large corporations concentrate the flow of money and credit that is so decisive for the Mexican financial system and its dynamics. The second element is the federal government's practice of using public funds to bail out large bankrupt domestic firms, especially financial firms—a practice that encourages ventures plagued by high "moral hazard." The third factor is the legal system's inability to regulate and oversee the domestic financial system, as well as its inadequate or wrongful application. And because large amounts of low-cost international financial resources are periodically channeled to countries like Mexico, a fourth variable—the international financial system—is needed to complete the analysis.

In general, the dynamic of the economic-financial cycle originates in the actions of national financial-industrial groups, the key actors in a private financial system that concentrates deposits and credit.[2] This system operates according to an informal mechanism that turns certain business losses—those resulting from excessive risktaking—into public debt and subjects large corporations to only very lax regulation and

---

[2] The present study does not address the subject of state actions to control the economic surplus and its impacts on the structure of the financial system.

supervision. This situation generates tensions by stimulating speculative financial ventures and raising the possibility of crises when the chains of debt created by such operations cannot be closed. Tensions develop when there is an abundance of low-cost international capital and international creditors are disposed to relax their risk analysis in order to grant loans to businesses and the government.

When crisis breaks out, financial and nonfinancial firms go bankrupt, and the government then bails them out. This raises the demand for public funds, which in turn has negative impacts on private financing and exacerbates the recession in the domestic market. The bankruptcy of a financial firm brings changes in its organizational structure and the property it controls, degrading the firm's institutional quality and producing losses in the capabilities and skills it had developed over previous decades. Similarly, as a result of this process, the financial system's overall capacity to meet productive needs is further weakened. This leads to a recession that ultimately deepens into financial paralysis. The expansionary phase of the cycle begins again when there is a new, favorable articulation of the relationships between domestic factors and the dynamic of the international financial system.

The financial-economic cycle that began in Mexico in 1995 marks a shift away from the longer evolutionary cycles that predominated between 1976 and 1994, in that this latest financial-economic cycle is characterized by market segmentation and foreign dependence. In the economic and financial structure presently developing in Mexico, a few large national conglomerates (which have generally lost their banking subsidiaries) participate primarily in international markets and look abroad for their project financing. They resort to local banks only as a source of complementary funding. In contrast, the majority of Mexican businesses operate within the domestic market, where modern and efficient financial services are unavailable. For these producers oriented toward the domestic market, macroeconomic conditions mean that they are dependent upon foreign short-term capital, and their needs tie the evolution of the domestic market to the macroeconomic equilibriums needed to sustain growth in the external sector. This economic and financial structure does not appear capable of supporting progressive and sustainable development for the economy as a whole. For this reason, it is essential to reform the economic structure and financial system if the goal of development is to be attained.

In developing this argument, the remainder of this chapter is divided into the following sections. The first part examines the four long-term institutional factors that determine financial-economic cycles. The second section reviews broad cycles and the financial crises that occurred in Mexico between 1976 and 1994. The third focuses on the massive banking crisis that developed in 1995, and the fourth outlines changes that occurred in the course of this cycle. The concluding section presents some reflections on the dilemmas posed by this new economic and financial configuration, as well as some general lines of action for confronting these challenges.

INSTITUTIONAL FACTORS IN MEXICO'S FINANCIAL CYCLES SINCE 1976

Corporate Structure and the Concentration of Bank Deposits and Credit

The corporate structure of Mexico's large, private national firms tends toward conglomerates (or financial-industrial groups) that often own both financial and nonfinancial businesses. This pattern has been evident since the 1970s, and it was reinforced when these groups purchased privatized banks in the early 1990s (see table 3.1). Moreover, large Mexican firms tend to be family owned, and the family heads of the financial-industrial groups often make investments in each other's conglomerates and sit on each other's executive boards. They thereby weave a complex network through which they can exercise varying degrees of control over all businesses in which they are involved.

This corporate structure is accompanied by high economic concentration in the markets where the companies operate. In the case of the financial system, this is an outcome of historical limitations on foreign banks' participation in the domestic market and of the government's policy of promoting concentration in the banking sector in order to achieve economies of scale. For their part, large national firms traditionally have maintained strong oligopolistic power in the productive sectors where they operate, as indicated by these conglomerates' changing share in Mexico's 500 largest corporations (see table 3.2).[3]

How these conglomerates make their net earnings reflects their corporate structure and the degree of concentration that characterizes them. Their earnings include those from regular business operations as well as those resulting from financial operations. What is significant here is not the fact that these firms combine both types of earnings; this is the norm for any relatively large corporation. Instead, what is im-

---

[3] This table is presented for illustrative purposes only. The sample has significant limitations, such as the severe underestimation of participation by foreign firms. Nevertheless, the sample does reflect the fact that private national firms represent a much larger proportion of all large national firms as a consequence of the privatization of state-owned enterprises.

portant is the effect that this mixing of operating and financial earnings has on financial relationships when it is done by firms with high degrees of concentration in both fields of activity.

Large, private national firms play a decisive role in the appropriation and assignment of funds within the national economic and financial system. This enhances their ability to compete with other firms, first, by allowing them to finance their own investments and, second, by granting the corporations power over the structure of the financial system. However, the same linkages between industry and finance that generate net earnings also produce periodic conflicts between the firms' own objectives and the broader goal of maintaining a sound relationship between the country's financial system and production and consumption activities. Tensions arise when the firms must choose between maintaining corporate earnings, preserving their owners' capital, and assuring the firms' survival, on the one hand, and the need to preserve the stability of the national financial system and its links with the international system, on the other. Such tensions have historically been resolved through massive capital flight, a severe crisis of the national financial system, and a credit crunch for other economic actors.

State Interventions to Socialize Losses

A second factor influencing the long-term evolution of the Mexican financial system has been an informal arrangement first established more than two decades ago among high-level federal government officials, managers of publicly owned financial firms, and owners of large, private national businesses. Under the unwritten terms of this arrangement, when risky or badly managed corporate ventures resulted in near-bankruptcy, the state would expropriate the firm and assume responsibility for covering the losses with public funds. If public funds were not available, the state would turn either to increases in public debt or the printing of money. This practice nullified market penalization of unsound corporate practices by allowing businesses to take risks in the knowledge that their losses could be passed along to the population as a whole via state action. Indeed, Acle Tomasini and Vega Hutchinson (1986) determined that over half of the firms in their sample of public enterprises established between 1970 and 1982 were created as a result of this dynamic.

This relationship between the state and large, private national corporations has favored—even engendered—a business attitude toward risk that is generally termed "morally hazardous." Under these circumstances, firms may make extraordinarily risky investments, or they may take risks they are not financially prepared to cover. They are inclined to

TABLE 3.1. Mexico's Privatized Banks, Listed by Territorial Coverage, 1990s

Territorial Coverage	Bank	Purchasing Group	Group's President	Origin of Purchaser	Region	Purchase Date
National	Banamex	Accival/regional groups	Roberto Hernández/ Alfredo Harp	Stockbroker	Federal District	1991
	Bancomer	Vamsa/regional groups	Eugenio Garza Laguera	Visa	Nuevo León	1991
	Serfín	OBSA/regional groups	Adrián Sada	Vitro	Nuevo León and Federal District	1991
	Banco Internacional	Prime	Antonio del Valle/ Juan Sánchez Navarro	Industry	Federal District	1992
	Multibanco Comermex	Inverlat	Agustín Legorreta	Stockbroker	Federal District	1992
	Banca Cremi	Firm in Jalisco	Raymundo Gómez Flores	Dina Trucks	Guadalajara	1991
	Unión[1]	Firm in Southeast	Carlos Cabal Peniche	Agroindustry	Southeast	1991
	Banco Mexicano Somex	Inverméxico	Carlos Gómez y Gómez	Grupo Industrial Desc	Federal District	1992

	Bank	Partner	Person	Sector	Region	Year
Multiregional	Multibanco Mercantil	Probursa	J. M. Madariaga	Stockbroker	Federal District	1991
	Banpaís	Mexival	Ángel Rodríguez	Transportation	Federal District and Northeast	1991
	Bancrecer	Firm in Federal District and Guanajuato	Roberto Alcántara	Transportation	Federal District and Guanajuato	1991
	Banco del Atlántico	GBM	Alonso de Garay	Stockbroker	Federal District	1992
	Banoro	Estrategia Bursatil	Rodolfo Esquerra	Stockbroker	Sinaloa	1992
Regional	Banca Confía	ábaco	Jorge Lankenau	Stockbroker	Nuevo León	1991
	Banco de Oriente	Grupo Margen	Marcelo Margáin	Stockbroker	North and Center	1991
	Banco Promex	Finamex	Mauricio López Velázquez	Stockbroker	Jalisco	1992
	Banco del Centro	Multivalores	Hugo Villa	Stockbroker	Federal District and Jalisco	1992
	Banorte	Maseca/Gamesa	Rorberto González Barrera/Alberto Santos de Hoyo	Agroindustry	Nuevo León	1992

Source: Secretaría de Hacienda y Crédito Público.

[1] Formerly BCH.

TABLE 3.2. Mexico's 500 Largest Corporations by Property Type, 1987, 1990, and 1996

Property Type	1987		1990		1996	
	Number of Firms	Percent of Total	Number of Firms	Percent of Total	Number of Firms	Percent of Total
State-owned	45	9.0	14	2.8	5	1.0
National private	366	73.2	411	82.2	404	80.8
Multinational	89	17.8	75	15.0	91	18.2
Total	500	100.0	500	100.0	500	100.0

Source: Expansión, several years.

do so because of their assumption that, pending successful negotiations, they will be bailed out by the state with public funds. Their losses will thus be socialized, in the sense that they are assumed by the community as a whole.

Such conduct can occur in both industrial and financial activities, but it is in the latter category that this "morally hazardous" conduct is most likely to take place—as when a financial agent deposits third-party funds in high-risk operations on the assumption that the state will reimburse the depositor if a loss is incurred. Following this logic, the Mexican state saved the nation's private banks and other financial intermediaries from bankruptcy twice in the twelve-year span between 1982–1983 and 1994–1995.[4] Table 3.3 summarizes the development stages and the principal operations carried out under this informal mechanism from the 1970s through the 1990s.

The information in table 3.3 demonstrates that there is a relationship between the state practice of implicitly guaranteeing "insurance coverage" for big corporations' business risks and the sometimes "morally hazardous" investment practices that are followed by some large corporations. This establishes a logical link between these corporations' capi-

---

[4] The common view is that the government's 1982 takeover of private banks was a seizure. This action should, however, be considered a government bailout, along the same lines as the 1995 bank bailout. More than a government response to continuing political conflicts with private bankers and the heads of Mexican conglomerates, the bank nationalization ensured the continuation of minimal financial intermediation. The aggressive tone of government statements issued at the time merely provided political cover for the bailout.

The 1982 bank nationalization was not the seizure of businesses operating normally; rather, it was a rescue of a number of banks that were essentially bankrupt. After the exchange-rate crisis and devaluation in mid-1982, Mexican banks had U.S. dollar-denominated liabilities ("mexdollar" deposits) totaling some US$12 billion—as well as significant amounts of debt denominated in other foreign currencies—that they could not cover. As part of the bailout, the government applied an old regulation that allowed bankers to pay these liabilities in pesos at the favorable exchange rate of 70 pesos per U.S. dollar, at a time when the free-market rate was more than 110 pesos per dollar.

An even more important factor behind the government's action was that, following the devaluation, many businesses and consumers were unable to repay their loans. Private banks thus faced the imminent prospect of borrowers defaulting on their obligations, making the probability of a major banking crisis very high. The bank nationalization transferred all these difficulties to the government. Over time, the government managed the problem of loan defaults via inflation and the rollover of bank credits. For a similar interpretation of the 1982 bank nationalization, see Tello 1984 and Aguilar, Carmona, and Hernández 1985.

TABLE 3.3. Evolution of the Mexican Federal Government's Corporate Bailouts, 1970s–1990s

1970s: Closed Economy with State Intervention	1980s: Closed Economy with State Intervention	1990–1994: Open and Unregulated Economy	Since 1995: Open and Unregulated Economy
Nationalization of bankrupt private firms	Nationalization of commercial banks and socialization of banks' foreign debt	Insider privatization of publicly owned industrial, commercial, and service firms[1]	FOBAPROA bailout of privatized commercial banks
Booming growth of public sector through appropriation of private enterprises	FICORCA program for bailout of large economic groups unable to pay their foreign debt	Insider privatization of banks, insurance companies, and savings banks	FEMEVAL bailout of stock brokerages
	Public debt increased to finance capital outflows ("capital flight") driven by fears of a devaluation		Highway bailout programs
			BANCOMEX bailout of large corporations
			IMF/U.S. Federal Reserve bailout of national and foreign investors in dollar-denominated government bonds

Source: Author's compilation using data from diverse sources.

[1] Socialization of the "moral hazard" facilitated unviable insider privatizations.

tal accumulation and the evolution of the public sector's domestic and foreign debt. The conditions of this accumulation dynamic lead to growing public-sector debt through the forced socialization of losses when investments fail, in addition to the costs incurred through state subsidies to private corporations.

It is important to note that, although this informal arrangement was established during the protectionist stage of Mexico's economic development, it was maintained and even extended during the economic liberalization process and downsizing of the government's role in the economy that began in the mid–1980s. Also noteworthy is the fact that the operation of this informal mechanism contributed to important changes in the structure of the banking system. As noted in table 3.3, the banks were nationalized in 1982 and then reprivatized in the early 1990s, only to undergo a later de facto nationalization. Over the course of this process, skills and knowledge that had been acquired over time were lost, severely undercutting the banks' institutional quality. When repeated through successive cycles, such a pattern creates an implicit institutional cost for state management of private firms that is equal to or greater than the financial costs implied in the bailouts.

The Legal Environment Regulating the Financial System

Between 1977 and 1999, the legislation establishing norms for the institutions, markets, and regulations that make up the financial system was revised seven times. These reforms have produced radical and sometimes contradictory changes, some of which hindered the development of financial institutions and practices (see table 3.4). Such far-reaching modifications in the legal and regulatory structure of the national financial system reflected changing relations between the Mexican government and financial-sector entrepreneurs (especially banks), the stock market, and, starting in the 1990s, pressure from foreign financial actors and the U.S. Federal Reserve. Throughout this period, government authorities often applied regulations in an irresponsible—even damaging—manner. When individuals' risky or irregular financial transactions went awry, the need for the government to cover their losses inevitably drove the Mexican financial system into deep crisis.

Institutional Conditions of the International Financial System

The fourth factor contributing to Mexico's cyclical financial-economic dynamic is the international financial system, which can periodically

TABLE 3.4. Evolution of Mexico's Banking System and Stock Market under Changing Financial System Regulations, 1980s–1990s

Before 1982	1982–1988	1989–1994	Since 1995
Mixed multiple banking and financial groups	Nationalized banks	Private national banks and financial groups	Private national and foreign banks and financial groups
A very small stock market closed to foreign capital	Stock market grows with public debt issues but is closed to foreign capital	Stock market grows rapidly with the entrance of foreign capital	Stock market continues to grow thanks to foreign capital inflows
Ministry of Finance and the dependent central bank, in conflict with the private national banking system, regulate financial markets	Ministry of Finance and the dependent central bank administer financial markets according to the government's financial needs	A dependent central bank and an unregulated banking system	Independent central bank and a deregulated banking system open to foreign capital
		Central bank regulates international capital flows by setting the rates on public securities, and it rigidly manages price stability	Central bank regulates international capital flows by setting the rates on public securities, and it rigidly manages price stability
		Very lax regulation of private intermediaries	Bank regulatory system reformed under U.S. influence, but it still remains very weak
The 1977 Financial Reform	Financial Reforms in 1982 and 1984	Financial Reforms in 1989–1990 and 1993	Financial Reforms in 1995 and 1998–1999

Source: Author's compilation based on the content of Mexican banking legislation.

detonate pent-up tensions within the Mexican financial system. This has been the case in successive cycles since 1982.

Since the dollar crisis of the early 1970s and the collapse of the gold standard, the international monetary system has had no established governmental regulatory mechanism, while the rapidly expanding Eurodollar market[5] has permitted the creation of private international liquidity that is unregulated by central banks or the International Monetary Fund (IMF). This market boosts the development of international financing through Eurocredits and Eurobonds. These processes have been accompanied, moreover, by ongoing financial innovation in the administration and transfer of risk through derivative products, as well as in the increasing liquidity of instruments and the supply of available credit to national financial systems.

These and related transformations have led to the globalization of international money and capital flows, along with the transnationalization of banks and other actors operating in these circuits. These new international monetary and financial relationships have given rise to an extraordinary growth in international liquidity under conditions of systemic instability and volatility.

Given these supranational forces, since the mid–1980s national financial and stock market authorities have come under continued pressure to liberalize financial markets and allow entry to foreign financial firms and investors. This takes the specific form of liberalizing the capital account, permitting foreign banks to operate in the country, and deregulating foreign investment in the stock market, changes that together gave rise to "emerging markets" in developing countries.

Destabilizing factors for the monetary, banking, and foreign exchange systems also appeared at the same time (especially in developing countries) because of the effects that large, speculative, short-term international capital movements have on these markets. An example of this is the correlation observed in a large number of countries between incoming short-term capital flows and bank crises, a relationship illustrated for selected cases in table 3.5. In Mexico's case, this factor operated from 1979 up to the bank nationalization in 1982, and again in 1990–1994, when it was followed by the 1995 banking crisis.

When the supply of low-cost international funds rises cyclically due to short-term financial stimuli, the pressures described above come to

---

[5] Originally this market consisted of dollar deposits established by U.S. banks in Europe, beyond the control of the U.S. Federal Reserve. Later the concept was extended to include other hard currencies, which is why we speak of eurocurrencies as private, supranational bank liquidity, beyond the control of all central banks.

TABLE 3.5. Credit Expansion and Banking Crises in Selected Developing
Countries, 1970s–1990s

Country	Period of Extensive International Capital Flows	Capital Flows as Percentage of Gross Domestic Product (GDP)	Banking Crises	Annual Rate of GDP Growth (percent)
Argentina	1979–1982	2.0	1980–1982	–1.8
	1992–1993	4.0	1994–1995	14.3
Brazil	1992–1994	2.2	1995	3.4
Chile	1978–1981	1.7	1981–1983	–3.4
	1989–1994	5.5	No crisis	7.4
Malaysia	1980–1986	6.7	1985–1988	3.5
	1989–1994	9.8	No crisis	7.3

Source: World Bank 1997.

bear on the dynamics of the local financial system. This influence appears to have been rising since Mexico sparked a series of crises in 1994 with the so-called tequila effect, and which continued with the Russian and East Asian economic crises. As a result of these events, it is now clear that the international financial system has become the central problem facing national economies, especially in developing countries. These characteristics of the international financial system also pose serious challenges for international financial institutions, particularly the roles played by the International Monetary Fund and the World Bank.

ECONOMIC AND FINANCIAL CYCLES IN MEXICO, 1976–1994

Based upon the elements discussed above, we can now analyze Mexico's recurrent economic and financial cycles, which are defined as the intervals between outbreaks of financial crisis. Since 1976, Mexico has experienced four such cycles. The first, from 1976 to 1982, ended with the country's foreign debt crisis and the nationalization of the banking system. The second, from 1983 to 1987–1988, culminated with a stock market crash, the threat of hyperinflation, and the launching of business-government-labor stabilization pacts. The third, from 1989–1990 to 1994, concluded with the crisis in *tesobono* (dollar-denominated) gov-

FIGURE 3.1. Economic and Financial Cycles in Mexico, 1970-1999

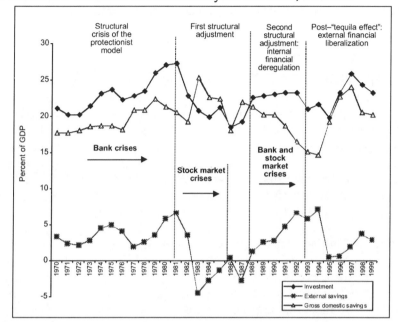

Source: Author's compilation based on data from the Instituto Nacional de Estadística,
Geografía e Informática (INEGI) and the Banco de México.

ernment bonds and the insolvency of the banking system. The fourth
such cycle began in 1995. These four cycles are presented schematically
in figure 3.1 according to the evolution of investment and foreign and
domestic savings.

The fact that these periodic financial crises have coincided with the
end of Mexico's six-year presidential terms has been interpreted as
demonstrating causality — that is, that a lack of political confidence at a
time of transition catalyzes a financial crisis. This connection has raised
expectations that changes in government will lead to crises in the future, stimulating economic policy measures (such as the Banco de México's "financial padding" package begun in 1999) to prevent such a crisis
in 2000.

In contrast to this short-term focus, the present study highlights the
structural character of these cycles. They should more appropriately be
viewed as financial-business cycles; their dynamic is a function of the
interrelationship among the four elements outlined above, as well as of
variations in those factors. The context for this analysis of Mexico's
changing economic structure is the period encompassing the collapse of

the import-substitution model and the shift toward an open, unregulated economy whose engine of growth is private enterprise.

The 1976–1982 Cycle

The first cycle began in 1976 following that year's international economic crisis and a deep devaluation of the peso; it ended in 1982 with a new domestic and international financial crisis of even greater proportions. This cycle was characterized by the impacts of rising international petroleum prices on Mexico's economy, private sector, and government. Not only did inflated foreign earnings from petroleum exports *not* stimulate sustained economic growth, but the loosening of external financial restrictions that they provoked is now viewed as the origin of Mexico's development difficulties in the 1980s and 1990s.

One explanation for this outcome is that the financial windfall accruing to Middle Eastern oil exporters from rising petroleum prices produced an extraordinary abundance of funds in international credit markets. These funds were offered to the Mexican government and to the country's major firms by international lenders, who saw a very low level of risk given that Mexico's petroleum could serve as de facto collateral for the loans.

Another factor was the multitude of conflicting ends to which Mexico's principal economic actors were trying to direct the new petroleum surplus. Locked in an escalating struggle to control these surplus funds, each actor took advantage of the favorable borrowing conditions in local and international financial systems. This meant that borrowed funds were dispersed broadly but without any positive impact on national development. Instead, there was an explosive increase in foreign debt, which had become the principal means for expending anticipated surpluses.

During this period, Mexico's large financial-industrial conglomerates grew at an accelerated pace as they diversified their activities in the domestic market, financing their expansion by contracting significant amounts of foreign debt through their own banks. These conglomerates — especially their banks — were increasingly involved in financial operations abroad. On the one hand, they acquired funds through interest rate arbitrage, taking advantage of the stability of Mexico's exchange rate and the significant differentials between local and foreign interest rates. On the other hand, they participated — together with transnational banks — in financing Mexico's foreign public debt through syndicated loans to the Mexican government.

This period also saw an increased government role in the economy, primarily through expanded state control over public enterprises under the impulse of deepening industrialization. Government interventions to absorb the losses incurred by private businesses contributed to the state's expanding presence. Business losses were mounting as the exhaustion of the import-substitution industrialization model began forcing firms into bankruptcy. Arguing that it needed to protect jobs, the state took control of a large number of these failed and failing private firms. According to Acle Tomasini and Vega Hutchinson (1986), 53 percent of a sample of 132 government-run companies created during this period were private firms absorbed by the state. Whole industries were taken over, including the sugar industry when market conditions forced many sugar mills into bankruptcy.

With respect to the financial system and its regulation, in the second half of the 1970s Mexican banks operated under a universal banking regimen. It covered both private and state-owned firms, but it also maintained the traditional restriction on foreign participation. The financing of large private and public businesses and of private consumption expanded under this system. However, the use of private bank deposits to finance the public deficit led to frequent confrontations between the government and financial groups. This led to domestic financial disintermediation, capital flight, bank speculation, an escalating trade deficit, and rapidly growing public-sector and private-sector foreign debt. Taken as a whole, this situation was one of "financial strangulation" (Quijano 1983). When petroleum prices fell and capital flight accelerated, this tension led to the nationalization of the banking system and the outbreak of the foreign debt crisis in 1982.

The 1983–1988 Cycle

The cycle that began in 1983 and ended in 1988 was marked by the effects of the 1982 crisis. As a result of the crisis, Mexico could not service its foreign debt and was barred from international financial markets. To avoid declaring a debt moratorium, the Mexican government accepted conditions imposed by its transnational bank creditors, who demanded that the country give priority to meeting its foreign loan commitments rather than to retaking the path to growth. This meant sinking the domestic market in stagnation and converting Mexico into a net exporter of capital.

At the start of this process, Mexican conglomerates faced two grave problems. The most immediate was that they were insolvent, both as large industrial corporations and as banks. This was the short-term result of the peso devaluation's effect on the cost of their foreign debt. At the same time, the 1982 bank nationalization meant that these groups lost control over the local financial system, imposing a major structural change on these groups as well as new conditions for their economic activities.

The Mexican state also found itself in severe difficulties. It was unable to service its foreign debt, making it insolvent in the short run even though the government's property rights over petroleum and the revenues it generated made the public debt manageable over the longer term.[6] However, because the government itself was the guarantor of all Mexican debt owed to transnational banks, it also had to reassure creditors that the foreign debts assumed by private corporations would be repaid.

The government adopted a fourfold strategy for handling the foreign debt crisis. It consisted of: (1) renegotiations with creditors and continued debt payments; (2) promotion of new, nontraditional exports in order to generate foreign earnings that could be used to service the debt; (3) a bailout of bankrupt large, private corporations and subsequent promotion of them as leaders in a new export-driven economy; and (4) reorganization of the country's financial relations so as to collect the economic surplus needed to service the foreign debt.

The government's renegotiation of the foreign debt was plagued with difficulties, but this goal was ultimately achieved because creditor banks wanted to avoid a moratorium by Mexico. There was also a new move toward exports, led by large national corporations and U.S. automakers with plants in Mexico. This shift was accompanied by a reduction in imports in order to produce a foreign trade surplus and the net export balance in the capital account that was needed to service the debt.

In contrast, the Mexican government handled the bailout of bankrupt conglomerates and the reorganization of financial relations for the repayment of foreign debt in a way that led to the domestic financial crisis that closed this cycle in 1988. The bailout meant that the government assumed large private-sector liabilities and converted them into public debt. The first step in this process was the nationalization of the banking system in 1982, through which the state assumed the obligation to pay the banks' foreign debt by absorbing their "mexdollar" accounts.[7] As a result, the conglomerates owning the banks were freed

---

[6] This became apparent during the 1994 tesobono crisis when the Mexican government had to turn over to the U.S. Federal Reserve "receipts" for its petroleum export revenues as collateral for funds provided to rescue U.S. investors holding nonconvertible Mexican bonds.

[7] "Mexdollar" accounts were U.S. dollar–denominated bank deposits that could be opened with pesos but which permitted withdrawals in dollars. These operated until 1982. The accounts left many depositors bankrupt because the banks ulti-

from assuming the costs of the bankruptcies.[8] A second important government initiative in the corporate bailout was the creation of the Exchange-Rate Risk Hedge Fund program (FICORCA), which covered large industrial and commercial firms' foreign debt and allowed them to restructure their foreign liabilities by taking advantage of public subsidies and the government's risk coverage.

The biggest demand for domestic savings came from the state, given its need to service both private and public foreign debt and sustain the costs of the corporate bailout. To obtain these funds, the state recurred to forced savings through inflation and to an increasing public-sector domestic debt. It did this by absorbing bank deposits through reserve requirements, and also by increasing its public bond issues in the stock market.

Furthermore, the expanded public bond issues were accompanied by stock market reforms, one of the most important of which was the privatization of brokerage houses. This measure allowed conglomerates to reassume a position in the financial system. As a result, they gained control over the market for the public sector's domestic debt, which was the primary source of financial profits during the period. The market for government bonds was driven by their supply and the private sector's demand, which found the yields on these financial issues attractive compared with the returns they could realize through productive investments in Mexico. National conglomerates were unique among bond purchasers because the pesos that they pumped into the market came from FICORCA. The profits obtained through these op erations in the stock market facilitated conglomerates' restructuring toward exports.

Financial regulation was extraordinarily lax during this cycle. On the one hand, the government was under pressure to increase deposits through the banks and the stock market. Likewise, as was later recognized when the banks were reprivatized, the government's supervision of the management of nationalized banks was very poor. This was also true of governmental supervision of brokerage houses, a fact that became evident in the 1987 stock market crisis.

---

mately paid depositors in pesos only, at an exchange rate far below the market's parity price.

[8] The government also undertook other, more general, initiatives to cover the risks of private businesses. For example, it absorbed the costs of banks' large nonperforming loan portfolios generated by debtor insolvency following the debt crisis and resulting economic recession. It also set up an implicit protection mechanism for exchange-rate risks by continuing to contract foreign debt to sustain the supply of dollars that allowed a large and continuous outflow of capital from Mexico during this period.

The state's reorganization of the financial system generated a domestic public debt–inflation spiral, which had a devastating impact on economic activity. The financial costs of public-sector domestic debt became the primary source of the public deficit, which is why the latter continued to grow despite cuts in government investment and a notable contraction in current expenditures. All of this produced a credit freeze for businesses and consumers, along with the rising threat of fiscal collapse and hyperinflation.

Following the stock market crash of October 1987, the federal government moved once more to assume the private sector's risks. The crash threatened to bankrupt brokerage houses and many large investors, and the government responded by purchasing large blocks of shares through Nacional Financiera (NAFIN), the national development bank). This action sustained share prices temporarily and allowed many large investors to exit the market before prices fell. However, as the cycle came to a close, there were mounting pressures to devalue the peso and indications of an accelerated increase in prices, all of which was controlled through the government's successful efforts in late 1987 to establish a stabilization pact among government, corporations, and labor unions.

The 1989–1994 Cycle

The third financial cycle began in 1989–1990 and ended with another crisis in 1994. Several radical changes marked its commencement. The first was the Brady Plan (named after U.S. Treasury Secretary Nicholas F. Brady) for restructuring Mexico's foreign debt, which allowed Mexican firms and the government to return to international financial markets. The second was a government reform that reprivatized the banks and authorized the formation of financial groups.[9] This reform retained a protectionist policy for the financial sector by limiting the number of banks to be privatized to eighteen and restricting participation in the auction to a small number of large national corporations. As a result,

---

[9] Analysts such as Herring and Santómero (1990) argue that the risks posed by industrial-financial groups can be controlled by creating institutional "firewalls" that impede the transmission of weaknesses from the financial to the nonfinancial divisions of these groups. In Mexico's case, the 1990 legislation that created financial groups established general arrangements to prevent this problem. Nevertheless, the new private owners' management of these groups and the lack of effective regulation by governmental authorities between 1990 and 1994 permitted the transmission of weaknesses across divisions. For an analysis of the conditions under which new financial groups began to form in the 1990s and the problems associated with this process, see Ejea et al. 1991.

national conglomerates purchased banks and were once again able to set themselves up as financial-industrial groups. Together with other bank purchasers, they benefited from the quasi-monopoly financial rents generated by the manner in which the privatization was carried out.

Second, at this time the government also privatized a significant number of publicly owned industrial and service-oriented firms. This meant transferring large amounts of assets to several national conglomerates, turning some of them into huge corporations as a result. The privatization of public nonfinancial firms and of banks and other financial institutions was carried out under conditions that were extremely favorable for the purchasers. This policy paved the way for the monumental bailouts that would come in the following financial cycle.

The third change was a legislative reform that allowed foreign investors to participate in the stock market. This resulted in a massive, sustained inflow of short-term foreign capital, which had two important consequences. First, foreign investors became the dominant holders of domestic public debt, displacing the large national corporations that had abandoned this market in order to participate in the privatizations of state-owned firms. Second, the massive influx of funds to the stock market generated a vertiginous increase in share prices. Because these transactions took place in the secondary market, they did not have a strong impact on net financing for the economy. They did, however, generate huge profits both for brokerage houses and for stock issuers (thanks to the revaluation of their stock).

Over the course of the 1989–1994 cycle, the developments outlined above produced several significant changes. On the one hand, Mexico's relations with short-term international capital changed after the country carried out financial liberalization and opened its stock market to foreign portfolio investment. This move led to a perverse articulation between macroeconomic equilibrium and short-term international capital flows. Maintaining equilibrium came to depend upon attracting the short-term capital flows needed to close the trade deficit that accompanied the shift toward an export-oriented economy. To achieve macroeconomic equilibrium under these conditions, incoming international capital flows were allowed to overvalue the exchange rate, and, in order to keep capital in the country, high real interest rates were offered on public debt issues in the stock market. In addition, the Banco de México applied a restrictive monetary policy designed to maintain price stability. All of this ended up promoting a segmented economy because it subjected the domestic market to stagnation while accelerating the expansion of export-oriented activities.

For their part, Mexican conglomerates' industrial branches consolidated their expansion in the international economy, not only by exporting commodities but also by making direct investments abroad. They thereby became regional multinational corporations, which significantly altered their relationship with the national economy. Of particular importance is the fact that these firms satisfied their financial needs for expansion by obtaining funds in international capital markets. As a result, they again took on large amounts of debt denominated in U.S. dollars and other foreign currencies. However, this debt differed significantly from these companies' pre–1982 foreign debt; at this later time the companies had incomes in these same foreign currencies with which to cover the debt. The conglomerates' connection with the Mexican financial system was reduced to taking advantage of the high, quasi-monopoly financial rents available through their banks. They did this by borrowing under favorable conditions, and then lending at much higher interest rates to consumers who lacked other borrowing options.

Regarding regulation of the financial system during this cycle, the government continued to be incredibly tolerant with the new bankers, helping them expand and consolidate even at the cost of allowing questionable or blatantly irregular transactions. Imbalances were already apparent in the banking sector in 1992, when the portfolio of bad consumer and home loans began to grow and capitalization fell sharply. At the same time, local banks made highly leveraged investments in highway concessions that proved unviable, forcing the banks into bankruptcy and destabilizing the banking system. Similarly, other debt chains—like the one generated in the credit union circuit through subsidized credits from NAFIN—became difficult to sustain without intervention by government authorities.

Finally, the Banco de México and the Ministry of Finance and Public Credit acted in a flagrantly irresponsible manner when, in order to keep foreign capital in the country during the change in presidential administration in late 1994, they expanded the issue of tesobonos far beyond the country's capacity to pay. They also maintained a stable exchange rate even when it was clear that it could no longer be defended.

On the whole, this cycle manifested rising tension between the evolution of the export sector and the dynamics of the domestic financial system. While the export sector grew steadily, the domestic financial system accumulated imbalances that ultimately brought about the 1994 peso devaluation and then the collapse of the market for government bonds—opening the way for the next financial crisis.

THE FAILURE OF THE BANKING SYSTEM AND GOVERNMENT
BAILOUTS: FROM FOBAPROA TO IPAB

The financial-economic cycle that began in 1995 differed from earlier ones in its complex evolution. The December 1994 devaluation set off a payments crisis in diverse public- and private-sector debt chains that portended the collapse of those debts.[10] The crisis in the Mexican banking system was explosive. Capitalization levels plummeted, and banks were threatened with insolvency as the number of loans in arrears continued to rise.[11] Payments on loans declined further as interest rates soared, and in early 1995 both incomes and economic activity in the domestic market declined sharply.

The government's strategy for dealing with the banking crisis did not seek a balanced distribution of losses between debtors and creditors, nor did it promote the rapid recovery of banking and productive activity in the national economy as a whole.[12] To the contrary, government policy followed a pattern established in previous cycles: the primary (though unstated) goals were to overcome the negative economic

---

[10] According to authorities at Federal Highways and Bridges (CAPUFE), the net liabilities of businesses participating in the privatization of highways reached a total of approximately US$8 billion by 2000. The insolvent development banks, whose net liabilities were estimated at US$10 billion in early 2000, were managed though another public organization — the Liquidation Fund for Credit Institutions and Supplementary Credit Organizations (FIDELIQ) (*Reforma*, February 2, 2000).

In the case of the stock market, the 1994–1995 crisis resulted in severe losses both because of falling output and because brokers had extended loans to clients on margin, using as financing funds provided by banks from the same financial groups. The government rescued these brokerage houses with monies from the Stock Market Rescue Program. One important reason for the rapid attenuation of the debt crisis's impact on the stock market was the integration of brokerage houses' obligations to banks into the credit packages absorbed by the bank rescue programs.

[11] This crisis basically affected the eighteen banks that were reprivatized in the early 1990s and a few banks that were created thereafter. After the bank privatization, the government authorized the creation of new private banks or subsidiaries of foreign banks. By May 2000, there were thirty-six banks operating in Mexico. Only two of these belonged to the group of eighteen reprivatized banks, which remain in the hands of the original buyers.

[12] The government's official position was that its strategy aimed to save private banks, not bankers. This was generally true for small shareholders who in some cases suffered a total loss of their capital. But it was not true for those shareholders who held controlling interests in the banks and who had recovered their investments prior to the crisis. For them, the bank rescue program offered an opportunity to detach themselves from the problem and eventually to realize profits through FOBAPROA (Garrido 1997).

effects generated when large corporations could not service their bank loans, and to keep bankruptcies of the groups' financial divisions from having an impact on their industrial enterprises.[13]

The banking crisis posed a fundamental problem for the Mexican government. The legal regimen of unlimited coverage of bank deposits (and even of the banks themselves in the interbank market) meant that the banking crisis could not be treated as a mere problem of insolvency. The fact that the state guaranteed deposits created a grave financial problem because deposit insurance was financed with monies accumulated in the Bank Savings Protection Fund (FOBAPROA), in place since 1990 and funded with bank contributions.[14] Given the magnitude of the crisis, these funds were clearly insufficient. Supplying the additional public funds meant generating public debt to be paid out of future taxes, and this required congressional approval. Neither the Ministry of Finance and Public Credit nor the Banco de México sought this approval; instead, they issued funds through FOBAPROA until 1998, without congressional approval and without any fixed limit on the amount of resources they could issue.

In the wake of the 1994–1995 crisis, bank losses from delinquent loans were handled by the government through the SHCP and the Banco de México, which together developed two programs based on FOBAPROA. The first program—the Temporary Capitalization Program (PROCAPTE)—was made available to commercial banks so that they could maintain the capitalization and reserves needed to meet their obligations with depositors. The program, which began in March 1995 and lasted five years, used loans granted by the Banco de México to FOBAPROA to finance bank capitalization and reserve formation. With the aim of keeping the banks' capitalization at a minimum of nine percent, FOBAPROA bought subordinate convertible obligations from the banks that would become shares in these institutions at the end of the program. A total of seven banks entered PROCAPTE. Once the capitalization process began, these banks gradually liquidated the obligations held by the Banco de México. However, the capitalization

---

[13] To service the bankers' foreign debt, the Banco de México implemented a short-term program through which it offered banks the means to service their obligations. Disbursements through this program reached almost US$4 billion by the end of 1996; they were financed through loans from the World Bank and the Inter-American Development Bank.

[14] In fact, the fund was set up at the beginning of the 1994 crisis through an agreement between the SHCP and the Banco de México, the latter acting as trustee. This version of FOBAPROA was developed from the Preventive Support Fund for Multiple Banking Institutions, created in November 1986 via a similar agreement between both institutions (SHCP–BANXICO 1996).

problem was to reemerge later on when the nonperforming loans crisis deepened.

The government's principal means of responding to the banking crisis was to buy delinquent loans from banks while postponing the implementation of plans for resolving debtors' repayment difficulties. The government launched the Portfolio Purchase Program through FOBAPROA, asserting that the asset side of the banks' balance sheets had to be addressed because the rise in nonperforming loans was weakening their portfolios. Under this program, FOBAPROA assumed banks' nonperforming loans in exchange for promissory notes maturing in 2005. These "FOBAPROA notes" paid interest to banks at a rate set by the central bank, thus providing banks with a positively valued asset that generated income. Furthermore, should the loans backed by these notes be paid off, the income generated would be applied directly to paying the debt with FOBAPROA. Under this arrangement, banks continued to administer the loans, but the risk of nonfulfillment was shared by the banks and FOBAPROA.

FOBAPROA initially bought a portfolio worth 143 billion pesos (approximately US$23.8 billion) from ten commercial banks.[15] However, the purchase of these loans proved to be extremely problematic. The program promoted a perverse distortion of banking practices because banks received interest on notes granted in exchange for nonperforming loans, yet the notes could not be traded in order to recover liquidity and issue new loans. Thus the banks corrected the problem with the asset side of their balance sheets and maintained their level of earnings, but they did not reinitiate lending to businesses and households.

Another element in the crisis was the implicit problem of accounting standards, the magnitude of which was initially underestimated. This became clear in early 1997 with the implementation of a 1995 accounting reform adopted under pressure from the U.S. government. This reform standardized the accounting of nonperforming loans in Mexico with USGAAP (U.S. generally accepted accounting principles) norms. The application of these criteria for determining the market value of a loan—and when it was to be considered nonperforming—resulted in a delinquent loan portfolio twice as large as previous estimates.

The problems produced by the Mexican government's highly selective approach to the bank rescue were aggravated by insufficient legislation and an inadequate regulatory framework. There was, for example, considerable discretion in the criteria guiding FOBAPROA purchases of

---

[15] The cost of FOBAPROA's purchase of bank loan portfolios stood in stark contrast to the 39 billion pesos the government received in 1990 from the privatization of the banks. See Garrido and Peñaloza 1996.

loans. Loans were purchased at 70 percent of their nominal value, on average, and in amounts that duplicated the fresh capital contributed by the banks' investors. However, the rates that were applied to the purchase of loans differed from bank to bank. The government's decisions to intervene in only eleven banks and twenty-four other financial institutions—including some of the largest in the system—and to allow the bankers who caused the problem to continue administering bank portfolios were also noteworthy. Moreover, governmental supervision of portfolio buyouts under FOBAPROA was lax, leading to an accelerated increase in large debtors' and private financial institutions' moral hazard problems. This contributed to a substantial increase in the volume of loans transferred to public ownership, independent of the debtors' real capacity to pay.[16]

The FOBAPROA dynamic was further complicated by the government's mismanagement of bank debtors' problems. Initially, and for a prolonged period, the banks tried to dismiss these problems, emphasizing that their first responsibility was to depositors. The government essentially adopted the bankers' perspective on debtors in its various unsuccessful bailout programs, and the banks' loan portfolios deteriorated further as the number of insolvent debtors rose.[17] The most significant program of the period was the Immediate Support Program for Debtors (ADE), to which was added the Additional Benefits for Mortgage Holders Program in May 1996. These programs, together with a new accounting unit called the "investment unit," were supposed to prevent an accelerated amortization of debts via inflation. The result, however, was that these programs increased debtors' obligations to banks, a situation that was exacerbated further by exchange-rate instability beginning in late August 1998.[18]

By mid–1998, FOBAPROA had become a heavy drag on the national financial system. The expense of "FOBAPROA notes" had not been formally incorporated into the public debt, which raised their issuing costs. Moreover, the conversion of overdue loans into notes escalated continuously, as did the irregularities in the conversion process itself. As a result, the cost of the bank rescue program shot from around US$40

---

[16] Guillermo Ortiz, governor of the Banco de México, recognized that some businesses had classified loans as unrecoverable even though the debtors still had the capacity to repay them (*Reforma*, May 26, 1998).

[17] An alternative would have been to renew loans in order to avoid a collapse of production and the skyrocketing growth of delinquent loans. Although it is difficult to render a cost estimate, it is probable that this strategy would have substantially reduced the fiscal costs of the banking crisis.

[18] Unstable exchange rates and fluctuations in interest rates resulting from the 1997–1998 international financial crisis generated new waves of insolvent bank debtors.

billion in 1996 to more than $60 billion in 1998, as calculated in the executive branch's proposal to the Congress to convert FOBAPROA notes into public-sector debt (table 3.6).[19]

It was only in December 1998 that a legal reform of the financial system was finally approved. This reform created the Bank Savings Protection Institute (IPAB), which among other things was responsible for administering the liabilities contracted by FOBAPROA and determining what approach would be used to deal with other banks in difficulty (especially Serfin and Bancrecer). Under the reform, FOBAPROA's liabilities were incorporated into the public budget, with FOBAPROA notes exchanged for IPAB bonds. IPAB simultaneously received funding to fulfill its principal task — resolving the FOBAPROA problem.[20]

Given the ADE's limited scope, the government and the banks together developed a new bailout program, "End Point" ("Punto Final"), which was designed to prevent large debtors from receiving FOBAPROA support. This program also significantly reduced debtors' burdens in order to compensate for rising interest rates. Over a million debtors participated in the program, which ended on March 31, 2000. Taken together, debt relief programs implemented since the beginning of the crisis carried a total fiscal cost of about US$1 billion (*El Financiero*, June 4, 2000).

Yet despite these new institutional arrangements, FOBAPROA liabilities continued to rise. By December 1999 they totaled US$98 billion (21.7 percent of 1999 GDP), or perhaps even more.[21] This meant that the inclusion of FOBAPROA obligations in the country's public finances raised the total public debt by between 50 and 90 percent.

---

[19] As part of a financial reform initiative, the executive branch informed the Congress of the need to incorporate FOBAPROA notes into the public-sector debt. It did so in a footnote to the document that proposed the financial reforms. It took a good deal of time for legislators to appreciate the extent of the problem and understand the procedure followed by the Banco de México.

[20] However, this change did not make the management of the banking crisis completely transparent. For example, given the large portfolio of delinquent loans, it was necessary to raise the capitalization index for these loans. This implied an expenditure of between US$5 and $7 billion for banks in difficulties, an amount that shareholders were unlikely to contribute. As a result, the Ministry of Finance and Public Credit granted the banks a deferment on their tax payments so as to facilitate their capitalization. This raised the banks' liabilities with the government, which by late 1998 were around US$4 billion. Another example involved the National Foreign Trade Bank, which operated credit programs to support large businesses in financial difficulty.

[21] Standard and Poor's estimated the total as high as US$105 billion (*Reforma*, August 31, 1999).

TABLE 3.6. Fiscal Costs of Mexico's Bank Rescue Programs, 1995–1998 (in billions of pesos and as percentage of gross domestic product)

	1995	1996	1997	1998
Debtors	30.4	74.7	96.3	112.8
Investment and rescue	32.0	70.5	187.3	312.6
Portfolio purchases[1]	7.4	39.0	77.4	98.3
Highway loans[1]	14.1	26.1	18.8	18.8
Total	83.9	210.3	379.8	542.5
Less amount already covered[2]				94.1
Total[1]				448.2
Total as percentage of GDP[3]	5.1	8.4	11.9	14.4[4]

Source: Author's compilation based on information from the Secretaría de Hacienda y Crédito Público, *Reforma*, and *El Financiero*.

[1] Operations related to FOBAPROA.

[2] Amounts reported for informational purposes only.

[3] Estimated gross domestic product for 1998 was 3,762.8 billion pesos.

[4] Includes 80 billion pesos for FOBAPROA operations already covered.

FOBAPROA liabilities also increased as a result of the IPAB's approach to rescuing banks in serious difficulties. The Serfin and Bancrecer cases were particularly noteworthy. In these cases the government's strategy consisted of capitalizing the banks and improving their balance sheets in order to resell them to private buyers at market price.[22] However, because of the huge amounts needed to capitalize these banks, there was heated debate about whether their sale could begin to recover these costs. For example, the government invested about US$12 billion in public funds in preparing Serfin for sale. The bank was purchased by the Banco Santander Central Hispano for US$1.4 billion, producing a loss of over US$10 billion.[23]

By 2000, five years after it erupted, Mexico's banking crisis was largely resolved. Yet commercial bank credit remained extremely limited, and salvaging the banking sector was only accomplished by con-

---

[22] According to IPAB reports, the choice between closing these banks or setting their finances aright was made on the basis of studies by international consulting firms, which recommended the latter option as being less costly.

[23] The cost of cleaning up Bancrecer's finances was around US$10 billion; in September 2001, Banorte purchased Bancrecer for only US$186 million.

verting bank losses into public debt. Setting up the IPAB did not solve the problem. Although interest payments on the assumed debts were supposedly scheduled into the federal budget, it was not clear how much debt would be issued, how it would be incorporated into the public debt, or what effects it would have on Mexico's fiscal and macroeconomic equilibrium. These issues were among the challenges that the administration of President Ernesto Zedillo (1994–2000) left for its successors.

MEXICO'S FINANCIAL-ECONOMIC CYCLE SINCE 1995

The explosive financial dynamic generated by the management of the banking crisis has dominated perceptions of the financial-economic cycle that began in 1995. Yet at the same time, the central features of traditional cycles have undergone transcendental changes. As a result, a new financial-economic configuration has developed.

The first change was in the structure of Mexico's national financial-industrial conglomerates. In the 1989–1994 cycle, conglomerates' financial divisions had supported the international and national growth of their industrial enterprises and, thereby, made a strong contribution to total earnings. However, since the 1994–1995 crisis, these conglomerates' financial and industrial divisions have evolved very differently. Their industrial arms faced the post–1995 cycle as midsize multinational firms with a consolidated international presence. Their expansion had been financed primarily through international capital markets, which meant that they had significant foreign debt. However, the 1994–1995 foreign-exchange crisis did not mean a payments crisis for them because these firms had earnings in foreign currencies derived from their international operations.[24] By mid–1995, these firms could once again count on international financing, along with funding from investors in the local capital market. As a result, they continued their international expansion through exports and investments, and they retained access to international financial markets.

In contrast, as noted earlier, the conglomerates' financial institutions—especially their banks—faced bankruptcy in the post–1995 cycle. As a result, they ceased to support the development of conglomerates' industrial divisions; to the contrary, they placed a heavy burden on

---

[24] This comment does not imply that these industrial firms did not face serious economic and financial problems as well, especially at the end of 1997. However, their problems are explained by the effects of the international financial crisis on their markets and foreign investments, which was an outcome of their own internationalization.

their successful industrial counterparts. This situation was resolved by the government's bank rescue, which gave substantial protection to the conglomerates as a whole while socializing their losses in the form of FOBAPROA–mediated public debt.

Nonetheless, losing their financial divisions did have a strategic impact on these conglomerates. After a long and tortured process that began in 1995, the government concluded in 1998 that domestic capitalists had neither the capacity nor the inclination to invest the capital needed to strengthen the banks. This meant that conglomerates lost one of the main means through which they had generated their own financing— that is, raising funds through direct participation in financial circuits. With these changes, conglomerates were forced to develop new financial relationships in order to sustain their investment projects in Mexico and abroad. It appears in retrospect that the most powerful of the large national conglomerates recognized this problem, as suggested by Banamex's bid to merge with Bancomer.

A second element that underwent radical change during this period was the legislation affecting the banking sector. At the end of 1998, following on the limited reforms implemented in January 1995 to deal with the currency crisis of that year, the Mexican Congress approved a new financial reform, which, as noted above, included the creation of the IPAB. The reforms eliminated the unrestricted guarantee on bank deposits and replaced it with a limited deposit insurance (to enter into effect in 2005) that will be financed with bank contributions and administered by the IPAB. The reforms also eliminated restrictions on foreign participation in bank ownership, even for the country's largest banks (Banamex, Bancomer, and Serfin).[25]

Another important reform initiative, promoted primarily by the banks and approved in early 2000, concerns legislation governing business bankruptcies. According to bankers, the obsolescence of this law contributed to the banks' growing difficulties because it hindered executive decisions and failed to protect banks' rights.

The third element that underwent important modifications during this cycle was the international financial system—which is why the 1994–1995 tesobono crisis was resolved differently than earlier Mexican debt crises and why only the bank crisis reached explosive levels.[26] The

---

[25] These three banks had been off limits in early 1995 because of their key role in the national payments system. The 1998 legislation gave no indication as to how to preserve the national interest in this matter.

[26] In addition to the considerations noted here, it has been pointed out that the handling of the 1994 crisis was strongly influenced by the web of interests created by the North American Free Trade Agreement (NAFTA).

main issue concerns the systemic imbalances created by the globalization of finance and the dominance of short-term international capital flows. Problems arise when an open-economy country that is receiving large short-term capital inflows does not have sufficient reserves to protect itself against the outflow of this capital. Not only does this scenario affect the investors involved, but in a global economy with high capital mobility, such problems could also infect other markets, including large world centers like New York. Ultimately, it could result in a global financial crisis.

In order to protect the stability of the international financial system when a country is facing insolvency, the IMF abandons its traditional role in order to come to the defense of international financial investors. Under these conditions, the IMF functions like a world lender of last resort, providing loans to the troubled country so that it can meet its obligations to investors. The counterpart of this is that the IMF gains new rights to intervene in the failing economy, including the right to prescribe economic controls and structural reforms.

Mexico played a pioneering role in the development of the IMF and international financial system's new dynamic when the "tequila effect" was identified as the first crisis of financial globalization. The problem began in early 1994 when then–Finance Minister Pedro Aspe, hoping to reassure foreign investors, pledged to pay short-term tesobono obligations in the same currency in which they were denominated—that is, U.S. dollars. There was an over-issue of tesobonos, and the December 1994 peso devaluation sparked a crisis of confidence among investors holding the bonds. The government could not renew the bonds because it lacked the reserves to do so, leading to the collapse of the bond market and ultimately to a serious international financial conflict. A powerful set of international interests moved quickly to find a solution to the problem so as to avert a world crisis, and tesobono investors were rescued through a credit line from the U.S. Department of the Treasury, the IMF, and the Bank of International Settlements.[27] In exchange, the United States withheld Mexico's petroleum receipts as collateral, and the Banco de México had to report weekly to the U.S. Federal Reserve on the state of the nation's accounts.

---

[27] Within the context of the negotiations headed up by the U.S. government, the Mexican government had its own selective rescue plan for bailing out some national investors who had invested heavily in tesobonos. The Banamex case was particularly noteworthy because the govenment sold this institution a package of these instruments at an exchange rate of 3.997 pesos per dollar, for a total of US$300 million, yielding Banamex a return of around 25 percent on the investment after parity devaluation the same day (*Reforma*, April 6, 1998).

This new international practice appears to have serious flaws. The IMF's role as lender of last resort has stimulated morally hazardous conduct on the part of international investors, which could lead to greater imbalances in world finances as a whole. This situation has generated fierce debates over the need to reform the international financial system and to develop a new financial architecture for globalization.

As a consequence of the 1994–1995 crisis, the Mexican government altered its relationship with the international financial system, allowing the exchange rate to be determined by supply and demand while accumulating hard currency reserves in order to support the overvalued parity. Similarly, the government avoided accumulating short-term debt in foreign currencies, and the Banco de México maintained a restrictive monetary policy in order to control prices. These policy measures were part of the "financial padding" framework developed jointly with the IMF, which was intended to prevent the crises that had recurred with the inauguration of each new Mexican president.

Overall, the Mexican economy's productive and financial sectors are increasingly segmented. There is also marked dependence upon short-term foreign capital, and the domestic market is conditioned to a recessionary evolution in order to achieve the macroeconomic equilibrium required to sustain growth under the present export model.

CONCLUSION

The post–1995 financial-economic cycle has produced results that pose extraordinary dilemmas for social development in Mexico. On the one hand, the government's handling of the banking crisis created a flow of long-term public debt obligations that will restrict growth in coming decades. Under optimal circumstances, this debt burden will be manageable. The assumption here, however, is that gross national product will expand at rates that permit the government to meet these obligations without weakening Mexico's ability to sustain economic growth over the long term.

Yet economic growth will run up against limitations imposed by other consequences of this cycle: a financial-economic configuration characterized by segmentation of the national economy and an extraordinarily high degree of foreign dependency. Under current conditions, economic sectors linked to the international market have experienced accelerated growth, but domestic production chains have deteriorated, putting a brake on domestic market expansion and impeding the reestablishment of banking services for the national population.

If international conditions remain unchanged, this economic configuration may be unable to generate a sufficiently large economic surplus to service the public debt over the long term.[28] Given that a significant proportion of the Mexican population already lives in extreme poverty, the future could well witness high levels of social conflict if servicing the public debt and maintaining the income of leading socioeconomic sectors worsen the pattern of national income distribution.

Taking a long-term economic perspective, there is a clear need to make Mexico's financial-economic configuration compatible with the management of the FOBAPROA–created debt. The spontaneous action of markets will not suffice to solve this problem; it will only take Mexico further down the path it is already on. For this reason, Mexico needs to extend the benefits derived from the country's gains in competitiveness while mitigating the distortions that the process of economic liberalization has caused.

This means, first, addressing the institutional factors that deepened the imbalances created by economic opening and that contributed to the present lack of articulation between finance and production. These changes would include legal reforms to break up the highly concentrated financial system so that the state could no longer cover private bankruptcies by incorporating them into the public-sector budget; a real financial reform comprising legislation and rules to support economic stability and growth; and strategies for avoiding excessive exposure to the volatility of the international financial system. Second, since the early 1970s Mexico has required a deep fiscal reform that not only ensures that all social sectors shoulder their share of the costs of servicing the public debt, but that also provides the government with the resources necessary to fund health care and education programs and to counteract a highly unequal pattern of income distribution. These fiscal needs have increased with each bailout program, culminating in the huge demands generated by FOBAPROA. Finally, Mexico must design policies that will promote integration of the productive sector, development of the domestic market and employment based upon innovation and technological advances in firms of all sizes, and a financial system that meets the needs of producers operating under the competitive conditions of the global marketplace, in which Mexico is now an active player.

---

[28] Nor should one forget the impact that rising U.S. interest rates or a slowdown in the U.S. economy might have on Mexico's public debt.

REFERENCES

Acle Tomasini, Alfredo, and Juan Manuel Vega Hutchinson. 1986. *La empresa pública: desde fuera, desde dentro.* Mexico City: Instituto Nacional de Administración Pública.

Aguilar, Alonso, Fernando Carmona, and Ignacio Hernández. 1985. *La nacionalización de la banca, la crisis y los monopolios.* Mexico City: Nuestro Tiempo.

Calvo, Guillermo, et al. 1996. "Special Issue on Mexico," *Journal of International Economics* 41 (3–4).

Ejea, Guillermo, Celso Garrido, Cristián Leriche, and Enrique Quintana. 1991. *Mercados de valores, crisis y nuevos circuitos financieros en México, 1970–1990.* Mexico City: Universidad Autónoma Metropolitana–Azcapotzalco.

Garrido, Celso. 1997. "El actor bancario y el poder financiero en México: incertidumbres y desafíos." In *El debate nacional*, vol. 4, edited by Estela Gutiérrez. Mexico City.

Garrido, Celso, and Tomás Peñaloza. 1996. *Ahorro y sistema financiero en México.* Mexico City: Grijalbo.

Herring, Richard J., and Anthony M. Santómero. 1990. "The Corporate Structure of Financial Conglomerates," *Journal of Financial Services Research*: 471–90.

Quijano, José Manuel, ed. 1983. "La banca pasado y presente." Ensayos del CIDE. Mexico City: Centro de Investigación y Docencia Económicas.

SHCP (Secretaría de Hacienda y Crédito Público). 1997. *Programa Nacional para el Financiamiento del Desarrollo, 1997–2000.* Mexico City: SHCP.

SHCP-BANXICO (Secretaría de Hacienda y Crédito Público–Banco de México). 1996. "Convenio para la creación del Fobaproa." Mimeo.

Tello, Carlos. 1984. *La nacionalización de la banca en México.* Mexico City: Siglo Veintiuno.

World Bank. 1997. "Private Capital Flows in Developing Countries." Washington, D.C.: World Bank.

4

Foreign Investment in Mexico after Economic Reform

Jorge Máttar, Juan Carlos Moreno-Brid, and Wilson Peres

INTRODUCTION

Since the mid–1980s the Mexican economy has undergone a process of deep economic reform designed to shift away from the more inward-oriented development model that Mexico had followed until then. The main purpose of these reforms was to privilege market mechanisms in economic activities, which meant reducing the state's direct and indirect involvement in the economy. Some of these economic reforms have been completed, some are still in process, and still others — those that encountered opposition — have not yet, or have only just, been implemented.

Economic liberalization had varying effects on the behavior of economic actors and therefore on the evolution of various economic sectors and the Mexican economy as a whole. Liberalizing reforms were intended to have a strong impact on the investment process. Under the previous development model — import-substitution industrialization (ISI) — the state played a fundamental role in directing investment; the reforms sought to shift that role by placing greater emphasis on domestic and foreign private investment, while at the same time orienting investment more toward exports and tradable activities and less toward non-tradable sectors. The expectation was that, as the reform process took its course and obstacles to free-market operations were reduced, investment decisions would increasingly be based on market signals, thus increasing both efficiency in the use of the factors of production and the potential for economic growth.

·The opinions expressed herein are not necessarily those of the Economic Commission for Latin America and the Caribbean. The authors gratefully acknowledge the valuable research assistance of Jesús Santamaría.

Mexico's liberalization process began in 1982, when collapsing petroleum prices and rising international interest rates highlighted the economy's vulnerability and the waning effectiveness of an import-substitution model characterized by high levels of protectionism and strong state participation. Those developments prompted the Mexican government to try to modulate the impact of international economic shocks, and they also paved the way for vigorous attempts to modify the country's development pattern.

Liberalizing reforms sought to convert the private sector into the axis of economic growth, ideally making it able to operate competitively (without subsidies) in world markets. The main elements of this reform process included opening the domestic market to foreign trade, attracting foreign investment, deregulating the economy, privatizing public enterprises, signing the North American Free Trade Agreement (NAFTA), and liberalizing financial markets.[1] The reforms' goals have been bolstered by a governmental commitment to continue stringent monetary and fiscal policies while eliminating preferential lending.

These efforts, particularly by the late 1980s, transformed a nearly closed economy into one that is highly open to foreign participation in trade and investment. State involvement in the economy was curtailed sharply, as shown by the downsizing of the public sector and the substitution of market forces for state intervention in determining key variables such as interest rates, nominal exchange rates, and prices of basic inputs.

In addition to their broad sweep and the speed with which they were implemented, the reforms displayed two other interesting features. The first is that, after some initial resistance to trade liberalization, they were largely accepted by key economic and political players. That is, the shift toward trade liberalization, the elimination of subsidies, and an expanded role for market forces in allocating funds did not encounter overly strong opposition from those who had benefited from the prior system of protection and subsidies, or from the workers and labor unions who were affected by productive restructuring and new conditions in the labor market. Even the currency crisis that erupted in December 1994 did not provoke a rejection of the new development model. In fact, in dealing with the crisis, the administration of President Ernesto Zedillo (1994–2000) reaffirmed its commitment to the reform process and to orthodox management of fiscal and monetary policy.

The second feature concerns the reforms' impact on economic growth. From 1983 to 1988, the Mexican economy was stagnant; from

---

[1] Mexico's reforms are well documented; for an overview, see Aspe Armella 1993; Lustig 1992; Ros 1991.

1989 to 1994, per capita gross domestic product (GDP) grew by only 0.8 percent a year on average; and in 1995, more than ten years after the reform process was launched, per capita GDP dropped 9 percent in real terms, its largest decline in sixty years. The consensus among observers is that Mexico received an international financial aid package and achieved a speedy, though moderate, economic recovery in 1996–2000 largely thanks to the NAFTA, the productive apparatus's focus on foreign markets, and sound fiscal policy—all central results of the economic reform process. Despite the recovery, however, Mexico's economy has yet to show the high and sustained growth rates required in order to generate sufficient jobs to curb national unemployment and underemployment.

The key role that capital formation plays in creating and expanding productive capacities, incorporating technology, and raising productivity makes it a fundamental factor in macroeconomic development. Yet despite its importance, there is little information available on the sectoral performance of capital formation in the Mexican economy.[2] In fact, empirical studies of investment in specific sectors have lagged behind the theoretical advances of recent years.

Against this background, this chapter analyzes the effect that Mexico's liberalizing reforms have had on fixed capital formation at the aggregate level and in the industrial sector.[3] The period under study begins with the aftermath of the 1982 economic crisis and continues to 2000. The following four sections review, respectively, the behavior of aggregate investment and its relationship to the growth process,[4] trends and performance of foreign direct investment (FDI), including the activities of in-bond processing plants (*maquiladoras*); the behavior and determining factors of investment in manufacturing; and the impact of investment patterns on the manufacturing industry's structure and export performance.

---

[2] The available data on capital formation tend to be highly aggregated.

[3] Commodity-producing sectors and public utility services are not included in this study. For a general overview of investment in these fields, see Máttar 2000. For the telecommunications sector, see Escobar de Medécigo 1999; on the electrical power sector, Rodríguez 1999; on highways and ports, Scheinvar 1999; and on the petroleum sector, Torres 1999.

[4] The section on the behavior of aggregate investment draws partly on Máttar 2000; the sections on investment in manufacturing and its impact on the industry's structure and export performance draw on Moreno-Brid 1999a.

THE DYNAMICS OF AGGREGATE INVESTMENT

The Mexican economy has grown slowly since 1982. GDP growth rates have been low, development has been unstable, and the economy has been subject to the effects of recurrent balance-of-payments crises. In the 1983–1987 period, productive activity stagnated, and the recovery that began in 1988 — with the reform process and domestic price stabilization fully under way — was limited. GDP growth reached 5.1 percent in 1990 but subsequently lost momentum. GDP grew just 2.0 percent in 1993, and the 4.4 percent growth in GDP in 1994 (bolstered by public spending) led to a major crisis in the foreign sector. On average, real annual GDP growth averaged 3.9 percent during the 1988–1994 period, much lower than the 6 percent that had been recorded consistently from the end of World War II until the beginning of the 1980s.

In 1995, GDP fell 6.2 percent in real terms, the sharpest drop since the early 1930s. Although growth resumed between 1996 and 2000, economic expansion stopped abruptly in 2001 (GDP fell by 0.3 percent). On average, over the 1985-2001 period GDP grew at an annual rate of just 2.3 percent, or barely half a percentage point above the rate of population growth. Furthermore, by the late 1990s per capita GDP in constant dollars was equal to 23 percent of the U.S. figure, a gap almost 8 percentage points wider than in 1981 and similar to the level recorded fifty years earlier (Moreno-Brid 1999b: 149–50).

The notable slowdown in economic growth was accompanied by — and largely due to — a weakening of investment, which hampered the growth and modernization of productive capacity while restricting the expansion of aggregate demand. Total gross fixed investment in real terms followed a trajectory similar to that of GDP, growing rapidly during the petroleum boom of the late 1970s and early 1980s, stagnating from 1982 to 1987, and recovering in 1988 (table 4.1). This rebound gained impetus in 1990–1992, when investment grew 11.6 percent on average due to high expectations generated by the NAFTA negotiations. However, because of uncertainty surrounding the U.S. Congress's approval of the NAFTA, capital formation fell off in 1993 in real terms. A recovery in capital formation in 1994 was followed by a 29.0 percent drop in 1995, and then by vigorous growth in 1996–2000 (13.1 percent per year on average). If one looks at the 1980s and 1990s as a whole, the investment process has performed poorly: in 2000 real gross fixed investment was only a little higher than in 1981.

For its part, the investment/GDP ratio fell from a historical high of 26.5 percent in 1981 to a low of 14.6 percent in 1995, and it stood at 20.5 percent in 2000 (table 4.1). This trend gives rise to concern over future growth. During the 1970s, the investment/GDP ratio showed a downward trend that was offset by the petroleum boom. The 1982–1983 re-

TABLE 4.1. Growth in Gross Fixed Capital Formation, Gross Domestic Product (GDP), and the Investment/GDP Ratio in Mexico, 1970–2000 (percentages)

Year	Growth in Gross Fixed Capital Formation	GDP Growth	Gross Fixed Capital Formation/GDP Ratio
1970–75	8.5	6.3	21.3
1976–80	9.3	7.0	22.3
1981–85	0.5	3.2	20.8
1986	-11.8	-3.8	16.4
1987	-0.1	1.9	16.1
1988	5.8	1.2	16.8
1989	5.8	4.1	15.8
1990	13.1	5.2	17.0
1991	11.0	4.2	18.1
1992	10.8	3.5	19.4
1993	-2.5	1.9	18.6
1994	8.4	4.5	19.3
1995	-29.0	-6.2	14.6
1996	16.4	5.2	16.1
1997	20.9	6.7	18.3
1998	10.3	4.8	19.3
1999	7.7	3.8	19.9
2000	10.0	6.9	20.5

Source: Comisión Económica para América Latina y el Caribe (CEPAL), based upon data from Mexico's Instituto Nacional de Estadística, Geografía e Informática (INEGI).

Note: Figures for 1970–1988 were calculated on the basis of data given in 1980 constant pesos; figures for 1989–2000 were based on data in 1993 pesos.

cession translated into a 10–point fall, which placed the ratio substantially below 20 percent for the first time in years. The ratio hovered around 18 percent for several years thereafter and only began rising consistently at the end of the 1980s. Its rise was sharply curtailed in 1995 when it dropped nearly 5 percentage points, and only in 2000 did it recover its 1980–1981 levels.

The period under study can be divided into four phases, in keeping with the behavior of investment and growth. Although the level of capital formation differed by sectors, the periodization employed here is nevertheless valid in general terms. The first period (1982–1987) was characterized by a drop in investment levels and generally slow growth. This was the period of the Mexican government's adjustment and stabilization programs, which, among other things, were designed to balance public finances and alleviate the foreign exchange constraint. As such, they had two complementary recessive effects. The first, fiscal discipline, led to a downturn in investment in some infrastructure sectors. The second was a reduction in multiplier effects in the rest of the economy, the outcome of which was stagnation.

By the end of the 1982–1987 period, national investment levels in real terms were no higher than they had been at the end of the 1970s. However, a significant recovery had begun in certain activities, particularly investment to modernize machinery and equipment in sectors such as auto parts, automobiles, petrochemicals, beer, glass, and certain processed foods. Conversely, the oil and gas, electrical power, highways and ports, and water and sanitation sectors—which depended almost entirely upon public investment—showed strong capital formation shortfalls, owing largely to the fiscal discipline that was part of the macroeconomic adjustment process.

The second period (1988–1994)—dating from the implementation in December 1987 of an unorthodox stabilization program known as the Economic Solidarity Pact—saw a fairly generalized recovery of investment. In some cases, this was the result of reforms aimed at specific sectors (including the highway concession program, privatization of the steel industry, and the divestiture of the state monopoly on telephone services). In other instances, investment recovery reflected reforms that had a broader impact on the economy, such as the initiation of the NAFTA negotiations and a more flexible approach to FDI. These developments had a positive impact on investment decisions, particularly in concentrated sectors where transnational companies had a strong presence. Conversely, the restructuring of the productive apparatus during these years led to a drastic decline in investment in numerous small-scale enterprises and even to their elimination from the market. This was especially the case in sectors (toys, clothing, textiles, footwear, and so on) that were slow to adopt a restructuring strategy to bring them into line with open markets and strong international competition.

At the beginning of the 1990s, many observers hoped that, after nearly ten years of stagnation, the Mexican economy would enter a new phase of sustained growth. The private sector was optimistic; privatization had generated favorable prospects for investment, and the NAFTA was expected to encourage large flows of FDI. Nevertheless, these growth expectations were shattered at the end of 1994 when a sharp devaluation of the peso led to Mexico's worst recession in sixty years.

During the third period (basically 1995), the government announced a number of initiatives to divest public assets. These actions, which were expected to generate significant flows of FDI, included the partial or total divestiture of the state-owned petroleum company's (Petróleos

Mexicanos, PEMEX) secondary petrochemicals industry, the electrical power sector, railways, satellite communications, ports, and airports. However, little progress was actually made in this new round of privatizations: a few railway lines were opened to bids, a bill to open the electrical power sector was sent to Congress in early 1999, the privatization of secondary petrochemicals was delayed, and the process of privatizing airports proved to be slow.

Coming in the midst of a deep recession (domestic demand fell 13 percent in 1995), the 31 percent devaluation of the peso in real terms gave extraordinary impetus to exports, which rose by 30 percent. Interviews with export-oriented companies show that not only did the pace of investment not drop, it held steady and even increased in some sectors.[5] This implies that the drop in aggregate capital formation that took place in 1995 was due to low investment by non-exporting companies.

The fourth period began in 1996. During this period, aggregate investment grew at two-digit levels following the drop in 1995, although only in the late 1990s did it overtake the peak it reached at the beginning of the 1980s. The vigor of foreign direct investment was remarkable, but it only focused on certain branches of the economy. Thus, while some sectors were able to restructure rapidly, others lagged severely and seemed incapable of surviving the onslaught of foreign competition.

The recovery of investment at the sectoral level has been markedly unequal. Although definitive figures for recent years are not available, qualitative data gathered in interviews point to an increase in the segmentation that has been visible in the Mexican economy since the mid–1980s. Export-oriented activities—including the maquiladora industry and indirect exporters—maintained their strong growth in the late 1990s, which helps to account for the penetration of Mexican exports in international markets. This segment of the economy comprises a small group of companies that are typically large or midsize, are either transnational or linked to leading foreign companies, and have access to foreign financial resources.

The structure of capital formation by source shows a growing tendency toward investment in machinery and equipment, which in turn indicates a trend toward modernized production. In the late 1990s this type of investment as a proportion of total investment was at one of its highest points in thirty years, reflecting the need for upgraded equipment to satisfy increased demand and to meet foreign competition.

---

[5] The lack of disaggregated information on investment after 1994 and the need to assess the impact of liberalizing reforms on the behavior of economic agents prompted the authors to conduct interviews with individual businessmen, companies, and business chambers, the results of which are set forth in Máttar 2000 and Moreno-Brid 1999a.

The trend by type of actor shows the decreasing importance of public investment, although the federal government still accounted for 25 percent of total investment in 1996. The destination of this investment has also changed: whereas in the mid-1980s nearly 10 percent of public investment went to industry, ten years later industry received less than 1 percent. This reallocation was an explicit aim of government policy — an effort to avert competition between the state and the private sector over financial resources and factors of production.

Although the slow formation of fixed capital in Mexico since the launching of the economic reform process can be attributed in part to the uncertainty inherent in any transition, it is nevertheless a matter for concern. Gross capital formation grew by an annual average of only 6.1 percent in real terms from 1988 to 2000. Assuming a capital depreciation rate of 5 percent a year, the net fixed capital stock in 2000 was at virtually the same level as a decade earlier, when the reforms had recently been implemented. Even taking into consideration the fact that comparisons at constant prices tend to underestimate investment drive (because they do not take into account the effects of modernizing capital stock and technological progress), it is clear that investment was slow to respond to the new, more competitive environment. This fragile capital formation process accounts in large part for the modest economic growth of the past ten years.

It is still too early to tell whether the strong recovery of aggregate investment from 1996 to 2000, when annual growth rates were generally in the double digits, signaled a new phase of vigorous fixed capital formation that will continue over the medium term and enable Mexico's economy to reach high growth rates over the long term. Although GDP, aggregate fixed capital, and foreign direct investment performed well during this period, certain factors are likely, sooner or later, to slow the pace of economic activity and weaken internal linkages within the national productive apparatus. These include the continuing appreciation of the real exchange rate, the critical state of the country's banking system, and the uncertainty that accompanies each change in presidential administration.

FOREIGN DIRECT INVESTMENT

Foreign direct investment has played an increasingly important role in the dynamics of investment in Mexico. The FDI/GDP ratio rose from 1.4 percent in the 1980–1985 period to 1.8 percent in 1986–1993 and 3.4 percent in 1994–2000, while the share of FDI in gross fixed capital formation increased from 3.2 percent to 9.1 and 16.3 percent, respectively, for these periods.[6]

These figures reflect the presence of two factors that have characterized FDI growth during the past two decades: the success of the Mexican government's efforts to attract greater flows of foreign investment in the context of the economic reform process that began in the mid-1980s, and Mexico's progressive integration into the North American economic bloc, which began gathering momentum during the first half of the 1990s. The liberalization of regulations governing foreign investment acted as a catalyst by opening up areas that were previously the domain of the state or of Mexican citizens, while also reducing transaction costs and increasing investors' security. Nevertheless, Mexico's investment regulations are not as liberal as those of other large and midsize countries in the region (Argentina, Chile, and Venezuela, for instance). Mayorga's review of national regulations (1996) shows that in some of these countries there is no obligation to provide information on investments, nor is there a government agency specializing in FDI control and supervision. Sectoral rules are also far less restrictive.[7]

The 1990s saw an upturn in FDI both in Mexico and in the other large economies of Latin America.[8] Its momentum was such that by the

---

[6] Authors' calculations based on Banco de México data. The means for 1980 and 1981 — the last two years of the petroleum boom — were 0.8 percent and 3.0 percent, respectively. These percentages were much lower than those for the 1986 - 1993 period.

[7] Mexico's December 1993 law on foreign investment prohibited foreign participation in nineteen activities. Thirteen of these were designated as the sole domain of the state: (1) petroleum and other hydrocarbons, (2) basic petrochemicals, (3) nuclear energy generation, (4) transmission and supply of electrical power as a public utility, (5) mining of radioactive minerals, (6) satellite communications, (7) telegraphy, (8) wireless telegraphy, (9) postal services, (10) railways, (11) issuing of bank notes, (12) coin minting, and (13) control, supervision, and surveillance of ports, airports, and heliports. Those areas reserved for Mexicans or Mexican companies — through a clause that excluded foreigners — were: (1) marketing of gasolines and natural gas, (2) broadcasting services, radio, and television (except cable television), (3) credit unions, (4) development banking institutions, (4) rendering of professional and technical services, and (6) overland passenger, tourist, and freight transportation.

The 1993 law was modified in December 1996 (together with laws and regulations governing specific sectors) to make the legislation compatible with decisions regarding the privatization of communications, railways, and airports, as well as to allow greater flexibility for investment in the financial sector. The regulations issued under this law were amended in September 1998 in order to expedite administrative procedures for investors (CEPAL 1998; Moreno-Brid 1999a).

[8] These are the members of the Latin American Integration Association (ALADI).

TABLE 4.2. Net Inflows of Foreign Direct Investment to Latin America, 1991–2000 (millions of U.S. dollars)

	1991	1992	1993	1994	1995	1996	1997	1998	1999	2000
Mexico	4,742	4,393	4,389	10,973	9,526	9,186	12,831	11,312	11,786	12,950
Brazil	1,103	2,061	1,292	3,072	4,859	11,200	19,650	31,913	32,659	30,250
Argentina	2,439	4,012	3,261	3,107	5,315	6,522	8,755	6,670	23,579	11,957
Total ALADI member countries[1]	11,841	13,390	12,783	26,280	27,789	41,301	61,125	66,025	85,571	67,191
Mexico's share of total (percent)	40.0	32.8	34.3	41.8	34.3	22.2	21.0	17.1	13.8	19.3

Source: CEPAL 1998 and 2001.

[1] The Latin American Integration Association (ALADI) includes Argentina, Bolivia, Brazil, Chile, Colombia, Ecuador, Mexico, Paraguay, Peru, Uruguay, and Venezuela.

year 2000, the total net inflow of FDI to the region was nearly six times higher than a decade earlier. Mexico and Brazil benefited significantly from this increase in FDI flows; their combined share of the Latin American total rose from 49.4 percent in 1991 to 64.3 percent in 2000 (see table 4.2).

Net flows of FDI to Mexico in the 1990s were the highest among Latin America's largest economies and were only surpassed by Brazil in 1996–2000, when the latter's privatization of state-owned companies reached its peak (table 4.2). As was the case in Mexico at the outset of the 1990s, Brazil's privatizations played a lead role in increasing FDI flows to that country.

Short-term capital flows to Mexico were also highly dynamic in the first half of the 1990s. Unlike direct investment, however, they collapsed in 1995. Portfolio investment (PI) reached a high of almost US$29 billion in 1993, seven times the level of FDI that year. However, the economic crisis that followed the peso devaluations of 1994–1995 led to a downward spiral in PI, producing a negative flow amounting to almost US$10 billion in 1995. From 1996 to 2000, flows turned generally positive again, although they fluctuated substantially and declined following the global financial crisis that erupted in Thailand in 1997. At any event, the contrary trends between direct investment and portfolio investment have made current-account financing sounder than it was at the beginning of the 1990s. In fact, the ratio between PI and FDI at the end of the 1990s — with nearly eight dollars of FDI entering Mexico for nearly every dollar of PI — was the opposite of the trend visible during the first half of that decade.

Although sales of state-owned assets have played a significant role in stimulating investment inflows to Latin America, purchases of private assets have also been important. In 1994–1996, foreign investors were inclined to invest in creating new assets for major investment projects and in modernizing companies they had already established in the region or had acquired as a result of privatizations. Thereafter, in contrast, investment focused mainly on acquiring existing assets, as it had at the outset of the decade. By the end of the 1990s, more than 70 percent of FDI inflows in the member countries of the Latin American Integration Association (ALADI) were for investment in existing assets (CEPAL 1998, 2000). In the case of Mexico, this trend was further reinforced in 1998-2001, when more than half of new FDI was linked to purchases of privately owned banks.

Information gathered at the firm level confirms this process of asset restructuring. A survey by *América Economía* found that the presence of national, privately owned companies in the sales of the one hundred largest industrial concerns in the region dropped from 45.9 percent in

1990 to 38.1 percent in the late 1990s, while foreign firms increased their share from 45.9 percent to 60.7 percent. Although the strong growth of the automobile industry accounts for the increased foreign presence in the period 1990 to 1994, during the following three-year period changes in equity were mainly the result of foreign investors' acquisitions of large national enterprises (Garrido and Peres 1998). This was particularly evident in Argentina, Brazil, and Mexico, but a similar process also took place in Chile when its growth rate dropped in 1998.

Foreign investors' acquisition of private assets was particularly significant in Argentina and Mexico in 1997, when such operations made up 97.5 percent and 62.3 percent, respectively, of total FDI inflows. Brazil accounted for the highest sales amount in absolute terms (US$19.7 billion, or 27.9 percent of total FDI), and Chile and Venezuela each accounted for over 30 percent of total FDI. In Mexico, an estimated US$7.8 billion (out of a total $12.5 billion) in foreign investment stemmed from net sales of local private companies. Acquisitions were mostly in the fields of telecommunications (38 percent) and beverages and tobacco (30 percent), and most (78 percent) were carried out by U.S. investors (CEPAL 1998).

In sectoral terms, the investment strategies that foreign companies follow in Latin America are driven by four factors: the search for raw materials, a desire to establish export platforms, the need for guaranteed access to national markets, and the quest for strategic advantages (such as long-term technological or marketing partnerships). Of these factors, the first three are by far the most powerful, given that strategic advantages are not a strong stimulus for investment decisions in the region. It is also important to differentiate between manufactured goods and services when considering the role of access to national markets (see table 4.3).

Despite its simplicity, table 4.3 reveals two significant trends. The first is Mexico's prominent role as an export platform (like Brazil and, to a lesser extent, Argentina in the MERCOSUR) for the automobile industry[9] and (together with the Greater Caribbean) for exports of ready-made clothing and electronic products to the United States. The second is the services sector's importance in foreign companies' regional strategies.

Manufactures predominate in the sectoral composition of FDI in Mexico, averaging 49 percent of the total in 1981–1993 and rising to

---

[9] It is important to bear in mind that MERCOSUR holds far less importance for Brazil-based automotive firms than North America does for Mexico-based exporters.

approximately 63 percent in 1994-2000.[10] The rise was mainly due to increased investment in maquiladora activities; imports of machinery and equipment rose from 17.8 percent of total FDI in 1994 to 28.3 percent in 2000. In 1993-2000, gross fixed investment in maquiladoras grew at an average of some 30 percent a year, for a cumulative total of US$22.2 billion (the great majority was foreign investment) or 12 percent of the national total.[11] In 1994-2000, foreign investment within the manufacturing industry focused on the machinery and equipment sector (47 percent of the total), particularly automobile and auto parts production, electronic goods, and electrical materials, while investment in food, beverages, and tobacco production saw a strong increase due to substantial sales of private domestic assets to foreign concerns.[12]

With regard to the sources of FDI, trends have been very stable. As in previous decades, the United States was the main country of origin, accounting for 60 percent of the total in 1981-2000, followed at a substantial distance by the countries of the European Union (18 percent). The most important changes that have taken place since the implementation of the NAFTA in 1994 are the United States' rising share (it accounted for 86.3 percent of total FDI in the year 2000) and the declining shares of Canada, the European Union, and Japan (4.8, 1.5, and 3.7 percent, respectively, in 2000). Notwithstanding the dynamism of

---

[10] These figures are not exactly comparable. The FDI registered in Mexico includes: (1) amounts reported to the National Foreign Investment Registry, (2) provision of capital for new companies, (3) foreign-investor trust funds, (4) transfers of stock from nationals to foreigners, (5) imports of capital assets (fixed assets) by maquiladora plants, (6) ploughing back of profits by FDI companies, and (7) the amounts involved in accounts between companies (debts and loans between parent companies). Prior to 1994, data were only available for the first three of these categories. The data in this paragraph are drawn from SECOFI, *Evolución de la inversión extranjera en México*, various years.

[11] The maquiladora export industry — the only sector that witnessed sustained growth in 1980-2000 — has been the most dynamic sector of the Mexican economy since the early 1980s. Its development has stemmed from the synergy derived from a combination of five strategic factors: (1) a highly deregulated legal framework in comparison to the rest of the national economy, (2) the wide gap between wages in the United States and Mexico, which has acted as a source of competitiveness, (3) its geographical location, which translates into low transport costs due to the proximity of U.S. production and consumption centers, (4) the NAFTA, and (5) the U.S. economy's high, sustained rate of growth during the 1990s.

[12] These include the sale of Cigarrera La Moderna to British American Tobacco, Anheuser-Busch's acquisition of 37 percent of the Modelo brewery, and the sale of 21 percent of Cigarrera La Tabacalera Mexicana (CIGATAM) to Phillip Morris (CEPAL 1998).

TABLE 4.3. Foreign Companies' Strategies in Latin America and the Caribbean, by Sector

	Business Strategy		
	Access to Raw Materials	*Export Platform*	*Access to National Market*
Commodity-producing sectors	*Petroleum and gas:* Argentina, Colombia, and Venezuela *Minerals:* Argentina, Chile, and Peru		
Manufacturing		*Automobiles:* Mexico and Mercosur *Electronics:* Mexico and Greater Caribbean *Clothing:* Mexico and Greater Caribbean	*Chemicals:* Brazil *Agroindustry:* Argentina, Brazil, and Mexico *Cement:* Colombia, Dominican Republic, and Venezuela
Services			*Financial:* Argentina, Brazil, Chile, Colombia, Mexico, Peru, and Venezuela *Telecommunications:* Argentina, Brazil, Chile, Mexico, and Peru *Electricity:* Argentina, Brazil, Central America, and Colombia *Gas distribution:* Argentina, Brazil, Chile, and Colombia

Source: CEPAL 1998.

Korean investments in maquiladora plants, Korea contributed only 0.2 percent of Mexico's FDI in 2000.[13]

Mexico's international position has been strongly determined by the growth of foreign companies' exports, a trend that became evident almost a decade before the NAFTA but that has been significantly reinforced by this trade agreement (Calderón, Mortimore, and Peres 1996). Sales by foreign companies have been the main component of Mexico's ever-increasing exports of manufactures since the mid–1980s. Between 1993 and 1996, manufactures rose from 47.8 to 56.2 percent of the total, approximately equal to all nonpetroleum exports in 1986–1987 (53.1 percent) (Peres 1990).

Firms with foreign investment also account for most of the exports with medium or high technological content, and as such they have been instrumental in paving the way for an international position based on higher technological quality. Nevertheless, there is still a long way to go in strengthening internal linkages in the Mexican economy to ensure that the impetus from FDI has a broad impact on the national productive apparatus and becomes an engine of sustained economic growth.

INVESTMENT IN THE MANUFACTURING SECTOR

Under the import-substitution industrialization model, fluctuations in GDP were more pronounced for manufacturing than for the economy as a whole. This cyclical behavior stemmed from the manufacturing sector's accelerating or constraining action on the economy via its backward and forward linkages. Gross fixed capital formation in manufacturing has historically been in line with GDP trends, but with broader fluctuations than in the economy as a whole.

Medium- and long-term trends regarding investment/GDP ratios have been similar for manufacturing and for the economy in general,[14] although manufacturing has displayed sharper fluctuations (figure 4.1).[15] In essence, these shifts reflect the different phases in Mexico's economic performance.

---

[13] These data are from the Secretaría de Comercio y Fomento Industrial's Comisión Nacional de Inversiones Extranjeras.

[14] The analysis of investment dynamics in manufacturing is based on data from the Banco de México's Survey of Fixed Capital Stocks and Formation (Banco de México n.d.) and on interviews with representatives of business chambers and executives whose companies have generally been successful in reconverting to a focus on exports.

[15] Because the survey was discontinued, no disaggregated data are available for the period since 1996. The total investment/GDP ratios in figure 4.1 are low because they are based solely on investment data taken from the Banco de México's capital

FIGURE 4.1. Fixed Investment as a Proportion of Total Gross Domestic
Product and Manufacturing-Sector Product in Mexico,
1970–1994 (percent)

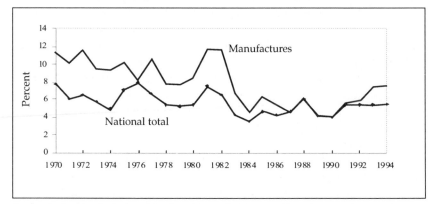

Source: Authors' calculations based on Banco de México n.d. and national accounts data
from the Instituto Nacional de Estadística, Geografía e Informática (INEGI).

Note: The values for total gross domestic product and manufacturing-sector product
were adjusted for inflation.

Investment and industrial output grew in a sustained manner from
the post–World War II period to the early 1980s, except for a brief period in 1976–1977 following a devaluation of the peso. During the first
half of the 1970s, the pace of manufacturing growth slowed and its in-
vestment/output ratio dropped owing to weak fixed capital formation
(figures 4.2 and 4.3). This was viewed as a symptom of the obsolescence
of the ISI model.

In the 1978–1982 period, manufacturing GDP grew at an average
annual rate of nearly 10 percent in real terms, and fixed investment
reached high levels both in absolute terms and in relation to GDP. This
growth period came to an abrupt halt in 1982, when the Mexican government responded to a new external-sector crisis with an adjustment
and stabilization program that led to several years of recession. Fixed
capital formation in the manufacturing sector plummeted by 50 percent
in 1983–1984.

Manufacturing GDP began to recover in 1987 but then lost momentum in 1990–1993, and its modest upturn in 1994 was more than offset
by a fall of nearly 8 percent during 1995. Its recovery in 1996–2000 was

stock survey and GDP data on the entire manufacturing industry, as reported in
national accounts data.

FIGURE 4.2. Ratio of Investment to Total Output and Growth of Manufacturing Product in Mexico, 1970–1996 (percentages based on data at 1980 prices)

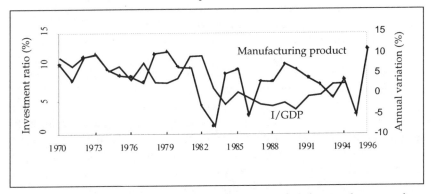

Source: Authors' calculations based on Banco de México n.d. and national accounts data from the Instituto Nacional de Estadística, Geografía e Informática (INEGI).

FIGURE 4.3. Gross Fixed Capital Formation in Mexican Manufacturing, 1970–1994 (at 1980 prices and as a proportion of manufacturing product)

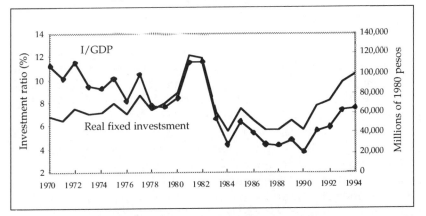

Source: Authors' calculations based on Banco de México n.d. and national accounts data from the Instituto Nacional de Estadística, Geografía e Informática (INEGI).

all the more remarkable given that, for the first time, GDP growth rates exceeded those achieved during Mexico's petroleum boom. For its part, manufacturing investment did not begin rising steadily until 1991, a trend that lasted until 1994. For the 1988–1994 period as a whole, the real gross fixed capital stock in manufacturing grew at an average annual rate of 5.3 percent, a slight increase over the 4.7 percent registered in 1985–1987 but several points below rates prior to the 1980s.

The crisis of 1995 led to a sharp drop in manufacturing investment, which was followed by a recovery in 1996–2000. Although complete data are not yet available for the most recent years, manufacturing investment is estimated to have dropped 5 percent in 1995 and to have increased 10 percent in 1996.[16]

Information from interviews and other sources indicates that manufacturing investment in new projects dropped off in 1995, although projects already under way (especially export-oriented projects) were continued. This suggests that investment by large companies with links to foreign markets and access to foreign-currency financing increased. There is also a consensus that firms not operating under such favorable conditions did not step up investment. This appears to have been the case with small enterprises, whose investment plans were blocked by a lack of competitively priced financing.

In the 1988–1996 period, manufacturing absorbed 30 percent of total gross fixed investment, or 16 points less than in 1980–1982, while the trade and services sectors increased their shares. Similar patterns appeared in investment in machinery and equipment for production, where manufacturing accounted for 46 percent in 1980–1982 but only 36 percent in 1988–1994 (Moreno-Brid 1995).

Investment as a share of real GDP had not recovered its 1982 level in most branches of the manufacturing sector, which suggests that an overall upturn in investment in the sector did not accompany the liberalizing reforms.[17] Of the nine branches where the performance of the investment/output ratio and the growth rate of fixed capital stock indicate a substantial accumulation of fixed capital during the 1988–1994 period, only four showed strong real GDP growth. These branches were food commodities, pharmaceuticals, electronics, and automobiles (Moreno-Brid 1999a: 89). These branches were also notable for the fact that their investment drive in GDP terms was higher in the 1983–1987 period than in 1970–1976 or even 1977–1982. In other words, even during periods of low domestic sales and weak economic activity, these branches focused on investing for export and adapted their operations to Mexico's increased openness to global competition and decreased dependence upon special treatment by the state. Three of these four

---

[16] This estimate is based on preliminary and partial figures from the Banco de México survey for 1995 and 1996, which were released in early 1999.

[17] Estimates of investment/output ratios and average annual growth rates of fixed capital stock, real GDP, and exports by manufacturing branch in Mexico prior to and after the reforms are drawn from Moreno-Brid 1999a: tables 2–7.

branches – pharmaceuticals, electronics, and automobiles – had been the object of special industrial promotion programs. Similarly, all three branches have significant amounts of foreign capital; indeed, electronics and automobiles are Mexico's highest FDI recipients.

The great majority of manufacturing branches that have received strong investment flows are characterized by the presence of foreign capital. Figures for 1994–1997 show that branches with the highest FDI shares were also the most dynamic in terms of investment. They produced foods, soft drinks, tobacco, iron and steel, electrical machinery and equipment, electronic appliances, and automotive industry goods. Other branches displaying intense capital formation during the period of liberalizing reforms included metal products; machinery and equipment (electronic appliances, automobiles, and other metal products, excluding machinery); and chemicals, petroleum by-products, rubber, and plastics (pharmaceuticals, soaps, detergents and cosmetics, and other chemical products).

As is the case for the economy as a whole, the sluggish growth of gross fixed investment in manufacturing, at least until 1995, is cause for concern. The meager formation of capital was consistent with growth in manufacturing, which averaged only 3.6 percent per year in 1988–1996.

In general terms, the virtually irreversible nature of fixed capital formation and its dependence upon events governed by uncertainty help explain why Mexico's economic reforms have had somewhat inconsistent impacts on investment.[18] The inconsistency arises because the investment response depends upon whether relevant agents believe that investment will improve the business climate and what activities and sectors they feel will be favored. Investment decisions are also influenced by whether agents perceive liberalizing reforms as being permanent or temporary.[19] Moreover, although the reforms entail changes that in principle favor private initiative, the transition from one macroeconomic policy approach to another leads to an uncertain business

---

[18] The conventional frame of reference offers an in-depth explanation of investment in advanced economies, but it is inadequate for developing economies, where institutional organization is relatively weak and certain key markets are incomplete and operate under sui generis conditions (Rama 1993; Agenor and Montiel 1996).

[19] Ibarra (1995) examines the impact of the "credibility" of trade liberalization on investment. His findings show the negative and significant effect of the "probability of reversing trade reform" on investment, and his conclusion is that actors' uncertainty concerning the permanence of market-oriented reforms dampened investment in Mexico. As long as investors believe that protectionist measures will again be enacted, they will have little incentive to carry out projects whose profitability depends upon the extent of trade liberalization.

climate, undermines stability, and can lead to the postponement or even cancellation of fixed capital formation projects.

In situations of great uncertainty, fixed capital investment can take a long time to be reactivated. Similarly, once projects to expand or modernize productive capacity have been launched, it may be difficult to put them on hold during temporary fluctuations in the pace of economic activity. According to the businessmen interviewed, in 1995 this inertia in investment was visible in the steel and auto parts industries, where, despite the drastic fall in output, various companies continued projects to expand and modernize their productive capacity.

In order to identify the factors that determine investment in manufacturing, this chapter draws on the results of a series of panel models estimated by Moreno-Brid (1999a), based on data on fixed capital formation by branch of activity. This analysis is based on an accelerator model, while also taking into account the effects of the cost of capital use and other variables viewed as pertinent in the literature on the process of fixed capital formation within the context of market-oriented reforms.[20]

The results suggest a significant positive effect of the accelerator — reflected in total manufacturing GDP — and of delayed investment. The real interest rate ratios were negative, in keeping with theory, but they were far from showing a significant influence on investment. This could be due in part to the use in the analysis of the ex post borrowing rate rather than the ex ante lending rate. The internal credit to the manufacturing sector that was deferred for a period showed a positive and significant influence on branches with a strong investment process.[21] In this regard, the entrepreneurs interviewed felt that credit avail-

---

[20] The panel analysis was conducted by presupposing "fixed effects." Although this makes it easier to establish estimates, it limits the analysis because it presupposes that the differential effect between the activities considered is only on constant term "α" and not on "β" slopes (Greene 1997: 615). The multicolinearity between certain explanatory variables made it necessary to estimate different alternative specifications for the linear model and contrast them so as to select the most appropriate one. The R^2 of the models estimated in the manufacturing-sector branches with the most dynamic process of capital formation ranged between 0.60 and 0.67, and between 0.40 and 0.50 in the remaining group. The size of the ratios estimated in the different models examined and their levels of significance are reported in Moreno-Brid 1999a: tables 13 and 14.

[21] Gelos and Werner (1998) studied the behavior of fixed capital investment in Mexican manufacturing and reached the conclusion that liquidity squeezes had a significant effect on capital formation, particularly in small companies, whereas access to credit did not have a significant influence on public enterprise investment. The study also detected the effect of the real exchange rate on capital formation and noted that exchange-rate depreciations tend to dampen formation. On

ability, rather than cost, was the financial variable that facilitated or constrained fixed investment, while most of the large companies or groups interviewed stated that foreign rather than domestic financing was most relevant to investment decisions.[22]

Moreover, the results of this econometric exercise show that prices of capital goods exert a significant influence on the prices of other goods. This suggests that, ceteris paribus, cheaper prices of machinery and equipment acted as an incentive for investment. It should be stressed, however, that to the degree that cheaper prices are accompanied by real exchange rate appreciation, this tends to discourage investment in tradable sectors, because in principle such changes run counter to the local productive apparatus's orientation toward the foreign sector.

With regard to the influence of FDI, the results also suggest that it had a positive, albeit not very significant, effect on total manufacturing investment. There was a complementary effect between public investment and fixed investment in the manufacturing industry, a finding that accords with studies of other developing economies.

The businessmen interviewed by Máttar (2000) and Moreno-Brid (1999a) consistently noted the sensitivity of investment in manufacturing to economic growth. They emphasized that the implementation of the NAFTA made the U.S. market more attractive, although they also stated that high and sustained economic growth in Mexico is a requisite for strong fixed capital formation. These entrepreneurs were of the opinion that, although the foreign market has become an important focus of corporate strategies, a growing domestic market is essential for strengthening fixed capital investment in manufacturing. Moreover, a high percentage of the individuals interviewed stated that ownership

---

that basis, the authors concluded that financial reform had a decisive impact on manufacturing investment because it broadened private firms' access to bank loans. These findings seem to confirm the conclusions of other studies, which indicate that the scarcity of financial resources acts as a strong constraint on private investment (World Bank 1994). Trigueros, however, states that if one takes into account the impact of foreign funds in Mexico, financial liberalization helped boost consumption more than investment (1997).

[22] Large companies have not sought loans from national banks for a long time and do not wish to, because the terms, rates, and amounts that national banks offer are not competitive with those available on international markets. Such companies have earned access to international financing (and the possibility of exchange-rate hedging) through their successful export penetration of world markets. They far prefer taking on foreign, dollar-denominated debt, and they only resort to national banks for very basic services, having stopped viewing them as a source of working capital or fixed investment financing some time ago. In fact, many of these firms are net creditors with domestic banks.

insecurity effectively discourages both national and foreign investment, while also skewing the capital formation process and reducing international competitiveness.

IMPACTS OF THE INVESTMENT PATTERN

The Change in Industrial Structure

Industrial investment is strongly concentrated in four branches, which together accounted for 84.0 percent of total gross fixed investment in manufacturing between 1988 and 1994 (table 4.4). These subsectors were: metal products, machinery, and equipment (29.4 percent of total investment); chemicals, rubber, and plastics (20.5 percent); food, beverages, and tobacco (20.3 percent); and basic metals (13.8 percent).

The concentration of investment in these branches was almost the same in 1983–1987 as in 1988–1994, and we estimate that the pattern remained steady in 1994–1998. These branches were also those receiving the most investment in 1977–1982 (the years of the previous upturn in manufacturing), accounting for 76.6 percent of investment in nonpetroleum manufacturing during those years. Despite this concordance, on comparing the composition of gross fixed investment in 1977–1982

TABLE 4.4. Composition of Fixed Investment in Mexico's Manufacturing Sector by Division, 1970–1994 (percentages)

	1970–1976	1977–1982	1983–1987	1988–1994
Food, beverages, and tobacco	15.9	16.0	15.1	20.3
Textiles, clothing, and leather	8.7	7.3	7.3	4.8
Wood and wood products	1.5	1.6	1.0	0.6
Printing and publishing	4.7	5.1	5.4	4.6
Chemicals, rubber, and plastics[1]	27.2	15.0	20.3	20.5
Nonmetallic mineral products	10.4	8.2	8.3	5.2
Basic metals	11.9	22.8	12.0	13.8
Metal products, machinery and equipment	18.8	22.8	29.6	29.4
Other manufactures	0.9	1.2	1.0	1.0

Source: Authors' calculations based on Moreno-Brid 1999a, using data in constant 1980 pesos.

Note: Percentages may not add to 100.0 because of rounding.

[1] Not including the petroleum and petroleum by-products, basic petrochemicals, and fertilizer branches.

and 1988–1994, certain changes indicate a shift in the structure of the productive apparatus to adapt to Mexico's new competitive environment. During the latter period, the metal products, machinery, and equipment branch increased its lead owing to the growth of the automobile industry, whereas the basic metals industries' share decreased, partly due to declining investment in the casting and iron and steel industries, which had been strongly promoted during the petroleum boom of the late 1970s and early 1980s.[23]

In more disaggregated terms, the composition of fixed investment in manufacturing has changed following Mexico's economic reforms. One might expect that this change and the rise in fixed capital formation would have led to a new industrial matrix in Mexico, one more in keeping with the country's open economy and the public sector's reduced involvement in the productive sphere. To estimate the magnitude of the change in the productive apparatus, Moreno-Brid (1999a) calculated the values for Mexico of the United Nations Industrial Development Organization's (UNIDO) structural-change index, which measures shifts in industrial structure between two points in time. The results, based on two-digit data, show a change in manufacturing GDP structure of 10.2 percent in 1984–1994 and 9.2 percent in 1987–1994. In other words, one-tenth of the structure of Mexico's total manufacturing GDP in 1984 or 1987 had changed by 1994. The scant difference between the structural-change index in 1984–1994 and 1987–1994 suggests that much of the manufacturing restructuring that took place following market-oriented reforms occurred after 1987.

The structural-change index was 10.2 percent for 1970–1981, the same as for 1984–1994. In view of the radically different economic policy approaches adopted in these two periods, it could be assumed that the structural recomposition of GDP would run in different directions. In other words, one would expect that the industrial branches benefiting most from the import-substitution development model would be different from those on the rise under the new model, based on open competition from abroad and a lack of state supports. However, the disaggregated results show that the manufacturing GDP share of two-thirds of all branches changed in the same direction in 1970–1981 as in 1984–1994. Furthermore, sixteen of the eighteen branches whose share changed the most in 1984–1994 moved in the same direction in 1970–1981 — that is, their previous trend was strengthened. For example, the three branches that most increased their GDP share in 1987–1994 — auto-

---

[23] Public-sector iron and steel enterprises were privatized in the early 1990s, and the industry has since become highly competitive as a result of investment in modernization, even though its size has been reduced in absolute terms.

mobiles, motors and accessories, and nonelectrical machinery and equipment—were also those whose share increased the most in the period
1970–1981.[24]

At that level of disaggregation, more than a decade of economic
reform appears not to have radically changed the momentum in the
makeup of manufacturing activity that had been under way since the
1970s and the oil boom. The figures presented above also seem to imply that the process of transformation and modernization has concentrated on large, export-oriented companies with access to international financing.

Export Performance

The sluggish growth of manufacturing GDP in recent years stands in
contrast with Mexico's dynamic export performance. During the first
years of the economic reform process, manufacturing exports increased sharply, spurred by exchange-rate depreciation, low domestic demand, and the pressing need for companies to focus on foreign
markets in order to secure foreign exchange. The growth rate for
manufacturing exports overtook that of manufacturing GDP in 1990,
although the export drive subsequently lost impetus, partly due to
the peso's appreciation. Exports regained their earlier momentum
from 1995 to 2000, this time as a result of a new peso devaluation and
strong foreign demand.

In the 1988–2000 period, manufacturing exports grew at an annual
average rate of 15 percent in real terms, four times the sector's average
GDP growth. Manufacturing exports (excluding maquiladoras) rose
from less than 10 percent of the sector's GDP in the 1970s to 27 percent
during the second half of the 1980s, 34 percent in 1994, and over 60
percent in the late 1990s. Exporters have focused on dynamic markets
in developed countries, which now absorb more than 90 percent of
Mexico's total exports. Several authors have found evidence of Mexican
manufacturing exports' increased international competitiveness in the
1980s and 1990s.[25]

In terms of specific sectors, industries in which foreign companies
have a strong presence (including maquiladoras) were very important
in boosting exports to the United States and Canada in the 1990s (tables
4.5, 4.6). Some export items—in particular, television sets, electricity-

---

[24] Disaggregated estimates of the structural-change index can be found in Moreno-
Brid 1999a: table 8.

[25] See, for example, Máttar 1996; Calderón, Mortimore, and Peres 1996.

distributing equipment, and measuring equipment—also held high market shares.[26] Such exports form part of a drive by U.S.–origin companies to increase efficiency, mainly in the automobile, data-processing, electronics, and clothing industries. Pressures to reduce costs and limit access to the North American market have been key factors in the expansion of productive capacity over the past decade, although some of these U.S.–origin companies (such as automobile manufacturers) had already made significant investments in Mexico.

The "Big Three" U.S. automakers began investing in plant construction and modernization in Mexico during the late 1970s in response to competition from East Asia, and from 1994 to 2000 their investments totaled US$1.3 billion a year on average. These companies, which are the largest car manufacturers in Mexico, built 1.08 million of the 1.82 million vehicles produced in Mexico in 2001; 85 percent of these vehicles were for export, mostly destined for the U.S. market (AMIA 2001). On average during 1997–1999 Mexico held 23.9 percent of the U.S. market in commercial vehicles, 10.7 percent in passenger vehicles, and 9.4 percent in auto parts.[27]

In clothing manufacturing, foreign firms have benefited from their preferential access to the U.S. market under the NAFTA (SECOFI 1994) to the extent that Mexico's garment exports to the United States have overtaken all international competitors, including China.[28] The NAFTA also stimulated electronics exports, owing to the immediate tariff reduction on imported office equipment and photocopier parts and components, and to the deferred tariff reduction (until 1998) on television sets, computers, and telephone equipment. These cuts, and the prospect of the full enforcement of the NAFTA's rules of origin in 2003, encouraged foreign companies to invest in Mexico as an export platform (CEPAL 1998).

Notwithstanding the importance of exports in foreign companies' strategies, Mexico's enormous domestic market holds a potential that did not disappear with economic liberalization. This potential is evident in three areas. First, except in crisis years like 1995, the domestic market absorbs between one-third and one-half of output—even in auto-

---

[26] Seven of the sectors in the table pertain to both the largest export industries and those with the largest market shares. Foreign companies and maquiladoras play a leading role in six of these sectors: television sets, electricity-distributing equipment, freight transport vehicles, electrical circuits, electricity-generating equipment, and other electrical power plants and machinery.

[27] Calculations based on ECLAC's CANPLUS software program. These market shares increased until 2000.

[28] By the late 1990s, Mexico supplied more than 13 percent of U.S. garment imports, compared to less than 2 percent in 1985.

TABLE 4.5. Mexico's Main Exports to the United States and Canada, 1985 and 1998 (percentage of total exports)

	1985	1998
Passenger motor cars (excluding public service types)	1.0	10.0
Crude petroleum (including from bituminous minerals)	31.5	7.2
Television sets	0.7	4.3
Motor vehicles for the transport of goods and materials	0.7	3.9
Automatic data-processing machines	0.0	3.9
Auto parts and accessories	3.2	3.8
Commodities not classified	2.8	3.7
Electrical apparatus for making and breaking electrical circuits	2.0	2.6
Furniture	0.8	2.5
Electrical machinery and apparatus	1.8	2.3
Electrical power machinery	1.3	1.8
Outer garments (women's and girls')	0.4	1.7
Outer garments (men's and boys')	0.5	1.5
Rotating electrical plant and parts thereof	0.8	1.5
Measuring and control instruments	0.6	1.4
Undergarments, knitted or crocheted	0.2	1.4
Outer garments, knitted or crocheted	0.0	1.4
Non-electrical parts and machinery	0.3	1.1
Other household equipment, electrical and non-electrical	0.5	1.1
Manufactures of base metals	0.6	1.0

Source: Authors' calculations based on ECLAC's CANPLUS software program.

Note: These were Mexico's twenty highest-ranking exports in 1998. The data reported for 1985 are the average of figures for 1984, 1985, and 1986; similarly, the data for 1998 are the average of figures for 1997 and 1998.

TABLE 4.6. Mexico's Share of U.S. and Canadian Import Markets, 1985 and 1998 (percentages)

	1985	1998
Television sets	7.2	69.5
Equipment for distributing electricity	37.7	58.0
Meters and counters	0.8	52.9
Rotating electrical plant and parts thereof	11.6	28.5
Electrical power machinery	17.6	24.9
Motor vehicles for the transport of goods and materials	1.4	23.9
Ores and concentrates of precious metals, waste, scrap	1.2	22.1
Electrical apparatus for making and breaking electrical circuits	13.7	17.6
Trailers and other vehicles (not motorized)	0.1	16.9
Medical instruments and appliances	5.5	16.3
Undergarments, knitted or crocheted	2.0	15.9
Outer garments (men's and boys')	4.2	15.8
Furniture	7.3	15.2
Glass	8.7	15.2
Other household equipment, electrical and non-electrical	3.2	15.0
Heating and cooling equipment	3.2	14.8
Fruit and nuts (other than oil nuts), fresh or dried	5.0	14.6
Electrical machinery and apparatus	7.0	14.5
Sugar confectionery (except chocolate)	0.8	14.3
Sanitary, plumbing, heating, and lighting fixtures	6.8	14.1

Source: Authors' calculations based on ECLAC's CANPLUS software program.

Note: These were the twenty Mexican export products with the largest U.S. and Canadian market shares in 1998. The data reported for 1985 are the average of figures for 1984, 1985, and 1986; similarly, the data for 1998 are the average of figures for 1997 and 1998.

TABLE 4.7. Technological Specialization Index for Latin America and Southeast Asia, 1977–1995

	Latin America and the Caribbean	Mexico	Argentina	Brazil	Chile	G7[1]	Hong Kong, Korea, Singapore, and Taiwan
1977–80	0.17	0.55	0.12	0.25	0.01	2.16	0.85
1981–85	0.22	0.51	0.13	0.29	0.01	2.12	0.96
1986	0.29	0.78	0.08	0.32	0.01	1.90	0.89
1987	0.32	0.97	0.07	0.32	0.01	1.82	0.93
1988	0.34	1.06	0.08	0.33	0.01	1.80	0.99
1989	0.35	1.13	0.08	0.32	0.01	1.78	1.05
1990	0.35	1.18	0.09	0.30	0.01	1.77	1.09
1991	0.38	1.29	0.09	0.27	0.01	1.76	1.16
1992	0.42	1.44	0.10	0.25	0.01	1.77	1.26
1993	0.45	1.57	0.09	0.23	0.01	1.73	1.41
1994	0.47	1.63	0.09	0.22	0.01	1.73	1.51
1995	0.48	1.62	0.07	0.23	0.01	1.67	1.80

Source: Alcorta and Peres 1998.

[1] The G7 countries include Canada, France, Germany, Great Britain, Italy, Japan, and the United States. (The European Union joined in G7 summits beginning in 1977.)

mobiles, the country's main export industry. Second, FDI has a strong presence in the food, beverage, and tobacco industries, both as a result of purchases of national enterprises and from added investment by foreign companies already established in Mexico (PepsiCo., Nestlé, and Coca-Cola, for example). Third, there is an important level of investment in the services sector, particularly in telecommunications and financial services, which were among the most attractive fields for FDI during the 1990s.[29]

In addition to FDI's sectoral dimensions in the Mexican economy and its outstanding role in promoting Mexico's integration into international markets through exports, it is important to assess the technological quality of the country's international integration. Alcorta and Peres (1998) developed a technological specialization index (TSI) that describes the extent to which a country (or a set of countries) adapts its export structure to changes in world trade in goods with greater or lesser technological content.[30] From a growth perspective, the TSI shows how a country's (or a set of countries') market share changes in high- and medium-technology activities in relation to its share in activities with lower technological content.[31] Table 4.7 shows the 1977–1995 TSI values for Latin America and the Caribbean as a whole and for Mexico, Argentina, Brazil, and Chile individually, as well as for two sets of countries that serve as a frame of reference (the G7 countries and four high-growth economies in East Asia).

Mexico's TSI values are surprising. They more than tripled during the nineteen years in question, whereas Brazil and Argentina show a negative trend over the long term and Chile shows a steady but very low level of technological specialization. Although Mexico's values are

---

[29] The privatization of Teléfonos de México and the opening up of the mobile telephone and long-distance markets during this period deserve special mention. Moreover, foreign investment in the banking sector rose sharply after the 1995 crisis; Spanish, Canadian, and U.S. banks played a dynamic role in this process.

[30] A country's (or a set of countries') TSI is calculated as the quotient of market share in sectors of high and medium technology, and market share in light technology sectors. Sectors are defined to three digits of the Standard International Trade Classification (SITC), revision 2. Because the aim is to measure technological specialization, the market used as a reference is that of the OECD member countries — that is, the market closest to the technological frontier. TSI was calculated using ECLAC's CANPLUS software program.

[31] Both absolute TSI values and changes in them are important. A value higher (lower) than 1.0 indicates that a country's export share of markets for goods with high technological content is higher (lower) than its export share of markets for goods with low technological content. An increasing (decreasing) TSI value over time indicates a relatively greater (lesser) share of markets for high-technology goods.

TABLE 4.8. Capital Formation in Mexico and Growth of Manufactured Exports, 1980s–1990s

Annual mean variation in manufactured exports, 1989–1996[2]	Annual Mean Variation in Gross Fixed Capital Stock, 1988–1994[1]		
	Less than 4.3 percent	*Between 4.3 and 6.3 percent*	*More than 6.3 percent*
Less than 10 percent	Hard-fiber spun goods and piece-goods Printing and publishing Rubber products Cement Nonferrous metals Structural metal products	Coffee processing and milling Alcoholic beverages Beer and malt Paper and cardboard Synthetic resins and artificial fibers Automobile motors, accessories	Sugar Other wood products Pharmaceutical products
From 10 to 20 percent	Basic chemicals Soft-fiber spun goods and piece-goods Sawmills	Leather and footwear Plastic articles Nonmetallic products Electrical appliances Other manufactures	Meat and dairy products Tobacco Other chemical products Other metal products (except machinery)
More than 20 percent	Nonelectrical machinery Transport equipment and material	Edible oils Clothing Glass Iron and steel Metal furniture Electrical machinery and appliances Household appliances	Fruit and vegetables Wheat milling Cornflour milling Animal fodder Other food commodities Refreshments and soft drinks Other textile products Soaps and cosmetics Electronic appliances Automobiles

Source: Moreno-Brid 1999a: table 12, based upon INEGI and Banco de México figures.

Note: Annual mean variation in manufacturing exports in 1989–1996 was 14.4 percent (1993 prices); annual mean variation in fixed capital stock in 1988–1994 was 5.3 percent (1980 prices).

[1] Calculations for gross capital formation are based on data in 1980 pesos.

[2] Export calculations are based on data in 1993 pesos.

strongly dependent upon the "maquiladora effect"[32] — exports of so-phisticated goods where only the least advanced stages of the assembly process are carried out in the country — its TSI levels and growth show increasing progress in the quality of its international integration. In this regard, at the beginning of the 1970s Mexico exported shrimp, coffee, cotton, and tomatoes; it became a petroleum exporter at the end of the 1970s; and by the beginning of the 1990s Mexico was exporting auto-mobiles, computers, and electrical and electronic equipment, although in many cases national content was rather low.

The central problem with this development is the sophisticated ex-ports' low level of integration with the rest of the national economy and the reduced linkage effect on other activities and nonexporting agents. Although this situation is undeniable, the starting point for such an integration is in place in Mexico, unlike the rest of Latin America. Whether or not it becomes the national economy's engine of growth will depend upon the development of more solid forward and back-ward linkages.

This point leads to interesting considerations regarding the maqui-ladora sector's potential to advance toward more complex activities, incorporating more national value-added into exports by using more domestically produced inputs or developing more sophisticated local activities. Efforts to incorporate domestic inputs and develop local sup-pliers have had extremely poor results. Nevertheless, recent studies (such as Buitelaar and Padilla 2000) show that some Mexican maqui-ladora establishments have begun to incorporate their own design ele-ments and research and development, giving rise to "third-generation" maquiladoras. These coexist with first- and second-generation plants, which focus, respectively, on assembly or industrial processing without engaging in technological endeavors. Although this dualism demon-strates the disparity that exists in the maquiladora industry, it also in-dicates the sector's potential to evade the trap of long-term specializa-tion based solely on comparative advantages stemming from unskilled labor.

Export performance has been closely associated with the vigor of investment at the level of industrial branches. Branches in which capital formation was more (less) dynamic have tended to be among those that stepped up exports more (less) rapidly (table 4.8). Thus ten of the sev-enteen branches in the group in which capital formation reacted rapidly

---

[32] The reforms had the effect of making nonmaquiladora manufacturers operate more like export maquiladoras. Under these conditions and in the context of fall-ing trade barriers, the ever-increasing imports of inputs (mainly by export-oriented industries) "maquiladorized" diverse production sectors.

TABLE 4.9. Capital Formation and Manufacturing Growth in Mexico, 1980s–1990s

Annual mean variation in manufacturing product, 1989–1996[2]	Annual Mean Variation in Gross Fixed Capital Stock, 1988–1994[1]		
	Less than 4.3 percent	*Between 4.3 and 6.3 percent*	*More than 6.3 percent*
Less than 2.5 percent	Soft-fiber spun goods and piece-goods Hard-fiber spun goods and piece-goods Sawmills Printing and publishing Rubber products Cement Nonferrous metals Structural metal products Nonelectrical machinery Transport equipment and material	Coffee processing and milling Edible oils Alcoholic beverages Clothing Leather and footwear Nonmetallic products Metal furniture Electrical appliances	Wheat milling Corn flour milling Animal feed Tobacco Other wood products
From 2.5 to 4.5 percent	Basic chemicals	Paper and cardboard Synthetic resins, artificial fibers Plastic articles Electrical machinery Automobile motors, accessories Other manufactures	Sugar Refreshments and soft drinks Pharmaceutical products Soaps and cosmetics Other chemical products Other metal products (except machinery)
More than 4.5 percent		Beer and malt Glass Iron and steel Household appliances	Meat and dairy products Fruit and vegetables Other food commodities Other textile products Electronic appliances Automobiles

Source: Moreno-Brid 1999b: table 11, based upon INEGI and Banco de México figures.

Note: Annual mean variation in manufacturing product in 1989–1996 was 3.5 percent (1993 prices); annual mean variation in gross fixed capital stock in 1988–1994 was 5.3 percent (1980 prices).

[1] Calculations for gross capital formation are based on data in 1980 pesos.

[2] Manufacturing product calculations are based on data in 1993 pesos.

between 1988 and 1994 were in the group that increased exports by more than 20 percent a year between 1989 and 1996 (table 4.8, bottom right block). Of these, fruits and vegetables, other food commodities, other textile industries, electronic appliances, and automobiles were among those branches in which output expanded fastest between 1989 and 1996 (table 4.9).

Similarly, most industrial branches with low fixed capital investment have been in the group with low export growth. Only two branches with low investment levels—nonelectrical machinery, and transport equipment and material—were among those that most increased exports in 1989–1996, probably because they had idle capacity at the outset of the period. A similar trend is evident when viewing GDP instead of exports: almost half of the branches are in the main diagonal (top left to bottom right) of table 4.9, suggesting a positive relationship between investment growth and GDP growth.

CONCLUSION

More than ten years after the implementation of reforms designed to make Mexico's private sector the engine of economic development in a market open to international competition, investment has only partially recovered from its collapse at the end of the petroleum boom in 1981. The upsurge in investment during the past decade has not been strong enough to ensure high levels of sustained economic growth

The moderate dynamism of investment during the reform process is reflected in modest GDP growth, with fluctuations that have prevented the consolidation of a sustained expansion. Short-lived upswings exert excessive pressure on the trade balance and ultimately stoke foreign-exchange crises. It is too early to tell whether the fall in aggregate investment in 2001 (-5 percent) meant that its dynamism during the 1996-2000 period—which exceeded 10 percent per annum—initiated a longer cycle of high investment in fixed capital, or whether it was merely an effort to replenish depleted capital stock. If the latter was the case, the Mexican economy will remain unable to consolidate the high, sustained growth platform that it badly needs.

Although total gross fixed investment, GDP, and foreign direct investment grew vigorously in 1996–2000, several factors still hamper economic growth. The most important of these are the real exchange rate, Mexico's financial system, a degree of continued uncertainty after the 2000 presidential transition, and the downturn in the U.S. economy.

A number of factors help explain investment's limited response to market-oriented reforms in Mexico. First, the reforms were implemented when the domestic economy was in deep stagnation, which was further aggravated by strong constraints on foreign and domestic financing. Second, the reforms explicitly aimed at sectoral neutrality and the elimination of all types of incentives, subsidies, or promotion programs for specific activities. The strategy shift also implied a refusal by government to establish measures to promote investment spending as opposed to consumption expenditure. The government's decision not to promote fixed capital formation during the transition period occurred in combination with the uncertainty arising from the change in economic development strategy, which led to the postponement or interruption of investment projects. Third, the elimination of sectoral incentives had a strong impact on the traditional lead sector in capital formation—manufacturing—because it had been the most favored under the model of import substitution and state intervention. The loss of preferential treatment thus placed pressure on manufacturing's relative rate of return, which curbed investment.

A fourth factor was the appreciation of the real exchange rate in 1988–1994. In theory, real exchange-rate appreciation in developing countries encourages fixed investment, because it lowers the relative prices of imported machinery and equipment. However, it also changes relative prices by encouraging the reassignment of factors toward the production of non-tradable goods and services. Finally, a fifth factor that also had a negative effect was the fall in public investment, because "crowding in" between public and private investment has historically been more predominant than "crowding out."

In general terms, then, economic reforms have not yet made it possible to raise long-term economic growth rates to satisfactory levels or to eliminate external imbalances and balance-of-payments crises.[33] Although the reforms have encouraged FDI in certain sectors, they have not led to a rise in fixed capital formation in the economy as a whole. The aim of making the private sector the pivot of economic development has only been partially achieved, and the economy has become more strongly segmented between large export-oriented companies with strong links to foreign capital and smaller producers focusing on domestic demand and facing significant constraints on their development. The result is a pattern of economic development that has yet to show sufficient strength to absorb the labor supply or to ensure that balance-of-payments crises will not recur.

---

[33] Some reforms had enormous negative economic and social costs and had to be reversed. For example, the privatization of the commercial banking system and the leasing of highways to the private sector soon resulted in a spectacular deterioration in these activities' performance, forcing the government to make special financial rescue arrangements.

The reforms have given rise to opportunities for simultaneously generating and destroying productive capacity. By opening markets and reducing state intervention, they have fostered activities favored by redefined price vectors and the relative profit margins derived from the new macroeconomic context. At the same time, however, liberalizing reforms have posed a threat to enterprises that have, in principle, become unprofitable. Real exchange and interest rates play a key role, and their evolution may act as an incentive or as an obstacle to increasing the international competitiveness of the manufacturing industry. The behavior of these variables will determine the reforms' impact on the long-term growth of the Mexican economy.

Without underrating the Mexican economy's export performance and the vitality of FDI in some sectors, it must be stressed that import penetration has also been remarkable. The increasing income elasticity of imports that began in the mid–1980s continued through the 1990s, and that high elasticity runs counter to expectations that the wave of imports would lose strength as Mexican consumers became accustomed to having access to foreign goods.

Behind the high foreign content in Mexico's exports lie disrupted domestic chains of production, arising from the displacement and elimination of companies that previously produced for the domestic market. Investment to rebuild these production chains or create others in different industrial sectors is crucial to the country's economic development.[34] Fixed capital formation and the intermeshing of the industrial fabric will determine to what extent the export orientation of industry contributes to the high, sustained growth of the economy as a whole, thereby averting recurring foreign-exchange crises. In this regard, market integration and growth are a requisite for fixed capital formation, to which end it will be essential for foreign investment to focus more on creating new productive activities than on acquiring established enterprises that can serve as outlets for imported goods.

The Mexican economy is still not registering growth rates on a par with the historically high rates of the past. Even though GDP growth resumed in the 1990s, the average rate of expansion was rather low, and the economy had already begun to lose momentum in late 1998 due to the impact of the East Asian crisis on international financial and trade markets. It is still too early to tell whether recent growth will be sus-

---

[34] Concern over this issue was reflected in renewed discussions on industrial policy during the Zedillo administration (Máttar and Peres 1997; SECOFI 1996).

tained over the medium term, or whether measures to curb demand will be needed to prevent the resurgence of balance-of-payments problems, particularly now that the U.S. economy's growth has been interrupted. Either way, giving impetus and continuity to fixed capital formation remains an indispensable condition of sustained economic growth in the medium and long term.

REFERENCES

Agenor, Pierre-Richard, and Peter J. Montiel. 1996. *Development Macroeconomics*. Princeton, N.J.: Princeton University Press.

Alcorta, Ludovico, and Wilson Peres. 1998. "Innovation Systems and Technological Specialization in Latin America and the Caribbean," *Research Policy* 26: 857–81.

AMIA (Asociación Mexicana de la Industria Automotriz). 2001. *Boletín de prensa* (December).

Aspe Armella, Pedro. 1993. *El camino mexicano de la transformación económica*. Mexico City: Fondo de Cultura Económica.

Banco de México. n.d. *Encuesta de acervos y formación bruta de capital*. Mexico City: Banco de México. Various years.

Buitelaar, Rudolf, and Ramón Padilla. 2000. "Maquila, Economic Reforms, and Corporate Strategies," *World Development* 28 (9): 1627–42. Special issue edited by Wilson Peres and Nora Reinhard.

Calderón, Álvaro, Michael Mortimore, and Wilson Peres. 1996. "Mexico: Foreign Investment as a Source of International Competitiveness." In *Foreign Direct Investment and Governments: Catalysts for Economic Restructuring*, edited by John Dunning and Rejeesh Narula. London: Routledge.

CEPAL (Comisión Económica para América Latina y el Caribe). 1998. *La inversión extranjera en América Latina y el Caribe: Informe 1998*. Santiago, Chile: CEPAL.

———. 2001. *Foreign Investment in Latin America and the Caribbean: 2000*. Santiago, Chile: CEPAL.

Escobar de Medécigo, Rebeca. 1999. *El cambio estructural de las telecomunicaciones y la inversión: el caso de México*. Serie Reformas Económicas, no. 17. Santiago, Chile: CEPAL.

Garrido, Celso, and Wilson Peres. 1998. "Grandes empresas y grupos industriales latinoamericanos en los años noventa." In *Grandes empresas y grupos industriales latinoamericanos: expansión y desafíos en la era de la apertura y la globalización*, edited by Wilson Peres. Mexico City: Siglo Veintiuno Editores.

Gelos, Gastón, and Alejandro Werner. 1998. "La inversión fija en el sector manufacturero mexicano, 1985-1994: el rol de los factores financieros y el impacto de la liberalización financiera." Documento de Investigación No. 9805. Mexico City: Banco de México.

Greene, William H. 1997. *Econometric Analysis*. 3d ed. Englewood Cliffs, N.J.: Prentice Hall.

Ibarra, Luis A. 1995. "Credibility of Trade Policy Reform and Investment: The Mexican Experience," *Journal of Development Economics* 47: 39–60.

Lustig, Nora. 1992. *Mexico: The Remaking of an Economy*. Washington, D.C.: Brookings Institution Press.

Máttar, Jorge. 1996. "Desempeño exportador y competitividad internacional: algunos ejercicios CAN para Mexico," *Comercio Exterior* 46 (3): 193–202.

———. 2000. "Inversión y crecimiento durante las reformas económicas." In *Reformas económicas en México, 1982-1999*, edited by Fernando Clavijo. Mexico City: Fondo de Cultura Económica.

Máttar, Jorge, and Wilson Peres. 1997. "La política industrial y de comercio exterior en Mexico." In *Políticas de competitividad industrial: América Latina y el Caribe en los años noventa*, edited by Wilson Peres. Mexico City: Siglo Veintiuno Editores.

Mayorga, Rebeca 1996. "Foreign Investment Regimes in Countries within the Hemisphere: Legal Challenges." Presented at the seminar "Políticas de inversión y reglas multilaterales de inversión en América Latina," Río de Janeiro, March.

Moreno-Brid, Juan Carlos. 1995. "Ahorro externo, inversión y crecimiento económico en México, 1989–1994." Santiago, Chile: CEPAL. Manuscript.

———. 1999a. "Reformas macroeconómicas e inversión manufacturera en México." Mexico City: CEPAL. Manuscript.

———. 1999b. "Mexico's Economic Growth and the Balance of Payments Constraint: A Cointegration Analysis," *International Review of Applied Economics* 13 (2): 149–59.

Peres, Wilson. 1990. *Foreign Direct Investment and Industrial Development in Mexico*. Development Centre Studies. Paris: Organisation for Economic Cooperation and Development.

Rama, Martin. 1993. "Empirical Investment Equations for Developing Countries." In *Striving for Growth after Adjustment: The Role of Capital Formation*, edited by Luis Serven and Andrés Solimano. Washington, D.C.: World Bank.

Rodríguez, Víctor. 1999. *Impacto de la reforma económica sobre las inversiones de la industria eléctrica en México: el regreso del capital privado como palanca de desarrollo*. Serie Reformas Económicas, no. 18. Santiago, Chile: CEPAL.

Ros, Jaime. 1991. *The Effects of Government Policies on the Incentives to Invest, Enterprise Behaviour, and Employment: A Study of Mexico's Economic Reforms in the Eighties*. Notre Dame, Ind.: University of Notre Dame.

SECOFI (Secretaría de Comercio y Fomento Industrial). 1994. *Tratado de Libre Comercio entre México, Canadá y Estados Unidos*. Mexico City: SECOFI.

———. 1996. *Política industrial y comercio exterior*. Mexico City: SECOFI.

———. 1998. "Informe estadístico sobre el comportamiento de la inversión extranjera directa en México." Mexico City: SECOFI.

Scheinvar, Isaac. 1999. *Las carreteras y el sistema portuario frente a las reformas económicas*. Serie Reformas Económicas, no. 20. Santiago, Chile: CEPAL.

Torres, Ramón Carlos. 1999. *México: impacto de las reformas estructurales en la formación de capital del sector petrolero.* Serie Reformas Económicas, no. 19. Santiago, Chile: CEPAL.

Trigueros, Ignacio. 1997. "Flujos de capital y desempeño de la inversión: México." In *Flujos de capital e inversión productiva: lecciones para América Latina,* edited by Ricardo Ffrench-Davis and Helmut Reisen. Santiago, Chile: McGraw Hill.

World Bank. 1994. *Mexico: Country Economic Memorandum – Fostering Private Sector Development in the 1990s.* Report No. 11823-ME. Washington, D.C.: World Bank.

Part III

Trade, Export-Led Growth, and Industrial Policy

5

Mexico's Trade Policy: Financial Crisis and Economic Recovery

Gustavo Vega and Luz María de la Mora

INTRODUCTION

In December 1994, Mexico experienced the most severe financial collapse in its contemporary history. The resulting recession in 1995 cost one million jobs and caused a 6.2 percent contraction of Mexico's gross domestic product (GDP). This domestic shock was followed by global financial instability unleashed by the 1997 Thai devaluation and the Asian crisis, and later by the 1998 collapse of the Russian economy and the Brazilian devaluation. In such a volatile economic environment, in which global investors shunned even the most promising emerging markets, few expected Mexico to recover rapidly. Yet Mexico recovered in a remarkably short period; GDP rose 5.2 percent in 1996, 7.0 percent in 1997, 4.8 percent in 1998, 3.8 percent in 1999, and 6.9 percent in 2000.

This chapter evaluates the role of trade policy in Mexico's economic development beginning in the 1980s, with special attention to the period since 1994 and the implementation of the North American Free Trade Agreement (NAFTA). The authors posit that trade policy and the successful promotion of an export-manufacturing sector have made important contributions to Mexico's financial recovery and economic growth. The chapter brings these contributions into relief not only by exploring economic performance since trade liberalization went into effect, but also by considering the domestic and global environment that Mexico confronted in the mid–1980s and in the second half of the 1990s.

Although the authors highlight trade policy's significant contributions to financial recovery and economic growth, they also recognize its

The authors gratefully acknowledge the research assistance of Marie Elliott in the preparation of this essay. The opinions expressed in this chapter are the authors' and should not be taken as a statement of Mexican government policy.

limitations. The export sector represents only a limited proportion of the whole economy, and it has just begun to create upstream linkages with a much larger non-export-producing sector. In order to achieve balanced and sustained development, Mexico must find mechanisms to make its domestic productive structure as dynamic as its export sector. Trade policy can be a powerful instrument to promote development, but it cannot be the only one. Nor can it be a substitute for domestic growth.

FROM IMPORT SUBSTITUTION TO EXPORT-LED GROWTH

Mexico's decision to adopt an export-oriented economic model was the result of a number of internal and external factors. From the early 1950s to the early 1980s, Mexico, like most countries in Latin America, employed a growth strategy based on import substitution, which emphasized expanding the internal market. The import-substitution industrialization model delivered results during the 1950s and 1960s. However, it began to stumble in the 1970s due to persistent inefficiency resulting from a protected industrial structure. Moreover, industrial growth did not match the demand for new jobs required by Mexico's expanding labor force.

By the early 1980s, Mexico had also become dangerously dependent upon petroleum export revenues. When international oil prices collapsed in 1982, the country could no longer service its foreign debt of almost US$100 billion, threatening both its own economy and the stability of the international financial system. Mexico was forced to negotiate a rescue package with the International Monetary Fund that emphasized fiscal and monetary stringency, deregulation, privatization, and liberalization of trade and investment policies.

Trade liberalization began in 1983 with a moderate unilateral reduction of import tariffs and a gradual elimination of official prices, quotas, licenses, and import permits. In 1986 Mexico became a member of the General Agreement on Tariffs and Trade (GATT), and its maximum tariff was bound at 50 percent, down from 100 percent (Story 1986; Torres and Falk 1989). In 1987 Mexico went even further in unilateral liberalization when it set its highest import duty at 20 percent. These policy decisions were consistent with the Pacto de Solidaridad Económica (Economic Solidarity Pact) negotiated by the government in late 1987, a corporatist arrangement that included business and labor. The pact aimed to stabilize the economy by reducing inflation, and it helped legitimize difficult economic policy choices, such as trade opening.

By 1994 Mexico's highest import tariff rate was 20 percent, and its import schedule was substantially simplified. Almost all import licenses had disappeared. In addition, restrictions on foreign investment had been eliminated for most industries, or else substantially reduced for many others.[1]

The dismantling of policy instruments that formerly had granted protection to Mexico's industry transformed the economy into one of the most open among developing countries.[2] By early 1994, Mexico's structural economic reforms had made it the darling of foreign investors, and few predicted anything but a promising future for the Mexican economy. The annual rate of inflation had fallen from 160 percent in 1987 to 7 percent in 1994. Over this same period, gross domestic product grew by 23 percent in real terms, after a decline of 8 percent between 1981 and 1987, and real wages increased nearly 20 percent

---

[1] Starting in 1984, Mexico began lifting restrictions on foreign ownership by changing the administrative regulations and guidelines established by the 1973 Law to Promote Mexican Investment and Regulate Foreign Investment. This law had empowered the National Foreign Investment Commission (CNIE) to waive restrictions on foreign investment when it deemed the foreign participation to be in the public interest. Following regulatory changes in 1989, the CNIE granted automatic approval for investment projects in "unrestricted industries" when the investments met guidelines designed to promote foreign trade and create jobs outside major industrial areas such as Mexico City, Guadalajara, and Monterrey. In December 1993, a new Foreign Investment Law was enacted that eliminated most of the restrictions in the 1973 law. By that time, according to the GATT's *Trade Policy Review*, the CNIE had approved 98.4 percent of the investment projects that it had reviewed since 1989.

The impact of the 1989 changes was evident in the subsequent increase in foreign direct investment (FDI). More impressive, however, than the increase in FDI was the surge in portfolio investment. In 1989 the CNIE and the National Securities Commission were authorized to approve trust funds through which foreigners could buy equities issued by Mexican firms without acquiring shareholder voting rights. Foreign investors were attracted to the Mexican stock market by the large returns available. Between 1991 and 1993, Mexico was able to offset its substantial current account deficit with inflows of foreign capital (GATT 1994; Kehoe 1995: 147).

[2] Economic openness, measured as the ratio of trade (exports and imports) in goods and non-factor services to GDP, increased from 33 percent in 1985 to 38 percent in 1993. The composition of trade changed dramatically during this period. In 1985, raw materials and mining products, led by petroleum, accounted for 62.4 percent of Mexican export earnings, but these materials' share began to decline in 1986 and had dropped to 19.6 percent by 1993, with petroleum representing 14.2 percent (WTO 1997). Manufactured exports, meanwhile, rose every year from 1986 to 1993 at levels surpassing growth of manufacturing output countrywide. Manufactured exports also showed a clear evolution toward more complex goods in terms of design, production, and marketing.

after having plummeted 30 percent between 1981 and 1987. The government's fiscal deficit, which in the early 1980s was as high as 15 percent of GDP, declined to 2 percent in 1994. Debt restructuring also strengthened national and international investors' confidence in the Mexican economy, and capital inflows rose to unprecedented levels until 1993 (Kehoe 1995: 141).

Despite these positive developments, however, there were signs of weakness in Mexico's economic foundations. Since 1989 Mexico had been accumulating growing current account deficits, which by 1994 reached US$28.5 billion. The country's semi-fixed exchange rate caused real appreciation of the currency from 1991 onward, which undermined competitiveness in the context of liberalized trade and increased the current account deficit. Critics questioned the model's sustainability and recommended a devaluation of the peso. However, the Mexican government argued that a devaluation would ignite inflation and damage international confidence. Besides, foreign capital inflows remained sufficient to finance the current account deficit and the growth of imports — mainly capital goods and inputs that would make the Mexican economy more competitive over time.

A series of domestic and external events led to a collapse of the Mexican peso in December 1994. Contributing events within Mexico were the January 1994 indigenous-based uprising in Chiapas and several highly publicized political assassinations. Externally, rapid growth in the United States caused the U.S. Federal Reserve to raise interest rates, which made investment in U.S. securities far more attractive (Kessler 1998). The cumulative result of destabilizing domestic political events and international economic trends was a dramatic reduction in foreign capital flows into Mexico, and nominal interest rates rose substantially. To prevent further interest rate increases, the Mexican government expanded domestic credit and converted about-to-mature, short-term, peso-denominated government liabilities to dollar-denominated government bonds. As several analysts noted, by late 1994 capital flight had depleted Mexico's foreign exchange reserves and made further defense of the peso unsustainable (Naím and Edwards 1997).

RECOVERY THROUGH TRADE

Thanks largely to trade, Mexico's economic recovery after the 1994–1995 peso collapse was far more rapid than expected. Although GDP contracted by 6.2 percent in 1995, if exports had remained stagnant, the

TABLE 5.1. Mexico's Total Trade, 1991–2000 (billions of current U.S. dollars and percentages)

	Imports		Exports		Total Trade	
Year	Value	Annual growth (percent)	Value	Annual growth (percent)	Value	Annual growth (percent)
1991	50.3	—	41.2	—	91.5	—
1992	64.0	27.2	46.2	12.1	110.2	20.4
1993	65.4	2.2	51.8	12.1	117.2	6.4
1994	79.3	21.2	60.8	17.4	140.1	19.5
1995	72.5	-8.6	79.5	30.8	152.0	8.5
1996	89.5	23.4	96.0	20.8	185.5	22.0
1997	109.8	22.7	110.0	14.6	219.8	18.5
1998	125.2	14.0	118.0	7.3	243.2	10.6
1999	141.9	13.3	136.4	15.6	278.4	14.5
2000	174.5	23.0	166.4	22.0	340.9	22.4

Sources: Data from the Banco de México and Secretaría de Comercio y Fomento Industrial.

decline could have been on the order of 11 percent.[3] Between 1994 and 1995, exports—mostly to the United States—grew by 30.8 percent, allowing Mexico to get back on the track to recovery (see table 5.1).

This recovery was much faster than the one following the 1982 devaluation, even though the 1995 recession was much deeper than that caused by the 1982 debt crisis. In 1982 Mexico's immediate response was a drastic cut in imports, combined with the imposition of heavy import quotas and prohibitive tariffs that erected a protective fortress around the domestic economy. Imports fell by more than 60 percent, from US$24 billion in 1981 to only US$9 billion in 1983. It took the country seven years to get back to pre-crisis import levels. In contrast, after the 1994 financial crisis Mexico's membership in the NAFTA guaranteed continuity in Mexican trade policy. Beyond these international commitments, however, the administration of President Ernesto Zedillo (1994–2000) was unwilling to reverse trade liberalization. Indeed, Mexico actually deepened liberalization, and it regained pre-crisis import levels in about eighteen months.[4] Something similar

---

[3] During the first six months of 1995, GDP actually fell more than 10 percent.

[4] Although macroeconomic stabilization has been the government's highest priority since the financial crisis hit, the increased openness of the Mexican economy (as measured by the ratio of trade to GDP) and the important structural reforms undertaken since the mid-1980s also facilitated recovery. Openness of the economy increased from 38 percent in 1993 to 62 percent in 1998. The government also reinforced structural reform, for example, through further liberalization of the foreign

occurred with production. After the 1982 debt crisis, it took Mexico almost nine years to recover pre-crisis industrial output; in contrast, less than two years after the deepest point of the 1995 recession, the country had recovered 1994 output levels (Heath 1998: 190).

As noted earlier, trade liberalization played a major role in this rapid recovery. Immediate pressures on financial markets eased; short-term nominal interest rates and inflation fell, and gross international reserves moved above their pre-crisis level. Mexico also improved its access to international capital markets.

Since 1997 Mexico has endured tremendous external shocks that have placed severe pressures on the economy. The international price of petroleum plummeted to its lowest level in decades—from an estimated US$18 per barrel in 1997 to an average of US$8.50 per barrel in the first quarter of 1999—and dramatically reduced Mexico's export earnings. In 1997 Mexico exported almost 2 million barrels of crude oil a day; in 1998 its export platform was a little over 1.7 million barrels per day, at an average price of US$10.50 a barrel. As a result, Mexican petroleum export revenues fell by US$4 billion (around 1 percent of GDP), lowering petroleum's share in total exports from 10 percent in 1997 to only 6.2 percent in 1998 and forcing three rounds of cuts in government spending during 1998.[5]

At the same time that Mexico was suffering the impact of declining petroleum revenues, the Asian financial crisis unleashed by the 1997 Thai devaluation put in question the viability of so-called emerging markets worldwide. The subsequent Russian financial crisis further undermined investor confidence in developing countries. Because Russia's defaulted loans were dragging down the portfolios of investors who also lent to Latin America, international capital markets seemed to be punishing emerging markets indiscriminately. When global inves-

---

investment regime, deepening of the already extensive privatization program, reforms in social security and the banking sector, and the creation of futures markets for foreign exchange (WTO 1997).

[5] Because Mexico's oil monopoly, Petróleos Mexicanos (PEMEX), is state owned, the public revenue loss prevented the government from playing a key role in stimulating economic growth. In a desperate move to raise revenue, Mexico's Ministry of Finance and Public Credit (SHCP) successfully lobbied Congress to approve a budget in December 1998 that raised import tariffs on products coming from countries that did not have free-trade agreements with Mexico, effectively raising Mexico's average import tariff for all non-free-trade partners from 13 to 16 percent. In 1995 Mexico had raised import tariffs to 35 percent on inexpensive Asian imports that competed with its own industries. This measure was not extended, however, to U.S. and Canadian products, nor to countries with which Mexico had free-trade agreements.

tors began to reduce their exposure in Latin American markets, many predicted that the Mexican peso would undergo another collapse. In fact, while almost every major economy in the world experienced a slowdown in 1998, Mexico's grew by 4.8 percent, the second-highest rate among the world's fifteen largest economies.[6]

Trade policy was one of Mexico's main growth engines throughout the 1990s, and in the late 1990s export activity accounted for half of Mexico's GDP growth and almost one-third of its overall GDP. In the year 2000 the country's GDP surpassed US$600 billion, and its total exports reached US$166.4 billion. Mexico has become the eighth-largest trading nation in the world and the first in Latin America, with total trade of US$340.9 billion in 2000, equivalent to over half of the country's GDP.[7] The bulk of these exports (88 percent in the year 2000) were manufactured products.

TRADE EFFECTS OF LIBERALIZATION

During the mid–1980s, Mexico liberalized trade without putting in place policies to help noncompetitive firms adjust to increased foreign competition. One resulting disadvantage for all but the largest national firms was (and still is) the lack of access to affordable credit. By reducing barriers to trade, the Mexican government told companies, in effect, that in order to become competitive they had to invest in technology, equipment, and training. However, most firms were left without access to the necessary resources to accomplish such modernization. In this case, the market alone was not enough.

Inefficient Mexican industries responded to trade opening in two ways. Thousands of small firms were unable to adapt and simply went out of business (Heath 1998: 196). Others stopped producing and became importers and distributors of consumer goods.[8]

---

[6] World GDP growth in 1998 was 2.4 percent, developed countries' economic growth averaged 2.1 percent, and developing countries' GDP growth was 3.0 percent. Mexico's growth outperformed every other country in Latin America (Federal Reserve Bank of Dallas 1999: 2).

[7] In 2000, Latin America's exports reached US$359 billion, and Mexico's exports accounted for 46 percent of that total (WTO 2001: table 1.5).

[8] A counterfactual analysis might suggest that, had the government's liberalization policy been more gradual and had it applied a prudent industrial policy, Mexican firms could have become as competitive as those of the East Asian "tigers." However, that argument assumes that Mexico's economic bureaucracy had the necessary experience and autonomy to guide its national firms, as well as the ability to withstand pressure from rent-seeking groups calling for privileges and protection.

As a result of business failures, unemployment increased and the informal sector expanded. Between 1988 and 1993, there was a continued drop in the number of manufacturing jobs. Heath (1998: 182) argues that although trade liberalization has been a factor in Mexico's slow rate of employment generation, other factors—such as capacity use, wages, and productivity—also explain the trend. Until 1995 most of the job losses in the manufacturing sector were absorbed by other sectors, especially services.

In addition to the microeconomic consequences for firms and workers, trade liberalization also forced the government to surrender a major source of income. While Mexico could tax imports at rates as high as 100 percent in the early 1980s, by the mid–1980s the maximum rate had declined to 20 percent. The consequences were mixed. On the one hand, lower tariffs translated into fewer resources for public investment and social spending; on the other, they reduced the government's ability to allocate funds for political purposes.

MEXICO'S NETWORK OF FREE-TRADE AGREEMENTS

During the 1990s, Mexico became an active player in international trade, seeking to open markets for its exports and to attract productive investment. Although Mexico had undertaken a unilateral trade liberalization during the 1980s to help recover macroeconomic stability, it needed agreements with its main trading partners in order to reap the full benefits of openness. Because its development strategy relied heavily upon exports, market access was essential.

At the multilateral level, Mexico participated in the Uruguay Round of the General Agreement on Tariffs and Trade (GATT), largely to counteract global protectionist trends. Later, World Trade Organization (WTO) membership gave Mexico a clear and transparent set of rules for its export activities, reducing the likelihood of unilateral trade restrictions and contributing to the durability, stability, and predictability of Mexico's liberalization reforms. Mexico's commitments under the GATT and WTO reduced its ability to use economic instruments, such as subsidies or production and export requirements, to promote industrialization.

Mexico's most important strategy, however, has been to negotiate bilateral trade agreements. During the 1990s, Mexican negotiators reached a series of free-trade agreements with the country's most important trading partners. Mexico also went about "aggressively dismantling its trade barriers" with other Latin American markets (Schrader 1999: A1) in an effort to become a global trade hub where producers can take advantage of preferential access to a large number of markets. Mexico's network of free-trade agreements gives a high degree of credibility and permanence to the domestic policy reforms undertaken since the mid–1980s, and it assures private investors that Mexico will not revert to economic isolation.

The North American Free Trade Agreement

In 1990 the Mexican government announced its intention to negotiate a free-trade agreement with the United States, a path-breaking decision that challenged all previous conceptions of Mexico–U.S. relations.[9] Mexico's decision to pursue such an accord resulted from a combination of international and domestic factors: the 1989 Canada–U.S. Free Trade Agreement, the scarcity of foreign capital outside North America, the emergence of regional economic blocs, and the limited potential of the multilateral trading system under the Uruguay Round[10] (Del Castillo and Vega Cánovas 1995; Lustig, Bosworth, and Lawrence 1992.)

Mexico pursued a free-trade agreement with the United States in order to secure long-term access to its most important market. In addition, Mexican officials anticipated that integrating with a rich country like the United States would yield benefits beyond trade efficiency, because it would stimulate foreign direct investment (FDI) and encourage technology transfers. Given Mexico's lack of domestic savings and its high level of foreign indebtedness, increased access to foreign capital became an indispensable resource for the country's productive activities (Poitras and Robinson 1994).

---

[9] The NAFTA was not the first attempt to promote economic integration between Mexico and the United States. Under the 1942 U.S. Reciprocal Trade Agreements Program, Mexico and the United States entered into a bilateral agreement that lasted until 1950. In 1980, Ronald Reagan proposed the creation of a North American common market during his campaign for the U.S. presidency. Given Mexico's historical suspicions about excessive U.S. influence in its domestic affairs, the project did not go forward; instead, a rather ineffective Joint Commission on Trade and Commerce was established in 1981. Later arrangements leading toward Mexico–U.S. economic integration included the 1985 Bilateral Understanding on Subsidies and Countervailing Duties, the 1987 Framework Agreement on Trade and Investment, and the 1989 Understanding Regarding Trade and Investment Facilitation Talks. Attracting U.S. capital and increasing access to the U.S. market were the bases for Mexico's involvement in international trade negotiations with the United States.

[10] The Uruguay Round, the eighth round of GATT negotiations, began in 1986 and ended in 1994. The Uruguay Round Agreements entered into effect on January 1, 1995.

The NAFTA was the first reciprocal free-trade treaty to join two industrialized countries with a developing country. It was based upon principles of equality and full reciprocity despite the fact that the Mexican economy is just one-twentieth the size of the U.S. economy. The agreement created the second-largest free-trade area in the world, with almost 400 million people and a third of world GDP (around US$8 trillion) in 1994. The NAFTA encourages foreign investment in its member countries (especially direct investment in plants and equipment) and promotes integration in North America through procedures to expedite dispute resolution. The NAFTA also includes supplemental cooperation agreements to enhance and encourage protection of the environment and to improve and enforce labor standards in the region (Mayer 1998).

Most economists and policy makers concur that the full effects of the formation of a free-trade area take time to manifest themselves. One important reason is that each member country must undertake structural adjustments, reducing capacity and employment in some sectors, increasing investment in other sectors, and developing a workforce with new skills. A second reason that the effects of trade liberalization emerge gradually is the deliberate inclusion in the agreement of phase-out periods for the full elimination of tariffs and the dismantling of nontariff barriers.[11]

NAFTA Update Since the NAFTA's implementation, trade and investment flows have surpassed the most optimistic predictions (Hufbauer and Schott 1993). Between 1993 and 2000, trade in the NAFTA region grew at an annual average rate of 12.5 percent, exceeding the average annual growth in trade worldwide. Over this same period, total trade among the NAFTA partners increased 128.2 percent, from US$288.9 billion to US$659.2 billion (table 5.2).

Under the NAFTA, U.S.–Mexico trade more than tripled between 1993 and 2000, rising from US$85.3 billion to US$263.5 billion. Mexico even displaced Japan as the United States' second-largest trading partner and export market. Indeed, of every dollar that Mexico spent abroad, 80 cents went for U.S. products, and Mexican products increased their share in the U.S. market from less than 7 percent in 1993 to more than 11 percent in 2000.

Mexico–Canada trade has increased under the NAFTA as well, despite the geographic distance and historical absence of economic inter-

---

[11] The NAFTA established a program for phasing out tariffs in four stages: some were eliminated upon implementation, and others are to be phased out at the five-, ten-, and fifteen-year marks.

action between these countries. Prior to the NAFTA, Canadian exports to Mexico faced a weighted average import tariff of 12.1 percent; by 2000 this tariff had dropped to approximately 2 percent. Moreover, the NAFTA increased awareness in both Mexico and Canada of new trade and investment opportunities in the other's market. In 2000, seven years after the implementation of the agreement, Canada–Mexico trade stood at US$12.1 billion, up from US$4.1 billion in 1993. Although this trade flow is small when compared to U.S.–Mexico trade, Canada–Mexico trade demonstrates a high degree of dynamism and potential for future growth.[12] Mexico has become Canada's main trading partner in Latin America and its fourth-most-important supplier of products worldwide. Likewise, Canada has become Mexico's fourth trading partner, after the United States, Japan, and the European Union.[13]

Sectoral Performance Under the NAFTA, foreign capital flows to Mexico have revitalized some older sectors and created new ones, helping establish state-of-the-art plants that are internationally competitive. Three industrial sectors—automobiles, electronics, and textiles, which represent core sectors from heavy, high-technology, and traditional industries—have become more dynamic and competitive since the NAFTA's implementation in 1994.

Sectors that have not received the same capital inflows have not enjoyed the same success. For example, Mexico's agricultural sector has shown mixed results under the NAFTA. A dynamic export-oriented agribusiness sector coexists with a traditional subsistence agriculture sector. The uneven performance of agriculture reveals the limits to what the NAFTA can deliver. The agreement is an instrument that creates opportunities for growth in certain economic sectors; it is not a tool that can transform the entire economy.

---

[12] Official statistics tend to underestimate the extent of Canadian trade under the NAFTA. For example, Canadian auto parts are typically incorporated into components produced in the United States that are then exported to Mexico and integrated into a final vehicle. Notwithstanding the Canadian component, the shipment is considered a U.S. product.

[13] Mexico's main exports to Canada are automobiles, auto parts, insulated wire, cable and insulated electrical conductors, automatic data-processing machines, televisions, and electrical apparatus for line telephony. Canada's main exports to Mexico are automobiles and auto parts, electrical apparatus for line telephony, textile fabrics, coal, sulfur, and machinery for working rubber or plastic. Canada's agricultural exports to Mexico include canola seeds, wheat, and milk and cream (SECOFI 1998a).

TABLE 5.2. Regional Trade under the NAFTA, 1993–2000 (billions of current U.S. dollars)

	1993	1994	1995	1996	1997	1998	1999	2000
U.S. imports from Canada	111.2	128.4	144.4	155.9	168.2	170.0	198.7	229.2
U.S. imports from Mexico	40.0	49.5	62.1	74.3	86.0	94.5	109.7	135.9
Canada's imports from the United States	88.3	100.5	109.8	115.4	132.5	135.2	144.9	154.4
Canada's imports from Mexico	2.9	3.3	3.9	4.4	5.0	5.1	6.4	8.1
Mexico's imports from the United States	45.3	54.8	53.8	67.5	82.0	93.5	105.2	127.6
Mexico's imports from Canada	1.2	1.6	1.4	1.7	2.0	2.2	2.9	4.0
Total	288.9	338.1	375.4	419.2	475.7	500.5	567.8	659.2

Sources: U.S. Department of Commerce, Statistics Canada, and Banco de México. Import data are the preferred source.

The Automotive Industry. The automotive industry plays a crucial role in the three NAFTA countries in terms of exports, employment generation, and technological and industrial development. Thus it is not surprising that the automotive sector was singled out as particularly sensitive during the treaty negotiations. For Mexico, the automotive sector is not only the largest exporter and importer of manufactured goods, but it is also a prime example of the kind of intra-industry trade the NAFTA was designed to boost. Free trade allows firms that sell throughout the entire North American market to relocate their production facilities to any NAFTA country and to take advantage of cost reductions as well as specialization and economies of scale.

Mexico's auto industry has taken full advantage of trade and investment policies established under the NAFTA.[14] It has gone through a restructuring process that enabled it to increase competitiveness and to integrate into the North American and the world automobile markets. By 2000, with total annual exports of almost 1.5 million vehicles and production approaching two million vehicles (up from 600,000 in 1993), Mexico had become the world's tenth-largest automobile exporter.[15]

Although the 1994–1995 peso crisis had a devastating effect on Mexican automobile production (with domestic sales falling 80 percent), the NAFTA made it possible for the industry to recover with remarkable speed. In the late 1990s, vehicle and auto parts production represented 2 percent of Mexico's GDP and more than 11 percent of Mexico's manufacturing GDP. The industry accounted for 20 percent of Mexico's total exports and 22 percent of total manufactured exports. In 2000, these exports reached US$33.9 billion, up from US$10.8 billion in 1993, an average annual growth rate of 30.5 percent.

The automotive industry is Mexico's main manufacturing-sector employer, providing jobs to around 12 percent of the country's manufacturing labor force. Over half a million Mexicans are involved in the production of auto parts and vehicles. In 2000, 260 *maquiladoras* (in-bond processing plants) produced automotive parts and components, employing close to 250,000 workers.

---

[14] The NAFTA's provisions will be fully implemented in 2003, when specific levels of local content and export requirements for automobile manufacturers in Mexico are eliminated. The provision in Mexico's 1989 automotive industry decree linking foreign vehicle imports to sales in the Mexican market will also be eliminated in 2003.

[15] In 2000, General Motors produced 444,000 vehicles in Mexico; DaimlerChrysler and Ford produced, respectively, 404,000 and 280,000 vehicles. In 2000, worldwide production of vehicles (cars, trucks, and buses) reached 58.4 million units; Organisation Internationale de Constructeurs D'Automobiles, Statistics Committee, Paris, May 2001.

Automotive products represent the largest component of NAFTA trade. U.S.–Mexico trade in vehicles and auto parts grew almost 223.6 percent between 1993 and 2000, from US$14.6 billion to $47.1 billion. Mexican vehicle sales to the United States account for almost 15 percent of all U.S. motor vehicle imports, which reached US$28.4 billion in 2000. Around 90 percent of Mexico's vehicle exports go to the U.S. market, followed by 6 percent to Canada and 2.5 percent to Germany. In addition, almost 25 percent of U.S. auto parts imports come from Mexico, which reflects an increasing level of integration and specialization of the North American auto industry.[16] Under the NAFTA, Mexico has become the second-largest export market (after Canada) for U.S. vehicles and auto parts. Although starting from a very low base, exports of U.S. vehicles to Mexico increased tenfold during the first seven years of the NAFTA. In 2000, U.S. car exports to Mexico totaled US$4.3 billion.

The NAFTA represented a major shift in Mexico's industrial policy toward vehicle production. Prior to 1994, Mexico's automobile industry enjoyed extensive protection. This protection began to be relaxed in the early 1990s, but the NAFTA ended the strict production and export restrictions on vehicle manufacturing that had undermined the industry's competitiveness and its capacity to adjust to changes in the industry worldwide.[17] Gradual deregulation and liberalization of the Mexican automobile industry under the NAFTA has promoted specialization in small and midsize cars, light trucks, and auto parts. In the late 1990s, Mexico produced nearly three million engines annually (exporting over two million of these), placing it seventh in engine manufacturing worldwide.

Consistent with the Mexican government's trade policy objectives, the NAFTA attracted significant new investment to Mexico's automotive sector, not only from firms already operating in Mexico but from newcomers as well.[18] This inflow of fresh capital allowed the Mexican

---

[16] Among the main auto parts that the United States buys from Mexico are wire harnesses, auto stereos, auto body parts, speedometers, engines, and air conditioning parts. For its part, Mexico buys from the United States engines, wheels, seat parts, and auto stereos. A similar integration has occurred between the Mexican and Canadian automotive sectors.

[17] For a detailed analysis of the automobile industry under the NAFTA by country and in North America as a whole, see Weintraub and Sands 1998.

[18] Seven major assemblers of passenger cars and light trucks (DaimlerChrysler, General Motors, Nissan, Ford, Volkswagen, Honda, and BMW) had operations in Mexico in the late 1990s. Eleven firms produced heavy trucks and buses (Daimler-Chrysler, Dina, Ford, General Motors, Kenworth, Masa, Navistar, Scania, Volvo,

automobile industry to restructure operations extensively and to reduce the gap in this two-tier industry between export-oriented facilities and plants producing for the domestic market. For example, between 1993 and 1995, the General Motors plant in Silao, Guanajuato, and the Chrysler plant in Saltillo, Coahuila, restructured production to engage in light truck manufacturing, and in 1998 Ford began a US$1 billion upgrade of its manufacturing plant in Chihuahua to build 400,000 engines annually on a new production line designed for small and midsize Ford vehicles (Lloyds 1998).

Volkswagen also invested heavily in upgrading its Puebla plant for production of its Jetta A4 model and the new Beetle, which is sold in Mexico and also exported to Canada, the United States, Germany, and Japan. The NAFTA's strict rules of origin encouraged non–U.S. manufacturers such as BMW, Mercedes-Benz, and Honda to establish new plants in the region, where they can build vehicles with North American auto parts.[19] For example, in 1999 DaimlerChrysler initiated a US$7 million expansion of its Mercedes-Benz plants in Monterrey and Santiago Tianguistengo, near Mexico City. Most of the new investment supported increased production of heavy trucks and buses. For its part, Honda also began vehicle assembly operations in Mexico, producing its midsize Accord model in its El Salto plant near Guadalajara.

As noted above, the NAFTA has encouraged greater rationalization and specialization of production, as well as improved competitiveness among vehicle and parts producers in North America. Several assembly plants in Mexico—such as the General Motors plants in Ramos Arizpe, Chihuahua, and Silao, Guanajuato—have been awarded international prizes for their competitiveness, product quality, and production processes. In fact, the plants that General Motors, Ford, and DaimlerChrysler operate in Mexico are among the most competitive in the world.

Since 1994, investments of about US$8 billion in the auto parts industry[20] have also helped Mexico become a highly efficient producer of

---

Omnibuses Integrales, Oshmex), and eight produced engines (DaimlerChrysler, General Motors, Ford, Volkswagen, Nissan, Renault, Perkins, and Cummins).

[19] The NAFTA gives preferential treatment only to automotive products that incorporate a specific level of North American content—for example, 56 percent for cars by 1998 (increasing to 62.5 percent in 2002) and 60 percent for most auto parts. Strict rules of origin for the automobile industry guarantee that only producers with substantial operations in North America enjoy preferential market access.

[20] The auto parts sector includes more than 800 firms. Of these, 600 are direct suppliers to vehicle producers, 220 are direct exporters, and 47 are "highly export-oriented companies."

transmission systems, glass, wheels, chassis, aluminum parts (including motor heads), alternators, engine parts, spark plugs, and axles. In 1998, Mexico's auto parts exports totaled US$6.5 billion, and the domestic market reached a value of over US$10 billion. The NAFTA's strict rules of origin have given Mexican auto parts producers an advantage in the North American market. The treaty has also promoted the creation of joint ventures and clusters among independent auto parts producers and vehicle assemblers that have enabled Mexican auto parts manufacturers to acquire the new technologies necessary to produce high-quality, competitive parts.[21]

The Apparel and Textile Industry. Under the NAFTA, the United States and Canada for the first time gave free market access to a developing country's textile and apparel industry (Hufbauer and Schott 1993: 45). Liberalization in textiles was particularly challenging. The protectionist Multi-Fiber Arrangement manages international trade in this sector through quota allocation, and the strong textile producers' lobby in the United States had succeeded in keeping the North American market highly protected.[22]

In 1995 the Mexican apparel and textile industry suffered from the collapse of the domestic market. However, like the automobile industry, the sector was able to export its way to recovery thanks to preferential market access provided under the NAFTA and other free-trade agreements. After a sharp 6 percent decline in Mexican textile production in 1995, the industry grew 15, 10, and 5 percent, respectively, in 1996, 1997, and 1998. New investments and reduced tariffs in export markets triggered the industry's growth and increased exports.

In 2000 Mexico's textile and apparel exports of US$11.0 billion accounted for 6.5 percent of Mexico's total exports. Mexico–U.S. trade in textiles increased from US$4.1 billion in 1993 to $15.3 billion in 2000, making Mexico, not China, the leading supplier of textile and apparel products to the United States.[23] Significantly, Mexico has also become the largest market for U.S. textile products. Indeed, approximately 75

---

[21] For example, one hundred Volkswagen suppliers invested half a billion dollars in Mexico to supply the firm more efficiently.

[22] The NAFTA disallows new quotas in the textile and apparel sector except under specific safeguard provisions. However, some products that do not meet the NAFTA rules of origin may still qualify for preferential treatment up to a "tariff preference level" or a specified import level negotiated among the agreement's three signatories.

[23] See www.economia-snci.gob.mx/PRESENTA/TEXTIL. Mexico's main textile exports to the United States are denim products, knit fabric, synthetic fabric, pants, T-shirts, sweaters, and underwear.

percent of Mexico's apparel production incorporates U.S. components (Kurt Salmon Associates 1999).

Upon implementation of the NAFTA, Mexico conferred duty-free access to approximately 20 percent of U.S. textile and apparel exports, and by 1999 almost all textile products enjoyed duty-free status. As in the case of the automotive sector, because preferential access depends upon textiles and apparel being made of yarn spun in North America or from textiles fabricated from North American fibers, the NAFTA's rules of origin have encouraged investment in new facilities throughout North America.

The NAFTA has stimulated substantial investments in the Mexican textile industry and increased its access to its main export market. The labor-intensive nature of certain stages in the textile production chain, combined with the advantages of geographic location and the market access guarantee, have encouraged regional and nonregional textile firms to establish plants in Mexico.[24] These factors have also stimulated suppliers and cutting and sewing firms to invest in Mexican operations.[25] As a result, foreign investment in the sector totaled US$1.7 billion between 1994 and 2000. Since the NAFTA's implementation, Chinese investment in Mexico's textile sector has increased steadily as Chinese businesses seek to gain easier access to the U.S. market. By the late 1990s, Chinese investors had channeled about US$43 million into Coahuila's textile industry, and they had entered into a joint venture — between Grupo Coppel (70 percent) and the Chinese Yang Tse River United Development Corporation (30 percent) — to produce cotton thread in Sinaloa. Another example of the sector's success is the Compañía Industrial de Parras in Coahuila, which has become the fourth-largest denim producer in the world. It exports more than 60 percent of its total output to the United States, Canada, Central and South America, and Europe.[26]

---

[24] The trends toward vertical integration, closer ties between supplier and customer, and low manufacturing costs have encouraged textile and apparel companies to relocate to Mexico (Kurt Salmon Associates 1999).

[25] U.S. textile and apparel companies such as Burlington, Cone Mills, Dan River, DuPont, Guilford Mills, and Tarrant have invested in Mexican operations. Guilford Mills and Cone have invested in a new "textile city" in Altamira, Tamaulipas, and the former firm has invested US$100 million in a knitting, dyeing, and finishing plant there (Smith and Malkin 1998: 52). Dan River has also established a joint venture with Grupo Industrial Zaga (Kurt Salmon Associates 1999: 3).

[26] The Compañía Industrial de Parras is the oldest Mexican company owned by a single family since its establishment (in 1899). Parras produced 16 million meters of cloth and fabric in 1990; its output in 2000 was 110 million meters. Employment increased from 2,100 to 3,579 workers over this same period (www.parras.com).

Thanks to Mexico's network of free-trade agreements, Mexican apparel exports to Latin America have almost doubled since 1994. These products have a considerable tariff advantage over U.S. and Canadian exports to Latin American markets. For example, Mexican hosiery exports enter Costa Rica, Bolivia, and Chile duty free, while Canadian and U.S. producers pay a 10 percent import duty. Mexican textile exports to Venezuela and Colombia enjoy reduced tariff rates of 12 and 10.5 percent, respectively, compared to the 20 percent tariff applied to Canadian and U.S. products.

Mexico's textile industry includes almost 1,200 maquiladora plants, which employ close to 286,000 workers.[27] Textile production is mainly concentrated in the central states of Hidalgo, Morelos, Puebla, the State of México, and Tlaxcala. However, states far removed from the U.S.-Mexico border, such as Yucatán, have also experienced a boom in textile production and exports. Wide geographic distribution of textile production has spread export activities to areas that traditionally had not participated in world markets.

The Electronics Industry. The electronics industry has become a leading export player in Mexico as a result of trade and investment liberalization, constituting almost one-third of Mexico's total trade in 2000. Under the NAFTA, Mexico has become the United States' main trading partner in electronics, surpassing such key markets as Japan, Canada, Taiwan, South Korea, and Singapore.[28] In 2000, Mexican exports of electronics products to the United States surpassed US$34.6 billion, while U.S. exports to Mexico amounted to US$33.7 billion. Electronics trade between Mexico and Canada during NAFTA's first seven years rose from US$210 million in 1993 to US$773 million in 2000. Tariff reductions have been a major factor in attaining these high trade levels. U.S. exports of electronics and computer products to Mexico faced an average import tariff of 13 percent in 1993, but by 2000 this tariff had dropped to 1.3 percent (it will reach zero in 2003). In 1993, Mexican computer and electronics exports to the United States faced an average import tariff of 1.6 percent; by 2000 this tariff was zero.

---

[27] Workers in textile maquiladoras account for 20 percent of total employment in Mexico's maquiladora sector.

[28] Mexico has become the United States' main supplier of televisions, electric motors, dielectric transformers, direct-current motors, cable and closed circuits, television converters, decoders, amplifiers, preamplifiers, and certain television tubes. For its part, Mexico has become the leading purchaser of U.S. electronic products: certain television tubes, printed circuits, electrical terminals, transformer parts, and parts of electronic integrated circuits and micro-assemblies (SECOFI 1999b).

Several factors have combined to pull foreign investment into this sector. An experienced workforce and existing industrial infrastructure have permitted Mexico to attract investment from throughout North America, and as a result of the NAFTA and Mexico's other trade agreements, Mexico has also received investment from Asian electronics producers seeking access to the North American and Latin American markets. Most of this investment has gone into the maquiladora sector. There are some 570 maquiladoras in the electrical and electronics sectors, representing almost 12 percent of the total number of maquiladoras operating in Mexico. In 2000 these firms employed approximately 350,000 workers, an increase of 80 percent over 1993 levels.

The NAFTA has encouraged production of more sophisticated electronic products that go beyond mere assembly, with significant research and development now conducted in Mexico (Carrillo and Hualde 1997). The 1970s stereotype of low-cost, labor-intensive assembly does not accurately characterize the new generation of electronics production (Lowe and Kenney 1999). In the 1980s, Mexico produced black-and-white televisions for the domestic market; today it produces color televisions, mostly for export (Jones 1997). Tijuana has become the world capital for television set production, with an annual output of around 25 million units. Companies like Sony and Samsung have made heavy investments in production facilities with state-of-the-art technology, and they are increasingly hiring Mexican engineers to develop and design new products for the North American and world markets.

To the south, meanwhile, far from the border, Guadalajara is becoming Mexico's "Silicon Valley." In 1995 a joint government–business partnership attracted investment from twenty-five foreign companies. The firms include IBM, which is now producing computer parts for export to its California operations. (Prior to the NAFTA, IBM shipped these components from Singapore, Taiwan, or Malaysia.) Similarly, Taiwan's Universal Scientific Industrial Co. has relocated operations to Guadalajara, where it produces computer motherboards (Smith and Malkin 1998: 53).

The Agricultural Sector. The NAFTA has had very different impacts on Mexico's two-tier agricultural sector, where booming agribusinesses coexist with a backward, traditional subsistence sector. While the former have increased exports as a result of improved access to the U.S. and Canadian markets, the latter has been unable to reap any benefit from the NAFTA.

Free trade in agriculture was one of the most sensitive and controversial issues in the NAFTA negotiations. For Mexico, the NAFTA represented a continuation of the opening of the country's agricultural sector that had begun in 1988. Reforms made to Article 27 of the Mexican Constitution in 1992 introduced substantive changes in the country's land tenure regime in an attempt to promote foreign and domestic private capital participation in agricultural production. However, the reforms also officially ended land distribution and changed the characteristics of the *ejido*, a form of tenure that since Mexico's postrevolutionary period had guaranteed peasants access to land on which they could make their own living.

Given the high political stakes involved in agricultural liberalization, Mexico argued that its farmers lagged far behind the productivity levels of Canadian or U.S. producers and that it would be years before the gap could be closed, even with increased investment. For these reasons, Mexico sought an exceptional fifteen-year transition period for very sensitive products like corn and beans. Similar political sensitivities in the other NAFTA countries prevented negotiators from reaching a trilateral agreement on agriculture. Mexico ultimately negotiated with the United States and Canada separately in order to overcome strong opposition to agricultural trade liberalization from these countries' producers, who had long benefited from substantial government subsidies.[29]

During the NAFTA's first seven years, U.S.–Mexico agricultural trade grew steadily, though it still accounted for less than 5 percent of all U.S.–Mexico trade. Mexican agricultural exports to the United States rose from US$3.1 billion in 1993 to $6.0 billion in 2000.[30] U.S. agricultural exports to Mexico, which measured $3.5 billion in 1993, reached US$6.5 billion in 2000. Despite predicted increases in domestic corn, sorghum, and wheat production, Mexico is not an efficient grain producer, and it is expected that Mexican imports of these basic products will remain high (Lloyds 1999). Notwithstanding some remaining restrictions on foreign investment in Mexico, U.S. agricultural producers have gained a foothold in Mexican agribusiness under the NAFTA.

---

[29] For political and economic reasons, agricultural production worldwide has been characterized by the presence of strong government subsidies and guarantees, as well as high levels of protection. The Uruguay Round of the GATT took the first steps toward liberalizing this sector. As a result, a built-in agenda for the further liberalization of agriculture was established within the new WTO. In the 1990s, the NAFTA was the only regional free-trade agreement to go one step beyond the GATT/WTO system in the liberalization of the agricultural sector.

[30] Most of Mexico's agricultural exports are fruits and vegetables grown in northern and western Mexico, where competitive growers enjoy access to credit. Traditional Mexican subsistence agriculture, in contrast, is heavily concentrated in central and southern Mexico. This dichotomy between *ejido*-type subsistence production and export-oriented agriculture prompted the Mexican government to introduce a variety of domestic support policies that sidestep the NAFTA in an effort to ensure the economic survival of the Mexican peasantry.

Mexico and the World: Trade Diversification

The promotion of Mexico–U.S. economic integration will continue to be Mexico's international economic policy priority. The size of the U.S. market, its proximity to Mexico, and U.S. leadership in technological innovation suggest that in the near future the United States will remain the main destination of Mexican exports and the main source of FDI in Mexico. At the same time, as a result of the NAFTA Mexican firms have developed an increasingly sophisticated knowledge of the U.S. market.

Nevertheless, it is imperative that Mexico not only have guaranteed market access in North America, but that it also diversify its export markets and foreign investment sources. A perennial goal of Mexican foreign economic policy in the post–World War II period, especially since the 1970s, has been opening new markets and diversifying the country's foreign trade. This goal has driven Mexico's membership in the Latin American Integration Association (ALADI), the GATT, and the WTO, as well as the establishment of a network of free-trade agreements in Latin America. This section analyzes Mexico's recent attempts to advance a free-trade agenda beyond North America.

Mexico and Latin America Although Latin America is a natural market for Mexico, Mexico's trade with other countries in the region has been low in absolute terms. To achieve a higher degree of integration, early in the 1990s Mexico proposed a new regional negotiation strategy. Seeking to overcome the limitations of previous trade agreements, Mexico promoted comprehensive free-trade agreements, as opposed to sector-by-sector accords. It pursued liberalization through the establishment of a maximum tariff among member countries and tariff phase-out schedules, as well as the total elimination of nontariff barriers for most products. Mexico was also committed to eliminating export subsidies, discriminatory and unequal tax charges, and obstacles to foreign trade in transportation. Clear rules of origin were required to prevent transshipment of goods, with transparency ensured by transitional safeguards. These agreements also incorporated rapid dispute settlement procedures. Because these agreements belonged to a new era of regionalism, they also incorporated the gradual liberalization of investment, trade in services, and intellectual property rights (Noyola 1991: 141–42).

By 2000, Mexico had negotiated free-trade agreements with nine Latin American countries: with Chile, Colombia, and Venezuela (the G-3), and with Bolivia, Costa Rica, Nicaragua, Guatemala, Honduras,

TABLE 5.3. Mexico's Trade with Selected Latin American Partners, 1991-
2000 (millions of current U.S. dollars)

Partner	Total Trade before Free-Trade Agreement	2000	Percent Change
Bolivia	32.5 (1994)	39.9	22.8
Chile	174.0 (1991)	1,325.1	661.6
Colombia	427.1 (1994)	735.2	72.1
Costa Rica	122.2 (1994)	466.3	381.6
Nicaragua	75.7 (1997)	120.3	58.9
Venezuela	471.2 (1994)	941.9	99.9

Source: Secretaría de Comercio y Fomento Industrial.

and El Salvador (these last three as a group).[31] These agreements liberalized trade in goods and services, granted protection to investors, incorporated protections of intellectual property rights, and established
dispute-settlement mechanisms. Mexico's trade with these countries
was at very low levels in the early 1990s, but it has risen notably since
then as a result of these agreements (see table 5.3).

Mexico negotiated a free-trade agreement with Chile in 1991. Although very limited in scope, it formed the basis for later agreements.
The agreement was subsequently revised in 1997 and implemented in
1998. As opposed to the 1991 version, the new agreement was comprehensive, covering investment, intellectual property rights, and services,
and deepening integration on technical issues such as rules of origin,
safeguards, market access, standardization measures, investment protection, and dispute settlement. Trade between Mexico and Chile increased by 661.6 percent between 1991 and 2000, reaching approximately US$1.3 billion in the latter year (see table 5.3). Mexico became
Chile's fourth-largest supplier; it ranked only sixteenth in 1992. Among
Mexico's main exports to Chile are automobiles and trucks, televisions,
and computers. Mexico imports copper products, grapes, peaches, and
fish meal from Chile (SECOFI 1998c).

Similarly, Mexico's trade with Costa Rica increased by 381.6 percent
between 1994 and 2000 (see table 5.3). Mexican trade with Bolivia rose
22.8 percent over this same period. Mexico–Colombia trade increased
by 72.1 percent between 1994 and 2000, and trade with Venezuela doubled over this period. Mexico's free-trade agreement with Nicaragua
went into effect in July 1998, and trade between the two countries rose
by 58.9 percent between 1997 and 2000.[32]

---

[31] In 2000 Mexico also negotiated an economic complementation agreement with
Uruguay that took effect in March 2001.

[32] Mexico's free-trade agreement with El Salvador, Guatemala, and Honduras took
effect in January 2001.

Mexican trade policy toward Latin America is pragmatic. More than any other country in the region, Mexico can offer preferential access to a number of markets in the hemisphere, making Mexico a highly attractive location for foreign direct investment. In fact, Mexico has become a hub that producers can use to obtain preferential access to several markets in the Western Hemisphere simultaneously.

Mexico also has strong political and security reasons—including concerns for political stability in Cuba, Haiti, and Central America—for advancing free-trade agreements with countries in the region. Equally important is the need to maintain Mexico's autonomy in commercial policy. The Mexican government's opposition to the Helms-Burton Law and the Torricelli Act—through which the U.S. government seeks to impose restrictions on foreign investors in Cuba and on the commercial activities of U.S. companies' foreign subsidiaries, respectively—indicates its commitment to maintaining independence in its foreign economic policy.

In the late 1990s, Mexico was also actively negotiating free-trade agreements with Ecuador, Panama, and Peru. For Mexico, this array of trade agreements with Latin American partners represents the beginning of a more ambitious hemispheric free-trade area in which it can play a pivotal role, attracting investors to Mexico as a strategic location for their corporate activities. In the negotiations for a Free Trade Area of the Americas, Mexico's network of free trade-agreements has helped it propose a comprehensive regional accord (see Pastor and Wise 1998: 24).

From NAFTA to MEFTA: Mexico–EU Trade Negotiations for a Mexico–European Union Free Trade Agreement (MEFTA) were concluded in November 1999.[33] The agreement was unique in several ways. It was the most inclusive free-trade accord ever negotiated by the European Union (EU) with any single nation, and it was also the EU's first such agreement with a Latin American country.

Mexico's negotiations with the EU were comprehensive, extending beyond the elimination of tariffs to include rules of origin, technical standards, sanitary and phytosanitary measures, safeguards, investment, services, government procurement policies, competition, intellectual property rights, and dispute-settlement mechanisms. The agreement provides for the elimination of tariffs by 2003 for Mexican products going to the EU market, and by 2007 for EU exports to Mexico.

---

[33] The Mexico–EU negotiations began in July 1998, lasting through nine rounds and sixteen months. The MEFTA went into effect on July 1, 2000, following ratification by the Mexican Senate and approval by the European Council of Ministers.

Mexico's heavy dependence upon the U.S. market and its intention to diversify sources of foreign direct investment provided an important impetus to its effort to establish a free-trade agreement with the European Union. The fall of the Soviet Union in 1989 made it difficult to generate European interest in any area distant from its own rapidly changing region, but by the late 1990s the EU was ready to enter into talks with Mexico. The NAFTA had demonstrated that Mexico had the technical capacity and political commitment to become closely integrated with a major industrial economic power, and it provided convincing evidence to European investors that Mexico was a stable and secure business partner.

The NAFTA also brought negative trade consequences for Europe, and these considerations prompted negotiation of the EU–Mexico accord as well. Although the European Union has remained Mexico's second-largest trading partner since the 1980s, its share of the Mexican market had been shrinking steadily, particularly after the mid-1990s. Between 1986 and 1992, Mexico's trade with Europe represented 13 percent of Mexico's average annual trade. By 1998, however, the EU share of Mexico's total trade had dropped to just 6 percent.[34] Given Mexico's large population, its tremendous potential for future market growth, and its strategic trade relationship with the key economies in the Western Hemisphere, the European Union wanted to guarantee a foothold for itself in the Mexican market.

Even though the United States will remain Mexico's most important trading partner and its largest export market, the MEFTA has long-term significance for the country's domestic and foreign economic policies. Mexican exporters who already sell to the United States now have a real opportunity to expand and diversify into another enormous and wealthy market.

Complementing its diversification strategy in Europe, Mexico in 2000 completed its negotiation of a free-trade agreement with members of the European Free Trade Area (EFTA): Iceland, Liechtenstein, Norway, and Switzerland. This was the tenth in Mexico's international network of free-trade agreements, linking it to countries with the highest per-capita income in the world. Mexico-EFTA trade totaled US$1.2 billion in 1999, with Mexican exports representing US$456 million. Effective July 2001, all Mexican industrial products exported to an EFTA country enjoy duty-free access. Mexico immediately eliminated tariffs on 60 percent of its EFTA imports; the remainder will be phased out by 2007.

---

[34] See table 5.4 for summary data on Mexico–EU trade between 1991 and 2000.

TABLE 5.4. Mexico-European Union Trade, 1991-2000 (billions of current U.S. dollars and percentages)

	Mexican Imports		Mexican Exports		Total Trade	
Year	Value	*Annual growth (percent)*	Value	*Annual growth (percent)*	Value	*Annual growth (percent)*
1991	6.2	—	3.4	—	9.7	—
1992	7.7	24.2	3.4	0	11.1	14.4
1993	7.8	1.3	2.8	-17.6	10.6	-4.5
1994	9.0	15.4	2.8	0	11.9	12.3
1995	6.7	-25.6	3.4	21.4	10.1	-15.1
1996	7.7	14.9	3.5	2.9	11.2	10.9
1997	9.9	28.6	4.0	14.3	13.9	24.1
1998	11.7	18.2	3.9	-2.5	15.6	12.2
1999	12.7	8.5	5.2	33.3	17.9	14.7
2000	14.7	15.7	5.6	7.7	20.4	14.0

Sources: Banco de México and Secretaría de Comercio y Fomento Industrial (www.secofi-snci.gob.mx/estadistica).

Further extending its free-trade network, in 2000 Mexico and Israel signed a free-trade agreement, Mexico's first with a Middle Eastern country. Mexico-Israel trade had been minimal, amounting to US$350 million in 2000.[35] However, like its free-trade negotiations with Japan and Singapore, the agreement with Israel forms part of Mexico's strategy of attracting foreign direct investment and strengthening its position as a world manufacturing hub.

Mexico's Network of Investment Agreements Attracting productive investment has been a cornerstone of Mexico's foreign economic policy since the reform process commenced in the mid–1980s. In pursuit of this objective, Mexico began negotiating bilateral investment agreements based on the investment chapter of the NAFTA. Their purpose is to promote and protect foreign investment while providing the same kinds of guarantees that the NAFTA gives to investors. As of 2001, Mexico had concluded bilateral investment agreements with Argentina, Greece, South Korea, Switzerland, and Uruguay, as well as with twelve of the fifteen members of the European Union (Austria, Belgium, Denmark, Finland, France, Germany, Italy, Luxembourg, the Netherlands, Portugal, Spain, Sweden). It also planned to negotiate such agreements with Israel, Japan, and the United Kingdom.

---

[35] Mexico's principal export to Israel was petroleum.

TABLE 5.5. Foreign Direct Investment (FDI) Flows to Mexico, 1994–2000 (billions of current U.S. dollars)

Year	Annual FDI Inflow	Cumulative FDI
1994	14.9	14.9
1995	9.5	24.4
1996	9.9	34.3
1997	13.9	48.2
1998	11.7	59.9
1999	12.1	72.0
2000	13.5	85.5

Source: Secretaría de Comercio y Fomento Industrial. Includes reinvested profits and internal company transfers.

Prior to the implementation of the NAFTA, Mexico attracted about US$4 billion of FDI annually. By 2000, that total had risen to US$13.5 billion, almost 60 percent of it coming from the United States and Canada (see table 5.5). Between 1994 and 2000, foreign direct investment totaled US$85.5 billion (compared to the US$23 billion of FDI that flowed into Mexico during the entire decade of the 1980s; Pastor and Wise 1998: 24). By the late 1990s, Mexico was the second-leading recipient of FDI among developing countries, after China.

TRADE'S CONTRIBUTIONS TO DEVELOPMENT

In the wake of the 1994–1995 peso crisis and ensuing economic debacle, many observers blamed trade liberalization for Mexico's difficulties. But trade policy is only one of the many instruments that governments can use to influence economic development. Trade policy is largely a matter of problem solving within a framework of domestic and international rules and of competing domestic and international political and economic pressures.

Ultimately, the solutions to these problems should improve national and international welfare. To achieve that end, trade policy can be used: (1) to promote access to foreign markets by reducing or eliminating barriers to exports imposed by foreign governments; (2) to increase the competitiveness of domestic producers by exposing them to the world economy and integrating them into global markets; and (3) to establish and preserve an effective international trade system based on clear and transparent rules and the principles of reciprocity and nondiscrimination. The first of these is a *business* objective—to maximize export opportunities for domestic producers already competing in the international market. The second is an *economic* objective, based on classical trade theory. The third is primarily a *political and bureaucratic* objective, grounded in the values and instruments of international law; its successful pursuit is the vehicle for achieving the other two objectives. By pursuing these three objectives, trade policy seeks directly to influence the scope and content of a country's foreign trade, and indirectly to influence a country's economic development.

Generally speaking, minor changes in the deployment of trade policy instruments will lead to minor changes in imports or exports or in industrial activity, while major changes may lead to more substantial transformations. From this perspective, Mexico's trade policy since the mid–1980s represents a radical change, and it has had strong impacts on the structure of trade and industrial activities. By the early 1990s, its achievements were impressive—a reduced rate of inflation, direct benefits to consumers through higher-quality, lower-cost products, and impressive adjustments by firms that had the resources or ingenuity to take advantage of new markets.

However, these successes led the Banco de México to relax monetary and credit policy in 1994 and to transfer an important part of the Mexican government's peso-denominated debt into dollar-denominated *tesobonos*. The combination of an excessively expansionary monetary policy and an enormous growth in external debt created the conditions for the currency crisis, lack of liquidity, and capital flight that ensued. The effects that the subsequent devaluation and restrictive monetary and fiscal policies had on the Mexican economy were dramatic; internal production declined drastically as a result of skyrocketing short-term interest rates, a spiraling inflation rate, and the collapse of the banking system.

Trade was the key factor in Mexico's macroeconomic recovery following the 1995 recession. Between August 1995 and August 1999, the Mexican economy generated two million new jobs, of which about half were related directly or indirectly to export activities.[36] Export activity also had a positive impact on wages. Workers in export-oriented firms are better paid than those working in non-export manufacturing activities. In 1999, for example, real wages in the maquiladora manufacturing

---

[36] After a decline of more than 4 percent in 1995, employment rose 4 percent in 1996, 8 percent in 1997, 7 percent in 1998, 7 percent in 1999, and 4.7 percent in 2000. According to data from Mexico's Institute of Statistics, Geography, and Informatics (INEGI) and analyses by the Federal Reserve Bank of Dallas of eleven unemployment measures, all of these indexes rose during the 1995 crisis and all fell again after the worst part of the shock had passed. Mexico's overall unemployment situation improved after 1995 (Federal Reserve Bank of Dallas 1999: 5). In January 1997, the country's open unemployment rate was 4.5 percent; by 2000, open unemployment had dropped to 2.2 percent (www.dgcnesyp.inegi.gob.mx/bdi.html-ssi).

sector rose by 3.0 percent, compared to only 1.8 percent in the non-maquiladora manufacturing sector.[37]

Maquiladora Plants

The debate regarding the contribution that maquiladora activities make to the Mexican economy has been dominated by ideology and stereotypes. Advocates of free trade view maquiladoras as generators of production, jobs, and technology, while opponents characterize them as low-wage assembly lines that add nothing to the domestic economy, fall short in terms of developing local management and technicians, and fail to incorporate local inputs. The reality, not surprisingly, lies somewhere in between. Moreover, that reality depends upon which part of the maquiladora sector one is examining.

According to Carrillo and Hualde (1997), the maquiladora sector is a dynamic and heterogeneous industry in which three types of production facilities coexist: traditional, labor-intensive assembly plants; plants oriented toward conventional manufacturing processes; and plants based on intensive knowledge competencies that emphasize production clusters. Most criticisms of maquiladoras derive from a stereotype based on the first generation of plants and fail to consider the sector's evolution. Maquiladoras were Mexico's second-most-important source of foreign currency earnings and of manufacturing employment during the 1990s.[38]

Maquiladora export activity has had a particularly significant impact on national development because it is geographically dispersed. In the past, Mexico's export operations were concentrated in major cities — Mexico City, Guadalajara, and Monterrey — and in the northern border region. By the late 1990s, even predominantly rural states like Aguascalientes, Campeche, Durango, and Yucatán participated in international trade. Between 1993 and 2000, the number of Mexican exporting firms increased by 78.5 percent, from 2,700 to 4,820. More than half of these new plants were located outside the Mexico–U.S. border region.[39]

The establishment of maquiladora plants has promoted the development of regional production centers. Much automotive-sector pro-

---

[37] www.economia-snci.gob.mx/PRESENTA/MAQUILA/sld010.htm.

[38] In 2000, maquiladoras employed more than 1.3 million Mexican workers, or more than 10 percent of the workers registered in the Mexican Social Security Institute (IMSS).

[39] The number of maquiladoras increased steadily after 1993, when there were 2,405 maquiladoras in Mexico. The total rose to 2,602 in 1994; 2,939 in 1995; 3,402 in 1996; 3,839 in 1997; 4,235 in 1998; 4,636 in 1999; and 4,820 in 2000 (SECOFI 1998d and www.economia-snci.gob.mx/PRESENTA/MAQUILA/sld010.htm).

duction has concentrated in the Saltillo–Monterrey area, and Tijuana–Mexicali has become the world leader in television manufacturing. In the late 1990s, Campeche had twenty maquiladoras producing textiles, food products, and watersports equipment, while Yucatán had over a hundred maquiladoras employing 26,000 people in textile production and food processing. The state of Aguascalientes was home to automotive producers like Nissan, and Jalisco hosted Hewlett-Packard, IBM, Lucent Technologies, and Xerox. Guadalajara had become a production center for electrical and electronics parts and components. The states of Puebla and Tlaxcala, along with the Laguna region (centered on the cities of Torreón, Coahuila, and Gómez Palacio, Durango), had become preferred locations for textile and apparel producers.

As state-level governmental authorities become more aware of the potential benefits that export activities can bring, they are working to attract these industries to their areas. For example, Guanajuato, a major producer of apparel and footwear, has opened trade offices in Chicago, Dallas, Los Angeles, New York, London, and Tokyo. Between 1995 and 1998, the state's number of exporting firms rose from 362 to 768 (Fox 1999). More than fifteen other Mexican states have trade offices abroad, mostly in the United States.[40] Trade has clearly offered subnational authorities new opportunities for bringing more national and foreign resources into their regions, and it has become an instrument for promoting each state's development agenda.

CHALLENGES

Mexico faces enormous economic and social difficulties that must be addressed in the near future. The country still has a dual economy that excludes the majority of the population from high-value-added productive activities. Integrating more small and midsize firms — the primary generators of employment — into the export sector presents a significant challenge, one that will not automatically be met by opening markets. Lack of access to credit continues to prevent small businesses from expanding and modernizing their plants.[41] In addition, firms undertaking modernization efforts often require technical help across a wide variety of activities, including inventory management, establish-

---

[40] For example, Campeche, Tabasco, and Yucatán have opened trade offices in Florida, and Jalisco has established close trade links with Idaho, Oregon, and Washington.

[41] In 1994, Mexico's import-export bank, BANCOMEXT, approved loans for more than US$15 billion; in 1995 these fell to $8 billion, in 1996 to $6 billion, and in 1997 to $5 billion, before recovering in 1998 to $6 billion and an estimated $7.5 billion in 1999 (*Wall Street Journal*, April 21, 1999). BANCOMEXT's loan program for 2000 was US$4.2 billion (BANCOMEXT annual report 2000).

ment of distribution channels, product development, quality control, packaging, and marketing. Such supports are not yet widely available to any but large firms.

In any case, long-term economic development will only be achieved by recovering robust, sustained economic growth. Given an anticipated annual growth of 2.3 percent in Mexico's labor force over the next several years, the country must grow at an inflation-adjusted rate of 6 to 7 percent in order to prevent further unemployment. This growth will have to be financed by increased exports and a higher rate of domestic savings if Mexico is to avoid an overdependence on foreign capital. Clearly this is no easy undertaking. For Mexico to achieve this rate of economic growth, exports would have to increase by 30 percent annually.

Assuring secure and open markets for Mexican exports will be a crucial factor in this effort, and Mexico will have to seize opportunities where it finds them. The challenge is to maintain and solidify Mexico's presence in the Canadian and U.S. markets, while simultaneously making every effort to increase exports to Latin America, Europe, the Pacific Rim, and elsewhere. Thus free trade has become a necessary condition (though not the only one) for Mexico's economic development.

REFERENCES

Carrillo, Jorge, and Alfredo Hualde. 1997. "Third Generation In-Bond Assembly Plants: The Case of Delphi-General Motors," *Comercio Exterior* 47 (9): 747–58.

Del Castillo, Gustavo, and Gustavo Vega Cánovas. 1995. *The Politics of Free Trade in North America.* Ottawa: Centre for Trade Policy and Law.

Federal Reserve Bank of Dallas. 1999. "The Mexican Economy." Federal Reserve Bank of Dallas, El Paso Branch.

Fox, Vicente. 1999. "Guanajuato: globalización y oportunidades." March 5.

GATT (General Agreement on Tariffs and Trade). 1994. *Trade Policy Review: Mexico.* Geneva: GATT.

Heath, Jonathan. 1998. "The Impact of Mexico's Trade Liberalization: Jobs, Productivity, and Structural Change." In *The Post–NAFTA Political Economy: Mexico and the Western Hemisphere,* edited by Carol Wise. University Park: Pennsylvania State University Press.

Hufbauer, Gary Clyde, and Jeffrey Schott. 1993. *NAFTA: An Assessment.* Washington, D.C.: Institute for International Economics.

Jones, Jeff. 1997. "Are Exports Unlimited?" *Business Mexico* 7 (6): 12–15.

Kehoe, Tim. 1995. "A Review of Mexico's Trade Policy from 1982 to 1994." In *The World Economy: Global Trade Policy 1995,* edited by Sven Arndt and Chris Milner. London: Blackwell.

Kessler, Tim. 1998. "Political Capital: Mexican Finance Reform under Salinas," *World Politics* 51 (1): 36–66.

Kurt Salmon Associates (New York). 1999. "Textile Transactions and Trends: Perspectives on Mergers and Acquisitions in the Textile Industry." Summer.

Lloyds. 1998. *Lloyds Mexican Economic Report*, January. At mexconnect.com/ MEX lloyds.

———. 1999. *Lloyds Mexican Economic Report*, May. At mexconnect.com/MEX-lloyds.

Lowe, Nichola, and Martin Kenney. 1999. "Foreign Investment and Global Geography of Production: Why the Mexican Consumer Electronics Industry Failed," *World Development* 27 (8): 1427–43.

Lustig, Nora, Barry P. Bosworth, and Robert Z. Lawrence, eds. 1992. *North American Free Trade: Assessing the Impact*. Washington, D.C.: The Brookings Institution.

Mayer, Frederick W. 1998. *Interpreting NAFTA: The Science and Art of Political Analysis*. New York: Columbia University Press.

Naím, Moisés, and Sebastian Edwards. 1997. *Mexico 1994: Anatomy of an Emerging-Market Crash*. Washington, D.C.: Carnegie Endowment for International Peace.

Noyola, Pedro. 1991. "El surgimiento de espacios económicos multinacionales y las relaciones de México con Europa, la Cuenca del Pacífico y América Latina y el Caribe." In *Hacia un tratado de libre comercio en América del Norte*, edited by Secretaría de Comercio y Fomento Industrial (SECOFI). Mexico City: Miguel Ángel Porrúa.

Pastor, Manuel, Jr., and Carol Wise. 1998. "Mexican-Style Neoliberalism." In *The Post–NAFTA Political Economy: Mexico and the Western Hemisphere*, edited by Carol Wise. University Park: Pennsylvania State University Press.

Poitras, Guy, and Raymond Robinson. 1994. "The Politics of NAFTA in Mexico," *Journal of Interamerican Studies and World Affairs* 36 (1): 1–35.

Schrader, Esther. 1999. "Mexico Learns Lesson Well in Pursuit of Trade Accords: Exports Pacts Similar to NAFTA May Hinder Clinton's Push to Form 34-Nation Free Trade Area of the Americas," *Los Angeles Times*, September 14.

SECOFI (Secretaría de Comercio y Fomento Industrial). 1998a. *NAFTA Works for Mexico–Canada Trade, 1993–1998*. Ottawa: SECOFI-Canada.

———. 1998b. "Latest NAFTA Tariff Reductions Benefit Textiles," *NAFTA Works* 3 (12): 3.

———. 1998c. "Mexico Exports and Increasingly Participates in International Trade," Spring. At www.naftaworks.org.

———. 1998d. "Maquiladoras Contribute to U.S.–Mexico Border Development," *NAFTA Works* 3 (3): 1–2.

———. 1999a. "Mexico's Auto Industry: A Remarkable Performance," *NAFTA Works* 4 (1): 1–2.

———. 1999b. *NAFTA Works for Textiles*. Sectoral Fact Sheet. At www.naftaworks.org.

————. 1999c. *NAFTA Works for Electronics.* Sectoral Fact Sheet. At www.-naftaworks.org.

Smith, Geri, and Elizabeth Malkin. 1998. "Remaking Mexico," *Business Week,* December 21, pp. 51–54.

Story, Dale. 1986. *Industry, the State, and Public Policy in Mexico.* Austin: University of Texas Press.

Torres, Blanca, and Pamela S. Falk, eds. 1989. *La adhesión de México al GATT: repercusiones internas e impacto sobre las relaciones México–Estados Unidos.* Mexico City: El Colegio de México.

U.S. General Accounting Office (GAO). 1997. *NAFTA Three-Year Report.* Washington, D.C.: GAO.

Weintraub, Sidney, and Christopher Sands, eds. 1998. *The North American Auto Industry under NAFTA.* Washington, D.C.: Center for Strategic and International Studies.

WTO (World Trade Organization). 1997. *Trade Policy Review, Mexico.* Geneva: WTO.

————. 2001. *International Trade Statistics.* Geneva: WTO.

6

Mexico's Industrial Development: Climbing Ahead or Falling Behind in the World Economy?

Gary Gereffi

Globalization has become the buzzword to characterize the international economy at the beginning of the twenty-first century. Although numerous authors have debated the precise meanings of globalization (Dicken 1998), its main dimensions (McMichael 1996; Jaffee 1998), and indeed whether global flows of goods, foreign direct investment, finance capital, and people (migrants) actually are greater today than in earlier periods (Wade 1996), no one disputes the centrality of globalization to contemporary development theory. There is, however, a sharp divide between two sets of theorists: those who see globalization as a *constraint* on the development prospects of non-core nations, and those who see the linkages implied by globalization as posing not only constraints but also *opportunities* for the advancement of developing countries.

This distinction parallels a controversy between the modernization and dependency perspectives that was in vogue some twenty-five years ago in development theory. Modernization theorists argued that the closer the ties between "modern" and "traditional" societies, the faster traditional societies would progress. In the 1950s and 1960s, when modernization theory was the leading development paradigm, the basic assumption was that the institutions and values of the United States, at least in their idealized forms, represented an appropriate model that other, less fortunate societies should emulate. In stark contrast, dependency theorists argued that the stronger the links between "core" and "peripheral" countries, the more retarded or distorted the development of the periphery. For orthodox Marxists like André Gunder Frank, the development of the core capitalist economies requires the "underdevelopment" of the periphery. For more moderate proponents of "dependent development" like Fernando Henrique Cardoso and Peter B. Evans, capitalist linkages can actually promote development in the periphery, but these ties to foreign capital and overseas markets compromise national autonomy in dependent societies, and they often lead to a truncated or distorted form of development.[1]

Although the fault lines in the debates about globalization and dependency may not have changed much in the past quarter-century, the same cannot be said of the international economy itself. There are two fundamental transformations in the global context that profoundly shape our contemporary perspectives on development theory. First, there has been a widespread shift in national development strategies from import-substituting industrialization (ISI) to export-oriented industrialization (EOI) throughout the developing world (Gereffi and Wyman 1990). Buttressed by the policy prescriptions of powerful international economic organizations like the World Bank and the International Monetary Fund, as well as the U.S. government, this preference for EOI rested heavily on the experiences of the East Asian "miracle economies" from the 1960s to the mid–1990s. During this period, Japan and a handful of other high-performing Asian economies (most notably, the "four little tigers" of Hong Kong, Singapore, South Korea, and Taiwan) attained booming exports and lofty per capita growth rates against the backdrop of relatively low income inequality, high educational attainment, and record levels of domestic saving and investment (World Bank 1993). East Asia has easily outdistanced other parts of the developing world on a wide range of economic and social development indicators, and these achievements are largely attributed to the adoption of export-oriented industrialization as the region's main development strategy. Export-oriented industrialization is the new development orthodoxy in much of the world, despite the financial crisis that wracked Asia in 1997.

Second, there has been a major transformation in how the international economy is organized. In the period when ISI development strategies prevailed, transnational corporations were the dominant economic actors. They were vertically integrated and had a global reach through the operations of wholly owned subsidiaries that extracted natural resources for export or engaged in local production for sale in domestic markets around the world (Barnet and Müller 1974). Now, however, the exchange between "core" and "peripheral" areas has become much more complex. The explosive growth of imports in industrialized countries suggests that the center of gravity for the production and export of many manufactures has moved to an ever-expanding

---

[1] See Gereffi 1983: chap. 1 for a detailed review of these theoretical controversies.

array of newly industrializing economies (NIEs) (Arrighi and Drangel 1986). As the East Asian and Latin American NIEs have moved toward more technology-intensive and skill-intensive exports, it has become clear that "cheap labor" alone is no longer an adequate explanation for industrialization in developing countries (Fröbel, Heinrichs, and Kreye 1981).

The globalization thesis sees a qualitative shift in the functional integration of internationally dispersed activities and a concomitant weakening of national institutions (Dicken 1998). This vision highlights a kaleidoscopic fragmentation of many production processes and their geographic relocation on a global scale in ways that slice through national boundaries. Core corporations are shifting from high-volume to high-value production. Instead of a pyramid, where power is concentrated in the headquarters of transnational firms and there is a vertical chain of command, global production networks today look more like a spider's web of independent yet interconnected enterprises. Core firms act as strategic brokers at the web's center, controlling critical information, skills, and resources needed for the overall global network to function efficiently (Reich 1991). In order for countries and firms to succeed in today's international economy, they need to position themselves strategically within these global networks and develop strategies for gaining access to the lead firms in order to improve their position.

Assessing Mexico's industrial development in this context requires us to use a different set of theoretical tools than might have been appropriate in the past. The approach taken in this chapter includes, first, a review of the basic changes in Mexico's development model during the past three decades, with an emphasis on how the change from ISI to a greater reliance on exports alters the way in which we need to study industrialization. This is followed by the author's proposal of a new theoretical framework, particularly applicable to the current era, that utilizes two key constructs: global commodity chains and industrial upgrading. A focus on global commodity chains assesses international industries in terms of where power is located in the inter-firm networks of buyers and sellers that make up the social structure of an industry. The concept of industrial upgrading helps us to understand more precisely how countries and firms try to improve their positions in these industries. The succeeding section offers the automobile and apparel industries as case studies in which to explore Mexico's industrial development since the 1970s. These are very telling cases because they are Mexico's two leading sectors in terms of both exports and employment. In addition, they represent two distinct kinds of commodity chains (producer-driven and buyer-driven, respectively), and they offer very different lessons about the role of the state, foreign capital, and local firms in Mexico's development.

MEXICAN INDUSTRIAL DEVELOPMENT: AN OVERVIEW

By any standards, Mexico is a highly industrialized country. It has a longer record of sustained economic progress than any of its East Asian or Latin American counterparts among the NIEs. From the mid-1930s until the late 1970s, while experiencing uninterrupted political stability under the dominant Institutional Revolutionary Party (PRI), the Mexican economy grew at an average annual rate in excess of 6 percent, and manufacturing output rose at about 8 percent per annum. Mexico's real gross domestic product (GDP) increased most rapidly from the mid-1950s until 1970 (averaging about 9 percent a year), a period of considerable prosperity and price stability known as "stabilizing development" (Gereffi and Wyman 1990: chap. 1). Mexico and Brazil were the first NIEs to move from "horizontal" ISI (1930–1955), a development phase that focused on the domestic production of consumer nondurable goods (such as textiles and apparel) and the local assembly of consumer durables (such as automobiles), to the subsequent phase of "vertical" ISI (1955–1970). In vertical ISI, the emphasis was on internalizing within the domestic economy all phases in the manufacture of consumer goods and integrating backwards in the direction of intermediate products and capital goods (Gereffi and Evans 1981).

The import-substitution model in Mexico was, however, plagued by recurrent trade deficits in the early 1970s and by an excessive reliance on petroleum exports to finance balance-of-payments shortfalls. In the early 1980s, Mexico became mired in a spiraling debt crisis that brought economic growth and Mexico's nascent "export promotion" initiatives to a grinding halt. Indeed, the debt crisis hit all of Latin America very hard. The high external debt burden required the allocation of 25 to 30 percent of the region's foreign exchange proceeds merely to cover interest payments, which led many to refer to the 1980s as Latin America's "lost development decade" (Urquidi 1991).

It was in this context that Mexico decided to reverse its longstanding allegiance to ISI and to push all-out economic liberalization and export expansion during the administrations of Miguel de la Madrid Hurtado (1982–1988) and Carlos Salinas de Gortari (1988–1994). There were two related trends here. De la Madrid began a process of economic liberalization that was heralded by Mexico's accession to the General Agreement on Tariffs and Trade (GATT) in 1986, and that included subsequent efforts to privatize state-owned companies and relax restrictions on foreign direct investment in Mexico. Salinas de Gortari accelerated these reforms and added regional integration as a new emphasis, culminating in Mexico's entry into the North American Free Trade Agreement (NAFTA) with the United States and Canada in 1994.

The impact of these changes on exports and foreign investment has been dramatic. Between 1990 and 1999, Mexico's exports more than quadrupled, from US$29.2 billion to US$143.5 billion (see table 6.1). Manufactured goods made up close to 90 percent of Mexico's sales abroad in 1998, compared to 77 percent in 1993. Petroleum exports declined from 22 percent to just 7 percent of exports during the same five-year period (*Business Week* 1998). The more internationalized Mexican economy received 19 percent of the US$65 billion that flowed into Latin America in 1997, making it the second most important (after Brazil) focus of foreign investment in the region (ECLAC 1998: 17–18).

Within Latin America, Mexico has surpassed all other nations in building its manufacturing export capacity. Between 1995 and 1999, foreign investment poured into Mexico at more than US$10 billion a year to create new export-driven factories (ECLAC 2001: 37). Productivity has risen steadily, and total-quality management systems are becoming the norm. Indeed, the number of exporting firms rose from 22,000 in 1994 to 34,000 in 1998, and employment in Mexico's thriving *maquiladora* industry (which primarily assembles imported U.S. inputs for re-export to the United States) passed the one million mark (Smith 1999). In 1997, the maquiladora industry accounted for over 40 percent of Mexico's total exports, and nearly 85 percent of those goods were shipped to the United States (ECLAC 1998: 74).

Given these features of Mexico's recent development trajectory, what criteria should we use to assess the country's performance in the past three decades? Rather than focusing on policies intended to promote industrialization, it may be preferable to stay closer to the ground, looking at what industrial firms located in Mexico actually do and addressing the question, "What is made where, by whom, and for whom?" *What* refers to types of products, including both industry classification and whether they are finished goods or intermediate inputs; *where* refers to the location of production, including countries as well as regions within a country; *by whom* refers to the kinds of companies that lead Mexico's industrialization efforts, including transnational firms, local private companies, and state enterprises; and *for whom* refers to whether production is for the domestic market or export.

This chapter focuses on Mexico's exports, rather than production for the domestic market. This is a stringent indicator of "industrial development" because it deals only with those products in which Mexico has demonstrated an international competitive edge. It is appropriate to use this standard because of Mexico's emphasis on export promotion as an essential ingredient in its current development strategy.

NAFTA and the Maquiladora Sector

The North American Free Trade Agreement has dominated discussion of the Mexican economy in recent years. It certainly alters the incentives regarding what will be made in Mexico because it removes tariff barriers for Mexican exports to the United States. Moreover, it changes the rules of origin for foreign investors seeking access to the U.S. market from a North American production base.

Nonetheless, it is important not to exaggerate the NAFTA's impact. Many of the trends toward regional economic integration involving Mexico and the United States were under way long before the NAFTA was signed. In addition, the NAFTA by itself does not guarantee that Mexican firms will become successful exporters. East Asia achieved its export success in large part without special access to the U.S. market; indeed, U.S. and European quotas and other trade barriers have actually made it more difficult for East Asian exporters to sustain their process of trade-led industrialization. One of the major advantages of the firm-level focus adopted in this chapter is that we can see how companies devise strategies to deal with recurrent obstacles to their trade and development objectives. The macroeconomic and industrial policies adopted by national governments play a major role in shaping international trade and production networks, but equally important are the ways in which firms respond to these policy changes by devising new strategies and arrangements to pursue their own interests.

One important feature of Mexico's economic landscape that will disappear with the NAFTA is the maquiladora program, which was officially terminated on January 1, 2001. Even here, however, a broader perspective is needed to see that the maquiladora sector has been changing in substantial ways during the past two decades. Although the onset of the NAFTA has removed the legislative rationale for the maquiladora industry, broader structural changes during the past ten to fifteen years have rendered obsolete many of the popular stereotypes concerning it. A recent study of Mexico's export manufacturing industry (MacLachlan and Aguilar 1998) challenges at least five of these outmoded generalizations:

- *Myth #1:* Maquiladoras are found almost exclusively along Mexico's northern border.

    Fact: Once true, this is no longer the case. Since the mid–1980s, maquiladoras have been expanding rapidly in other parts of Mexico, and in 1996 these non-border plants accounted for one-third of national maquiladora employment.

- *Myth #2:* The maquiladora labor force is dominated by young women.

  Fact: The proportion of female workers in maquiladora plants has plunged, and the gender structure of maquiladora employment is approaching parity.

- *Myth #3:* Labor compensation in maquiladoras is extremely low and exploitative.

  Fact: Although maquiladora wages are abysmal in relation to U.S. standards, they compare quite favorably to industrial wages in Mexico. Furthermore, there appears to be little difference between working conditions in maquiladora plants and domestic manufacturing facilities in Mexico.

- *Myth #4:* Maquiladoras are primarily foreign-owned plants.

  Fact: The origin of capital invested in maquiladoras is almost evenly divided between the United States and Mexico.

- *Myth #5:* Maquiladoras are export enclaves, totally dependent upon imported components.

  Fact: Although maquiladoras still import an average of 98 percent of their material inputs, those maquiladoras located in Mexico's interior regions show a greater propensity to use domestic inputs than those along the Mexico–U.S. border, and there has been a sharp growth in inter-maquila trade in certain sectors (such as the electronics and automobile industries). These trends, along with the loosening of trade restrictions implied by the NAFTA, suggest a greater integration of maquiladoras into the Mexican economy.

Given these transformations in the maquiladora sector, we need to look more closely at how the export-oriented automobile and apparel plants in Mexico, Canada, and the Caribbean Basin are shaping the competitive performance of these economies vis-à-vis the United States. But first we need to have a clearer sense of how the automobile and apparel industries are organized at the international level.

GLOBAL COMMODITY CHAINS

In global capitalism, economic activity is both international in scope and global in organization. "Internationalization" refers to the geographic spread of economic activities across national boundaries. As such, it is certainly not a new phenomenon. Indeed, it has been a prominent feature of the world economy since at least the seventeenth century, when colonial powers began to carve up the globe in search of raw materials and new markets for their manufactured exports. "Globalization" is much more recent than internationalization because it implies functional integration between internationally dispersed activities (Dicken 1998: 5).

Industrial and commercial capital have promoted globalization by establishing two distinct types of international economic networks. These can be called, respectively, "producer-driven" and "buyer-driven" global commodity chains (Gereffi 1999). A commodity chain refers to the whole range of activities involved in the design, production, and marketing of a product.[2] Producer-driven commodity chains are those in which large, usually transnational, manufacturers play the central roles in coordinating production networks (including their backward and forward linkages). This is characteristic of capital- and technology-intensive industries such as automobiles, aircraft, computers, semiconductors, and heavy machinery. The automobile industry offers a classic illustration of a producer-driven chain, with multilayered production systems that involve thousands of firms (including parents, subsidiaries, and subcontractors).

Buyer-driven commodity chains are characteristic of those industries in which large retailers, marketers, and brand-name manufacturers play the pivotal roles in setting up decentralized production networks in a variety of exporting countries, typically located in developing areas. This pattern of trade-led industrialization has become common in labor-intensive consumer goods industries such as garments, footwear, toys, housewares, consumer electronics, and a variety of handicrafts. Production is generally carried out by tiered networks of developing-country contractors that make finished goods for foreign buyers. The specifications are supplied by the large retailers or marketers that order the goods.

One of the main traits of the firms that fit the buyer-driven model (including retailers such as Wal-Mart, Sears Roebuck, and J.C. Penney; athletic footwear companies such as Nike and Reebok; and fashion-oriented apparel companies such as Liz Claiborne and The Limited) is that they design and/or market—but do not make—the brand-name products they order. They are, then, part of a new breed of "manufacturers without factories" that separate the physical production of goods from the design and marketing stages of the production process. Profits in buyer-driven chains derive not from scale, volume, and technological advances as in producer-driven chains, but rather from unique com-

---

[2] See Gereffi and Korzeniewicz 1994 for an overview of this framework.

binations of high-value research, design, sales, marketing, and financial services which allow retailers, designers, and marketers to act as strategic brokers in linking overseas factories and traders with evolving product niches in their main consumer markets.

There is an affinity between commodity chains and development strategies. The ISI development strategy, which prevailed in Latin America for nearly five decades until the 1970s, was based on producer-driven commodity chains. Transnational corporations—which have actively tapped Latin America's mineral and agricultural resources since the nineteenth century—were invited to establish more advanced manufacturing industries in the region, beginning with automobile assembly plants in large countries like Mexico, Brazil, and Argentina in the 1920s. By the 1950s and 1960s, ISI factories were spread throughout the region in diverse industries such as petrochemicals, pharmaceuticals, automobiles, electrical and non-electrical machinery, and computers. Output was mainly destined for the domestic market, although beginning in the 1970s more attention was given to manufactured exports in order to offset the costly import bills associated with ISI "deepening" (Gereffi and Wyman 1990). In contrast, buyer-driven commodity chains have been virtually ignored in Latin America because the transnational firms that established ISI were primarily interested in Latin America's domestic markets, not exports. This pattern allowed local exporters in East Asian NIEs to gain the lion's share of U.S. and European markets for the profitable consumer goods that are only supplied via buyer-driven chains.

Both buyer-driven and producer-driven commodity chains are useful in analyzing and evaluating global industries. As with traditional supply-chain perspectives, the commodity chains framework is based on the flow of goods involved in the production and distribution of products. However, the global commodity chains approach has at least four distinctive elements:

- it incorporates an explicit *international* dimension into the analysis;
- it focuses on the *power* exercised by the lead firms in different segments of the commodity chain, and it illustrates how power shifts over time;
- it views the *coordination* of the entire chain as a key source of competitive advantage that requires using networks as a strategic asset; and
- it looks at *organizational learning* as one of the critical mechanisms by which firms try to improve or consolidate their positions within the chain.

One of the major hypotheses of the global commodity chains approach is that development requires linking up with the most significant "lead firms" in an industry. Indeed, one of the keys to a nation's industrial upgrading is access to the resources and networks controlled by the lead firms in global industries. These lead firms are not necessarily the traditional vertically integrated manufacturers, nor do they even need to be involved in making finished products. They can be located upstream or downstream from manufacturing (such as the fashion designers or private-label retailers in the apparel industry), or they can be involved in the supply of critical components (such as microprocessor companies like Intel and software firms like Microsoft in the computer industry). What distinguishes lead firms from their followers or subordinates is that they control access to major resources (such as product design, new technologies, brand names, or consumer demand) that generate the most profitable returns in the industry.

DIMENSIONS OF INDUSTRIAL UPGRADING

The concept of industrial upgrading encompasses several related levels of analysis: intersectoral shifts, intrasectoral shifts, economic roles, and product characteristics (Gereffi and Tam 1998). At the most general level, industrial upgrading may be viewed as *intersectoral* shifts from primary products to manufactured goods and services (the so-called secondary and tertiary sectors), and within manufacturing, from low-value, labor-intensive industries to capital- and technology-intensive ones (such as from clothes to cars to computers). A second type of industrial upgrading involves an *intrasectoral* progression, typically from the manufacture of finished items to the production of higher-value goods and services involving forward and backward linkages along the supply chain. At the level of *economic roles*, there are various types of activity that involve increasingly sophisticated production, marketing, and design tasks. One typology includes: assembly, original equipment manufacturing (OEM), original brand-name manufacturing (OBM), and original design manufacturing (ODM). Finally, at a *product* level, one can talk about the movement from simple to more complex goods of the same type (as from cotton shirts to men's suits). Although firms typically are the agents of industrial upgrading activities, the spatial context in which this activity occurs includes local, national, and regional economies, and government policies at each of these levels can facilitate (or impede) the upgrading process.

Industrial Upgrading as Intersectoral Shifts: From Primary Products to Manufactures

One of the most basic indicators of industrial development is the shift from primary products to manufactured goods. Table 6.1 illustrates this transition for Mexico. In 1980, Mexico's top ten exports to the world were dominated by primary products: food (vegetables and fruit, coffee, and seafood), raw materials (textile fibers and metalliferous ores), and fuels (petroleum and natural gas). By 1999, Mexico's export profile was dramatically transformed. Only two of its top ten export items were primary products (petroleum, and fruits and vegetables), and eight were manufactured goods. Six of the manufactured items were in the relatively advanced machinery and transport equipment sector, and another was apparel.

Table 6.1 also shows that Mexico has become a much more diversified exporter in the past two decades. In 1980, Mexico's leading export (petroleum) accounted for 61.6 percent of total export revenues, while in 1999 its top export item (motor vehicles) represented only 17.2 percent of the total. Similarly, the top ten exports in 1980 were 87.3 percent of total exports, while in 1999 this proportion had fallen to 76.2 percent.

If we compare Mexico with its North American neighbor Canada, we see that Mexico arguably underwent a more significant degree of industrial upgrading between 1985 and 1999, as measured by both countries' exports to the United States (see table 6.2). Canada's exports to the United States are far larger than Mexico's (US$213.7 billion and $122.5 billion, respectively, in 1999), although the gap has shrunk very rapidly since 1990, when Canada's export total to the United States (US$100.8 billion) was five times larger than Mexico's (US$20.4 billion). Canada's top exports remained very stable during the 1990s, while Mexico showed considerable diversity and upgrading in its export profile. Motor vehicles, petroleum, and paper were Canada's top three export items in 1985, 1990, and 1999, and four other products (gas, cork and wood, non-ferrous metals, and power-generating machinery) were in the top ten all three years. By contrast, Mexico made more significant strides in moving from primary products to manufactured goods.

A fuller understanding of the causes and consequences of intersectoral upgrading shifts would require us to look at government policies toward each of these sectors in Mexico, the United States, and Canada; international market conditions; and the kinds of firms that are doing the exporting. However, at a minimum we should recognize that

TABLE 6.1. Mexico's Top Ten Exports to the World, 1980–1999 (millions of current U.S. dollars and percentage of total exports)

	1980				1990				1999		
Rank	SITC[1]	Product	Value	Per-cent	SITC	Product	Value	Per-cent	SITC	Product	Value	Per-cent
1	33	Petroleum	10,114	61.6	33	Petroleum	10,285	35.2	78	Road vehicles	24,637	17.2
2	34	Gas, natural and manufactured	690	4.2	78	Road vehicles	3,444	11.8	77	Electrical machinery and appliances	22,895	16.0
3	05	Vegetables and fruit	685	4.2	71	Power-generating machinery	1,696	5.8	33	Telecommunications and sound-recording apparatus	15,104	10.5
4	68	Nonferrous metals	566	3.5	05	Vegetables and fruit	1,651	5.7	76	Petroleum	10,111	7.0
5	07	Coffee, tea, cocoa, spices	541	3.3	68	Nonferrous metals	918	3.1	75	Office machines and automatic data-processing equipment	10,078	7.0

	SITC				SITC				SITC			
6	03	Fish, crustaceans, mollusks	479	2.9	67	Iron and steel	828	2.8	84	Apparel	8,188	5.7
7	78	Road vehicles	362	2.2	77	Electrical machinery and appliances	659	2.3	71	Power-generating machinery	6,057	4.2
8	26	Textile fibers	347	2.1	51	Organic chemicals	593	2.0	89	Miscellaneous manufactures	4,667	3.2
9	52	Inorganic chemicals	280	1.7	75	Office machines and automatic data-processing equipment	572	2.0	74	General industrial machinery and parts	4,231	2.9
10	28	Metalliferrous ores	260	1.6	89	Miscellaneous manufactures	515	1.8	05	Vegetables and fruit	3,392	2.4
Top ten products			14,324	87.3			21,161	72.5			109,360	76.2
Total exports			16,408				29,180				143,502	

Source: World Trade Analyzer, based on United Nations trade data.

[1] SITC refers to Standard International Trade Classification categories.

TABLE 6.2. Industrial Upgrading Scorecard: Category Distribution of Canada's and Mexico's Top Ten Exports to the United States, 1985–1999

SITC Category[1]	Canada			Mexico		
	1985	1990	1999	1985	1990	1999
0 - Food	0	0	0	3	1	1
1 - Beverages	0	0	0	0	0	0
2 - Crude materials	2	2	1	0	0	0
3 - Fuels, lubricants, and related materials	2	2	2	1	1	1
4 - Animal and vegetable oils, fats, and waxes	0	0	0	0	0	0
5 - Chemicals and related products	0	0	0	0	0	0
6 - Manufactured goods	3	2	2	1	3	0
7 - Machinery and transport equipment	3	3	4	4	4	6
8 - Miscellaneous manufactured articles	0	0	0	1	1	2
9 - Commodities not classified elsewhere	0	1	1	0	0	0
Total value (billions of current U.S. dollars)	74.2	100.8	213.7	16.6	20.4	122.5

Source: World Trade Analyzer, based on United Nations trade data.

Note: Table 6.1 contains more detailed information concerning Mexico's top ten export products.

[1] SITC refers to Standard International Trade Classification categories.

Mexico's export sector has been both dynamic and diversified, especially since 1990.

Industrial Upgrading as Intrasectoral Shifts: Forward and Backward Linkages

Sustaining the upgrading process within a particular sector or industry involves both forward and backward linkages from production and the kind of learning that occurs across these segments. In the apparel industry, for example, one upgrading option is to move forward along the supply chain from production to marketing. Prominent U.S. apparel companies like Levi Strauss and Sara Lee have chosen to lessen their commitment to manufacturing in order to put more resources into building global brands, which are the most profitable part of the soft-goods value chain (Black 1998). Textile manufacturers like Burlington Industries, beginning one step further back in the chain, are integrating forward into apparel supply precisely to enhance their manufacturing capabilities and enlarge their potential customer base (Bonner 1997).

Intrasectoral industrial upgrading can also be seen from a country perspective. The progressive removal of U.S. tariff restrictions under the NAFTA has encouraged U.S. textile and apparel companies to locate more and more stages of apparel manufacturing (such as textile production, cutting, and washing of finished garments) within Mexico. Conversely, the Caribbean Basin economies that were not granted "NAFTA parity" by the U.S. government have been severely hindered in their upgrading efforts.

In the automobile industry, many of the most significant intrasectoral upgrading shifts have also occurred as a result of government policies. In Mexico, the automobile industry has been regulated by a series of governmental decrees (issued in 1962, 1972, 1977, 1983, and 1989). The two main goals of these decrees were to make Mexico an automobile producer rather than a mere assembler, and to lower the automobile industry's perennial trade deficit (Truett and Truett 1994). A variety of specific industrial policy objectives were incorporated into Mexico's automobile decrees in order to push transnational automakers to contribute more to the local development of the industry. These included: (1) increasing the local content of finished vehicles; (2) ensuring that engines and drive trains would be made in Mexico; (3) regulating the proliferation of models; and (4) reducing the industry's trade deficit by imposing export requirements intended to balance an automobile firm's imports with an equal or greater amount of exports. Although some of these policies could not be implemented, and others have since been rescinded, the state's role in the automobile industry was critical in establishing a relatively sophisticated auto parts sector in Mexico.

Industrial Upgrading as Economic Role Shifts: From Assembly to OEM to OBM/ODM

In the specific historical context of the global apparel industry, one of the clearest qualitative indicators of industrial upgrading is the role shift involved in moving from assembly (using imported inputs) to more integrated forms of manufacturing and marketing associated with the OEM and OBM export roles (Gereffi 1999). Participation in assembly networks (often associated with export-processing zones) is considered the first step in the upgrading process because it teaches apparel exporters about the price, quality, and delivery standards used in global markets. Thus entry into the apparel commodity chain via the assembly role requires learning how to work with organizational buyers (including manufacturers, trading companies, and brokers) that supply the exporting firm with fabric and other inputs needed to assemble garments.

The most typical upgrading move following assembly is full-package production (also known as OEM). Why is full-package production so important to the success of a country in a global commodity chain? Compared with the mere assembly of imported inputs, full-package production fundamentally changes the relationship between buyer and supplier in a direction that gives the supplier far more autonomy and learning potential. Full-package production is necessary because the retailers and marketers that order the garments do not know how to make them. Thus suppliers must learn how to do everything, and they frequently do so in a relatively long-term relationship with buyers. Moreover, if the buyer is a marketer, the supplier can closely observe its client's behavior in response to changing market conditions. The more stable and open the relationship between the buyer and the supplier, the more favorable is the environment for observing and learning from the buyer.

The East Asian NIEs (Hong Kong, Singapore, South Korea, and Taiwan) have used the OEM role to create an enduring edge in export-oriented development. However, East Asian producers confront intense competition from lower-cost exporters in various developing countries, and the price of their exports to industrialized nations was further elevated by sharp currency appreciations during the 1990s. Under these circumstances, it is advantageous to establish forward linkages to developed-country markets, where the biggest profits are made in buyer-driven commodity chains. Therefore, a number of firms in the

East Asian NIEs that pioneered OEM are now pushing beyond it to the OBM role by integrating their manufacturing expertise with the design and sale of their own brand-name merchandise (Gereffi 1995).

In the case of the automobile industry, the typical upgrading trajectory is different. The lead firms have traditionally been the transnational automakers that engage in final assembly of complete vehicles. This is a very capital intensive process, and typically it is carried out in or close to the major markets where the vehicles will be sold. The way auto parts companies have tried to improve their position in the automobile commodity chain is by advancing within the tiered hierarchy of suppliers. An elite corps of large "Tier 1" suppliers is now vying for the role of "systems integrator" in the automobile supply chain. This represents one type of industrial upgrading via the creation of a new role. Another shift would be to move from being an OEM supplier for a particular automaker to developing one's own global brand. This would allow a company to become a global supplier that could deal with multiple assemblers simultaneously and on an equal footing (such as Denso electronic systems, Lear seats, and Johnson Controls).

Industrial Upgrading as Product Shifts: From Simple to Complex Products

The ability to move from simple to complex products is often a by-product of industrial experience, as well as the result of shifting from less demanding to more demanding customers. However, government policies can play a role here, too. A classic example is the European and U.S. quota system, which is a limit placed on the quantity (rather than the value) of goods shipped. This arrangement, chosen in part because it was easier for importing countries to enforce, had an unforeseen effect. In the words of Kenneth Fang, one of Hong Kong's leading apparel exporters, "[Quotas] encouraged the Hong Kong manufacturers to move from textiles to clothing and then from simple to fancy clothing, in order to generate more income and employment per square yard" (Lardner 1988: 46). This process of quota-induced industrial upgrading was repeated throughout East Asia. U.S. voluntary export restraints and other non-tariff barriers had a similar effect on cars. Japanese automakers, faced with a limit on the maximum number of vehicles they could ship to the United States, moved quickly and surely from low-value to high-value vehicles, beginning with compacts, then shifting to midsize and luxury cars, and now exporting minivans and light trucks. Thus government policies and corporate strategies are often closely intertwined.

THE AUTOMOTIVE SECTOR IN MEXICO

Producer-driven commodity chains like those in the automobile industry offer numerous insights into how the Latin American NIEs are
making the transition from import-substituting to export-oriented development strategies. Under ISI, the state's strongest bargaining chip
with transnational firms was access to the domestic market. The Latin
American NIEs were quite successful from the 1950s through the 1970s
in using this bargaining leverage to move from the assembly stage of
automobile production to manufacturing stages involving higher levels
of local content, joint ventures with foreign partners, and sectoral export initiatives. After 1980, this old pattern was replaced by a new internationalization, one involving a strong commitment to exports, substantial amounts of vertically integrated local manufacturing, and a
growing number of alliances between transnational automobile companies and domestic firms. Government decision makers' emphasis
under EOI shifted from industrial policy to macroeconomic policy, and
from favoring domestic linkages to facilitating international ones. In
many ways, the new internationalization built on the foundations laid
by ISI strategies, given that many domestic industries were developed
through local-content requirements.

Since the early 1980s, the automobile industry has been marked by
intensifying competition and increased globalization, processes that
have resulted in both lower costs and improved product quality. With
the advent of "lean" production by the principal Japanese automakers
(led initially by Toyota), "just-in-time" systems emphasized close as-
sembler-supplier relations and flexible forms of production in which
quality control (or total quality management) was viewed as an essential element at all stages of the production process (Womack, Jones, and
Roos 1990; Dicken 1998: chaps. 5 and 10). U.S. and foreign motor vehicle assemblers now employ supply chains to diffuse lean production
methods and high-performance work organization practices into the
broader automotive industry.

Supply-chain management is central to the efforts of U.S. automakers to restructure, rationalize, and integrate the automotive supplier
industry across Canada, the United States, and Mexico. In particular,
the "Big Three" — DaimlerChrysler Corporation, Ford Motor Company,
and General Motors Corporation — initiated three key changes during
the 1990s that have redefined their relationship with suppliers (Kumar
and Holmes 1997). First, automakers have shifted more of the responsibility for product design and inventory control to their suppliers. This
has allowed the assemblers to focus their resources on their "core capa-

bilities," which include overall system design, drive trains, final assembly, and the marketing of the completed vehicle. Second, those portions of the vehicle that are sourced from suppliers have grown in size and complexity, from individual parts and components to entire subassemblies (such as acceleration, braking, steering, handling, and seating systems) or even larger modules (such as integral automobile interiors that include carpets, headliners, and dashboards). The outsourcing of complete systems and modules offers important cost savings to the assembler through reductions in the size of the plant and workforce needed to assemble vehicles. Third, automotive assemblers are reducing the number of direct suppliers and offering them longer contracts, which lowers the overhead costs of managing and coordinating the entire system.

The automotive supply chain has always been organized hierarchically into tiers, but in recent years the tiered structure has become much more pronounced. There has been a drop in the number of suppliers at all levels of the supply chain, with each assembler relying on a core group of highly competent Tier 1 suppliers. To meet the automakers' ever-increasing demands for cost reductions, enhanced productivity, and quicker delivery times, automotive parts suppliers have continued to consolidate. This has resulted in the emergence of a relatively small number of "systems integrators" among the ranks of Tier 1 suppliers. These firms are capable of designing, manufacturing, and delivering complete modules to motor vehicle assembly plants (Kumar and Holmes 1997). Sophisticated parts firms like Delphi, Bosch, Denso, Johnson Controls, Lear, Federal-Mogul, and Dana are consolidating across subsystems, which is leading to a significant degree of vertical integration in what had been a relatively fragmented industry. Systems integrators are beginning to assume prime responsibility for selecting lower-tier suppliers and for coordinating key segments of the automotive supply chain at a global level. Thus these top Tier 1 suppliers are challenging the assemblers for control over the key high-value activities in automotive production. Because many of the leading auto suppliers make parts in Mexico, this is another avenue for Mexico to improve its position in the industry.

Automotive exports from Mexico rose dramatically during the 1980s and 1990s. Virtually all of these exports were controlled by transnational companies; indeed, while foreign firms accounted for two-thirds of Mexico's total manufactured exports in the early 1990s, they supplied 99 percent of automotive exports. Transnational firms' exports of vehicles, engines, and auto parts were supplemented by exports from maquiladora plants, which rocketed from US$100 million in 1982 to US$5.8 billion in 1992 (ECLAC 1995a: 4–8).[3]

Mexico's economic hardships of the 1980s and 1990s paved the way for an important policy initiative, the "popular car" regime (ECLAC 1995a, 1995b). This policy—driven by the government's goal of making cheap, fuel-efficient, "no-frills" automobiles widely available for domestic consumption—consisted of providing tax deductions and tariff breaks for small cars (less than 1,000cc engines) that could be sold cheaply (in the late 1990s, around US$7,500). Mexico introduced this policy in 1989, and by 1990 popular cars accounted for 25 percent of all automobile sales.[4] The boom in popular cars represented a striking contrast with the past, when automobile producers focused on luxury models with higher profit margins for a restricted market. As they turned to more austere vehicles, the assemblers reintroduced a mass-production logic of scale economies for the domestic market. This is quite the opposite of the lean-production logic and high levels of specialization being pursued by transnational automobile firms in export markets.

By the late 1990s, the automobile industry had become Mexico's single most important manufacturing business. More than 500,000 workers were employed making parts and assembling vehicles for eight of the world's biggest automakers, including the U.S. Big Three, Nissan, Honda, Volkswagen, BMW, and Mercedes-Benz. In large part because of the post-devaluation collapse of Mexico's internal market in the face of recession and high interest rates, 90.6 percent of the vehicles produced by the Big Three in Mexico in 1995 were for export, compared with 74.5 percent in 1994 (see table 6.3). The NAFTA's rules of origin, which require high North American–made content in cars, have forced European and Asian parts suppliers to follow their automakers to Mexico. Some seventy parts suppliers cluster around Volkswagen's sprawling factory in Puebla, which churns out 600 "new Beetles" and 900 other Volkswagen cars per day (*Business Week* 1998). Induced by the

---

[3] In the case of Brazil, the half-dozen vehicle assembly companies that exist in the market are subsidiaries of transnational corporations from the United States, Germany, Italy, and Sweden. Although three-quarters of the 750 firms in Brazil's auto parts industry are of national origin, the largest and most dynamic of the auto parts firms are foreign-owned (ECLAC 1995c, 1995d).

[4] In Brazil, popular cars had an even more dramatic impact on the market. The program was officially established in April 1993, and by September 1994 these compact models accounted for over 50 percent of all domestic car sales. Each transnational assembler in Brazil has its own popular car model, with Fiat shifting 75 percent of its production in Brazil to compact cars.

NAFTA, many other U.S., Asian, and European auto parts firms have also set up manufacturing operations in Mexico.

North American passenger car production in the 1990s showed considerable variation by country. U.S. and Canadian car production remained relatively steady or declined from 1994 onward. Mexico suffered a major drop in car production—from 839,939 units in 1994 to 698,028 units in 1995—as a result of the peso devaluation and subsequent collapse of the domestic market, but it recovered to 956,354 units in 1998 and 1,130,488 units in 2000 (see table 6.3). The U.S. Big Three account for three-fourths of car production in Canada and two-thirds of U.S. output, but they represent just over one-third of the automobile industry in Mexico (36.7 percent in 2000), where Volkswagen and Nissan have a particularly strong presence.

The performance of each of the eight automobile assemblers located in Mexico is highlighted in table 6.3. In 1995, when the peso devaluation hit the hardest, 85.4 percent of Mexico's total production of 698,028 cars were exported and 14.6 percent were sold in the domestic market. Three years later, the share of Mexico's car output that was destined for the domestic market more than doubled to 37.2 percent. In 2000, Volkswagen (340,054 cars) and Ford (178,877 cars) led all of the automakers in Mexico in terms of export volume. General Motors and Nissan were relatively more committed to the Mexican market.

The NAFTA should play a major role in promoting the industrial upgrading of the Mexican motor vehicle industry. From 1994 to 1999, Mexico's motor vehicle exports to the United States tripled (from US$7.3 billion to US$21.2 billion), while Canada's U.S. exports rose by only 46.5 percent. The most dynamic sector for Mexico was light trucks (SITC 782), which grew by 495.0 percent from the 1994 level, while auto parts exports increased by 114.4 percent (see table 6.4). If we focus on the most sophisticated subassembly being made in Mexico, internal combustion piston engines, Mexico increased its exports to the United States by 158 percent between 1994 and 1998, while Canada's percentage increase in engine exports was a comparatively modest 76 percent (U.S. Department of Commerce, official statistics).

Focusing only on exports, it seems clear that Mexico has improved its position in the North American automobile commodity chain. It has attracted all the major assemblers to Mexico, and despite the economic recession of the mid–1990s, vehicle exports have returned to pre-devaluation levels. In addition, the prospects for further growth are good because three new assemblers (Honda, Mercedes-Benz, and BMW) entered Mexico in the 1990s. The logic of industrial upgrading would dictate that two routes for continued development seem particularly promising. One option is to use the most dynamic manufac-

TABLE 6.3. Mexico's Car Production, Domestic Market and Exports, 1994–2000 (units produced and percentages)[1]

	1994	Percent	1995	Percent	1996	Percent	1998	Percent	2000	Percent
Ford	176,004		205,337		168,545		163,767		191,588	
Mexico car[2]	26,804	15.2	9,317	4.5	13,889	8.2	16,767	10.2	12,711	6.6
Export car	149,200	84.8	196,020	95.5	154,656	91.8	147,000	89.8	178,877	93.4
General Motors	112,345		139,791		143,455		167,214		185,216	
Mexico car	41,962	37.4	15,088	10.8	42,261	29.5	94,862	56.7	102,398	55.3
Export car	70,383	62.6	124,703	89.2	101,194	70.5	72,352	43.3	82,818	44.7
Chrysler[3]	164,668		80,131		144,362		132,724		38,111	
Mexico car	46,816	28.4	15,624	19.5	19,566	13.6	43,424	32.7	7,022	18.4
Export car	117,852	71.6	64,507	80.5	124,796	86.4	89,300	67.3	31,089	81.6
Volkswagen	243,389		190,206		231,078		338,959		425,703	
Mexico car	144,517	59.4	33,784	17.8	53,105	23.0	91,360	27.0	85,649	20.1
Export car	98,872	40.6	156,422	82.2	177,973	77.0	247,599	73.0	340,054	79.9
Nissan	143,533		82,563		107,516		143,829		269,475	
Mexico car	92,286	64.3	27,863	33.7	32,104	29.9	99,384	69.1	122,112	45.3
Export car	51,247	35.7	54,700	66.3	75,412	70.1	44,445	30.9	147,363	54.7

Honda	0		0		1,194		7,194		18,801	
Mexico car					1,194	100.0	7,194	100.0	11,524	61.3
Export car									7,277	38.7
Mercedes-Benz	0		0		1,043		722		0	
Mexico car					1,043	100.0	722	100.0		
BMW	0		0		487		1,945		1,594	
Mexico car					487	100.0	1,945	100.0	1,594	100.0
Total	839,939		698,028		797,680		956,354		1,130,488	
Mexico car	352,385	41.9	101,676	14.6	163,649	20.5	355,658	37.2	343,010	30.3
Export car	487,554	58.0	596,352	85.4	634,031	79.5	600,696	62.8	787,478	69.7

Source: Ward's Communications, *Ward's Motor Vehicle Facts and Figures*, various issues.

[1] Percentages may not add to 100.0 because of rounding.

[2] "Mexico car" indicates units produced for sale in Mexico.

[3] In 1998, Chrysler merged with Daimler-Benz. The company subsequently reduced production in Mexico in response to slumping consumer demand.

TABLE 6.4. U.S. Imports of Motor Vehicles and Parts from Canada and Mexico, 1980–1999 (millions of current U.S. dollars)

Canada	1980	1985	1990	1994	1999	Percent change, 1994–1999
SITC 78–Motor vehicles[1]	8,942	24,910	28,098	40,610	59,476	46.5
781–Passenger motor cars	3,958	12,907	14,775	24,224	35,892	48.2
782–Motor vehicles for transport of goods and materials	2,287	4,829	6,894	8,501	12,224	43.8
784–Parts and accessories of motor vehicles	2,563	7,046	5,987	7,155	10,055	40.5
Other (783, 785, 786)	135	127	442	730	1,305	78.8

Mexico	1980	1985	1990	1994	1999	Percent change, 1994–1999
SITC 78–Motor vehicles	192	426	3,169	7,271	21,156	191.0
781–Passenger motor cars	1	110	2,696	4,140	10,537	154.5
782–Motor vehicles for transport of goods and materials	5	29	55	945	5,623	495.0
784–Parts and accessories of motor vehicles	183	280	393	2,003	4,294	114.4
Other (783, 785, 786)	4	7	25	183	702	283.6

Source: World Trade Analyzer, based on United Nations trade data.
[1] SITC refers to Standard International Trade Classification categories.

turers (Volkswagen and Ford) as a basis for developing more integrated supplier networks in Mexico because they can tap export demand in the U.S. market. A second option would be for Mexico to encourage top Tier 1 suppliers to set up advanced manufacturing and research and development facilities in the country.[5] The importance of this approach lies in the fact that these systems integrators are becoming the new drivers of change in the global automobile industry. Although there are no Mexican systems integrators as yet, a growing number of second-tier suppliers are Mexican firms.

THE APPAREL SECTOR IN MEXICO

The apparel industry best captures the development dilemmas that beset Mexico's regional integration efforts in the 1990s. It is an industry that is simultaneously very traditional (many of its antiquated sewing factories are a throwback to sweatshops at the onset of the Industrial Revolution) and ultramodern (the global sourcing networks managed by today's large apparel companies connect dozens of countries, hundreds of factories, and thousands of retail outlets, and they are linked by the most advanced transportation, communications, and information technologies available). As they did in the East Asian NIEs two decades earlier, apparel shipments from Mexico and the Caribbean Basin countries to the United States are pacing the boom in manufactured exports from these economies, generating plenty of jobs and foreign exchange. Yet complaints abound about the quality of these jobs, the stability of the export earnings, and apparel workers' standard of living.

In particular, there is acrimonious debate about whether the NAFTA should be considered a good deal or not, and for whom. The dispute galvanizes strong vested interests in the United States and Mexico, as well as in the Caribbean Basin. U.S. critics of the agreement claim that it has accelerated the destruction of the U.S. manufacturing base in textiles, and they bolster this view with estimates of very substantial job losses in the U.S. apparel and textile sector because of the passage of the NAFTA. Although consolidation, automation, and enhanced productivity have contributed to these job losses in the United States, the NAFTA is seen as the primary culprit because producing apparel products in Mexico dramatically increases U.S. corporate profits: "U.S. corporations in Mexico can pay workers $30 per week, provide little or no benefits, avoid U.S. laws that protect the health and safety of workers, and then discharge waste into the local river or ditch without having to worry about meeting the stringent government regulation that exists in the United States" (Castelli 1999).

---

[5] See Carrillo 1998 on Delphi.

This critical perspective is sharply challenged by NAFTA boosters, who see the regional trade agreement as a defensive "survival strategy" intended to protect the North American market against a flood of Asian imports. Since the NAFTA went into effect on January 1, 1994, Mexico has overtaken China as the top U.S. supplier of apparel. More generally, the NAFTA has precipitated a profound regional shift in where apparel is made. Before the NAFTA, most U.S. clothing imports came from Asia. By the late 1990s, most U.S. apparel came from the Americas—Mexico, Central America, the Caribbean, and Canada, all places that use U.S. yarn and fabric (unlike Asian clothing imports, which contain virtually no U.S. yarn or fabric). Using impeccable supply-chain logic, Carlos Moore of the American Textile Manufacturers Institute concludes that the NAFTA has indeed benefited the U.S. textile industry and its workers:

> [W]hen apparel imports from the Far East increase, textile production in this country decreases. When production drops, that means fewer jobs for American textile workers. Simply put, apparel imports from Mexico help our industry and our workers; apparel imports from the Far East hurt us. . . . I'm not claiming all is rosy in our industry. Like manufacturing industries all across the United States, the textile industry has consolidated and increased its productivity, which has resulted in job losses. The industry also has faced growing imports from Asia, much of which violates trade rules, and this has added to job losses. But keep in mind, if we didn't have NAFTA, job losses in the textile industry would have been far more drastic because U.S. garment-making would have continued to move to the Far East and we would not have nearby markets for our textiles. (Moore 1999)

Unraveling the North American restructuring paradox requires us to take a global perspective on trade and investment patterns in the textile and apparel sector. In the context of the NAFTA, East Asia is being pitted against Mexico as a competing source of supply for the U.S. market. However, a closer look reveals that Asian and Mexican exporters have played very different roles in U.S. apparel sourcing, in terms of both product niches and production networks. Despite Asia's financial crisis in the late 1990s, the East Asian NIEs are still viewed as export success stories, and many in the development field are trying to identify the most appropriate lessons to draw from their experience. Thus the questions to be addressed are what Mexico can learn from East Asia in terms of its sustained success in global apparel markets, and in what ways does the Mexican context remain distinct.

Global Sourcing via Full-Package Supply: The East Asia Story

The world textile and apparel industry has undergone several production shifts since the 1950s, and they all involve Asia. The industry's first migration took place from North America and Western Europe to Japan in the 1950s and early 1960s, when a sharp rise in imports from Japan displaced Western textile and clothing production. The second supply shift was from Japan to the "Big Three" Asian apparel producers (Hong Kong, South Korea, and Taiwan), which permitted the latter group to dominate global textile and clothing exports in the 1970s and 1980s. Since the mid–1980s, there has been a third migration of production—this time from the Asian Big Three to a number of other developing economies. In the 1980s, the principal shift was to mainland China, but it also encompassed several Southeast Asian nations and Sri Lanka. In the 1990s, the proliferation of new suppliers included South Asian and Latin American apparel exporters (Khanna 1993).

The most important policies shaping U.S. apparel imports have been quotas and preferential tariffs. Since the early 1970s, quotas on apparel and textile items have been regulated by the international Multi-Fiber Arrangement (MFA). The MFA has been used by the United States, Canada, and various European nations to impose quantitative import limits in numerous product categories. Although the clear intent of the MFA was to protect developed country firms from a flood of low-cost imports that threatened to disrupt domestic textile and apparel industries, the result was exactly the opposite. Protectionism led developing country manufacturers to heighten their competitive capabilities, learning to make sophisticated products that were more profitable than simple ones. Industrialized country protectionism also diversified the scope of foreign competition, as booming North American and European demand called forth an ever-widening circle of exporters. The creation of the European Union and the NAFTA heightened preferential tariffs in these trade blocs and promoted a growing consolidation of supply chains within regions.

The ability of the East Asian NIEs to sustain their export success over several decades, and to develop a multilayered sourcing hierarchy within Asia, is only partially related to wage rates and state policies. From a commodity chain perspective, East Asia must be viewed as part of an interrelated regional economy (Gereffi 1999). Industrial restructuring in northern-tier East Asian NIEs has to a significant extent driven the apparel export boom in the less developed southern tier of Asia. As Northeast Asian firms began moving their production offshore, they devised ways to coordinate and control their sourcing networks. Ultimately, they focused on the more profitable design and marketing segments within the apparel commodity chain to sustain their competitive edge. This transformation can be conceptualized as a process of industrial upgrading, based in large measure on building various kinds of economic and social networks between buyers and sellers.

Modalities of Export-led Growth: The Mexico and Caribbean Basin Story

Our analysis of the apparel commodity chain in Asia suggests two main trends relevant to the future of the textile and apparel sector in North America. First, the relative decline of finished apparel exports from the East Asian NIEs is producing a "supply gap" in the North American apparel commodity chain. This is due partly to the greater geographical distances and logistical complexity involved in managing Asia's OEM production networks, as well as to the trend toward more direct marketing in Asia as local manufacturers shift from OEM to OBM. Second, apparel manufacturers in Mexico and the Caribbean Basin will need to develop the capability to carry out full-package production if they hope to compete for the large, dynamic brand-name and private-label segment of the U.S. market, especially more fashion-oriented products such as women's wear. Ready-to-wear garments had previously been produced only in the East Asia NIEs (for the U.S. mass market) or in the fashion centers of Europe (for *haute couture*).

Three Models of Competition Between 1990 and 2000, U.S. apparel imports rose from $25.0 to $64.4 billion. Figure 6.1 is an import map that identifies trade shifts among the main suppliers to the U.S. apparel market. Those nations in the innermost circle each accounted for 10 percent or more of the total value of U.S. clothing imports in 2000, while each of those in the outer ring made up only 1.0 to 1.9 percent of total imports. In other words, as countries move from the outer rings to the inner ones in this import map, their relative importance in the U.S. apparel import market increases.

Figure 6.1 reveals several key aspects of the direction and magnitude of change in U.S. apparel trade. First, there are striking regional differences in the pattern of U.S. apparel imports. The NIEs in Northeast Asia are becoming much less important in U.S. apparel sourcing; South and Southeast Asia are growing slowly or not at all; and imports from the Caribbean Basin, China, and especially Mexico are booming. Second, despite considerable mobility during the 1990s, there is a strong core-periphery pattern that dominates the geography of export activity in the U.S. apparel sourcing matrix. Only four economies (China,

FIGURE 6.1. Shifts in the Regional Structure of U.S. Apparel Imports, 1990–2000

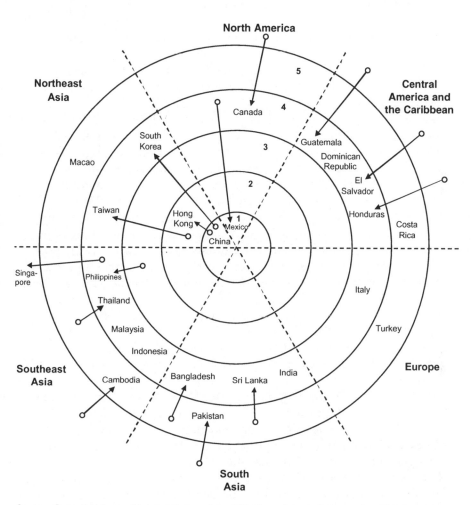

Source: Compiled from official statistics of the U.S. Department of Commerce (U.S. imports for consumption, customs value).

Note: The numbered rings indicate the share of total U.S. imports in U.S. dollars by partner country: (1) more than 10 percent; (2) 6.0–9.9 percent; (3) 4.0–5.9 percent; (4) 2.0–3.9 percent; (5) 1.0–1.9 percent. The 2000 position corresponds to the ring where the country's name is located; the 1990 position, if different, is indicated by a small circle. The arrows represent the magnitude and direction of change over time.

Hong Kong, Mexico, and South Korea) were core U.S. suppliers during the 1990s, and only China and Mexico still held that distinction in 2000. Third, although most countries experienced a relatively modest degree of change from 1990 to 2000 (they changed their position by only one ring or not at all), only Mexico improved its position substantially, moving from the fourth ring in 1990 (with 2.8 percent of all U.S. apparel imports) to the core (13.6 percent of U.S. imports) a decade later (see figure 6.1).

These patterns of U.S. sourcing highlight three distinct models of competition in the North American apparel industry. First, there is an *East Asian model* in which companies in the East Asian NIEs offer full-package apparel exports to U.S. buyers, allowing them to dominate the higher-value, mainly women's fashion-apparel market. Second, there is an emerging *Mexican model* in which the NAFTA's rules of origin create an incentive for more integrated apparel production in Mexico, although diverse U.S. firms are vying for the lead role in coordinating this full-package option. Third, there is a *Caribbean Basin model* in which the traditional form of production sharing prevails, based on a mixture of low wages, an export-processing-zone format, and preferential access to the U.S. market through Caribbean Basin Initiative (CBI) production-sharing provisions. However, Caribbean Basin apparel producers still confront U.S. quotas that offer none of the benefits of the NAFTA rules of origin. Although Mexico has graduated beyond simple assembly, it has not yet achieved the full-package status of East Asian export firms.

The remainder of this chapter will examine the dynamics and regional development implications of these three models in greater detail.

The United States, Mexico, and the Caribbean Basin: Who Benefits from Regional Integration? If one envisions the complete apparel commodity chain as encompassing raw materials, yarn and synthetic fibers, textiles, apparel, and the distribution of apparel to retailers (Appelbaum and Gereffi 1994), then the Mexican and U.S. commodity chains are quite distinct. Mexico has several large, reasonably successful synthetic fiber companies, a multitude of export-oriented assembly firms that use U.S. inputs to produce apparel products destined for the United States, and an emergent retail sector that is fashioning a number of strategic alliances with U.S. counterpart firms. By far the weakest link in the Mexican production chain is the textile segment. The vast majority of Mexico's textile companies are undercapitalized, technologically backward, and inefficient, and they produce goods of poor quality. By contrast, the United States is very strong in synthetic fibers, textiles, and retailing, but limited in its garment production capability, especially for women's and children's apparel. The Mexican apparel chain thus appears to be strongest where the U.S. chain is relatively weak: garment production.[6]

This picture becomes more complex if we expand the borders of North America to include Central America and the Caribbean.[7] The most common form of export activity in Latin America is the labor-intensive assembly of manufactured goods from imported components in export-processing zones (EPZs). These zones are disproportionately concentrated in Mexico (where they are known as the maquiladora industry) and the Caribbean Basin (where they are called free-trade zones) because of the area's low wages and proximity to the U.S. market, where over 90 percent of their exports are sold. Virtually all EPZ production in the region is of a very low value-added nature.[8] This is a direct result of U.S. policy. Under U.S. Harmonized Tariff Schedule provision 9802.00.80 (formerly clause 807), enterprises operating in EPZs have an incentive to minimize locally purchased inputs because only U.S.-made components are exempt from import duties when the finished product is shipped back to the United States. This constitutes a major impediment to increasing integration between activities in the zones and the local economy, and it limits the usefulness of EPZs as stepping-stones to higher stages of industrialization.

Mexico relied heavily on a handful of apparel exports to gain a strong foothold in the U.S. market during the 1990s. Table 6.5 shows that over three-fourths (75.9 percent) of Mexico's US$8.4 billion in total apparel exports to the U.S. market in 2000 were accounted for by just

---

[6] Additional empirical support for the arguments in this section appears in Gereffi, Spener, and Bair 2002.

[7] Canada is a niche player in the North American apparel sector. Canada's considerable textile strengths are oriented to the home furnishings market (upholstery, rugs, and curtains). Within the apparel sector, Canada's main export niche to the United States is wool suits.

[8] Mexico's maquiladora industry, which was established in 1965, comprises assembly plants that mainly use U.S. components to make goods for export to the U.S. market. In 1993, the industry generated US$22 billion in exports and employed 540,000 workers; by 1996, employment had grown by 50 percent to 811,000 workers, while exports rose by 54 percent to US$34 billion (USITC 1997: 4.3). Until relatively recently, Mexico's maquiladora sector typified low value-added assembly, with virtually no backward linkages (local materials typically accounted for only 2 to 4 percent of total inputs). In the late 1980s, however, a new wave of maquiladora plants began to push beyond this enclave model to a more advanced type of production, making components for complex products like automobiles and computers (Carrillo 1998).

TABLE 6.5. Mexico's Top Apparel Exports to the U.S. Market, 1990–2000 (millions of current U.S. dollars and percent)

Product[1]	1990 Value	Percentage of Total Imports[2]	1993 Value	Percentage of Total Imports	1996 Value	Percentage of Total Imports	1998 Value	Percentage of Total Imports	2000 Value	Percentage of Total Imports
Cotton trousers	194	28.6	458	33.4	1,259	29.7	2,285	30.7	3,218	38.2
Men's (347)	111	16.4	297	21.6	758	17.9	1,222	16.4	1,670	19.8
Women's (348)	83	12.2	162	11.8	501	11.8	1,063	14.3	1,548	18.4
Cotton knit shirts	16	2.4	81	5.9	456	10.8	952	12.8	1,374	16.3
Men's (338)	3	0.4	53	3.9	261	6.2	601	8.1	793	9.4
Women's (339)	13	1.9	27	2.0	195	4.6	350	4.7	581	6.9
MMF[3] knit shirts	9	1.3	65	4.7	384	9.1	598	8.0	666	7.9
Men's (638)	1	0.1	4	0.3	190	4.5	263	3.5	424	5.0
Women's (639)	7	1.0	61	4.4	194	4.6	334	4.5	242	2.9
MMF trousers	55	8.1	64	4.7	257	6.1	466	6.3	638	7.6
Men's (647)	42	6.2	36	2.6	113	2.7	215	2.9	382	4.5
Women's (648)	13	1.9	27	2.0	144	3.4	250	3.4	256	3.0
Cotton underwear (352)	6	0.9	38	2.8	120	2.8	248	3.3	228	2.7
MMF brassieres (649)	49	7.2	97	7.1	167	3.9	239	3.2	262	3.1
Top six products	329	48.5	803	58.5	2,644	62.5	4,787	64.2	6,386	75.9
Total Multi-Fiber Arrangement apparel imports from Mexico	678		1,372		4,229		5,928		8,413	

Sources: U.S. International Trade Commission, *Annual Statistical Report on U.S. Imports of Textiles and Apparel,* various years; "Major Shippers Reports" on the U.S. International Trade Administration's Office of Textiles and Apparel website www.otexa.ita.doc.gov.

[1] Identified by Multi-Fiber Arrangement category.

[2] Percentage of total U.S. apparel imports from Mexico.

[3] MMF: man-made fiber

six products: cotton trousers (38.2 percent of the total), cotton knit shirts (16.3 percent), man-made fiber (MMF) knit shirts (7.9 percent), MMF trousers (7.6 percent), cotton underwear (2.7 percent), and MMF brassieres (3.1 percent). The relative importance of these top six products has increased substantially since 1990, when they represented less than half (48.5 percent) of Mexico's total of US$678 million in exports to the United States. Thus, while Mexico's total apparel exports to the United States increased more than twelvefold from 1990 to 2000, the value of the top six export products grew by a factor of more than nineteen over this same period.

The lack of NAFTA parity for the Caribbean Basin in the 1990s dramatically truncated the growth of export-oriented apparel assembly in these smaller economies. In 1995 and 1996, more than 150 apparel plants closed in the Caribbean, and 123,000 jobs were lost "as a direct result of trade and investment diversion to Mexico," according to the Caribbean Textile and Apparel Institute in Kingston, Jamaica (Rohter 1997). Momentum is currently building within the U.S. Congress for some kind of a CBI trade enhancement bill. Proposed NAFTA parity legislation for the CBI economies was defeated in 1997, but lingering concern over the effects of two hurricanes (Mitch and Georges) that devastated huge parts of Central America and the Caribbean in the fall of 1998 led Congress to debate legislation providing short-term funding for hurricane relief projects. Amidst reports that Central American immigration through Mexico to the United States increased by more than 30 percent in the first few months of 1999 alone, attention has turned to longer-term reconstruction projects that will generate and sustain employment for the Central Americans who can no longer work in industries wiped out by the storms (AAMA 1999a). On May 4, 2000, the U.S. House of Representatives voted 309 to 110 to pass a Caribbean/Sub-Saharan Africa trade bill that extended preferential treatment to imports from up to twenty-four CBI countries. Under the terms of this legislation, these countries would receive the same tariff treatment on imports as those received by Mexico under the NAFTA. The U.S. Senate approved the bill on May 11, effectively granting the CBI countries NAFTA parity.

Corporate Restructuring among U.S. Apparel and Textile Firms: A Struggle for Power, Profits, and Jobs

Given the power shifts that are occurring among North American textile, apparel, and retail firms, a key question is: Who will be the main "organizing agents" in modernizing Mexico's apparel commodity chain? The notion of organizing agents is used here to refer to those firms—foreign and domestic—that could enhance the competitiveness of the Mexican apparel sector through backward or forward linkages with major producers and retailers.

Large firms (mainly from the United States) in different segments of the apparel chain are vying to become coordinating agents in new North American networks that would strengthen Mexico's capabilities to carry out full-package supply:

- *Synthetic fiber companies* in the United States and Mexico have been lobbying downmarket with U.S. apparel manufacturers and retailers, attempting to persuade apparel firms to develop products using their fibers and trying to get retailers to bring these orders to Mexico.

- *Textile mills* have been forging alliances with apparel suppliers that could allow for more integrated textile and apparel production in different regions of Mexico. In addition, textile firms are exploring the possibility of creating their own product development teams for select apparel categories.

- *Brand-name apparel manufacturers* are rationalizing their supply chains in Mexico, looking for smaller numbers of more capable suppliers. Some firms are "de-verticalizing" their domestic and offshore production operations by divesting themselves of manufacturing assets in favor of building up the marketing side of their business, with an emphasis on global brands.

- A handful of *Mexican integrated apparel manufacturers*—companies that own modern plants that go from spinning and weaving through apparel production and finishing—are beginning to develop strong reputations with U.S. retailers and marketers seeking to place full-package orders in Mexico.

- *Latin American retailers* are beginning to set up sourcing networks in Mexico, aided by government-supported vendor certification programs.

- *Mexican sourcing agents* are emerging to serve as intermediaries for U.S. buyers and Mexican factories, a pattern already widespread in East Asia.

Spurred by intense competition, the major U.S. apparel and textile firms are currently undergoing extensive restructuring. This restructuring involves several related aspects: (1) a shift from domestic manufacturing to foreign sourcing; (2) divestment of manufacturing facilities in order to become consumer-driven and develop marketing expertise; (3) consolidation by retailers and manufacturers alike; and (4) the blurring of boundaries between firms in adjacent segments of the apparel commodity chain. A major consequence of these corporate restructuring initiatives is that they tend to increase the salience of U.S. firms' Mexican and Caribbean Basin operations and simultaneously decrease employment in the United States.

Table 6.6 summarizes a number of these changes for leading companies in the U.S. apparel industry. The table includes information on five of the top U.S. apparel manufacturers and two of the biggest U.S. textile firms, all of which have extensive linkages to Mexico and the Caribbean Basin region. Levi Strauss, Fruit of the Loom, Burlington Industries, and Cone Mills have experienced substantial decreases in U.S. employment since the NAFTA took effect in 1994. In most cases, sales and employment declines mirrored each other during the 1994-2000 period. The exceptions were Warnaco, which grew through acquisitions, and Sara Lee, where apparel represented only 44 percent of total corporate sales.

These same trends characterize the U.S. apparel sector as a whole. During 1993–1997, restructuring by U.S. apparel companies caused an estimated loss of 176,000 jobs in the domestic industry (Jones 1998: 37). In 1998 the U.S. apparel industry shed an additional 74,000 jobs, and the textile labor force dropped by 30,000. Apparel employment in 2000 stood at just over 633,000 workers, and U.S. textile employment was at an all-time low of 541,000 (U.S. Bureau of Labor Statistics 2001). However, these job declines in the United States have been accompanied by two related and less well recognized phenomena: improved productivity and higher U.S. wages. Between 1995 and early 1999, the productivity of the average U.S. apparel worker increased by about 11 percent because of advances in technology, production practices, and inventory management, and average weekly wages increased by about 12 percent during the same period (AAMA 1999b). The hourly earnings of the average U.S. apparel worker increased from $7.34 in 1994 to $9.09 in 2000, while the hourly wages of U.S. textile workers rose from $9.41 to $10.95 over the same period (AAFA 2000). Thus, contrary to much popular opinion, competitiveness and wage levels in the U.S. textile and apparel industries have actually improved since the NAFTA went into effect, despite continuing job losses.

Mexico's Transition to the Full-Package Model in Apparel

The global apparel industry has gone through a series of transformations in production, trade, and corporate strategies during the past several decades that have fundamentally altered the distribution of basic

TABLE 6.6. Restructuring by Major Firms in the U.S. Apparel and Textile Industry[1]

Firm	Sales (U.S.$ millions)	Employees	Market Niche — Product Type	Market Niche — Economic Role	Main Brands	Foreign Activity	Recent Restructuring Activity
Levi Strauss (San Francisco, CA)	6,074 (1994) 4,600 (2000)	36,500 (1994) 17,300 (2000)	Jeans and trousers	Branded manufacturer and retailer	Products include jeans, dress pants, and casual sportswear under Levi's, Dockers, and Slates brands.	One-third of Levi's global sales are in Europe and the Asia-Pacific region. Most production is being moved to contract operations in Mexico and the Caribbean.	Levi's announced in February 1999 that it would close 11 U.S. plants and lay off 5,900 workers (30% of its total workforce), leaving only 11 plants remaining in the U.S. Firm is stressing consumer-focused brand management, as well as moving to Internet sales.
VF Corp. (Greensboro, NC)	4,972 (1994) 5,748 (2000)	68,000 (1994) 75,000 (2000)	Jeans and intimate apparel	Branded manufacturer	Holds 27% of jeans market under the Wrangler, Lee, Riders, Britannia, and Rustler labels; produces intimate apparel under Vanity Fair, Bestform, and Vassarette labels; also workwear and Jansport daypacks.	Formed VF Global Sourcing Organization in 1996. Offshore production accounted for 57% of production in 1998, with plans to increase to 80% in the near future. Eight plants in Mexico; six in Costa Rica; one in Honduras.	In 1997, firm launched "consumerization" plan: 17 decentralized divisions consolidated into five product-based coalitions in order to become more flexible, efficient, and competitive. It acquired Britannia jeans from Levi Strauss in 1997, and in 1998 VF moved from Pennsylvania to North Carolina, closer to the company's production facilities.

Company					Products	Foreign operations	Strategy
Sara Lee Corp. (Chicago, IL)	6,449 (1994) 7,598 (2000)	137,100 (1997) 154,200 (2000)	Intimate and athletic apparel	Branded manufacturer and marketer	Apparel is 44% of total sales. Products include underwear, intimate apparel, hosiery, and athletic and casual apparel under the Hanes, Playtex, Bali, and L'eggs brands and Champion label.	In 1997, foreign operations accounted for 42% of apparel sales and 47% of profits. Firm announced plans in February 1999 to spend US$45 million to expand Puerto Rico apparel plants, where it already owns 12 plants and is Puerto Rico's largest employer.	A "de-verticalization" plan was announced in 1997, resulting in divestiture of nine U.S. textile plants to allow for a greater focus on product development and brand marketing. Firm's goal is to own fewer fixed assets and to use knowledge-based skills to develop and market its goods.
Fruit of the Loom (Chicago, IL)	2,298 (1994) 1,550 (2000)	37,400 (1994) 27,000 (2000)	Intimate apparel	Branded manufacturer and marketer	Leading producer of underwear and basic casual family apparel under Fruit of the Loom, BVD, Gitano, Munsingwear, and Wilson brands.	Firm performs 95% of its sewing in Mexico and Caribbean Basin countries. Firm's 14 company-owned offshore plants accounted for 50% of all offshore sewing in 1998.	Since 1995, firm has closed 9 U.S. sewing plants, employing more than 7,000 workers, and moved most operations to Mexico and the Caribbean Basin in an effort to reduce costs.
Warnaco (New York, NY)	789 (1994) 2,250 (2000)	14,800 (1994) 21,440 (2000)	Intimate apparel	Manufacturer of licensed goods	Leading marketer of bras to U.S. department and specialty stores, with more than 30% of the market. The company boasts a diverse port folio of its own and licensed women's and menswear brands, including Calvin Klein, Warner's, and Chaps by Ralph Lauren.	Firm has subsidiaries and manufacturing facilities in North and South America, the Caribbean Basin, and Asia. Its operations in Mexico are primarily production-sharing arrangements. Firm owns 20 Calvin Klein stores in Asia.	Firm continues to acquire licenses for major brand names to consolidate branded share of intimate wear and sleepwear market. In 1997 it acquired Designer Holdings, Ltd., holder of a 40-year extendable license for Calvin Klein jeans and jeans-related sportswear.

TABLE 6.6 continued

| Burling-ton Indus-tries (Greens-boro, NC) | 2,127 (1994) 1,620 (2000) | 23,800 (1994) 17,900 (2000) | Textiles | Textile production and full-package apparel services | Firm produces textiles, including synthetic fabrics, denim, polyesters and blends, and worsted wool blends. In recent years it has added apparel service operations to each of its textile divisions in order to meet booming demand in private-label apparel market. | Mexico is a key growth area. Firm is involved in NuStart, a planned "textile city" south of Mexico City. In 1998 it announced plans to invest US$80 million in five garment-making facilities coordinated by its garment service center in Chihuahua; these plants will employ 2,000 workers and are expected to add US$225 million to Burlington's annual sales. In 1999 three new plants opened in Morelos. | Firm is undergoing reorganization. U.S. plant production capacity will decrease 25%, and seven plants will close. Sportswear division will be absorbed as a unit within the Global Denim division. Sportswear, recently moved to Mexico, produces men's shirts and slacks with some fabrics coming from Mexican weaving plants, with sewing contracted to apparel manufacturers around Mexico City. Firm is adopting full-package assembly in various stages in all divisions. |
| Cone Mills (Greens-boro, NC) | 806 (1994) 617 (2000) | 5,500 (1998) 4,300 (2000) | Textiles | Textile production | Firm produces denim for jeans makers such as Levi Strauss. | Company formed a joint venture in 1995 with Compañía Industrial de Parras in Coahuila, the largest producer of denim in Mexico. Firm announced in 1998 that it would build a manufacturing plant as part of a new textile city in Altamira, Mexico. | In February 1999 the firm announced a restructuring plan to deal with losses stemming from Levi's troubles (Cone's largest customer), hoping to save US$20-30 million annually through a 20% reduction of its workforce. Its real estate subsidiary was sold in order to concentrate on core denim production. |

Sources: Compiled from Hoover's company profiles, corporate web sites and annual reports, Jones (1998: 36–37), and other sources.

[1] This table reflects major developments in the U.S. apparel industry through December 2001.

economic benefits for countries (exports), companies (profits), and workers (jobs). We have used the global commodity chains framework to help explain these changes both because it is dynamic and global and because it seeks to identify the driving forces behind industrial upgrading at multiple levels. Industrial upgrading is conceptualized as shifts in apparel suppliers' export roles in the world market; the corporate strategies of the leading firms in the apparel commodity chain are the main drivers of change. Important regulatory events such as the Multi-Fiber Arrangement, the NAFTA, and the Caribbean Basin Initiative alter the political and institutional environment that conditions corporate strategies, while new technological developments in communications, transportation, and inventory management are enabling factors that facilitate industrial upgrading (but do not determine it).

As noted above, three models of competition—the East Asian model, the Mexican model, and the Caribbean Basin model—stand out in examining the current situation of the North American apparel sector and its prospects for change. It would be misleading, however, to think of these as inherently national or regional patterns. Rather, the success and limitations of East Asian, Mexican, and Caribbean Basin apparel producers are determined by two factors: their location (not nationality per se) and the transnational networks in which they are enmeshed. Ultimately, success in the contemporary global economy requires understanding how to use organizational networks to penetrate international markets. Indeed, these three models of competition use networks and markets quite differently.

The *East Asian model* is based on highly successful textile and apparel exporters from Hong Kong, South Korea, and Taiwan (preceded by Japan, and now followed by China) that have progressed through a sequence of export roles, from assembly to OEM to OBM. The East Asian NIEs developed and refined their OEM capabilities in the 1960s and 1970s by establishing close ties with U.S. retailers and marketers, and then they engaged in "learning by watching" in order to use these foreign partners as role models to build East Asia's export competence. The performance trust built up through many successful business transactions with these U.S. buyers enabled suppliers in the East Asian NIEs to internationalize their OEM expertise via "triangle manufacturing"—that is, the East Asian manufacturers became intermediaries between U.S. buyers and hundreds of apparel factories in Asia and other developing regions in order to take advantage of lower labor costs and favorable quotas all around the world (Gereffi 1999). The creation of these global sourcing networks helped the East Asian NIEs sustain their international competitiveness when domestic economic conditions and quota constraints threatened the original, bilateral OEM relationships. The East Asian NIEs are now moving beyond OEM in multiple ways: shifting to higher-value "upstream" products in the apparel commodity chain (such as exports of textiles and fibers rather than apparel); moving "downstream" from OEM to OBM in apparel; and switching to new commodity chains where the export success in apparel can be replicated.

The emerging *Mexican model* involves an ongoing transition from assembly to full-package (OEM) production. The key factor in Mexico's shift has been the NAFTA, which removed the trade restrictions that virtually locked Mexico into an assembly role. The maquiladora system effectively conditioned Mexico's access to the U.S. market on the use of U.S. inputs. The phase-in period for the NAFTA allows one to see, step by step, how more of the apparel supply chain (such as cutting, washing, and textile production) is relocating to Mexico as specific tariff restrictions on each of these stages is eliminated (Bair and Gereffi 2001).[9]

Yet the NAFTA does not guarantee Mexico's success. Although the massive peso devaluation of 1994–1995 made Mexico very attractive as a production site for U.S. apparel manufacturers with international subcontracting operations, Mexico has traditionally lacked the infrastructure of related and supporting industries needed to undertake full-package garment production. However, U.S. textile and apparel companies have been expanding their investments in Mexico at a rapid and accelerating pace (see table 6.6). Thus Mexico is now better positioned to provide the quantity and quality of inputs needed for OEM production of standardized apparel items like jeans, knit shirts, trousers, and underwear (see table 6.5). Mexico is, nevertheless, still lagging in the fashion-oriented, women's wear categories. From a commodity chains perspective, the solution to the problems of how to complete the transition to full-package supply, and of how to develop new production and marketing niches, is to forge ties to the lead firms that can supply the needed resources and tutelage. In other words, Mexico needs to develop new and better networks in order to compete with East Asian suppliers for the U.S. full-package market.

U.S. firms have already shown a strong interest in transferring missing pieces of the North American apparel supply chain to Mexico.

---

[9] The East Asian NIEs did not employ the production-sharing provisions established by the 807/9802 U.S. trade regime in apparel because their great distance from the United States made U.S. textile inputs impractical. Moreover, U.S. textile mills did not have the production capability (nor were they inclined) to supply the diverse array of fabrics favored by the designers of women's wear and fashion-oriented apparel, which became the specialty of East Asian exporters. Both of these factors created an OEM niche for East Asian apparel companies that these firms adroitly exploited.

One real problem that must be confronted, however, is who controls critical nodes of the chain and how to manage the dependency relationships that such control implies. Thus far, U.S. firms are in clear control of the design and marketing segments of the apparel chain, while Mexican companies are in a good position to maintain and coordinate the production networks in apparel. Yet textile manufacturers in the United States (and, to a lesser degree, in Mexico as well) are making strong bids to integrate a broad package of apparel services that would increase their leverage vis-à-vis smaller garment contractors. For the foreseeable future, Mexico is likely to retain a mix of assembly plants linked to U.S. brand-name manufacturers and a new set of full-package producers linked to private-label retailers and marketers. As more critical apparel inputs become available in Mexico, U.S. inputs will decline and traditional Mexican assembly plants will be replaced either by vertically integrated manufacturers or else by clusters of related firms that compete through localized networks, such as companies producing jeans in Torreón, Coahuila (Bair and Gereffi 2001).

The *Caribbean Basin model* is almost exclusively limited to EPZ assembly using the 807/9802 trade regime. Because the CBI economies previously lacked NAFTA parity, they encountered quota restrictions, higher tariffs, and more limited possibilities for vertical integration compared to Mexico. Nonetheless, the CBI countries have enjoyed considerable success within the export assembly role, continuing to expand their position in the U.S. apparel market (see figure 6.1) through large assembly plants linked to the production-sharing operations of U.S. apparel transnationals. CBI exporters are, however, losing ground to Mexican firms that can export similar goods to the United States more cheaply and quickly. Trade parity vis-à-vis the NAFTA for the CBI economies places them on a more level footing with Mexico in terms of the regulatory and economic environment. Nevertheless, success in industrial upgrading still requires the CBI countries to develop new networks with U.S. retailers and marketers if they are to acquire the skills and resources needed to move into the more diversified activities associated with full-package production.[10]

The United States continues to define the terms of change in the North American apparel commodity chain. U.S. global brands dominate the industry, and these must be created in the U.S. market because demand is consumer-driven and fluctuates rapidly. Mass customization and agile manufacturing represent the next-generation challenges

---

[10] There are a few companies in the CBI region that engage in full-package production. One is Davon Corporation in Jamaica, which has successfully entered the hospital uniform market in the United States.

in manufacturing, and U.S. firms are taking a leadership role in trying to deliver highly personalized products at mass production prices (see table 6.6). This requires appropriate integration of information technology, automation, and short-cycle, team-based management systems. Giant U.S. retailers have raised the bar for domestic as well as overseas suppliers with state-of-the-art "quick response" systems that place stricter inventory management demands and bigger financial risks on producers, which must be able to supply consumer goods more quickly, more cheaply, and in greater variety than in the past. In this context, it is not surprising that U.S. job losses in textiles and apparel have been accompanied by record gains in productivity and higher compensation levels for those U.S. employees that remain in the sector.

Sustained competitiveness in the international apparel industry involves continual changes in economic roles and capabilities. New exporters are constantly entering the global supply chain, a development that compels existing firms to cut costs, upgrade, or exit the market. Industrial upgrading to adjust successfully—indeed, to survive—in a volatile, export-oriented sector such as apparel typically requires organizational linkages to buyers and suppliers in developed country markets. Mexico is attempting to use networks with U.S. firms to occupy niches that previously have been the stronghold of East Asian suppliers, and the CBI economies are trying to keep pace with Mexico. Sewing up the North American apparel market requires Mexico both to learn from U.S. lead firms in the chain and to seize control of opportunities that permit it to expand its domestic and regional capabilities and options.

CONCLUSION

Mexico's industrial development since the mid–1970s has been marked by a shift from ISI to a more export-oriented strategy of economic growth. The country has clearly progressed from primary products to manufactured exports, and its exports have become more diversified. Three broad factors are linked to these changes: globalization, liberalization, and regionalization. Globalization dates from the 1970s; it refers, among other things, to the increased significance of decentralized international trade and production networks. Liberalization refers to Mexico's creation in the 1980s of an "open economy" with fewer trade and investment restrictions, a policy that promoted the entry of record amounts of foreign direct investment. Regionalization refers to the process in the 1990s whereby Mexico became officially linked to the U.S. economy through the NAFTA. All of these factors, but especially the last, have greatly accelerated the pace of Mexico's industrial development.

Nonetheless, there are still significant problems to confront. Productivity gains in Mexico have not yet translated into higher real wages for workers, who often are less well off than their parents were. Although total trade between the United States and Mexico has doubled since the enactment of the NAFTA (placing Mexico ahead of Japan and behind only Canada as the United States' leading trade partner), most Mexican consumers were worse off at the end of the 1990s than they were a decade earlier in terms of what they could buy for themselves. In the years following Mexico's major currency devaluation of 1994–1995, when the peso lost over half of its value in a matter of months, Mexican consumers suffered a staggering 39 percent drop in their purchasing power (Millman 1999).

There remains a sharp division between two Mexicos: the "Dollar Mexico" tied to the international market, which produces about one-quarter of the country's output, and the "Peso Mexico," which makes goods for local consumers who are barely scraping by. Mexico is faced with the daunting task of creating one million *new* jobs a year just to keep up with the annual entry of young workers into the labor force. In order to maintain a rapid pace of growth, Mexico has no choice but to link up to global chains that are the conduits for the resources and learning needed to become internationally competitive.

However, this by itself is not enough to solve Mexico's most pressing development dilemmas: chronic poverty and a shortage of jobs. The economy cannot be expected to solve all of a society's problems. Education, especially for women, remains a top priority, and Mexico's ongoing political reforms will continue to be slow and painful — but necessary. Modernizing the economy through export linkages is an important step in the development process, but Mexico has to maximize the spillover effects to local firms. Here, as in the social arena, government policy can be very helpful. But the pace of economic change will be deeply affected by the willingness and ability of Mexican firms to learn how to succeed in international markets, as well as by the society's commitment to further reforms on the social and political fronts.

REFERENCES

AAFA (American Apparel and Footwear Association). 2000. *2000 Footwear and Apparel Industry Data.* Arlington, Virginia: AAFA.

AAMA (American Apparel Manufacturers Association). 1999a. "Momentum Builds for CBI Bill," *AAMA News*, March–April, pp. 1–2.

―――. 1999b. "1998: The Year in Numbers," *Apparel Industry Trends*, March.

Appelbaum, Richard P., and Gary Gereffi. 1994. "Power and Profits in the Apparel Commodity Chain." In: *Global Production: The Apparel Industry in the Pacific Rim*, edited by Edna Bonacich et al. Philadelphia, Penn.: Temple University Press.

Arrighi, Giovanni, and Jessica Drangel. 1986. "The Stratification of the World Economy: An Exploration of the Semiperipheral Zone," *Review* 10: 9–74.

Bair, Jennifer, and Gary Gereffi. 2001. "Local Clusters in Global Chains: The Causes and Consequences of Export Dynamism in Torreón's Blue Jeans Industry," *World Development* 29 (11): 1885-1903.

Barnet, Richard J., and Ronald E. Müller. 1974. *Global Reach: The Power of the Multinational Corporations.* New York: Simon and Schuster.

Black, Phil. 1998. "Megabrands: Firms Consolidate, Leverage to Stay in the Game," *Bobbin* 39 (10): 48–63.

Bonner, Staci. 1997. "Convergence: One-stop Shopping in the Apparel Supply Chain," *Apparel Industry Magazine* 58 (9): 82–93.

Business Week. 1998. "Mexico's Makeover," December 21 (international edition).

Carrillo, Jorge. 1998. "Third Generation Maquiladoras? The Delphi-General Motors Case," *Journal of Borderlands Studies* 13 (1): 79–97.

Castelli, Pete D., III. 1999. "Agreement Escalated Destruction of U.S. Manufacturing Base," *Greensboro News & Record* [Greensboro, N.C.], February 21.

Dicken, Peter. 1998. *Global Shift: Transforming the World Economy.* 3d ed. New York: Guilford.

ECLAC (Economic Commission for Latin America and the Caribbean). 1995a. *Restructuring and International Competitiveness: The Mexican Automobile Industry.* LC/R.1550. Santiago, Chile: ECLAC.

―――. 1995b. *Technology and Work Organization in Latin American Motor Vehicle Industries.* LC/R.1517. Santiago, Chile: ECLAC.

―――. 1995c. *International Competition and Globalization Challenging the Brazilian Automotive Industry.* LC/R.1536. Santiago, Chile: ECLAC.

―――. 1995d. *Restructuring and Changing Market Conditions in the Brazilian Auto Components Industry.* LC/R.1484. Santiago, Chile: ECLAC.

―――. 1998. *Foreign Investment in Latin America and the Caribbean.* LC/G.2042-P. Santiago, Chile: ECLAC.

―――. 2001. *Foreign Investment in Latin America and the Caribbean.* LC/G.2125-P. Santiago, Chile: ECLAC.

Fröbel, Folker, Jürgen Heinrichs, and Otto Kreye. 1981. *The New International Division of Labor.* New York: Cambridge University Press.

Gereffi, Gary. 1983. *The Pharmaceutical Industry and Dependency in the Third World.* Princeton, N.J.: Princeton University Press.

————. 1995. "Global Production Systems and Third World Development." In *Global Change, Regional Response: The New International Context of Development*, edited by Barbara Stallings. New York: Cambridge University Press.

————. 1999. "International Trade and Industrial Upgrading in the Apparel Commodity Chain," *Journal of International Economics* 48 (1): 37–70.

Gereffi, Gary, and Peter Evans. 1981. "Transnational Corporations, Dependent Development, and State Policy in the Semiperiphery: A Comparison of Brazil and Mexico," *Latin American Research Review* 16 (3): 31–64.

Gereffi, Gary, and Miguel Korzeniewicz, eds. 1994. *Commodity Chains and Global Capitalism*. Westport, Conn.: Praeger.

Gereffi, Gary, David Spener, and Jennifer Bair, eds. 2002. *Free Trade and Uneven Development: The North American Apparel Industry after NAFTA*. Philadelphia, Penn.: Temple University Press.

Gereffi, Gary, and Tony Tam. 1998. "Industrial Upgrading through Organizational Chains: Dynamics of Rent, Learning, and Mobility in the Global Economy." Paper presented at the annual meeting of the American Sociological Association, San Francisco.

Gereffi, Gary, and Donald Wyman, eds. 1990. *Manufacturing Miracles: Paths of Industrialization in Latin America and East Asia*. Princeton, N.J.: Princeton University Press.

Jaffee, David. 1998. *Levels of Socio-economic Development Theory*. 2d ed. Westport, Conn.: Praeger.

Jones, Jackie. 1998. "Apparel Sourcing Strategies for Competing in the U.S. Market," *Industry, Trade, and Technology Review*, December: 31–40.

Khanna, Sri Ram. 1993. "Structural Changes in Asian Textiles and Clothing Industries: The Second Migration of Production," *Textile Outlook International* 49 (September): 11–32.

Kumar, Pradeep, and John Holmes. 1997. "Diffusion of HR/IR Practices under Lean Production and North American Economic Integration: The Case of the Canadian Automotive Parts Industry." Manuscript, Queen's University, October.

Lardner, James. 1988. "Annals of Business: The Sweater Trade" (Part 1), *The New Yorker*, January 11, pp. 39–73.

MacLachlan, Ian, and Adrián Guillermo Aguilar. 1998. "Maquiladora Myths: Locational and Structural Change in Mexico's Export Manufacturing Industry," *Professional Geographer* 50 (3): 315–31.

McMichael, Philip. 1996. *Development and Social Change*. Thousand Oaks, Calif.: Pine Forge.

Millman, Joel. 1999. "Is the Mexico Model Worth the Pain?" *Wall Street Journal*, March 8.

Moore, Carlos. 1999. "NAFTA: A Good Deal or Not?" *Greensboro News & Record* [Greensboro, N.C.], February 21.

Reich, Robert B. 1991. *The Work of Nations: Preparing Ourselves for 21st–Century Capitalism*. New York: Alfred A. Knopf.

Rohter, Larry. 1997. "Impact of NAFTA Pounds Economies of the Caribbean, Jobs Flowing to Mexico," *New York Times*, January 30.

Smith, James F. 1999. "Mexico: Sweeping Changes of Last Decade Translate into a Tale of Two Economies," *Los Angeles Times*, January 10.

Truett, Dale B., and Lila J. Truett. 1994. "Government Policy and the Export Performance of the Mexican Automobile Industry," *Growth and Change* 25 (Summer): 301–24.

Urquidi, Víctor L. 1991. "The Prospects for Economic Transformation in Latin America: Opportunities and Resistances," *LASA Forum* 22 (3): 1–9.

U.S. Bureau of Labor Statistics. 2001. Data available at www.bls.gov.

USITC (United States International Trade Commission). 1997. *Production Sharing: Use of U.S. Components and Materials in Foreign Assembly Operations, 1992–1995*. USITC Publication 3032. Washington, D.C.

Wade, Robert. 1996. "Globalization and Its Limits: Reports of the Death of the National Economy are Greatly Exaggerated." In *National Diversity and Global Capitalism*, edited by Suzanne Berger and Ronald Dore. Ithaca, N.Y.: Cornell University Press.

Womack, James P., Daniel T. Jones, and Daniel Roos. 1990. *The Machine That Changed the World*. New York: Macmillan.

World Bank. 1993. *The East Asian Miracle*. New York: Oxford University Press.

7

Industrial Policy, Regional Trends, and Structural Change in Mexico's Manufacturing Sector

Enrique Dussel Peters

INTRODUCTION

The constancy and coherence of Mexico's macroeconomic and industrial policies since 1994 have made the country an international showcase for structural adjustment and quick recovery from economic crisis. Vindicated by the actions of multilateral agencies and in international public opinion, during the late 1990s Mexico experienced significant growth in exports, productivity, and foreign investment, along with increased integration with the U.S. economy following implementation of the North American Free Trade Agreement (NAFTA).

This chapter has two broad goals. On the one hand, it outlines the development strategy that Mexico adopted in 1988 and continues to follow. This topic is important because other policy issues, including those concerning the manufacturing sector, are integral and functional parts of this overall socioeconomic strategy. On the other hand, the chapter analyzes industrial policy instruments along with conditions and changes in the manufacturing sector since 1988. In this context, it also examines several emerging regional trends that shed light on issues of economic sustainability.

The discussion proceeds in four sections. The first overviews Mexico's development strategy since 1988. Along with the logics, objectives, and context of liberalization, this section highlights the functional role of industrial policy since 1988 and reviews the key principles that guided it during the 1995–2000 period. This section concludes with a brief examination of contemporary industrial policy instruments. The second section draws on available data to analyze the general conditions of Mexico's manufacturing sector from 1988 through the late 1990s. The discussion covers trade, productivity, employment, and real wage issues. The third section examines recent regional development patterns in Mexico, focusing on foreign direct investment (FDI) data, gross domestic product (GDP), and GDP per capita. The fourth and final section considers the increasing regional polarization of manufacturing, as well as the implications of this development for economic sustainability and the impact on Mexico's macroeconomy.

ECONOMIC LIBERALIZATION AND INDUSTRIAL POLICY

Mexico's economic crisis of 1982, whose immediate catalyst was the inability of the private and public sectors to service their foreign debt, was not so much a "liquidity" crisis as a crisis of the import-substitution industrialization (ISI) model. Mexico's agricultural trade surpluses since the 1940s,[1] petroleum export revenues, and massive international credits since the late 1970s were insufficient to finance the crisis posed by ISI's growing unsustainability (Brailovsky, Clark, and Warman 1989; Ros 1991). Beginning in 1982, international conditions (particularly in the United States) prevented Mexico from "recycling" old international loans into new ones. Paradoxically, it was the demand for capital that the U.S. economy generated in international markets that drove interest rates up and changed the direction of capital flows toward the United States and other Organisation for Economic Co-operation and Development (OECD) nations. This situation resulted in a worldwide inability to service external debt, provoking the international debt crisis of the 1980s (Dussel Peters 1993). Moreover, a doubling in petroleum prices in 1979–1980 prompted overly optimistic estimates of Mexico's future oil revenues (Gurría Treviño 1993), an anticipated income that disappeared when petroleum prices began to fall in 1981 and eventually collapsed in 1986.

Mexico's efforts to manage the impact of economic crisis during the 1982–1987 period—including pursuing a policy of gradual economic liberalization—proved inadequate, and by 1987 the country had an annual inflation rate of 159 percent and a fiscal deficit of 16.1 percent of GDP. Investment and overall economic activity were in a free fall, while the country was simultaneously feeling increasing pressure from multilateral lending agencies and from the weight of external debt service. It is from this perspective that December 1987 stands as the end of the ISI crisis and the beginning of a new socioeconomic development strategy—liberalization.[2]

---

[1] These surpluses gave way to deficits in the late 1960s.

[2] Of course, as subsequent parts of this discussion make clear, some elements of liberalization appeared before 1987. These included tariff reduction, a relaxation

The attractions of export-oriented industrialization, in combination with Mexican policy makers' numerous links with U.S. academic institutions and government officials, favored the adoption of a liberalization strategy, which was implemented by the administration of President Carlos Salinas de Gortari (1988–1994) beginning in 1988. The policy shift was consolidated through a series of "economic pacts" negotiated jointly by the government, union officials, and the private sector. The pacts—which included wage ceilings and allowed for a retrospective indexing of wages—became the centerpiece of the Salinas administration's liberalization strategy. This strategy—carried forward by President Ernesto Zedillo (1994–2000)—was based on the following pillars (Aspe Armella 1993; Córdoba 1991; Gurría Treviño 1993; Martínez and Fárber 1994; Zabludovsky 1990; and Zedillo 1994):

- Macroeconomic stabilization was to induce a process of micro-economic and sectoral growth and development. All sector-specific development policies were to be abolished in favor of sector-neutral policies. Significant savings were expected from the resources previously destined for direct or indirect economic subsidies.

- As an extension of the preceding point, the government's top priority was to stabilize the macroeconomy. Starting in 1988, the government made controlling inflation[3] (or relative prices) and the fiscal deficit and attracting foreign investment the main macroeconomic priorities in its liberalization strategy, backed by the Banco de México's restrictive monetary and credit policies.[4]

---

of some controls on foreign direct investment, and membership in the General Agreement on Tariffs and Trade (GATT). However, it was with the announcement of the first of a series of "economic pacts" in December 1987 that liberalization measures were presented as a new development path.

It is important to recall that liberalization's conceptual core is export-oriented industrialization. The model generally assumes that export growth is linked to economic growth and development, and that the private manufacturing sector—through exports—is an engine driving growth and development. For an in-depth analysis of the liberalization model, see Dussel Peters 1997.

[3] As Aspe Armella (1993) stresses, lowering inflation was the crucial variable given that high inflation rates, caused in general by domestic demand but particularly by the inertial tendencies of real wages, did not allow for improvements in the fiscal deficit during the 1982–1987 period.

[4] Controlling inflation and attracting investment were to finance the new strategy because other sources—petroleum revenues and extensive foreign credits—were either unavailable or insufficient.

- Nominal and real exchange rates are a result of controlling the rate of inflation ("the real exchange rate as an anti-inflationary anchor"). That is, because controlling inflation is the main macroeconomic priority under liberalization, the government will not permit devaluations, which push up inflation rates because they raise the costs of imported inputs.

- Supported by the reprivatization of the banking system beginning in the mid–1980s and the massive privatization of state-owned industries, the Mexican private sector was to lead the economy out of the "lost decade" of the 1980s through exports. The wholesale import liberalization process (initiated at the end of 1985) was supposed to support private manufacturers—who were losing the domestic market to cheaper imports—and orient them toward exports.

- Finally, government policies toward organized labor were of the utmost importance. As reflected in the economic stabilization pacts, only government-friendly labor unions were deemed sufficiently worthy to negotiate with private-sector firms and the government; other unions were marginalized. This process, which included harsh government attacks on politically independent labor unions, made national wage negotiations possible within the framework of successive economic pacts.

The Mexican government persisted in this liberalization strategy with few interruptions or exceptions.[5] The overall elimination of subsidies (culminating in early 1999 with the suspension of subsidies on tortillas and other basic commodities), public services, and credits reflects this process.

Industrial Policy since 1988

There are several reasons why the general context of economic liberalization is significant for industrial policy. First, Mexico's export-oriented manufacturing sector is viewed as the motor for this new development strategy. Its specific form of integration into global markets is, therefore, crucially important for the economy. Second, given inflation and

---

[5] Probably the most significant inconsistency in the liberalization strategy has been the government's bailout of the financial sector, at an estimated cost of about 20 percent of GDP in 1999. From the strict perspective of liberalization strategy, this massive public intervention ran contrary to the socioeconomic model implemented beginning in 1988.

fiscal deficit constraints, the government is not expected to provide supports that negatively affect these macroeconomic variables. Thus for the manufacturing sector, as for any sector, the government will prefer industrial policy instruments that do not involve direct expenditures. Third, controlling inflation will result in an overvaluation of the real exchange rate.[6] This is particularly significant for inter-industry trade, where an overvalued exchange rate will have a negative effect on exports. Finally, dependence upon foreign investments (both portfolio investment and FDI) is significant because, at least until 1994, Mexico attracted these funds by offering high real interest rates in U.S. dollars. Yet these rates carried great costs for the Mexican economy. Although they succeeded in attracting foreign investment, they generated negative incentives for domestic investment in Mexico.

Until the late 1970s, Mexico's industrial and foreign trade policies were strongly interlinked, and together they formed an important part of import-substitution industrialization. Developing the manufacturing sector was considered essential for Mexico's modernization, and foreign trade policy was understood to be a tool that could enhance import substitution and thus promote industrial self-sufficiency and economic independence in the long run. "Peaceful coexistence" with transnational corporations (TNCs) and an array of trade policy instruments — preferential exchange rates, import licenses, and price controls, which in many cases resulted in the prohibition of certain imports — were of crucial importance for supporting the private manufacturing sector. Direct government interventions in "strategic" industries were also key because they provided infrastructure and other vital inputs. Labor laws and Mexico's overall political stability were also important underpinnings of the relatively successful period of ISI growth that culminated in the late 1970s.

However, industrial and trade policies under ISI proved increasingly ineffective in both microeconomic and macroeconomic terms. This "truncated" industrialization was the result of the Mexican private manufacturing sector's inability to develop beyond the first stage of import-substitution industrialization. In the 1980s, after more than thirty years of government support, Mexico's domestic manufacturers were still significantly outperformed by transnational corporations in terms of profit rates, GDP growth, and labor productivity (Blomström and Wolff 1989; Maddison 1989). Nevertheless, it was the dynamic

---

[6] Independent of tight monetary and credit policies, the real exchange rate must be overvalued as a result of controlling the rate of inflation. Otherwise, depreciation of the real exchange rate will not allow for inflation control because Mexico's economy depends heavily upon imported goods.

TNC sector that produced most of the country's current account deficit, accounting for a minimum of 48.9 percent of the total trade deficit in various years between 1970 and 1980 (Peres 1990: 23ff.).[7] Thus the industrial structure that had evolved after the 1940s, producing impressive growth in labor and capital productivity, also created a substantial deficit in the balance of trade. The 1980–1981 trade deficit became one of the main sources of Mexico's current account deficit that threatened the country's ability to service its foreign debt (Dussel Peters 1997: 133ff.).

Industrial and trade policies after 1988 were designed to serve the objectives of liberalization, especially controlling the fiscal deficit and eliminating subsidies to permit a "market-friendly" allocation of resources. "Horizontal" policies—that is, policies that affect all firms and sectors equally and avoid preferences or subsidies—became the catchword among those who made industrial and trade policy.[8] Assuming that macroeconomic changes would induce microeconomic and structural transformations in manufacturing, the government's industrial and trade policies aimed to liberalize imports, achieve overall economic deregulation, and abolish price controls, subsidies, direct state ownership of firms, and preexisting sectoral programs.

Most notably, the government reduced average import tariffs to 11.8 percent (from 24.5 percent in 1986), and overall tariff levels fell dramatically. The privatization of state-owned companies generated revenues of US$30 billion, and by 1993 the number of state-owned enterprises had been reduced from 1,155 to just 217. The Salinas administration reformed the 1973 foreign investment law to make it substantially more flexible, granting automatic approval for majority foreign investment in activities not specifically reserved by the 1973 law for Mexican control and introducing a faster approval process for new investment projects. These amendments, in addition to other measures to promote foreign investment in Mexico, were formally incorporated into a new investment law in 1993 (Dussel Peters 1997; Máttar and Peres 1997).

Although such measures had been recasting the Mexican economy since 1988, the NAFTA brought significant changes, particularly for the

---

[7] The TNCs accounted for a high proportion of intra-industry trade, reflecting their specialization in sectors in which Mexico did not have traditional comparative advantages, such as electronic goods, automobiles, and auto parts (Ros 1991; Ruiz Durán, Dussel Peters, and Taniura 1997). These industries had been characterized since the 1970s by economies of scale and favorable access to the U.S. and world markets.

[8] For a detailed description of issues presented in this chapter, see Poder Ejecutivo Federal 1996.

manufacturing sector. First, the NAFTA commits its members to overall trade and investment deregulation, which for Mexico has meant continuing its liberalization strategy. By the year 2008, most goods that Mexico imports from the United States and Canada will enter duty free, providing a strong incentive to increase trade with its NAFTA partners. Second, the NAFTA requires its signatories to treat all firms and investors equally. That is, the Mexican government no longer has the discretionary power to implement policies that favor national firms with specific characteristics (such as geographic location, sector, size, degree of local content, and so on).

In the aftermath of Mexico's December 1994 financial crisis, the new Program for Industrial and Foreign Trade Policy (PROPICE) highlighted the need to achieve macroeconomic stabilization and make exports the engine of GDP and job growth.[9] PROPICE pointed to the challenges presented by globalization, import liberalization, and rising foreign investments, and it recognized that events like China's and India's integration into world markets held important implications for Mexico, in the form of an excess supply of labor-intensive products and a consequent negative impact on prospects for raising workers' wages in these sectors (Poder Ejecutivo Federal 1996: 15). Finally, the policy documents announcing PROPICE emphasized the need to generate productive linkages and to relocate geographically portions of the manufacturing sector in Mexico.

Several of the recommendations outlined in the PROPICE documents are worth highlighting:

- Exports will continue to constitute the basis for Mexico's future economic growth, making a positive contribution to productivity, employment, and income distribution. The export-promoting mechanisms established during 1988–1994, including those affecting the *maquiladora* (in-bond processing) sector and direct financial support for manufacturing, will be continued. The government will collaborate with private firms in selecting priority sectors and markets for promotion (Poder Ejecutivo Federal 1996: 141).

- There is a need to build production linkages and manufacturing clusters and to recover the domestic market, particularly through the promotion of micro, small, and medium-size firms (pp. 49ff).

---

[9] PROPICE 1995–2000 stressed that industrial and trade policies cannot "be accomplished successfully through the spontaneous action of market forces. Instead, they require an active industrial policy that generates the coordinating social mechanisms; collaboration; and support for individual actions through the concertation of the factors of production" (Poder Ejecutivo Federal 1996: 33).

Substitution of imports in sectors like electronics and automobiles could produce up to US$10 billion in savings.

- Regional perspectives on industrial promotion are important. For example, nonexporting regions could become suppliers of raw materials and consumption goods for cities and regions actively engaged in export production (p. 56).

- Business institutions and chambers of industry and commerce should be included as active participants in decision making regarding industrial policy, as well as in the implementation of such policies (p. 174).[10]

Since 1988, though, Mexico's liberalization strategy has at best given secondary importance to industrial and trade policy; indeed, for many government economic officials, the best industrial policy was none at all. Given that liberalization's core priority has been macroeconomic stabilization, Mexico's "new" trade and industrial policies were perfectly consistent with the overall goal of generating a market-friendly environment for the private export-oriented sector. Although some more focused programs were developed in response to the 1994-1995 financial crisis, most of them were set aside after 1996 as economic growth resumed.

Industrial Policy Instruments

Mexico's industrial policy since 1988 has, with few exceptions, been consistent with a strategy of economic liberalization. Traditional export-support programs have been eliminated and replaced by "self-financing" programs. The most important policy tools have been information services for production and marketing (especially of exports), along with programs to pair potential suppliers or exporters with international buyers (Dussel Peters 1997).[11] The elimination of price controls has been another important measure.[12] Moreover, after

---

[10] However, most of these proposals were sidelined when the economy began to recover in 1996, as reflected in rising GDP and booming exports.

[11] It must be remembered that Mexico's governmental institutions generally have not been strictly accountable to the public, and this extends to the policies and instruments that have been applied in manufacturing since the late 1980s, including the performance of Mexican development banks. Thus any evaluation of these mechanisms and instruments must be limited in nature until additional information becomes available.

[12] Some analysts argue that price controls "impose high costs on producers and limit competition through unjustifiably elevated prices; discriminate among eco-

1988 Mexico's established development banks—BANCOMEXT and NAFIN, which in preceding periods financed company-level and sectoral-level projects according to the industrial priorities and sectors identified as "strategic"—shifted to lending under market conditions (CEPAL 1992).[13] Local-content requirements for automobiles, auto parts, and electronics were being phased out gradually before 1994, and eventually they will be eliminated altogether under the NAFTA rules.[14]

Most of the industrial promotion programs in place in the late 1990s did not place a direct fiscal burden on the government. Instead, they sought to facilitate firms' access to inputs for products to be reexported, including the maquiladora program and the Program of Temporary Imports to Produce Export Goods (PITEX). The following is a listing of other programs that merit special mention:[15]

- The Program to Promote Industrial Clusters (Programa para Promover Agrupamientos Industriales), initiated by the Ministry of Commerce and Industrial Development (SECOFI) in 1998, was one of the most significant programs established after 1988. Based on a study of nine clusters in several Mexican states,[16] the program sought to promote a common vision among business, state governments, and the federal government, as well as to take advantage of local and regional specialization patterns and to strengthen linkages with other firms and sectors. This program generally did not include financing, but it did not prevent firms from participating in other programs.

---

nomic actors; discourage productivity; and result in an inefficient allocation of resources" (Martínez and Fárber 1994: 11). Also see Sánchez Ugarte, Fernández Pérez, and Pérez Motta 1994; SECOFI 1994.

[13] Between 1994 and 1998, Mexico's development banks reduced their staff by 34.4 percent and cut their lending by 4.2 percent (data obtained by the author from development banks; see also *El Financiero*, March 16, 1999, p. 3A).

[14] Interestingly, the several programs that remained in effect during 1988–1994 were directed to sectors dominated by transnational corporations, such as automobiles and computers.

[15] Most of the information on these programs was obtained directly from SECOFI and Nacional Financiera. Also see http://www.spice.gob.mx, http://www.centro-crece.org.mx, and http://www.nafin.gob.mx/desarrollo.html.

[16] These clusters included the garment industry (in Durango, Hidalgo, Jalisco, Oaxaca, and other states), seafood processing (Baja California Sur, Chiapas, and Sinaloa), the automobile and auto parts industries (Nuevo León and Aguascalientes), machine tools (San Luis Potosí), and construction materials (Chihuahua).

- Beginning in the mid–1990s, the network of Regional Centers for Business Competitiveness (CRECE) offered consulting support to micro, small, and midsize enterprises that were 100 percent Mexican owned, established in Mexico, and had at least two years in operation. CRECE's overall objective was to solve these firms' technical and organizational problems. It offered financial consulting that included an evaluation and overall diagnosis of the firm, as well as suggestions to increase competitiveness. Regional business chambers and SECOFI together provided the financing for CRECE. By June 1999, CRECE was established in all Mexican states and had provided support to more than 5,150 small and midsize firms — an average of about 160 firms per state. These firms increased their income by 33 percent on average, preserved some 20,000 jobs, and created almost 2,000 new jobs.

- The National Committee for Productivity and Technological Innovation (COMPITE) was created in 1996. It offered specialized courses for manufacturers, of which the firm paid half the cost (about US$1,500 in 1999). By 1999, COMPITE had conducted more than 800 of these courses — on just-in-time inventory, inventory optimization, new equipment, and space- and cost-saving measures. In some cases, firms participating in the program increased their productivity by over 100 percent.

- The Program for Subcontractor Development (Programa de Desarrollo de Proveedores), established in March 1999 by SECOFI and NAFIN, was one of Mexico's most important new industrial programs. To speed the development of forward and backward value-added linkages, this program provided quick working capital for subcontracting firms. NAFIN also provided automatic guarantees for commercial banks as well as direct loans for demonstration processes or products.[17] The program initially offered these options to firms subcontracting to the government. Forty-three such agreements were signed in 1999–2000.

STRUCTURAL CHANGES IN MEXICO'S MANUFACTURING SECTOR

Mexico's macroeconomic and industrial policies since 1988 have accorded particular importance to export promotion for all economic units (firms, regions, and the country as a whole). The following sections analyze the performance of Mexico's manufacturing industry from

---

[17] These loans were limited to 50 percent of the value of the contract or approximately US$650,000.

FIGURE 7.1. Exports of Goods and Services as a Proportion of Mexico's Gross Domestic Product, 1980–2000

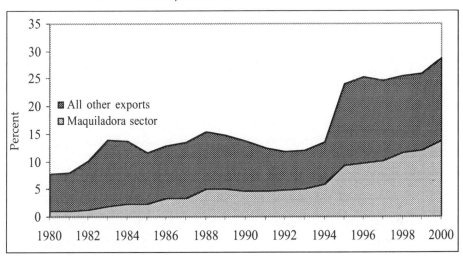

Source: Author's calculations based on INEGI data (www.inegi.gob.mx).

this perspective, with a special focus on exporting sectors. The first of the following subsections examines general trends in Mexican manufacturing, and their relevance for macroeconomic evolution; sectoral and firm-level data reflect some of these trends. The second subsection describes key characteristics of Mexico's export-oriented subsectors.

General Trends, 1988–2000

Since 1988, exports have been the leading—indeed, practically the only—component of Mexico's economic growth. GDP rose at an annual average inflation-adjusted rate of 3.6 percent from 1988 to 2000; exports increased at an average annual rate of 15.1 percent over the same period. Moreover, exports as a share of GDP have increased substantially since 1988, from less than 20 percent in the 1980s to over 25 percent since 1995 (see figure 7.1). This contrasts with domestic demand,[18] which has remained relatively flat or increased only moderately since 1994 (see figure 7. 2).

Mexico's export performance as a result of liberalization should be viewed from at least two different perspectives: firms' performance acc-

---

[18] Domestic demand was calculated as the coefficient of GDP minus exports and imports.

FIGURE 7.2. Index of Mexico's Exports and Domestic Demand,
1988–2000 (1988=100)

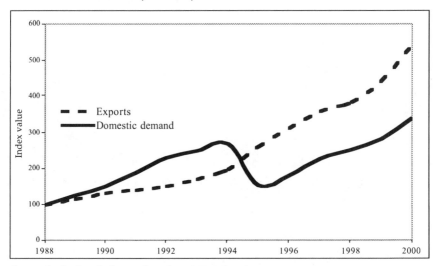

Source: Author's calculations based on INEGI data (www.inegi.gob.mx).

ording to their size, and aggregated firm-level data. Data from the
Mexican Social Security Institute (IMSS) concerning employment in
micro, small, midsize, and large manufacturing firms permit us to draw
some preliminary conclusions regarding the impact of liberalization
policy (see tables 7.1 and 7.2).[19]

- Micro, small, and midsize firms accounted for 97.9 percent of all
  manufacturing firms in operation during the period 1988–1998.

---

[19] IMSS data have several advantages (and limitations) vis-à-vis those from other
sources. By definition, IMSS–affiliated workers include both independent workers
and those employed under a collective contract. IMSS employment data allow for
comparisons of changes in employment patterns since 1980 at the regional and
national levels, and they can be disaggregated into employment in micro, small,
midsize, and large firms and then correlated with the number of firms. However,
IMSS figures only include a fraction of total employment. Whereas INEGI's figure
for total employment in 1996 was 28.3 million (INEGI 1999), the IMSS figure was
11.3 million, covering only Mexico's "most formal" labor market. Nevertheless,
these differences largely disappear for manufacturing, where INEGI counted 3.3
million employed in 1996, versus 3.4 million according to the IMSS.
    The 1988–1998 IMSS classifications of micro, small, midsize, and large firms
appear as notes in tables 7.1 and 7.2. In March 1999, IMSS revised the classification as follows: micro firms, 1–30 workers; small firms, 31–100 employees; midsize firms, 101–500 workers; large firms, more than 500 employees.

- In general, employment rose at an annual average of 3.6 percent in 1988–1998, significantly below the annual growth rate of Mexico's economically active population, which has been above 5 percent since 1988 (Dussel Peters 2000).

- Large firms accounted for significantly more job creation than micro, small, and midsize firms. During the 1988–1998 period, employment in large firms rose at an average annual rate of 4.9 percent, more than twice the 2.0 percent found in micro, small, and midsize firms.

- As a result, the share of total employment corresponding to micro, small, and midsize firms fell from 49.8 percent in 1988 and 51.0 percent in 1992 to 42.8 percent in 1998. This dramatic shift in employment patterns reflects the difficulties that liberalization has posed for smaller firms.

- On the other hand, large firms (which numbered 3,165, or 2.5 percent of total manufacturing establishments, in 1998) accounted for 57.2 percent of total employment in 1998, some seven percentage points above 1988 levels.

- Even in terms of the creation of new business establishments, large firms outperformed micro, small, and midsize firms, with an average annual growth rate of 4.2 percent over the 1988–1998 period.

An examination of the structure and dynamics of Mexico's leading exporters — most of them manufacturing firms, including maquiladora plants — for 1993–1999 reveals the following (see tables 7.3 and 7.4):

- Mexican exports are highly concentrated. During the 1993–1999 period, between 264 and 302 firms accounted for 93.1 percent of total exports.

- The maquiladoras' share of exports has increased importantly. Maquiladora exports for the period increased by 17.5 percent annually and accounted for 46.7 percent of all exports in 1999.

- Majority-foreign-owned manufacturing firms represented the most dynamic part of the export sector. They increased their share of total exports from 14.4 percent in 1993 to 16.9 percent in 1999. In contrast, the leading domestic firms' share of total exports dropped from 35.8 percent in 1993 to 25.3 percent in 1999.[20]

---

[20] Falling petroleum prices accounted for part of this decline during the 1997-1999 period.

TABLE 7.1. Business Establishments and Employment, by Firm Size, in Mexico's Manufacturing Sector, 1988–1998 (percentage of total)

	1988	1989	1990	1991	1992	1993	1994	1995	1996	1997	1998	1988–1998 average
Business Establishments												
Micro	77.1	77.4	78.5	79.3	79.9	80.5	80.6	81.2	79.9	79.4	78.8	79.4
Small	17.8	17.4	16.7	16.1	15.7	15.1	14.8	14.2	15.0	15.3	15.6	15.7
Midsize	3.0	3.0	2.8	2.7	2.6	2.6	2.7	2.7	2.9	2.9	3.0	2.8
Subtotal	97.9	97.8	98.0	98.1	98.1	98.2	98.1	98.0	97.8	97.6	97.5	97.9
Large	2.1	2.2	2.0	1.9	1.9	1.8	1.9	2.0	2.2	2.4	2.5	2.1
Total	100.0	100.0	100.0	100.0	100.0	100.0	100.0	100.0	100.0	100.0	100.0	100.0
Employment												
Micro	11.0	10.9	11.8	12.2	12.7	12.8	12.2	11.9	10.9	10.4	9.9	11.5
Small	23.0	22.2	22.6	22.4	22.7	22.2	20.9	19.9	19.1	18.7	18.2	21.0
Midsize	15.8	16.1	15.7	15.6	15.6	15.7	15.7	15.6	15.3	14.8	14.7	15.5
Subtotal	49.8	49.3	50.0	50.2	51.0	50.8	48.9	47.4	45.4	48.3	42.8	47.9
Large	50.2	50.7	50.0	49.8	49.0	49.2	51.1	52.6	54.6	56.2	57.2	52.1
Total	100.0	100.0	100.0	100.0	100.0	100.0	100.0	100.0	100.0	100.0	100.0	100.0

Source: Author's calculations based on Instituto Mexicano del Seguro Social (IMSS) data.

Note: In the IMSS classification, micro firms are defined as those employing between 1 and 15 workers; small firms, 16 to 100 employees; midsize firms, 101 to 250 workers; large firms, more than 250 employees.

TABLE 7.2. Annual Growth Rate in Business Establishments and Employment in Mexico's Manufacturing Sector, 1988–1998[1]

	1988	1989	1990	1991	1992	1993	1994	1995	1996	1997	1998	1988–1998 average
Business Establishments												
Micro	—	6.3	13.8	7.7	1.8	-2.1	-1.3	-4.9	0.4	4.1	2.6	2.7
Small	—	3.5	7.7	3.0	-1.9	-6.3	-3.0	-9.9	7.8	6.9	5.9	1.2
Midsize	—	9.1	1.8	3.0	-2.0	-4.0	2.1	-5.6	10.9	5.8	7.9	2.8
Subtotal	—	5.9	12.3	6.8	1.1	-2.9	-1.5	-5.7	1.8	4.6	3.3	2.5
Large	—	8.3	4.7	1.7	-2.5	-4.1	3.4	-2.6	15.1	11.6	7.9	4.2
Total	—	5.9	12.2	6.7	1.0	-2.9	-1.4	-5.6	2.0	4.8	3.4	2.5
Employment												
Micro	—	6.7	13.6	7.3	0.8	-3.3	-2.0	-7.4	2.7	4.7	3.5	2.5
Small	—	4.0	6.7	2.6	-2.1	-6.0	-3.2	-9.4	7.7	7.6	5.9	1.2
Midsize	—	9.2	2.3	2.4	-2.7	-3.4	2.7	-5.4	9.9	6.2	8.6	2.8
Subtotal	—	6.2	6.8	3.6	-1.6	-4.5	-1.1	-7.6	7.2	6.4	6.2	2.0
Large	—	8.4	3.8	2.5	-4.5	-3.6	6.7	-2.1	16.4	13.3	10.7	4.9
Total	—	7.3	5.3	3.1	-3.0	-4.1	2.7	-4.8	12.0	10.2	8.7	3.6

Source: Author's calculations based on Instituto Mexicano del Seguro Social (IMSS) data.

Note: In the IMSS classification, micro firms are defined as those employing between 1 and 15 workers; small firms, 16 to 100 employees; midsize firms, 101 to 250 workers; large firms, more than 250 employees.

[1] Percent change on preceding year.

TABLE 7.3. Aggregate Sales and Employment in Mexico's Export Sector, 1993–1999 (millions of current U.S. dollars and thousands employed)

	1993	1994	1995	1996	1997	1998	1999	1993–1999 average
Maquiladora sector								
Exports	21,853	26,269	31,103	36,920	45,166	53,083	63,749	39,735
Employment	547	601	681	799	938	1,039	1,197	829
Principal exporting firms[1]								
Exports	26,008	32,011	44,811	56,795	56,976	55,121	57,657	47,054
Employment	1,002	994	1,243	1,348	1,276	1,391	1,440	1,242
Foreign[2]								
Exports	7,452	10,084	12,878	20,308	22,310	22,761	23,091	16,983
Employment	147	169	216	239	227	200	155	193
National[3]								
Exports	18,556	21,927	31,933	36,487	34,667	32,360	34,566	30,071
Employment	855	825	1,027	1,110	1,049	1,191	1,285	1,049
Total exports	51,886	60,882	79,542	96,000	110,431	117,460	136,391	93,227
Total employment[4]	32,534	33,208	33,881	35,226	37,360	38,618	39,069	35,699

Sources: Author's calculations based on Banco de México 1999, *Expansión* (several years), Poder Ejecutivo Federal 1999, and Dussel Peters 2000.

[1] The number of firms in this category varied from year to year, ranging from 264 (1993) to 312 (1996) and averaging 293 for the 1993–1999 period.

[2] Firms with majority foreign capital. The number of firms in this category varied from year to year, ranging from 54 (1993 and 1994) to 78 (1995) and averaging 66 for the 1993–1999 period.

[3] Firms with majority national capital. The number of firms in this category varied from year to year, ranging from 210 (1993) to 246 (1996) and averaging 226 for the 1993–1999 period.

[4] Total employed population, as defined in Poder Ejecutivo Federal 1999. Data for 1994 are the author's estimates based on this source.

TABLE 7.4. Export Sales and Employment as a Proportion of Mexico's Total Export Activity, 1993-1999 (percentages)[1]

	1993	1994	1995	1996	1997	1998	1999	1993–1999 average
Maquiladora sector								
Exports	42.1	43.2	39.1	38.5	40.9	45.2	46.7	42.6
Employment	1.7	1.8	2.0	2.3	2.5	2.7	3.1	2.3
Principal exporting firms[2]								
Exports	50.1	52.6	56.3	59.2	51.6	46.9	42.3	50.5
Employment	3.1	3.0	3.7	3.8	3.4	3.6	3.7	3.5
Foreign[3]								
Exports	14.4	16.6	16.2	21.2	20.2	19.4	16.9	18.2
Employment	0.4	0.5	0.6	0.7	0.6	0.5	0.4	0.5
National[4]								
Exports	35.8	36.0	40.2	38.0	31.4	27.6	25.3	32.3
Employment	2.6	2.5	3.0	3.2	2.8	3.1	3.3	2.9

Sources: Author's calculations based on Banco de México 1999, *Expansión* (several years), Poder Ejecutivo Federal 1999, and Dussel Peters 2000.

[1] Percentages calculated on the basis of totals reported in table 7.3. These values do not add to 100.0 percent because not all exports or employment were accounted for by *maquiladora* (in-bond processing) firms or the principal exporting firms identified by *Expansión*.

[2] The number of firms in this category varied from year to year, ranging from 264 (1993) to 312 (1996) and averaging 293 for the 1993–1999 period.

[3] Firms with majority foreign capital. The number of firms in this category varied from year to year, ranging from 54 (1993 and 1994) to 78 (1995) and averaging 66 for the 1993–1999 period.

[4] Firms with majority national capital. The number of firms in this category varied from year to year, ranging from 210 (1993) to 246 (1996) and averaging 226 for the 1993–1999 period.

TABLE 7.5. Evolution of Mexico's Manufacturing Sector, 1988–2000

	1988	1989	1990	1991	1992	1993	1994	1995	1996	1997	1998	1999	2000
Growth rate of manufacturing product[1]	3.5	7.9	6.8	3.4	4.2	-0.7	4.1	-4.9	10.8	9.9	7.4	4.2	7.1
Manufacturing product as share of gross domestic product (GDP) (percent)	22.1	20.2	19.1	18.9	18.5	17.5	17.2	19.0	19.6	19.4	19.5	19.3	19.3
Growth rate of manufacturing employment[1]	NA	4.4	3.4	1.0	2.2	-2.1	-2.1	-5.3	6.9	8.8	5.8	3.7	3.0
Manufacturing employment as share of total employment (percent)	12.6	12.8	12.6	12.4	12.4	12.0	11.5	11.2	11.6	12.2	12.3	12.4	135.0
Index of manufacturing labor productivity[2]	100.0	103.4	106.7	109.3	111.4	113.0	120.2	120.7	125.1	126.4	128.3	129.0	135.0
Comparative index of manufacturing labor productivity[3]	100.0	101.3	101.5	102.8	104.8	105.6	107.6	104.0	105.7	108.8	109.4	110.8	115.0

	1988	1989	1990	1991	1992	1993	1994	1995	1996	1997	1998	1999	2000
Index of manufacturing capital productivity[2]	100.0	111.1	124.0	127.5	129.5	120.4	116.7	105.5	115.0	NA	NA	NA	NA
Comparative index of manufacturing capital productivity[3]	43.2	46.0	48.6	49.8	50.8	48.1	46.4	46.2	49.5	NA	NA	NA	NA
Growth rate of manufactured exports[1]	17.7	6.7	13.5	117.4	12.0	17.5	20.2	31.9	20.2	18.0	11.5	15.3	18.3
Manufactured exports as share of total exports (percent)	59.7	57.3	55.4	75.7	78.3	81.9	83.9	84.7	84.4	86.5	90.7	90.0	87.3
Index of manufactured exports[2]	100.0	106.7	121.1	263.3	294.8	346.4	416.3	549.2	660.4	779.0	868.5	1,001.1	1,184.1
Growth rate of imports[1]	52.9	26.0	24.9	64.7	24.0	5.7	20.9	-9.3	20.2	25.2	14.6	14.4	24.0

TABLE 7.5 continued

	1988	1989	1990	1991	1992	1993	1994	1995	1996	1997	1998	1999	2000
Manufactured imports as share of total imports (percent)	89.4	89.8	91.2	94.0	93.7	94.2	93.8	93.2	90.7	92.5	92.9	93.8	94.7
Index of manufactured imports[2]	100.0	126.0	157.4	259.2	321.4	339.8	410.7	372.5	447.8	560.6	642.6	735.0	911.5
Trade balance (million US$)	-5,852	-9,740	-13,662	-14,660	-22,066	-19,068	-23,350	-117	-124	-6,023	-9,881	-10,363	-19,889
Trade balance as share of GDP (percent)	-14.0	-21.2	-25.0	-23.8	-32.0	-26.3	-30.4	-0.2	-0.2	-7.2	-11.2	-10.7	-17.9

Sources: Author's calculations based on Instituto Nacional de Estadística, Geografía e Informática (INEGI, www.inegi.gov.mx) and Banco de México data (www.banxico.mx). All trade data were calculated in U.S. dollars, based on the peso/dollar exchange rate published by the Banco de México. After 1991, trade data include *maquiladora* (in-bond processing) activities. Data for the year 2000 on the growth rate of manufacturing employment and manufacturing employment as a percentage of total employment are the author's estimates.

Note: The data in this table include information concerning the *maquiladora* (in-bond processing) industry. However, trade data include maquiladora activities only beginning in 1991.

[1] Percent change on preceding year.

[2] 1988 equals 100.

[3] Average productivity in the economy as a whole equals 100.

NA = Not available

- Despite earlier trends, major exporting firms and maquiladoras accounted for only 5.8 percent of total employment on average from 1993 to 1999. In fact, one of the most striking features of Mexico's export sector is its inability to absorb the country's growing economically active population. For the 1993–1999 period, the main exporting firms and maquiladoras accounted for only 16.7 percent of new employment growth. Even more striking, the leading majority-foreign-owned exporting firms accounted for only 0.5 percent on average of total employment during 1993–1999.

For Mexico's manufacturing sector more generally, the period since 1988 has been characterized by the following trends (also see table 7.5):

- GDP growth in manufacturing fluctuated markedly between 1988 and 2000, averaging 4.3 percent annually (compared to 3.4 percent for the economy as a whole). As a result, manufacturing's share of total GDP increased slightly over the period, remaining at around 19 percent of total GDP since 1995.

- Manufacturing employment as a share of total employment fell slightly, from 12.6 percent in 1988 to 12.4 percent in 1999. This trend reflected the sector's relatively high capital intensity, but it also demonstrated its limited capacity to generate jobs.

- In terms of productivity, manufacturing outperformed the rest of the economy. Labor productivity increased by 35.0 percent over the 1988-2000 period, rising at a higher annual rate than labor productivity in the economy as a whole.

- The manufacturing sector performed most successfully in terms of exports. Including maquiladora activities, manufacturing's share of total exports increased from 59.7 percent in 1988 to 87.3 percent in 2000.

- However, despite GDP and export growth, manufacturing has not been able to overcome its most severe structural limitation since the ISI period: a persistent trade deficit. Although exports have expanded, so have imports, resulting in a high, increasing, and unsustainable trade deficit. Indeed, Mexico's trade deficit rose from US$6.3 billion in 1988 to US$32.6 billion in 1994. It began dropping in 1995 as a result of the country's severe economic crisis, but with macroeconomic recovery in 1996, the trade deficit in manufacturing resumed its sharp upward pattern. Because the trade deficit has no automatic financing mechanism, these deficits must be financed either by achieving a trade surplus in other sectors (petroleum, agriculture, tourism or other services, and so on) or by attracting foreign investment through high real interest rates.

- Independent of the absolute value of the manufacturing trade deficit, it is important to relate the trade deficit to manufacturing GDP—that is, as a coefficient that reflects the penetration of net imports in the manufacturing sector. For the manufacturing sector as a whole, the trade balance (exports less imports)/GDP coefficient rose from –14.0 percent in 1988 to –30.4 percent in 1994 (that is, net imports increased very rapidly). Import penetration in the 1990s reached levels not seen in Mexico since the 1960s.

Trends in Manufacturing Subsectors

Mexico's national accounting system divides the manufacturing sector into forty-nine branches, not including maquiladoras (INEGI 1999). For the purposes of this analysis, these subsectors were classified in three groups according to their export performance during the 1988–1996 period, and these groups were further subdivided according to their GDP performance over this period. Six subsectors (group I.A in table 7.6) are the leaders within both Mexico's manufacturing sector and the economy as a whole. The main characteristics of these manufacturing subsectors are:

- With the exception of soft drinks and flavorings, the subsectors in group I.A—particularly automobiles, electronic equipment, and machinery and electrical equipment—are strongly influenced by transnational corporations and foreign firms.

- Subsectors in groups I and I.A markedly increased their share of total GDP over the 1988–1996 period. Indeed, group I.A's share of manufacturing GDP rose from 10.6 percent in 1988 to 18.3 percent in 1996. This trend was driven by the automobile and electronic equipment sectors, whose annual average rates of GDP growth were 12.8 percent and 9.8 percent, respectively.

- As noted earlier, export-oriented subsectors generate much less employment than might be expected given their export and GDP performance. The subsectors in group I, which represented 37.7 percent of manufacturing employment in 1996, increased their share by less than 2 percent over the preceding eight years. However, subsectors such as those in group III.A did better, increasing their employment share from 14.0 percent in 1988 to 17.0 percent in 1996, mainly as a result of job creation in automotive engines and auto parts, fruits and vegetables, and other food products. Yet the automotive sector as a whole generated only 1.3 percent of manufacturing employment during 1988–1996 and 0.1 percent of total employment during this period.

- Trends in real wages in export-oriented subsectors are striking. Real wages for the subsectors in group I, particularly those in group I.B, were the lowest in all of Mexico's manufacturing sector. Even the automotive sector, which had the highest real wages in manufacturing after basic petrochemicals, fell from an index value of 246.3 percent in 1988 (100 = average real wages in the manufacturing sector as a whole) to 188.8 in 1996. In contrast, the subsectors in groups III and III.B (that is, those with the lowest export levels and GDP growth) had the highest real wages for the period. Although further analysis is needed, these data demonstrate that there is no automatic, positive association between export-oriented activities and real wages. Instead, these wage trends paralleled the pattern of dramatically falling wages throughout the period.[21]

- As a result of trends in GDP and employment, the most dynamic groups in terms of GDP and exports have increased capital and labor productivity substantially. Nevertheless, capital productivity fell after 1991 for subsectors in group I, dropping in 1996 to a level below that for manufacturing overall and for the other groups included in this analysis.[22] Labor productivity, on the other hand, showed impressive growth for manufacturing as a whole and for each of the groups examined here.[23] Most notable in 1996 were groups I and I.A, with labor productivity levels 30.0 percent and 49.1 percent, respectively, above 1988. Iron and steel and the automotive sector led the rise in labor productivity.

- Manufacturing-sector exports (excluding maquiladoras) increased by 92.9 percent from 1988 to 1996, and groups I and I.A increased their share significantly, from 23.6 percent and 18.6 percent, respectively, of all exports in 1988 to 49.1 percent and 41.0 percent in 1996. The automotive sector alone increased its share from 11.3 percent of manufacturing exports to 29.6 percent over the 1988–1996 period. Although all these groups increased exports by at least 30 percent, none compared with the dynamism of groups I and I.A, particularly the automotive sector.

---

[21] The minimum wage in 1998 was less than 30 percent of its 1980 value, and the average real wage in 1998 was at less than 60 percent of its 1980 value (Dussel Peters 2000).

[22] Capital productivity was measured as net capital stock over GDP. The author obtained data for net capital stock from the Banco de México.

[23] Labor productivity was measured as GDP over employment.

TABLE 7.6. Typology of Mexico's Manufacturing Sector by Growth Rate of Exports, 1988–1996[1]

	Annual Average Growth of Exports (percent)	Annual Average Growth of GDP (percent)
Group I	25.2	5.1
Group I.A	25.6	8.5
Automobiles	27.3	12.8
Electronic equipment	22.9	9.8
Other textile products	23.2	6.4
Household appliances	24.2	6.0
Machinery and electrical equipment	21.8	5.6
Soft drinks and flavorings	21.1	4.4
Group I.B	23.0	2.2
Apparel	21.3	3.9
Soaps, detergents, cosmetics	20.7	3.4
Fats and oils	23.6	2.5
Milled corn	21.3	1.8
Non-electrical machinery	21.2	1.8
Other transportation equipment	21.1	1.3
Milled wheat	23.5	1.1
Pesticides and fertilizers	36.4	0.3
Metal furniture	36.1	-0.1
Animal feeds	28.5	-0.4
Group II	14.4	3.2
Group II.A	15.2	5.2
Steel and iron	16.0	6.0
Other manufactured goods[2]	15.4	5.6
Glass and glass products	10.2	5.2
Meat and milk products	16.8	5.1
Other metal products	16.7	4.2
Group II.B	13.8	1.6
Other chemicals	14.4	3.3
Plastic products	10.5	3.2
Basic inorganic chemicals	13.0	3.0
Basic petrochemicals	12.0	2.4
Electrical equipment	15.5	2.3
Ceramics	15.5	2.3
Tobacco	18.0	1.3
Leather and footwear	12.7	0.8
Cotton, wool, and synthetic textiles	12.4	-1.4
Lumber and plywood	10.5	-3.5

TABLE 7.6 continued

	Annual Average Growth of Exports (percent)	Annual Average Growth of GDP (percent)
Group III	4.8	3.4
Group III.A	3.4	4.8
Fruits and vegetables	9.0	7.3
Other food products	6.5	5.1
Beer and malt	5.8	5.0
Automotive engines and autoparts	3.0	4.4
Paper and paperboard	0.9	4.4
Sugar	-4.9	4.1
Group III.B	6.7	2.1
Medicinal products	9.0	3.8
Plastic resins, synthetic fiber	9.3	3.6
Cement	4.2	2.4
Alcoholic beverages	7.6	2.3
Other wood products	4.3	2.0
Structural metal products	8.8	1.8
Rubber products	8.7	1.7
Non-ferrous metals	8.2	1.6
Coffee	6.2	1.6
Jute, rough textiles	-3.6	1.6
Refined petroleum	3.8	1.3
Printing	3.3	0.7
Agriculture	5.4	1.9
Mining	0.9	1.9
Manufacturing	14.4	3.9
Total economy	13.4	2.7

Source: Author's calculations based on Instituto Nacional de Estadística, Geografía e Informática (INEGI) data.

[1] Average annual growth rate for the 1988–1996 period. *Maquiladora* (in-bond processing) activities are not included.

[2] This category includes such products as jewelry, musical instruments, weight-lifting and other sports equipment, office and drawing accessories, toys, and brooms and brushes.

- Just as noteworthy as the dynamism of exports was that of imports. For the manufacturing sector as a whole, imports increased by 179.4 percent from 1988 to 1994 and then declined following the 1994–1995 economic crisis. Although the import share of group I increased by only 1.6 percent over 1988–1996, the figure for the six subsectors in group I.A was 3.6 percent. Sectors such as soft drinks and flavorings, textiles, and automobiles increased their imports by more than 350 percent over this period.

- As a result of earlier trade trends, Mexico's manufacturing sector amassed a trade deficit of US$161 billion for the entire 1988–1996 period. For most groups (with the exception of group I.A for certain years) and for manufacturing in general, the trade deficit increased sharply from 1988 to 1994, fell during the 1994–1995 crisis, and then rose once again after the economy regained momentum. Groups II.A and III.A contributed more to the trade deficit than did the B groups.[24] These patterns reappeared in the trade balance/ GDP coefficient, demonstrating the dramatic structural changes that occurred in the subsectors in groups I and I.A. These subsectors generated a significant surplus after 1995 while, with few exceptions, the other groups generated a deficit. Thus, excepting group I, all subsectors significantly increased their coefficient during the 1988–1996 period.

REGIONAL TRENDS

The polarization of the Mexican economy that has occurred among companies and subsectors has also taken place at the regional level since the adoption of economic liberalization policies. In the context of liberalizing the flows of capital, goods, and services, two features of globalization merit special note in the Mexican case. One is the emergence since the 1980s of global commodity chains, a worldwide trend in which transnational corporations (but not only transnationals) have come to depend increasingly upon the international organization of inputs, production, and distribution. Global commodity chains have become a leading mechanism for maximizing flexible production processes, increasing quality, implementing just-in-time strategies, reducing inventories, and integrating production operations with problem-

---

[24] With the exception of the automobile industry, no branch of Mexican manufacturing generated a significant trade surplus during the 1988–1996 period. The automobile industry had a surplus of US$39.6 billion for the period, but if we include engines and auto parts (which import most of the inputs for the automotive sector), the trade surplus fell to US$3 billion for 1988–1996.

solving and benchmarking approaches (Dussel Peters 1999; Gereffi 1994). Thanks to global commodity chains, firms are much freer in deciding where to locate their operations and facilities, and they can avoid duplicating their efforts in several regions or countries.

On the other hand, flexible production has brought important changes in industrial organization. Fordism has been replaced by a tendency to transform products and services in an increasingly diversified manner. Diversified demand requires significant changes in industrial organization, including an abbreviated production cycle, "lean production," just-in-time inventory management, and the ability to change supplier and production systems to meet demand (Dussel Peters, Piore, and Ruiz Durán 1997).

Global commodity chains and flexible production are extremely important from an international perspective because networks, not firms, are increasingly the competitors in world markets (Borrus and Zysman 1998). In a context of greater national liberalization of goods, capital, and services, global commodity chains and flexible production can generate strong but geographically contained regional- and local-level impacts. For example, were IBM to increase its investments for producing liquid-crystal displays at its El Salto, Jalisco, plant, this would have minimal impact, if any, in Chiapas. In like manner, policy challenges also appear at the local and regional levels. Thus a single national industrial policy will have little effect on most regions given their increasing differentiation as a result of global commodity chains and flexible production.[25]

What, then, has been the impact of liberalization on Mexico's regions? Ruiz Durán (1997, 1999) argues that since 1988 Mexico's states have experienced different degrees of economic concentration and have been exposed to different types of state intervention and foreign investment (oriented to the domestic market, exports, and maquiladoras).[26] For the 1980–1993 period, the foreign investment model (characterized by a high degree of industrialization and higher GDP growth in the manufacturing sector) was far more dynamic than other models. Other studies (Dávila Flores 1998, among others) have found that, based on specialization coefficients of employment, Mexico's states were characterized by a process of relative convergence in terms of GDP growth during 1980–1993, although variability coefficients were very high. The performance of micro, small, and midsize firms particularly varied across states. Although some of these firms were able to

---

[25] The same holds for policies concerning education, poverty reduction, technological development, and so on.

[26] See also Mungaray 1998.

FIGURE 7.3. Gross Domestic Product per Capita for Selected
Mexican States, 1970–1996 (Federal District = 100)

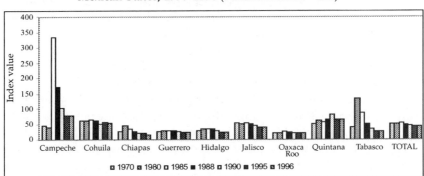

Sources: Author's estimates based on Poder Ejecutivo Federal 1999; author's estimates for
population (1985, 1988) and gross domestic product (1990).

enter the supplier networks of large exporting firms, most still lacked
financial and technological support, and they suffered from an overall
lack of coordination among federal programs and mechanisms (Kuri
Gaytán, Pacheco Ibarra, and Noriega Valdez 1999). Finally, there is an
increasing consensus that economic and social disparities and polarization have increased at the regional level since 1988 (Asuad Sanén 2000;
Ruiz Durán 1999).

Data for the 1970–1996 period on regional GDP, employment, and
GDP per capita depict several important trends in this regard (INEGI
1999; Poder Ejecutivo Federal 1999).[27] First, the share of GDP accounted
for by the four leading states — the Federal District, the State of México,
Nuevo León, and Jalisco — fell significantly between 1970 and 1985,
from 49.2 to 44.7 percent. Yet since 1988 these four states — along with
the northern border states of Baja California, Coahuila, Chihuahua, Sonora, and Tamaulipas, all of which have very significant maquiladora
and export activities (Mendiola 1997) — have increased their share of
total GDP substantially (see figure 7.3). Second, other states (Campeche
and Tabasco) showed strong economic fluctuations over the 1970–1996
period, resulting primarily from the petroleum boom of the 1980s and
the activities of Mexico's state-owned oil company, Petróleos Mexicanos (PEMEX). Meanwhile, Quintana Roo was able to increase its
share of national GDP from 0.2 percent in 1970 to 1.2 percent in 1996,
mainly as a result of tourism. Third, during the 1970–1988 period, the

---

[27] Unfortunately, there are no homogeneous data available on regional GDP before
1999. INEGI and Poder Ejecutivo Federal have published data on GDP in current
pesos, but one cannot calculate growth rates for the earlier period.

Mexico City area—Mexico's economic and political center—lost its primacy of place in terms of GDP per capita to the northern border states, to petroleum-producing states, and to Quintana Roo, though it has recovered its position since 1988.

Polarization at the regional level is particularly significant for states like Chiapas, Guerrero, and Oaxaca, where per capita GDP levels have declined since 1988 and were 20 percent below those for Mexico City in 1996. In Chiapas, for example, GDP per capita declined from an index value of 25.5 in 1988 to 18.4 in 1995 and 17.5 in 1996, when measured against the comparable figures for the Mexico City area (Federal District = 100).

These data suggest an increasing North–South polarization in Mexico. Whereas the country's traditional economic and political centers (the Mexico City area, the State of México, Jalisco, and Nuevo León) and states with strong export and maquiladora activities have increased their share of total GDP, states south of Mexico City have been excluded from regional and global integration. This territorial polarization in the distribution of the benefits of liberalization could have serious economic, social, and political implications for Mexico in the future.

CONCLUSION

Trends in Mexico's manufacturing sector reflect impressive structural change within a small group of firms—transnational corporations, maquiladoras, and large Mexican industrial groups (Garrido 1998)—that have been able to integrate into global markets through exports and that display a high degree of intrafirm and intra-industry trade (León González Pacheco 1999). As one might have anticipated under liberalization, they have also increased their overall productivity and promoted GDP growth as a result of increased exports. Several of these success stories have been studied in depth, including the automobile and auto parts industries (Carrillo and González López 1998; CEPAL 1998; Ruiz Durán, Dussel Peters, and Taniura 1997), the electronics industry (Dussel Peters 1998; Mortimore 1999), and the apparel industry (Gereffi and Bair 1998). *Expansión*'s 1998 phrase—"*Exporto, luego existo*" ("I export, therefore I am") is certainly a reality for a small number of firms, sectors, and regions.

Unfortunately, however, most government and academic sources overstate the importance of export-oriented activities, while paying relatively little attention to the remainder of the Mexican economy. Exports are clearly important. Nevertheless, it is also true that exporting firms are generally characterized by low levels of job creation. One of the most striking features of Mexico's liberalization experience is the manufacturing sector's inability to generate endogenous growth conditions, as reflected in the balance of trade/GDP coefficient. This has led to increasing polarization in the Mexican economy, particularly in its manufacturing sector. The lack of integration has meant that benefits from liberalization have accrued to only a small number of firms, sectors, and regions—a fact that is reflected in the increasing disparity between domestic demand and export growth.

The export sector's overall inability to generate linkages with the rest of the economy—in terms of employment, learning processes, and technological innovation, among many other aspects—creates unsustainable macroeconomic conditions in the medium and long term. As soon as the economy (particularly manufacturing) grows in terms of GDP and exports, it requires larger quantities of imports for capital accumulation. This cycle has operated since 1988, and it helped produce the 1994–1995 crisis. Imports fell as a result of the crisis, but they surged again as soon as the economy recovered.

The industrial organization that has emerged since Mexico liberalized its economy has proven to be macroeconomically unsustainable. Economic polarization has increased as only a small number of firms and sectors have been able to integrate themselves into the world market through exports. Unsustainability refers not only to the size of the trade deficit but also to its tendency to spiral upward in absolute terms and relative to GDP. Macroeconomic unsustainability also raises a financial—and political and social—question: which sectors are able and willing to pay for these growing external shortfalls? Not only has dependence upon foreign capital since 1988 made Mexico vulnerable to a variety of international disruptions, but it has also revealed the fragile nature of the country's export-oriented industrialization and liberalization strategy.

The implication, of course, is that continued liberalization will have significant economic and social costs for Mexico. Either the economy expands at a rate that enables it to absorb some or most of the growing economically active population (but at the cost of unsustainable trade and current account deficits), or growth is much lower (leaving most would-be job market entrants without employment). This rather perverse situation, in which the economic sectors that are most dynamic in terms of exports and GDP growth are also relatively high in capital intensity and relatively low in real wage levels, merits much further discussion.

Mexico's list of priority macroeconomic and industrial policy needs should include generating linkages between the dynamic export sector and other parts of the economy, "recovery" of the domestic market, national and regional policies designed to produce endogenous growth conditions in a globalized context, and programs to promote micro, small, and midsize firms (De Maria y Campos 1999; Dussel Peters 2000). However, any effort to promote a higher degree of economic integration of export-oriented firms, sectors, and regions carries costs, which must be paid by either the public or the private sector. Because of continuing budgetary constraints, economic and political priorities will compete for funding: spending for industrial policies and public higher education, for example, versus a bailout of the financial sector.

Nonetheless, one must recognize that Mexico's liberalization strategy has been relatively successful on its own terms—that is, in promoting exports, raising productivity, and, to a lesser degree, stimulating economic growth. Thus any discussion of Mexico's emerging industrial organization since 1988 must necessarily go beyond industrial policy. The vision, logic, and assumptions of export-oriented industrialization and of liberalization more generally are theoretically and empirically questionable, and they should be subjected to critical review. Otherwise, even though generating domestic economic linkages might become a key feature of Mexico's liberalization program, this objective might be sacrificed to macroeconomic priorities such as control of inflation and the fiscal deficit.

REFERENCES

Aspe Armella, Pedro. 1993. *El camino mexicano de la transformación económica.* Mexico City: Fondo de Cultura Económica.

Asuad Sanén, Normand E. 2000. "Aspectos básicos que debe atender la política de desarrollo regional y urbano en México en el corto, mediano y largo plazo," *Investigación Económica* 231: 71-107.

Banco de México. 1999. *The Mexican Economy, 1999.* Mexico City: Banco de México.

Blomström, Magnus, and E. N. Wolff. 1989. "Multinational Corporations and Productivity Convergence in Mexico." Working Paper Series, No. 3141. Cambridge: National Bureau of Economic Research.

Borrus, Michael, and John Zysman. 1998. "Globalization with Borders: The Rise of Wintelism as the Future of Industrial Competition." In *Enlarging Europe: The Industrial Foundations of a New Political Reality,* edited by John Zysman and Andrew Schwartz. Berkeley: International and Area Studies, University of California, Berkeley.

Brailovsky, Vladimiro, Roland Clark, and Natán Warman. 1989. *La política económica del desperdicio.* Mexico City: Universidad Nacional Autónoma de México.

Carrillo, Jorge, and Sergio González López. 1998. "Mercedes-Benz, BMW y Volkswagen en México: proveedores y estrategias," *Comercio Exterior* 48 (10): 849–57.

CEPAL (Comisión Económica para América Latina y el Caribe). 1992. *Estructuras institucionales y mecanismos de promoción de exportaciones: las experiencias de México y Colombia.* LC/L.722. Santiago, Chile: CEPAL.

———. 1998. *La inversión extranjera en América Latina y el Caribe.* Santiago, Chile: CEPAL.

Córdoba, José. 1991. "Diez lecciones de la reforma económica en México," *Nexos* 158: 31–49.

Dávila Flores, Alejandro. 1998. "Globalización económica y diferencias regionales en la industria manufacturera en México." Manuscript.

De Maria y Campos, Mauricio. 1999. "Necesidad de una nueva política industrial para el México del siglo veintiuno." Paper presented at Centro Lindavista, Mexico City.

Dussel Peters, Enrique. 1993. "Quo Vadis, Señor Brady? The Brady Initiative: A Way Out of the Global Debt Crisis?" *Union of Radical Political Economy* 25 (1): 81–107.

———. 1997. *La economía de la polarización: teoría y evolución del cambio estructural de las manufacturas mexicanas (1988–1996).* Mexico City: Editorial Jus/Universidad Nacional Autónoma de México.

———. 1998. *La subcontratación como proceso de aprendizaje: el caso de la electrónica en Jalisco (México) en la década de los noventa.* Santiago, Chile: CEPAL/Gesellschaft für Technische Zusammenarbe.

———. 1999. "Reflexiones sobre conceptos y experiencias internacionales de industrialización regional." In *Dinámica regional y competitividad industrial,* edited by Clemente Ruiz Durán and Enrique Dussel Peters. Mexico City: Universidad Nacional Autónoma de México/Fundación Friedrich Ebert/ Editorial Jus.

———. 2000. *Polarizing Mexico: The Impact of Liberalization Strategy.* Boulder, Colo.: Lynne Rienner.

Dussel Peters, Enrique, Michael Piore, and Clemente Ruiz Durán. 1997. *Pensar globalmente y actuar regionalmente: hacia un nuevo paradigma industrial para el siglo XXI.* Mexico City: Universidad Nacional Autónoma de México/Fundación Friedrich Ebert/Editorial Jus.

Garrido, Celso. 1998. "El liderazgo de las grandes empresas industriales mexicanas." In *Grandes empresas y grupos industriales latinoamericanos,* edited by Wilson Peres. Mexico City: Siglo Veintiuno.

Gereffi, Gary. 1994. "The Organization of Buyer-Driven Global Commodity Chains: How U.S. Retailers Shape Overseas Production Networks." In *Commodity Chains and Global Capitalism,* edited by Gary Gereffi and Miguel Korzeniewicz. Westport, Conn.: Praeger.

Gereffi, Gary, and Jennifer Bair. 1998. "U.S. Companies Eye NAFTA's Prize," *Bobbin Magazine* 39 (7): 26–35.

Gurría Treviño, José Ángel. 1993. *La política de la deuda externa.* Mexico City: Fondo de Cultura Económica.

INEGI (Instituto Nacional de Estadística, Geografía e Informática). 1999. *Banco de datos INEGI*. Mexico City: INEGI.

Kuri Gaytán, Armando, Daniel Pacheco Ibarra, and Alejandro J. Noriega Valdez. 1999. "Experiencias de desarrollo territorial en México," *Comercio Exterior* 49 (8): 679–89.

León González Pacheco, Alejandra. 1999. "El comercio intraindustrial en México." Bachelor's thesis, Universidad Nacional Autónoma de México.

Maddison, Angus. 1989. *The World Economy in the 20th Century*. Paris: Organisation for Economic Co-operation and Development.

Martínez, Gabriel, and Guillermo Fárber. 1994. *Desregulación económica (1989–1993)*. Mexico City: Fondo de Cultura Económica.

Máttar, Jorge, and Wilson Peres. 1997. "La política industrial y de comercio exterior en México." In *Políticas de competitividad industrial*, edited by Wilson Peres. Mexico City: Siglo Veintiuno.

Mendiola, Gerardo. 1997. "La empresa maquiladora de exportación, 1980–1995." In *Pensar globalmente y actuar regionalmente: hacia un nuevo paradigma industrial para el siglo XXI*, edited by Enrique Dussel Peters, Michael Piore, and Clemente Ruiz Durán. Mexico City: Universidad Nacional Autónoma de México/Fundación Friedrich Ebert/Editorial Jus.

Mortimore, Michael. 1999. "The Colour TV Receiver Industry in Mexico, Malaysia and Thailand." UNCTAD Study of Industrial Restructuring and International Competitiveness.

Mungaray, Alejandro. 1998. "Desarrollo industrial y subcontratación en el Norte de México." *El Mercado de Valores* 58 (March): 3–11.

Peres, Wilson. 1990. "Foreign Direct Investment and Industrial Development in Mexico." Paris: OECD Development Centre.

Poder Ejecutivo Federal. 1989. *Plan Nacional de Desarrollo, 1989–1994*. Mexico City.

———. 1995. *Plan Nacional de Desarrollo, 1995–2000*. Mexico City.

———. 1996. *Programa de Política Industrial y Comercio Exterior, 1995–2000*. Mexico City.

———. 1999. *Quinto Informe de Gobierno*. Anexo. Mexico City.

Ros, Jaime. 1991. "Mexico's Trade and Industrialization Experience since 1960: A Reconsideration of Past Policies and Assessment of Current Reforms." Paper presented at United Nations University/WIDER conference "Trade and Industrialization Reconsidered," Helsinki.

Ruiz Durán, Clemente. 1997. "Lo territorial como estrategia de cambio." In *Pensar globalmente y actuar regionalmente: hacia un nuevo paradigma industrial para el siglo XXI*, edited by Enrique Dussel Peters, Michael Piore, and Clemente Ruiz Durán. Mexico City: Universidad Nacional Autónoma de México/Fundación Friedrich Ebert/Editorial Jus.

———. 1999. "Territorialidad, industrialización y competitividad local en el mundo global." In *Dinámica regional y competitividad industrial*, by Clemente Ruiz Durán and Enrique Dussel Peters. Mexico City: Universidad Nacional Autónoma de México/Fundación Friedrich Ebert/Editorial Jus.

Ruiz Durán, Clemente, Enrique Dussel Peters, and Taeko Taniura. 1997. "Changes in Industrial Organization of the Mexican Automobile Industry by Economic Liberalization." Joint Research Program Series, no. 120. Tokyo: Institute of Developing Economies.

Sánchez Ugarte, Fernando, Manuel Fernández Pérez, and Eduardo Pérez Motta, eds. 1994. *La política industrial ante la apertura*. Mexico City: Fondo de Cultura Económica/SECOFI.

SECOFI (Secretaría de Comercio y Fomento Industrial). 1994. "Informe especial de avances de los programas sectoriales para el mejoramiento de la productividad." Mexico City: Comisión de Seguimiento y Evaluación del Pacto para la Estabilidad, la Competitividad y el Empleo, SECOFI.

Zabludovsky, Jaime. 1990. "Trade Liberalization and Macroeconomic Adjustment." In *Mexico's Search for a New Development Strategy*, edited by Dwight S. Brothers and A. E. Wick. Boulder, Colo.: Westview.

Zedillo, Ernesto. 1994. "La propuesta económica de Ernesto Zedillo: palabras de Ernesto Zedillo Ponce de León, candidato del Partido Revolucionario Institucional a la Presidencia de la República," presented in the forum "Crecimiento económico para el bienestar familiar," Mexico City, June 6.

Part IV

Social Policy and Rural Development

8

Education and Development in Mexico: Middle and Higher Education Policies in the 1990s·

Lorenza Villa Lever and Roberto Rodríguez Gómez

INTRODUCTION

The last educational reform in Mexico that involved an overall review of the system was carried out during the administration of Carlos Salinas de Gortari (1988–1994), when Ernesto Zedillo was secretary of public education. The reform began with the presentation of the 1989–1994 Program of Educational Modernization (PME). One of its main instruments was the modification of Article 3 of the Mexican Constitution in March 1993, establishing the principles for national education. A new General Law on Education governing the operation of the educational system as a whole took effect in July 1993.

The PME established a series of policies for the national educational system. Among other changes, it gave priority attention to elementary education, sought to reduce educational lags, federalized basic education, increased compulsory education to ten years, and attempted to improve the quality of education as a whole. For the reform of post-basic education, the PME took Mexico's demographic and occupational changes as its point of departure. In demographic terms, a significant increase in the demand for middle and higher education could be foreseen as a result of the population growth of the 1970s and because of increased efficiency at the basic education level. At the same time, the number of young people in a position to demand jobs overwhelmed the capacity of the urban occupational structure to accommodate all of them. On the basis of this diagnosis, what the PME emphasized for middle education was the link between the educational and production systems. For higher education, the emphasis was on the relationship

·Translated by Aníbal Yáñez-Chávez.

between university schooling and national scientific and technological development. In tune with President Salinas's economic policy focus, the PME's more general objective was to include the national educational system in the changes required for Mexico's desired entry into the developed world.

When he became president and announced his educational program, President Zedillo (1994–2000) expressed his intention of continuing along the general lines established by the PME. He did, however, add other goals. For example, in the case of middle education, his government sought to improve the forms of institutional coordination and to make the curriculum more flexible, and in the case of higher education, to broaden educational coverage and deepen the process of institutional diversification already under way. Thus, over the course of the Salinas and Zedillo administrations, educational policies were designed with the aim of improving the quality of middle and higher education and paying attention to the links between learning at these educational levels and transformations under way in the employment market.

During both administrations, the economic development model that was promoted fostered industrial restructuring, favored openness to foreign investment in various forms, and gave support to the export production sector. The strategies deployed involved deregulation and privatization of sectors and firms that remained in state hands, including parastatal manufacturing industries, banking, transportation, and telecommunications. Moreover, the Salinas and Zedillo governments fostered private investment in health services, education, and housing. Within the framework of a development model inspired by neoliberal economic theses, post-basic education was assigned the function of providing students with the knowledge and the skills demanded by integrated and globalized economies.

In this essay we will analyze government policies aimed at middle and higher education in the 1988–2000 period and, to the extent possible, the way in which those actions have shaped Mexico's development. The basic hypothesis is that, despite the government's stated intentions and efforts, strengthening secondary and higher education in Mexico was not a real public policy priority during the last decade of the twentieth century. Indeed, to a very real extent, the Salinas and Zedillo administrations did not consider education to be an important element for Mexico's development.

This hypothesis is backed by two arguments:

- First, once it was declared that universal basic education had been attained, the state's attention turned to the middle and higher levels of the national educational system. But this was done in a reactive manner, more in response to growing social pressures than to changes in the world of work or desired development goals.

- Second, since the 1982 economic crisis and particularly since the 1994–1995 financial crisis, the educational sector has not fared well in its competition for resources with other governmental priorities. This has resulted in a decline in the amount of public subsidies to middle and higher education, hampering the possibilities for reform and development beyond a few changes in the normative and organizational area.

As a consequence, Mexico's secondary and higher educational systems are still inadequate. To demonstrate this, we will analyze some of the factors that affect the quality, equity, efficacy, and relevance of the educational services offered. An analysis of these elements will bring us closer to an understanding of the relationship between education and social development.

This chapter is comprised of four sections. The first considers the characteristics of "knowledge society" and the educational changes that developing countries must undertake if they are ever to close the gap with the industrialized world. The next section assesses secondary education in Mexico, and the third examines the higher educational system. The final part offers a series of reflections on the tendencies that we are now witnessing, outlining the changes that are required to achieve better articulation between middle and higher education policy and Mexico's options for growth and development in the near future.

EDUCATION AND KNOWLEDGE AS THE AXIS OF DEVELOPMENT

The category "knowledge society" is a central notion in the discussion of twenty-first-century education policies, as well as in academic debates about the role of contemporary education. It should be made clear at the outset that this notion is above all a qualitative idea and not a name that serves descriptive, analytic, or explanatory purposes. However, precisely because of its utopian quality, it is guiding processes of change in many spheres of reality—or, rather, it is bringing about the convergence of diverse innovations originating in the areas of production, technology, science, and culture around the question of educational policy.

As a prospective scenario, the knowledge society can be viewed as the cultural result of the global economy. It is characterized as an environment in which science and technology inform all areas of life. In this sense, the notions of a knowledge-based economy, a knowledge society, and a learning society describe ideal-type production and cultural systems in which knowledge becomes the driving force behind economic growth and social cohesion.

In a knowledge society, middle and higher education are very important because of the role that they play in three areas: (1) providing the skills for global competitiveness, democracy, and citizen participation in decision making; (2) fomenting the ability to work in a team, solve problems, and develop capacities to reflect, analyze, and reason in a logical manner; and (3) increasing the capacity to reduce poverty. However, even in the developed world, the processes that point in these directions have not been free of problems, tensions, or resistance. Among the sources of conflict identified so far, the following should be mentioned: the tendencies toward polarization unleashed by an inequitable distribution of educational opportunities (Colclough 1996; Gorostiaga 1999); the patterns of labor exclusion arising from technological and organizational changes, as well as the displacement of labor and productive sectors with limited capacities for adaptation (Hyman 1998); the differentiation between economies with greater or lesser opportunities to promote innovation (Johnson and Bearg Dyke 2000); the confrontation between the logic of producing knowledge in academic centers and its appropriation and use in firms (Cohen, Nelson, and Walsh 1996; Akyeampong 1998); pressures on universities in terms of curricular and research agendas (Bowie 1994; Slaughter and Leslie 1997); and the tendency toward the privatization of teaching institutions, in which they are viewed principally as suppliers of commodities for a price (Schugurensky 1995).[1]

In addition to these problems, we must realize that real societies are characterized by their heterogeneity. Globalization has increased societal differences in terms of the distribution of both income and educational opportunities. Moreover, these differences occur not only between countries but also within them. This is why, now more than ever, it is necessary to recognize the capacity of education to improve individuals' income and living conditions.

---

[1] To this list of problems we can add the instability of the information technology market. In addition to the financial losses registered by the major technology firms during 2000, the drop in the share value of electronic commerce firms (dot.com sites) resulted in the loss of more than 40,000 jobs in that year. This crisis of the Internet industry may have important effects on the course of the "new economy." In fact, figures on investment in equipment and software by U.S. firms already reflect it. According to data from the U.S. Department of Commerce, investment in that area declined from 20 percent to 5 percent between the first and last quarters of 2000.

Mexico, for example, is very close to reaching universal coverage in primary education at the national level, but there are some states (Chiapas, Guerrero, and Oaxaca) where that indicator has not yet reached 60 percent. The states in the middle range in terms of development, where at least 60 percent of the population has completed primary schooling, have poor secondary school enrollments and poor completion rates. Meanwhile, the Mexican states with higher schooling levels are at a point where barely 50 percent of the population has completed secondary education.

According to criteria established by the Economic Commission for Latin America and the Caribbean (ECLAC), the number of years of education necessary to have a 90 percent assurance that the population does not fall into poverty is 10 to 11 years for Latin American urban areas, and it is more than 10 years for wageworkers between the ages of 35 and 54 (CEPAL 1997). According to Inter-American Development Bank estimates (IADB 1997), it was expected that by the mid-1990s the average level of schooling in Latin America would be 7 years. However, it only reached 5.2 years. In Mexico, average schooling (7.9 years) was above the level of Latin America as a whole, although still below that of countries with similar levels of development; Argentina and Chile, for example, have crossed the threshold of 10 years of average schooling. Furthermore, even though the 1980s and 1990s in Mexico were characterized by the rapid growth of secondary and higher education, by the year 2000 secondary education only covered 46 percent of the corresponding age group, while higher education covered only 19 percent.

There are many dimensions to the relationship between education and development. In general, the quantity and quality of education available, as well as the articulations between the educational and productive systems, express the role that education plays as the axis of economic and cultural development. In practice, the relationships between educational demand and supply; between schooling, jobs, and wages; between the needs of the productive sector (expressed as a demand for competencies and skills) and the educational sector's capacity to respond; as well as the relationship between schooling and social mobility, form a complex arrangement that is not without its paradoxes and unforeseen effects.

Thus, in the case of Mexico, the average level of schooling increased by two years between 1980 and 1990, the percentage of workers with less than a primary school education dropped from almost half in 1984 to 36 percent in 1994, and the proportion of workers with secondary education rose from 26 to 39 percent (Lächler n.d.). Nevertheless, in Mexico as in much of Latin America, the 1980–1990 period was one of nearly zero growth in gross domestic product (GDP), which would support the hypothesis that schooling and macroeconomic indicators are relatively independent variables.

Of course, the contributions of education to economic growth and social equity are neither simple nor linear. The increase in the average educational level of the population, particularly of the workforce, has precipitated an inflationary rise in schooling requirements in the formal sector of the economy (from 6–8 to 10–12 years of study), while at the same time it has devalued some educational degrees. It is also true that levels of schooling have increased because of a social perception that education provides the indispensable tools to improve one's quality of life and to achieve entry into labor markets whose requirements are ever more demanding and complex.

In fact, during the 1984–1994 period, the Mexican workforce with less than a primary school education, those who completed primary school, and even those who completed junior high school saw their real economic possibilities decline. At the same time, workers who completed high school or had some university education were able to increase their wages and incomes in real terms. According to Lächler (n.d.), the most feasible explanation for income inequality among workers is that provided by Hernández Laos, Garro, and Llamas (1998), who show that shifts in the demand for workers in Mexico, based on their level of schooling, are rooted in changes in the labor market and in technology. The result—an increase in demand for higher-skilled workers and a decline for those with lower levels of schooling—suggests that wage dispersion originates in a structure of production within a sector that favors better-educated workers over those who have lower educational levels (and not in changes in patterns of wage negotiation or agreements between sectors).

Thus the upward trend in educational levels benefits those who are able to enter the schooling circuit and remain there until they reach its higher levels. At the same time, the population excluded from educational benefits is also deprived of job opportunities and decent wages. Here, then, is a paradox by which education operates simultaneously as a means of achieving social equality and as a mechanism for reproducing inequalities. This paradox, well known to sociology and the economics of education (Boudon 1973; Halsey et al. 1997), has no formal solution. The only responses are circumstantial ones involving educational policies that affect the market by shaping the distribution and diversity of educational opportunities, or strategies that assure the equity, quality, and relevance of the education that is imparted.

Let us examine this last point in greater detail. The theses in vogue on economic growth (Drucker 1993; Foray and Lundvall 1996; Woolcock 1998) concur in emphasizing the micro- and macroeconomic links between an increase in the knowledge base and growth in productivity. In developed economies there is substantial evidence that the sectors that systematically use knowledge inputs (that is, the results of research and development and an educated and skilled workforce) grow more rapidly and generate higher profits (Scarpetta et al. 2000). Nevertheless, the valorization of knowledge-based goods and services takes place in a competitive environment, which means that knowledge and skills, insofar as they are economic factors, are subject to relationships of supply, demand, and competition (that is, to the rules of the market). This means that not all investment in knowledge results directly in growth, and that the rate of economic growth is variable and relative as a function of investments in knowledge. This conclusion, for which there is much empirical evidence worldwide, highlights the need to distinguish between the weight of education as a factor in economic growth and the significance of education as a component of national development.

In a general sense, it is well recognized that, by supporting public and private education, the state responds to societal demands for participation. Yet this is both an economic response and a political and cultural one (UNESCO 1999; World Bank/UNESCO 2000). In addition to being a factor that affects individual and social productivity, education is a positive instrument for modernization and social change and for countries' democratic development.

For these reasons, educational systems—particularly secondary and higher education—are faced with new requirements, demands, and opportunities, as are scientific and technological research systems as well. These new demands emphasize the key role of educational systems in the generation and mobilization of knowledge (Castells 1994), and the possibilities they have of imbuing individuals with creative abilities and the capacity to adapt to change. Among the courses often charted for the modernization and adaptation of educational systems, it is worth noting the following: general expansion of enrollment; diversification in terms of types of institution, their functions, and sources of financing (Meek, Huisman, and Goedegebuure 2000; Cook and Lasher 1996); decentralization and federalization; creation of regulatory and coordinating bodies (Gove and Stauffer 1986; Neave 1998; Glenny 1995); implementation of planning, assessment, and accountability formulas (Goedegebuure et al. 1994; Meek et al. 1996); updating the structure and operating methods of university governance and administration (Higgerson and Rehwaldt 1993); implementation of mechanisms to ensure quality (El-Khawas 1998; Harman 1998); and increased flexibility in the curriculum and use of distance learning (Trow 1999).

In countries with comparatively solid economies, the priority given to secondary and higher education, as well as to scientific research, is reflected in the trend toward universal secondary education, a new wave of expansion in university enrollments (El-Khawas 1998), and significant growth of public and private investment in research and development activities. In the 1990s the rate of coverage of potential demand (represented by the 20– to 24–year age group) increased in these countries from 45 to 60 percent. In Latin America, covered demand only rose from 16 to 20 percent, mainly due to the sustained expansion of private educational institutions (UNESCO 2000).

There is also a worrisome gap in research and development capacity and spending between the economically powerful countries and underdeveloped countries. In terms of the number of scientists and technicians per 10,000 inhabitants, the former countries outstrip the latter by a factor of nearly ten (3.8 compared to 0.4 in 1998). In terms of research and development spending, the difference is between 2 percent of gross domestic product for the former compared to 0.4 percent of GDP for the latter, which means that on average the developed countries spend five times as much. In Mexico total spending on science and technology is approximately 0.45 percent of GDP (Poder Ejecutivo Federal 2000).

In addition to these quantitative differences, assessments of the quality of secondary and higher education systems and of science and technology systems in Latin America are generally disheartening (although there are significant exceptions, which is why the Inter-American Development Bank speaks of a "mixed performance"; IADB 1997). On the one hand, there is evidence of overcrowding, lack of funds, deficiencies in the administration and coordination of systems, and a lack of relevant curricula (World Bank/UNESCO 2000). On the other hand, there are universities and academic centers that carry out high-level teaching and research, with appropriate standards of quality. The problem, of course, lies in the small proportion that these institutions constitute within the universe of Latin American higher education (García Guadilla 1996).

The development of secondary and higher education and of science and technology systems in Mexico, as in most countries in Latin America, has taken place amidst conflicting forces. In the first place, the expansion of these systems responded more to social demands than to the direct requirements of the productive apparatus or the labor market (Brunner 1994). Second, although public universities continue to be the places par excellence where links are made between scientific research and higher learning, they are usually at a disadvantage in the competition for resources with other governmental priorities. Third, until well into the 1990s, multilateral banks and other intergovernmental agencies recommended to the governments of underdeveloped countries that they channel their educational investments toward primary education, leaving to private actors the expansion of higher and postgraduate education (World Bank 1994, 1995). This policy stance truncated public universities' possibilities for growth and development (Rodríguez Gómez 1999).

These patterns have begun to change in recent years. As a result of the worldwide debate on the strategic value of knowledge (UNESCO 1999; OECD 2000), a consensus of sorts appears to be on the horizon regarding the need to increase coverage and transform both secondary and higher education systems and science and technology systems. The principal goal is to expand their capacities to better adapt to the challenges posed by the dynamics of globalization (Yarzábal 1999).

Considering the transformations facing secondary and higher education worldwide, what have been the major challenges confronting Mexico's secondary and higher education systems? What have been the dynamics of expansion and diversification? What changes have been carried out for the educational system's qualitative improvement? And, in sum, what results were achieved in these areas during the 1990s? These questions are taken up in the following sections of this chapter.

SECONDARY EDUCATION IN MEXICO

This section considers the issue of secondary education in Mexico. The discussion focuses first on the principal modalities by which the system is organized. It then examines secondary educational policies, considering processes of change during the 1970s and 1980s and the lines of development proposed during the 1990s. Finally, we analyze the main problems faced by this educational level. The section concludes by emphasizing the idea that reforms of secondary education in Mexico have not considered knowledge as a generator of development.

General Characterization

In Mexico, middle education[2] is coordinated by two agencies of the Ministry of Public Education (SEP): the Undersecretariat of Higher

---

[2] "Higher middle education" is the official term, referring to a time when primary school was considered basic education (six years), secondary school was termed basic middle education (three years), and the baccalaureate or preparatory school was higher middle education (three years). Because secondary school now makes

Education and Scientific Research (SESIC) and the Undersecretariat of Education and Technological Research (SEIT). SESIC has responsibility for the baccalaureate, including the general and the university programs,[3] both of which are propaedeutic (that is, aimed principally at satisfying the academic and disciplinary requirements of the professions). The SEIT coordinates technological education, including the technological or bivalent baccalaureate, which in addition to propaedeutic studies offers work training and technical education. This is a terminal certificate and is directly oriented toward work.[4]

Each of these middle education modalities embraces different types of institutions. For example, the general or propaedeutic baccalaureate includes baccalaureate colleges (*colegios de bachilleres*), baccalaureate studies centers, the Lázaro Cárdenas Federal Preparatory School, privately incorporated preparatory schools, baccalaureate programs affiliated with universities, military baccalaureates offered through the Ministry of National Defense, arts baccalaureates affiliated with the National Institute of Fine Arts (INBA), and distance-learning baccalaureate programs. The technological and bivalent baccalaureates include the National College of Professional-Technical Education (CONALEP); various technological and industrial institutes; nursing and obstetrics programs; art studies centers coordinated by the INBA; oceanographic, agricultural, fresh-water, and forestry technological institutes; and various state government-coordinated science, technology, and industrial institutes. This institutional differentiation is supposed to satisfy the diverse needs, interests, and capabilities of a heterogeneous population.

Middle education includes public and private institutions. The federal government is fundamentally in charge of the public institutions. However, the autonomous or university middle schools that are part of institutions of higher education are also public institutions, as are those that are dependencies of individual Mexican states. Private institutions have private owners.

---

up part of basic education (nine years), when we refer to middle education we will be speaking of the baccalaureate level.

[3] Middle education has a duration of three years in all its modalities, although there are some university baccalaureate programs that take two years.

[4] There is also a General Directorate for the Baccalaureate that coordinates the general baccalaureate and falls under the SESIC. It currently coordinates the following institutions: the baccalaureate studies centers, the Lázaro Cárdenas Federal Preparatory School, the baccalaureate colleges, private preparatory schools incorporated with the Ministry of Public Education and private preparatory schools incorporated with the Ministry of Public Education by special agreement, the Open Preparatory School, the part-time baccalaureate (*bachillerato semiescolarizado*), and Distance Higher Middle Education.

Middle Education Policies in the 1970s and 1980s

The Mexican government's interest in middle education is long-standing. Indeed, the first institutions that fulfilled the function of linking elementary education with a university education date to the colonial period. For example, San Ildefonso College, established in the seventeenth century, offered an education to youths who sought the bachelor's degree granted by the Royal University of Mexico (Real Universidad de México). The National Preparatory School (Escuela Nacional Preparatoria) was established in 1867 and later became part of the new National University of Mexico, created in 1910. In 1925, middle education, which covered the whole educational span between primary school and the *licenciaturas* in the university, was divided into two cycles: secondary school (lasting three years) and preparatory school (also lasting three years). The former was left under the supervision of the Ministry of Public Education, while the latter remained in the hands of the National University. Outside of Mexico City, the development of middle education took place principally in arts and sciences institutes at the state level, which in turn would give rise to public universities in the individual states of the federation.

Over time, the baccalaureate cycle took on two general dimensions, one of a propaedeutic type (as an education in preparation for the university cycle) and another of a technological type (linked to higher education institutions in the technical area, such as the National Polytechnic Institute and the regional technological institutes). However, the process of curricular diversification that resulted from the system's expansion lacked the planning and coordination mechanisms necessary to build satisfactory standards of quality. Thus, beginning in the 1960s there was a thorough review of the content and structure of the baccalaureate in Mexico.

In 1971 the National Association of Universities and Institutions of Higher Education (ANUIES), concerned about middle education in Mexico, established a discussion forum that engaged the participation of autonomous universities, state and private universities, the National Polytechnic Institute, and the various technological institutes. The first ANUIES meetings that took up the topic of the baccalaureate were in Villahermosa, Tabasco, and in Tepic, Nayarit, both in 1972. There the participants agreed that the baccalaureate would be propaedeutic and terminal, that it would be delivered in semester courses, that it would take three years, and that it would follow the credit system. The ANUIES convened a second meeting in 1975 at which it was agreed to establish a common curricular core for middle education.

Similar meetings followed, among which the one held in Cocoyoc, Morelos, in 1983 was noteworthy. The Cocoyoc Congress had as its main concerns: (1) the characterization of the baccalaureate as a "formative and integral" cycle, not just a propaedeutic one; (2) the design of a curriculum structure that offered students the basic educational elements (a common core) and at the same time allowed for a certain diversity, in line with different institutions' interests and objectives; and (3) the diversity of institutional policies, which prevented "horizontal permeability," or movement between institutions (Castrejón Díez 1997). Moreover, the goal of the baccalaureate was defined as the need to "generate in youth the development of an initial personal and social synthesis that will allow them access both to higher education and to an understanding of their society and their times, as well as the possibility of undertaking productive work" (Castrejón Díez 1997).

In order to accomplish all this, specialists concluded that it was necessary for middle education to orient young students toward the adoption of their own value system, critical participation in the culture of their time, the acquisition of methodological knowledge that would enable them to have access to scientific knowledge, the development of their personality and their capacity for abstract thinking and independent learning, and an interest in the applied aspects of science in the institutions oriented toward occupational training. At the 1983 meeting, the profile of the student with a baccalaureate was defined as someone able to: express himself or herself correctly and efficiently; speak various languages; use cultural, scientific, technical, and axiological tools to solve problems; understand and criticize the ecological, socioeconomic, and political context of her or his community and country in a rational manner, thus participating in its improvement; learn independently; evaluate and solve situations corresponding to her or his age and development; and undertake higher studies or productive work.

Middle Education Policies in the 1990s

In the framework of the 1989–1994 national Program of Educational Modernization, the Mexican government sought to achieve more effective coordination so as to allow inter-institutional collaboration with the aim of improving the functioning and development of middle education. The first National Meeting on Higher Middle Education was held in 1991. The National Commission for Planning and Programming of Higher Middle Education (CONPPEMS)[5] was established at that meeting, and soon after a State Commission for Planning and Pro-

---

[5] The CONPPEMS became the National Commission for Higher Middle Education (CONAEMS) in 1994, with the objective of coordinating student demand, programs and courses of study, and assessment efforts.

gramming of Higher Middle Education (CEPPEMS) was established in each state. The objective was to address the deficiencies that existed in each state and—as a result of the government's policy of educational decentralization, which was not actually implemented until 1998 for middle education—encourage the states to participate more actively in financing middle education by having different institutions (particularly the professional-technical schools) seek external funding sources (Villa Lever 1990). However, it should be noted that alongside these new coordinating bodies, the various types of institutional arrangements that have always controlled the resources for middle education continued to function: federal, state, autonomous, and private.

The national education policy framework articulated in the 1995–2000 Educational Development Program[6] emphasized the need to: consolidate a system of higher middle education that makes it possible to improve indicators of quality, relevance, and equity; connect technological and scientific change with educational change; make academic structures more flexible; develop a basic profile for the student and another for the teacher upon which to base educational and continuing education programs; bring supply and demand into balance to avoid competition between different institutions; link technological education with productive sectors, taking into account shifting trends in labor markets and thus strengthening the relevance of education for national development; establish the competency-based education model (*modelo de educación basado en competencias*) through the application of work-competency technical norms (*normas técnicas de competencia laboral*) in both formal and non-formal education; and provide greater autonomy and transparency in the management and spending of resources.

In the curriculum area, the education that is offered is made up of: (1) a common core of courses that fosters a general culture, based on several fields of knowledge (language and communication, mathematics, natural sciences, and socio-historical studies); (2) subjects that pre-

---

[6] The assessment on which this program was based stated that, in the case of higher middle education, "the plans and programs still retained their content and characteristics more than fifteen years after the complete modification of the technological baccalaureate's common core and after only partial modifications had been made to the structure of the curriculum during the previous decade. The baccalaureate options that were available had not been able to offer sufficient and effective responses to their general and propaedeutic demands, and they did not offer students a renewed education that would make them better able to enter new professional areas. The bivalent modality (the technical-professional option), despite the diversification of the areas that make up the curricular offerings, did not always correspond in a relevant way to the needs of the world of work" (Ortega 2000: 316).

pare youths to continue with higher education; and (3) a core of occupational education that orients the student with regard to labor processes in a specific field and encourages positive attitudes toward them. Among the elements that inform the curriculum, which has as its aim contributing to the full development of young people, are the following: the development of thinking skills; logical reasoning; values such as liberty, justice, solidarity, national identity, democratic responsibility, and love of truth; environmental education; human rights; and, finally, the quality or path that leads to excellence.

In both the Salinas and Zedillo administrations, together with enrollment expansion and the development of infrastructure to serve middle education students, some actions were carried out to improve the quality and relevance of middle education.[7] However, everything seems to indicate that these actions have had a very limited effect in terms of the system's retention capacity and the quality and relevance of the education that is offered.

Efficiency, Equity, and Relevance: Middle Education's Main Problems

The problems facing middle education have to do with the efficiency with which the system operates, the equity with which the service is distributed, and its relevance to individual and social needs. In other words, at the start of the third millennium, middle education in Mexico continues to be burdened with many of the problems it faced two or three decades ago. Among them the following should be noted:

Very Low Efficiency of Middle Education The middle education system grew constantly during the last half of the twentieth century. According to Ministry of Public Education figures (SEP 2000), enrollment rose from a little more than 37,000 students in 1950 to 2.1 million students in 1990. In 1998, 2.8 million students were enrolled in middle education, and in the 2000–2001 cycle there were just over 3.0 million. Among the most important reasons for the increase in enrollment are the country's strong demographic growth, the expansion of enrollments at the basic education level, and an increase in recent years in the rate of absorption of secondary students by middle education (table 8.1), a

---

[7] The most important measures were the updating of educational plans, programs, and methods; linking schools with productive sectors (in the case of the technological modalities); decentralization of services (particularly in the baccalaureate colleges system); and some training courses for teachers and administrators.

TABLE 8.1. Profile of Mexico's Middle Education System, 1990–2001

School Year	Secondary School Graduates	Middle Education Absorption Rate (percent)	Entrants into Middle Education	Total Middle Education Enrollment	Percentage Increase on Previous Year
1990–1991	1,176,290	75.4	899,653	2,100,520	—
1991–1992	1,169,556	79.3	933,117	2,136,194	1.7
1992–1993	1,162,311	80.9	945,766	2,177,225	1.9
1993–1994	1,174,446	82.5	958,979	2,244,134	3.1
1994–1995	1,189,307	87.9	1,032,854	2,343,477	4.4
1995–1996	1,222,550	89.6	1,065,274	2,438,676	4.1
1996–1997	1,272,675	94.3	1,152,724	2,606,099	6.9
1997–1998	1,277,300	94.4	1,187,678	2,713,897	4.1
1998–1999	1,335,625	94.5	1,206,872	2,805,534	3.4
1999–2000	1,369,109	93.0	1,242,361	2,892,846	3.1
2000–2001	1,448,505	93.3	1,277,105	3,001,377	3.8

Source: Secretaría de Educación Pública (SEP), *Perfil de la educación en México*, 3d ed. (Mexico City: SEP, 2000).

Note: Data on secondary school graduates in 1999–2000 and all data for 2000–2001 are preliminary.

figure that rose from 75.4 percent in 1990 to 89.6 percent in 1995 and 93.3 percent for the 2000–2001 school cycle. Despite this, at the start of the twenty-first century, only 46 percent of the population between 16 and 18 years old is enrolled in middle education. This situation is the result of three other problems burdening middle education: (1) a very low completion rate, which in the professional-technical options is below 45 percent and in the propaedeutic baccalaureate is 57 percent, (2) high failure rates (73 percent), and (3) high dropout rates (46 percent) (SEP 1999).

However, efficiency also has to do with spending. Of the three main levels of education in Mexico (basic, middle, and higher education), middle education is the least important in terms of aggregate financing. In 1999, 9.5 percent of the Ministry of Public Education's spending went to middle education, 65.1 percent went to basic education, and 13.7 percent and 11.7 percent of total spending were dedicated to, respectively, university and postgraduate education. Despite efforts to decentralize middle education, the federal government still finances the education of the largest number of students in Mexico. In 1996, for example, the states contributed only 18.3 percent of the total budget (ranging from 15.2 percent of the total budget for middle and higher education, to 19.5 percent for basic education).[8]

The pattern of spending on middle education raises two issues. First, it is clear that middle education has not been a high budgetary priority; it has not, for example, achieved the importance of basic education and higher education (Villa Lever 2000). However, during the Salinas and Zedillo administrations, technical middle education services expanded significantly. The number of schools, classrooms, laboratories, and workshops doubled in ten years. Enrollment increased by almost one-third, and the size of the teaching staff rose by 24 percent (SEP/SEIT 1998).

In middle education in general, there was also a significant growth of enrollment during the Salinas and Zedillo presidencies, and during 1997–1998 alone 35 baccalaureate colleges were created in the states. However, the second major problem that middle education faces has to do with the capacity to retain in school young people from diverse social groups. What is required to achieve this goal is quality education, which principally implies attention to academic variables, especially the curriculum and teacher training.

According to figures from the National Institute of Statistics, Geography, and Informatics (INEGI 2000), Mexican youth between 15 and 19 years old (the age group that corresponds to middle education) are the ones who are most likely to be enrolled in school (44.7 percent). However, more than half of them are no longer studying. According to the same source, among youth from 15 to 19 years of age, 2.2 percent have no education at all, nearly two-thirds have barely a basic education, and only one-fourth are currently studying or have completed middle education. Of this last group, 14 percent are students following a professional-technical career and the rest are in the baccalaureate. Only 2.5 percent of this age group is enrolled in higher education.

Very few youths in this age group are full-time students. A substantial number of them are engaged in other activities in addition to studying, mostly working and/or helping with household chores. Even more unfortunate, however, the majority of youths between the ages of 15 and 19 do not go to school because they work or help with household chores.

The youths who do not continue their schooling give as their main reasons a lack of motivation to study (60.6 percent of males and 54.3

---

[8] Authors' calculations based on data in SEP 1999.

TABLE 8.2. Distribution of Mexico's Middle Education Enrollments by Program Type, 1970–2001 (percentages)

Year	General Baccalaureate	Technological	Professional/ Technical
1970–1971	68.8	20.4	10.8
1980–1981	70.4	19.2	10.4
1990–1991	61.5	20.5	18.0
1995–1996	57.8	26.3	15.9
2000–2001	59.7	27.7	12.6

Source: Secretaría de Educación Pública, *Estadística básica del sistema educativo nacional: inicio de cursos*, various years.

percent of females) and the need to work to help provide for their families or themselves (29.2 percent of males and 18.6 percent of females). For women, family responsibilities (12.4 percent) and marriage and household chores (9.3 percent) are significant barriers; among men, these factors tend not to be major reasons for dropping out of school (4.3 percent and 0.5 percent, respectively) (Observatorio 51).

In sum, the choice that is posed in Mexican middle education is not whether the general or the technical educational option should receive a greater commitment of resources. This is a false dilemma; any quality education costs money. What is clear is the absolute need to improve the quality of middle education in all its modalities so that there is a real comparative advantage for whoever studies, thereby altering the current perspective of young people that it does not make much of a difference. To the extent that the majority of those who complete middle education must enter the labor market, it would be important to include a heightened appreciation of the culture of work in all the system's modalities, even in the general educational option, thus avoiding the false specializations that exist in school but not in the world of work (Villa Lever 2000).

Low Levels of Equity in Middle Education Inequality in society is reproduced in education through schooling paths of differing qualities aimed at various publics. The distribution of middle education enrollment across its various modalities changed during the 1990s; the relative weight of the propaedeutic or general option in enrollments gradually decreased, the bivalent or technological option grew substantially, and enrollments in the professional-technical option declined (table 8.2). However, the strong orientation toward propaedeutic middle education in its three options (the general baccalaureate, the university baccalaureate, and the bivalent baccalaureate), along with the low

TABLE 8.3. Private Middle Education in Mexico, 1998–1999 School Year

Program Type	Enrollment			Institutions			Academic Personnel		
	Private Schools (000s)	*National Total (000s)*	*Private as Percent of National Total*	*Private Schools*	*National Total*	*Private as Percent of National Total*	*Private Schools (000s)*	*National Total (000s)*	*Private as Percent of National Total*
Baccalaureate	465.8	2,430.9	19.2	2,804	7,340	38.2	49.1	157.4	31.2
Professional/ technical	86.8	410.2	21.2	1,070	1,864	57.4	9.2	38.0	24.2

Source: Secretaría de Educación Pública (SEP), *Perfil de la educación en México,* 2d rev. ed. (Mexico City: SEP, 1999).

social status of a technical education as a terminal degree, have devalued the latter in relation to both socioeconomic development and personal development.

If we take those who presented the middle education entry test (*concurso de ingreso*) in the Mexico City metropolitan area in 1998 and 1999 (SEP 1999: 74; 2000: 58–59) as a sample characterizing middle education applicants, we can conclude that:

- Of the total number of applicants, 66.2 percent in 1998 and 65.8 percent in 1999 came from a general secondary school, while only 27.9 percent and 28.0 percent, respectively, came from a technical secondary school. In 1998 and 1999, 2.7 percent and 2.9 percent had studied in a *telesecundaria* (secondary school via television). Both years, 1.4 percent had graduated from a secondary school for workers, and 1.6 percent and 1.8 percent, respectively, came from an open secondary school.[9]

- Of the total number who took the test, graduates of private schools had on average 80 and 81 correct answers in 1998 and 1999, respectively, out of a total of 128, while graduates of public schools had only 67 and 66 correct answers out of the same total.

In other words, the fact that the majority of middle education applicants came from a propaedeutic secondary school suggests that quite probably they were from families in better socioeconomic circumstances than those from technical secondary schools, to the extent that a greater proportion of these children were able to continue their studies. Similarly, the data from the entry test indicate that those students who come from a private secondary school have greater access to the codes of modernity that permit them to have greater success in their studies, compared to students from public schools.

Finally, private schools play an important role in Mexico's middle education system because of the size of their enrollments (table 8.3). One-third of all preparatory schools are in private hands, as are more than half of all technical schools in the country. One-fifth of all baccalaureate and professional-technical students attend these schools. But are the efficacy, relevance, and equity of the educational services provided by these private institutions satisfactory? In general, the so-called consolidated private schools provide services that have won them their good reputation. However, it is necessary to underscore that there are many small private institutions, born out of the demand for educational credentials, whose quality leaves much to be desired.

---

[9] The secondary education background of the remaining applicants was not specified.

A large majority of middle education students in Mexico are oriented toward the general or technological baccalaureate and very few toward the professional modality. Although the available evidence indicates that youths who graduate from the professional option are able to find employment, it is clear that this modality is still not attractive for most of them. Therefore, if there are so many youths who need work, it is fair to ask why so few of them choose the professional-technical path in middle education.

Of course, the solution is not to close down the occupational training modalities, but rather to eliminate their discriminatory connotations. For this to occur, it is crucial to move from the concept of "preparation for work" (which has an instrumental meaning and refers to training in specific technical and manual skills) to "preparation for a working life" (emphasizing versatile and adaptable training for the middle and long run). In this sense, more than simply transmitting information, education should generate competencies for analysis, reflection, innovation, solving unforeseen problems, and dealing with contingencies—privileging general subjects and giving students the opportunity to continue studying. In addition, it is indispensable to create procedures that will permit those who complete the middle cycle in the professional option to go on to higher education if they so desire and if they have the required academic ability.

Furthermore, both the general baccalaureate and the technological baccalaureate options are characterized by low levels of efficiency and relevance. Less than half of those who start studies at this level are able to complete them, and still fewer go on to university studies. Complaints persist in institutions of higher education regarding the insufficient preparation of arriving students, while work alternatives for those who interrupt the cycle are minimal. Thus it is evident that problems of relevance are present throughout the middle education system, whether as a place where youths are prepared for university or technological studies, or as a place that provides training in competencies for the world of work.

Low Relevance of Middle Education The centralism with which middle education programs (particularly the professional-technical options) have been designed has made it difficult to link schools with regional production sectors, and this creates a problem in terms of their relevance to employment possibilities for young graduates. The lack of effective links between schools and firms, as well as the high rates of dropout and failure, result in an education whose quality must be questioned.

In addition to the diversity of modalities and, within them, the variety of institutions with specializations aimed at various sectors, middle education in Mexico is burdened by a selection process that places clear limits after grade 10 on different school and work paths. Moreover, the difficulties that graduates face in finding employment and the stigma associated with the professional-technical options reinforce the social and regional inequalities that themselves help determine the quality of the paths open to various segments of the population. This closes the circle in terms of a loss of prestige for technical schools, while at the same time propitiating the growth of the propaedeutic baccalaureates.[10]

As an educator of future professionals, the middle education system itself defines a false choice that counterpoises study and work: the general baccalaureate and the technological baccalaureate, on the one hand, or professional-technical education, on the other. The system has long since ceased to provide an adequate response to the needs of the increasingly diverse social groups involved. These problems have resulted in many youth abandoning their studies before completion, generally because they need to work. These young people will be left with a precarious education and poor wages.

In synthesis, because professional-technical education in Mexico has the stigma of being the option open to those who belong to the most downtrodden social classes, this potentially important modality is not valued by either parents or students. Instead, they struggle to pursue the baccalaureate, which offers what to many will remain an illusion: entry into the university (Villa Lever 1991a, 1991b, 1986).

What Should Be the Orientation for Middle Education?

The tendency toward early educational differentiation in the middle levels, which in many countries begins as early as the age of 11 or 12 and is closely connected to graduates' subsequent path and their future opportunities, was questioned in the developed world during the 1970s. What was proposed instead was a comprehensive school organized into a first-year common core (basic secondary), leaving the separation into modalities or specializations for the second year (upper secondary). The main arguments in favor of these changes were that early selection reinforced inequalities, low educational coverage, and the

---

[10] It should be noted that the National College of Professional-Technical Education (CONALEP) carried out a reform that considerably reduced the number of technical specializations offered, made it possible to obtain a general baccalaureate by completing one additional semester, and reorganized management, which apparently resulted in an increase in enrollment.

disparity of opportunities, as well as not promoting the adequate intellectual or social development of students.

In the 1980s, technological advances and the world's new political configuration oriented the welfare state toward the roles of coordinator and regulator. Educational reforms sought to improve the quality and efficiency of mass middle education, without neglecting the relationship between education and social demand. In many (especially European) countries, centralized educational systems were decentralized with the objective of bringing decision making closer to the schools.

More recently, many countries have increasingly focused on educational integration. No matter how middle education is defined, it is widely recognized that the system has a number of objectives having to do with personal, social, and civic development, as well as preparation for a life of work. The tendency toward convergence of the general baccalaureate, the technological baccalaureate, and professional-technical education has as its main objective exploiting the possibilities and resources that are available and offering opportunities that emerge from the system itself, allowing students to follow different educational and occupational training options as well as the academic or general one.

The Mexican state has responded reactively to enrollment growth in middle education. However, it has not seriously occupied itself with the problems of efficiency, relevance, and inequity that persist in the system, nor has it adequately defined the objectives and goals of middle education or created a body responsible for coordinating the efforts of the diverse actors in charge of it.

A further important omission concerns middle-level teachers. There are no clear academic requirements for certification, promotion, or tenure; instead, what prevails are bureaucratic categories and clauses in union contracts. Each modality offers its teachers different types of continuing education courses, generally of short duration. But these measures do not offer an adequate response to the rapid evolution of knowledge and the need for teachers with a solid education, in tune with the highly heterogeneous needs of a middle education system characterized by its curricular diversity, the breadth of the professional-technical specializations that it offers, and the plurality of social groups that it serves. In order for middle-level teachers to be able to respond with quality teaching in the diverse situations that characterize those who demand the service at this level, professionalization of teacher education is crucial. This requires resources and clear objectives, but above all it takes the political will to arrive at basic agreements among the various types of coordinating bodies involved in middle education.

The great challenge, then, is to reconceptualize middle education so that the system can respond to massive, heterogeneous demand. This necessarily means remedying a major shortcoming: insufficient meaningful knowledge to serve the requirements of a productive citizenry for the twenty-first century. An effective middle education must provide the basic competencies that allow young people to become a part of society as citizens and as workers, with the ability to communicate and place themselves in the context and space in which they live (socio-historically) and with reasoning, scientific, technological, ecological, critical, and creative competencies (De Ibarrola and Gallart 1994).

There are necessarily limits to the tendency to allow market forces a free hand and to decentralize educational services. All countries must bring their technological education systems closer to the evolution of educational needs, with the aim of improving the quality and efficacy of teaching. Both private firms and the state have important roles to play in this regard. Indeed, at the school level this responsibility may be shared with families and representatives of the local community.

Even though some might think that private firms are best suited to define the needs of professional education, in practice they may have a narrow, short-term view that favors technical knowledge and practical know-how, to the detriment of a general education. Therefore it is important that educational objectives be defined from a sufficiently broad perspective, one that takes into account not only the interests of firms but also the needs of workers and of society in general.

The middle education system must be flexible in both its contents and structure if it is to succeed in offering youth educational opportunities that are diversified and capable of adapting to changing needs. Its contents must be reformulated according to the changing demands of the labor market, reducing the number of educational specializations, broadly conceived. Nonetheless, while education must be oriented toward serving labor market needs, there is neither a linear nor a mechanical connection between supply and demand. Rather, the educational system must help individuals achieve the general competencies that will help them have an active work life, whatever the particular opportunities that might arise.

In today's world no initial education can prepare youth for their whole life. Life-long learning has been recognized as a necessity because, although it cannot be said that education guarantees employment, in the long run a country that has workers with a solid education will find it easier to generate new industries. It will also be able to apply accumulated knowledge to production in industries that generate wealth on the basis of information, rather than simply importing technologies for assembly-processing. Furthermore, as the general educational level increases, the youths who leave school without minimum qualifications are increasingly threatened with economic and social exclusion. It is therefore necessary to create programs oriented toward serving this population by alternating periods of study with periods of work.

HIGHER EDUCATION AND POSTGRADUATE STUDIES IN MEXICO

This section offers a general description of higher education in Mexico, including data on how it is organized and its current enrollment. It then examines the recent evolution of the system, beginning with the application of higher education policies during the Salinas and Zedillo administrations.

General Overview

The higher education system in Mexico covers all educational institutions at the professional-technical, undergraduate (licentiate or *licenciatura*), and postgraduate levels. It includes both public institutions (those supported primarily by the federal government, although state and municipal funding is increasingly important) and private institutions. The main modalities are technical, university, and normal school education, but the higher educational system also includes research centers and institutes that may or may not be part of universities.

In the 2000–2001 academic year there was a total of 2,073,500 students enrolled in higher education (SEP 2001). Of these, 67,838 (3.3 percent) were in the non-university technical cycle; 1,878,962 (90.6 percent) in undergraduate and normal schools; and 126,700 (6.1 percent) in postgraduate programs. The public higher educational system covered 67.8 percent of total enrollment. In the non-university technical sphere, public education covered 85.8 percent of the total enrollment. In the undergraduate cycle (universities, technical institutes, and normal schools), public education covered 69.0 percent, and in postgraduate programs the figure was 59.8 percent.

Within each of these cycles there are educational modalities that represent diversified curricular offerings:

- *The non-university technical cycle.* This cycle, which follows middle education, offers education of a technical character in areas of production and services. It takes two years to complete the courses and receive a degree as an associate professional or technical professional. Almost half of all enrollments in this cycle are concentrated in 43 "technological universities," recently created public institutions that currently offer 22 advanced technical careers.[11] The first three of these were established in 1991, three more in 1994, and another 37 were added between 1995 and 2000. It should be underlined that all of the technological universities are located outside of Mexico City, mostly in midsize cities. The other programs in this cycle are located in public universities and in some private institutions.

- *The undergraduate (licenciatura) cycle.* The licenciatura cycle covers university degrees, advanced technical education programs, and teacher education programs (normal schools). The largest enrollments are in the university undergraduate modality, with 1,346,425 students (71.7 percent of the total) in 2000–2001 (SEP 2001). Of these, some 70 percent were in a public university.[12] The technical modality covers enrollments in technological-university institutes and schools;[13] all enrollments in this modality are part of the public system of technical institutes distributed across the country.[14] The normal school modality, which is responsible for educating professional teachers, was composed of 213,800 students, 61.5 percent of whom were in the public system. The remainder of enrollments in this cycle were made up of: 24,174 students in public professional schools administered by non-university government bodies such as the National Institute of Fine Arts (INBA) and the National Institute of Anthropology and History (INAH); 3,348 students in schools operated by the army and navy; and, finally, 189,754 students enrolled in non-university private schools that offer an undergraduate education in some area of specialization.

- *The postgraduate cycle.* Postgraduate education covers all specializations, master's, and doctoral programs imparted in public and private universities and institutes. The total postgraduate enrollment in 2000–2001 was 126,700 students (SEP 2001), 21.4 percent of them in specializations, 71.6 percent in master's programs, and the re-

---

[11] Beginning with the 2000–2001 academic year, university careers (in chemistry) were launched in technological universities in Tabasco and San Juan del Río.

[12] The public university system includes federal universities, state universities, and public universities with "solidarity support" (*universidad pública con apoyo solidario*).

[13] The public technological system is organized into a general modality (technical institutes) and specialized modalities (agricultural, forestry, and oceanographic studies). It also includes the National Polytechnic Institute (IPN).

[14] There are a total of 189 institutions of this type, 23 of which were created in the year 2000.

maining 7.0 percent in doctorates. Federal universities[15] absorbed 16.2 percent of total postgraduate enrollment; state universities, 27.4 percent; private universities, 25.5 percent; technical institutes, 6.0 percent; public normal schools, 2.5 percent; and private normal schools, 0.6 percent. The remainder was in public or private schools that are authorized to offer education at this level even though they are not part of a university, such as healthcare training institutions.

Growth and Diversification of the Higher Education System in the 1990s

During the 1990s, Mexico's higher education system underwent major transformations in its organization, size, distribution, and performance. In 1990, total enrollment in higher education was 1,245,532 students, including all educational modalities (see table 8.4). In 1999, enrollment reached 1,803,790, for a total expansion of 44.8 percent of the student body. Over the same period, the number of university professors rose from 129,092 to 192,406 (table 8.5), equivalent to a 49.0 percent increase in ten years, and the number of higher education institutions grew from 760 to 1,250 (an increase of 64.5 percent).

Other changes in the system included:

Increased coverage of potential demand. In 1990, Mexico's higher education system served 13.8 percent of the population between the ages of 20 and 24; by the end of 2000, it reached 19 percent of that age group.

Changing patterns of enrollment in public higher education. In the public sector, expansion during the 1990s was due almost exclusively to growth of the technical education segment. Through the creation of 51 institutes and 38 technological universities, enrollment in the technical subsystem grew by more than 60 percent (from 166,500 students in 1990 to more than 260,000 in 1999), and the subsystem's share of public higher education offerings went from 20 to 36 percent. In contrast, overall enrollment in universities grew by less than 7 percent over the decade. Enrollment in public normal schools increased from 9,067 students in 1990 to 11,209 in 1999 (equivalent to an overall growth of 23.6 percent), thus maintaining its share of public higher education at around 10 percent.

---

[15] The National Autonomous University of Mexico (UNAM) and the Metropolitan Autonomous University (UAM) are called "federal" universities because they are subsidized with funds from the federal budget.

TABLE 8.4. Higher Education Enrollments in Mexico by Program Type, 1980–2000

Year	Colleges and Technical Schools	Normal Schools	Postgraduate Programs	Total Enrollment
1980	731,147	96,590	25,503	853,240
1985	961,468	125,236	37,040	1,123,744
1990	1,078,191	123,376	43,965	1,245,532
1991	1,091,324	110,525	44,946	1,246,795
1992	1,126,805	105,662	47,539	1,280,006
1993	1,141,568	110,241	50,781	1,302,590
1994	1,183,151	120,996	54,910	1,359,057
1995	1,217,431	138,048	65,615	1,421,094
1996	1,286,633	160,036	75,392	1,522,061
1997	1,310,229	188,353	87,696	1,586,278
1998	1,392,048	206,292	107,149	1,705,489
1999	1,481,999	210,544	111,247	1,803,790
2000	1,629,158	215,506	118,099	1,962,763

Source: Asociación de Universidades e Instituciones de Enseñanza Superior (ANUIES), *Anuarios estadísticos*, 1980–2000.

TABLE 8.5. Academic Personnel in Mexico's Higher Education System by Program Type, 1980–1999

Year	Colleges and Technical Schools	Normal Schools	Postgraduate Programs	Total Personnel
1980	69,214	3,588	1,072	73,874
1985	95,779	7,849	9,046	112,674
1990	105,058	12,488	11,546	129,092
1991	109,475	12,103	11,009	132,587
1992	113,238	12,002	11,467	136,707
1993	120,183	11,222	9,406	140,811
1994	123,290	12,026	10,053	145,369
1995	132,222	12,730	10,934	155,886
1996	133,598	12,759	14,531	160,888
1997	138,052	14,724	14,992	167,768
1998	143,325	16,359	18,304	177,988
1999	158,539	16,836	17,031	192,406

Source: Asociación de Universidades e Instituciones de Enseñanza Superior (ANUIES), *La educación superior en el siglo XXI* (Mexico City: ANUIES, 2000).

TABLE 8.6. Enrollments in Mexico's Public and Private Higher Education Systems, 1980–2000

Year	Undergraduate[1]			Postgraduate		
	Public	Private	Total	Public	Private	Total
1980	632,307	98,840	731,147	NA	NA	25,503
1985	810,391	151,077	961,468	29,513	7,527	37,040
1990	890,372	187,819	1,078,191	34,435	9,530	43,965
1991	891,524	199,800	1,091,324	35,460	9,486	44,946
1992	910,257	216,548	1,126,805	37,018	10,521	47,539
1993	908,480	233,088	1,141,568	38,131	12,650	50,781
1994	936,646	246,505	1,183,151	41,574	13,336	54,910
1995	943,245	274,186	1,217,431	47,390	18,225	65,615
1996	989,448	297,185	1,286,633	52,822	22,570	75,392
1997	990,729	319,500	1,310,229	61,210	26,486	87,696
1998	1,036,935	355,113	1,392,048	69,408	37,741	107,149
1999	1,073,098	408,901	1,481,999	70,589	40,658	111,247
2000	1,118,731	466,677	1,585,408	71,246	46,853	118,099

Source: Asociación de Universidades e Instituciones de Enseñanza Superior (ANUIES), *Anuario estadístico,* 1980–2000.

[1] *Licenciatura* programs

NA = Not available

Increased presence of the private sector in higher education. The participation of the private sector in higher education became very significant over the course of the decade. In 1990 private institutions covered 17.4 percent of the demand for undergraduate education; by 1999, their participation had risen to 27.6 percent (table 8.6). Enrollment increased at a rate of nearly 10 percent per year over the 1990–1999 period. The expansion of private higher education has been most extraordinary at the postgraduate level; in 1990 there were 9,530 students in that modality, while in 1999 there were 40,658. Moreover, there was evidence of increased differentiation among private-sector educational options. For instance, there was consolidation among the set of higher educational institutions ruled by market conditions (that is, those that do not carry out research or cultural functions and do not have an adequate academic infrastructure, even though they offer professional training that is in high demand). It is estimated that, of the more than 700 currently existing private institutions, barely one-fifth of them may be considered universities; the rest are institutes, centers, advanced training schools, and other non-university modalities. On the other hand, during the 1990s the more solid private universities developed strategies for territorial growth, establishing regional sites throughout Mexico.

Greater concentration of educational demand in areas and professional careers associated with services. As a general tendency during the 1990s, enrollments in higher education declined in the agricultural and livestock sciences, as well as in natural and exact sciences. This continued a trend in place since the 1980s. The health sciences and education, on the one hand, and the humanities, on the other, remained constant as a percentage of educational offerings (27 percent and 4 percent of total enrollment, respectively, not counting enrollment in normal schools). In contrast, the social and administrative sciences continued to expand, to the point that this area covered practically half of all undergraduate enrollments (counting both public and private institutions, including the technical, university, and normal school modalities). In 2000, one-third of total enrollment was concentrated in only three options: law (12 percent), accounting (11 percent), and administration (10 percent) (ANUIES 2001). According to the ANUIES classification, approximately 70 percent of total higher education enrollment is associated with the tertiary sector of the economy, which is out of proportion with indicators of the employed population (53 percent of the labor force belongs to the tertiary sector) and gross domestic product (GDP) (the tertiary sector accounts for 66 percent of GDP). This disproportionality is considerably more acute in those states with the highest levels of economic backwardness, such as Chiapas, Guerrero, Hidalgo, Nayarit, and Oaxaca. In each of these states, enrollment in tertiary sector professions is considerably higher than the national average.

Growth of postgraduate education. In 1990, national enrollment in postgraduate education was slightly above 40,000 students; in 2000, there were 120,000 students enrolled in specialized courses of study, master's programs, and doctorates. The near tripling of enrollment was due both to progressive increases in the educational requirements of the modern sector of the labor market and to an explicit policy of strengthening the academic faculty of higher educational institutions. However, this expansion also reflected the constriction of the job market for professionals, a phenomenon that made the option of continuing in school more attractive (a significant portion of postgraduate students are protected by scholarships) than going out to find a job.

Changing gender balance in university undergraduate programs. By the end of the 1990s, the number of women in the higher educational system was practically equal to the number of men. This shift was due both to the greater presence of women in undergraduate, normal school, and technical education and to slowing growth in the number of men in university enrollments. By the end of the decade, the proportion of women in the areas of health sciences, social and administrative sciences, and education and humanities (which together made up nearly 70 percent of total enrollments) was higher than the proportion of men.

Along with the changes outlined above, the 1990s witnessed trends toward diversified financing, more rigorous evaluation and accreditation, greater accountability, strengthened infrastructures, and quality assurance. As previously noted, these changes were accompanied by the Zedillo administration's efforts to promote growth in the coverage of the higher educational system and strengthen the academic profile of the teaching faculty.

Although the tendencies toward change that developed in the higher educational system during the 1990s were partly the result of government strategies, they were also the product of new arrangements between governmental agencies and the various higher education subsystems. No less important were the transformations promoted from within the institutions themselves, in areas such as academic organization and educational content. Added to this were the changes resulting from private educational actors and, lastly, the shifts that took place in the orientation and preferences of educational demand. Viewed in this way, the dynamic of change originated at the intersection of multiple political and social logics whose convergence is contingent and not without tension. However, from a general perspective, it can be said that in addition to the dynamic of expansion and diversification already noted, Mexico's public universities experienced fundamental changes in three areas of their organization: norms, preparation of faculty, and evaluation.

Higher Education Policies in the 1990s

The Salinas Administration Beginning with his presidential campaign in 1987–1988, Carlos Salinas de Gortari underscored the need to foster quality in higher education as the basis for the system's transformation (Melgar Adalid 1994). This idea was also stressed in the National Development Plan (PND) adopted for the 1989–1994 period. In 1989, the federal government inaugurated a Program of Educational Modernization (PME) and defined the general principles that would guide educational policy during Salinas's term. Among other goals, it advocated the revitalization of the system of indicative planning derived from the interactions between the Ministry of Public Education and ANUIES, and it stated that the Integral Program for the Development of Higher Education (approved by the ANUIES in 1986) was a part of the government's general strategy. It also established as programmatic lines evaluation and institutional reform, and it indicated that the growth and distribution of educational offerings would be guided by three principles: better use of installed capacity, gradual growth of institutions that had not reached their optimal size, and the opening of new options, principally in the open education system. In addition, the system's growth would be administered through the decentralization and regionalization model derived from the PND. The PME especially emphasized the need for policies that would make it possible for low-income students to have access to higher education.

At the level of concrete actions, the PME suggested: the expansion of educational offerings in school and open modalities; reconciling career offerings that are a priority for development with student preferences; a territorial balance in enrollments; the simplification of the catalog of careers to avoid excessive specializations; the establishment of national criteria for academic excellence; and promoting evaluation processes in higher education in order to determine levels of performance, productivity, efficiency, and quality. In fact, the PME's proposals took up the recommendations made in the document ("Statements and Contributions for the Modernization of Higher Education") approved by the ANUIES general assembly, with which the association responded to the federal executive's charge to develop a consensus proposal that could be incorporated into government policy.

Between 1989 and 1991, the definition of the political course of higher education unfolded in open convergence between the SEP and the ANUIES, with the supplemental participation of other federal government agencies. The rapprochement that took place between these two bodies—the former representing governmental interests and the latter the interests of the autonomous universities—was decisive for the smooth development of higher education policy. Without the participation of the ANUIES, the state's dialogue with universities would have depended upon bilateral arrangements made on a case-by-case basis. Through the Association's consensus-building procedures, the corresponding government agency (the Undersecretariat of Higher Education and Scientific Research, SESIC) could reach agreement on overall models and strategies to be applied.

Thus, as a first step, in 1989 the National Commission for Higher Educational Planning (CONPES) was reactivated and a series of national commissions were established comprised of federal government functionaries (SEP, the National Council for Science and Technology [CONACYT], and the Ministry of Budget and Planning [SPP]) and the rectors or directors of higher educational institutions. These included national commissions for the evaluation of higher education, the promotion of open higher education, linking research with the social and productive sectors, the evaluation and improvement of postgraduate education, the evaluation and stimulus of research quality, and participation in the National Solidarity Program (PRONASOL, the Salinas administration's hallmark anti-poverty program). Each one of these commissions was chaired by the secretary of public education. Although they met throughout 1990 and 1991, in practice the only commission that produced results that could be implemented was the one for the evaluation of higher education.

Later, in 1990, the ANUIES approved a document articulating a higher educational strategy based on seven programs: academic improvement, upgrading of research, postgraduate education, continuing education, cultural extension, administration, and support to the baccalaureate. In 1991, the CONPES defined "priority lines of action for improving the quality of higher education in Mexico": bringing the curriculum up to date; improving quality in the training of teaching and research professionals; establishing an institutional identity in research and postgraduate studies; updating academic infrastructure; reorganizing educational administration and norms; developing an institutional information system; diversifying funding sources; and promoting the participation of social and productive sectors in higher education.[16] The same CONPES statement established "priority lines of an institutional character": training of academic personnel; development of academic infrastructure and a national network of libraries; diversification of wage policies (differentiated salary scales); improvement of procedures for granting subsidies and for other transactions with agencies of the federal government; and strengthening inter-institutional research programs.

Progressively and through a complex process of negotiations and agreements, the Salinas administration's policy action lines took shape: modifying the inertial model of financing, differentiating academic salaries, and introducing a culture of evaluation. The emphasis placed on evaluation was translated into a series of initiatives and measures that without doubt will, over time, change canonical practices in academia, as well as traditional forms of administration.

The new emphasis on evaluation in higher education appeared in a proposal for multipronged institutional evaluation adopted by the ANUIES in July 1990. It consisted of three modalities: (1) institutional self-evaluation, (2) evaluation to be carried out by inter-institutional committees for evaluation of higher education (*comités interinstitucionales de evaluación de la educación superior*), and (3) evaluations of the higher education system and its subsystems carried out by the SEP and ANUIES. Although all three modalities were operationalized in the course of the Salinas administration, only program evaluations carried out by peer-review committees occurred in a more or less regular fashion. However, a culture of evaluation became firmly established in the academic management of educational institutions, above all through the variety of programs designed to stimulate academic productivity that spread through Mexico's universities beginning in the early 1990s. Similarly, the Salinas government continued the National System of Researchers (SNI) administered by CONACYT; the SNI constitutes another mechanism for the evaluation and selective promotion of university researchers and teaching faculty.

In 1993, the ANUIES General Assembly approved the creation of the National Center for the Evaluation of Higher Education (CENEVAL). The CENEVAL took the form of a nonprofit organization (*asociación civil*) charged with designing and administering entrance exams for higher middle education, higher education, and postgraduate edu-

---

[16] See "Prioridades y compromisos para la educación superior en México, 1991–1994." In 1994, ANUIES published a study entitled "Avances de la universidad pública en México" ("Progress in Public University Education in Mexico"), which reported on institutions' progress in meeting the goals set by the CONPES agreements.

cation, as well as having responsibility for the quality of graduates. At that same meeting, the ANUIES approved the use of two procedures for the accreditation of studies: a national indicative exam before entering undergraduate studies (*licenciatura*) and a general exam of professional qualifications.

During the 1990–1991 period, the SEP began distributing complementary funds by means of the Fund for Educational Modernization (FOMES). Through the FOMES, the SEP set out to guide institutions of higher learning toward the objectives put forward in the PME. Similarly, in 1993–1994 the ANUIES established the Program for the Improvement of Academic Personnel (SUPERA), through which the SEP distributed grants to improve the academic level of university teaching faculty.[17] The activities of FOMES and SUPERA began to restructure traditional methods of financing public institutions of higher education, which involved assigning budgets on the basis of enrollments and through negotiations between the SEP and each one of the institutions.

The strategy of redistributing and reorganizing educational financing was also pursued in another public policy instrument, the so-called development agreements (*convenios únicos de desarrollo*) through which federal and state authorities establish the bases for coordinating budgetary actions. These development agreements were part of the Salinas government's more general federalization strategy. Through them, the country's institutions of higher education began to diversify their sources of subsidy, achieving more (or less) advantageous combinations according to the system of alliances and political relations between federal and local powers that emerged in each case.

In addition to the strategies already mentioned, all of which arose principally from the SEP–ANUIES policy axis, the Salinas administration pushed for important changes in technical higher education. The project to create technological universities began in 1991 with the establishment of the Nezahualcóyotl, Tula-Tepeji, and Aguascalientes units, and in 1993 the government initiated the academic reform of technical institutes.

In keeping with the objectives outlined in the PME, the Salinas government did not neglect the reform of various legal frameworks. Most noteworthy in this area were the reform of Article 3 of the Mexican Constitution (March 1993) and the new General Law on Education (July

---

[17] Between 1994 and 1996, SUPERA provided a total of 1,593 postgraduate scholarships to tenure-track professors working at institutions affiliated with the ANUIES. Beginning in 1998, SUPERA focused its efforts on providing postgraduate scholarships to academic personnel from technological institutes under the jurisdiction of the SEP, public universities affiliated with the Ministry of Agriculture and Livestock, and private institutions affiliated with the SEP.

1993).[18] The reform of Article 3 added (as section V) new language obligating the state to "promote all the educational types and modalities necessary for the country's development," including higher education. However, this amendment removed the phrase stating that "the state provides higher education," thus loosening the state's legal obligation to finance fully public higher education. The same reform established the state's obligation to "support scientific and technological research" and to "foster the strengthening and dissemination of national culture." Moreover, the 1993 General Law on Education introduced a section that regulates the evaluation of systems covering public universities and other institutions of higher education.

What stands out in a balance sheet of the achievements and limitations of higher education policy during the Salinas administration is the government's commitment to introduce efficiency criteria and values (quality, competitiveness, and productivity) to guide the activities of university institutions. The government's ability to do so reflected its capacity to develop multiple spaces of negotiation and agreement, although it was also based on the implementation of more aggressive instruments (above all financial ones) designed to align the educational programs with the government's goals. Nevertheless, some of the government's objectives were not met or were abandoned in the course of the Salinas administration, including the program to support low-income students, the promotion of open education systems, the reorientation of educational demand, and the redefinition of career offerings.

Some analysts note that a typical feature of President Salinas's administration was the tendency to modify agreed-upon strategies through selective interventions that reflected conjunctural political interests. This style of government was indeed the outstanding characteristic of the Salinas government's higher education policies. Perhaps because of this, by the end of the Salinas administration there were clear signs that the discourse of modernization had worn thin.

One of the greatest shortcomings of the Salinas education program was its underestimation of the demand for university education. This underestimation resulted in absurd limits being placed on the supply of new educational openings precisely in the areas of greatest demand, Mexico's metropolitan areas. Demand pressures would very quickly force the succeeding administration to revise its plans.

---

[18] The Salinas administration did not, however, reform the Law for the Coordination of General Education.

The Zedillo Administration In January 1995, President Ernesto Zedillo announced his 1995–2000 Program of Educational Development (PDE). In keeping with the terminology in fashion, the document placed emphasis on the "equity, quality, and relevance" of education as the main educational challenges facing the new administration. The section having to do with higher education started by recognizing the need to meet increasing demand and, in this manner, broaden the system's social coverage. The document set the goal of 1.8 million higher education students for the year 2000, equivalent to a 30 percent increase requiring the creation of nearly 100,000 new places per year.

Among other objectives, the PDE proposed forging closer links between higher education and the job market for professionals, having the states share responsibility for both financing and orienting educational offerings so as to take account of the needs of the local and regional environment, and improving the training of academic personnel. Like the PME under Salinas, the PDE advocated academic quality, based on the improvement of study plans and programs and the supply of appropriate equipment, especially laboratories, libraries, computing centers, and workshops. In terms of research activities, the PDE underlined the role of research as an input for the improvement of teaching and its importance as a resource for technological innovation. It stressed, therefore, that research projects should in all cases have a practical application.

Furthermore, the PDE established a commitment to improve the incomes of professors and researchers based on their professional performance, as well as to double the number of professors with postgraduate degrees by the year 2000. In addition, the PDE was explicit in giving continuity to, and deepening, the evaluation policies established during the previous administration. It also sought to improve coordination among institutions, organizations, and subsystems. Finally, the document signaled the intention of fostering advisory boards drawn from society as a whole in order to include the points of view of diverse organizations and social and productive sectors in professional training programs and in adjustments or modifications to study plans.

Some of the PDE's guidelines and orientations overlapped with the planning efforts of the ANUIES, in particular those of the Consejo de Universidades Públicas e Instituciones Afines (Council of Public Universities and Related Institutions). The ANUIES's 1994 document titled "Progress in Public University Education in Mexico" defined objectives that, from the point of view of university rectors, would allow for the continuity of policies from one presidential term to the next. Specifically, it called for the "redefinition of the general mission of the university in Mexico and of the mission of each university institution in particular; creation of a national accreditation system; institutionalization of minimum quality benchmarks for the functioning of universities; establishment of new bases for making budgetary allotments and assigning special project funds; definition of status quo criteria concerning the academic careers of teaching and research personnel."[19]

Meanwhile, as a result of Mexico's entry into the Organisation for Economic Co-operation and Development (OECD) in 1994, the Mexican government contracted with that organization for it to carry out a diagnosis of the conditions prevailing in the country's higher-middle and higher education systems. The ensuing report, published in 1996 as "An Examination of Education Policy in Mexico," included a diagnostic section and another with operational recommendations. The diagnostic part underlined the heterogeneous, complex, fragile, poorly articulated, and rigid character of the great majority of higher-middle and higher education institutions. In other words, it is a system divided into various subsystems, but without internal integration or opportunities for horizontal student mobility; with different forms of coordination with educational authorities and different legal frameworks; with significant growth of private institutions; and with enrollments that are highly concentrated in the social and administrative sciences. The report indicated that "the weight of scientific and technical education is modest compared to Mexico's current level of economic development." In the chapter on recommendations, the OECD experts pointed to five critical areas in which "reforms are patently necessary," namely: flexibility, relevance, quality, academic personnel, and financial resources. For each of these areas there were recommendations ranging from generic objectives to very specific proposals. The OECD report was distributed to public universities through the SEP's Undersecretariat of Higher Education and Scientific Research, with the request that it be acted upon and that the actions taken in response to the OECD recommendations be reported to the SEP.

Thus, during the early years of the Zedillo administration a relatively new scenario emerged for the definition and negotiation of higher education policy guidelines. In addition to the traditional actors (SEP and ANUIES), a prominent role would be played by the state commissions for higher educational planning that were reactivated by the SEP in 1997, and by the organization that brings together Mexico's private universities, the Federation of Mexican Private Institutions of Higher Education (FIMPES).

---

[19] "Avances de la universidad pública en México," *Revista de la Educación Superior* no. 89 (January–March 1994).

One marked difference between the Salinas and Zedillo administrations in this field was that, despite continuity in strategies for educational evaluation and the diversification of financing, the Zedillo government intervened less in such areas as academic reform and institutional reorganization. To the contrary, the agencies of the SEP concentrated on the development of selected projects,[20] on managing complementary resource funds, and on the design of administrative reform programs.

It is also important to note that, during its early years, the Zedillo administration had to face the effects of the economic crisis brought on by the sharp devaluation of the peso in 1994–1995. The federal budget for higher education did not recover until 1999–2000, so that the objectives established in the PDE were constrained by financial limitations. These considerations shifted the government's priorities toward strengthening scholarship programs for the professional development of academic personnel in institutions of higher learning (principally those outside of Mexico City); bolstering the technical education subsystem; consolidating the evaluation and financing systems for public universities; and, finally, allowing private investment in the field of university education. The first of these initiatives resulted in the creation of the Program for the Improvement of the Professoriate (PROMEP) in 1996. This program mandated self-evaluations and institutional development programs as a condition for eligibility, and it required participating bodies to define specific needs for the development of their faculty, which would be met by providing scholarships for professors to obtain postgraduate degrees in academic programs of excellence.[21] In addition, in 1998 the government established the Program of Incentives for Performance of Career Teaching Personnel, which provided salary supplements for those institutions that lacked their own incentive programs for teaching performance. Meanwhile, the FOMES program remained in place and became the SEP's main instrument for financial redistribution.

Throughout the Zedillo administration, the private higher education system exhibited a great deal of dynamism in both quantitative and qualitative terms. In early 2000, the proportion of students in private schools exceeded 30 percent of the total, and the number of private establishments exceeded that of public ones. As part of this expansion, some well-established private universities (such as the Universidad

---

[20] The most important of these were the program for technological universities, the reform of the normal school system, and expansion of the system of technological institutes, which took shape as a federal system starting in 1997.

[21] The PROMEP replaced the earlier SUPERA in public universities.

Iberoamericana, the Instituto Tecnológico de Estudios Superiores de Monterrey, and the Universidad La Salle) instituted schemes for the regional distribution of their professional career offerings, as well as curriculum renewal initiatives. At the same time, the professional establishment oriented toward serving those excluded from higher education opportunities consolidated itself. In general terms, private institutions relieved the pressures of growing demand and limited resources under which the Zedillo administration was operating. In exchange, they benefited from a deregulation policy that culminated in SEP Accord 279 (July 10, 2000), which streamlined accreditation procedures. The accord practically eliminated the SEP's supervision and evaluation of institutions, programs, and academic personnel, in contrast to what takes place in the public sector.

Lacking indicators that would permit an objective evaluation of the impact of public policies in areas such as the quality and relevance of higher education, it would be foolhardy to end this presentation with conclusive judgments on the effectiveness of the strategies and instruments implemented during the Zedillo administration. As in the case of the Salinas administration, the Zedillo record was mixed in terms of goals accomplished (for example, those having to do with growth and coverage of the higher education system and doubling the number of professors with postgraduate degrees) and unfulfilled. Among the latter, though, the following should be noted: the establishment of links between the various higher education subsystems; linking educational offerings with job market openings for professionals; and the establishment of civilian advisory boards. It is no coincidence that the unmet objectives require the development of non-corporatist linkages among the state, educational institutions, and society. This may be the main challenge in designing a new higher education policy.

CONCLUSION

In the introduction to this chapter, we stated that policies put in place during the 1990s favored the expansion and diversification of the middle and higher education systems. However, these processes were not accompanied by changes that would produce greater academic quality, social relevance, or even a better fit between labor market needs, on the one hand, and the academic quality of technical, baccalaureate, and professional studies, on the other. Although some advances are indisputable—such as having overcome the stagnation in enrollment growth experienced in the 1980s, having experimented with new modalities of middle and higher education, and having strengthened postgraduate education—it is clear that the major unfinished task for middle and higher education in Mexico is the academic reform of these educational levels.

What is needed is academic reform characterized by flexibility, focused on learning, and aimed at achieving higher levels of social relevance. By flexibility, we mean the creation of procedures that facilitate students' schooling trajectories and which allow student mobility among the different modalities that make up the system. In addition, students should also be able to participate in the design of their own curriculum plans, in line with their interests and vocational preferences. Despite the good intentions of educational planners, the prevailing pedagogical approach is one based exclusively on teaching that privileges rote learning and leaves little room for creativity and independent learning. There is, then, a need for new pedagogical models centered on students' learning needs, models that foster independent learning and recognize that those who are being educated can generate knowledge. Finally, there should be a thorough going review of study plans and programs to make sure that each educational level (technical, baccalaureate, undergraduate, and postgraduate) really responds to Mexico's development needs and the challenges of globalization. Achieving improved levels of efficiency, relevance, and equity is the fundamental priority facing Mexico's educational systems, and the only chance for education to participate in addressing the country's development challenges.

REFERENCES

Akyeampong, Daniel. 1998. "Thematic Debate on Higher Education and Research: Challenges and Opportunities," UNESCO (United Nations Educational, Scientific, and Cultural Organization) World Conference on Higher Education. ED-98/CONF.202/8.

ANUIES (Asociación Nacional de Universidades e Instituciones de Enseñanza Superior). 2001. *Anuario estadístico 2000*. Mexico City.

Boudon, Raymond. 1973. *La inegalité des chances*. Paris: Colin.

Bowie, Norman E., ed. 1994. *University-Business Partnerships: An Assessment*. Boston: Rowman and Littlefield.

Brunner, José Joaquín. 1994. "Estado y educación superior en América Latina." In *Prometeo Encadenado: estado y educación superior en Europa*, edited by Guy Neave and Frans van Vught. Barcelona: Gedisa.

Castells, Manuel. 1994. "The University System: Engine of Development in the New World Economy." In *Revitalizing Higher Education*, edited by Jamil Salmi and Adriaan M. Verspoor. Oxford: Pergamon.

Castrejón Díez, Jaime. 1997. "El bachillerato." In *Un siglo de educación en México*, vol. 2, edited by Pablo Latapí. Mexico City: Fondo de Cultura Económica.

CEPAL (Comisión Económica para América Latina y el Caribe). 1997. *La brecha de la equidad.* Santiago, Chile, CEPAL–UNESCO.

Cohen, Wesley, Richard Nelson, and John Walsh. 1996. "Links and Impacts: New Survey Results on the Influence of University Research on Industrial R&D." Pittsburgh, Penn.: Department of Social and Decision Sciences, Carnegie Mellon University.

Colclough, Christopher. 1996. "Education and the Market: Which Parts of the Neoliberal Solution Are Correct?" *World Development* 24 (4): 589–610.

Cook, W. Bruce, and William F. Lasher. 1996. "Toward a Theory of Fund Raising in Higher Education," *Review of Higher Education* 20 (1): 33–51.

De Ibarrola, María, and María Antonia Gallart, eds. 1994. *Democracia y productividad: desafíos de una nueva educación media en América Latina.* Lecturas de Educación y Trabajo, no. 2. Mexico City: UNESCO/Organización Regional para la Educación en América Latina y el Caribe.

Drucker, Peter. 1993. *The Post-Capitalist Society.* Oxford: Butterworth Heinemann.

El-Khawas, Elaine. 1998. "Quality Assurance in Higher Education: Recent Progress, Challenges Ahead." Latin America and the Caribbean Social and Human Development Paper Series, no. 23, Washington, D.C.: Human Development Department, World Bank.

Foray, Dominique, and Bengt-Åke Lundvall, eds. 1996. *Employment and Growth in the Knowledge-based Economy.* Paris: Organisation for Economic Co-operation and Development.

García Guadilla, Carmen. 1996. *Situación y principales dinámicas de transformación de la educación superior en América Latina.* Paris: UNESCO.

Glenny, Lyman A. 1995. *Autonomy of Public Colleges: The Challenge of Coordination.* New York: McGraw-Hill.

Goedegebuure, Leo, et al., eds. 1994. *Higher Education Policy: An International Comparative Perspective.* Oxford: Pergamon.

Gorostiaga, Xabier. 1999. "En busca del eslabón perdido entre educación y desarrollo: desafíos y potencialidades para la universidad en América Latina y el Caribe." Paper presented at the meetings of the Working Group on Education and Society, Consejo Latinamericano de Ciencias Sociales (CLACSO), Recife, Brazil.

Gove, Samuel K., and Thomas M. Stauffer, eds. 1986. *Policy Controversies in Higher Education.* New York: Greenwood.

Halsey, A. H., Hugh Lauder, Phillip Brown, and Amy Stuart Wells, eds. 1997. *Education: Culture, Economy, and Society.* New York: Oxford University Press.

Harman, Grant. 1998. "Quality Assurance Mechanisms and Their Use as Policy Instruments: Major International Approaches and the Australian Experience since 1993," *European Journal of Education* 33 (3): 331–48.

Hernández Laos, Enrique, Nora Garro, and Ignacio Llamas. 1998. "Productividad y mercado de trabajo en México." Background paper for the World Bank Country Economic Memorandum on Mexico: Enhancing Factor Productivity Growth. Washington, D.C.: World Bank.

Higgerson, Mary Lou, and Susan S. Rehwaldt. 1993. *Complexities of Higher Education Administration: Case Studies and Issues.* Bolton, Mass.: Anker.

Hyman, Richard. 1998. "La teoría de la producción y la producción de la teoría," *Trabajo* 1 (1): 8–31.

IADB (Inter-American Development Bank). 1997. "Higher Education in Latin America and the Caribbean: A Strategy Paper." EDU-101. Washington, D.C.: IADB

INEGI (Instituto Nacional de Estadística, Geografía e Informática). 2000. *Los jóvenes en México.* Mexico City: INEGI.

Johnson, Elmer, and Nancy Bearg Dyke, eds. 2000. *The International Poverty Gap: Investing in People and Technology to Build Sustainable Pathways Out.* Report of the Aspen Institute Conference. Atlanta, Ga.: Aspen Institute.

Lächler, Ulrich. n.d. "Education and Earnings Inequality in Mexico." Paper prepared for the World Bank.

Meek, V. Lynn, Leo Goedegebuure, Osmo Kivinen, and Risto Rinne, eds. 1996. *The Mockers and Mocked: Comparative Perspectives on Differentiation, Convergence, and Diversity in Higher Education.* Oxford: Pergamon.

Meek, V. Lynn, Jeroen Huisman, and Leo Goedegebuure. 2000. "Understanding Diversity and Differentiation in Higher Education: An Overview," *Higher Education Policy* 13 (1): 1–6.

Melgar Adalid, Mario. 1994. *Educación superior: propuesta de modernización.* Mexico City: Fondo de Cultura Económica.

Neave, Guy. 1998. "The Coordination of Higher Education Systems," *Higher Education Policy* 11 (1): 1–2.

Observatorio Ciudadano de la Educación #51. 2001. *La Jornada,* March 23.

OECD (Organisation for Economic Co-operation and Development). 2000. *Knowledge Management in the Learning Society. Education and Skills.* Paris: OECD.

Ortega, Víctor Manuel. 2000. "Educación e investigación tecnológicas: imagen y realidad." In *SEP: Memoria del quehacer educativo, 1995–2000.* Vol. 1. Mexico City: Secretaría de Educación Pública.

Poder Ejecutivo Federal. 2000. *Sexto informe de gobierno.* Mexico City: Poder Ejecutivo Federal.

Rodríguez Gómez, Roberto. 1999. "La universidad latinoamericana en la encrucijada del siglo XXI," *Revista Iberoamericana de Educación* 21: 55-57.

Scarpetta, Stefano, Andrea Bassanini, Dirk Pilat, and Paul Schreyer. 2000. "Economic Growth in the OECD Area: Recent Trends at the Aggregate and Sectoral Level." Working Papers, no. 248. Paris: Economic Department, Organisation for Economic Co-operation and Development.

Schugurensky, Daniel. 1995. "La reestructuración de la educación superior en la era de la globalización: ¿hacia un modelo heterónomo?" In *Educación, democracia y desarrollo en el fin de siglo,* edited by Armando Alcántara, Ricardo Pozas, and Carlos Alberto Torres. Mexico City: Siglo Veintiuno.

SEP (Secretaría de Educación Pública). 1999. *Perfil de la Educación en México.* Mexico City: SEP.

———. 2000. *Informe de labores, 1999–2000.* Mexico City: SEP.

———. 2001. *Programa Nacional de Educación 2001–2006.* Mexico City.

SEP/SEIT (Secretaría de Educación Pública/Subsecretaría de Educación e Investigación Tecnológicas). 1998. *Estadística básica: sistema nacional de educación tecnológica, 1997–1998.* Mexico City: SEP/SEIT.

Slaughter, Sheila, and Larry L. Leslie. 1997. *Academic Capitalism: Policy, Politics, and the Entrepreneurial University.* Baltimore, Md.: Johns Hopkins University Press.

Trow, Martin. 1999. "Lifelong Learning through the New Information Technologies," *Higher Education Policy* 12 (2): 201–12.

UNESCO (United Nations Educational, Scientific and Cultural Organization). 1999. *Higher Education in the Twenty-First Century: Vision and Action.* Final Report of the World Conference on Higher Education, October 1998. Paris: UNESCO.

———. 2000. *World Education Report 2000.* Paris: UNESCO.

Villa Lever, Lorenza. 1986. "Escolaridad versus experiencia: la calificación del obrero y del técnico en la industria jalisciense." In *Cambio regional, mercado de trabajo y vida obrera en Jalisco,* edited by Guillermo de la Peña and Agustín Escobar. Guadalajara: El Colegio de Jalisco.

———. 1990. "La educación media superior ante la modernización educativa." In *La modernización educativa en perspectiva: análisis del Programa para la Modernización Educativa, 1989–1994,* edited by Teresa Bracho. Mexico City: Facultad Latinoamericana de Ciencias Sociales.

———. 1991a. "La educación media superior: antesala de la universidad y aproximación al futuro laboral." In *La formación de profesionistas ante los retos del siglo XXI,* edited by C. M. Zataráin. Guadalajara: Universidad de Guadalajara.

———. 1991b. "El mercado de trabajo de los técnicos." In *Perspectivas de la investigación en educación,* edited by Lorenza Villa Lever. Guadalajara: Universidad de Guadalajara.

———. 2000. "La educación media en México." In *México 2010: pensar y decidir la próxima década.* 2 vols. Mexico City: Centro de Estudios Estratégicos Nacionales/Instituto Politécnico Nacional/Universidad Autónoma Metropolitana.

Woolcock, Michael. 1998. "Social Capital and Economic Development: Toward a Theoretical Synthesis and Policy Framework," *Theory and Society* 27 (2): 151–207.

World Bank. 1994. *Higher Education: The Lessons of Experience.* Washington, D.C.: World Bank.

———. 1995. *Priorities and Strategies for Education: A World Bank Sector Review.* Washington, D.C.: World Bank.

World Bank/UNESCO Task Force on Higher Education and Society. 2000. "Higher Education in Developing Countries: Peril and Promise." At www.tfhe.net/report/.

Yarzábal, Luis, ed. 1999. *Consenso para el cambio en la educación superior.* Caracas, Venezuela: UNESCO/Instituto para la Educación Superior en América Latina y el Caribe.

9

The Transformation of Social Policy in Mexico

Asa Cristina Laurell

SOCIAL REFORM OF THE STATE

The debt crisis of 1982 marked the starting point of a new economic and social project in Mexico, a project proposing a wholesale reorganization of society based on neoclassical economic theory and neoliberal ideology (Sader and Gentili 1995; McMurtry 1998). This goal implied a profound transformation not only of the economy but also of the role of the state. Although the neoliberal reform project is internally unified precisely because it seeks to establish a different social order, for analytic purposes it is useful to separate out its political, economic, and social dimensions. Differentiating these dimensions allows for a better understanding of the complexities involved in a process that, if successful, will create a distinct social rationality and a new set of priorities. Among these new priorities, the satisfaction of human needs occupies a secondary position and no longer qualifies as a "common interest." This shift in values is most evident in the social reform of the Mexican state.

This reform project is based on translating ideas about ways to satisfy social needs (George and Wilding 1994: 35–39) into specific social policies. The agenda goes far beyond simple pragmatic or technical adjustments that increase efficiency in social programs and diminish their costs in order to reduce the public budget deficit. Instead, the main thrust is to commodify social services and benefits—that is, to move them into the sphere of private capital accumulation (Laurell 1991), increasing the role of the family and reducing the state's responsibilities in the provision of welfare (Esping-Andersen 1996: 3–5). Consequently, the reform implies reduced social rights for citizens and a social policy with a strong individualistic and market orientation.

This new conceptualization corresponds to the neoliberal definition of the satisfaction of social needs as an individual responsibility within the family or in the marketplace (C. Pierson 1991: 40–48). Social services and benefits are defined as "private" goods that obey market forces that, it is assumed, distribute resources efficiently. Following this logic, the state's actions must neither nullify the neoliberal project nor destroy the legitimacy of the state itself. This is achieved by following two complementary strategies. One is to promote the transfer of potentially profitable social-service financing and provision to the private sector. The second, essentially a legitimization device, is to create selective, means-tested, low-cost public programs targeted to persons in extreme poverty (Laurell and Wences 1994). Another important characteristic of this policy approach involves surrendering employment and income (wages, salaries, or agricultural prices) to market forces, in marked contrast with an approach that sees full employment and reasonable incomes as the foundation of any social policy (Esping-Andersen 1999: 13–14).

Under the terms of the neoliberal project, government intervention is appropriate in four areas: (1) the provision of narrowly defined "public" goods according to the principles of nonrivalry (use by one person does not make the good unavailable to others) and nonexclusion (no one is excluded from access); (2) certain activities directed toward the individual but that imply large externalities; (3) regulation to compensate for market failures; and (4) certain cost-effective services and subsidies for poverty alleviation. These interventions can be justified because they increase human capital and the productivity of the poor, do not provoke political resistance from powerful economic groups, and are compatible with fiscal orthodoxy (World Bank 1993). All other social services and benefits should be managed according to a market logic and gradually transferred to the private sector. In this scenario, the state's tasks would be to regulate markets, establish norms, and certify companies' and professionals' capacities.

What is usually not stated is that the implementation of this scheme requires further strong state intervention in the form of new legislation and considerable subsidies to sustain privatization and markets. Such subsidies represent a regressive redistribution of public social funds, and such a policy places a heavy burden on the families that are supposed to bridge the social gap between the retrenched state and the inaccessible market.

Social reform is more difficult to implement than economic reform because social policies affect people's everyday lives; as a direct consequence, there tends to be more popular resistance to the former than the latter. The successful implementation of social reform requires specific political conditions and depends upon the strength of social institutions (P. Pierson 1996; Navarro 1998), and thus it generally tends to be gradual. In Mexico and other Latin American countries, however, the process has been both rapid and profound, reflecting the limitations of previous welfare policies, different political regimes' authoritarian traits, and countries' decreasing margin for maneuver with international lending institutions such as the International Monetary Fund (IMF) and the World Bank.

In Mexico, institutions to protect social well-being were created over a half-century as part of a broad-based social pact among the state, private enterprises, and unions that set the scene for growth based on the import-substitution industrialization development model. Even a cursory historical analysis demonstrates that this type of development—focusing on expansion of the domestic market, employment creation, and some wage protections—established social entitlements and extended a wide range of social services and benefits to growing fractions of the population, along with supports for those outside the formal labor market (Vilas 1995: 9–29; Laurell 1996). The social reform of the Mexican state aims to abolish this regime (Esping-Andersen 1990) and replace it with one based on a neoliberal approach.

The process has unfolded in two phases: a preparatory phase, from 1983 to 1988, and the actual reform phase, from 1989 to the present. The preparatory phase of social reform was built into the logic of structural adjustment, given that fiscal adjustment, wage cuts, and unemployment together lead to the deterioration of public social institutions and programs (Laurell 1991; Iriart, Leone, and Testa 1995; Cohn 1995; Vergara 1997). This is the case because these factors put social institutions and programs under severe financial strain; at the same time, they devalue work and working conditions within these institutions. This erosion prepares the ground for an ideological attack that presents public institutions and social programs as intrinsically inefficient, bureaucratic, inhumane, and so on. And because social services and benefits are not universal and equitably distributed, the discourse alleging corporate and middle-class privileges at the expense of the poor has permeated even progressive thought (Vilas 1995: 193–201).

The discrediting of established social institutions legitimizes the social reform of the state. This began gradually in 1989 with the implementation of the anti-poverty National Solidarity Program (PRONASOL). Three important legislative reforms followed in the period between 1991 and 1994. One was the reform of Article 27 of the 1917 Constitution—the pillar of postrevolutionary rural development—to allow for the privatization of *ejido* lands, in effect commodifying them (Calva 1993). Article 3 was amended to give private and public institutions equal access to state subsidies for higher education and to exempt public universities from the principle that public education is free of charge. The third legal innovation was the introduction of a complementary mandatory pension system, the Retirement Savings System (SAR), based on privately administered individual retirement accounts (Laurell 1996).

The economic crisis of 1994–1995 accelerated the social reform process for two interrelated reasons. First, funds made available through the financial rescue package put together by the U.S. government and the IMF had to be replaced with longer-term, lower-cost international loans, prompting the Mexican government to negotiate "adjustment" loans (World Bank 1995, 1998). Second, the Mexican government and the World Bank saw reform of social welfare policies as a means to expand financial and service markets (Poder Ejecutivo Federal 1995). Despite broad opposition, the Mexican Congress passed a new Social Security Law in December 1995. Poverty alleviation programs were restructured initially as part of a fiscal adjustment and later to tighten targeting, monetarize benefits, and reorganize social "participation." Moreover, health and education services were decentralized.

When attempting to assess the impact of the social reform project in Mexico, it is useful to examine two key areas: the social security reform that lies at the heart of the commodification of services and benefits, and the poverty alleviation programs designed to soften the effects of structural adjustment and to reduce social and political conflict. Focusing on these two areas also aids in understanding the financial, institutional, and operational arrangements implicit in the reform project and their impacts on redistribution and social stratification—that is, the problems of privilege, inequity, and inefficiency.

SOCIAL WELFARE REFORM

The neoliberal social policy reform agenda in Mexico addresses pensions, workers' compensation, health services, and child care. Under the Mexican Constitution, all wage-earning and salaried workers are guaranteed access to basic welfare services provided by public institutions and guided by principles of comprehensiveness, solidarity, and redistribution. The Mexican Social Security Institute (IMSS) addresses these needs in the case of private-sector workers; the Social Security Institute for State Workers (ISSSTE) does so for public employees. To date, the reform project has only affected the former, which covers about 85 percent of Mexico's insured population. However, official documents indicate that a similar reform of the ISSSTE is on the agenda (Poder Ejecutivo Federal 1995).

Before 1997, when the new social welfare legislation came into force, the IMSS and the ISSSTE were decentralized state institutions with responsibility for the financing and delivery of services. Each institution had its own staff and infrastructure, and subcontracting with the private sector was extremely rare. These institutions represent by far the most important network of health care facilities in Mexico, with centers distributed throughout the country.[1] This health service network was constructed by investing a portion of pension funds in health centers, clinics, and hospitals, according to the principle that common social funds should meet important social needs.

Mexico's social welfare system is comprehensive: it includes old-age and disability pensions for insured workers; pensions for widows and dependent children; workers' compensation; medical care for insured workers and their families; child care for insured female workers; cultural, sports, and recreation centers; and low-cost housing financed with low-interest funds. Its underlying principle of solidarity is understood as solidarity between active and inactive (retired and disabled) workers, between workers in good health and those who are unwell, and between all workers and women with preschool-age children.

The main restriction in the Mexican welfare system is that, because of the structure of the Mexican labor market, it covers only about 55 percent of the national population (Poder Ejecutivo Federal 1999: 253). Self-employed and informal-sector workers are excluded, and this represents a serious inequity because those who are excluded are generally the poorest of the poor. Yet it would not be accurate to assume that workers covered by the IMSS constitute a privileged group; about 70 percent of them earn only three times the Mexican minimum wage or less (that is, US$300 per month or less in the late 1990s) (IMSS 1999: 3.3.5.1), an income that places them below the poverty line (Boltvinik 1995). Although coverage is contingent upon formal employment and is provided by different institutions depending upon whether the worker is employed in the private or the public sector, this is not a benefit that was established through collective or individual bargaining agreements. And prior to the reform, within each institution all workers had equal access to services.

The IMSS and ISSSTE were central to Mexico's effort to build a universal welfare state. The number of insured workers increased annually by 13 percent during the 1960s, by 11 percent in the 1970s, and by 5 percent in the 1980s. Furthermore, beginning in the 1970s, the IMSS

---

[1] The IMSS and ISSSTE together have approximately 400 hospitals (including 64 medical centers), 40,000 hospital beds, 1,400 operating rooms, 70,000 physicians, and a total of 300,000 employees (Poder Ejecutivo Federal 1999: 247–48).

developed a separate state-subsidized rural health care system for the uninsured poor. Health care centers in this system, known as IMSS–Solidaridad, were much more efficient and comprehensive than those operated by the Ministry of Health, and they reached an estimated 10.5 million Mexicans (Laurell and Ruiz 1996: 21).

Yet by the mid–1980s, the social welfare system had begun to deteriorate. A decade later, the IMSS and ISSSTE were commonly said to be "in crisis." Pensions had been eroded by inflation, and the quality of health services was in dramatic decline. Although there is general agreement that the key problem was a lack of funding, explanations for the deficit differ.

Government officials argued that the funding shortfall stemmed from demographic and epidemiological trends and, further, that it was exacerbated by an inefficient use of resources (IMSS 1995). Employers agreed on this last point, alleging that public institutions are inefficient by nature. This inefficiency, when combined with overly generous entitlements, supposedly had burdened employers with high labor costs,[2] which, in turn, had made them noncompetitive in global markets (Laurell 1995: 24–26). The government's and employer organizations' arguments helped justify the reform of the welfare system, which aimed to reduce entitlements, shift costs away from employers, and encourage the privatization of service provision.

However, a more objective look at the funding situation reveals a very different picture, one that suggests a close link between the decline in social welfare programs and the adoption of neoliberal economic policies beginning in 1983. The two principal causes of the drop in funding for social welfare programs were the steady decline in real wages and the failure to create jobs in the formal sector. Between 1983 and 1994, the IMSS lost approximately 215 billion pesos (about 5.4 times its total budget for 1994) because of falling wages (Laurell 1997: 29), and government subsidies were simultaneously reduced. Stagnant employment in the formal labor market and an explosion in informal-sector jobs had a dual impact on social welfare funding. First, the rate at which the IMSS–insured population grew dropped from a yearly average of 9.7 percent in the 1970s, to 5.1 percent in the 1980s, and to –0.8 percent in the early 1990s (Laurell 1999: 378–79). In other words, the earlier strategy of expanding the base of contributors in order to extend coverage and to finance social well-being was reversed.

---

[2] This argument has no objective basis. The average monthly industrial wage in Mexico was about US$300 in 1999, and indirect labor costs amounted to 24.7 percent of total labor costs. This compared to 35 percent in Japan, 45 percent in the United States, 65 percent in Germany, and 74 percent in Sweden (Laurell 1997).

Despite government claims, this situation had little to do with demographic or epidemiological changes. Mexico's total dependency ratio has actually declined over the last three decades—from 1.05 in 1970 to 0.66 in 1997—as a result of falling birth rates. The broad dependency ratio has changed very slowly, from 0.07 in 1980 to 0.08 in 1997 (Laurell 1997: 34).[3] This means that if all Mexicans with the potential to be economically active were employed in formal-sector jobs and contributing to the social security system, Mexico would be on a firm footing in terms of the well-being of its population. The failure of the current economic model to create even a modest increase in formal employment during periods of growth has produced an imbalance between active workers and retired workers. In 1980, the ratio was 38 active workers to each retiree; that ratio had dropped to 16.7 to 1 in 1997 (Poder Ejecutivo Federal 1999: 253). Finally, there is no consistent empirical evidence to demonstrate a negative impact on health care costs caused by epidemiological trends; the pattern of diseases treated at hospitals has changed very little (INEGI 1999: 15).

The IMSS initially offset the decrease in its funding by dramatically cutting the salaries of its personnel (Herrera 1990). Combined with normal equipment wear and tear and a lack of medical supplies, these cuts undermined the quality of institutional services. At the same time, demand for service was rising as the insured population became poorer, and the increased demand created logjams that barred timely access to service. Nevertheless, despite having to function under adverse conditions, the IMSS and ISSSTE remain Mexico's most important providers of health services, serving at least 40 percent of the population in low or lower-middle income brackets. Estimates based on official data also show that these institutions are making optimal use of their existing resources, in contrast to a low utilization of resources in private health care establishments (Laurell 1997: 39).

The 1995 Social Security Law marked a radical shift away from the principles of Mexico's previous social welfare policy. The basic scheme moves from public financing and provision to private administration; from comprehensive coverage to different plans for retirement insurance, life and disability insurance, and workers' compensation insurance; from solidarity to individualism; and from redistribution and equal rights to correspondence between the premium paid and the amount of the entitlement. The new law is an example of direct state

---

[3] The total dependency ratio is the ratio between the population below 15 years of age and over 65, on the one hand, and the population group between the ages of 15 and 64 years, on the other. The broad dependency ratio is that between the population over age 64 and the 15–64 age group.

intervention to create new markets and to favor special interest groups —
in this case, financial trusts.

Pensions for Profit

The shift in goals and methods is clear in Mexico's pension reform,
which was modeled on a World Bank proposal (1994). The new program eliminates the pay-as-you-go scheme based on publicly administered common funds with guaranteed annuities; it replaces it with a
mandatory program of individual retirement accounts managed by
private financial intermediaries, the Retirement Fund Administrators
(AFOREs)[4] The amount in the account varies depending upon an individual's savings and is therefore uncertain. The accounts must be used
at retirement to purchase old-age and survivor annuities from private
insurance companies. Although disability pensions and workers' compensation insurance continue to be funded collectively, these annuities
must also be purchased from an insurance company, and the worker's
individual retirement account is expropriated in the process even though
it is a separate insurance.

The new scheme emphasizes privatization, domestic saving, and
expansion of the financial market. It also tightens eligibility rules and
establishes a strict equivalence between the amount saved and the annuity received. The shift to individual retirement accounts eliminates
intergenerational transfers and risk sharing among workers. However,
the law does guarantee a minimum annuity (equal to the minimum
wage) for eligible retirees. In other words, the state will eventually
complement individual assets with public funds.[5]

Every formal-sector worker in Mexico must now sign a contract with
an AFORE. Monies that Mexican workers paid into pension funds prior to
the implementation of the new law are not recognized, presumably because
their inclusion would substantially increase transition costs. Government
officials argue that this virtual expropriation of workers' funds is redressed
by the fact that eligible workers who contributed under the old program
may, on retirement, choose between annuities calculated under the old
and the new rules. In the interim, however, private pension funds will
continue to receive premiums and charge commissions for years.

The Social Security Law created three special financial entities to
manage the pension program: AFOREs, Specialized Investment Retire-

---

[4] A mandatory quota for housing (5 percent of a worker's wage) is also deposited in
the individual retirement account, but it is not subject to variable interest rates.

[5] The tripartite premium for this insurance is 6.5 percent of the worker's wage, with
a state subsidy corresponding to 5.5 percent of the legal minimum wage.

ment Funds (SIEFOREs), and special insurance companies to handle annuities. The emerging trend is that financial groups establish an AFORE–SIEFORE and an insurance company, thus gaining control over the entire pension cycle. The AFORE manages the retirement accounts and invests the savings in financial markets through one or various associated SIEFOREs. The role of the specialized insurance companies is to sell old-age, survivor, and/or disability pensions to the insured workers. Thus the new financial organisms will replace the IMSS in all functions related to pensions except in the administration of funds collected for life and disability insurance and for workers' compensation.

This pension scheme will effect the largest transfer of public funds to private financial groups ever experienced in Mexico. The IMSS has estimated that these funds will equal 25 percent of gross domestic product (GDP) in ten years, 45 percent in twenty years, and 60 percent in thirty years (IMSS 1996). Control over these vast amounts of capital confers unprecedented economic—and political—power on private financial agents, which can be only partly moderated by legislation (Ruiz-Tagle 1996).

In December 2001, banks or insurance companies owned thirteen AFOREs. Five were controlled by foreign capital, and six others had important foreign partners (such as Aegon, Citibank, Santander, and Zurich Insurance). Only two belonged to Mexican financial groups, one of which was associated with the IMSS.[6] Despite rules designed to guarantee competition, a process of concentration is under way: 57 percent of registered workers belonged to five AFOREs, which together controlled 65 percent of pension funds and two of which controlled 37 percent (CONSAR 2001: 1.2, 1.14).

Apart from controlling large amounts of capital, the AFOREs also benefit because they charge insured workers a commission. This fee may be a percentage of the premium, a percentage of accumulated assets in the account, a percentage of revenues from the invested funds, or some combination of these.[7] According to estimates by the National Commission on Retirement Savings (CONSAR), the average commission that is charged, recalculated as a percentage of the premium, is 1.71 percent of a worker's wage (CONSAR 2001: 1.8). This means that

---

[6] By late 1999, four AFOREs had already gone out of business.

[7] All AFOREs but one charge a fee based on the premium; this ranges from 1.45 to 1.7 percent of the worker's wage, or between 24 and 26 percent of the amount paid into the account. Most AFOREs also charge a percentage fee (ranging from 0.2 to 1 percent) based on accumulated assets. And one AFORE levies a charge of 33 percent of revenue.

the AFOREs charged insured workers about US$1.5 billion between July 1997 and June 1999 alone.

These figures conclusively disprove the claim that private management of pension funds is more efficient; the IMSS spent only 0.63 percent of workers' wages on administration (IMSS 1995). The fees paid to the AFOREs have gone to cover these companies' high marketing and advertising costs, but the companies have also turned a 24 percent profit (CONSAR 2001: 4.2). Although the commissions that the AFOREs charge may decrease over time, this has not happened in Chile, where competition has tended to increase expenses (BANAMEX 1996). Thus one of the main objections to individual retirement accounts—that they are a very expensive pension alternative (Ruiz-Tagle 1996; Hazas Sánchez 1996; Bonilla 1995; López 1995)—has been confirmed in Mexico.

Under the 1995 Social Security Law, the specialized insurance companies that manage annuities are even more favored than the AFOREs because workers must purchase from them not only old-age pension insurance but also survivors', disability, and workers' compensation insurance. This will have a radical impact on the Mexican insurance market, where the premiums paid for all other private insurance are roughly equivalent to the mandatory pension premiums to be transferred (Laurell 1997: 72).

The state, as underwriter of the pension reform, is committed to subsidizing the privatization of pensions over the long term. Thus the transition costs, estimated by the Ministry of Finance and Public Credit at about 1 to 1.5 percent of GDP per year for six decades,[8] must be paid by the federal government (SHCP 1996). These costs are an inevitable result of the shift from a pay-as-you-go scheme to fully funded private retirement accounts. The former scheme is built on a match between income and disbursements—that is, part of workers' contributions are used to pay pensions—and the system need not accumulate assets equal to future pensions. It need only have sufficient actuarial reserves to cover annuities in the event that contributions fall below immediate pension commitments.

The new system of private retirement accounts follows a completely different logic. Under this scheme, the premiums paid by active workers cannot be used to pay current annuities. Instead, the basic goal is to capitalize these accounts at a level sufficient to cover the holders' future annuities. The accounts are managed by private trust funds, and they are invested in financial markets with the objective of maximizing profits.

---

[8] Because of the large number of uncertain events (wage and employment levels, GDP growth, interest rates, and so on) potentially affecting transition costs, a more precise forecast is impossible.

In the meantime, the state—that is, insured and uninsured taxpayers— must cover the transition costs. These include the payment of current pensions as well as any additional amounts needed to purchase annuities for workers who paid premiums into the pay-as-you-go scheme.

The retirement program also includes some additional state-subsidized guarantees that were adopted to quiet strong public opposition to the new legislation (Laurell 1995). These include a "social quota," a guaranteed minimum annuity, and the right of retiring workers who contributed under the old plan to select between annuities calculated under the old and the new rules. The Mexican state also contributes an "invisible" subsidy when it issues high-interest government bonds that return high yields on retirement accounts (Beattie and McGillivray 1995).

Establishing private retirement accounts is not a feasible option unless the state is willing to underwrite the costs of transition and additional subsidies. This is why opponents contend that the state is subsidizing private financial groups and that workers would be better off under the old system. The estimated transition cost of 1 to 1.5 percent of GDP per year is substantial when one considers that total government social expenditures—including education, health care, social welfare programs, poverty alleviation programs, and housing—equal less than 10 percent of GDP (Poder Ejecutivo Federal 1999: 73). And because a balanced budget remains one of the Mexican government's top priorities, it is likely that other social programs will be cut in the future to finance the new social security plan.

In this new system, financial trusts are the winners and uninsured taxpayers and insured workers are the losers. Taxpayers are obliged to subsidize a system that gives them nothing in return, and insured workers lose because some of them will be ineligible under the new plan. The size of the pensions for those who are eligible is not certain, though it will probably be small. Contrary to government claims, the new scheme is likely to reduce the size of the insured population. Under the previous scheme, a worker who had made 500 weekly payments into the system had the right to a life-long pension and free medical care at age 65. Under the provisions of the 1995 Social Security Law, a worker qualifies for a pension only after making 1,250 weekly contributions, and the right to medical care after retirement is contingent upon having made 750 weekly contributions. Because the instability of the labor market makes it more difficult for workers to make continuous contributions, the number of workers eligible to participate in the new pension program will likely be restricted.

Under the new plan, the size of an annuity by definition depends upon accumulated individual savings. None of the components—the size and number of weekly deposits, fees and commissions charged, and the interest rate on the account—can be predicted over a working lifetime.[9] Most uncertain is the average interest rate that financial markets will deliver. Because of this uncertainty, AFORE contracts state explicitly that the insured accepts that his or her fund may decrease or increase in value due to market fluctuations (Laurell 1997: 70). Some optimistic experts estimate real annual interest rates of 4 to 5 percent, while more cautious observers predict rates between 2 and 3 percent.[10] As of mid-1998, the return on pension funds was negative after factoring in inflation and commissions. This trend was reversed when the federal government issued special development bonds, which are indexed against inflation and are available for sale only to pension funds and SIEFOREs. In 2001, these bonds made up 69 percent of SIEFORE investments (CONSAR 2001: 2.1–2.3).

The formal labor market is a second source of uncertainty regarding the ultimate value of a pension. Slow economic growth and frequent layoffs make it difficult to predict the average time a worker may be unemployed during his or her working life. While unemployed, a worker does not make contributions to his or her retirement account, but the AFORE continues to charge a commission. Both of these factors reduce the value of the fund at retirement. It is revealing in this regard that, on average, more than 20 percent of registered workers were inactive between mid-1997 and mid-1999 (CONSAR 2001: 2.1).

The most technically precise estimate of future annuities under the new pension scheme comes from the National Association of Actuaries.[11] Depending upon the worker's "wage career," the annuity would range from 16 to 37 percent of the individual's pre-retirement annual income, which in most cases means that the insured would receive the minimum annuity of one minimum wage guaranteed by the federal government. By contrast, under the former pay-as-you-go scheme, a worker who had contributed to the pension fund for thirty-five years would receive an annuity that equaled no less than 98.75 percent of his or her pre-retirement income, and as much as 99.7 percent (IMSS 1993).

These data confirm that future annuities will fall short of an acceptable standard of income security for senior citizens, given that an in-

---

[9] Beattie and McGillivray 1995; Ruiz-Tagle 1996; Bonilla 1995; Kurczyn 1996; Lo Vuolo 1996; Du Boff 1997.

[10] Bonilla 1995; Du Boff 1997; Ruiz-Tagle 1996; Gillion and Bonilla 1992; Bustos Castillo 1993.

[11] This study assumed thirty-five years of continuous contributions of 11.5 percent of wages (which includes a contribution to the housing fund), commissions equal to 25 percent of the total premium, and an average real interest rate of 5 percent per year.

come of one minimum wage (about US$100 per month in 1999) falls below the poverty line. The data also show that payments into the retirement accounts are insufficient and must be complemented with additional funds if the new scheme is to be sustainable. If the social insurance payroll tax is maintained at its same level (a commitment the government has made to employers), the 5 percent contributed for housing must be incorporated into the retirement account, even though this means that workers would forfeit their constitutional right to adequate housing. And even with this supplement, a reasonable annuity could only be achieved if accounts earn average real interest rates of at least 7 or 8 percent per year.

Although the 1995 legislation established that annuities are to be adjusted annually for inflation, pension experts are skeptical whether this is feasible under a private and individualized scheme. Under conditions of high inflation, the federal government would have to intervene, subsidizing insurance companies either directly or indirectly by issuing government bonds with a guaranteed interest rate above the rate of inflation (Beattie and McGillivray 1995; Du Boff 1997). Furthermore, the legislation does not establish clear-cut rules for computing the purchase cost and annuity amount in pension contracts. This oversight might lead to discriminatory practices against certain segments of the population, especially women, who live longer on average (Beattie and McGillivray 1995; Ruiz-Tagle 1996).

Supporters of pension reform assert as their closing argument that the reform is beneficial overall because the large increase in domestic savings will produce rapid investment, economic growth, more jobs, and higher wages. It is not clear, however, whether mandatory retirement savings produce an increase in national savings or just change the balance between private and public savings. The negative public savings implicit in the transition cost might, in fact, lead to a decrease in public investment, with negative effects on growth. Furthermore, there is no consistent empirical evidence to prove a causal relationship between rates of saving, investment, and economic growth (Gillion and Bonilla 1992; Kurczyn 1996), for the simple reason that a supply of financial assets does not automatically generate a demand for productive activities. Given the prolonged contraction that has occurred in the Mexican domestic market in response to falling real wages, there is little convincing evidence that an increase in domestic savings will quickly reinvigorate the economy (López 1995). Some studies on the dynamics of the Mexican economy (Huerta 1991; Valenzuela 1995) show that large profits, obtained primarily through wage depression, have not increased the rates of productive investment or job creation. Rather, the scarcity of profitable investment opportunities in the national economy has provoked capital flight, along with a boom in luxury consumption (generally of imported goods) among the tiny minority of the population that is favored by the neoliberal model.

This evidence challenges the assumption that mandatory pension savings, channeled through new financial intermediaries, will create a virtuous circle of "saving–investment–employment." What is clear is that Mexican financial markets do not have the capacity to absorb the expanded supply of credit, forcing the federal government to issue bonds at interest rates that are high enough to generate the expected rate of return on retirement accounts. In late 2000, 88 percent of pension funds were invested in government bonds with yields above those available in financial markets (CONSAR 2001: 2.1). The only other option would be a legislative reform to allow the trusts to invest pension funds abroad (as has happened in Chile; see Ruiz-Tagle 1996) or to relax regulations. However, such a move would subvert the objective of stimulating domestic economic growth or run higher risks.

Health Reform: Stratified Health Insurance and Minimum Public Assistance

The second important aspect of social welfare reform in contemporary Mexico concerns health services. This element of the reform project is linked to an overall transformation of the health care system, including social security health services, private health services, and public services for the uninsured.

The government's blueprint for structural reform of the health sector is found in the "Program for Health Sector Reform" (Poder Ejecutivo Federal 1996). It is strikingly similar to a 1993 World Bank proposal that embodies the essence of neoliberal social reform (World Bank 1993). It establishes, on the one hand, a market-driven system for those who can afford to pay for their own health care or have access to health insurance through mandatory social security and, on the other, a decentralized system of publicly provided basic services for the "uninsurable" — that is, the poor.

Social welfare reform is a core element in a market-driven health system because it lays the foundation for the commodification of services and gives private businesses access to mandatory social security health funds and to the most advanced hospital facilities. The three most relevant changes in legislation affecting the health sector are: (1) a new formula for calculating premiums, (2) the possibility of choosing between public and private health insurance and services within the mandatory system, and (3) a new form of voluntary health insurance,

Salud para la Familia (Family Health), designed to incorporate unin-sured individuals with purchasing power.

The new financing scheme is based on "equal pay for equal ser-vices," with all insured individuals paying the same premium. (Under the previous health care system, individuals paid a fixed percentage of their income and received services according to need; on average under the old "solidarity" system, 80 percent of insured workers received more health services than they paid for [Laurell 1997: 24]). Conceptu-ally, the uniform premium policy implies putting a price on the health services offered through the IMSS mandatory health insurance pro-gram. Proponents view this as a necessary step toward introducing a market logic into health care provision.

Another element in the financing scheme is a government contribu-tion of 13.9 percent of one minimum wage for each member of the population covered by health insurance, thereby increasing the state's contribution from 5 to about 30 percent of total premium costs (17,428 million pesos in 1998 [IMSS 1999: 3.4.6]). These funds mainly constitute a subsidy to big private employers who will, therefore, be able to re-duce their health care contributions substantially.[12] However, the total income that the IMSS will receive under the new plan will remain ap-proximately the same because the government subsidy only compen-sates for the decrease in employer and employee premiums (Laurell 1997: 97). This means that the financial problems of the IMSS health care system — which in the late 1990s was operating at a 10 percent deficit — will remain. Moreover, shortfalls can no longer be covered with monies from pension funds because those are now in the hands of AFOREs. And following the logic of separate accountability for each type of insurance, the IMSS also began to be charged rent for medical facilities that were built with pension funds (IMSS 1999: 3.4.7).

The main changes in health care services derive not from new leg-islation but from a complex institutional reorganization affecting finan-cial management and service provision for about 45 million people.[13] It began by separating regulation, financing, and service provision, all of

---

[12] For example, the fee an employer pays for five minimum wages drops from 8.75 to 5.22 percent, and for twenty-five minimum wages, it falls from 8.75 to 2.48 per-cent, while the employer fee for one minimum wage (corresponding to workers in small companies) increases from 8.88 to 21.53 percent. Estimated from IMSS data (IMSS 1999: 3.4.4–3.4.5) and articles 25, 106, 107 and transitory article 19 of the 1995 Ley del Seguro Social.

[13] Although the Mexican federal government was reluctant to publicize details of this reorganization, it provided an outline to the World Bank in May 1998 when requesting a US$700 million adjustment loan (see World Bank 1998).

which used to be managed by the IMSS. In the contemporary model, a central administration will collect contributions and transfer these monies to an autonomous fund, the Social Security Health Fund (SSHF). This fund has two basic functions. One is to set and maintain a budgetary ceiling, which implies establishing maximums for total and per person health care expenditures. The other is to transfer health care funds to public and private managed care organizations (MCOs) using a universal capitation formula (payment per insured adjusted for age and sex) and, eventually, to compensate for "catastrophic" expenditures. A first essential step is to define the set of services to be covered by the mandatory premium — the "comprehensive health package" — and its cost. Given that the package does not cover all services, it will be necessary to offer supplemental insurance through the IMSS or private insurance companies.

Health care for the insured population will be provided directly by MCOs or subcontracted by MCOs from other providers. To cover the costs of service delivery, each MCO will receive funds from the SSHF according to the size and characteristics of the population it serves. The MCOs, which are patterned on U.S.-style health maintenance organizations (HMOs), will compete for insured "clients." Initially, MCOs will be "internal markets" equivalent to the 139 IMSS medical area units (MAUs) that will provide primary and secondary health care, and they will purchase specialized medical care from the 41 IMSS specialized hospitals, which will also become self-supporting. However, the formation of private MCOs is being encouraged through new legislation affecting the private insurance industry. Private MCOs will have an equal opportunity to compete for clients and an equal right to receive funds from the SSHF and purchase services from specialized IMSS hospitals. Government planners anticipate a gradual transition from internal markets to a free market in which health care users can choose freely among MCOs.

All MCOs are administratively independent, which should encourage efficiency and cost control. All will be required to provide the comprehensive health package and to comply with established quality norms. To be competitive, MAUs must be free to provide services directly or to purchase them. And they must be able to hire and fire staff and to introduce productivity-based incentives, things they cannot do under existing federal labor law. To survive, MCOs must attract clients and keep costs within budget. Nevertheless, it is not yet clear how MCO profits might be regulated or how any surplus in a MAU would be used. Nor has a source of financing been identified for covering the severe deficits that exist in IMSS infrastructure and equipment (Laurell and Ruiz 1996: 49–52). The MAUs' competitiveness will be hampered by the ongoing deterioration of the IMSS system, which, together with the system's fragmentation into self-sufficient units, presages a dismantling of the largest public health care system in Latin America.

The private actors that will profit from this new arrangement are insurance companies and international HMOs, on the one hand, and large for-profit hospitals, on the other. The former are the same financial groups that control pension funds, but given the Mexican companies' relative inexperience in health care insurance, large U.S. HMOs are likely to enter this lucrative market,[14] as they have done elsewhere in Latin America (Stocker, Waitzkin, and Iriat 1999). It is important to emphasize that the key activity in the reform model is the management of health funds, which imposes its own logic on service provision. Although there are over 2,000 private clinics and hospitals in Mexico (INEGI 1999: 151), the vast majority are small and are unlikely to meet the new certification requirements. This leaves about 100 large private hospitals as managed care providers. Previous experience suggests that they are likely to stress financial management over care provision, with deleterious consequences for patients (Working Group 1994). And as they become increasingly powerful, insurance companies and MCOs will also gain greater influence over policy decisions (Bodenheimer 1995; Navarro 1997).

The market logic underlying this scheme undermines solidarity among the insured and reduces entitlements. This is so because the range of supplemental health plans (with different premiums and copayments) will lead to a stratification in access and in quality of service that did not exist under the previous system, in which all insured patients had the same rights regardless of their contribution (Laurell 1997). Furthermore, the available empirical data do not confirm that the complementary insurance programs will rapidly increase coverage. One such voluntary insurance, Salud para la Familia, had enrolled fewer than 200,000 families two years after the new social welfare legislation had been implemented (IMSS 1999: 3.3.2). The annual premium in effect in the late 1990s (about 2,000 pesos) was beyond the reach of most Mexican households.

Because mandatory health insurance covers only about half of the population, the Mexican Ministry of Health operates a complementary public assistance service for the uninsured poor. This service was both reorganized as part of the overall health care reform and reoriented ac-

---

[14] The estimated size of the market in the late 1990s was approximately US$6 billion (IMSS 1999: 3.4.6).

cording to the principles of Mexico's poverty alleviation programs —
targeting, decentralization, and cost-effectiveness. The federal government decentralized services to the state level, a process that was completed in 1997. During the transition, the federal government transferred funds to state governments according to their past levels of
expenditure.

However, under the terms of the health care reform (Poder Ejecutivo Federal 1996: 32), the federal government only has a long-term
commitment to finance a "basic package" of public health interventions
and cost-cutting outpatient care. The package covers household hygiene; family planning and Pap smears; prenatal, perinatal, and post-
natal care; child nutrition and development; immunizations and control
of parasites; mobile medical care for persons with acute respiratory
disease; prevention and control of tuberculosis, hypertension, and dia-
betes; accident prevention and first aid; and community training for
self-care. This package will be provided free of charge, but it contains
substantially fewer services than those the Ministry of Health previously provided to the poor. This means that, in the future, all services
not included in the basic health care package must be paid for by the
patient or by the state government. This arrangement will intensify
the inequality in health status that already exists between individuals
and regions because of an inequitable distribution of resources.

This two-pronged health care reform strategy — the commodification
of health care financing and services and a selective benefits package
for the poor — is likely to add to social distress. It reverses the historical
trend in Mexico toward universal and comprehensive health care. It
also implies a redistribution, rather than a reduction, in public funding
for health care, with some share of these monies going to private
health-care providers and insurance companies. Moreover, there is no
solid evidence that this market-driven reform will actually achieve its
goals of equity, efficiency, and quality; in fact, most empirical evidence
suggests the opposite.[15] And the privileging of a market logic over the
logic of meeting health needs raises serious ethical questions (Doyal and
Gough 1991).

Viewed from this perspective, Mexico's contemporary social welfare
reform is actually a counterreform. It does not solve any of the problems that supposedly inspired it. There is no empirical evidence that it
will increase pension or health service coverage or grant old-age income security. The alleged positive impact on economic growth and job

---

[15] Dahlgren 1994; Diderichsen 1995; Health Policy Network 1995; Cárdenas Rivera
1997; Vergara 1997.

creation is equally uncertain. The values of solidarity and income redistribution through public action are being replaced by the values of
the marketplace, individual capacity, and private profits. By using its
legal authority to promote private goals at the expense of the common
interest, the federal government is conceding to a tiny minority the
right to exercise economic power so as to socialize risks and losses and
privatize profits—an orientation that is alien to classical liberal thought
and to prevailing ethical and social values.

THE POVERTY OF POVERTY PROGRAMS

Narrowly focused poverty programs—as opposed to integrated, comprehensive, and universal social policies—are being promoted in Mexico because they are compatible with neoliberal economic policies and
the state's withdrawal from its traditional role as the primary funder
and manager of social services. The argument goes as follows: given the
scarcity of public resources, the state should direct its efforts toward
ensuring a minimum level of well-being for the poor through selective,
carefully targeted, and cost-efficient poverty alleviation programs that
complement market and family mechanisms. That is, the federal government should intervene only when the market and family networks
"fail."

The explicit principles that guide the new poverty programs are targeting, decentralization, and participation; the implicit one is a low and
inflexible budget ceiling. There is an immediately apparent contradiction here: poverty is increasing while the resources channeled to poverty alleviation programs are being reduced. In this context, targeting is
nothing more than a device for distributing insufficient resources. Resource needs are no longer calculated on the basis of the unmet basic
needs of the population, but rather according to the logic of fiscal adjustment and neoliberal priorities. "Decentralization" of poverty alleviation programs means, at best, that state and municipal authorities or
community groups can select from among a preestablished menu of
programs, and "participation" means that those involved are expected
to contribute financial and/or human resources or, alternately, to adopt
prescribed behaviors. In this scheme, welfare assistance is not a "right"
that citizens can claim, but something bestowed at the discretion of
government officials.

The cost-savings strategy, which derives from a management logic,
has been applied particularly to programs that invest in the human
capital of the poor (IADB 1996). This approach has some serious conceptual limitations because it extracts simple causal relationships from
complex processes (Laurell 1997: 87). Although advocating social in-

vestment and the rational use of resources has merit, these criteria are frequently used to justify restrictions on welfare services and to transform social priorities into numerical values that are alien to human values.

Mexico has a long history of social programs directed to the poorest of the poor. The key characteristic of these previous programs was that they were based in the public institutions responsible for social welfare. Thus, even though such programs are, in theory, temporary efforts, past logic dictated that they be incorporated into the established national welfare structure (Laurell 1996). The first poverty program of a new type was the National Solidarity Program (PRONASOL), initiated in December 1988 by the administration of Carlos Salinas de Gortari (1988–1994). Defined as a discretionary program of the federal government (*Diario Oficial* 1988), PRONASOL was innovative in that it bypassed established institutional mechanisms and instead concentrated authority for the program in the hands of the president. The rationale for this arrangement was that it supposedly would allow more flexibility in the allocation of funds, increase sensitivity to community demands, and, therefore, stimulate popular participation (SEDESOL 1993: 8).

Funding for PRONASOL rose from 0.3 percent of GDP in 1989 to 0.8 percent in 1994, far below the level of funding allocated for similar purposes prior to 1983. The amount and distribution of the PRONASOL budget belie any claim that the government intended to use the program to provide a safety net for poor families and children. In fact, the correlation between regions with high poverty indices and regions receiving PRONASOL funding and benefits was very low. Moreover, the program created very few employment opportunities, and the subsidies to peasants in high-risk, low-yield agriculture were insignificant (Laurell and Wences 1994).

Despite extensive publicity about the accomplishments of PRONASOL, regular institutional programs have been far more important in providing social services to the Mexican population. It is now widely acknowledged that PRONASOL was created, not to aid the poor, but to strengthen political support—especially electoral support—for Salinas and the governing Institutional Revolutionary Party (PRI) (Molinar Horcasitas and Weldon 1994). It was also intended to create a stable popular base for Salinas's neoliberal project (Dresser 1994) and to organize a new, neocorporatist mechanism for political negotiation that bypassed existing labor and peasant organizations. PRONASOL failed on this last point, however, because the ad hoc local organizations it fostered proved to be unstable (Laurell and Wences 1994).

TABLE 9.1. Selected Poverty Programs in Mexico, 1995–1999

Category/Program	1995	1996	1997	1998	1999
Income opportunities ("temporary jobs")					
Jobs created[1]	662,145	851,296	848,403	907,073	1,031,623
240-day-equivalent jobs	223,252	287,027	286,052	305,833	347,827
Equivalent jobs with one annual minimum wage	150,157	151,497	233,497	232,692	310,900
Average total income per job (current pesos)	1,072.4	1,167.3	1,204.6	1,515.9	1,667.4
Average total income per job (1994 pesos)[2]	645.8	527.3	473.7	501.1	509.1
Unemployment and underemployment[3]	8,385,828	8,294,359	7,965,583	6,949,896	
Human capital development ("Progresa")					
Families receiving benefits			404,200	1,909,900	2,298,600
Children with scholarships			101,100	1,690,900	2,172,800
Annual scholarship (current pesos)			221.9	322.0	1,041.6
Families receiving food support			300,700	1,595,600	2,298,600
Total food support (millions of current pesos)			64.8	790.7	2,778.8
Total food support (millions of 1994 pesos)[2]			25.5	261.5	848.5
Average annual value of food support per family (current pesos)			215.4	495.5	1,208.9
Human capital development (other "food programs")					
Millions of current pesos	9,989.1	10,455.2	8,171.6	6,729.6	5,595.3
Millions of 1994 pesos[2]	6,015.7	4,723.4	3,213.4	2,224.7	1,708.4

Source: Poder Ejecutivo Federal, *Quinto informe de gobierno,* Anexo estadístico, 1999.

[1] One temporary job equals 88 working days.

[2] Deflated by the changing value of a basic consumption basket.

[3] Number of persons in "alternative open unemployment" or "critical employment conditions" as defined in Poder Ejecutivo Federal, *Quinto informe de gobierno,* Anexo estadístico, 1999: 53.

Mexico's 1994–1995 financial crisis led to a generalized repudiation of Salinas, ended PRONASOL (which had been closely identified with the former president), and resulted in a 15 percent cut in social expenditures. The budget allocation for "social welfare and basic goods" fell from 0.8 percent of GDP in 1995 to 0.4 percent in 1996, 0.3 percent in 1997, and 0.2 percent in 1998 (Poder Ejecutivo Federal 1999: 72–73).[16] Poverty alleviation programs were restructured under three main headings: human capital development, physical capital development, and income opportunities. A change in program names was accompanied by even narrower targeting, the elimination of subsidies and price controls for basic foods, and the decentralization of some resources to municipalities, conditional on approval of specific projects (Poder Ejecutivo Federal 1999).

It is also very important to consider the scope of these programs in relation to need. Following a neoliberal logic, the labor market should obey the law of supply and demand and the state should not play an active role in the labor market. The data on unemployment and underemployment suggest that, conservatively, about 8 million individuals a year in 1995–1997 and 7 million individuals in 1998 were looking for work, wanted to work but were not actively seeking a job, were underemployed (working less than 35 hours per week), were working more than 35 hours a week and earning less than the minimum wage, or were working more than 48 hours and earning less than two minimum wages. In the face of this critical situation, a program to create temporary employment (lasting 88 working days) generated fewer than 10 percent of the jobs needed, and the positions that did materialize paid an average annual income of about 10 percent of a single minimum wage (see table 9.1). And if one raises the bar to consider positions that lasted 240 days, the number of jobs created drops by two-thirds. Although the temporary employment program clearly failed to meet the needs of Mexico's potential workforce, it did comply with the neoliberal policy of a free labor market.

The most important program that the administration of President Ernesto Zedillo (1994–2000) initiated under the "human capital development" rubric was the Program on Education, Health, and Nutrition (PROGRESA), which replaced PRONASOL in 1997 and expanded rapidly thereafter (table 9.1). It claimed to integrate health, education, and food

---

[16] Several ministries besides the Ministry of Social Development (SEDESOL) allocate a portion of their budgets to poverty alleviation programs. The federal government claimed that, when these contributions were taken into account, 1.1 percent of GDP was allocated to poverty alleviation in the late 1990s (Poder Ejecutivo Federal 1999: 265).

TABLE 9.2. Selected Poverty Indicators for Mexico, 1994 and 1996

	1994	1996	Change, 1995–1996
Households in extreme poverty	7,873,200	11,256,850	3,383,650
Indigent families	6,473,520	8,868,351	2,394,831
Children aged 7 to 15	19,370,650	19,677,296	306,645
Children in extreme poverty	7,845,113	10,822,512	2,977,399
Indigent children	6,450,426	8,526,172	2,075,746

Sources: Data for households in extreme poverty and for indigent families were esti-mated from Boltvinik 1998. The data on children between the ages of 7 and 15 are projections by the Consejo Nacional de Población. The data on children in extreme poverty and indigent children were estimated from Boltvinik 1998, assuming the same number of children per household, which gives a conservative estimate of the number of poor children.

components. In 1999, 2.17 million children received PROGRESA schol-arships averaging 1,041 pesos (US$110) a year (approximately one month's minimum wage), and 2.3 million families received food sup-port averaging 1,209 pesos per year (also approximately one month's minimum wage). The allocation for scholarships and food support was approximately US$140 million (0.04 percent of GDP) in 1998 and US$540 million (0.11 percent of GDP) in 1999 (Poder Ejecutivo Fede-ral 1999: 266).

A comparison of these numbers with data on poverty in 1996 (table 9.2) indicates that one of every four indigent children or one of every five children in extreme poverty received a scholarship in 1999.[17] Moreover, the number of children receiving scholarships was approxi-mately equal to the increase in the population of indigent children be-tween 1994 and 1996. Similarly, one of every four households living in poverty or one of every five households in extreme poverty received benefits. These numbers do not even rise to the rate at which house-holds in extreme poverty increased between 1994 and 1996. These data confirm that PROGRESA fell far short of constituting a social welfare program able to ensure a minimum standard of living for Mexicans living in poverty or in extreme poverty.

Other food programs, primarily the subsidies for tortillas and milk, should be evaluated in this context. Resources directed to those pro-

---

[17] Poverty data are calculated from the federal government's survey of family in-come and expenditures. These data are not available for the post–1996 period.

grams dropped steadily in both absolute and relative terms from 1995 to 1999, losing 62 percent of their economic value by the end of the period (table 9.1). PROGRESA food supports did not come close to offsetting this decrease, which meant that many families lost part of this fundamental social assistance. General subsidies for basic foods were also eliminated during this period, despite the fact that between half and three-fourths[18] of the population lived in poverty (Boltvinik 1998).

Because it was implemented in poor rural municipalities (*municipios*), PROGRESA was a more carefully targeted program than PRONASOL. However, villages within these municipalities that did not have a school or health services—presumably the poorest ones— were excluded. The program's second, individual level of targeting selected some families with children as beneficiaries but excluded others, which created divisions within poor communities. Furthermore, poor urban areas were entirely excluded from PROGRESA, despite the fact that extreme poverty has grown very fast in cities (Boltvinik 2000: 20).

At best, then, Mexico's poverty alleviation programs have been able to manage poverty—but not overcome it (Boltvinik 1998). The basic reason for this failure is that they do not change the overall dynamics of poverty, which are rooted in the logic of a neoliberal political economy that has destroyed jobs, reduced income, and concentrated wealth. The minimal level of resource allocation demonstrates that these programs are not committed to satisfying basic human needs. They do, however, establish a social discourse that demonstrates the government's concern for the well-being of the impoverished and directs attention away from the decay of public welfare institutions.

It is precisely the selective allocation of social assistance under these programs that indicates how they can be used as a means of political control and electoral patronage—something political, civil, and human rights organizations have systematically claimed to be the case. Despite the paltry amounts involved, being included in a program such as PROGRESA, for instance, carries the possibility of a 10 percent increase in income for a family surviving on a single minimum wage.

PROGRESA acquired its full meaning as an expression of a political reform of the state that aims to destroy the institutional space for intermediation between government and organized social actors (Zermeño 1996). In its place, the government intends to organize new forms of conflict resolution in which the federal government conducts negotiations and strikes short-term agreements with individual actors. Women beneficiaries of PROGRESA pledged their political loyalty to

---

[18] Estimates vary depending upon the methodology used.

the government in exchange for a minimal amount of foodstuffs that was meaningful only because of the distressing circumstances of a family in extreme poverty. By accepting PROGRESA food aid, these women took on the social assistance responsibilities formerly borne by public institutions. In practice, such new forms of social participation — "co-responsibility" — do not mean more decision-making power for the citizenry; they mean new obligations for the family. A careful reading of the governmental discourse on participation reveals that the empowerment of the individual is understood as his or her freedom to choose in the marketplace (Bennett 1994), a "right" with little concrete meaning for a population in poverty.

CHALLENGES IN SOCIAL POLICY

The challenges to social policy in Mexico lie in the unsatisfied needs that have accumulated since the early 1980s as the proportion of the population in poverty has exploded and income and wealth have become increasingly concentrated (Boltvinik 1998). An institutional reorganization premised on a reduced role for the state, the promotion of open markets, and increased family responsibilities is not a suitable tool with which to address social issues. One might even suggest that we are witnessing a simultaneous failure in all three components of the "welfare triangle" — state, market, and family (Esping-Andersen 1999).

Any meaningful response to this social crisis must attack the extremely unequal distribution of income and wealth and also redefine national priorities.[19] Although resources are scarce, this does not mean there are no resources, or that available resources are being used appropriately. Is it justifiable, for example, for the Mexican government to spend US$93 billion to save the banking sector[20] and then claim that only US$540 million is available to meet the basic social needs of the poor? And does it make sense to subsidize the privatization of social

---

[19] In the year 2000, spending on social programs only amounted to about 9 percent of GDP, a very low level compared to other middle-income countries. There is a growing consensus in Mexico that there must be tax reform to increase the government's budgetary resources. However, even if additional resources become available, the basic structure of the budget must change in order to meet the country's social needs.

[20] This is the amount that the Mexican government expended to save the nation's banks from bankruptcy. It was converted into public debt in 1999 (López Obrador 1999). Furthermore, in November 1999, US$10 billion went to rescue a single bank.

benefits and services with public funds while public institutions and programs are suffering from severe budgetary cutbacks?

Falling real wages and rising underemployment have eroded the foundations of social welfare in Mexico for two reasons. First, jobs and wages are the normal means by which people satisfy a large part of their social needs—shelter, food, clothing, transportation, and so on. Second, all social welfare or insurance schemes (whether public, private, or mixed) are sustained to a large extent by the wages and salaries of employed workers through general or payroll taxes or through insurance premiums.

This means that an integrated anti-poverty policy should incorporate an effective labor market policy and measures to improve and protect the purchasing power of wages in a sustained effort to redistribute income. With the majority of Mexico's population living below the poverty line, the concept of "targeting" would be inappropriate even if sufficient resources were available to meet every need. Although programs directed toward specific groups are needed, it is unlikely that they can be sustained unless they are integrated into a broad public effort to meet human needs based on social citizenship. Such an effort would include programs that reach all in need through subsidies for basic food products and public transportation, nutritional programs in public schools, and so on. Furthermore, such an initiative would establish criteria for receiving social assistance (that is, access to social welfare programs might be means-tested, but these programs would not be discretionary in focus) and it would always maintain as its key objective preserving and expanding social rights such as health, education, economic security for senior citizens, and housing. Such an initiative would, moreover, work to strengthen public institutions in order to extend social services.

Such an effort is economically feasible. Expenditures for a universal minimum pension for all senior citizens—estimated to cost 0.8 percent of GDP—would be less than the transition costs involved in the highly selective scheme of private retirement accounts established in Mexico (Laurell 1997). Similarly, universal health coverage could be achieved at a cost of 4.2 percent of GDP, with an additional 2 percent of GDP invested in health infrastructure over a period of something like five years. Such a system could be created by unifying the present IMSS and Ministry of Health systems into a national health service (Laurell and Ruiz 1996: 57–65). This national service could be funded by combining those general tax revenues currently allocated for health care (1.35 percent of GDP) with monies derived by maintaining the previous payroll tax for health care (1.86 percent of GDP) and eliminating the tax exemption for private medical care (equivalent to 0.6 percent of GDP), yielding a total 3.81 percent of GDP. The remaining funds required—only 0.31 percent of GDP—could easily be collected from higher taxes on tobacco and alcohol.

The challenges are enormous, but they can be overcome. Failing to meet them will create severe polarization, social disintegration, and a crisis of governance in Mexico. Even more important, it will deny millions of Mexicans the opportunity to develop the individual and collective capabilities that underlie a creative and productive participation in society.

REFERENCES

BANAMEX. 1996. "Administradoras de fondos para el retiro: reforma en México y los ejemplos chileno y argentino," *Examen de la Situación Económica de México* 884: 102–14.

Beattie, Roger, and Warren McGillivray. 1995. "A Risky Strategy: Reflections on the World Bank Report 'Averting the Old Age Crisis.'" In *Proceedings of the Conference on Financial Security in Retirement.* Geneva: International Labour Office/International Social Security Association.

Bennett, Robert J. 1994. *Local Government and Market Decentralization.* Hong Kong: United Nations University Press.

Bodenheimer, Thomas. 1995. "The Industrial Revolution in Health Care," *Social Justice* 22: 26–42.

Boltvinik, Julio. 1995. *Pobreza y estratificación social en México.* Mexico City: El Colegio de México/INEGI/Instituto de Investigaciones Sociales, Universidad Nacional Autónoma de México.

———. 1998. "Pauperización zedillista," *La Jornada,* October 11.

———. 2000. "El diseño de Progresa," *La Jornada,* June 2.

Bonilla, Alejandro. 1995. "Reformas de los sistemas de pensiones." In *Memorias de la reunión internacional de expertos en seguridad social.* Mexico City: Centro de Desarrollo Estratégico para la Seguridad Social.

Bustos Castillo, Raúl. 1993. "Analysis of a National Private Pension Scheme: The Case of Chile," *International Labour Review* 133: 3.

Calva, José Luis. 1993. *Alternativas para el campo mexicano.* Mexico City: Fontamara.

Cárdenas Rivera, Miguel Eduardo. 1997. "La reforma de la seguridad social colombiana: entre la competencia y la solidaridad." In *La seguridad social en América Latina: ¿reforma o liquidación?* edited by Jaime Ensignia and Rolando Díaz. Caracas: Nueva Sociedad.

Cohn, Amélia. 1995. "Mudanças econômicas e políticas de saúde no Brasil." In *Estado e políticas sociais no neoliberalismo,* edited by Asa Cristina Laurell. São Paulo: Cortez–Centro de Estudos de Cultura Contemporanea.

CONSAR (Comisión Nacional del Sistema de Ahorro para el Retiro). 2001. Statistical information available at www.consar.gob.mx.

Dahlgren, Göran. 1994. *Framtidens Sjukvardsmarknade – Vinnare och Förlorare.* Stockholm: Natur och Kultur.

Diderichsen, Finn. 1995. "Market Reforms in Health Care and Sustainability of the Welfare State: Lessons from Sweden," *Health Policy* 32: 141–53.

Diario Oficial de la Federación. 1988. "Acuerdo de creación de la Comisión del Programa Nacional de Solidaridad," December 6.

Doyal, Len, and Ian Gough. 1991. *A Theory of Human Need.* London: Macmillan.

Dresser, Denise. 1994. "Bringing the Poor Back In: National Solidarity as a Strategy for Regime Legitimation." In *Transforming State-Society Relations in Mexico*, edited by Wayne A. Cornelius, Ann L. Craig, and Jonathan Fox. La Jolla: Center for U.S.–Mexican Studies, University of California, San Diego.

Du Boff, Richard B. 1997. "The Welfare State, Pensions, Privatization: The Case of Social Security in the United States," *International Journal of Health Services* 27: 1–23.

Esping-Andersen, Gøsta. 1990. *The Three Worlds of Welfare Capitalism.* Princeton, N.J.: Princeton University Press.

———. 1996. "After the Golden Age? Welfare States' Dilemmas in a Global Economy." In *Welfare States in Transition*, edited by Gøsta Esping-Andersen. London: Sage.

———. 1999. *Social Foundations of Postindustrial Economies.* Oxford: Oxford University Press.

George, Vic, and Paul Wilding. 1994. *Welfare and Ideology.* London: Harvester Wheatsheaf.

Gillion, Colin, and Alejandro Bonilla. 1992. "Analysis of a National Private Pension Scheme: The Case of Chile," *International Labour Review* 131: 2.

Hazas Sánchez, Alejandro. 1996. "Futuro del sistema pensionario de los trabajadores sujetos a la nueva ley del IMSS." In *Alternativas de reforma de la Seguridad Social*, edited by María Luisa Mussot. Mexico City: Universidad Autónoma Metropolitana/Fundación Friedrich Ebert.

Health Policy Network. 1995. "In Practice: The NHS Market in the United Kingdom," *Public Health Policy* 16: 452–91.

Herrera, Martín. 1990. "Austeridad y lucha sindical en el IMSS," *Chemizal* 3: 57–66.

Huerta, Arturo. 1991. *La economía mexicana más allá del milagro.* Mexico City: Diana/Universidad Nacional Autónoma de México.

IADB (Inter-American Development Bank). 1996. *Economic and Social Progress in Latin America.* Baltimore, Md.: Johns Hopkins University Press.

IMSS (Instituto Mexicano del Seguro Social). 1993. *Ley del Seguro Social.* Mexico City: IMSS.

———. 1995. *Diagnóstico.* Mexico City: IMSS.

———. 1996. *Aportaciones para el debate.* Mexico City: IMSS.

———. 1999. *Reporte de gestión.* Mexico City: IMSS.

INEGI (Instituto Nacional de Estadística, Geografía e Informática). 1999. *Información estadística del sector salud y seguridad social*, number 15. Mexico City: INEGI.

Iriart, Celia, Francisco Leone, and Mario Testa. 1995. "Las políticas de salud en el marco del ajuste," *Cuadernos Médico Sociales* 71: 5–22.

Kurczyn, Sergio. 1996. "Reforma del sistema de pensiones mexicano: principales aspectos macro-económicos," *Comercio Exterior* 46: 741–54.

Laurell, Asa Cristina. 1991. "Crisis, Neoliberal Health Policy, and Political Processes in Mexico," *International Journal of Health Services* 21: 457–70.

———. 1995. *La reforma de los sistemas de salud y seguridad social: concepciones y propuestas de los distintos actores sociales.* Mexico City: Fundación Friedrich Ebert.

———. 1996. "La política social del pacto posrevolucionario y el viraje neoliberal." In *Hacia una política social alternativa,* edited by Asa Cristina Laurell. Mexico City: Instituto de Estudios de la Revolución Democrática/Fundación Friedrich Ebert.

———. 1997. *La reforma contra la salud y la seguridad social.* Mexico City: Era.

———. 1999. "The Mexican Social Security Counter Reform: Pensions for Profit," *International Journal of Health Services* 29: 371–91.

Laurell, Asa Cristina, and Liliana Ruiz. 1996. *¿Podemos garantizar el derecho a la salud?* Mexico City: Fundación Friedrich Ebert.

Laurell, Asa Cristina, and María Isabel Wences. 1994. "Do Poverty Programs Alleviate Poverty?" *International Journal of Health Services* 24: 381–401.

Lo Vuolo, Rubén. 1996. "Reformas previsionales en América Latina: el caso argentino," *Comercio Exterior* 46: 692–702.

López, Amancio C. 1995. "El ahorro interno en los planes de ajuste estructural." In *Memorias de la reunión internacional de expertos en seguridad social.* Mexico City: Centro de Desarrollo Estratégico para la Seguridad Social.

López Obrador, Andrés Manuel. 1999. *FOBAPROA: expediente abierto.* Mexico City: Grijalvo.

McMurtry, John. 1998. *Unequal Freedoms: The Global Market as an Ethical System.* Toronto: Garamond.

Molinar Horcasitas, Juan, and Jeffrey A. Weldon. 1994. "Electoral Determinants and Consequences of National Solidarity." In *Transforming State-Society Relations in Mexico,* edited by Wayne A. Cornelius, Ann L. Craig, and Jonathan Fox. La Jolla: Center for U.S.–Mexican Studies, University of California, San Diego.

Navarro, Vicente. 1997. *Neoliberalismo y estado de bienestar.* Barcelona: Ariel.

———. 1998. "Neoliberalism, 'Globalization,' Unemployment, Inequalities, and the Welfare State," *International Journal of Health Services* 28: 607–82.

Pierson, Christopher. 1991. *Beyond the Welfare State?* Cambridge: Polity.

Pierson, Paul. 1996. *Dismantling the Welfare State?* Cambridge: Cambridge University Press.

Poder Ejecutivo Federal. 1995. *Plan Nacional de Desarrollo, 1995–2000.* Mexico City: Poder Ejecutivo Federal.

———. 1996. *Programa de reforma del sector salud.* Mexico City: Poder Ejecutivo Federal.

———. 1999. *Quinto informe de gobierno.* Anexo estadístico. Mexico City: Poder Ejecutivo Federal.

Ruiz-Tagle, Jaime. 1996. "El nuevo sistema de pensiones en Chile: una evaluación preliminar," *Comercio Exterior* 46: 703–709.

Sader, Emir, and Pablo Gentili. 1995. *Pósneoliberalismo: Las políticas sociais e o estado democrático.* São Paulo: Paz e Terra.

SEDESOL (Secretaría de Desarrollo Social). 1993. *La solidaridad en el desarrollo nacional.* Mexico City: SEDESOL.

SHCP (Secretaría de Hacienda y Crédito Público). 1996. *Informe sobre la situación económica, las finanzas públicas y la deuda pública.* Mexico City: SHCP.

Stocker, Karen, Howard Waitzkin, and Celia Iriart. 1999. "The Exportation of Managed Care to Latin America," *New England Journal of Medicine* 340: 1131–36.

Valenzuela, José Carlos. 1995. "Estancamiento económico neoliberal." In *México DF ¿Fin de un régimen?* edited by José Carlos Valenzuela. Mexico City: Universidad Autónoma Metropolitana.

Vergara, Pilar. 1997. "In Pursuit of 'Growth with Equity': The Limits of Chile's Free-Market Reform," *International Journal of Health Services* 27: 207–15.

Vilas, Carlos. 1995. *Estado y políticas sociales después del ajuste.* Caracas: Nueva Sociedad.

Working Group on Managed Competition. 1994. "Managed Competition: An Analysis of Consumers' Concerns," *International Journal of Health Services* 24: 11–24.

World Bank. 1993. *Investing in Health.* Washington, D.C.: World Bank.

———. 1994. *Averting the Old Age Crisis.* New York: Oxford University Press.

———. 1995. "Mexico: Country Strategy and Implementation Review Meetings." Summary minutes. Washington, D.C. Unpublished.

———. 1998. "Mexico: Health System Reform." Washington, D.C.: Unpublished.

Zermeño, Sergio. 1996. *La sociedad derrotada.* Mexico City: Siglo Veintiuno Editores.

10

The Agricultural Sector and Rural Development in Mexico: Consequences of Economic Globalization

Hubert C. de Grammont

INTRODUCTION

Prior to the late 1960s, Mexico's agricultural and livestock sector functioned largely to support the take-off of the country's industrial activities. Following an "inward-oriented" economic model, agriculture—both market-oriented peasant agriculture and commercial agriculture—produced staple foods (maize, beans, and sugar) for the urban population, as well as raw materials (cotton, vegetable oils, and leather) for the manufacturing sector. Agriculture also generated foreign exchange earnings thanks to exports of grains, coffee, sugar, vegetables, and livestock. During this period, Mexico's agricultural and livestock gross domestic product (GDP) grew at a faster rate than did the national population.

However, the "Mexican miracle" in the countryside could not endure. Because natural conditions (climate, soil, and topography) on most of the country's arable land did not permit the application of the intensive-growth technological package (mechanization, agrochemicals, and irrigation), rising production depended mainly upon opening new lands to cultivation (extensive growth) rather than upon productivity gains achieved through the adoption of "Green Revolution" technologies (intensive growth). But when there was no more land available for redistribution, all of the agricultural sector's inefficiencies became readily apparent, especially under the spotlight of Mexico's opening to international markets. The sector's problems included marked inequalities in the social and regional distribution of wealth, inefficient government institutions, and a significant fraction of the rural population with little likelihood of receiving land or finding employment.

in the social and regional distribution of wealth, inefficient government institutions, and a significant fraction of the rural population with little likelihood of receiving land or finding employment.

Throughout the 1980s, a radical transformation took place in rural Mexico, a process that was driven by two main factors. First, national economic crisis forced the federal government to limit its various forms of support to the countryside and to begin a unilateral process of trade opening following Mexico's entry into the General Agreement on Tariffs and Trade (GATT) in 1986. Second, Mexican agriculture was increasingly forced to compete within a global framework of comparative advantages, and it had to adopt new international quality norms that intensified demands on firms' competitiveness (Lara Flores 1998). In this context, the agricultural and livestock sector's role in national economic development was profoundly transformed. It ceased to be the main lever for urban-industrial development because agricultural products imported from advanced economies were cheaper than domestic ones. For this reason, the government lost interest in fostering national agricultural production, and its policies were rapidly reoriented toward fighting inflation and reducing the public account deficit.

The federal government drastically reduced its financial support to the countryside during the administration of President Miguel de la Madrid (1982–1988). Public spending targeted to the agricultural and livestock sector dropped from an 11.7 percent share of total spending in 1980 to a 6.4 percent share in 1987 (Escalante Semerena and Talavera Flores 1998: 78-93). Federal public investment aimed at fostering the agricultural and livestock sector made up 16.6 percent of total investment in that sector in 1980, but it dropped to 7.8 percent in 1989. The budget for the Ministry of Agriculture and Livestock (SAG) was cut by some 70 percent in real terms during this same period. Subsidies (price supports, as well as inputs, credit, and consumption subsidies), which made up fully 10.9 percent of agricultural and livestock GDP in 1982, dropped to 3.2 percent in 1988.

In addition, the agricultural sector's terms of trade[1] deteriorated sharply, dropping from an index of 100 in 1980 to 83.8 in 1989 (Escalante Semerena and Talavera Flores 1998). With Mexico's entry into the GATT, the government eliminated most livestock sector tariffs to facilitate meat imports. This provoked such a crisis among domestic producers that protective tariffs had to be reestablished in 1992, even in the face of strong U.S. pressure not to do so.

---

[1] Terms of trade are equal to the relative prices of the agricultural sector's products divided by the relative prices of inputs acquired by that sector.

Important institutional and legal changes were undertaken after Carlos Salinas de Gortari assumed the presidency (1988–1994). One of the principal architects of these reforms summarized their rationale in the following terms:

> As long as peasants cling to a marginal plot of land, without resources and with low productivity, they will remain impoverished, a dead weight on society. The solution is for this population to find work in better-paid activities and for agricultural production to be left to those who have what it takes to make it profitable and dynamic. (Téllez Kunzler 1994: 153)

In 1990, Mexico's National Program for the Economic Modernization of the Countryside diagnosed the main problems affecting rural areas as follows: excessive state intervention; insecure land tenure arrangements and the proliferation of small, unproductive properties (*minifundia*); financing without profitability as a criterion; and excessive subsidies (SARH 1990). To remedy this situation, the federal government undertook four main institutional changes. First, it thoroughly reformed the agro-financial system in order to ensure its profitability (Cruz Hernández 1995; Santoyo Cortés 1998; Martínez 1998). Second, state enterprises were privatized (De la Fuente and Mackinlay 1994). Third, the government abandoned price guarantees in favor of market prices (Escalante Semerena and Talavera Flores 1998). Fourth, the Salinas government ended land distribution, and the reform of Article 27 of the Mexican Constitution (January 6, 1992) and the promulgation of implementing legislation in 1993 permitted the privatization of *ejido* lands (Diego Quintana 1995). The reactivation of the economy and modernization of the countryside were supposed to create the employment needed to absorb persons displaced from rural production. At the same time, neoliberal economic reformers assumed that a decline in agricultural and livestock GDP was desirable because, following the pattern established in the evolution of industrialized countries, it was a clear indicator of economic development.[2]

Thus, in the period from Mexico's entry into the GATT up to the approval of the North American Free Trade Agreement (NAFTA) in late 1993, the Mexican countryside experienced drastic changes. For the countryside, NAFTA, far from being the start of a new process, was the last phase of a long transformation (C. de Grammont, Lara Flores, and Rubio 1996). These changes resulted in enormous polarization of the agrarian structure, a sharp increase in poverty, and an acute crisis of

---

[2] Agriculture and livestock activities account for a mere 3 percent of the economically active population in the United States and 9 percent in Western Europe.

failed loans among commercial agricultural producers. But they also strengthened agricultural exporting firms able to compete in international markets. Although rural employment increased significantly, it still fell far short of actual needs. Equally important, inadequate pay levels and unstable forms of work in the countryside are obstacles to reinvigorating domestic consumption and reducing poverty.

This chapter constructs a balance sheet of the situation in Mexico's agricultural and livestock sector at the end of the twentieth century. Several key economic and social dimensions will be examined in order to evaluate the degree to which the Mexican government's economic policies adequately address rural development problems. The author's interest lies in analyzing the problem of development and not just economic growth. Thus, instead of focusing on macroeconomic indicators, the analysis addresses the concrete effects that economic policies have on the structure of production and on agricultural employment—in other words, on the population living in the countryside.

There are a number of key questions to be answered. Although it is true that agricultural exports increased markedly during the 1990s, what is the real weight of the agricultural exporting sector within the Mexican economy? For example, what is the agricultural exporting sector's true importance in terms of generating employment, and has it acted as a dynamic axis for rural development? Although there has been a clear decline in the economically active population engaged in agricultural and livestock activities in recent decades, the tendency has slowed in recent years. What does this population trend (one that does not show up in developed countries) mean for Mexico, given that the end of land distribution in the early 1990s had supposedly curtailed the countryside's potential to absorb what were once called "landless peasants"? What limits or possibilities for balanced regional development are contained within this singular phenomenon?

The first of the following sections examines contemporary tendencies toward polarization in Mexico's agrarian structure and toward the economic exclusion of nearly half of the rural population. The discussion focuses on three indicators: access to land, the destination of production, and the evolution of financing. The second section analyzes the conditions of rural employment. This is a crucial problem because rural employment has become the main source of income for the greater part of the population living in the countryside. The third section examines population dynamics in the agricultural sector, a vital element for understanding the processes unfolding in the Mexican countryside. Addressing the question of population dynamics also provides a means for linking the idea of agricultural development with the broader concept of rural development.

POLARIZATION AND ECONOMIC EXCLUSION

Land

In the early 1990s, only 13 percent of Mexico's national territory was classified as being for agricultural use; 25 percent was identified as forest land and 54 percent as pasture.[3] The rest was made up of urban land, communication routes, unproductive land, or bodies of water. However, 64 percent of the 35 million hectares[4] classified as being for agricultural use were of poor quality because of low moisture, infertile soil, or adverse slope conditions. Furthermore, 14 million of those hectares were considered unfit for agricultural production (SEDESOL/INE 1994). This yielded an effective agricultural area of just over 22 million hectares.

The distribution of this land was highly polarized, a situation that neither Mexico's decades-long agrarian reform nor rural development policies have been able to redress. In the past, the government made efforts to limit polarization, but by the 1990s the phenomenon had increasingly become accepted as a "necessary evil" of economic development. The government shifted its policy emphasis to fighting polarization's "undesirable" social effects through targeted policies, especially anti-poverty policies.

The extent to which this polarization process has increased cannot be measured using available statistical data,[5] but the 1991 agricultural census showed enormous differentiation in access to land (table 10.1). Firms controlling more than 1,000 hectares made up only 0.3 percent of the total number of firms (10,439 units) with agricultural and forestry production, yet together these firms covered 45.6 percent (41,687,544 hectares) of Mexico's total agricultural and forest land area. At the other extreme, 59.2 percent of production units (2,263,683 in number) had fewer than 5 hectares (their national average was 2.2 hectares), and they covered only 5.4 percent (4,953,011 hectares) of Mexico's agricultural and forest lands.[6]

---

[3] Contemporary estimates suggested that expanding livestock ranching in tropical areas accounted for over 60 percent of deforestation in Mexico (SARH 1992).

[4] One hectare equals 2.47 acres.

[5] Based on data on 2,600,531 producers in the 1970 agricultural census, one can deduce that social differentiation in 1970 was similar to that in the early 1990s. Subsistence farmers made up 54.7 percent (1,422,896) of all producers in 1970 (CEPAL 1982: 114). The difference is that, by the early 1990s, poor peasants' subsistence production made up a smaller proportion of their total income, and the big firms were larger.

[6] Differentiating agricultural and forest activities by type of land tenure (ejido and private), one finds that in the early 1990s there were 1.4 million private units with

TABLE 10.1. Agricultural, Livestock, and Forestry Production Units in Mexico by Size of Holdings, 1991

Size of Landholding	Production Units (number)	Total Area (hectares)	Average Area (hectares)
Up to 2 hectares	1,305,345	1,494,003	1.1
2–5 hectares	958,338	3,459,008	3.6
5–20 hectares	1,193,865	12,606,815	10.6
20–50 hectares	208,594	6,559,552	31.4
50–100 hectares	72,068	5,243,247	72.8
100–1000 hectares	74,414	20,363,223	273.6
1000–2500 hectares	5,709	9,060,803	1,587.1
More than 2500 hectares	4,730	32,626,741	6,897.8
National total	3,823,063	91,413,395	23.9

Source: INEGI 1991.

Note: This area included all land under cultivation by agricultural firms, whether owned or leased. It was the area that actually corresponded to these firms, whatever its origin or legal form of land tenure. According to the same census, 69.7 percent of the lands cultivated under indirect rights (leases, sharecropping, loan arrangements, and so on) were in the hands of the private sector.

According to neoliberal views, the free operation of market forces should lead to the disappearance of peasant producers because they are inefficient. However, available information suggests that this has not happened. Firms that ceased production between 1986 and 1991 (the five years preceding the 1991 agricultural census) represented 13 percent (584,817) of all firms in the census and 16 percent (16,932,688 hectares) of total agricultural and forest area. The average size of these units often exceeded the average for their state. At the national level, the average area of firms that were still producing was 23.9 hectares

a total area of more than 71 million hectares. On average, each firm's area was 50.8 hectares. In the ejido sector, 2.8 million producers had a total area of 33.5 million hectares, or an average of 11.7 hectares per producer. There was strong social polarization in both cases, but minifundia were more widespread in the ejido sector, while large firms predominated in the small private property sector. Also, while 108 million hectares of land had been distributed through the 1980s, only 33.5 million of these were fit for agriculture, livestock raising, or forestry activities. The rest of the area given to *ejidatarios* (73 million hectares) was unfit for productive activities and made up the common lands (for collective use) that served basically for gathering activities (wood and medicinal or edible plants) and extensive grazing, or they lay abandoned. They were basically forests that could not be commercially exploited, hillsides, grasslands unfit for livestock raising, deserts, or wetlands.

per unit, while the average area of firms that ceased production was 28.9 hectares per unit (INEGI 1991). This indicates that it was mainly the midsize and large firms that abandoned agricultural activity during this period.

This phenomenon demonstrates, once again, that domestic producers (in this case, peasant producers) do not respond directly to capitalist market laws. Rather, they obey the needs of their own social reproduction. Under adverse market conditions, they increase their investment in labor (insofar as they are able) and reduce their level of well-being, but capitalist firms are obliged to quit producing as soon as marginal costs exceed profits. Clearly, the crisis of production broadly affects midsize and large producers.[7]

Production

If one analyzes the components of Mexico's trade balance, one finds that the NAFTA negotiators' bet on agricultural trade paid off: Mexico now imports more grains—particularly maize, soybeans, and cottonseed—but it exports more fresh fruits and vegetables (tables 10.2 and 10.3).

Maize imports began in the late 1960s, toward the end of Mexico's "inward-oriented" development period, but they remained low throughout the 1970s. They shot up with the importation of 2 million tons (about 20 percent of total agricultural imports) in 1985, and they expanded even more rapidly in the 1990s. In this regard, it is widely known that the Mexican government has not followed the rules established under the NAFTA to protect domestic maize production. Those rules provided for a gradual market liberalization over fifteen years, with successive reductions in quotas and tariffs until fully free trade was achieved in the year 2009 (C. de Grammont 1995). This mechanism was designed to allow Mexico time to modernize maize production and to mitigate the negative social effects of free trade. Maize accounts for approximately 40 percent of the country's harvested area and a similar proportion of the value of total agricultural production. Additionally, about 72 percent of all agricultural production units are devoted to maize production, and they employ about 34 percent of all labor in the agricultural sector—equal to about 10 percent of the employed population nationwide (Fritscher Mundt 1995: 48).[8]

---

[7] Other aspects of this phenomenon are discussed in a later section of this chapter on bad loans in the agricultural sector.

[8] Mexico's maize production has remained stable because international prices do not have direct effects on subsistence production.

Beginning in 1994, Mexico made enormous purchases of maize in the United States, well above the quotas that had been agreed to in the NAFTA (Fritscher Mundt 1995: 45–58; Suárez Carrera 1995: 59–66).[9] In 1996, Mexico imported close to 6 millions tons of maize, or more than 30 percent of its national consumption (*Boletín de Información Oportuna del Sector Alimentario*, February 1999).[10] There are two explanations for the decision to import maize on this scale: one emphasizes the importance of lower-cost food in Mexico's struggle against inflation, while the other stresses pressures from the United States, which sought to sell its surplus production.[11]

One of the most serious aspects of the NAFTA gamble in the countryside is that there is still a large negative balance in agricultural and livestock trade, as well as in food products (see table 10.4). Clearly the trade deficit in food products is greater than the trade deficit in agricultural and livestock products. However, if we include imported inputs for agriculture in the agricultural and livestock trade balance, the trade deficit increases from US$1.178 billion to $1.570 billion in 1998 (INEGI 1999).[12] These data show that Mexico has not developed its own

---

[9] This meant that an ambitious project launched in the late 1980s to modernize maize cultivation in Mexico, the National High-Technology Maize Program, was effectively scrapped.

[10] One infrequently mentioned issue is the nutritional value of imported maize. Imported maize (known as yellow corn or feed corn) is basically used to feed livestock. Although it has higher yields, it is nutritionally inferior to the white corn traditionally grown in Mexico. A fair price should take into account these differences in nutritional quality. Another serious problem is that some of the imported maize is genetically modified (5 million tons in 1998), and its effects on biodiversity and human health are unknown (*La Jornada*, December 2, 1999, p. 54).

[11] The U.S. surplus was due to the drastic drop in purchases from the Soviet bloc and then from Asia, as well as to the food self-sufficiency policies of the European Union. "The United States, as the largest producer and supplier of maize in the world, has had to suffer the consequences of this debacle. Its exports have fallen dramatically (from 8 billion dollars to approximately 5 billion between 1980 and 1992), and because of this large subsidies had to go to maize growing farms in order to avoid economic catastrophe for the more than 700,000 producers engaged in that activity. . . . Maize is by far the most important product [in the United States]: it occupies first place in terms of area, value, and production. In 1992, with a cultivated area of nearly 30 million hectares, it produced the equivalent of 237 million tons, with an approximate value of 19 billion dollars. In terms of agricultural volume and value, maize also occupies first place" (Fritscher Mundt 1995: 47–48).

[12] Imported inputs for agriculture include tools (plows, harrows, seeders), farm machinery (tractors, harvesters), fertilizers, herbicides, fungicides, inputs for cattle-raising, and so on.

TABLE 10.2. Mexico's Agricultural and Livestock Imports, 1982–2000 (millions of 1982 U.S. dollars and percentages)

	1982		1988		1994		2000	
	Value	Percent	Value	Percent	Value	Percent	Value	Percent
Agricultural imports	926.6	84.3	1,138.8	78.8	1,948.6	88.8	2,343.5	89.7
Maize	37.7	4.1	321.2	28.2	240.4	12.3	299.2	12.8
Beans	98.3	10.6	11.0	1.0	24.9	1.3	22.5	1.0
Soybeans	155.8	16.8	274.3	24.1	417.0	21.4	426.3	18.2
Sorghum	194.7	21.0	112.8	9.9	257.0	13.2	255.5	10.9
Wheat	87.0	9.4	112.0	9.8	123.1	6.3	181.6	7.7
Cottonseed	0.7	0.1	9.6	1.0	165.5	8.5	320.9	13.7
Other seed and fruit oils	203.0	21.9	104.5	9.2	188.5	9.7	239.5	10.2
Other	149.4	16.1	193.4	17.0	532.2	27.3	598.0	25.5
Livestock imports	172.4	15.7	307.1	21.2	246.1	11.2	268.9	10.3
Total	1,099.0	100.0	1,445.9	100.0	2,194.7	100.0	2,612.4	100.0

Source: Author's calculations based on INEGI/SHCP/BANXICO 1982, 1988, 1994, 2000.

TABLE 10.3. Mexico's Agricultural and Livestock Exports, 1982–2000 (millions of 1982 U.S. dollars and percentages)

	1982		1988		1994		2000	
	Value	*Percent*	*Value*	*Percent*	*Value*	*Percent*	*Value*	*Percent*
Agricultural exports	1,096.8	88.9	1,400.9	83.8	2,221.0	82.9	3,585.0	90.7
Cotton	183.8	16.8	114.0	8.1	42.3	1.9	54.6	1.5
Coffee	345.1	31.5	434.2	31.0	359.7	16.2	635.7	17.7
Fresh fruits	72.0	6.6	165.8	11.8	470.7	21.2	732.2	20.4
Vegetables	332.3	30.3	510.7	36.4	1,084.1	48.8	1,758.7	49.0
Other	163.6	14.9	176.2	12.6	264.2	11.9	403.8	11.3
Livestock exports	136.4	11.1	270.9	16.2	457.4	17.1	369.3	9.3
Total	1,233.2	100.0	1,671.8	100.0	2,678.4	100.0	3,954.3	100.0

Source: Author's calculations based on INEGI/SHCP/BANXICO 1982, 1988, 1994, 2000.

Note: Silviculture exports are insignificant and are included under "other" agricultural exports.

TABLE 10.4. Mexico's Trade Balance in Agricultural and Food Products, 1990-2000 (millions of current U.S. dollars)

Year	Agriculture and Livestock[1]	Food Products[2]
1990	48	−1,400
1991	162	−960
1992	−167	−2,608
1993	−152	−1,990
1994	−643	−2,646
1995	1,093	686
1996	−1,057	−1,416
1997	−331	-613
1998	-559	-1,178
1999	-499	-795
2000	-468	-1,006

Sources: For the 1988-1996 period, Poder Ejecutivo Federal 1998; for 1997 and 1998, SAGAR 1998; for 1999, Poder Ejecutivo Federal 2000; for 2000, Secretaría de Agricultura, Ganadería, Desarrollo Rural, Pesca y Alimentación (SEGARPA) information and statistics service.

[1] Corresponds to the primary producer sector.

[2] Corresponds to the food-processing sector, including canned goods, frozen food, beverages, and so on.

agroindustrial sector, nor has it developed its own technology for agricultural production. Rather, based on exports of fresh fruits, vegetables, and livestock on the hoof, it continues to play its traditional role as a supplier of raw materials, now for the international consumer market.

The destination of agricultural and livestock production offers clear indications of the polarization in Mexico's agrarian structure. In 1991, only 0.3 percent of agricultural production units (11,744) reported that they sold their products in the domestic market or exported them. Meanwhile, 45.9 percent (1,757,611 units) reported that they produced only for family consumption, and 43.4 percent (1,663,308 units) produced for family consumption but also sold a portion of their production in local or national markets (see table 10.5).[13] However, if we exclude coffee-producing states (home to minifundia that reported exporting their production), we find that only 3,451 agricultural enterprises exported part or all of their production, making up a mere 0.09 percent of all agricultural production units in Mexico. Together they covered just over 500,000 hectares, or about 2 percent of the total area under

---

[13] About 10 percent did not report the destination of their production.

cultivation (C. de Grammont 1998).[14] These are the firms that can compete successfully in the international market; the future for the rest of the agricultural sector is extremely uncertain.[15]

Credit

The credit picture can also illuminate contemporary trends in the agricultural and livestock sector. The level of loan "delinquencies" began to increase among producers in 1989, almost doubling over five years. Producers' indebtedness, far from facilitating increased profit levels for their firms (as would be the case with healthy debt), corresponds to a severe structural crisis. Agricultural and livestock GDP fell in real terms while debt levels rose. In 1987, overdue loans in the agricultural and livestock sector equaled 1.4 percent of agricultural and livestock GDP; by 1994, overdue loans had increased to 7.6 percent (C. de Grammont 2001).

One way to measure the crisis in commercial agricultural production is to compare the ratio of overdue loans to credits granted. With some year-to-year fluctuations, this ratio rose drastically, from 6.7 percent in 1984 to 33.5 percent in 1997 (table 10.6). These numbers point both to the crisis of production in the countryside and to the financial crisis of the Mexican banking system.

However, as Schwentesius et al. (1995) note, money that appears as credit includes both the portfolio of unpaid overdue loans and the portfolio of restructured loans (unpaid overdue loans that have been renegotiated with new terms and new interest rates). To have a clearer view of the money actually provided to producers each year—in other words, "fresh" money—one must subtract the portfolio of unpaid overdue loans and the portfolio of restructured loans. Looking at the problem in this way, one finds that, beginning in 1989, fresh money dropped sharply as a share of total credit, plummeting to only 53 percent of the total amount that appears as credit (Schwentesius et al. 1995: 13).

---

[14] SECOFI reports that, circa 1997, there were 802 fruit and horticultural exporters (ASERCA 1997).

[15] The polarization is even sharper in the livestock subsector (including all types of livestock raising). In 1991, 75.4 percent (2,386,927) of the units that stated they were engaged in livestock production consumed all of their own production (backyard producers); 24.3 percent (769,941) sold in local and national markets; and only 0.23 percent (7,391) also exported their products. In the forest subsector, out of the 1,219,166 production units that declared being engaged in forest activities, 97.4 percent (1,188,109) did so for their own consumption; 2.5 percent (30,529) sold products in the national market; and 0.04 percent (528) were exporters (INEGI 1991).

TABLE 10.5. Destination of Mexico's Agricultural Production, 1991

State	Total Production Units	Units Producing for Family Consumption	Units Producing for Domestic Market	Units Producing for Domestic Market and Export	Main Export Crops[1]
Aguascalientes	19,343	6,340	8,038	80	F
Baja California	11,211	1,606	6,883	356	V
Baja California Sur	3,652	640	2,237	338	V
Campeche	37,114	14,799	16,800	36	F
Coahuila	51,633	14,008	28,873	144	F
Colima	13,606	3,150	8,580	114	F
Chiapas	304,920	113,300	174,959	1,022	C-F
Chihuahua	92,096	36,775	48,592	389	F
Durango	85,010	34,785	43,312	64	F
Federal District	20,180	10,950	5,417	4	
Guanajuato	136,746	52,148	71,883	149	V
Guerrero	203,357	126,680	59,966	259	C
Hidalgo	200,609	111,180	50,133	28	V
Jalisco	150,292	49,040	82,400	554	V
México State	299,510	205,708	65,935	146	FI

Michoacán	185,168	76,750	88,216	757	F-V
Morelos	48,167	12,610	30,728	67	F
Nayarit	60,890	14,318	43,623	703	F-V
Nuevo León	42,951	16,690	15,063	31	F
Oaxaca	344,229	209,667	98,946	3,111	C
Puebla	338,496	198,189	110,575	624	C
Querétaro	46,250	27,344	11,891	33	V
Quintana Roo	27,999	15,562	10,357	10	F
San Luis Potosí	145,116	67,459	62,372	129	V
Sinaloa	95,349	20,216	67,595	591	F-V
Sonora	39,617	8,846	24,612	660	F-V
Tabasco	88,710	26,503	40,968	83	F
Tamaulipas	85,324	14,342	61,047	387	F-V
Tlaxcala	68,301	44,703	21,066	22	F
Veracruz	377,185	141,521	202,159	771	C-F
Yucatán	86,754	38,196	39,719	28	F
Zacatecas	117,802	42,586	60,363	54	F
National total	3,827,587	1,757,611	1,663,308	11,744	F-V-Fl-C

Sources: INEGI 1991. Main export crops for each state based on author's fieldwork.

Note: The difference between the total number of units nationwide and the sum of the units that declared the destination of their production is made up of the units that did not specify the destination of production.

[1] C = coffee, F = fruit, Fl = flowers, V = vegetables

TABLE 10.6. Credit and Overdue Loans in Mexican Agriculture, 1984–1997 (thousands of current pesos)

Year[1]	Credit	Overdue Loans	Overdue Loans as Percent of Credit
1984	801,220	53,977	6.7
1985	1,267,009	93,378	7.4
1986	1,818,204	149,161	8.2
1987	3,691,702	227,463	6.2
1988	8,185,751	395,144	4.8
1989	13,533,619	1,398,581	10.3
1990	21,388,759	2,785,564	13.0
1991	24,849,693	2,362,231	9.5
1992	33,392,599	3,357,567	10.0
1993	39,847,472	5,288,029	13.3
1994	50,526,642	6,255,784	12.4
1995	53,516,000	13,064,000	24.4
1996	63,668,000	14,373,000	22.6
1997	68,384,000	22,903,000	33.5

Source: Banco de México economic indicators.

[1] Data to December of each year.

Even though it is extremely difficult to ascertain the impact of the financial system on the countryside,[16] the best way to measure the real presence of credit is through the land area that benefited from it. In 1988, the last year before the drastic overdue loan crisis, 9.4 million hectares were planted with the support of bank financing. By 1993 the area was down to 3.8 million hectares, and in 1995 fewer than 2 million hectares were planted with the support of bank credit (Cruz Hernández 1995: 107). At the same time, BANRURAL provided credits for 3 million hectares of maize in 1987, but for only 154,000 hectares in 1994 (Schwentesius et al. 1995: 12). Throughout the remainder of the 1990s, this situation remained unchanged

A crucial question to be answered is whether private banks are willing to accept the role that new governmental policies would have them play. For nearly half a century, state banks granted agricultural credit. With a few exceptions in Mexico's northern states, commercial banks had nothing to do with the countryside. Their presence became important in the 1980s, but this occurred under the responsibility of the government as it lent money discounted by the Investment Fund for

---

[16] Moreover, government and private banks have shown an enormous ability to disguise the real state of the national financial system.

Agriculture (FIRA) (see table 10.7). In other words, commercial banks received money from the Banco de México and did not have to risk their own capital.

With the privatization of commercial banks and the intensified application of neoliberal policies in the countryside, private-sector lending accelerated. Much of this lending was discounted by the FIRA, and it often went to showy but shaky production projects—as in the case of Banco CREMI and the Del Monte corporation, both controlled by Carlos Cabal Peniche.[17] Although it appears as if commercial banks lent three times as much money to the countryside in 1993, of the 39.8 billion pesos in credit going to the countryside, nearly 18 billion (46 percent) was money discounted by FIRA (FIRA 1994: 77). Thus the private sector's commitment to the countryside has been much less significant than it appears at first glance. This lack of interest in investing is in part the result of the current penury of the Mexican financial system. But it reflects one overwhelming fact: beyond the small number of agro-exporting businesses that have achieved competitiveness in the international market, under current conditions agriculture is not a profitable business for the majority of producers.

EMPLOYMENT

Data from the National Employment Survey (ENE) show that—probably as a reflection of the overdue loans crisis—the number of agricultural producers dropped from 43.9 percent to 39.7 percent of the national population between 1991 and 1999. The number of agricultural workers rose in those years, from 56.1 percent of all individuals in the agricultural and livestock sector (5,526,967) to 60.3 percent (5,708,186) (see table 10.8). With the end of land distribution, it is fundamentally important that new public policies recognize that the population employed in agriculture is comprised mainly of workers (who may or may not be wage earners), not independent producers.

More than fifty percent of agricultural workers are unpaid. They are family members or peasants who contribute labor to one another. Although unpaid labor diminished in relative importance between 1991 and 1999, it nevertheless remains very significant, providing a place for

---

[17] Cabal Peniche was one of the most successful entrepreneurs during the administration of Carlos Salinas de Gortari. His business empire first grew by creating trading companies to export fresh fruits and vegetables (particularly from Tabasco, his home state) to the United States. He was then able to put together a business group to buy Banco CREMI and another group to buy one of the largest agro-exporting businesses in the world, Del Monte Fresh Fruit.

TABLE 10.7. Agricultural and Livestock Credit in Mexico, 1978–1997 (thousands of current pesos)

Year[1]	BANRURAL Credit	Commercial Bank Credit	Commercial Credit as Percentage of BANRURAL Credit	Total Credit in Current Pesos	Total Credit in 1978 Pesos[2]
1978	48,121	280	0.6	48,401	48,401
1979	57,741	52,989	91.8	110,730	93,680
1980	104,548	73,155	70.0	177,703	119,024
1981	109,386	109,103	99.7	218,489	114,332
1982	150,651	120,334	79.9	270,985	89,257
1983	237,087	193,361	81.6	430,448	70,231
1984	390,910	410,310	105.0	801,220	79,008
1985	647,537	619,472	95.7	1,267,009	79,228
1986	1,028,237	789,967	76.8	1,818,204	61,030
1987	1,799,257	1,892,445	105.2	3,691,702	53,452
1988	4,133,922	4,051,829	98.0	8,185,751	55,342
1989	5,654,653	7,878,966	139.3	13,533,619	76,243
1990	8,121,337	13,267,422	163.4	21,388,759	95,139
1991	6,456,968	18,392,725	284.8	24,849,693	90,112
1992	8,119,442	25,273,157	311.3	33,392,599	104,834
1993	10,444,048	29,403,424	281.5	39,847,472	113,983
1994	11,535,788	38,990,854	338.0	50,526,642	140,085
1995	15,269,000	38,247,000	250.5	53,516,000	91,000
1996	18,010,000	45,658,000	253.5	63,668,000	85,000
1997	19,723,000	48,661,000	246.7	68,384,000	79,000

Source: Banco de México economic indicators.

[1] Data are to December of each year.

[2] Deflated by the consumer price index to December of each year, with 1978 = 100.

the fraction of the rural population that cannot find work any place else.

According to the 1999 ENE, the number of agricultural day laborers and wage employees rose notably (by 333,489 people). However, 91 percent of them received less than twice the monthly minimum wage, demonstrating that agriculture is not viable as a means for the rural population to make a living.[18] Perhaps for this reason, there is a tendency in Mexican agriculture, among both poor peasants and agricultural laborers, toward the feminization of work. In overall terms, the proportion of women among the agricultural workforce rose slightly (table 10.9).

Let us consider in more detail the situation of women working in agriculture. On the one hand, there are women who replace men in the fields while the latter migrate temporarily to urban areas or to the United States. To the extent that absent men continue to be formal owners of the land, these women's work is counted as unpaid family help even if the women have full responsibility for the family's agricultural and livestock activities. In 1991, for example, 51 percent of women occupied in agriculture did not receive remuneration; by 1999, the number had risen to 70 percent (INEGI–STPS 1991, 1999).

On the other hand, a 1997 study found that 17 percent of those who were in possession of ejido lands were women who received plots via inheritance from their husband. (This number was only 1.3 percent in 1970; Procuraduría Agraria 1997: 152.)[19] Moreover, women played an important role in producer organizations, constituting 42 percent (of a total 6,258) of those who participated in Social Solidarity Societies and 14 percent (of a total 2,423) of the Rural Producer Societies registered in the ejido sector (Procuraduría Agraria 1997: 158).

According to the National Employment Survey (INEGI/STPS 1999), in the late 1990s some 15 percent of agricultural wage earners were women. More particularly, several studies have shown that women were important as wage workers in the fruit-producing and horticultural regions of Mexico's Northwest (horticulture, grapes, and citrus in Baja California, Baja California Sur, Sinaloa, and Sonora), on the Pacific Coast (Jalisco and Nayarit), in the Northeast (citrus in northern Veracruz and horticulture in Tamaulipas), and in the North (fruit in Chihua-

---

[18] This situation is even more dramatic than it sounds because, in most cases, these incomes are earned through the work of all available members of the agricultural day laborer's family.

[19] However, women occupy leadership positions in only 10 percent of all ejidos (Procuraduría Agraria 1997: 157).

TABLE 10.8. People Employed in Mexico's Agricultural and Livestock
Sector, 1991 and 1999

People in Agriculture	1991		1999	
and Livestock Raising	*Number*	*Percent*	*Number*	*Percent*
Total	9,845,020	100.0	9,465,174	100.0
Independent producers	4,318,053	43.9	3,756,988	39.7
Workers	5,526,967	56.1	5,708,186	60.3
Workers		100.0		100.0
Day laborers	2,236,822	40.5	2,516,113	44.1
Employees	109,738	2.0	163,936	2.9
Unpaid workers	3,180,407	57.5	3,028,137	53.0

Sources: INEGI/STPS 1991, 1999.

hua, fruit and citrus in Montemorelos, Nuevo León) (Barrón 1993; Lara Flores 1995, 1998; Sifuentes 1996).

Child labor is another extremely important phenomenon. In the late 1990s, children under the age of 19 made up 45 percent of all unpaid family help in agriculture.[20] More than one-fourth of all day laborers (26 percent) were under the age of 19 (INEGI/STPS 1999).[21] This is a population that in past decades was probably counted as inactive, participating in household tasks or studying. Now they are agricultural workers hired by the day.

A study conducted in the mid-1990s in Sinaloa found that close to 50 percent of agricultural day laborers in horticulture (totaling approximately 100,000 people) were women. Of these, some 47 percent were between 5 and 19 years of age. This means that nearly one-fourth of all agricultural day laborers were female children or adolescents. In the packinghouses, where horticultural products are sorted and crated, 90 percent of workers were women. Other crops, such as cut flowers for export, provided employment for more than 5,000 women as permanent, year-round workers (Lara Flores 1998).

---

[20] Because the age groups employed in the National Employment Survey (ENE) are from 12 to 14 and from 15 to 19, it is not possible to draw the line at 16, the age at which it is legal to work under the terms of Mexican federal labor law.

[21] There is some debate about the impact of a U.S. food safety law that would force Mexican agro-exporters to maintain minimum field hygiene conditions for the handling of fresh fruits and vegetables and that would ban child labor. This law was devised by U.S. producers to raise their Mexican competitors' labor costs and thus restrict competition.

The lack of employment opportunities for rural residents in the areas where they live produces significant out-migration. However, migratory flows that were traditionally established from the countryside to the city have taken a new course, with many people now headed toward midsize cities or other rural localities. In the 1995 population census, 12.4 percent of people in localities with fewer than 2,500 inhabitants were born in another state; this proportion rose to 17.3 percent in localities with between 2,500 and 15,000 inhabitants.[22] As to the composition of migratory flows, there is increasing migration of entire families from Mexico's poorest states. Moreover, most of this migrant population is made up of indigenous peoples.

A survey by the Instituto de Investigaciones Sociales at the National Autonomous University of Mexico (UNAM) examined rural-rural national migration patterns in 326 villages and towns in the state of Oaxaca.[23] It found that emigration varies a great deal by village. In some villages, temporary migration involves more than a quarter of the total population, but this proportion can rise to 90 percent. One outcome is the appearance of "ghost towns" and villages that remain empty for several months of the year, stripped of their entire economically active population.

As to the composition of migratory flows, this same study found that migration by the entire family was the most widespread type of migration for most of the localities surveyed (173 out of 326). It was more common than the migration of single men and heads of families. Notably, the migration of single women was important in some localities. The principal migration destinations for the villages surveyed were, first, the fruit and horticultural fields of Sinaloa, and second, those of Baja California.

Migration means that significant amounts of money can flow from developed areas (both within Mexico and abroad) to poor areas. Both the importance and the instability of this relationship were demonstrated in 1991, when a hurricane destroyed most of the horticultural crops about to be harvested in Sinaloa. Not only did the Mexican government have to repatriate tens of thousands of agricultural day laborers to their home villages, but it also had to implement emergency

---

[22] In total, 5.1 million out of 33 million people in localities with fewer than 15,000 inhabitants were born in another state. Obviously, the rate of migration is greater in cities; whereas the national average was 23.7 percent, it was 30.3 percent in localities with more than 15,000 residents (INEGI 1995).

[23] The author carried out this survey ("Empresas, mercado de trabajo rural y migración") during 1997–1999. The first results appear in C. de Grammont and Lara Flores 2001.

TABLE 10.9. Employment Patterns in Mexico's Agricultural and Livestock Sector, 1991 and 1999

	1991			1999		
	Total	With Income	Without Income	Total	With Income	Without Income
Men						
Number	7,127,838	5,140,677	1,696,824	6,796,015	4,270,151	2,359,914
Percentage	87.9	91.7	77.1	85.4	92.9	74.2
Women						
Number	982,529	464,941	502,941	1,161,424	324,875	819,424
Percentage	12.1	8.3	22.9	14.6	7.1	25.8
Total						
Number	8,110,367	5,605,618	2,199,765	7,957,439	4,595,026	3,179,338
Percentage	100.0	100.0	100.0	100.0	100.0	100.0

Sources: INEGI/STPS 1991, 1999.

Note: Discrepancies between totals and the categories "with income" and "without income" are due to cases in which this factor was not specified.

employment programs (basically local public works projects) in the sending areas (Oaxaca, Guerrero, and Michoacán, among others) in order to mitigate the effects of job losses in Sinaloa.

The following examples are typical of the kinds of financial flows that result from international migration.[24] The state of Oaxaca received US$45 million via postal money orders from the United States in 1991, a total equal to the state's annual budget (Carrasco 1999: 97). The money basically went to the poorest areas, which are also those with large indigenous populations (39.8 percent to the Mixteca, 37.1 percent to the Valles Centrales, 12.2 percent to the Sierra Norte, and 8.4 percent to the Sierra Sur). Similarly, a 1998 report by the Migratory Affairs Commission of the Mexican Senate found that remittances to the state of Zacatecas totaled US$211 million in 1996, an amount equal to 166 percent of the federal funds that went to the state that year (Senado de la República 1998). Another study of remittances to Zacatecas found that these monies represented an average monthly income of 1,500 pesos for the receiving families and that 90 percent of these families used this money for basic consumption needs (Fideicomiso 1998).

This situation indicates how some rural regions are becoming increasingly dependent upon income from abroad, primarily because they lack local alternatives. However, it is also an indication of the tremendous economic polarization that characterizes contemporary rural Mexico.

REGIONAL DEVELOPMENT AND POPULATION DYNAMICS IN THE AGRICULTURAL SECTOR

Mexico's national accounts system divides economic activities into three sectors: primary, secondary, and tertiary. This sectoral—or even bipolar (countryside versus city)—vision that is the framework for economic analysis obscures the connections that exist between various branches of the economy in regional spaces. One fundamental issue in this regard is the relationship between population dynamics and regional development. The data available for Mexico portray five important phenomena.

---

[24] Remittances from the United States to Mexico totaled an estimated US$3.6 billion in 1995 (*La Jornada*, September 19, 1995), nearly equal to the total value of agricultural, livestock, and forest exports for that same year (approximately US$4 billion) (INEGI/SHCP/BANXICO). A report by the Mexican Senate found that remittances via banks, currency exchange brokers, and wire transfers totaled more than US$2 billion during the first half of 1997 (Senado de la República 1998).

TABLE 10.10. Population Employed in Agriculture and Livestock Raising in Mexico, 1960–1999

	1960	1970	1990	1995	1999
Agricultural employment	6,144,930	5,103,519	5,300,114	7,768,640	8,208,709
Total employment	11,332,016	12,955,057	23,403,413	34,466,017	39,069,095
Agricultural employment as percentage of total	54.2	39.4	22.6	22.5	21.0

Sources: INEGI 1960, 1970, 1990, 1995; INEGI/STPS 1999.

Note: The 1980 census is not used because its data are unreliable.

First, agricultural activity should be considered a branch, not a sector, of the economy. As a branch, agriculture occupies an intermediate position in terms of its direct contribution to Mexico's GDP (6.4 percent of total GDP in 1995).[25] However, if one considers that the agricultural and livestock sector and the agroindustrial sector (food, beverages, and tobacco) together make up a single agroindustrial production chain, we find that the proportion of GDP derived from primary economic activities rises to 37.7 percent of the total (the agricultural and livestock sector's 6.4 percent plus the agroindustrial sector's 31.3 percent). This is relevant to understanding the dynamics of regional development because practically all agroindustries are located in areas of agricultural and livestock production (ASERCA 1997), with significant impacts on outlays for local wages.[26]

Second, although it is true that over the last half-century the tendency has been toward a decline in the population engaged in agriculture in both relative and absolute terms, there was a shift in this tendency beginning in 1990 (table 10.10). However, even from 1960 to 1990, it is necessary to distinguish between two phases. From 1960 to 1970, the population in agriculture and livestock raising declined both absolutely and relatively (by 1.4 percent per year). Yet between 1970 and 1990, the decline in relative terms was only 0.8 percent per year, and the agricultural population remained more or less constant in absolute terms. In the second stage, from 1990 to the present, the population engaged in agriculture and livestock raising expanded significantly in absolute terms and remained stable in relative terms. It is this enormous growth of the agricultural population—occurring at the same time that agricultural and livestock GDP was stagnating (it grew by little more than 1 percent in real terms during the 1990s)—that has caused a rapid spread of poverty to close to half of the rural population.

Third, it merits noting that in 1970 and 1990 agriculture was the main source of employment for localities with fewer than 10,000 in-

---

[25] In 1995, textile, clothing, and leather manufacturing's contribution to GDP was 8.4 percent; paper, printing, and publishing, 5.0 percent; chemicals, 16.5 percent; nonmetallic minerals, 7.5 percent; metal products, machinery, and equipment, 23.4 percent; construction, 3.9 percent; electricity, gas, and water, 1.7 percent; trade, restaurants, and hotels, 19.5 percent; transportation, storage, and communications, 9.5 percent; and so on (Sistema de Cuentas Nacionales, INEGI).

[26] Of the 421 fruit and horticultural agroindustries surveyed by ASERCA in 1997, 409 were located in agricultural and livestock-producing areas, while 12 were in the Federal District (ASERCA 1997). The national accounts system classifies these agroindustries under manufacturing, which obscures the economic relationship that exists at the local level with the primary sector.

TABLE 10.11. Mexico's Employed Agricultural Population by Activity and Size of Locality, 1970 and 1990

	1970		1990	
	Number	*Percentage of Total*	*Number*	*Percentage of Total*
Localities with fewer than 2,500 inhabitants				
Total employment	5,058,964		5,621,802	
Primary activities	3,889,318	76.9	3,807,638	67.7
Manufacturing	307,345	6.1	481,219	8.6
Trade	139,649	2.8	223,682	4.0
Services	225,601	4.4	405,400	7.2
Other	497,051	9.8	703,863	12.5
Localities with 2,500 to 4,999 inhabitants				
Total employment	1,064,751		1,160,833	
Primary activities	484,191	45.5	500,590	43.1
Manufacturing	174,156	16.4	177,894	15.3
Trade	84,856	8.0	103,499	8.9
Services	134,375	12.6	172,434	14.8
Other	187,173	17.6	206,416	17.8
Localities with 5,000 to 9,999 inhabitants				
Total employment	984,542		1,100,216	
Primary activities	269,507	27.4	325,513	29.6
Manufacturing	220,482	22.4	190,486	17.3
Trade	105,560	10.7	127,665	11.6
Services	175,234	17.8	224,652	20.4
Other	213,759	21.7	231,900	21.1

Localities with 10,000 to 49,999 inhabitants

Total employment	1,855,433		2,548,630	
Primary activities	263,012	14.2	392,316	15.4
Manufacturing	458,512	24.7	508,247	19.9
Trade	253,572	13.7	391,563	15.4
Services	433,147	23.3	663,312	26.0
Other	447,190	24.1	593,192	23.3

Localities with 50,000 inhabitants or more

Total employment	3,991,367		12,971,932	
Primary activities	197,491	4.9	274,057	2.1
Manufacturing	1,008,579	25.3	3,135,433	24.2
Trade	613,241	15.4	2,261,719	17.4
Services	1,189,818	29.8	4,248,527	32.8
Other	982,238	24.6	3,052,196	23.5

National total

Total employment	12,955,057		23,403,413	
Primary activities	5,103,519	39.4	5,300,114	22.6
Manufacturing	2,169,074	16.7	4,493,279	19.2
Trade	1,196,878	9.2	3,108,128	13.3
Services	2,158,175	16.6	5,714,325	24.4
Other	2,327,411	18.0	4,787,567	20.5

Sources: INEGI 1970, 1990.

Note: For purposes of simplification, the following have been grouped under "other": petroleum production and other extractive industries, construction, electrical power generation, government transportation, and the "insufficient information" category. Individually, each of these branches is of minor importance in terms of the population employed. For example, the petroleum industry – which is strategic in terms of the national economy – represented no more than 0.8 percent of employment in 1990. Percentages may not add to 100.0 because of rounding.

habitants (see table 10.11). The precise impact of agriculture on regional economies cannot be measured, but it is very significant for the 33.7 million inhabitants (37 percent of Mexico's population) who live in these small towns and villages.[27] In localities of 10,000 to 49,999 inhabitants, it is the third most important economic activity.

Fourth, rural population growth has created new, often isolated, small localities. Between 1990 and 1995, nearly 5,000 small settlements with a total population of 262,440 inhabitants grew up near highways, and an additional 6,342 small, isolated localities (with 316,365 inhabitants) were created. In addition, nearly 50,000 micro-settlements (with fewer than three houses) sprang up over this same period (CONAPO 1998: 78).

Finally, the countryside includes significant numbers of residents who are not peasants. When the ejidos were established, they were strictly peasant communities. By the late 1990s, however, one-quarter of the families living in ejidos were residents who had a small piece of land in the ejido's urban zone but who had neither an agricultural parcel nor use rights to common lands (Procuraduría Agraria 1999: 13).[28]

These facts indicate the great social complexity of the Mexican countryside, a situation that must be taken into account in order to formulate appropriate public policies. This rural population is the poorest fraction of the national population, and it poses enormous challenges for the generation of endogenous rural development processes.

CONCLUSION

The preceding discussion has demonstrated that the Mexican countryside is in the midst of a profound process of change. A few thousand large agroindustries (exporting fruits, vegetables, and some livestock) have found considerable success; meanwhile, a significant proportion of commercial producers (in the main, those producing grains, meat, and milk for the domestic market) are bankrupt. The peasant maize economy is battered by free trade, but it will not disappear because there is a dearth of alternative employment except for the limited op-

---

[27] A total of 184,153 of the 201,138 localities counted by the 1990 census had fewer than 10,000 inhabitants.

[28] This population is so significant that the 1992 agrarian law had to create a new institution in the ejidos, the council of settlers (*junta de pobladores*). Ejidatarios and residents participate in these councils to address issues having to do with the settlement, public services, and community works. In some ejidos, the ejido assembly grants settlers certain rights to common lands, mainly when they are children of ejidatarios.

portunities provided by modern fruit and vegetable producers (or job opportunities in the cities or in the United States). The rise in unpaid family labor is the best evidence of this situation.

Even if the free-trade model promotes an agricultural sector in Mexico that can compete in the international market, this sector has not been able to incorporate more than a fraction of existing producers. The impact of free trade on Mexican agriculture as a whole has been negative. Not only has this exclusionary model been unable to solve the problems of subsistence producers, but it has also left out a significant number of midsize and large production units.

One thus finds an illogical situation in which good agricultural lands go uncultivated because farmers cannot compete with imports from the United States, while poor peasants deplete natural resources on lands poorly suited for agriculture. Supporters of sustainable regional development hold that this population has positive potential, but from a productive standpoint, it represents a threat to the environment.

It is also clear that agricultural and livestock production remains very important in terms of the population the sector employs, particularly in localities with up to 10,000 inhabitants. This suggests that, given the lack of other employment options, agriculture functions as a "refuge" for a significant fraction of the population. The employment issue cannot be reduced to determining if overall employment will rise or fall; instead, attention must also focus on labor market conditions.

It is important to note that commercial agriculture (particularly exporters of fruits and vegetables) has generated salaried employment. However, it is even more significant to highlight the fact that this has been accomplished by extending family and female labor, massive migration processes that include school-age children, and wage levels that keep families trapped in extreme poverty. This state of affairs produces a ceaseless migratory flow to the United States, so that the labor market for poor Mexican peasants is increasingly an international one.[29]

In order to develop innovative policy proposals that combine productivity with development, it is necessary to rethink—in both theoretical and practical terms—the whole set of issues related to the countryside. Two topics are especially important in this regard. The first is the role of the peasantry in Mexican society. The concept of peasant—a producer who lives from his or her own labor on his or her own land—

---

[29] It is common even in Mexico's most remote peasant communities to find young people who speak English, or to see signs in English ("beer" instead of "cerveza" in the saloons, for example). Even in regions with indigenous populations, men often wear the checkered shirts, boots, and Texan hats of the *norteño* ("cowboy"). And airlines now offer a weekly direct flight from Oaxaca to Tijuana, a favored point of departure to the United States.

no longer adequately describes rural realities. It does not fit subsistence producers who produce only for their own consumption and who cannot envision ways to expand their production for the marketplace. Nor does it fit those who survive thanks to income obtained through complex processes of temporary migration, processes that create a clear division between an individual's community—a place of social or family reproduction—and a place of work hundreds or thousands of miles away.

Although temporary migration has an important impact on local cultural change, its ability to capitalize the family production unit is very limited. The money saved is insufficient to stimulate processes of regional development—the dream of the migrant who returns to his or her hometown with new knowledge and a bit of money to start a business. The bottom line is that the migrant, even if paid in dollars, earns a wage that must be divided up to meet his or her own needs in his or her place of work and those of family members who stayed behind. Thus a migrant's wages can only buffer the effects of poverty, and migration is but one among several survival strategies for the poor peasant family experiencing de-capitalization.

Experiences in other parts of the world indicate that it is possible to establish savings institutions among the poorest strata of the population. However, these must be created with the intervention of external agents (including nongovernmental organizations), and they require a high level of organization among members. In Mexico, government actions during the 1980s and 1990s to fight poverty did not contemplate the possibility of promoting new processes of capitalization and local development; instead, they were limited to undertaking specific actions to provide the marginal population with basic services (health care, education, and so on).

The second important issue is the notion of rural space as a strategic factor in rethinking the role of agriculture vis-à-vis other sectors of the economy and vis-à-vis the issue of environmental conservation. Until now, development has been based on large-scale industrial (or agroindustrial) expansion, resulting in capital concentration and territorial polarization. Mexico's neoliberal development model has assumed that "development poles" would have beneficial impacts on their surroundings, but reality has proven otherwise. This obliges us to look for new models. Following Alexander Schejtman, "adequately understanding the issue of rural development means placing it in the framework of local economic development—that is, to emphasize economic linkages between the urban center and its rural hinterland, analyzing how markets are interwoven at this scale. Within this framework it is possible to deal not only with issues of transforming production, but also with poverty and the environment, all with the specificity that is needed to assure effectiveness and participation under a given institutional framework" (1998: 151).

REFERENCES

ASERCA (Apoyo y Servicios de la Comercialización Agropecuaria). 1997. *Directorio de exportadores de productos hortifrutícolas*. Mexico City: SECOFI.

Barrón, María A. 1993. "Los mercados de trabajo rurales: el caso de las hortalizas en México." Ph.D. thesis, Universidad Nacional Autónoma de México.

C. de Grammont, Hubert. 1995. "Nuevos actores y formas de representación social en el campo." In *El impacto social de las políticas de ajuste en el campo mexicano*, edited by Jean-François Prud'homme. Mexico City: Plaza y Valdés/ Instituto Latinoamericano de Estudios Transnacionales.

———. 1998. "Análisis de la estructura de las empresas agroexportadoras mexicanas en el contexto del TLC." Presentation at Asociación Latinoamericana de Sociología Rural, Universidad Autónoma de Chapingo, Texcoco, Mexico, October.

———. 2001. *El Barzón: clase media, ciudadanía y democracia*. Mexico City: Plaza y Valdés/Instituto de Investigaciones Sociales, Universidad Nacional Autónoma de México.

C. de Grammont, Hubert, and Sara María Lara Flores. "Encuesta a hogares de jornaleros migrantes en regiones hortícolas de México," mimeo, Instituto de Investigaciones Sociales, Universidad Nacional Autónoma de México, 2001.

C. de Grammont, Hubert, Sara Lara Flores, and Blanca Rubio. 1996. "La política agropecuaria mexicana: balance y alternatives." In *Políticas públicas alternativas en México*, edited by Enrique de la Garza Toledo. Mexico City: La Jornada Ediciones.

Carrasco, Tania. 1999. "Los productores del campo en Oaxaca," *Alteridades* (Universidad Autónoma Metropolitana–Iztapalapa) 17 (9): 95–104.

CEPAL (Comisión Económica para América Latina y el Caribe). 1982. *Economía campesina y agricultura empresarial*. Mexico City: Siglo Veintiuno.

CONAPO (Consejo Nacional de Población). 1998. *La situación demográfica de México*. Mexico City: CONAPO.

Consejo Nacional Agropecuario. 1996. *Estadísticas básicas, 1987–1996*. Mexico City: Dirección de Estudios Económicos, Consejo Nacional Agropecuario.

Cruz Hernández, Isabel. 1995. "Transformaciones en el financiamiento rural mexicano durante el sexenio salinista: balance y tendencias," *Cuadernos Agrarios* 11–12: 95–120.

De la Fuente, Juan, and Horacio Mackinlay. 1994. "El movimiento campesino y las políticas de concertación y desincorporación de las empresas paraestatales: 1989–1994." In *Campo y ciudad en una era de transición*, edited by Mario Bassols. Mexico City: Universidad Autónoma Metropolitana–Iztapalapa.

Diego Quintana, Roberto. 1995. "El paradigma neoliberal y las reformas agrarias en México," *Cuadernos Agrarios* 11–12: 13–26.

Escalante Semerena, Roberto, and Diana Talavera Flores. 1998. "La política macroeconómica en el sector agrícola." In *El sector agropecuario mexicano después del colapso económico*, edited by Felipe Torres Torres. Mexico City: Plaza y Valdés.

Fideicomiso para Estudios de la Región Norteamericana. 1998. "Migrantes internacionales: cambios en el patrón migratorio y sus limitantes para el crecimiento económico regional en Zacatecas." Mimeo.

FIRA (Fideicomiso Instituido en Relación con la Agricultura). 1994. *Informe anual*. Mexico City: FIRA.

Fritscher Mundt, Magda. 1995. "Las políticas de maíz en el salinismo," *Cuadernos Agrarios* 11–12: 45–58.

———. 1998. "Incertidumbre en los mercados de maíz: las tendencias internacionales," *Revista Mexicana de Sociología* 4: 39–62.

INEGI (Instituto Nacional de Estadística, Geografía e Informática). 1960. *Censo de Población y Vivienda*. Mexico City: INEGI.

———. 1970. *Censo de Población y Vivienda*. Mexico City: INEGI.

———. 1990. *Censo de Población y Vivienda*. Mexico City: INEGI.

———. 1991. *VII Censo Agropecuario-forestal*. Mexico City: INEGI.

———. 1995. *Conteo de población*. Mexico City: INEGI.

———. 1999. *Balanza Comercial de México*. Mexico City: INEGI, March.

INEGI/SHCP/BANXICO (Instituto Nacional de Estadística, Geografía e Informática/Secretaría de Hacienda y Crédito Público/Banco de México). 1982. *Estadísticas del comercio exterior de México*. Mexico City.

———. 1988. *Estadísticas del comercio exterior de México*. Mexico City.

———. 1994. *Estadísticas del comercio exterior de México*. Mexico City.

———. 2000. *Estadísticas del comercio exterior de México*. Mexico City.

INEGI/STPS (Instituto Nacional de Estadística, Geografía e Informática / Secretaría del Trabajo y Previsión Social). 1991. *Encuesta Nacional de Empleo*. Mexico City.

———. 1999. *Encuesta Nacional de Empleo*. Mexico City.

Lara Flores, Sara María. 1995. *Jornaleras, temporeras o bóias-frías: el rostro femenino del mercado de trabajo rural en América Latina*. Caracas, Venezuela: Nueva Sociedad.

———. 1998. *Nuevas experiencias productivas y nuevas formas de organización flexible del trabajo en la agricultura mexicana*. Mexico City: Juan Pablos/Procuraduría Agraria.

Martínez, Aurora Cristina. 1998. "El crédito al sector agropecuario." In *El sector agropecuario después del colapso económico*, edited by Felipe Torres Torres. Mexico City: Plaza y Valdés.

Poder Ejecutivo Federal. 1998. *Cuarto informe de gobierno*. Mexico City.

———. 2000. *Sexto informe de gobierno*. Mexico City.

Procuraduría Agraria. 1997. *La transformación agraria*. 2 vols. Mexico City.

———. 1998. *Los tratos agrarios en ejidos certificados*. Mexico City.

———. 1999. "Perspectivas del campo mexicano." Mexico City. Mimeo.

SAGAR (Secretaría de Agricultura, Ganadería y Desarrollo Rural). 1998. *Análisis coyuntural.* Mexico City: Subsecretaría de Planeación, Dirección de Análisis Económicos, SAGAR, November–December.

Santoyo Cortés, Horacio. 1998. "Apertura comercial y reforma del sistema financiero rural mexicano: consecuencias y tendencias." In *El sector agropecuario después del colapso económico,* edited by Felipe Torres Torres. Mexico City: Plaza y Valdés.

SARH (Secretaría de Agricultura y Recursos Hidráulicos). 1990. *Programa Nacional de Modernización del Campo, 1990–1994.* Mexico City: SARH.

———. 1992. *Inventario Nacional Forestal de Gran Visión.* Mexico City: SARH.

Schejtman, Alexander. 1998. "Alcances sobre la articulación rural-urbana y el campo institucional," *Políticas Agrícolas* (Brazil), special issue, pp. 139–66.

Schwentesius, Rita, et al. 1995. "La cartera vencida del sector agropecuario: evolución, causas, soluciones." Reporte de Investigación, no. 25. Mexico: Centro de Investigaciones Económicas, Sociales y Tecnológicas de la Agricultura y la Agroindustria Mexicana, Universidad Autónoma de Chapingo.

SEDESOL/INE (Secretaría de Desarrollo Social/Instituto Nacional de Ecología). 1994. *Informe de la situación general en materia de equilibrio ecológico y protección al medio ambiente, 1993–1994.* Mexico City.

Senado de la República. 1998. "Remesas que envían los mexicanos residentes en los Estados Unidos a México." Mexico City: Comisión de Asuntos Migratorios. Mimeo.

Sifuentes, Emma L. 1996. "Los mercados de fuerza de trabajo en la agricultura de Nayarit en el período 1970–1994 y la participación femenina." Master's thesis, Universidad Nacional Autónoma de México.

Suárez Carrera, Víctor. 1995. "Ni autosuficiencia alimentaria ni ventajas comparativas: los saldos del neoliberalismo en granos básicos y oleaginosas," *Cuadernos Agrarios* 11–12: 59–66.

Téllez Kunzler, Luis. 1994. *La modernización del sector agropecuario y forestal.* Mexico City: Fondo de Cultura Económica.

Part V

Inequality, Employment and Wage Problems, and Poverty

11

Welfare, Inequality, and Poverty in Mexico, 1970–2000

Julio Boltvinik

This chapter examines the evolution of welfare, inequality, and poverty in Mexico from 1970 through 2000. The essay begins with a contextual and conceptual introduction that briefly compares the so-called new poverty agenda that Mexican policy makers adopted in the 1990s with the "development and social justice" approach pursued up until 1982. This introduction also identifies the six sources that determine an individual's and a household's welfare: current income; basic assets (housing and consumer durable goods); non-basic assets (including households' borrowing capacity); access to publicly provided goods and services (including household services such as piped-in water, sewerage, and electricity; education; health care; and social security); free time; and knowledge (education).

The second section turns to calculations of the opportunities for social welfare in Mexico between 1981 and the year 2000, an exercise that links at the macro-social level five of the six welfare sources and their distributive dimensions. In pointing to a deterioration in what can be termed the opportunity set for social welfare, the results of these calculations prefigure the evolution of various dimensions of poverty and their impact on mortality. The following section succinctly analyzes the evolution of income distribution between 1963 and the year 2000.

The fourth part of the chapter examines the evolution of income poverty and of a group of specific poverties (understood as deprivation in specific needs) during the 1970–2000 period. Income poverty is primarily associated with the first source of welfare (current income); poverties of health care and social security are also partly associated with this source.[1] The specific poverties that are analyzed relate to all of

---

[1] Deprivation of health care and social security services is determined, via the integrated poverty measurement method, by reviewing whether households without social security have sufficient income to allow them to meet these needs through

the other sources of welfare except non-basic assets. The central finding here points to an apparent paradox: there was both an *increase* in income poverty and a *reduction* in specific poverties during the 1980s, although specific poverties declined at a slower pace than in the 1970s. During the 1970s, income poverty—as well as all specific poverties—decreased rapidly. Income poverty fluctuated during the 1990s but ended above its initial level. At the same time, most specific poverties decreased at a pace that was slower than in the 1970s but faster than in the 1980s.[2] This examination shows, then, that the periods 1970–1981, 1981–1989, and 1989–2000 are appropriate ones for analysis, although the last period might be conveniently divided into three stages (1989–1994, growth; 1994–1996, recession; 1996–2000, growth).

The next section focuses on an important determinant of the evolution of specific poverties: social expenditure. The analysis discloses that the usual reading of the evidence—that is, that public social expenditure dropped dramatically during the 1980s in Mexico and elsewhere in Latin America—is based upon the use of inappropriate price indices to deflate current expenditure figures. This discussion shows that when a correct price index is used as a deflator, social expenditures per capita stabilized during the 1980s but did not drop. This finding is consistent with the slower decline (but no increase) in the incidence of specific poverties noted above.

The empirical analysis presented in the sixth part of the chapter shows that the paradox identified above also holds when partial poverty measures are combined via the integrated poverty measurement method, which gauges poverty by income and by specific needs within each household. The evidence confirms that, although the periods of analysis are different, the trends are similar in both sets of poverty measures.

The penultimate section introduces a dimension of welfare not yet taken into account: the length of the life span, or the "quantity" of life. Evidence for Mexico reveals a strong association between poverty and early death. In general, individuals who suffer in terms of the quality of life also suffer in terms of the quantity of life, in the form of premature death. This part of the analysis then identifies periods in the evolution of mortality rates by age group from 1970 to 1999. The resulting periodization coincides in many ways with previous findings regarding the

the market. For a discussion of poverty measurement methodology and the integrated poverty measurement method, see the appendix included at the end of this chapter.

[2] The notable exceptions were poverties of health services and social security, which decreased at a rate that was slower than in the 1980s.

evolution of poverty. Within the context of an overall decline in mortality rates, there were periods of stagnation in the rates for all younger age groups, a pattern that was associated with the economic recessions that Mexico experienced throughout the years under consideration.

The chapter concludes with some reflections on the relationships among the opportunities for social welfare, the heterogeneous evolution of the various dimensions of poverty, the evolution of integrated poverty, changes over time in mortality rates by age group, and the evolution of public social expenditure. This discussion links changes in welfare and poverty over time to an assessment of the public policies associated with the adoption of the new poverty agenda in Mexico.

CONTEXTUAL AND CONCEPTUAL INTRODUCTION

Mexico and the New Poverty Agenda

Official public policy rhetoric in Mexico increasingly revolves around the struggle against poverty. This trend reflects the simultaneous presence of various factors. The first is the Mexican government's abandonment of public policies in several areas of economic and social development, areas now made subject (at least rhetorically) to the sway of market forces.[3] Second, the ascendance of anti-poverty policies reflects the agenda imposed by the so-called Washington Consensus, according to which one of the few areas requiring active governmental intervention (because markets are recognized as inadequate in this area) is the struggle against extreme poverty. The Mexican government has patterned its anti-poverty policies on the "new poverty agenda" promoted by the World Bank (Moore and Devereaux 1999). Third, this policy emphasis denotes the minimum that a government can do if it aims to keep social conflict at a manageable level in the face of the population's increasing pauperization.

The first two elements are reflected in government expenditures. Mexico's proposed federal budget for the year 2000 (Poder Ejecutivo Federal 1999: 1–3) stated that 60.7 percent of government expenditures (excluding debt service) were to be allocated to social expenditures, a proportion similar to that in previous and subsequent budgets. According to the same document, an increasing though still small proportion (10.8 percent) of government expenditures specifically targeted poverty. At the same time, the federal government has sought to trans-

---

[3] For example, Jaime José Serra Puche, who headed the Ministry of Commerce and Industrial Development (SECOFI) during the administration of President Carlos Salinas de Gortari (1988–1994), maintained that "the best industrial policy was no industrial policy."

fer responsibility for basic infrastructure development to the private sector and to reduce public investment in this area.[4]

The Mexican government's approach to poverty changed radically in the 1990s. In previous decades, the government intervened vigorously to alter the basic parameters that determine poverty. In particular, the government increased asset endowments of the poor through, among other measures, agrarian reform, land and livestock improvement, credit, technical assistance, health services, social security, and educational programs. The government also acted to influence relative prices for the goods and services the poor buy and sell by providing price guarantees and input, basic goods, and consumer subsidies; by increasing minimum and public real wages and thereby indirectly raising average wages; by providing public services; and by intervening in basic goods markets to prevent excessive and speculative profits.

This old agenda developed autonomously in Mexico, although it was undoubtedly influenced by Keynesian theories and by the ideas promoted by the Economic Commission for Latin America and the Caribbean (ECLAC). It was more an agenda for development and social justice than a poverty agenda per se. The implicit reasoning was that, because poverty arose from multiple causes, development policies designed to redress it should impinge upon all factors of production and correct the asymmetries that gave rise to poverty. Social programs—especially education—were predominantly universalistic and free. Although there were some targeted programs, their role was always secondary.[5] The government operated such programs directly and distributed their benefits in kind.

In sharp contrast, under the so-called new poverty agenda, government interventions must not alter market signals—and only demand (never supply) may be subsidized, preferably through monetary transfers. In order to avoid "distorting economic incentives," relative prices must not be altered. Growth should be subject to the free play of the market; the state's only role is to help those who cannot participate in the "market game" on their own—that is, the extremely poor. This new agenda does not consider poverty other than extreme poverty to be a problem that merits state intervention. Indeed, it recommends against directing social expenditures to the population that is not in extreme poverty; instead, it concentrates resources on targeted programs that benefit only the extremely poor. Moreover, the agenda recommends

---

[4] The World Bank has identified the abandonment of basic infrastructure investment as one cause of slow growth in the Mexican economy (World Bank 1998).

[5] One example is Industrialized Milk CONASUPO (LICONSA), which is still in operation. It sells subsidized milk to low-income (mainly) urban households.

user fees for preexisting universal programs both to help finance them and to prevent benefits from going to those who do not need them. Whenever possible, the private sector should operate such programs within a competitive framework, with benefits distributed in cash or quasi-cash (vouchers for specific goods that can be used to choose among different private suppliers).

The diagnosis underlying this approach is that extreme poverty arose because undue state intervention distorted market signals, and because insufficient human capital among the poor prevents them from participating effectively in the market. Whatever extreme poverty remains after the elimination of these distortions and after the provision of public support to those in extreme poverty is to be attributed to individual failures. It is not, therefore, the concern of the state.

A thorough evaluation of this new agenda is beyond the scope of this chapter. The purpose of the preceding paragraphs is to help the reader understand the basic orientation of this poverty agenda and the role it is playing in Mexico. It is within this framework that the empirical analysis presented in this chapter should be interpreted. The chapter's empirical findings do not support the contention that social policy was inefficient or inefficacious during the 1970s. Therefore, substituting the new poverty agenda for the previous "development and social justice" agenda was unjustified.

As noted above, this chapter analyzes the evolution of the basic macro-social parameters that determine welfare and poverty, examining from various angles the evolution of poverty in Mexico from the 1970s through the 1990s, as well as the association between mortality rates and poverty. The starting point for this analysis is a conceptual understanding of the sources of individual and household welfare.

The Sources of Welfare

The welfare of individuals and households depends upon the following sources of well-being: (1) current income; (2) family patrimony, understood as the set of durable goods and assets that provide households with basic services; (3) non-basic assets and households' borrowing capacity; (4) access to publicly provided free goods and services; (5) available time for rest, domestic work, education, and leisure; and (6) individual knowledge, conceptualized not as a means to obtain income but as direct satisfaction of the human need for understanding. The first three categories represent either flows or stocks of private economic resources; the fourth category embodies the flow of public economic resources (the so-called social wage). Together, the first four categories constitute economic resources that can be expressed in mone-

tary terms. The fifth and sixth categories have their own units of measurement, which are not reducible to monetary value. In sum, economic
resources, free time, and knowledge are the three irreducible dimensions of the sources of welfare.

These six sources of welfare display two notable characteristics. The
first is their degree of *substitutability*. Consuming non-basic assets or
borrowing can substitute for low current income without affecting the
satisfaction of other present needs. However, the same is not true for
basic assets because selling or pawning basic assets in order to compensate for low current income would affect the satisfaction of other needs.
Thus, if an individual draws down bank savings (a non-basic asset), he
or she can maintain current private consumption. But if that individual
takes his or her television, refrigerator, or bed to the pawnshop, the
gain in liquidity is offset by a loss in terms of the basic services these
assets provide. More current income can substitute for a lack of access
to free services (for example, by paying for private education and
health care) and for a lack of family patrimony (by renting a house or a
furnished apartment). Nevertheless, this substitutability has its limits.
More income cannot compensate for ignorance or the absence of free
time.

The fact that there is not a perfect substitutability among sources of
welfare is related to their second characteristic: their *specificity*. Generally speaking, these sources are not generic; they do not satisfy all
needs. However, there are diverse degrees of specificity among different sources. Welfare sources such as current monetary income and non-
basic assets permit the satisfaction of a broad range of needs (in principle, any need that can be satisfied through the consumption of goods
and services available on the market), but other sources are more specific. Non-monetary current income and basic patrimony take the form
of specific goods that provide defined services (for example, corn, a
house, a table, and so forth). Therefore, they can only satisfy specific
needs. Government social programs usually provide goods and services in kind (education, health care, food, and so forth) associated with
a specific need.[6]

From another perspective, several sources of welfare may be required in order to meet each need. For example, increasing a child's
knowledge requires the child to attend school. This, in turn, implies
devoting personal time to this effort. The government may provide free

---

[6] In the language of classical political economy and Marxism, monetary incomes are
exchange-values expressed in amounts of the general equivalent that can be transformed into almost any use-value through a market exchange. Non-monetary income, basic patrimony, and goods and services provided free by the government
are specific use-values.

school services, but the child will also need school supplies, appropriate clothing, and transportation—needs usually met through the market and financed by current family income or accumulated savings.
Feeding family members usually requires both income and domestic
work, which involves the use of time.

Welfare trends in a society are a function of the level and distribution among individuals of the six sources of welfare outlined above. At
the same time, the level and distribution of each source have specific
determinants. For example, a household's average real income in any
given year is determined by prevailing conditions in the broader economy and the factors that shape them, including macroeconomic policy.
Access to free government goods and services, in terms of both level
and distribution, depends almost entirely upon social policy (expressed
in public expenditures for social welfare) and its supporting legislation.
The availability of free time depends, on the one hand, upon customs
regarding the length of the workday, weekly and annual rest periods,
and so forth, and, on the other, upon household income (households
with less income will feel pressure to extend the workday) and individual preferences. Although the determinants of the level and distribution of each welfare source are quite different, this does not mean
that they are fully independent of one another. Social policy and free
time, for instance, may be influenced (although not mechanically determined) by trends in the economy. The welfare of the population is,
in turn, the fundamental determinant of mortality rates for specific age
groups, as demonstrated by the cross-national empirical relationship
between living standards and life expectancy at birth.

To summarize, social welfare is determined by multiple sources, the
evolution of which may vary over time because their determinants are
diverse. Therefore, when studying welfare trends in a society (whether
from a micro-social or a macro-social perspective), one must take into
account the diverse sources of human welfare and their determinants.

THE EVOLUTION OF OPPORTUNITIES FOR SOCIAL WELFARE

Evaluating development requires a vision other than the predominant
view, which reduces "development" to expanding gross domestic
product (GDP). To address this problem, Desai, Sen, and Boltvinik
(1992) developed an alternative approach—called the social progress
index—that, while not denying the importance of economic growth,
defines human welfare as the sole objective of development. The index
embraces two complementary perspectives: the *opportunity* set and the
achievement set for social welfare. The opportunity set focuses on the
availability of goods, services, free time, and knowledge—as well as the

fairness of their distribution—in relation to needs, providing a macro-social view of the *potential* for welfare. The achievement set is a micro-social evaluation of the welfare actually achieved at the household level. This section presents calculations of the opportunity set in Mexico during the period from 1981 through 2000. The analysis of different dimensions of poverty and of mortality rates in subsequent sections of this chapter (especially those performed via the integrated poverty measurement method) may be taken as an approximation of the achievement set.[7]

In order to quantify the opportunity set for social welfare, one must consider several factors: (1) the available volume of goods and services in relation to the population's needs, along with equality in the distribution of access to them; (2) available free time (or its complement, working time) and its social distribution; and (3) the level and distribution of knowledge in the population. The author explored two possible options for weighting these different dimensions. The first is to give them equal weight; the second is to accord half the weight to the first dimension because of its broader nature, with the other two dimensions comprising the other half. The second option (the one chosen here) is more faithful to the actual circumstances affecting social welfare.

The calculation of the opportunity set presented here incorporates the following variables: (1) total consumption, rather than the more usual GDP, as a measure of the availability of goods and services (the "size of the pie"); (2) the standardized size of the population, expressed as the number of adult equivalents, as an indicator of the magnitude of needs (the "hunger" of those at the table); (3) the Gini coefficient of income distribution among households as a proxy of inequality in the distribution of total consumption (how the pie is distributed); (4) a measurement of free time based upon observed extra-domestic excess work and on domestic work requirements; (5) an indicator of equality in access to free time; (6) a measure of educational achievement; and (7) an indicator of equality in the distribution of educational achievement.[8]

Total consumption—the sum of private and governmental (public) consumption, as defined in national accounts—is a better indicator than

---

[7] The approach adopted here differs in some respects from that developed by Desai 1992. The main difference is that the term "achievement set" is employed here to refer to the living conditions of one part of the population (namely, people living in poverty), whereas Desai's use of the term covered the entire population.

[8] The set of variables originally presented in Boltvinik 1992a included the first five elements but not the last two. In that work, the author suggested that the indicator of the availability of goods and services be adjusted so as to reflect environmental degradation and to exclude the production of harmful or destructive goods (such as cigarettes or weapons). These issues are not addressed in this chapter.

GDP of the size of the pie because it excludes asset depreciation (the consumption of fixed capital) and the income received by non-residents. It approximates national disposable income, which is the sum of private consumption, public consumption, and net savings.[9] Total consumption is an expression of the social capacity to attain a certain living standard. It embraces the first four sources of welfare, all of which are material resources that can be expressed in monetary terms.

The number of adult equivalents[10] is a better indicator than population size of the evolution of needs because, in addition to the overall number of people, it takes into account age and gender structures. To the extent that adults have greater needs than children or infants, the aging of the Mexican population means a faster growth in needs than what demographic expansion alone would suggest. Dividing total consumption by adult equivalents yields the size of the pie by unit of need, or total consumption per adult equivalent (TCAE). The values of this indicator for selected years between 1981 and 2000 appear in table 11.1. If TCAE increases, the availability of goods and services per unit of need rises.

The Gini coefficient is the best known and most widely used measure of income inequality. When the coefficient equals 1, there is total inequality in the distribution of income (one household receives all the income); when it equals 0, there is total equality. Its complement—the value that results from 1 minus the Gini coefficient—is a measure of equality in income distribution (table 11.1). Multiplying TCAE by the Gini complement produces the egalitarian total consumption per adult equivalent (ETCAE). In other words, ETCAE is the volume of consumption that would be needed, were it distributed with total equality, to generate the same level of welfare as the observed total consumption generates with the observed degree of inequality. It synthesizes the three variables considered up until this point in the discussion.[11]

---

[9] The difference between total consumption and national disposable income is only net savings.

[10] Because of the way in which caloric requirements for age groups and genders have been employed in this calculation, in a strict sense the measure is an adult *male* equivalent. Transforming the number of people into adult equivalents is a standard procedure in poverty and welfare studies. For a very good review of the (huge) literature on the topic, see Deaton and Mullbauer 1991.

[11] In ideal terms, this indicator should be based on the Gini coefficient of total consumption, not of household income. Although data exist concerning the distribution of private consumption among households, it is very difficult indeed to distribute public consumption among households—which is what would be required to calculate the Gini coefficient that corresponds to TCAE. The proxy used in the text is quite a good one.

TABLE 11.1. Opportunity Set for Social Welfare in Mexico, 1981–2000

	1981	1984	1989	1992	1994	1996	1998	2000
Total consumption per adult equivalent (TCAE, in constant 1993 pesos)	15,561	14,279	13,785	14,967	15,232	13,660	14,651	15,858
Index of total consumption per adult equivalent (1981=100)	100.0	91.8	88.6	96.2	97.9	87.8	94.2	101.9
Income distribution (Gini coefficients)	0.429	0.429	0.469	0.475	0.477	0.456	0.476	0.481
Income equality[1]	0.571	0.571	0.531	0.525	0.523	0.544	0.524	0.519
Egalitarian total consumption per adult equivalent (ETCAE, in constant 1993 pesos)[2]	8,885	8,153	7,320	7,858	7,967	7,431	7,677	8,231
Index of egalitarian total consumption per adult equivalent (1981=100)	100.0	91.8	82.4	88.4	89.7	83.6	86.4	92.6
Free time[3]	0.936	0.936	0.942	0.915	1.009	0.970	0.954	0.895
Free-time equality[4]	0.706	0.706	0.726	0.696	0.721	0.759	0.748	0.651
Egalitarian free time[5]	0.660	0.660	0.684	0.636	0.727	0.736	0.714	0.583
Educational achievement[6]	0.700	0.700	0.764	0.783	0.789	0.821	0.832	0.874
Educational equality[7]	0.679	0.679	0.663	0.632	0.605	0.620	0.625	0.625
Egalitarian educational achievement[8]	0.476	0.476	0.507	0.494	0.477	0.509	0.520	0.547

	1981	1984	1989	1992	1994	1996	1998	2000
Combined egalitarian free time and egalitarian educational achievement[9]	0.568	0.568	0.595	0.565	0.602	0.622	0.617	0.565
Opportunity set for social welfare (in constant 1993 pesos)[10]	5,046	4,630	4,358	4,443	4,798	4,625	4,736	4,648
Index of the opportunity set for social welfare (1981=100)	100.0	91.8	86.4	88.0	95.1	91.6	93.8	92.1

Source: Author's calculations based on Instituto Nacional de Estadística, Geografía e Informática national accounts data and national household income and expenditures surveys.

[1] Calculated as 1 minus the value of the Gini coefficient.

[2] This is the product of the TCAE value multiplied by the income equality value.

[3] Calculated as 2 minus the value for excess extra-domestic work.

[4] This is the quotient of the free time of the poor (defined as the poorest 75 percent of the population) divided by the free time of the non-poor (defined as the richest 25 percent of the population).

[5] This is the product of the free-time value multiplied by the free-time equality value.

[6] Calculated as 1 minus the educational gap.

[7] This is the ratio of the educational achievement of the poor to the educational achievement of the non-poor.

[8] This is the product of the educational achievement value multiplied by the educational equality value.

[9] Simple average of the values for these two categories.

[10] This is the product of the ETCAE value multiplied by the value reported in the preceding category.

The egalitarian free time indicator is constructed in two steps. The first step is to create a measure of extra-domestic excess work, the amount of which expresses a household's excess non-domestic work in relation to the social norm. It takes into account each household's domestic work requirements, according to the household's size, age structure, and resources available to support domestic work.[12] Because the value of this indicator ranges from 0 to 2 (with the norm at 1), subtracting its value from 2 yields a new variable, free time (FT), which also ranges from 0 to 2 with a norm of 1. FT is an indirect measure of available free time; at a value of 0, households have no free time, while at a value of 2 they reach a level of free time beyond which there is no further increase in welfare (that is, they reach the maximum welfare that free time can provide).

The second step is to construct an indicator of equality in free time. This is the quotient of the free time of the poor divided by the free time of the non-poor (FT_P/FT_{NP}), calculated according to the integrated poverty measurement method. The product of the average value of FT for the whole population and this quotient (called free-time equality) is egalitarian free time (EFT).[13] This measure also ranges from 0 to 2, with a norm of 1.

The egalitarian educational achievement (EEA) indicator serves as a proxy for the average level and equality of access to knowledge. It is obtained by multiplying educational achievement (EA, equal to 1 minus the educational lag) by a simple measure of distributive equality, defined as the ratio of the educational achievement of the poor (defined as the poorest 75 percent of the population) to the educational achievement of the non-poor (the richest 25 percent of the population) (EA_P/EA_{NP}). Educational lag is one of the indicators of unsatisfied basic needs that make up the integrated poverty measurement method. It is obtained by comparing each household member's educational level with the norm of completed secondary schooling for adults and school attendance (at an age-appropriate grade) for minors. In EA, the norm is 1 and the worst situation is 0; the maximum that can be reached has been reduced to 2.

---

[12] The methodology for calculating extra-domestic excess work is discussed in Damián 2000: 113. For a previous version of this methodology, see Boltvinik and Hernández Laos 1999 (Methodological Appendix).

[13] To avoid the bias that would have been introduced in the time series if free-time equality were to be calculated each year with the changing proportion of poor/non-poor in the population, EFT has been calculated defining the wealthiest 25 percent of the population as "rich" and the poorest 75 percent as "poor." These figures reflect the most frequent level these proportions have taken in the period under study, as calculated via the integrated poverty measurement method.

The indicators, combined in the following equation, yield the opportunity set for social welfare (OSSW):

$$OSSW = [(TCAE) (E_Y)] [\{(FT) (E_{FT}) + (EA) (E_{EA})\} / 2] \qquad (1)$$

where E_Y, the measure of income equality, is equal to $(1 - G_Y)$; E_{FT}, the indicator of free-time equality, equals (FT_P / FT_{NP}); and E_{EA}, the measure of educational equality, equals (EA_P / EA_{NP}).

Therefore, (1) may be rewritten as follows:

$$OSSW = [(TCAE) (1 - G_Y)] [\{(FT) (FT_P / FT_{NP}) + (EA) (EA_P / EA_{NP})\} / 2] \qquad (1')$$
$$= (ETCAE) [(EFT + EEA) / 2] \qquad (2)$$

given that $(ETCAE) = (TCAE) (1 - G_Y)$; $(EFT) = (FT) (FT_P / FT_{NP})$; and $(EEA) = (EA) (EA_P / EA_{NP})$.

TCAE is national total consumption per adult equivalent; G_Y is the Gini coefficient of households' current income (monetary and non-monetary); ETCAE is the product of TCAE and $(1 - G_Y)$ (that is, the egalitarian national total consumption per adult equivalent); FT is the average free time in Mexico's households, and FT_P and FT_{NP} are the average values of this same variable in poor and non-poor households (as defined above); and EA is the average educational achievement of the population older than seven years of age, while EA_P and EA_{NP} are the respective indicators for the poor and the non-poor (as defined).

ETCAE is multiplied by the simple average of EFT and EEA. Given that these last two indicators are both indices expressed in pure numbers that take a value between 0 and 2, with the norm at 1, this operation leaves intact the unit of measurement in which ETCAE is expressed (constant 1993 pesos). Thus, in a society in which everyone is at the maximum welfare that free time can provide, FT would be equal to 2 and E_{FT} equal to 1, so that EFT would also equal 2. If, in that same society, everyone were at the educational maximum, EA would be 2 and E_{EA} would be 1. Therefore, the arithmetic mean for the egalitarian indicators of free time and educational achievement would be 2. If one were to multiply egalitarian total consumption (ETCAE) by 2, its value would double as a consequence of the high results reached in terms of free time and education.

With values at the level of the norm in FT and EA and with total equality in both, the value of EFT is 1 and egalitarian consumption remains the same when multiplied by 1. What is most common is for the

TABLE 11.2. Non-Egalitarian Opportunity Set for Social Welfare in Mexico, 1981–2000

	1981	1984	1989	1992	1994	1996	1998	2000
Total consumption per adult equivalent (TCAE, in constant 1993 pesos)	15,561	14,279	13,785	14,967	15,232	13,660	14,651	15,858
Index of total consumption per adult equivalent (1981=100)	100.0	91.8	88.6	96.2	97.9	87.8	94.2	101.9
Free time[1]	0.936	0.936	0.942	0.915	1.009	0.970	0.954	0.895
Index of free time (1981=100)	100.0	100.0	100.7	97.8	107.8	103.6	101.9	95.6
Educational achievement[2]	0.700	0.700	0.764	0.783	0.789	0.821	0.832	0.874
Index of educational achievement (1981=100)	100.0	100.0	109.2	111.8	112.8	117.3	118.8	124.9
Combined free time and educational achievement[3]	0.818	0.818	0.853	0.849	0.899	0.895	0.893	0.885
Index of combined free time and educational achievement (1981=100)	100.0	100.0	104.3	103.8	110.0	109.5	109.2	108.2
Non-egalitarian opportunity set for social welfare (in constant 1993 pesos)[4]	12,726	11,677	11,760	12,701	13,696	12,228	13,079	14,030
Index of the non-egalitarian opportunity set for social welfare (1981=100)	100.0	91.8	92.4	99.8	107.6	96.1	102.8	110.2

Source: Table 11.1

[1] Calculated as 2 minus the value for excess extra-domestic work.

[2] Calculated as 1 minus the educational gap.

[3] Simple average of the values for these two categories.

[4] This is the product of the TCAE value multiplied by the value reported in the "combined free time and educational achievement" category.

empirical values of EFT and EEA to fall between 0 and 1. In this case, the closer their average is to 0, the greater the reduction entailed in making the shift from ETCAE to OSSW.

The final result, the OSSW, is the amount of national total consumption per adult equivalent, adjusted by three factors: equity in income distribution, egalitarian free time, and egalitarian educational achievement. These three adjustments preserve the ETCAE unit of measurement (constant 1993 pesos), but the amount declines (as one can see by reading table 11.1 vertically).[14] For example, in 1989 the TCAE of 13,785 pesos dropped to an ETCAE of 7,320 pesos as a consequence of income inequality. Conceptually, this means that the welfare effects were equivalent; 13,785 pesos distributed in the actually observed pattern (1 minus the Gini coefficient of 0.469) would produce the same aggregate welfare as 7,320 pesos distributed equally (1 minus a Gini coefficient of 1, or an E_Y value equal to 0). Table 11.2 reports the non-egalitarian opportunity set for social welfare, which only considers average achievement indicators in consumption, free time, and education.

Something similar occurs when one combines ETCAE with the average of egalitarian free time and educational achievement. The resulting OSSW value is 4,358 pesos. This indicates that 4,358 pesos, with total equality of income distribution and an egalitarian distribution of free time and education and no educational or free-time poverty, would generate the same welfare as 13,785 pesos with the actually observed degree of income equality and levels and distribution of free time and education.

The central conclusion to be drawn from table 11.1 is that in the year 2000, seventeen years after Mexico took the first steps toward implementing the neoliberal economic model, Mexicans' opportunities for social welfare had not only failed to increase, but they were actually 7.9 percent below their level in 1981. This situation was the result of negative trends in four of the six indicators employed here: the three measures of equality (in household income, E_Y; free time, E_{FT}; and educational achievement, E_{EA}) and the free-time average achievement indicator, FT. The only indicator that displayed a clear upward trend was

---

[14] This is a particularity of the social progress index that was consciously sought. The starting point was a diagnosis postulating that alternative indices of development had proved inadequate in part because "when they arrive at a single figure, it is usually expressed in artificial units which do not correspond to the units of daily life" (Boltvinik 1992a: 34). In developing this idea, the author postulated that the new index has the property of being expressed "in units of measurement that are dealt with by people on a daily basis and this allows them to be socially adopted in a generalized way" (Boltvinik 1992b: 8).

educational achievement. Total consumption per adult equivalent (TCAE) was practically stagnant over the 1981–2000 period (an overall increase of only 1.9 percent and an average annual rate of growth of only 0.1 percent). Throughout the 1982–1998 period, the TCAE measure was below its 1981 level.[15] Thus the data point to the inability of the Mexican economy and of government economic policy to attain a steady growth in consumption per unit of need.

This flow of resources was, moreover, generated with a greater working effort by the population. There was, therefore, less available free time. The average value of FT for the entire population attained a peak in 1994 and has been dropping since then. The level in the year 2000 was the lowest level in the 1981–2000 period (table 11.2), thus causing opportunities for welfare to shrink even further. If the non-egalitarian opportunity set for social welfare (NEOSSW) had been calculated only with these two indicators (consumption and free time), the level in 2000 would still have been 3.5 percent below the 1981 level.

However, in terms of achievements in average values for the population as a whole, education registered a significant advance of 24.8 percent (table 11.2). This advance explains the fact that when the three measures of mean achievement are combined (without taking inequality indicators into account) to obtain the non-egalitarian opportunity set (NEOSSW, table 11.2), the resulting indicator rose 10.3 percent over the 1981–2000 period as a whole, an increase that is basically explained by the important improvement that occurred in educational achievement and by the dramatic change between 1998 and 2000 in total consumption per adult equivalent.

The data reflect increased levels of inequality under Mexico's new economic model. The values for equality in income, free time, and education were between 8 and 9 percent lower at the end of the 1981–2000 period than at the beginning (table 11.1). Income equality worsened systematically from 1984 to 1994, improved temporarily from 1994 to 1996, and then worsened again through the year 2000, a year at which it attained its lowest level in the whole period under analysis. The period ended with the indicator for income equality 9.1 percent below its 1984 level (which was used as an estimate for 1981 as well). Free-time equality improved, with fluctuations, from 1984 to 1996 and then worsened. Educational equality reached its lowest level in 1994. Even though the

---

[15] Growth in the TCAE indicator was quite fast in the 1998–2000 period (4 percent annually, well above the rate of GDP growth per adult equivalent) because of an expansion in consumption credit. The 1996–2000 period of economic expansion ended with a 0.3 percent decline in GDP in 2001, although consumption apparently continued to grow. It is likely, therefore, that total consumption per adult equivalent stagnated in 2001.

FIGURE 11.1 Opportunities for Social Welfare in Mexico, 1981-2000

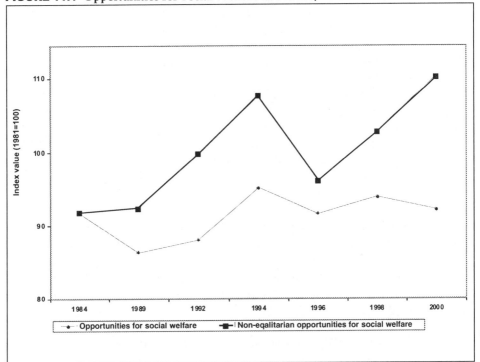

Sources: Tables 11.1 and 11.2.

indicator for educational equality rose again in subsequent years, the value for 2000 was much below the 1981/1984 level.

In other words, not only was Mexico's new development model unable to expand the economy, but it also furthered the concentration of income, free time, and education, thereby shrinking the population's welfare opportunities. Figure 11.1 summarizes the role of inequality in the evolution of opportunities for social welfare in Mexico. The area between the two lines may be interpreted as the inequality effect. As one can see, this area attained its maximum width in the year 2000, indicating the peak of inequality at which Mexican society had arrived.

In terms of mean achievements, the advocates of Mexico's economic reform process might argue that, once past the initial period of strong adjustment, the model's performance has been positive. After all, in 1996 — even after the 1995 economic crisis — the index value of the non-egalitarian opportunity set for social welfare (NEOSSW) was 96.1, above its level of 91.8 in 1984. Moreover, the level attained in the year 2000 was 18 index points above the 1984 level. However, only 10 of the points in this recovery were explained by economic performance (growth in TCAE); the rest were explained by evolution in education.

In fact, including measures of social inequality — as it is appropriate to do — produces a very different story, as demonstrated by the evolution of the opportunity set for social welfare. The OSSW indicator continued to fall after 1984, reaching its lowest level in 1989 and separating significantly from the NEOSSW indicator, especially during periods of economic expansion (figure 11.1). Without doubt, then, the overall result of Mexico's economic reform process is a socioeconomic system that offers fewer opportunities for welfare than it did two decades ago. This is a consequence of its meager capacity for growth and its intrinsic tendencies toward the concentration of its benefits.

TRENDS IN INCOME DISTRIBUTION

Although the opportunity set for social welfare takes all three dimensions of inequality (in income, in free time, and in education) into account, income inequality appropriately receives the greatest weight. For this reason, it is worth observing some features of this variable's evolution.

Income distribution in Mexico had moved in a very positive direction between 1963 and 1984. Indeed, Hernández Laos (1999: 177) concluded that the Gini coefficient fell from 0.606 in 1963 to 0.586 in 1968, 0.518 in 1977, and 0.501 in 1984.[16] He emphasized that "this trend is consistent with what is postulated by the Kuznets-Lydall-Robinson hypothesis. It holds that, as an effect of the transfer of the workforce from low- to high-productivity sectors (technology), in the early stages [the 1930s and 1940s] income distribution tends to become more unequal, eventually reaching a peak. Thereafter, once the majority of the workforce is in the nontraditional (or technologically modern) sector of the economy, income distribution becomes less unequal" (1999: 180). Hernández Laos noted that this trend was interrupted in Mexico after 1984, and that between 1984 and 1989 income distribution worsened dramatically, with the Gini coefficient rising from 0.501 to 0.549. He argued that this change was a consequence of both interrupted growth and the implementation of economic adjustment programs that sought to reduce domestic demand by limiting internal credit creation, raising taxes, and reducing government expenditure and transfers. In making this point, he highlighted the major changes that occurred after the early

---

[16] Hernández Laos developed the only available long-term series of Gini coefficients, calculated on the basis of income and expenditure surveys and adjusted to national accounts for comparability.

TABLE 11.3. Household Income Distribution in Mexico, 1984-2000 (Gini coefficients)

Year	Total Income Deciles		Per Capita Monetary Income Deciles
	Total Income	*Total Monetary Income*	
1984	0.429	0.456	0.466
1989	0.469	0.489	0.504
1992	0.475	0.509	0.521
1994	0.477	0.514	0.528
1996	0.456	0.489	0.503
1998	0.476	0.509	0.523
2000	0.481	0.503	0.516

Sources: Data concerning total income are from the Instituto Nacional de Estadística, Geografía e Informática's (INEGI) national surveys of household income and expenditure for each of the years reported. Data concerning per capita monetary income deciles are from Cortés 1997 and the author's communication with Cortés.

1980s in the relative prices of factors of production, especially reductions in wages and increases in real interest rates.

There is no Gini coefficient series with data adjusted to national accounts for the years after 1989. The unadjusted data, which must be viewed with caution, indicate that the rise in total income (the sum of monetary and non-monetary income) concentration continued through 1994, declined in 1996, and then started growing again, reaching its maximum in the year 2000. Table 11.3 presents Gini coefficients for monetary and total income drawn from published survey data on household income and expenditure collected by Mexico's Institute for Statistics, Geography, and Informatics (INEGI), as well as those coefficients calculated for monetary income by Cortés (1997) using the databases of the same surveys. Whereas the INEGI data were ranked based on total household income, Cortés's Gini coefficients were calculated from a ranking of households based on income per capita.

Despite the methodological differences, both data sets show the same trends. The Gini coefficient increased strongly and in a sustained way not only during the 1984–1989 period (a finding that coincides with the Hernández Laos data adjusted to national accounts), but also through the 1989–1994 and 1996–2000 periods. In other words, with the exception of the years between 1994 and 1996, the change in trend that Hernández Laos noted for the 1984–1989 period continued through 2000. This conclusion is important because it means that income concentration has increased in periods of both economic stagnation (1984–1989) and recovery (1989–1994 and 1996–2000). The exception came in the 1994–1996 period, when inequality decreased as income fell for all deciles but most dramatically for the tenth (richest) decile. It would appear, then, that greater inequality is intrinsic to Mexico's new economic model.

INCOME POVERTY AND SPECIFIC POVERTIES: A CONTRADICTORY EVOLUTION

Income poverty in Mexico decreased systematically in the 1960s and 1970s, until 1981 (Boltvinik and Hernández Laos 1999). The same trend

FIGURE 11.2. Three Versions of the Evolution of Poverty in Mexico, 1968–2000

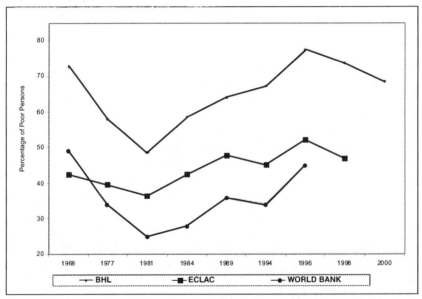

Sources: The Boltvinik-Hernández Laos (BHL) data for 1968-1984 are from Hernández Laos 1992; the remaining data in the BHL series are the author's estimates. ECLAC (Economic Commission for Latin America and the Caribbean) data for 1968 are from Altimir 1979; for 1977, CEPAL-PNUD 1990; for 1981, the author's own estimate; for 1984 and 1989, INEGI-CEPAL 1993; and for 1994 through 1998, CEPAL 2001. The World Bank data are from World Bank 1999: 52-53, except for 1981, which is the author's estimate.

Note: The BHL data estimates for the 1968-1984 period are based on income data adjusted to national accounts, while the estimates from 1989 onwards are based on household income data not adjusted to national accounts. Therefore, the estimations are not strictly comparable and should be analyzed as separate series.

is evident in a reconstruction of the ECLAC's and the World Bank's figures (see figure 11.2).[17] The trend was reversed in the 1980s as income poverty rose significantly, especially between 1981 and 1989. The increases in income poverty tended to level off toward the end of the 1980s and early 1990s (1989–1994). However, there was a further substantial rise during the 1994–1996 period. Finally, income poverty again decreased during the 1996–2000 period.

According to ECLAC estimates, the incidence of income poverty was greater in 1998 than the 1968 level and very similar to the 1989 level. In the author's own reconstruction of the ECLAC calculations, three periods can be identified: decrease (1968–1981); increase (1981–1996); decrease (1996–1998) (figure 11.2). The World Bank, whose series ends in 1996, identifies the same first two periods as the ECLAC. The Boltvinik-Hernández Laos (BHL) series, which extends through 2000, identifies the same three periods as did the ECLAC, but it extends the last period of declining income poverty to the year 2000. Thus, although there are large differences in the level of poverty incidence among the four series analyzed,[18] there is a high degree of consensus regarding the directions of change.[19]

---

[17] In order to compare the ECLAC and World Bank series with the Boltvinik-Hernández Laos series (which estimated the level of poverty in 1981, a year in which INEGI did not conduct a household income and expenditure survey), the author estimated poverty levels in 1981 in both the ECLAC's and the World Bank's series.

[18] The main reason why the BHL series and the ECLAC and World Bank series on the incidence of poverty vary so much from each other is the huge distance between their respective poverty lines. This distance, in turn, is explained by a different concept of poverty implicit in these analyses. In contrast to the ECLAC and the World Bank, which define poverty as not having enough income to buy food for a specified diet (for ECLAC, a socially generalized diet, and for the World Bank, a poor man's diet), Boltvinik and Hernández Laos define human needs in terms of much more than food (they include housing, clothing, transportation, energy, and so on), and they base the poverty line level on a complete budget. This approach, developed by a group of researchers working for the General Coordination of the National Plan for Depressed Areas and Marginalized Groups (CO-PLAMAR) during the 1980–1982 period, employs the normative basket of essential satisfiers (NBES). The methodological appendix to this chapter includes a brief explanation (with further references) of the procedure followed to derive the NBES. For an analytic criticism of the ECLAC and World Bank approaches, see Boltvinik 1996a, 1999, and 2000.

[19] Setting aside studies by international organizations (see Altimir 1979 and Bergsman 1980), the first poverty estimates made by Mexican researchers were CO-PLAMAR's calculations for 1977 (COPLAMAR 1982a). Hernández Laos (1992) was the first Mexican researcher to construct a data series on poverty evolution in Mexico. Levy (1991) estimated poverty in Mexico for the World Bank, but he only did so for 1984, using a very low extreme poverty line and COPLAMAR's moder-

Tables 11.4 and 11.5 present an overview of the evolution of specific poverties in Mexico between 1970 and 2000.[20] In these series as well, we can distinguish three periods in the evolution of the satisfaction of specific needs. However, because of differing dates for the available data, these periods are not the same as those for income poverty.

During the 1970s the evolution of specific poverties paralleled the very rapid decline in income poverty. In the 1980s, however, specific poverties and income poverty diverged. Specific poverties continued to decline (albeit more slowly), but the trend in income poverty changed dramatically. Income poverty continued to increase during the early 1990s (although at a lower rate), before experiencing some decline at the end of the period (1996–2000). In contrast, most of the specific poverties fell during the 1990s at a faster rate than in the 1980s. The notable exception was social security poverty, which worsened during the early 1990s and closed in 1999 at the same level as in 1989.

The first part of table 11.4 presents measures of the incidence and equivalent incidence of educational poverty for both adults and school-age children. Incidence is defined as the proportion of poor people in a given population, while intensity tells us how deprived the poor are and is measured as the relative gap in relation to the norm. Equivalent incidence, in turn, is defined as the product of incidence and intensity. The general pattern in the equivalent incidence of adult educational poverty and in the incidence of child educational poverty (non-attendance at school) was a rapid decline during the 1970s, followed by

---

ate poverty line. Alarcón (1994) made similar estimates for 1989. Pánuco-Laguette and Székely (1996) estimated the incidence of extreme and moderate poverty during the 1984–1992 period using (implicitly) similar conceptual definitions as the ECLAC but not the same poverty lines. They arrived at the rather strange conclusion that poverty decreased between 1984 and 1989 (a period characterized by stagflation) and then remained constant during the 1989–1992 period (years characterized by economic growth and lower inflation levels). Later, Székely worked with Lustig (Lustig and Székely 1997) and corrected this odd result for the 1984–1994 period using the ECLAC's poverty lines and adjusting income survey figures to national accounts. More recently, Damián (2000), Romero (1999), and Escotto (n.d.) have undertaken analyses that develop the integrated poverty measurement method in various directions. Damián, for example, has developed the time-poverty aspect of this method, while Escotto has enriched the methodology.

[20] In some instances, 1999 was the most recent year for which data were available.

The indicators designed for adult education, housing space, and housing services are such that they capture both the incidence and intensity of poverty, which, when combined, measure the equivalent incidence of poverty. The notes at the foot of tables 11.4 and 11.5 define the concepts and explain the specific procedures employed.

a slower decrease in the 1980s, and then a partial recovery in the rate of decline in the 1990s.

It should be noted, however, that in the adult equivalent incidence indicator the differences among these decades were not as marked as in the case of child educational poverty. The incidence of moderate adult educational poverty (adults who have completed six or more, but less than nine, years of schooling) tended to increase when the first two measurement categories—educational indigence (zero schooling) and extreme educational poverty (adults with less than six years of schooling)—decreased. This is what happened in the 1970s, for instance, indicating changes in the composition of educational poverty.

Changes such as these make it clear that poverty incidence by itself cannot be an appropriate indicator because it does not take into account how poor the poor are. This characteristic is disclosed by the equivalent incidence indicator, which (as noted) combines poverty incidence and intensity.[21] It shows a decline in the three main periods, with the 1970s being the fastest and the 1980s the slowest. The average equivalent incidence indicator for both adult and child educational poverty shows the same pattern.

The data in the second part of table 11.4 refer to poverty in living space and housing services. These measures include one indicator of overcrowding (poverty of living space, which has been constructed as an equivalent incidence indicator) and an equivalent incidence indicator for poverty in housing services, which is decomposed into one measure of the overall incidence of housing services poverty and specific measures of incidence in three different strata (indigence, extreme poverty, and moderate poverty). These strata measures are summed to obtain the overall incidence of poverty in housing services.

The indicators for both overcrowding and the equivalent incidence of housing services poverty show a similar pattern of deceleration in the downward trend from the 1970s through the 1980s. In the 1990s, in

---

[21] Because the figures on education and housing services reported in table 11.4 have been calculated without access to the original databases, it was not possible to calculate effective poverty intensities (gaps) at the household level. For this reason, the intensities used to obtain the values in row 5 are the average intensities that would result if all households in a given poverty stratum (extreme poverty, for example) were at the midpoint of the stratum's gap range (6/9 in the case of extreme educational poverty; see the explanatory note in table 11.4). In the case of education, this procedure misses improvement over time within each stratum. In the case of housing services, the procedure correctly captures the number of services below the norm, but it misses the intensity (when applicable) of poverty within each housing service category.

TABLE 11.4. Equivalent Incidence of Educational, Living Space, and Housing Services Poverties in Mexico, 1970–2000 (percentages)

Category	Year						Average Annual Rate of Change				
	1970	1980	1990	1995	2000		1970–1980	1980–1990	1990–2000	1980–2000	1990–1995
Education											
Incidence of adult educational indigence	31.6	16.1	13.7	10.4	8.7		−6.5	−1.6	−4.4	−3.0	−5.4
Incidence of adult educational extreme poverty (excluding indigence)	38.9	32.1	23.3	21.0	18.3		−1.9	−3.2	−2.4	−2.8	−2.1
Incidence of adult educational moderate poverty (excluding indigence and extreme poverty)	20.6	27.9	25.9	24.0	24.3		3.1	−0.7	−0.6	−0.7	−1.5
Incidence of educational poverty[1]	91.1	76.1	62.9	55.4	51.3		−1.8	−1.9	−2.0	−2.0	−2.5
Equivalent incidence of adult educational poverty[2]	62.1	43.7	35.0	29.7	26.3		−3.5	−2.2	−2.8	−2.5	−3.2
Child educational poverty[3]	36.1	13.5	13.1	6.4	5.4		−9.4	−0.3	−8.5	−4.5	−13.3
Equivalent incidence of adult and child educational poverty[4]	53.4	33.6	27.7	22.0	19.3		−4.5	−1.9	−3.5	−2.7	−4.5

Category	Year					Average Annual Rate of Change			
	1970	1980	1990	1995	2000	1970–1980	1980–1990	1990–2000	1980–2000	1990–1995
Living Space and Housing Services										
Equivalent incidence of living space poverty[5]	43.3	27.2	21.9	17.8	18.6	-4.5	-2.1	-1.6	-1.9	-4.1
Incidence of housing services indigence[6]	35.8	19.1	10.7	5.8	3.7	-6.1	-5.6	-10.1	-7.9	-11.5
Incidence of housing-services extreme poverty[7]	20.4	20.4	23.2	20.3	18.0	0.0	1.3	-2.5	-0.6	-2.6
Incidence of housing-services moderate poverty[8]	12.8	20.8	20.6	22.2	23.8	5.0	-0.1	1.5	0.7	1.5
Incidence of housing services poverty[9]	69.0	60.3	54.5	48.3	45.5	-1.3	-1.0	-1.8	-1.4	-2.4
Equivalent incidence of housing services poverty[10]	53.7	39.6	33.0	26.7	23.6	-3.0	-1.8	-3.3	-2.6	-4.1
Equivalent incidence of living space and housing services poverty[11]	48.5	33.4	27.5	22.3	21.1	-3.7	-1.9	-2.6	-2.3	-4.1

TABLE 11.4 continued

Sources: COPLAMAR 1982b; Boltvinik 1998; and the author's calculations based on Instituto Nacional de Estadística, Geografía e Informática data from the 2000 national population and housing census.

Note: For the measurement of educational poverty, the poor population was divided into three disjointed strata: indigents (those without instruction), the extremely poor (those with some degree of instruction but without complete elementary school), and the moderately poor (those who have completed the six years of elementary education but who have not completed the nine years of secondary education). To obtain a measure of the equivalent incidence of adult educational poverty, each stratum's incidence was weighted by its educational "gap." Thus educational indigents were weighted by 1 (their gap is total and includes the nine years of secondary education), and the extremely poor and the moderately poor were weighted by 6/9 and 2/9, respectively (in each instance, the proportional gap midway in the range of the stratum's variation).

The proportion of the population that exceeds the normative housing capacity of the dwellings in which they live (the relative housing deficit) was selected as the indicator of living space poverty because it expresses both the incidence and intensity of overcrowding – that is, its equivalent incidence. (In contrast, an indicator reflecting the proportion of people who live in overcrowded houses expresses only the incidence of overcrowding.) For the measurement of poverty in housing services (indoor piped water, sewerage, electricity), poor households were divided into three strata: indigents (those without any of the three specified services); the extremely poor (those with one service); and the moderately poor (those with two services). To measure the equivalent incidence of poverty in housing services, each stratum was weighted by its housing services "gap" (1 for indigents, 2/3 for the extremely poor, and 1/3 for the moderately poor).

[1] These values are the sum of the three preceding categories.

[2] These values are the product of incidence multiplied by intensity.

[3] Proportion of school-age children (6 to 14 years of age) not attending elementary school.

[4] Weighted average of "equivalent incidence of adult educational poverty" and "child educational poverty." The indicator for adults was weighted by 2/3 and the indicator for children was weighted by 1/3 to reflect their approximate numerical importance.

[5] Proportion of the population that exceeds the normative capacity of the dwellings in which they live.

[6] Proportion of the population with none of the specified housing services (piped-in water, sewerage, electricity) at or above the norm.

[7] Proportion of the population with one housing service at or above the norm.

[8] Proportion of the population with two housing services at or above the norm.

[9] These values are the sum of the three preceding categories.

[10] These values are the product of incidence multiplied by intensity.

[11] Simple average of "equivalent incidence of living space poverty" and "equivalent incidence of housing services poverty."

contrast, the declining trend in the overall incidence of housing services poverty accelerated slightly, whereas the declining trend in overcrowding further decelerated. On average, the indicator of equivalent incidence in living space and housing services poverty followed the same pattern as the indicator of educational poverty: a decrease in all three periods, with the fastest decline occurring in the 1970s and the slowest in the 1980s.

The data presented in table 11.5 refer to the equivalent incidence of health care and social security poverties.[22] In this instance, the years 1981 and 1989 were used as cut-off dates because both were years of change; 1981 marked the end of sustained economic growth in Mexico, and 1989 was the end of the economic crisis of the 1980s and the beginning of an economic recovery that lasted until 1994. Health services poverty decreased rapidly during the 1978–1981 period (at an average annual rate of 6.4 percent). It fell at a moderate rate between 1981 and 1989 (an average of 2.4 percent per year), and it decreased at a slightly faster average rate (3.5 percent per year) during the 1990s. Social security poverty declined at a moderate rate (an annual average of 3.4 percent) between 1970 and 1981 and at a slower average rate (2.5 percent per year) between 1981 and 1989. Between 1989 and 1999 it ceased to decline. This constancy is explained by the radical shift toward an increase in social security poverty that occurred between 1989 and 1995 (the last year showing the same level of social security poverty as in 1981) and then a sharp fall from 1995 to 1999.

In sum, the following patterns emerged in the three summary indicators employed in this analysis (the last row in the first and second parts of table 11.4 and the last row in table 11.5):

- Looking first only at the average rates of change for longer periods (decades or periods of similar length), all signs for the measures of specific poverties were negative. This indicates that the equivalent incidence of all specific poverties declined during the 1970s, 1980s, and 1990s.

- For all three summary indicators, the rate of decline slowed during the 1980s, and in two instances it accelerated again in the 1990s (albeit without recovering the rates of the 1970s).

- When the rates of decline are calculated for the 1980–2000 period and are contrasted with the rates achieved in the 1970s, the latter were on average 100 percent greater.

---

[22] The available data here are yearly figures drawn from the administrative records of Mexican social security institutions, allowing one to set any cut-off years. Unfortunately, the earliest available year for the health care indicator is 1978.

TABLE 11.5. Equivalent Incidence of Health Care and Social Security Poverties in Mexico, 1970–1999 (percentages)

Category	Year					Average Annual Rate of Change				
	1970/ 1978[1]	1981	1989	1995	1999	1970/78– 1981[1]	1981– 1989	1981– 1999	1989– 1995	1989– 1999
Equivalent incidence of health-care services poverty[2]	58.9	48.4	39.9	37.0	28.0	-6.4	-2.4	-3.0	-1.3	-3.5
Equivalent incidence of social security poverty[3]	74.3	50.9	41.5	50.8[4]	41.5[4]	-3.4	-2.5	-1.1	3.4	0.0
Equivalent incidence of health care and social security poverty[5]	66.6	49.7	40.7	43.9	34.8	-4.9	-2.5	-2.1	1.1	-1.7

Sources: COPLAMAR 1982b, Boltvinik 1998, and the author's calculations based on Instituto Nacional de Estadística, Geografía e Informática (INEGI). *Cuadernos de salud y seguridad social,* various years.

[1] The data series for health services poverty begins in 1978; the series for social security poverty begins in 1970.

[2] Proportion of the population that is not adequately protected by public-sector health institutions, which is calculated by subtracting from the total population the average population that can receive appropriate attention from the available number of doctors, nurses, hospital beds, laboratories, and operating and x-ray facilities.

[3] Proportion of the population not covered by public-sector social security institutions, implying a lack of income protection against sickness, incapacity, old age, or other covered risks.

[4] The INEGI's *Conteo de población,* 1995 and *XII Censo general de población y vivienda,* 2000 indicate values of 62.5 and 58.6, respectively, for 1995 and 2000.

[5] Simple average of the preceding two categories.

Therefore, our stylized (or simplified) conclusion is that specific poverties continued to decline from the 1970s through the 1990s — with the highest rates of decline in the 1970s, the next highest during the 1990s, and a much slower rate of decline in the 1980s.

One reason why this pattern contrasts so strikingly with the trends in income poverty during the 1980s has to do with the nature of the variables being analyzed. The income variable is a flow variable, while the others are stock variables. With flow variables, today's level is not tied (at least not strongly) to yesterday's level. One's income today may be zero even though yesterday it was very high. With stock variables, however, yesterday's level largely determines today's level. Houses that had indoor plumbing yesterday almost certainly will have it today. In order to reduce the weight of this feature, tables 11.4 and 11.5 include some flow variables (such as the proportion of the school-age population attending elementary school) and rates of change for stock variables. Even so, the nature of a variable cannot be changed; an adult with a secondary education will be at that level for her or his entire life.

A second reason for these observed differences derives from the fact that a non-commodity form of access (in the form of public transfers or self-production) is predominant in the needs analyzed in tables 11.4 and 11.5. Public transfers clearly constitute the main route of access in areas such as education, health care, and water and sewerage. In other words, the determinant source of welfare here is the fourth welfare source identified at the beginning of this chapter: access to free government-provided goods and services. In the case of other needs, access occurred primarily through self-production (for example, self-built housing). The so-called social wage behaved differently than current income during periods of economic crisis. Public social expenditure was not cut during the 1980s, even in per capita terms.[23] Structural adjustment in education and health services did not proceed by reducing the volume of employment and services; rather, it occurred by depressing the real wages of teachers, doctors, and nurses.[24]

Given the worldwide fashion of privatizing the social sphere and Mexican attempts to "rationalize" public expenditure and eliminate subsidies, one should value the fact that — despite the pauperization of their parents — children did not stop going to school in the 1980s or in

---

[23] See the discussion in later sections of this chapter and in Boltvinik 1998.

[24] There was, nevertheless, a marked slowdown in the growth of services compared to the 1970s, and it is very likely that in many instances there was a decline in the quality of services as well. A question for political scientists to answer is why the administration of President Miguel de la Madrid (1982–1988) did not adjust social expenditure more dramatically, as it did with such important areas of expenditure as rural development and infrastructure investment.

1995, because education is free (that is, it has been decommodified). Thus institutions in the social sphere continued to provide protection — even though it was insufficient, uneven, and sometimes contradictory — during these periods of economic crisis.

In sum, the data in figure 11.1 and tables 11.4 and 11.5 demonstrate that:

- Educational and housing poverties maintained the same dominant temporal profile — rapid decline, slowdown, and partial acceleration — in the three periods studied, with poverty levels diminishing throughout.

- Trends in health care and social security poverty followed a downward trajectory that slowed between the first and second periods, and then changed sign and increased during the first half of the 1990s (for social security) and continued slowing (for health services). However, recovery of the downward trend in the second half of the 1990s brought health services into line with the common pattern, while it brought social security poverty to a zero rate of change during the 1989–1999 period.

- Income poverty declined between 1968 and 1981, increased between 1981 and 1989, and approached stabilization between 1989 and 1994. However, it again grew very fast between 1994 and 1996 as a consequence of renewed economic crisis and the way it was managed, before decreasing between 1996 and 2000.

The two noteworthy exceptions to the general pattern of declining poverty were income poverty and social security poverty. Both may be considered types of poverty that are determined more by market forces and government economic policy than by social policy.

Thus the 1981–1989 period cannot be characterized simplistically as a retreat on all fronts. Because of the continuation of government social welfare expenditure, several policy measures that promoted the horizontal expansion of social security protection, and the maintenance of minimum conditions for improvements in housing, all of the specific poverties examined here continued to decline, albeit at a slower rate than in the 1970s. At the same time, income poverty increased at the alarming average rate of 3.5 percent annually.

The 1989–1994 period (or 1990–1995, depending upon data availability) should not be viewed as a return to the dynamics of the 1970s, despite the notable recovery in the rates of decline for specific poverties (except social security and health care), because income poverty continued to rise (although asymptotically) until 1994 and then jumped sharply with the 1994–1995 financial crisis. Moreover, for the first time in Mexico, a historic reversal occurred in social security coverage.

The second half of the 1990s witnessed a general recovery and renewed downward trends in all specific poverties, including income and social security poverties. However, economic recovery came to an end in 2001, reversing some of these trends. For instance, the population covered by the Mexican Social Security Institute (IMSS) decreased in absolute terms during 2001.

THE EVOLUTION OF SOCIAL EXPENDITURE

The evidence presented in the preceding section demonstrates that in a time-series analysis the correlation between income poverty and specific poverties is very low, sometimes approaching zero. Indeed, an analysis of the evolution of both types of poverty over time reveals different (sometimes diametrically opposed) patterns. The obvious explanation is that the factors that determine the satisfaction of some needs—such as education, living space, housing services (access to piped water, sewerage, and electricity), and access to health services—are not the same as the factors that determine the evolution of households' current income. The correlation is also imperfect when cross-sectional analyses are performed at a given moment in time; a significant proportion of households is income-poor but not poor in terms of the satisfaction of basic needs, or vice versa (Boltvinik and Hernández Laos 1999: section 5.4).

Public social expenditure is a fundamental determinant of most of these specific needs (except ownership of durable household goods and, partially, access to housing). Figure 11.3 illustrates the yearly evolution of per capita public social expenditure between 1970 and 2000, using four alternative price indices to deflate the expenditure series in order to express them in constant prices. Using generic deflators (such as the national consumer price index or the price index implicit in the gross domestic product) yields abrupt declines in social expenditure in 1983 and in the 1985–1988 and 1994–1995 periods. The index values (1980 = 100) in 1988 were 68.6 using the price index implicit in GDP and 55.2 using the national consumer price index, representing a drop in social expenditure of 43.3 and 53.7 percent, respectively, from 1981—the year in which per capita social expenditure reached its peak. Such circumstances would signal a true catastrophe, but in fact these are not appropriate indices to use as deflators of social expenditure.

Two other indices were tested to obtain a more accurate picture of the evolution of public social expenditure during this period. In contrast to the national consumer price index and the price index implicit

FIGURE 11.3. Real Per Capita Social Public Expenditure in Mexico, 1970–2000

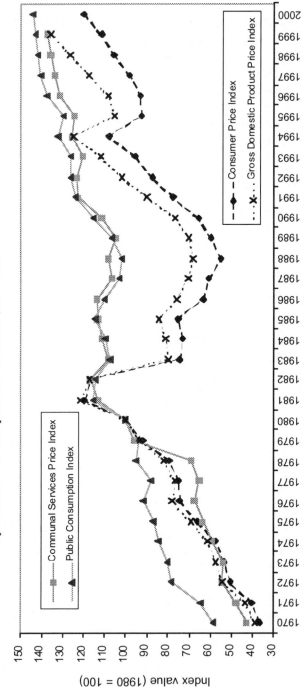

Sources: Author's calculations based on Instituto Nacional de Estadística, Geografía e Informática (INEGI) data regarding current social public expenditures. For 1970–1999, INEGI, *Anuario estadístico de los Estados Unidos Mexicanos,* various years; for 2000, INEGI, *El ingreso y el gasto público en México 2001* (Aguascalientes: INEGI, 2001). Consumer price index data are from www.inegi.gob.mx; data for the other indices are from INEGI, *Sistema de cuentas nacionales: cuentas del sector público,* various years, and *Sistema de cuentas nacionales: cuentas de bienes y servicios,* various years.
Note: The graph shows four series of the evolution of real per capita public social expenditure. Each series is the result of deflating current per capita public social expenditure by a specific price index. The consumer price index and the index of implicit gross domestic product prices are general, while the other two indices are specific to social expenditure. See the text for a fuller explanation of these indices and their meanings.

in GDP (which reflect, respectively, the evolution of consumer prices and prices for the economy as a whole), these alternative indices — both of which refer to the public sector — are based on the basket of specific goods and services that are acquired with public social expenditure.

The first, the implicit index in public-sector value added in communal services (or the communal services value-added price index, CSVAPI) only takes into account value added. In practical terms, therefore, this index is limited to wages and salaries paid, although in principle it also includes the consumption of fixed capital while omitting intermediate consumption (government purchases). The slower evolution of the CSVAPI reflects the pattern of wages and salaries paid to public servants (doctors, teachers, and nurses, among others), which during the period under analysis rose far more slowly than inflation in general. Selecting the CSVAPI as the deflator is equivalent to underestimating the rise in the cost of what is paid to provide public services; therefore, using it to deflate the expenditure series entails an overestimation of public social expenditure in real terms. Nevertheless, these biases should not be empirically important given that government purchases represented only about 20 percent of total government consumption during the 1988–1996 period and only 4 to 6 percent of education expenditure (which, in turn, represented close to 50 percent of total public social expenditure).

The public consumption price index (PCPI) is the most appropriate index to reflect changes in the cost of public consumption because it includes gross value added and the purchase of current goods and services. There are enormous differences between the evolution of the index of purchases and the index of value added; in fact, in years of strong inflation, the index of purchases is almost twice the index of value added. For this reason, the proportion of wages (value added) in total expenditure determines the level of its price index. In education, where purchases represented 4 to 6 percent of total expenditure, trends in teachers' salaries were the principal determinant. In the health care sector, government purchases represented between 20 and 25 percent of public expenditure. We can conclude, therefore, that it makes a great deal of sense to choose the average of the indices of public consumption in health care and education as the provisional deflator for public social expenditure. The choice of the simple average is based on the fact that the amounts of public expenditure in education were similar to those in health care during the period under consideration.

The pattern of real social expenditure after 1983 changes radically if we use the PCPI to adjust for inflation. Even in the worst year (1988), the index expressing the evolution of per capita social expenditure (1980=100) stayed slightly above 100, meaning that social expenditure

per capita did not decline in comparison to 1980. Even when the 1988
values (the lowest attained) are compared with those for 1981 (a year of
exceptionally high expenditure, well above the trend), the declines are
far from catastrophic — 11.7 percent using the PCPI and 4.3 percent employing the CSVAPI. Thus the trend in social expenditure during the
1983–1988 period can be regarded as one of stagnation, a view entirely
consistent with the deceleration in the downward trend of specific
poverties that was noted in the preceding section of this chapter.

THE INTEGRATED POVERTY MEASUREMENT METHOD AND THE PARADOX OF UNEVENLY EVOLVING POVERTIES

The Evolution of Poverty as Measured by the Integrated Poverty Measurement Method and Its Components

Table 11.6 presents information concerning the incidence, intensity, and
equivalent incidence of poverty in Mexico in the period between 1984
and 1998, calculated by applying the integrated poverty measurement
method (IPMM) to databases in which household income data have
already been adjusted to national accounts. It also presents disaggregated
data on unsatisfied basic needs and poverty line–time components.

These data show that the proportion of poor people in Mexico's total population rose from 68.5 percent in 1984 to 73.4 percent in 1989,
74.2 percent in 1992, and 75.3 percent in 1998. In other words, there was
a relatively rapid rise in the incidence of poverty between 1984 and
1989 and an apparent stabilization between 1989 and 1998. In fact, this
last period is comprised of three subperiods: stabilization, 1989–1994;
rapid increase, 1994–1996; and substantial decrease, 1996–2000.

Comparably quantified evidence is missing for 1994, 1996, and
2000.[25] In 1996 the incidence of poverty (as calculated by the IPMM)
might have approximated 80 percent, and it might have declined to 72
percent by 2000. However, information about the level of poverty
(again, as calculated by the IPMM) prior to the 1982 debt crisis is lacking.

---

[25] The author has in fact used the integrated poverty measurement method to
quantify the incidence of poverty for 1994, 1996, and 2000, but these calculations
were performed without adjusting household income to national accounts. The
results show that poverty increased sharply from 75.8 percent in 1994 to 81.9 percent in 1996, then grew slowly during the following two years (reaching a level of
80.3 percent in 1998), and fell significantly between 1998 and 2000, ending the period at 77.0 percent. If the 1994–1996 and 1998–2000 trends thus depicted were to
be reproduced in the adjusted series, adjusted poverty calculated by the integrated poverty measurement method would have been 80.1 percent in 1996 and
72.3 percent in 2000.

TABLE 11.6. Incidence, Intensity, and Equivalent Incidence of Poverty in Mexico, 1984–1998[1]

	Year				Percent Change			
					1984– 1989	1989– 1992	1992– 1998	1984– 1998
	1984	1989	1992	1998				
Integrated Poverty								
Incidence	0.685	0.734	0.742	0.753	7.2	1.1	1.5	9.9
Intensity	0.391	0.435	0.455	0.479	11.3	4.6	5.3	22.5
Equivalent incidence	0.268	0.319	0.338	0.361	19.0	6.0	6.8	34.7
Unsatisfied Basic Needs Poverty								
Incidence	0.750	0.701	0.707	0.677	−6.5	0.9	−4.2	−9.7
Intensity	0.466	0.454	0.467	0.479	−2.6	2.9	2.6	2.8
Equivalent incidence	0.349	0.318	0.330	0.313	−8.9	3.8	−5.2	−10.3
Income-Time Poverty								
Incidence	0.508	0.628	0.649	0.694	23.6	3.3	6.9	36.6
Intensity	0.484	0.536	0.547	0.572	10.7	2.1	4.6	18.2
Equivalent incidence	0.246	0.336	0.355	0.397	36.6	5.7	11.8	61.4

Source: Author's calculations from databases from the Instituto Nacional de Estadística, Geografía e Informática's national surveys of household income and expenditure for each of the years reported. Household income data have been adjusted to national accounts.

[1] Calculated via the integrated poverty measurement method. See this chapter's methodological appendix for a discussion of this method.

A huge increase must have occurred between 1981 and 1984, so that the 1984–1989 rise is only part of the growth that occurred—which might have been as large as 10 percentage points over the 1981–1989 period. If this is in fact the real picture (and the strong income evidence presented in figure 11.2 points in this direction), then the incidence of integrated poverty experienced a very substantial increase during the 1981–1989 period, followed by stabilization (with some fluctuations) in the 1990s. This, then, is a pattern similar to the one previously discussed concerning income poverty.

Not only did the incidence of poverty expand during the 1984–1998 period, but there was also a change in its structure, with more people in extreme poverty and more indigence (strata not included in table

11.6).[26] The growth in indigence in fact explains the entire increase in the number of the poor. This implies a rise in the average intensity of poverty, and as table 11.6 shows, poverty intensity did grow much faster than the incidence of poverty. Poverty intensity (or the average gap for integrated poverty) rose throughout the period, from 0.391 in 1984 to 0.435 in 1989, 0.455 in 1992, and 0.479 in 1998. Indeed, the whole structure of social stratification worsened. This change can be succinctly expressed: in 1984 there were four indigents for every member of the upper class, while in 1998 there were almost seven; in 1984 there were two indigents for every member of the middle class, and in 1998 there were three.

Because not all the poor are equally poor, simply adding up the number of poor is like adding apples and oranges. It is useful, therefore, to shift our focus from the incidence of poverty to the equivalent incidence of poverty, using instead of the number of poor people the number of equivalent poor (that is, the standardized number of poor individuals). If we multiply the number of poor individuals in a household or in a stratum by their average gap, we estimate the equivalent incidence of poverty for the group; dividing this product by the total population, we derive the equivalent incidence. Table 11.6 shows that the equivalent incidence of poverty (as measured by the IPMM) grew very rapidly over the 1984–1998 period, from 0.268 in 1984 to 0.361 in 1998. This represented a substantial 19.0 percent increase between 1984 and 1989 and smaller increases between 1989 and 1992 and between 1992 and 1998.

In the author's view, the IPMM is the poverty measurement method that most appropriately grasps the magnitude of poverty. It does so because it considers five of the six sources of welfare outlined at the beginning of this chapter. On the other hand, the best practice for quantifying poverty whenever income or consumption expenditures are involved is to adjust survey income data to national accounts. Finally, the equivalent incidence of poverty is the most adequate measure of poverty for a nation or any given set of households.[27] On all these

---

[26] Indigence is defined here as a situation in which a household meets less than half of social norms. Extreme poverty is defined as being below two-thirds of those norms.

[27] This is not a fashionable statement. Indices like those constructed by Sen (1981: chap. 3 and appendix C) and by Foster, Greer, and Thorbecke (1984), which take into account income distribution among the poor, give the gap of the poorest a greater weight than its numerical value would grant directly. Both indices assume decreasing marginal welfare (or utility) at all levels of income. This is implicitly formulated in the "weak transfer" axiom (one of the three axioms from which Sen derived his index), which states that a pure transfer of income from a richer per-

grounds, one must conclude that poverty grew substantially (by 34.7 percent) in Mexico between 1984 and 1998 (table 11.6).

The basic components of integrated poverty, as calculated by the IPMM, are unsatisfied basic needs (a direct measure of the actual dissatisfaction of a set of needs) and income-time poverty (an indirect measure of potential satisfaction of another set of needs, whose welfare source is current income, combined with actual dissatisfaction of free-time needs). Table 11.6 disaggregates the incidence, intensity, and equivalent incidence of unsatisfied basic needs and income-time poverty for the 1984–1998 period. Most notable are the inverse trajectories of unsatisfied basic needs and income-time poverty. The incidence of poverty as measured by the unsatisfied basic needs indicator declined significantly between 1984 and 1989 (from 75.0 to 70.1 percent), stabilized between 1989 and 1992, and then decreased again to 67.7 percent in 1998. Its 1998 level was substantially (9.7 percent) below the 1984 level. In contrast, both the incidence of income poverty (not shown in table 11.6) and the incidence of income-time poverty rose throughout this period, especially between 1984 and 1989.[28]

In which components of the integrated poverty measure did the equivalent incidence increase? Although the intensity of unsatisfied basic needs declined slightly between 1984 and 1989 (from 0.466 to 0.454 in 1989), the relative gap for income-time poverty grew substantially, from 0.484 in 1984 to 0.536 in 1989 (table 11.6). Intensities in both categories increased slightly between 1989 and 1992, and between 1992

---

son to a poor person below the poverty line — without making either cross the poverty line — must reduce the poverty measure (Sen 1981: 186). The transfer implies an increase in the richer person's level of poverty and a decrease in the poverty level of the poorest. If the richer person is also below the poverty line (the only case of interest, as otherwise the equivalent incidence indicator meets the axiom), the only valid reason to argue that the decrease in the poverty level of the poorer person will be larger than the increase in the poverty level of the richer person is that marginal welfare (utility) is a decreasing function throughout. This, however, is disputable. For arguments along these lines and for alternative positions, see Desai 1992 and Boltvinik 1993: 636–38.

[28] The incidence of income poverty rose abruptly between 1984 and 1989, from 41.3 to 55.6 percent. Income poverty as measured here, using a poverty line derived from the normative basket of essential satisfiers (NBES), differs from that measured by applying the poverty line method in its NBES variant, as in figure 11.2. The difference results from subtracting from the NBES the total cost of those items in the budget (such as housing) that were directly accounted for in the measurement of unsatisfied basic needs. At the same time, expenses for these categories were subtracted from household income, so that what is being contrasted is disposable income for a set of needs versus the cost of satisfying those needs at the normative level. See this chapter's methodological appendix for more details.

and 1998 the intensity of unsatisfied basic needs rose slightly while the intensity of income-time poverty increased substantially. Over the 1984–1998 period as a whole, although the intensity of unsatisfied basic needs poverty remained almost constant (a 2.8 percent increase), the intensity of income-time poverty increased significantly (18.2 percent). As a result of these changes, while poverty intensity in these two dimensions was quite similar in the initial year (less than a 4 percent difference), there was a wide gap by the end of the period (19.4 percent higher for income-time poverty).

Table 11.6 summarizes the average annual rate of change in the incidence, intensity, and equivalent incidence of integrated, unsatisfied basic needs, and income-time poverties in Mexico for the 1984–1989, 1989–1992, and 1992–1998 subperiods and for the 1984–1998 period as a whole. The data show that the equivalent incidence of integrated poverty increased by 34.7 percent over the entire period, and that this shift resulted from a 61.4 percent increase in the income-time equivalent incidence and a 10.3 percent drop in the unsatisfied basic needs equivalent incidence. In other words, the decline in the latter was insufficient to offset the brutal increase in the former. Because the increase in the intensity of integrated poverty (22.5 percent) was much greater than the growth of its incidence (9.9 percent), the magnitude of the increase in intensity explains a larger proportion of the overall change.

This conclusion highlights the limitations of employing the incidence of poverty as an isolated indicator, as well as the importance of taking intensity and equivalent incidence into account. Between 1984 and 1989, when unsatisfied basic needs poverty and income-time poverty followed very different trajectories, these differences appeared in both the incidence and intensity measures. While the incidence of unsatisfied basic needs poverty declined by 6.5 percent, the incidence of income-time poverty rose by 23.6 percent. And while the intensity of unsatisfied basic needs poverty fell by 2.6 percent, the intensity of income-time poverty rose 10.7 percent. In this case, too, the decline in the unsatisfied basic needs category was not sufficient to compensate for the rise in income-time poverty, so that both the incidence and the intensity of the integrated poverty measure rose (by 7.2 percent and 11.3 percent, respectively). Once again, the greatest increase was in intensity, which turned out to be the foremost contributor to the increase in equivalent incidence.

The IPMM and Fragmented Analysis: A Comparison of Findings

Up until this point in the analysis, we have obtained results that are consistent with the findings in the fourth section of this chapter. There we found that, during the 1980s, different components of poverty evolved in contradictory fashion. Income poverty trends changed course and the incidence of income poverty began to increase, while specific poverties (defined in terms of basic needs, including education, living space, piped-in water, sewerage, electricity, and access to health care and social security) continued to decline, albeit more slowly than in the 1970s. We also found that, during the decade of the 1990s as a whole, educational and housing services poverties decreased rapidly, at rates above the pace of the 1980s but below the pace in the 1970s. Moreover, we found that the indicator for social security poverty rose during the first half of the 1990s for the first time in modern Mexican history, and that it was stagnant over the 1989–1999 period as a whole.

What the analysis in that previous section illustrated "externally" (using independent measures for each dimension) has been "internalized" and ratified in this section via the integrated poverty measurement method. Income poverty grew and unsatisfied basic needs poverty declined between 1984 and 1998. In the earlier, fragmented analysis there was no way to synthesize the totality of changes in poverty.[29] The most we could do was to point out the contradictions in the evolution of different poverties. In contrast, the integrated poverty measurement method has allowed us, first, to synthesize the entire set of indicators for specific poverties in terms of incidence, intensity, and equivalent incidence of unsatisfied basic needs as a whole.[30] Second, the IPMM has allowed us to include the income dimension, which was combined with free time to form the income-time dimension. The integrated poverty indicator is constructed as a weighted average of income-time and unsatisfied basic needs, expressed in the measures for incidence, intensity, and equivalent incidence.

Disaggregating unsatisfied basic needs into the specific poverties that comprise it confirms the following trends:

- The incidence of living space and housing quality poverty declined from 86.3 percent in 1984 to 78.8 percent in 1989 and to 76.4 percent in 1992,[31] ratifying the findings presented in the preceding section

---

[29] The inability to synthesize is present in most poverty studies by international organizations such as the World Bank or the ECLAC. A similar problem characterizes the work of the vast majority of researchers who study poverty.

[30] Among the specific poverties included in the overall indicator for unsatisfied basic needs were health care and social security poverty. These were constructed as mixed indicators that take into account both access to health care and social security and the income of households lacking such access.

[31] This analysis has not been performed for the 1992–1998 period.

of this chapter concerning overcrowding in the 1980s.[32] The indicators for intensity and equivalent incidence declined as well.

* The incidence of sanitation deprivation poverty dropped sharply between 1984 and 1989, from 63.3 to 55.9 percent. It fell once again between 1989 and 1992, closing at 50.4 percent. Although intensity increased slightly during the 1989–1992 period, the final value was lower than in 1984, so that between 1984 and 1992 the intensity of sanitation deprivation poverty fell from 0.40 to 0.30.

* The proportion of the poor without sufficient access to durable household goods fell from 58.0 percent in 1984 to 53.0 percent in 1989 and to 51.9 percent in 1992. The intensity indicator also declined.[33]

* The proportion of the poor with an educational lag dropped dramatically, from 83.5 percent in 1984 to 74.7 percent in 1989 and 74.1 percent in 1992. Despite the high incidence of this form of poverty, it must be noted that the intensity was the lowest of all the indicators evaluated here. Moreover, the intensity measure declined from 0.40 in 1984 to 0.39 in 1989 and 0.38 in 1992.

* Health care and social security poverty behaved differently. Its incidence remained almost constant between 1984 and 1989, after which it changed course and increased to 48.1 percent by 1992—far above the 1984 figure. Intensity increased over the period examined, rising from 0.85 in 1984 to 0.88 in 1989 and 0.90 in 1992.[34] The equivalent incidence remained virtually unchanged from 1984 to 1989, after which it rose significantly in the 1989–1992 period to a level far above the initial year. The deterioration in this dimension of welfare during the 1989–1992 period coincided with the evolution of health care and social security poverty indicators between 1990 and 1995, although the time periods do not match. The trend in this area also contrasts with the decline in all the other indicators of unsatisfied basic needs.

---

[32] Besides overcrowding, this measurement includes an evaluation of the quality of dwellings in terms of the materials with which walls and ceilings are constructed and floors are covered.

[33] Change in this indicator depends upon household income, as does (but only partially) change in the indicator for housing poverty. The fact that it declined requires further explanation.

[34] These intensity levels have no parallel in the other categories examined here.

THE EVOLUTION OF POVERTIES AND MORTALITY RATES

In the mid–1980s, in the aftermath of the 1982 debt crisis, some observers of Mexico's social reality (including this author) expected that infant mortality rates would rise as a result of the brutal drop in the population's standard of living. Surprisingly, however, vital statistics for 1982, 1983, and subsequent years showed that infant mortality rates continued to decline. What observers did not understand at the time was that the satisfaction of certain needs such as education, health care, piped water and sewerage, and housing had not declined along with income. This section analyzes the evolution of mortality rates by age groups and outlines an overall hypothesis that links specific poverties and income poverty to mortality rates.

Poverty Kills

Countries with significantly different standards of living are also separated by enormous gaps in life expectancy. For example, in 1994 life expectancy in Japan was 79.8 years, but in Haiti it was only 54.4 years. The conclusion to be drawn is that there is a clear link between standard of living and average years of life. In other words, poverty kills.

Two specific pieces of evidence from Mexico show that, indeed, poverty does kill. Poor women in Mexico have more children, but these children are less likely to survive than the children of non-poor women.[35] This means that the poor die younger than the non-poor, which also means that they have a higher mortality proportion.

Table 11.7 presents information concerning the survival proportion (the number of surviving children divided by the number of live births) and its complement (1 minus the survival proportion), an indicator we label the mortality proportion. The data are stratified by standard of living and by urban and rural areas, and they are ranked from greater to lesser mortality proportion.[36] The survival proportion increases and

---

[35] The first piece of evidence draws upon results derived from a one-percent sample of the 1990 population census. The second is derived from the 1995 National Family Planning Survey. Details regarding the methodology employed in these studies can be found in Boltvinik 1996b: 17–19 and Romero 1999.

[36] There is a methodological problem in the calculation of mortality proportions. The events (births and deaths) used for the calculation of this proportion occurred over a relatively long period, but they are compared on the basis of a current social stratification. The evidence, however, suggests that this methodological difficulty is not an important problem in practice. The indigent/non-poor and poor/non-poor quotients for mortality proportions according to mother's age showed a surprisingly narrow range of variation. If we eliminate the 12–20 age group (which had very few observations in the non-poor strata), the indigent/non-poor quotient

the mortality proportion decreases as one goes from the poorer to the better-off strata and from the rural to the urban environment—showing that the expression "poverty kills" is not a metaphor but a crude reality. Variation in the mortality proportion in 1990 ranged from 12.8 percent among rural indigents to 4.0 percent among the urban upper class, a ratio of 3.2 to 1. If we adopt the urban upper class as a reference point, more than two-thirds of the deaths of rural indigents' children were avoidable.

Among all strata of the rural poor—and even in the "satisfaction of basic needs and income requirements" stratum—one can observe a mortality proportion that is more than twice that of the urban upper class. As a result, the average rural mortality proportion was 12.2 percent, over three times higher than the one corresponding to the urban upper class; the mortality proportion for the rural poor as a whole was 12.3 percent. This figure means that two-thirds of rural deaths—basically deaths of poor people—were avoidable.

The mortality proportion of the total rural population was substantially higher in 1990 than that of the total urban population (12.2 versus 7.5 percent). However, only part of this difference can be explained by the rural population's greater poverty. Comparing the same social strata in both environments, we note that there was always a difference in favor of the urban population. Part of the difference in mortality proportions must stem, then, from factors that are not measured by the poverty index. These would include, for example, access to health services.[37] Indeed, the ratio of mortality proportions among rural and urban indigents was 1.4 to 1; it was 1.3 to 1 among the very poor, and 1.5 to 1 among the moderately poor. Even among the population whose basic needs and income requirements were satisfied, the ratio was 1.9 to 1. If there were no significant measurement errors, these figures would indicate that rural-urban mortality differences sharpened at higher standard-of-living levels.

---

ranged from 1.48 among mothers over 70 years of age to 2.73 among those aged 31 to 40, while the poor/non-poor quotient varied from 1.40 to 2.28. If the group of mothers above 70 years of age is eliminated, the range of variation in the quotients becomes very narrow (ranging from 2.13 to 2.73 in the first case and from 1.86 to 2.28 in the second instance). Thus the conclusions presented in the text would not be altered if we calculated mortality proportions only for the youngest group of women, thereby shortening the time gap between the events (births and deaths) and the stratification employed in this analysis.

[37] The calculations presented here using the integrated poverty measurement method employed data from the 1990 population census (see Boltvinik 1994), which did not include any questions on access to health services.

TABLE 11.7. Mortality and Survival Proportions in Rural and Urban Mexico, by Standard-of-Living Stratum, 1990

Environment and Stratum	Mortality Proportion[1] (percent)	Survival Proportion[2] (percent)	Relative Mortality Proportion[3]
Rural indigents	12.8	87.2	3.2
Rural very poor	9.8	90.2	2.5
Rural moderately poor	9.7	90.3	2.4
Rural satisfaction of basic needs and income requirements	9.4	90.4	2.4
Urban indigents	8.8	91.4	2.2
Urban very poor	7.4	92.6	1.9
Urban moderately poor	6.4	93.6	1.6
Urban satisfaction of basic needs and income requirements	4.6	95.3	1.2
Urban middle class	4.2	95.8	1.1
Urban upper class	4.0	96.0	1.0
Total rural poor	12.3	87.7	3.1
Total rural population	12.2	87.8	3.0
Total urban poor	8.0	92.0	2.0
Total urban population	7.5	92.5	1.9
Total poor	9.4	90.6	2.4
Total population	8.7	91.3	2.2

Source: Boltvinik 1994: chap. 12.

[1] Calculated as non-survivors among live births, multiplied by 100.

[2] Equal to survivors among live births, multiplied by 100.

[3] Equal to each stratum's proportion of mortality, divided by the urban upper-class proportion.

Romero (1999) used micro-level data from the 1995 National Family Planning Survey and the integrated poverty measurement method to stratify Mexico's population. He presented results for nine priority states (Chiapas, Guanajuato, Guerrero, Hidalgo, the State of México, Michoacán, Oaxaca, Puebla, and Veracruz, states that include the country's poorest areas) and for Mexico as a whole, calculating infant mortality for each stratum. Romero's findings confirmed a strong link between infant mortality and social stratum. Indigents had an infant mortality proportion of 41.3 for every 1,000 live births; the corresponding figure for the non-indigent poor was 26.5, and for the non-poor it was 22.0. Thus the infant mortality proportion among the non-poor was approximately half that of indigents.

Yet if poverty kills and the poor die at a younger age, why did the expected change in mortality statistics not materialize in the mid-1980s, despite obvious signs that poverty was increasing? Is what can be verified in a cross-sectional analysis (such as that presented above) also true over time? We know that mortality rates have declined in virtually all countries where there has been sustained improvement in living standards, but is the opposite also true? In other words, when poverty increases in a society, do mortality rates also rise? The following section analyzes the evolution of mortality rates in Mexico.

The Evolution of Mortality Rates in Mexico by Age Group

Table 11.8 presents a synthesis of the evolutionary stages of mortality rates by age group between 1970 and 1999. In the case of mortality rates in the population between the ages of 0 and 14 years, it distinguishes among seven periods defined in terms of the economy's overall performance. In operational terms, an economic crisis existed whenever the average annual rate of change in GDP per capita was negative in most years (1982–1988, for example). Average GDP per capita growth of less than 2 percent per year defined a mild recession (1976–1977, for instance), whereas a per capita GDP rate above 2 percent annually in most years defined a growth period (1996–2000, for example). Mortality rates were calculated for periods that approximate (but do not always precisely overlap with) economic periods.

Despite underreporting and other problems,[38] the overall tendency in the infant (under one year of age) mortality rate appears reliable. During the 1970s (up to 1981), the rate fell slowly during the years from 1974 to 1977 (a period of mild recession) and experienced very rapid drops during two periods (1970–1974 and 1977–1986) that partially coincided with eras of strong economic growth. Infant mortality rates continued decreasing despite the outbreak of Mexico's debt crisis in 1982 and the collapse of oil prices, but the decline ended suddenly in 1986. Whereas the rate of decrease had been 7.3 percent per year be-

---

[38] See the explanatory note in table 11.8 for further details.

tween 1977 and 1986, infant mortality rose at an average rate of 0.9 percent annually between 1986 and 1990. This might be interpreted as a lagged response to the 1982 debt crisis, or as a consequence of the new recession in 1986 and its impact on the already deteriorated income levels of the population.

As we have seen in the analysis of opportunities for social welfare, total consumption per adult equivalent (TCAE) reached its lowest level in 1989. When TCAE began growing again during the 1989–1994 period, infant mortality again declined quickly. The infant mortality rate experienced a new period of slow growth during the 1993–1995 period (one that partially coincided with the period of economic contraction), but it then improved during the 1996–2000 period of economic recovery. In fact, all the drop in the 1994–1999 period came between 1997 and 1999 when strong economic growth resumed. Therefore, except for the 1982–1986 period, there was an almost perfect (negative) correlation between the rate of decline in infant mortality and growth in total consumption per adult equivalent.

From 1970 to 1999, infant mortality rates declined from 74.9 to 18.8 per thousand live-birth children. Of the total decline of 56.1 points that occurred over these three decades, the 1970s contributed more than half (30.3 points). The 1980–1999 period included ten years of mortality stagnation or slower decline (1986–1990 and 1993–1999), a period when the net decrease in infant mortality rates totaled only 2 percentage points.

In general, mortality rates for the pre-school population (ages 1 to 4) displayed a pattern similar to infant mortality rates. However, instead of a slow drop, this rate increased during the 1974–1977 period. The second very rapid decline in pre-school mortality rates coincided closely with the 1978–1981 oil boom. There was no lagged response to the start of the 1982 debt crisis, and the period of stagnation in mortality rates was longer. During the lengthy period of economic stagnation from 1982 to 1990, the pre-school mortality rate fell by a cumulative total of only 14.4 percent. Yet the rate of decline during the economic recovery of the early 1990s was the highest recorded in table 11.8. This phase lasted only two years, but the drop in mortality rates (from 2.2 to 1.2 per thousand inhabitants) meant an absolute decrease equivalent to that achieved during the whole of the 1980s. The accelerated decline in pre-school mortality rates during the 1996–2000 period of economic recovery was also sharper than for infant mortality rates.

Mortality rates for the school-age population (ages 5 to 14) showed almost identical periods and patterns of evolution as those for the pre-school group. The principal exceptions were the absence of positive

TABLE 11.8. Evolution of Mortality Rates by Age Group and Economic Growth in Mexico, 1970–1999[1]

	Final Import-Substitution Period, 1971-1918			Economic Crisis, 1982-1988	New Economic Model, 1989-2000		
	Growth, 1971–1975	Mild Recession, 1976–1977	Oil Boom, 1978–1981		Recovery, 1989–1994	Crisis, 1995	Recovery, 1996–2000
Infant mortality	−6.3 (1970–1974)	−1.7 (1974–1977)	−7.3 (1977–1986)	0.9 (1986–1990)	−8.6 (1990–1993)	−1.7 (1993–1995)	−3.0 (1995–1999)
Pre-school mortality	−15.6 (1970–1974)	1.0 (1974–1977)	−12.3 (1977–1982)	−1.7 (1982–1990)	−25.8 (1990–1992)	−1.3 (1992–1996)	−8.1 (1996–1999)
School-age mortality	−8.1 (1970–1975)	−2.4 (1975–1979)	−8.1 (1979–1983)	−1.6 (1983–1990)	−10.0 (1990–1994)	−0.6 (1994–1997)	−3.1 (1997–1999)
Younger-age mortality trends	Very rapid drop	Slow drop	Very rapid drop	Stagnation	Very rapid drop	Slow drop	Average drop
Productive-age mortality	←------- −2.0 -------→ (1970–1981)			−3.3 (1981–1991)	←------- −1.4 -------→ (1991–1999)		

Sources: Author's calculations using corrected population data from the Consejo Nacional de Población (CONAPO), except for the 0–1 and 1–4 age-group disaggregations for the 1970–1994 period, which are the author's own calculations. For the 1970–1979 period, data concerning the number of deaths in each age group are from Camposortega 1992: tables 3.9, 3.10; for the 1980–1999 period, these data are from the Secretaría de Salud and the Instituto Nacional de Estadística, Geografía e Informática (INEGI). Data concerning gross domestic product per capita (see below) are the author's calculations based on data in INEGI, "Banco de información económica" (www.inegi.gob.mx) and CONAPO's population series.

Note: The average annual rate of change in real gross domestic product per capita for the economic sub-periods identified at the top of the table were as follows: 1971–1975, 3.3 percent; 1976–1977, 1.1 percent; 1978–1981, 6.6 percent; 1982–1988, –2.1 percent; 1989–1994, 2.0 percent; 1995, –8.0 percent; 1996–2000, 3.9 percent.

Population statistics are troubled by many problems. The number of both live births and deaths, especially at younger ages, is a matter of dispute. For a strong criticism of CONAPO estimates, see Ordorica 2001. Nonetheless, the only coherent long-term population figures are from CONAPO. Thus, rather than using census data and interpolating for intermediate years (the result of which would not be a smooth series), CONAPO estimates were used for the calculations reported in this table.

Infant mortality rates were calculated using as the denominator the population of less than one year of age, rather than the more usual number of births (which fluctuate abruptly from year to year). Before adopting this decision, the author compared three sets of infant mortality rates for the 1985–1999 period, all of them using the same numerator (the number of deaths) but with three different denominators: (1) population 0–1 years of age; (2) total births registered each year; and (3) registered births of babies born in the same calendar year (excluding babies registered with a time lag). This exercise showed that the infant mortality rate is lowest (that is, the denominator is at its maximum) with the second option; it is highest with the third option. The first option (the one adopted in this analysis) yielded an intermediate rate. The trends are, nevertheless, determined more by the numerator than by the denominator. As a result, the series derived by using the first and third options are completely parallel, but their distance diminishes progressively from 3 deaths per thousand in 1985 to 1 in 1999. The series derived by using as the denominator the total births registered each year generally moves in parallel with the other two, but it moves in the opposite direction in several years.

[1] Average annual rate of change for each period indicated.

rates during the mild recession of 1976–1977 and some differences in the speed of decline during the 1990s. There was a very rapid drop in school-age mortality between 1979 and 1983, when the rate fell from 8.3 to 6.3 per thousand school-age children (a 25.3 percent decline in just four years). As in the case of the infant and pre-school populations, the school-age mortality rate stagnated between 1983 and 1990; the rate fell from 6.3 to 5.6 per thousand, representing an 11.1 percent decline over seven years. During the 1990s, there was a period of especially rapid decline between 1990 and 1994, a period of stagnation between 1994 and 1997, and a period of average decline in mortality rates from 1997 to 1999.

In contrast to these trends for Mexico's younger age groups, changes in mortality rates for the productive-age population (15–65 years) coincided with just three longer economic periods: the last phase of import-substitution industrialization (1970–1981), economic crisis (1981–1991), and the shift to a new economic model (1991–1999). Despite the impact of the post–1982 economic crisis, the rate of decline accelerated from the 1970s to the 1980s. However, it then decelerated substantially during the 1990s. The overall drop in the productive-age mortality rate was from 5.5 to 2.8 deaths per thousand (a decline of 49.1 per cent). Somewhat surprisingly, the largest drop occurred during the 1980s.[39]

The Relationship between Poverties and Mortality Rates

The preceding discussion identified phases in the evolution of mortality rates by age group. Trends in mortality rates for infants, pre-schoolers, and school-age children each defined seven successive phases from 1970 to 1999 with the same sequence: very rapid decline, slow decline, very rapid decline, stagnation (during the 1980s), very rapid decline, slow decline, and average decline. Rates for the productive-age group stagnated in the 1990s.

This pattern presents a double challenge. The first task is to explain the interruptions or decelerations in the downward trend in mortality rates at three moments in time: the mild recession of the mid–1970s, a part of the 1980s (associated with the debt crisis and the fall in oil prices), and the 1995 recession. The second challenge is to explain why mortality rates for the productive-age population do not seem to be affected by economic ups and downs (as the rates for younger age groups are), and why these rates decelerated during the 1990s when the rates for other age groups were recovering their earlier pace of decline.

---

[39] The following subsection offers a preliminary interpretation of this pattern.

On the basis of the evidence presented earlier, it is perfectly valid to hold that two forces acting in opposite directions came into play in the determination of mortality rates during the 1980s. On the one hand, the increase in income poverty eroded some aspects of the population's living standards. Several of these aspects are directly linked to the chances of becoming ill and dying: nutritional intake, access to health services for individuals not covered by social security (who had, therefore, to pay for such services), and housing for persons who did not own a home and had to pay rent. The worsening of conditions in these areas drew mortality levels upward. On the other hand, living conditions whose satisfaction depends mainly upon public expenditures (school attendance, education, public health care, piped water, sewerage, and the availability of household electricity) or which are a stock variable (such as housing) continued to improve during the 1980s. These improvements pushed mortality rates downward. As a result, mortality rates during the decade were simultaneously subjected to upward and downward forces—forces that nearly canceled each other out and produced stagnating mortality rates.

The 1990–1994 period (or a similar one, depending upon the precise years for which data are available) was noteworthy for the simultaneous recovery of trends toward rapidly declining mortality rates among the three youngest age groups. This development was linked to the favorable evolution of some specific poverties and to the stabilization of income poverty. It is also likely that some technological advances in medicine (such as oral rehydration and an increased emphasis on improved health care for mothers and infants) and changes in reproductive patterns (see below) may have shifted the relationship between living standards and mortality rates. This may have been particularly true for infant and pre-school mortality rates, although it is very difficult to establish the quantitative impact of such changes.

Since the 1970s, then, living conditions have been the principal determinant of mortality rates by age group, especially at younger ages. These forces lagged in the case of infant mortality, but pre-school and school-age mortality rates stagnated almost immediately in the 1980s as a result of a drop in family income levels. Rapid declines in mortality rates promptly reappeared in the 1990s when living conditions began to improve and income poverty tended to stabilize.

Mexican demographers (Hernández Bringas 1998; Romero 1999) have identified certain factors that can be interpreted as causing a downward trend in infant mortality rates independent of living conditions. Three sets of factors appear especially important in this regard: women's reproductive patterns and maternal health care, the mother's level of education, and whether the mother breast-feeds her baby. In the first set of factors (the most important of the three), the interval between births, the number of children, and the mother's age are the determining variables. According to Hernández Bringas, the reproductive pattern of Mexican women underwent great changes during the 1980s, and he concluded that this shift largely explained why infant mortality rates continued to decline despite the severity of the country's economic crisis.[40]

The behavior of productive-age mortality rates is more difficult to unravel. It is particularly hard to explain why, despite falling incomes, mortality rates continued to drop during the economic crisis of the 1980s. Part of the explanation surely lies in the fact that social security coverage continued to expand at a steady pace during that period – in stark contrast to the sharp shrinkage of coverage during the early 1990s.

It is important to note that a complex process of economic restructuring between 1990 and 1995 displaced many people from their jobs, which was a factor underlying the contraction of social security coverage during this period. Mexico's adoption of the neoliberal economic model brought free trade, privatization, and the rule of the market. In terms of labor, it encouraged businesses to decentralize many activities, a shift that often transformed contractual employees with social security coverage into unprotected independent contractors and freelancers. Layoffs did not necessarily appear in unemployment statistics because there is no unemployment insurance in Mexico, but in practice they meant the loss of social security benefits. This change, in addition to the loss of access to organized, prepaid, and subsidized health services, worsened the impact of losing a stable income. Job loss also entails stress that can manifest itself as cardiovascular problems or alcoholism – factors related to a very significant proportion of deaths in the productive-age group.

POVERTY, MORTALITY, AND OPPORTUNITIES FOR SOCIAL WELFARE

As noted earlier, the tendency for mortality rates to decline stagnated in both the 1980s and the two other periods of economic recession we have identified (1976–1977 and 1995), particularly among younger age groups. The relationship between the two sets of welfare indicators (household income and satisfaction of specific basic needs) and mortal-

---

[40] Perhaps because he based his analysis on demographic surveys (rather than the administrative records employed in the present study), Hernández Bringas did not identify the period of stagnation in infant mortality rates.

ity requires much more analysis. Nevertheless, there is a discernible functional relationship; both sets of indicators affect mortality. When they move in the same direction, as they did in the 1970s, mortality drops rapidly; when they move in opposite directions, as occurred in the 1980s, mortality rates remain stagnant. This allows us to postulate the following counterfactual hypothesis: if public expenditures had declined rapidly in the 1980s, mortality rates in Mexico would have increased.

Two sets of public policies were important determinants (although they were not the only ones) in the evolution of each set of welfare indicators. Economic policy was a crucial determinant of household income, while social policy significantly influenced the satisfaction of specific basic needs. Thus our findings in this area highlight the joint action of economic and social policy. In the 1970s, economic and social policies acted in the same direction, improving both dimensions of welfare (income poverty and specific poverties) and producing an accelerated decline in mortality rates. This pattern contrasts with the 1980s, when economic policy (and economic crisis) produced an increase in income poverty but social policy maintained basic social services (education and health care); extended water, sewerage, and electricity coverage to households; and supported the consolidation of households in poor neighborhoods by regularizing land ownership and providing support services. In the 1990s, there was a partial return to the virtuous circle of the 1970s, as manifested by a renewed decline in mortality rates among younger age groups. The picture was clouded, however, by stagnation in mortality rates within the productive-age group.

The examination of opportunities for social welfare in Mexico that was presented earlier in this chapter included only the 1981–2000 period. However, on the basis of the many indicators presented in the course of this analysis, we can conclude with a high degree of confidence that opportunities for social welfare increased rapidly between 1970 and 1981. There is also sufficient indirect evidence to estimate the direction and rate of change for other indicators even when the period of analysis did not include the 1970s. Thus this concluding section summarizes in qualitative terms what occurred over the course of the three periods analyzed: 1970–1981, 1981–1989, and 1989–1999. The following paragraphs present this information through a vertical reading of table 11.9.

From 1970 through 1981 or 1982 (the last phase of inward-oriented development), there was positive synergy in all aspects of social welfare in Mexico. The central objective of public policy was to maintain economic growth despite the exhaustion of the import-substitution model (Boltvinik and Hernández Laos 1981) and to generate well-paying

TABLE 11.9. Overall Assessment of the Evolution of Well-Being in Mexico, 1970s–1990s

Category	1970s	1980s	1990s
Opportunity set for social welfare	Rapid increase	Rapid decline	Slow increase, with fluctuations
Non-egalitarian opportunity set for social welfare	Rapid increase	Decline	Increase, with fluctuations
Equality (income)	Rapid increase	Rapid decline	Slow decline, with fluctuations
Equality (free time)	NA	Increase	Rapid decline, with fluctuations
Equality (education)	NA	Slow decline	Decline
Poverties of education, living space, and housing services	Very rapid decline	Decline	Rapid decline
Poverties of health care and social security	Very rapid decline	Decline	Slow decline
Income poverty	Very rapid decline	Very rapid increase	Increase, with fluctuations
Integrated poverty	Very rapid decline	Rapid increase	Slow increase, with fluctuations
Mortality in young age groups	Very rapid decline	Stagnation (part of period)	Rapid decline (except for years around 1995)
Public social spending per capita	Rapid increase	Stagnation	Increase
Character of public policies	Final phase of import-substitution development	Stabilization and introduction of the neoliberal model	Structural adjustment and consolidation of the neoliberal model

NA = Not available

jobs. Wage policies protected real wages, which continued to rise until 1981 (Boltvinik 1998: 259–70). However, the high point in wages' share in gross national product (the so-called functional distribution of income) came in 1976.

Opportunities for social welfare increased as a result of both rising average achievements and greater income equality (the only dimension of equality with data available for this period). The government contributed significantly to the growth of these opportunities through greater public social expenditure, which expanded public social consumption rapidly (table 11.9 and figure 11.3). These increased opportunities translated into a very rapid decline in all the specific poverties analyzed. Improved living conditions and wider access to health care explain the very rapid drops in mortality rates for younger age groups. The articulation between economic and social policy was positive; both contributed to the improvement of living conditions. However, the pattern of growth that was achieved — based in part on the petroleum boom and foreign borrowing between 1978 and 1981 — clearly could not be sustained in the face of radical changes in external parameters (the sudden drop in oil prices accompanied by the simultaneous rise in international interest rates). The period ended with the onset of a severe economic crisis in 1982.

During the 1980s Mexico abandoned the import-substitution industrialization model in favor of the neoliberal model, reversing nearly every positive result achieved in the previous period. The principal goal of economic policy — to which all other objectives were subordinated — was to service Mexico's foreign debt. The debt crisis did not just interrupt the flow of foreign capital; it actually reversed the flow, and Mexico found itself having to transfer substantial quantities of capital abroad. The country financed these transfers with large trade surpluses, which economic policy achieved by reducing aggregate demand via peso devaluations, accelerating inflation, and holding nominal wage increases below the rate of inflation. These policies produced drastic declines in real wages and in wages' share of national product, placing the costs of economic adjustment almost entirely on workers (Boltvinik and Torres 1987). Opportunities for social welfare suffered a rapid decline as a result of both the deterioration of average achievements and the increase in income inequality, despite the favorable but very slow change in educational equality and free-time equality that occurred between 1984 and 1989.

The decline in opportunities for social welfare did not, however, translate into widespread increases in all poverties. Although income poverty rose very rapidly, specific poverties continued to decline. This was a result of public social expenditure, which did not fall despite the severe financial crisis in the public sector. Indeed, per capita social expenditure grew (albeit slowly) in real terms during this period. The worsening of some aspects of the Mexican population's standard of living (aspects that were satisfied through the market and that depended upon families' monetary income) and the continuing improvement in other aspects (elements that were not dependent upon families' monetary incomes) translated into stagnation in mortality rates for younger age groups. Although the government's economic policy pauperized the population, its social policy acted in the opposite direction.[41]

The 1990s witnessed the consolidation of the neoliberal model, with rather mixed consequences for welfare and equality. Real per capita public social expenditure grew at a moderate pace (below the rate of the 1970s but above that of the 1980s). Average achievements, which constitute the non-egalitarian opportunity set for social welfare, halted their decline and (with some ups and downs) expanded substantially. Yet equality in income, free time, and education decreased. Indeed, in the year 2000 income and free-time equality reached their lowest levels ever. As a result, opportunities for social welfare grew very slowly, ending the century at levels below those attained in 1981.

In the 1990s the evolution of specific poverties underwent a change compared to the 1980s. Although education, housing, and housing services poverties resumed a rapid decline, the average of health care and social security poverties experienced only a slow decrease as a result of zero change in social security poverty and an average decline in health care poverty. In other words, both sets of specific poverties fell at a similar pace and behaved in a uniform manner during the 1980s, but their evolution was not uniform during the 1990s.

During this same period, the trajectory of mortality rates showed a rapid decline positively associated with the favorable, though slow, increase in opportunities for social welfare. A number of trends favored the decline in mortality rates in the 1990s, including significant growth in non-egalitarian opportunities for social welfare; the slow but positive growth in opportunities for social welfare; the very rapid fall in educa-

---

[41] Paradoxically, this period included the De la Madrid administration, which ended some of the anti-poverty programs in operation during the administration of President José López Portillo (1976–1982). It discontinued completely the Mexican Food System (SAM) but maintained those elements of COPLAMAR that had been institutionalized. These included IMSS–COPLAMAR, which continues operation under the name IMSS–Solidaridad and provides free health care services to the rural population not protected by the IMSS. Similarly, CONASUPO–CO-PLAMAR, a joint program with the National Basic Foods Company (CO-NASUPO), continues to provide basic supplies in rural areas.

tion, housing, and housing services poverties; the slow decrease in health care poverty; and the average increase in public social expenditure. The unfavorable elements were increases in all the inequalities measured here; the stagnation in social security poverty; and growth in income and integrated poverties.

Whether these changes were sufficient to explain the very rapid fall in children's mortality rates is an open question. It is likely that changing medical treatments and emphases in health care, as well as shifts in the reproductive patterns of Mexican women, also contributed to this decline.

There is nothing in this analysis to suggest, even indirectly, that social policy during the 1970s was inefficient or inefficacious. The simplistic view upon which the shift to targeted social welfare programs was based—a perspective that maintains that non-targeted expenditure represents a waste of resources—does not take into account the complexity of social dynamics. Radically transforming large population groups' access to goods and services can provoke a cultural change that converts the goods and services in question into a social need. In sum, the analysis presented in this chapter has yielded nothing that justifies the Mexican government's shift in the mid-1990s to the so-called new poverty agenda.

METHODOLOGICAL APPENDIX

The Methodology for Measuring Poverty: The Normative Basket of Essential Satisfiers and the Integrated Poverty Measurement Method

This appendix provides a brief explanation of two principal methods used in this chapter to measure poverty: the poverty line procedure based on the normative basket of essential satisfiers (NBES), and the integrated poverty measurement method (IPMM).

The Poverty Line Procedure Based on the Normative Basket of Essential Satisfiers

This poverty line methodology is known as the budget approach. The first step is to determine the basket of goods and services required by a given household during a particular period (a year, for instance). In the case of consumer durable goods, one needs to distinguish between the quantities required and their annual use by the household, the former being larger than the latter. For example, a household requires a stove but uses, consumes, or depreciates only 0.10 stoves each year (if the stove's useful life is estimated to be 10 years). In the case of nondurable goods such as food, both quantities are equal. The basket is defined by the vector of quantities of annual use. This vector must be multiplied by the prices of goods and services in order to obtain the annual cost of each item. The sum of the annual cost of all items yields the annual cost of the normative basket of essential satisfiers, which constitutes the poverty line. This cost is compared with a household's income or consumption to determine whether or not the household is poor.

There are two main problems involved in calculating normative requirements. The first consists of defining the foundations for those normative requirements. In constructing the NBES, two main criteria were employed: Mexico's social reality, as reflected in the list of goods and services frequently consumed by households; and Mexican law, which reflects a combination of reality and goals. The NBES is thus an operational definition expressing a concept of relative poverty.

The second difficulty is that the list of total requirements must be classified into two groups: those satisfiers that must be met through private consumption (that is, the satisfiers that must be produced by, or whose cost must be paid for by, households), and those satisfiers that are to be met through public expenditures (via government programs, public social security institutions, and so forth). Only satisfiers in the first group should form part of the poverty line, because this is to be compared with a household's current income or private consumption expenditures.

At this point, there are two possibilities. The simplest one consists of defining a unique classification of satisfiers in both groups, which is then applied to all households. The second, though more laborious, option consists of specifying for each household a classification according to its particular circumstances where access to public transfers is concerned. The first approach was adopted when the NBES measure was constructed under the auspices of the General Coordination of the National Plan for Depressed Areas and Marginalized Groups (CO-PLAMAR) in the early 1980s. The satisfiers that are to be met through public expenditures or social security were primary and secondary education, for both the school-age population and adults; health-care services; and water supply and sewerage infrastructure. Access to these services would then be through public transfers. Households would have to take care of all other satisfiers, which means that access to these is through the market or through self-production. Applying this single classification to all households facilitated the necessary calculations but underestimated the level of the poverty line because, for example, a household lacking free access to public health services has to pay for such expenses — even though these are not contemplated in the poverty line.

The resulting poverty line is then compared with household income. Here again, COPLAMAR's procedure was a simplified one. The poverty line was defined for the national average household size and age structure. A better and more accurate alternative would have been to define a poverty line for each household, which can be done by calculating the NBES per person or per adult equivalent so that the poverty line applied to each household is the result of multiplying this unitary cost by the number of persons or equivalent adults in each household.

The Integrated Poverty Measurement Method

The integrated poverty measurement method combines two previously existing methodologies: the poverty line procedure based on the normative basket of essential satisfiers, and the improved version of the unsatisfied basic needs method (see Boltvinik 1992c and Government of Bolivia 1994). Its foundation is the conception of a household's sources of welfare (set forth in the first section of this chapter) and the consequent critique of the poverty line and unsatisfied basic needs methodologies.

In brief, this critique holds that the main limitation of both the poverty line and unsatisfied basic needs methods is that they proceed as if satisfaction of basic needs depended only upon a couple of welfare sources. The poverty line method, for instance, assumes that needs satisfaction depends only upon current income or households' current private consumption. Similarly, in its usual applications in Latin America, the unsatisfied basic needs method assumes that need satisfaction depends only upon basic asset holdings (housing) or rights of access to free or subsidized services (piped water, sewerage, children's attendance at a primary school). Implicitly, therefore, it does not consider any of the other sources of welfare.

The integrated poverty measurement method was developed to account fully for all welfare sources. In order to achieve full complementarity of the two methods on which the IPMM rests, it is necessary to specify which needs are to be assessed by the unsatisfied basic needs method and which are to be assessed by the poverty line method. In principle, all needs whose satisfaction in most households depends predominantly upon public expenditure (consumption and investment), household patrimony (accumulated assets), and available time should be assessed directly by the unsatisfied basic needs method. Needs whose satisfaction depends essentially upon current private consumption should be assessed by the poverty line method.

In applying the IPMM, the analysis assessed six dimensions of welfare via the unsatisfied basic needs or direct method, and one dimension (health care and social security) via a mixed procedure. The six dimensions assessed by the unsatisfied basic needs method were: (1) *inadequacy of housing quality and quantity*, an indicator constructed by multiplying the values for two component elements: inadequacy of the building materials used in walls, roofs, and floors; and insufficiency of housing space per dweller (overcrowding), as measured by the relationship between the total number of rooms and the total number of dwellers while taking into account the different types of household space (kitchen, bedrooms, living rooms, and so forth); (2) *inadequacy of sanitary conditions*, the weighted average of indicators for water supply, sewerage, and single-household toilet facilities; (3) *inadequacy of other services*, the weighted average of indicators for electricity and telephone (in the latter case, only in metropolitan areas); (4) *inadequacy of basic patrimony* (as in the case of income, an indicator of one of the sources of welfare rather than of a particular need), including appliances used for food preparation and conservation, personal hygiene, and recreation; (5) *educational deprivation* (the educational gap), measured by child school attendance and adult educational levels (where literacy acts as a controlling element); and (6) *excess working time*, an inverse indicator of available time for education, recreation, and domestic work, as well as an indicator of one of the sources of welfare.

As noted above, a mixed procedure was used to construct an indicator for inadequate access to health care and social security. For the population lacking access to social security, the poverty line was increased to include the cost of private health care and insurance. The satisfaction of all other needs was identified by the poverty line or indirect method, comparing households' income per adult equivalent (with the poverty and extreme poverty lines also defined in terms of adult equivalents).

When applying the improved unsatisfied basic needs method, one starts by building an achievement indicator, which involves assigning scores to variables such as those mentioned above and defining the minimum norm for each dimension. This indicator is then standardized by dividing it by the normative score, so that the variable is expressed as a multiple of the norm. The variable thus loses the original unit of measurement in which it was expressed and becomes a pure number. The next step is to make uniform (insofar as it is possible) the range of variation in the standardized indicators by rescaling all values above 1 (the normative score) when there are values above 2, so that these values will range from 1 up to 2. The goal is for all indicators to vary from 0 to 2, with 1 as the normative value. The final step is to transform this achievement indicator into a deprivation indicator, which is done by subtracting its value from 1. Deprivation indicators will thus vary from

–1 to 1, with 0 as the normative value. It follows that positive values express deprivation and negative values express welfare. Unfortunately, because of the limited options built into survey questionnaires, it was not possible to achieve the complete range for all indicators. Therefore, the values of some deprivation indicators vary only from 0 to 1.

Following this approach, one obtains for each household six indicators of deprivation by the unsatisfied basic needs method, one by the poverty line method, and the mixed indicator. The synthesized indicators for each of the first five dimensions of unsatisfied basic needs (inadequacies of housing quality and quantity, sanitary conditions, other services, basic patrimony, and education) and the mixed indicator for health care and social security are combined as a weighted arithmetical mean to obtain the overall unsatisfied basic needs indicator for each household, which indicates the degree of dissatisfaction of the set of needs that is verified directly (or the intensity of unsatisfied basic needs poverty). The excess work and the income indicators are combined into a time-income indicator. This measure is constructed by dividing income by an excess working time index, before comparing it with the poverty line to obtain a measure of the intensity of income-time poverty. A system of cost-based weights, derived from the cost structure provided by the normative basket of essential satisfiers, is then used to integrate all of the indicators described above.

By thus integrating the poverty line–time and the intensity of poverty line–time measures, and the unsatisfied basic needs and intensity of unsatisfied basic needs measures, one obtains an integrated poverty indicator for each household, which shows both whether the household is poor (or not poor) and the intensity of its poverty. Once the poor and the non-poor populations have been identified by each of the partial methods and by the integrated method, one proceeds to (1) define three strata each for the poor population (according to the intensity of their poverty) and the non-poor population (according to their degree of wealth), and (2) calculate the main poverty indices (incidence, intensity, and equivalent incidence) for each stratum and for the poor population as a whole.

REFERENCES

Alarcón, Diana. 1994. *Changes in the Distribution of Income in Mexico and Trade Liberalization*. Tijuana: El Colegio de la Frontera Norte.

Altimir, Óscar. 1979. *La dimensión de la pobreza en América Latina*. Cuadernos de la CEPAL, no. 27. Santiago, Chile: Comisión Económica para América Latina.

Bergsman, Joel. 1980. *Income Distribution and Poverty in Mexico*. World Bank Staff Working Paper No. 395. Washington, D.C.: World Bank.

Boltvinik, Julio. 1992a. "Towards an Alternative Indicator of Development." In *Social Progress Index: A Proposal*, by Meghnad Desai, Amartya K. Sen, and Julio Boltvinik. Regional Project to Overcome Poverty, United Nations Development Programme. Bogota: United Nations Development Programme.

———. 1992b. "Introduction: An Overview." In *Social Progress Index: A Proposal*, by Meghnad Desai, Amartya K. Sen, and Julio Boltvinik. Regional Project to Overcome Poverty, United Nations Development Programme. Bogota: United Nations Development Programme.

———. 1992c. "El método de medición integrada de la pobreza: una propuesta para su desarrollo," *Comercio Exterior* 42 (4): 354–65.

———. 1993. "Indicadores alternativos del desarrollo y mediciones de pobreza," *Estudios Sociológicos* 33: 605–40.

———. 1994. *Pobreza y estratificación social en México*. Aguascalientes: Instituto Nacional de Estadística, Geografía e Informática/Instituto de Investigaciones Sociales, Universidad Nacional Autónoma de México/El Colegio de México.

———. 1996a. "Poverty in Latin America: A Critical Analysis of Three Studies," *International Social Science Journal* 148: 245–60.

———. 1996b. "Pobreza y comportamiento demográfico: la importancia de la política social," *Demos: Carta Demográfica sobre México* 9: 17–19.

———. 1998. "Condiciones de vida y niveles de ingreso en México, 1970–1995." In *Deuda externa mexicana: ética, teoría, legislación e impacto social*, edited by José Antonio Ibáñez Aguirre. Mexico City: Plaza y Valdés/ Universidad Iberoamericana.

———. 1999. "Métodos de medición de la pobreza: conceptos y tipología," *Socialis: Revista Latinoamericana de Política Social* 1: 35–74.

———. 2000. "Métodos de medición de la pobreza: una evaluación crítica," *Socialis: Revista Latinoamericana de Política Social* 2: 83–123.

Boltvinik, Julio, and Enrique Hernández Laos. 1981. "Origen de la crisis económica de México: el agotamiento del modelo de sustitución de importaciones. Un análisis preliminar." In *Desarrollo y crisis de la economía mexicana: ensayos de interpretación histórica*, edited by Rolando Cordera. Mexico City: Fondo de Cultura Económica.

———. 1999. *Pobreza y distribución del ingreso en México*. Mexico City: Siglo Veintiuno.

Boltvinik, Julio, and Fernando Torres. 1987. "Concentración del ingreso y satisfacción de necesidades en la crisis actual," *El Economista Mexicano* 19 (3): 15–36.

Camposortega, Sergio. 1992. *Análisis demográfico de la mortalidad en México, 1940–1980*. Mexico City: El Colegio de México.

COPLAMAR (Coordinación General del Plan Nacional de Zonas Deprimidas y Grupos Marginados). 1982a. *Necesidades esenciales y estructura productiva en México*. Mexico City: Presidencia de la República.

———. 1982b. *Serie necesidades esenciales en México*. 5 vols. Mexico City: Siglo Veintiuno.

Cortés, Fernando. 1997. "La distribución del ingreso en México en épocas de estabilización y reforma económica." Ph.D. dissertation, Centro de Investigaciones y Estudios Superiores en Antropología Social–Occidente.

Damián, Araceli. 2000. *Adjustment, Poverty, and Employment in Mexico*. Aldershot, England: Ashgate.

Deaton, Angus, and John Mullbauer. 1991. *Economics and Consumer Behavior*. Rev. ed. Cambridge: Cambridge University Press.

Desai, Meghnad. 1992. "Well-Being and Lifetime Deprivation: A Proposal for an Index of Social Progress." In *Social Progress Index: A Proposal*, by Meghnad Desai, Amartya K. Sen, and Julio Boltvinik. Regional Project to Overcome Poverty, United Nations Development Programme. Bogota: United Nations Development Programme.

Desai, Meghnad, Amartya K. Sen, and Julio Boltvinik. 1992. *Social Progress Index: A Proposal*. Regional Project to Overcome Poverty, United Nations Development Programme. Bogota: United Nations Development Programme.

Escotto, Teresita. n.d. "La conducta heterogénea de los pobres." Mexico City: Centro de Estudios Sociológicos, El Colegio de México. Manuscript.

Foster, James, Joel Greer, and Eric Thorbecke. 1984. "A Class of Decomposable Poverty Measures," *Econometrica* 52 (3).

Government of Bolivia. 1994. *Mapa de pobreza de Bolivia*. La Paz: Unidad de Análisis de Políticas Sociales (UDAPSO).

Hernández Bringas, Héctor Hiram. 1998. "Algunos determinantes de la mortalidad infantil," *Demos: Carta Demográfica sobre México* 11: 12–13.

Hernández Laos, Enrique. 1992. *Crecimiento económico y pobreza en México: una agenda para la investigación*. Mexico City: Universidad Nacional Autónoma de México.

———. 1999. "Evolución de la distribución del ingreso de los hogares, 1963–1989." In *Pobreza y distribución del ingreso en México*, by Julio Boltvinik and Enrique Hernández Laos. Mexico City: Siglo Veintiuno.

INEGI–CEPAL (Instituto Nacional de Estadística, Geografía e Informática–Comisión Económica para América Latina). 1993. *Magnitud y evolución de la pobreza en México, 1984–1992: informe metodológico*. Aguascalientes: INEGI.

Levy, Santiago. 1991. *Poverty Alleviation in Mexico*. Washington, D.C.: World Bank.

Lustig, Nora, and Miguel Székely. 1997. "México: evolución económica, pobreza y desigualdad." Washington, D.C.: Inter-American Development Bank and Brookings Institution.

Moore, Mick, and Stephen Devereaux. 1999. "Introduction: Nationalising the Anti-Poverty Agenda?" *IDS Bulletin* 30 (2): 1–5.

Ordorica, Manuel. 2001. "Hoy. Un momento importante para revisar las estimaciones demográficas. Hoy," *Carta sobre Población* 43. Mexico City: Grupo Académico de Apoyo a Programas de Población.

Pánuco-Laguette, Humberto, and Miguel Székely. 1996. "Income Distribution and Poverty in Mexico." In *The New Economic Model in Latin America and Its Impact on Income Distribution and Poverty*, edited by Victor Bulmer-Thomas. New York: St. Martin's.

Poder Ejecutivo Federal. 1999. *Proyecto de presupuesto de egresos de la federación, 2000*. Mexico City: Poder Ejecutivo Federal.

Romero, David. 1999. "La pobreza y la mortalidad infantil en México." Master's thesis, Centro de Estudios Demográficos y de Desarrollo Urbano, El Colegio de México.

Sen, Amartya K. 1981. *Poverty and Famines: An Essay on Entitlement and Deprivation*. Oxford: Clarendon Press.

World Bank. 1998. "Enhancing Factor Productivity Growth." Country Economic Memorandum. Washington, D.C.: World Bank.

12

Income Distribution and Poverty Alleviation in Mexico: A Comparative Analysis

Diana Alarcón

INTRODUCTION

Deteriorating living conditions throughout most of Latin America during the 1980s, along with the negligible improvements that occurred in the 1990s, brought renewed attention to issues of poverty and inequality. Although Mexico has been among the Latin American countries implementing a new wave of structural economic changes to recover its growth potential, the evolution of poverty and inequality is far from satisfactory.

Early in the 1980s, low petroleum prices and rising international interest rates forced the Mexican government to adopt radical stabilization and structural adjustment programs in order to restore macroeconomic stability. In the mid-1980s a second round of reforms aimed to trigger major structural changes in the economy. Although Mexico made rapid progress in altering the composition of exports—away from petroleum and into more diversified manufactured exports—macroeconomic instability remains a problem. Trapped by a heavy burden of foreign debt and highly dependent upon international capital flows, the performance of the Mexican economy has followed cyclical changes in the expectations of international investors. Almost two decades after the adoption of major reforms, Mexico's economic growth is highly unstable and subject to recurrent crises of confidence.

The most controversial aspect of Mexico's neoliberal reform program has been its failure to improve the living conditions of large sectors of the population. The adoption of broad social programs has failed to reverse the sharp deterioration in living conditions that took place in the 1980s. Indeed, all available measures reveal unfavorable trends in poverty and income distribution.

This chapter argues that the evolution of living conditions, in any country, depends not only upon the adoption of good social policies but also upon the structure of production. That is, the social impact of economic reform depends upon the country's poverty profile—who the poor are and the economic sectors in which they are found—and the expansion of the poor's economic opportunities. In this sense, the social impact of economic reform depends upon the level of coherence achieved between economic and social policies.

The main focus of this chapter is on the social implications of macroeconomic reform in Mexico. The underlying argument is that, over the long run, living standards depend upon: (1) the basic development strategy that a country adopts, (2) its macroeconomic policies, and (3) the characteristics of social policy, including targeted interventions specifically designed to mitigate social exclusion and poverty.

The first section provides a brief summary of Mexico's macroeconomic performance during the period of neoliberal reform, outlining overall trends in employment, agricultural development, poverty, and income distribution. The second section examines the characteristics and impact of two of Mexico's largest social programs. The third briefly describes the experiences of Costa Rica and Chile in order to illustrate the relationship between macroeconomic policy and poverty reduction in those countries. The conclusion offers some observations concerning criteria for evaluating social and economic policy in Mexico.

MEXICO'S NATIONAL DEVELOPMENT

Mexico's performance under import-substitution industrialization (ISI) was one of Latin America's success stories. Between 1950 and 1970, average annual increases in gross domestic product (GDP) of 6 percent supported rapid per capita growth—between 3 and 4 percent a year—as well as significant improvement in the indicators of human development. By 1999, Mexico was among the group of countries classified as having high human development, with relatively high rates of life expectancy and adult literacy (see table 12.1)

A dynamic manufacturing sector—growing at a rate above 7 percent a year—was a key determinant of Mexico's overall economic performance. Import-substitution policies and substantial government intervention promoted rapid industrialization by protecting domestic producers from international competition. These policies fostered the development of a fairly complex industrial sector, but failure to reduce tariff barriers and other forms of protection following the first stages of industrialization created substantial inefficiencies.

TABLE 12.1. Indicators of Human Development for Selected Latin American Countries, 1999

	Human Development Index, 1999	HDI Rank	Gross Domestic Product per Capita, 1999 (US$)[1]	Life Expectancy at Birth, 1999 (years)	Adult Literacy Rate, 1999 (percentages)
Argentina	0.842	34	12,277	73.2	96.7
Uruguay	0.828	37	8,879	74.2	97.7
Chile	0.825	39	8,652	75.2	95.6
Costa Rica	0.821	41	8,860	76.2	95.5
Mexico	0.790	51	8,297	72.4	91.1
Panama	0.784	52	5,875	73.9	91.7
Venezuela	0.765	61	5,495	72.7	92.3

Source: UNDP 2001.

[1] Calculated in terms of purchasing power parity.

Import-substitution industrialization in Mexico had important distributional consequences. First, overvaluation of the exchange rate led to a relatively capital intensive structure of production that failed to generate productive employment commensurate with the rate of expansion of the labor force. Employment growth was restricted to the most dynamic segments of manufacturing and related services, while large numbers of workers were forced into lower-productivity, informal-sector activities with low wage levels. Second, because job creation in the modern sector failed to keep pace with a fast-growing labor force, wage increases fell behind productivity gains. Third, overvaluation of the exchange rate, relatively high prices for manufactured goods, and the urban bias in government policies eventually led to the stagnation of the once-dynamic agricultural sector. Income differentials between residents in urban and rural areas remained large, and there was a high incidence of rural poverty.

Although attempts were made in the 1970s to remove some of the most obvious bottlenecks created during the decades of fast economic growth, the discovery in the mid–1970s of large petroleum reserves at a time of rising oil prices transformed the country into a major exporter of crude oil and postponed significant structural reforms. Petroleum revenues financed a short-lived economic expansion, with average annual growth rates of 8.4 percent between 1978 and 1982. But the headlong drilling of new oil wells and overly optimistic expectations about petroleum revenues led to growing external indebtedness, overvaluation of the exchange rate, and large trade deficits.

In 1982, following the collapse of petroleum prices and an upswing in international interest rates, Mexico was forced to adopt radical stabilization policies. In 1985 the government supplemented this policy with a more comprehensive program of structural adjustment whose essential features were rapid trade liberalization, privatization of state enterprises, deregulation of the domestic market (including the elimination of various subsidies to targeted groups of consumers and producers), and the liberalization of restrictions on international investors.

Underlying these measures was the idea that stabilization policies — as implemented in the early 1980s — were insufficient to produce the conditions for long-term growth in an economy that had accumulated large structural imbalances and economic inefficiencies during decades of protectionism. Freeing domestic markets would force Mexico's producers to improve their productivity and increase their competitiveness, provide new investment opportunities, and generate employment. The liberalization of external trade would create incentives to increase the labor intensity of production in Mexico, leading to job crea-

TABLE 12.2. Economic Growth Rates in Mexico, 1970–2000 (percentages)

	1970–1980	1980–1985	1985–1990	1990–1995	1995–2000
Average annual growth of GDP (constant 1993 pesos)	6.7	1.9	1.8	1.5	5.4
Average annual growth of GDP per capita	3.2	-0.5	-0.3	-0.4	3.8

Sources: For 1970–1980, author's calculations based on data in INEGI 1985; for 1980–2000, author's calculations based on data in Cárdenas 1996: 214-15, and the Instituto Nacional de Estadística, Geografía e Informática's (INEGI) "Banco de información económica" (www.inegi.gob.mx).

tion, rising wages, and a better distribution of income. General equilibrium models simulating the effects of the North American Free Trade Agreement (NAFTA) predicted negative consequences for maize producers but a net positive impact on agricultural producers once exchange-rate equilibrium was restored and access to larger international markets had improved.

So far, Mexico's stabilization and structural adjustment policies have not succeeded in restoring the conditions required for long-term economic growth. Most recently, a short-lived boom was followed by Mexico's deepest recession since the Great Depression of the 1930s. In 1995 GDP contracted by 6 percent. Beginning in 1996 the economy started to recover (GDP growth measured 5.4 percent per year in real terms from 1995 to 2000, and GDP per capita equaled 3.8 percent per year), but the rapidity of the recovery primarily reflected the depth of the economic contraction that had occurred in 1995. In 1998, the real value of GDP per capita (US$3,537) was only slightly higher than the level achieved in 1980 (US$3,424) (tables 12.2 and 12.3).[1]

The evolution of social conditions has been a highly controversial issue throughout this reform process. Yet in Mexico, economic instability clouds any attempt to assess the social implications of structural reform. Economic stagnation, currency devaluations, and restrictions on government spending obviously lead to unemployment and wage losses, low levels of investment, and credit restrictions—and hence low growth. Stabilization policies, by their very nature, have negative social consequences.

---

[1] In 1990 U.S. dollars, Mexico's GDP totaled $252.1 billion in 1981 and $338.1 billion in 1998.

TABLE 12.3. Economic Indicators for Mexico, 1980–2000

	1980	1985	1990	1995	2000
GDP per capita (1990 US$)	3,424	3,370	3,195	3,138	3,537[1]
Domestic investment (percentage of GDP)	38.1	23.4	23.1	19.8	23.3
Domestic savings (percentage of GDP)	30.9	28.9	22.3	19.3	20.2
Ratio of export earnings to GDP (percentage)	11.3	16.2	18.6	30.5	31.4
Annual rate of inflation (percentage increase in consumer price index)	26.4	57.8	26.6	35.0	9.5
Ratio of total external debt to GDP (percentage)	25.7	53.1	41.7	59.3	26.1
Ratio of debt service to export earnings (percentage)	48.5	51.6	132.7	40.1	20.8

Sources: For 1980 and 1985, Inter-American Development Bank Statistics and Qualitative Analysis Unit; for 1990-2000, author's calculations based on data in Poder Ejecutivo Federal 2001: 212, 235, and the INEGI's "Banco de información económica" (www.inegi.gob.mx).

[1] 1998 data.

It is more relevant, though, to identify the social impacts of structural reform itself because those are the changes that will have lasting effects on living conditions. Any reform process has winners and losers. Some sectors will not survive competition from abroad and will go bankrupt, with corresponding losses in employment and income. At the same time, opportunities will expand in other, potentially larger markets. Thus the social impact of economic reform will depend upon the net balance resulting from the employment and income gains from expanding sectors, minus the employment and income losses that occur in contracting sectors. If job creation and income gains in expanding sectors exceed the loss of jobs and income in contracting sectors, economic reform would be welfare enhancing; otherwise, it would have a negative social impact. A discussion of these issues for the Mexican case follows.

Manufactured Exports and Employment Trends

One of the criticisms levied against import-substitution industrialization in Mexico was the capital-intensive structure of production that emerged from trade protectionism. Because the United States is Mexico's largest trade partner, the expectation was that trade liberalization would intensify employment creation, especially in exporting sectors where Mexico's comparative advantage was its labor abundance.

Exports—particularly manufactured exports—have indeed expanded rapidly. However, manufacturing employment has not followed the same trend. Although available sources are limited with respect to their ability to illustrate solid employment trends over the course of the adjustment period, recent research clearly points to poor job market performance since the mid–1980s (Alarcón and Zepeda 1998; Salas and Zepeda, this volume). Official statistics based on a monthly industrial survey identify a contraction of employment throughout the adjustment period. In 1993 the number of workers in manufacturing was 22 percent below its 1980 level. The contraction of production in 1995 led to a further decrease in employment, and in the first half of 1995 there were 30 percent fewer manufacturing jobs in Mexico than in 1980.

Other sources—including quarterly information from the National Institute of Statistics, Geography, and Informatics (INEGI) and the National Urban Employment Survey (ENEU)—suggest that manufacturing employment increased by some 20 percent between 1987 and 1993. A comparison of the 1988 and 1993 economic censuses produces similar estimates. These differences in employment trends are related to differences in the coverage of the respective surveys. INEGI's monthly industrial survey reports employment trends in the largest manufacturing plants (which account for some 80 percent of total industrial production), whereas the other sources refer to total employment. The implication is that employment in midsize and large manufacturing firms contracted, and the increasing employment identified by the ENEU and the economic censuses refers mainly to employment created in micro and small enterprises, many of which would qualify as informal-sector activities. Thus the expansion of manufacturing-sector employment identified by more comprehensive data sources has been generated mainly in micro and small enterprises.

Another important source of employment in this period was the *maquiladora* (in-bond processing) sector. Mainly concentrated along Mexico's border with the United States, these off-shore production or assembly plants are typically large-scale operations that are relatively intensive in their use of labor. Since the mid–1980s, maquiladoras have been responsible for almost one-third of the new jobs created in manufacturing. They represented 14 percent of manufacturing employment in 1988 and 17 percent in 1993—an addition of over a half-million workers. But the problem with maquiladora operations is their low level of integration with the rest of the economy. Some 98 percent of inputs used in these plants are imports, so the plants have very little impact on employment creation in other sectors of the economy beyond the increased demand among low-paid maquiladora workers for domestic goods and services.

The informal sector is another area of the economy that has registered rapid employment growth. The ENEU reports that the proportion of workers in micro enterprises increased from 38.6 percent in 1987 to 44.2 percent in 1995.[2] Estimates from the Latin America regional office of the International Labour Office (ILO 1998) indicate an increasing trend toward informality in Mexico, rising from 55.5 percent of total nonagricultural employment in 1990 to almost 60 percent in 1997. A survey specifically designed to capture employment trends among micro enterprises also reported an increase in the proportion of people engaged in low-productivity, informal-sector activities (INEGI–STPS 1992, 1994).

To date, then, economic reform has had a very controversial impact on labor market performance in Mexico. Although the fastest-growing manufacturing sectors are indeed linked to export activities, employment creation in these sectors has slowed except in the maquiladoras — and, as noted above, the fact that the maquiladoras have few production links with the rest of the economy limits their contribution to job creation. The second source of employment creation in manufacturing is micro and small enterprises. Everywhere else, manufacturing employment has contracted in relative—and sometimes in absolute—terms.

The growth of employment in micro and small enterprises is more indicative of the contraction of employment in the higher-productivity formal sector than of the dynamic growth of small-scale enterprises. Although micro, small, and midsize enterprises have been a dynamic source of growth and employment expansion in other countries, in Mexico there is little experience with creating small enterprise associations, subcontracting arrangements, or production conglomerates that could become alternative sources of employment with rising productivity and higher incomes.

Agricultural Production

Agriculture is another area of the Mexican economy where a large proportion of the poor is concentrated. Production in this sector has been declining in per capita terms since the mid–1960s. Economic instability

---

[2] Micro enterprises are defined as production units with fewer than five workers.

and sudden trade liberalization during the adjustment period further undercut the conditions of agricultural production and employment. In fact, agricultural value added as a share of GDP decreased from 9.7 percent in 1975–1980 to 8.2 percent in 1986–1993.

There are several examples of companies that have responded to trade liberalization by becoming successful exporters of nontraditional agricultural products. However, these successes generally have been concentrated among relatively large farms and associated with foreign firms. The possibility of expanding and exporting agricultural production has not touched the traditional, small-scale producers and campesinos in central and southern Mexico, where most poor rural producers live. Their capacity to substitute more profitable products for traditional crops and to reach larger markets is restricted by their own deteriorated conditions of production, lack of credit, deficient infrastructure, lack of technical assistance, and insufficient information on new market opportunities. In this context, reduced government subsidies for staple crops, increased imports of staples at lower prices, high interest rates, lack of infrastructure development and maintenance, and a contraction of nonagricultural employment combined to widen the already substantial urban-rural gap. These factors also contributed to the intensification of poverty in rural areas.

POVERTY AND INEQUALITY

The available evidence suggests that poor job market performance in Mexico has produced a large contraction in workers' income, especially among blue-collar workers. The share of wages in manufacturing value added decreased systematically throughout the period — from 36.7 percent in 1975–1980 to 27.8 percent in 1981–1985 and to 19.6 percent in 1986–1993. A divergence in the evolution of wages for blue-collar and white-collar workers has given rise to a widening wage gap. Research confirms the existence of increasing inequalities in the distribution of labor income that have contributed to greater income inequality among households.[3]

Although there is no uniform information that would allow for a comparison of income distribution trends before and after the implementation of structural adjustment policies in Mexico, reliable sources for 1984–1994 reveal a systematic deterioration in the distribution of

---

[3] See, for example, Alarcón and McKinley 1994, 1997a, 1997b; Feenstra and Hanson 1994; Zepeda and Ghiara 1996.

TABLE 12.4. Total Income per Capita in Mexico by Decile, 1989–1994 (constant pesos, 1994 = 100)

Deciles	1989	1992	1994	Percent Change, 1989–1994
I	240.8	239.6	244.1	1.4
II	434.3	421.9	434.2	0.0
III	592.6	591.9	606.5	2.3
IV	761.8	762.4	790.2	3.7
V	954.8	958.6	997.7	4.5
VI	1,204.9	1,215.3	1,250.5	3.8
VII	1,519.7	1,552.2	1,598.6	5.2
VIII	1,991.3	2,053.2	2,113.3	6.1
IX	2,830.3	3,015.9	3,083.9	9.0
X	7,435.8	7,819.8	8,067.0	8.5

Source: Author's calculations based on INEGI 1989, 1992, 1994.

Note: Households ranked by per capita income.

income.[4] The Gini coefficient for total household income, grouped by deciles, increased from 0.43 in 1984 to 0.48 in 1994 (INEGI 1984, 1989, 1992, 1994). A comparison of the evolution of real per capita income by deciles reveals a widening gap between the poorest 20 percent of the population and the richest 20 percent (see table 12.4). Between 1989 and 1992, the income of the poorest 30 percent of households declined in real terms, while the income of wealthy families increased. By 1994, a year of growth, the income of the poorest 30 percent had roughly recovered its 1989 level, while the income of the richest 20 percent of households had gained more than 8 percent.[5]

Determining the precise evolution of poverty over the course of the economic adjustment process remains controversial. One study (Alarcón 1994) found that the proportion of the population living in extreme poverty increased from 19.5 percent in 1984 to 23.6 percent in 1989, yet a study sponsored by the Economic Commission for Latin America and the Caribbean and Mexico's INEGI reported a slight decrease in extreme

---

[4] Although there is an income expenditures survey for 1977 — prior to the structural adjustment — the survey's coverage and the definition of income it employed were different from those in subsequent surveys. Between 1984 and 2000, however, INEGI produced seven income expenditure surveys that are mutually comparable.

[5] Trends were similar in 1984–1989, when the real income of most households decreased between 10 and 15 percent, except for the richest 10 percent of households, whose income increased by 3.2 percent (Alarcón 1994: 85).

TABLE 12.5.　Estimates of Extreme Poverty in Mexico, 1984–1994
(percentage of population living in poverty)

	Pánuco & Székely	Alarcón	Mejía & Vos	CEPAL/ INEGI	Lustig & Székely	Londoño & Székely
1984	10.3	19.5	14.0	15.4	13.9	10.1
1989	10.7	23.6	19.0	18.8	17.1	13.5
1992	10.8		20.0	16.1	16.1	10.4
1994			21.0		15.5	10.6

Sources: Pánuco-Laguette and Székely 1996; Alarcón 1994; Mejía and Vos 1997; CEPAL–INEGI 1993; Lustig and Székely 1998; Londoño and Székely 1997a.

Note: Estimates from Pánuco-Laguette and Székely correspond to extreme poverty. The poverty line was defined as the monetary cost of a basket of goods that satisfies the "basic needs" of an average family (equivalent to US$30 per month). Londoño and Székely used a similar procedure, but the value of the poverty line was adjusted to purchasing-power-parity prices to allow for international comparisons. Alarcón estimated extreme poverty based on the cost of a consumption basket that would provide a minimum of 2,082 calories and 35.1 grams of protein a day to an average family. CEPAL–INEGI estimates were based on an extreme poverty line that represents the value of a minimum consumption basket. Adjustments were made to determine the nutritional requirements of individuals based on their age, gender, and work intensity.

poverty by 1992 (CEPAL–INEGI 1993). Other studies found a further deterioration in living standards in the 1990s, especially among the poorest segments of the population, and a corresponding increase in extreme poverty. Using a relatively low poverty line, Pánuco-Laguette and Székely (1996) found a slight increase in extreme poverty between 1984 and 1992—from 10.3 to 10.8 percent of the population. Lustig and Székely (1998) found a larger increase, from 13.9 percent of the population in 1984 to 15.5 percent in 1994. Additional estimates by Mejía and Vos (1997), using income data adjusted to national income accounts (see table 12.5), also reported a larger increase—from 14.0 percent of the population in 1984 to 21.0 percent in 1994.

The controversy with respect to the evolution of poverty goes back to differences in the methodologies used for estimating poverty. Results depend upon the chosen poverty line, the definition of income or expenditures, differences in adjusting the sample to national income accounts or to adult equivalent units, and so on. Yet despite the different results produced by contending methodologies, one may conclude with confidence that poverty in Mexico did not decrease significantly from 1984 to 1994, before the 1994–1995 economic crisis. This outcome is disappointing in view of the fact that the Mexican government implemented large-scale poverty reduction programs during this period. In fact, most estimates of poverty show an increase—frequently a large increase—in the incidence, intensity, and severity of poverty since 1984. Studies that found declining trends report a minor drop in one or two of the dimensions of poverty but an increase in others (see, for example, Pánuco-Laguette and Székely 1996).

Poverty Profile

Although Mexico is a relatively urban country, rural areas account for a large proportion of the poor. In 1989, 42.1 percent of the population living in what are defined as low-density areas (a proxy for rural areas) were classified as poor, compared with an incidence of poverty in high-density areas (a proxy for urban areas) of 11.8 percent (Alarcón 1994). Those figures represented over five million poor people in urban areas and over twelve million in rural communities.

All available estimates of the evolution of poverty in Mexico have found that the largest increase in poverty took place between 1984 and 1989. An important factor behind this trend was a sharp income drop among the rural poor. On average, incomes in rural areas decreased by 20.2 percent over this period. Once adjusted for population shares, the contribution of rural areas to the incidence of poverty increased from 66.9 percent in 1984 to 69.4 percent in 1989. Moreover, the rural population's contribution to total poverty increased even more if the poverty gap and income distribution among the poor are taken into account. That is, not only is rural poverty more widespread, but the average income of the poor in rural areas is much below that of the urban poor. It is also more unequally distributed (Alarcón 1994: chap. 7). By 1997, 59.2 percent of families, representing 64.1 percent of people living in rural areas, were extremely poor (Poder Ejecutivo Federal n.d.).

If one examines the occupations of heads of poor households and adjusts for population size, one finds that in 1989 agricultural workers and campesinos contributed 58.6 percent of the FGT index,[6] followed

---

[6] The FGT index measures three dimensions of poverty: poverty incidence, the poverty gap, and the distribution of income among the poor. It is calculated as

$$P\alpha = \frac{1}{n}\sum_{i=1}^{q}\left(\frac{z-y_i}{z}\right)^{\alpha}$$

where n is the number of people in the country, z is the poverty line, Y_i is the income of the Y_i person, q is the number of people below the poverty line, and α is a parameter that takes different values depending upon the society's "aversion" to poverty. When $\alpha = 0$, the FGT index is a simple measure of the incidence of poverty—the proportion of people whose income is below the poverty line, in relation to the total population. When $\alpha = 1$, the FGT index measures the difference be-by industrial workers and workers in services (each of which contributed 6.8 percent) and workers in construction and commerce (with 5.5 and 4.6 percent, respectively).

Although there are methodological limitations to estimating poverty by region, state-level indicators point to a disproportionate incidence of poverty in three rural southern states—Chiapas, Guerrero, and Oaxaca, where 40 percent of households are extremely poor.[7] In seven other states (Guanajuato, Hidalgo, Michoacán, Puebla, San Luis Potosí, Veracruz, and Zacatecas), 30 percent of households are extremely poor (Poder Ejecutivo Federal n.d.).

Education is another important determinant of poverty in Mexico, especially among the poorest of the poor. Over one-third of the heads of poor households have no education whatsoever, and over three-quarters have incomplete primary education or less (McKinley and Alarcón 1995).

POVERTY REDUCTION STRATEGIES

In Mexico as elsewhere, undertaking structural adjustment and transitioning from import-substitution industrialization to a more open economy brought important changes in the design of social policy. The traditional concept of the welfare state that prevailed during the ISI period—a view that saw the state as the provider of universal coverage of basic social services—was replaced by a more focused approach to poverty alleviation, an approach that was more consistent with the goal of reducing the scale of government intervention in the economy. However, the following discussion shows that the two principal governmental initiatives undertaken in this area have had only a limited impact on poverty alleviation.

PRONASOL

In 1989, the Mexican government launched a major poverty reduction program, the National Solidarity Program (PRONASOL, also known as Solidarity). PRONASOL was designed as an umbrella organization that would serve as the federal government's principal instrument in the

---

tween the average income of the poor and the poverty line—the poverty gap. When $\alpha = 2$, the FGT index becomes more sensitive to the income gap of the poorest among the poor.

[7] The income expenditure surveys on which estimates of poverty are based are not statistically representative at the level of individual states.

fight against extreme poverty (González Tiburcio and De Alba 1992). Government documents identify its objectives as improving income distribution and reducing regional disparities. Resources for Solidarity were allocated according to three categories: (1) Solidarity for Social Welfare, which accounted for about 60 percent of PRONASOL resources in 1990, (2) Solidarity for Production, accounting for about 24 percent of total PRONASOL spending in that year, and (3) Solidarity for Regional Development, accounting for 13 percent.[8] Each of these groupings included a large number of specific programs, ranging from infrastructure development (electricity, road paving, potable water, sewerage, health clinics, and so on), to assistance to producers (coffee growers, fishermen, and others), to the selection of poor states for special assistance programs.

Solidarity was conceived as an integrated poverty alleviation program. It was demand-driven and designed to facilitate the organization of the poor in "solidarity committees" that would define their own priorities and articulate their own demands for infrastructure and services. Although most Solidarity resources came from the federal government, the program also intended to mobilize additional resources both from state and local governments and from poor communities themselves (usually in the form of labor contributions).

Given its multiple dimensions, Solidarity has not been easy to evaluate. Some analysts have claimed that "PRONASOL is so large, dynamic, complex, and variegated that many different, and even contradictory, claims about it can be true" (John Bailey, quoted in Graham 1994: 324). This discussion is restricted to evaluating Solidarity's effectiveness in reaching the poor.[9]

Volume of Resources Federal funding for Solidarity rose throughout the administration of Carlos Salinas de Gortari (1988–1994), from 0.4 percent of GDP in 1989 to 1.1 percent in 1994.[10] Using the poverty gap in 1984 and population and GDP figures for 1990, Lustig (1994) has argued that to eradicate moderate poverty in Mexico would have required 2.2 percent of GDP, and eradicating extreme poverty would

---

[8] Proportions for the different programs changed over time, but their relative importance remained the same.

[9] Many studies have evaluated other dimensions of Solidarity. For an overview of the program, with references to other sources, see Cornelius, Craig, and Fox 1994.

[10] These figures refer to resources allocated by the federal government only; they do not include the contributions of state and local governments, which were substantial. In 1989, for example, the Solidarity budget increased from 0.3 to 0.4 percent of GDP once state and local government contributions were included. In 1992, those figures were 0.7 and 1.1 percent, respectively.

have required resources equivalent to 0.2 percent of GDP. Thus the eradication of extreme poverty in Mexico was well within the program's reach. What was lacking was adequate targeting.

Two issues merit mention with respect to the volume of resources. First, it is well known that once administrative costs and leakages are included, poverty reduction programs are more expensive than the preceding figures would suggest. And second, not all funds listed under the PRONASOL rubric were for poverty reduction. An important fraction of the program's resources consisted of a simple reclassification of social expenditures from the regular federal budget. For example, Bailey and Boone (1994) found that about 50 percent of the programs listed under Solidarity were already part of the regular budget—not all of whose resources were necessarily allocated for poverty reduction (also see Zepeda 1994; Laurell 1994).

Implementation of PRONASOL Although Solidarity was defined explicitly as a program for alleviating extreme poverty through well-targeted interventions, there were no clear criteria in official documents for identifying extreme poverty or for differentiating it from moderate poverty. Nor were there any explicit criteria about priority programs, target groups, or the selection of policy instruments to achieve objectives. Although there were some references to geographical criteria to identify poverty, no systematic methodology was used. Resources were allocated to organized groups—Solidarity committees—that applied for resources under the specific project headings.

Two issues have been raised in this regard. First, the most organized and vocal groups were not necessarily the poorest. Second, resource allocation was demand-driven and self-defined, yet local communities were not necessarily the best-equipped actors to set priorities (see Lustig 1994). Barrón and Trejo (1995) illustrate the problems in resource allocation by questioning the relevance of some large programs sponsored by Solidarity: the construction of urban freeways in Aguascalientes and Zacatecas and border bridges in Nuevo León; the extension of airport facilities within the "Nueva Laguna" program; the construction of sport complexes in Michoacán; and a comprehensive program of health care, housing, and scholarships for journalists and their children.

The Allocation of Resources Studies of the regional distribution of PRONASOL resources show a somewhat close relationship between the incidence of poverty in broadly defined regions and the allocation of Solidarity funds (Pánuco-Laguette and Székely 1996: 208). More disaggregated data, however, contradict these results. Numerous studies have found large inconsistencies between the geography of poverty and the distribution of PRONASOL resources.[11]

Using human development indices (HDI) calculated for Mexico's states, Laurell (1994) found an inverse correlation between PRONASOL resources for poverty reduction and the HDI by state; that is, resources for poverty alleviation tended to concentrate in states with a high HDI. Using a rank correlation, Zepeda (1994) found a weak relationship between PRONASOL expenditures and poverty incidence as measured by the FGT index (see note 6) and an inverse relationship between PRONASOL expenditures and several indices of marginality. He also found that the allocation of PRONASOL resources by state was very similar to the way in which federal public investment had been allocated during the 1960s and 1970s. In addition, Zepeda and Castro (1996) found a negative correlation between PRONASOL expenditures and poverty as measured by the three dimensions of the FGT index (the incidence, intensity, and severity of poverty) over the period 1989–1994.

Solidarity was designed as a comprehensive poverty alleviation program. It included twenty-three programs in different areas of social spending, infrastructure, and regional development. Zepeda and Castro (1996) found that at least four programs that were relevant for poverty reduction—focused on education, health care, food subsidies, and production credits, which together accounted for 12.2 percent of total PRONASOL resources in 1994—did follow the geography of poverty. That is, their distribution was positively correlated with the incidence, intensity, and severity of poverty by state. However, the allocation of 70 percent of resources in other PRONASOL programs was inversely correlated with the incidence of poverty. Similar results were obtained when the allocation of resources per program was evaluated with respect to the lack of specific services (water, sewerage, schooling, electricity, and so on) instead of income poverty. Zepeda and Castro's study also included an evaluation of the allocation of resources over time and found that from 1992 to 1994 the allocation of Solidarity funds diverged increasingly from the incidence of poverty.

---

[11] There are several problems in evaluating the allocation of resources for poverty alleviation. There are many ways to measure poverty, none of which is unambiguously better than the others. Measurement of poverty at the regional level requires large data sources, which are rarely readily available. An additional problem relates to the nature of targeted programs. Perfect targeting can occur when it is possible to identify conditions at the household level, but that kind of information is generally not available. Thus attempts to evaluate Solidarity's effectiveness in reaching its target population are based on different approximate poverty measures.

One objection raised by Solidarity's critics is that poverty reduction resources were used for electoral objectives. Molinar Horcasitas and Weldon (1994) correlated the allocation of the program's resources with its explicit objectives. The expectation was that more funds would be "allocated to the poorest states, the states with lower educational indices, to states with higher proportions of indigenous populations, and to states with higher proportions of rural population." Their analysis, however, produced negative correlation coefficients for both the poor and the illiterate for the three large program groupings (social welfare, production, and regional development) and for different specifications of both variables. Moreover, they found a strong correlation between resources spent by Solidarity and electoral results. "[T]he government usually allocated more PRONASOL funds to those states that were loyal to the PRI [Institutional Revolutionary Party], while it punished states that had voted for the opposition. However, when state elections were scheduled concurrently with the federal balloting, the slope of the [correlation] coefficient for Cárdenas [support for the political opposition candidate in the 1988 elections] becomes strongly positive." Their findings, then, are an indication that Solidarity resources were used not only to support loyal PRI voters, but also to regain support in areas recently lost to the opposition. The authors concluded by arguing that the "allocation of federal resources to the states through PRONASOL cannot be explained solely on the basis of the explicit goals of the program, but that electoral considerations had weight in the minds of the decision makers" (1994: 125–39).

Several questions have also surfaced about the implementation of PRONASOL programs at the more micro level. Gershberg (1994) defined a welfare function to analyze the distribution of resources for Solidarity's two educational programs—Escuela Digna ("Schools with Dignity") and Niños en Solidaridad ("Children in Solidarity")—in the State of México. He found that, although PRONASOL appeared to redistribute educational resources to poorer municipalities, the programs failed to reach the poorest of the poor. In the State of México, indigenous people were systematically excluded. According to Gershberg, this result cast doubt on the efficacy of resource allocation mechanisms that required the organization of Solidarity committees: "if indigenous populations are less capable—because of technical capabilities, language barriers, or other social or economic factors—of organizing, lobbying, and submitting proposals properly through these committees, then the government may be failing to recognize this and support such groups productively" (p. 250).

Another evaluation of Solidarity in three northern states (Coahuila, Durango, and Tamaulipas) reached similar conclusions. First, a large fraction of Solidarity resources "leaked" to nonpoor groups. Second, some of the programs with potentially large impacts on poverty reduction—such as education—were restricted to school remodeling rather than expanding school capacity to house more students, even though the schools' principals (who were also members of Solidarity committees) clearly identified inadequate school capacity as their major constraint. Third, within programs that provided credits to agricultural producers, resources were allocated mainly as a consumption buffer to peasants who had lost their harvests to natural disasters, rather than being used to extend productive capacity (Alarcón 1993).

Solidarity had a number of merits. It was designed explicitly for the alleviation of poverty, with an emphasis on extreme poverty; it incorporated geographical criteria that guided the selection of beneficiaries from the poorest regions; it involved poor communities in the identification of funding and investment priorities; and it adopted a multidimensional perspective on poverty that encompassed the provision of various social services and income-support programs. In its execution, however, the program often appeared to operate in a fashion directly contradictory to its expressed objectives. Its critics have provided evidence that political, rather than technical, criteria determined the allocation of Solidarity resources and that program resources were used for projects that were not necessarily related to poverty reduction. Overall, there is no evidence to support the conclusion that Solidarity—a very large-scale poverty reduction program—had a commensurably large impact on poverty reduction. At the end of the Salinas administration, poverty remained at high levels and the income of large population segments remained unstable, as evidenced by the rapid deterioration of living standards following the 1994–1995 peso crisis.

PROGRESA

The administration of President Ernesto Zedillo (1994–2000) introduced a new poverty alleviation program for the period 1995–2000. The Program on Education, Health, and Nutrition (PROGRESA) took a more integrated approach to poverty alleviation. Its objective was to reach the extremely poor, especially in rural areas, with simultaneous interventions in the areas of health, education, and nutrition. PROGRESA granted scholarships (which also covered the purchase of school supplies) to poor children eighteen years old or younger, with the goal of stimulating school attendance and retention through the first nine years of schooling. Scholarships increased with school level; they were slightly larger for girls in an attempt to reverse gender segmentation in rural education. According to official PROGRESA documents, the actual value of scholarships was equal to the monetary contribution that children made to household income.

In the area of health, PROGRESA sought to increase coverage of a basic health care package; to prevent malnutrition among children, including at the prenatal stage; and to provide training programs in basic health, nutrition, and hygiene to poor families. To fight malnutrition, PROGRESA emphasized prenatal care, including regular visits to a health clinic during pregnancy, as well as nutritional supplements that provided 20 percent of caloric requirements and 100 percent of micronutrients to pregnant women and to nursing mothers and their children aged four months to two years. In addition, beneficiaries received a monetary subsidy for food purchases if they met their scheduled medical checkups and attended health training programs. Estimates placed the overall monetary value of all PROGRESA benefits at 34 percent of the average household income of families in extreme poverty. The food subsidy alone represented 29.3 percent of their expenditures for food.[12]

Although PROGRESA proposed to incorporate both demand and supply factors in the fight against poverty, program documents did not elaborate on specific programs for social infrastructure construction, nor did they address the issue of differential quality of services by region and socioeconomic group. There were only vague references to the need to "de-phase" social programs traditionally managed by other government offices in order to avoid duplicated efforts (Poder Ejecutivo Federal n.d).

A key issue in the design of precisely targeted programs like PROGRESA is the selection of beneficiaries. PROGRESA employed a complex methodology to identify its subject population, a methodology that was refined over time to correct for previous errors in selection. For example, under the revised methodology, regions were first selected based on an index of segregation that included seven indicators: the proportion of literate adults in the locality; the share of dwellings without potable water, drainage systems, and electricity; the average number of occupants per room in each dwelling; the proportion of dwellings with a dirt floor; and the share of the population employed in the primary sector.

Once priority rural areas were identified, PROGRESA used a multivariate model (discriminant analysis) to identify families' socioeconomic characteristics, including "number of children in the household, rate of economic dependency, available water supply, household floor (dirt versus cement), and education and occupation of the head of

---

[12] PROGRESA had a maximum allocation of 695 pesos (approximately US$70) per household per month in 1998.

household," along with other variables such as the presence of disabled persons in a household, ownership of durable goods, and ownership of land and animals (Gómez de León 1998). This last step involved confirming the identity of selected families in a community assembly. Using this procedure, PROGRESA had, by December 1998, incorporated over 1.9 million beneficiary households in 35,688 localities, distributed among 1,488 municipalities in 28 states (Skoufias, Davis, and Behrman 1999).

PROGRESA's capacity to alleviate poverty in Mexico will have depended upon several factors: (1) the extent to which the revised methodology used to identify the poor minimized errors of inclusion and exclusion—that is, the incorrect selection of nonpoor beneficiaries and the exclusion of poor households; (2) the efficient delivery of benefits in ways that avoided bureaucratic obstacles that could have restricted access to benefits; (3) cost-efficiency, in the sense of reducing administrative, delivery, and monitoring costs as a proportion of benefits delivered; (4) the total amount of resources allocated to the program; and (5) the level of coordination the program achieved among the governmental institutions responsible for building infrastructure and providing the services needed for optimal program operation.

Although the methodolgy for selecting beneficiaries evolved in response to PROGRESA's initial problems of unintentionally excluding some of the poor, there remained significant concerns regarding the program's implementation. These included: (1) the lack of information regarding PROGRESA activities, including a long delay in the dissemination of the results of an evaluation conducted by the International Food Policy Research Institute (IFPRI), which raised questions about the program's political motivations; (2) PROGRESA's highly centralized decision-making and implementation processes, which weakened the role of municipal authorities and limited possibilities for promoting coordination among the various governmental agencies involved in poverty reduction efforts; (3) the potentially high proportion of total spending devoted to implementation costs (versus direct benefits); (4) the fear that program requirements may have led to the exclusion of the poorest children;[13] and (5) the concern that the practice of designating someone from the beneficiary community to certify compliance with the program's conditions may have reproduced the clientelism that plagued similar programs in the past.

The IFPRI's 1999 report limited itself to an evaluation of the target-

---

[13] In towns where there were no health care facilities, the cost of getting regular checkups (a program requirement) at the nearest clinic may have exceeded the value of the scholarship available to poor children.

ing methodology, identifying some of the problems that a program like PROGRESA will face when trying to expand its coverage beyond the narrowest definition of extreme poverty. According to the IFPRI report, PROGRESA was relatively successful at identifying extremely poor rural households, but errors of exclusion increased substantially when less narrow definitions of poverty were employed.[14] The IFPRI evaluators also concluded that PROGRESA's strict targeting may have had unintended (and significant) social and political costs when targeting criteria led it to make apparently arbitrary distinctions in the distribution of funds among beneficiaries in rural indigenous communities (Skoufias, Davis, and De la Vega 1999).

POVERTY REDUCTION AND MACROECONOMIC POLICIES

Even though the Salinas and Zedillo administrations made poverty alleviation programs a priority, the macroeconomic context in the 1980s and 1990s was not conducive to poverty reduction. First, economic growth was weak and unstable. Government efforts to stabilize the economy led to high interest rates, which put additional negative pressure on investment. As a consequence, investment as a proportion of GDP declined. Second, economic contraction and the corresponding drop in investment rates led to very slow employment growth in the most dynamic sectors and a disproportionate increase of informality in the labor market. Third, trade liberalization, closer integration with the rest of North America, and the contraction of the domestic market during the adjustment period produced rapid expansion in sectors engaged in manufacturing for export. However, the export-oriented manufacturing sector, including maquiladora plants, has been relatively capital intensive and heavily dependent upon imports of intermediate and capital goods. Thus these firms have had a fairly limited impact on employment creation, either directly or indirectly through additional demand for domestic inputs.[15] Fourth, weak demand for labor, coupled with explicit government wage control policies to reduce inflation, led to large losses in real wages, especially among unskilled workers. And fifth, the agricultural sector (where a large proportion of the poor is

---

[14] The IFPRI estimated that only about 6.6 percent of households were incorrectly excluded from program benefits. However, when the poverty line rose, errors of exclusion increased to 10.8 percent and 16.3 percent, respectively, at the 50th and 78th percentiles.

[15] As noted earlier, most inputs used in maquiladora plants (approximately 98 percent) are imported.

concentrated) is contracting, and nonagricultural rural activities have not shown signs of dynamism.

One of the most critical problems to be addressed in Mexico's economic reform process is the lack of correspondence between the objectives of poverty alleviation programs and a prevailing macroeconomic context that has hindered efforts to reduce poverty. In the case of PRONASOL, problems in the program's design and implementation prevented it from identifying the extremely poor and undertaking well-defined interventions that would effectively reduce poverty. Clearly, however, there is no social policy or poverty alleviation program, no matter how well designed it may be, that can effectively counter the negative impact of macroeconomic policy. Living conditions improve with the expansion of people's regular sources of income, and this depends, in turn, upon the expansion of economic opportunities. In a market economy, the only way to reduce poverty on a permanent basis is to incorporate the poor into well-functioning, expanding markets in a position in which they can compete effectively. Wage earners' real income reflects their access to productive assets (including physical, financial, and human capital) and the market price of the goods and services produced, varying with the level of asset productivity and depending upon the proper operation of goods and labor markets. In this sense, macroeconomic policy is most relevant in determining the economic opportunities of the poor, and social policy is crucial for expanding the incorporation of the poor into the market by increasing their access to productive assets and the level of productivity of such assets. Unless there is good articulation between macroeconomic and social policy, poverty alleviation will remain an elusive goal.

MACROECONOMIC POLICY AND POVERTY REDUCTION IN COSTA RICA AND CHILE

Costa Rica and Chile provide interesting examples in terms of the linkages between macroeconomic policy and poverty reduction.[16] Macroeconomic policy affects not only the rate of economic growth, but also the distribution of the benefits of growth across economic sectors and social groups. Its distributional effect depends heavily upon the economy's initial conditions and structure. Devaluing the currency to promote exports, for example, could benefit the poor if the exporting sectors generate employment and income for them. But if agricultural exports are grown on large landholdings and manufactured exports are

---

[16] This section draws on Alarcón 1997a, 1997b, 1997c.

produced by capital-intensive industrial firms, the benefits will accrue to the large landowners and the industrialists.

A country's development strategy is often shaped by the evolution of macroeconomic policies, which typically focus, by necessity, on the instabilities and imbalances that arise in the economy. If a country's basic development strategy and its associated macroeconomies are constantly reproducing poverty, there is little that targeted interventions against poverty can achieve, except as short-term palliatives to mitigate the worst aspects of deprivation.

Patterns of Development

Although both Costa Rica and Chile implemented policies of import-substitution industrialization during the post-World War II period, there were important differences in the degree and timing of their reorientations to a more open economy. Because Costa Rica is a relatively small country, it relies more heavily upon external trade and has maintained a relatively open economy. Costa Rica protected its domestic industrial producers, but the export of primary commodities provided a large part of its total revenues. What has been distinctive about Costa Rica is that since the democratic revolution of 1948, the public sector has spent extensively on human development. As a consequence, the country ranks relatively high on human development indicators.

Chile began building a comprehensive system of social security in the 1920s, and by the 1970s it had a relatively high level of human development. Like many other Latin American countries, Chile adopted a development strategy of import substitution, but its pattern of development underwent an abrupt change of direction in the mid–1970s when a military government instituted a radical reform program that emphasized rapid trade liberalization and deregulation of the economy. Economic reform carried high social costs; the traditional social security system was dismantled, and employment and incomes declined drastically. However, the military regime expanded its regulatory role after the mid–1980s, and in the 1990s democratic governments implemented more comprehensive social policies.

The Evolution of Poverty

Costa Rica The incidence of poverty in Costa Rica increased sharply during the economic recession of the early 1980s. The situation began to improve when the economy started growing again, but the recovery's

TABLE 12.6. Estimates of Poverty in Costa Rica, 1971–1995
(percentage of population living in poverty)

	Sauma	Morley & Álvarez	Trejos & Sauma	Mejía & Vos (nonadjusted)	Mejía & Vos (adjusted)
1971	25				
1977	13				
1980			16.6		
1981		25.4		44.0	15.0
1983	30		34.1		
1985			22.7		
1986	17	26.8			
1987			23.0		
1989		10.2		26.0	4.0
1990			21.1	24.0	10.0
1991				29.0	10.0
1992			19.9	25.0	9.0
1993				21.0	8.0
1994				18.0	8.0
1995				17.0	7.0

Sources: World Bank 1990; Morley and Álvarez 1992; Trejos and Sauma n.d.; Mejía and Vos 1997.

Note: Sauma's estimates referred to the proportion of households with incomes below the poverty line and were reported in World Bank 1990: 73. The income poverty line was defined as the cost of a minimum food basket that provided 2,900 calories per day to an average Costa Rican family, taking into account local consumption patterns and the demographic composition of families. Morley and Álvarez estimated poverty based on an income poverty line that was two times the cost of a basket of basic nutrients estimated by the United Nations Economic Commission for Latin America and the Caribbean (ECLAC) in 1971; in subsequent years the consumption basket was updated by the corresponding consumer price index. Calculations by Trejos and Sauma were based on a poverty line that was 1.57 times the cost of the minimum food basket. In this estimate, income used to calculate poverty only included wages and salaries and self-employed income; it excluded transfer payments, capital income, and all forms of nonmonetary income. Income reported in household surveys was adjusted to national income accounts and corrected for nonreported income and the proportion of the population in rural and urban households. Mejía and Vos estimated poverty in relation to a poverty line of US$60 per capita per month at 1985 purchasing-price-parity prices. Their first estimate corresponded to nonadjusted income as reported by household surveys; the second estimate was adjusted to match the level of income reported in national income accounts.

impact on poverty reduction is still being debated. Some studies report that poverty was reduced to levels much lower than those of the early 1980s, while others contend that the incidence of poverty in 1992 was higher than it had been in 1980. Most studies agree, however, that there

TABLE 12.7. Headcount Indices of Poverty in Costa Rica, 1981 and 1989

	1981		1989	
	Headcount Index	*Share of Total Poverty (percentages)*	*Headcount Index*	*Share of Total Poverty (percentages)*
By geographical area				
Metropolitan	19.5	16.7	10.0	21.8
Urban	20.4	18.6	8.8	23.2
Rural	29.8	64.7	11.0	55.0
Total	25.4	100.0	10.2	100.0
By economic sector				
Agriculture	30.7	37.7	13.9	36.3
Industry	11.0	5.1	7.1	9.3
Construction	9.6	3.2	1.5	1.0
Commerce	12.0	5.3	8.1	10.0
Services	9.4	4.7	6.0	10.3
Total	25.4		10.2	

Source: Morley and Álvarez 1992.

Note: The total contribution to poverty by economic sector in which the head of household was employed does not add to 100.0 due to nonapplicable or nonspecified economic sectors.

was a substantial decline in rural poverty, particularly among producers of nontraditional agricultural products.

Poverty measures are sensitive to the methodology used. Relevant factors in this regard include the welfare variable chosen to define poverty (usually income or expenditures), the threshold selected, whether income (or expenditures) reported in household surveys is adjusted to national income accounts, and so on. Several authors have calculated the incidence of poverty in Costa Rica, and each has produced a different set of estimates for various years (see table 12.6).

Despite the sizable differences in these estimates, there is some consensus on trends. All of the researchers listed in table 12.6 concluded that the incidence of poverty in Costa Rica increased sharply during the recession years of the early 1980s. Poverty began to decrease when economic growth was restored, but as noted above, there is still controversy regarding the recovery's impact on poverty reduction. Although Morley and Álvarez (1992) and Mejía and Vos (1997) identified fairly rapid progress in poverty reduction—to levels much below those of the

TABLE 12.8. Incidence of Poverty in Costa Rica by Socioeconomic Group, 1980–1992 (percentages)[1]

	1980	1985	1992
Traditional agriculture	39.8	42.1	42.9
Traditional agriculture for export	26.6	35.9	29.1
Nontraditional agriculture for export	30.3	31.7	29.1
Small industry	14.8	21.2	25.0
Midsize and large industry	6.3	12.7	10.0
Construction	9.7	22.9	21.1
Social services	5.5	9.3	9.9
Tourism	4.1	21.4	18.2
Business services	5.5	9.4	10.8
Personal services (microenterprises)	18.0	20.1	23.6
Personal services (small and midsize enterprises)	7.8	15.1	13.1
Total	16.6	22.7	19.9

Source: Trejos and Sauma n.d.

[1] Percentage of each socioeconomic group in poverty.

early 1980s — the incidence of poverty found by Trejos and Sauma (n.d.) in 1992 was still higher than the 1980 level. In order to elucidate the origin of changes in poverty trends, we turn to a review of the incidence of poverty by sector and each sector's contribution to total measured poverty.

Poverty in Costa Rica was highly concentrated in rural areas (see table 12.7). Almost one-third of rural residents were poor in 1981, and they accounted for 64.7 percent of the country's poor households. In that same year, 30.7 percent of household heads worked in the agricultural sector, and they represented 37.7 percent of the poor. According to Morley and Álvarez, poverty reduction in Costa Rica between 1981 and 1989 was due mainly to a substantial reduction in the incidence of rural poverty, particularly among agricultural producers. In 1989, only 11.0 percent of rural families were below the poverty line, and they represented 55.0 percent of Costa Rica's poor households. With respect to economic sectors, only 13.9 percent of household heads in agricultural activities were considered to be poor in 1989; they contributed 36.3 percent of total poverty.

These results were confirmed by Trejos and Sauma, who found that the incidence of poverty in 1992 was still higher than its level in 1980.

They did, however, find that the incidence of poverty decreased from 22.7 to 19.9 percent between 1985 and 1992 (table 12.8). They attributed this reduction to the substantial decline in poverty among producers of agricultural commodities (especially producers of nontraditional agricultural products). According to their calculations, this was the only sector of the economy in which the incidence of poverty actually declined between 1980 and 1992.

These different conclusions about changes in the incidence of poverty during Costa Rica's adjustment period are important, and this matter will undoubtedly be the subject of further research. Based on the available information, however, it is possible to draw at least one conclusion with respect to the evolution of poverty in Costa Rica. Economic recovery had a strong impact on the income of poor agricultural households, where most of the poor were located in the early 1980s. Poverty reduction was associated with the rapid growth of agricultural exports in both traditional products (bananas, coffee, and sugar) and nontraditional commodities (pineapples, cut flowers, and so on).

Chile Poverty increased in Chile during the period of market-oriented economic reforms in the 1970s and 1980s. High and persistent unemployment and wage deterioration led to a severe decline in living standards for large segments of the population. The poor were, moreover, adversely affected by changing patterns of government expenditures. During the military regime, targeted programs to generate temporary employment and provide basic health services helped prevent an even sharper drop in the living standards of the extremely poor. But such strict targeting within the context of reduced government spending and economic recession worsened the quality and coverage of basic services, and it heightened the vulnerability of broad segments of the population to economic fluctuations.

The resumption of growth in the late 1980s led to a substantial decline in the incidence of both moderate and extreme poverty, although these gains merely moved the country back to the lower levels of poverty that had prevailed in the 1970s. In the 1990s, democratically elected governments sought to enhance the complementarities between economic growth and poverty-reduction programs. Social spending increased, and the government implemented new poverty-alleviation programs that benefited groups beyond the ranks of the extremely poor.

How poverty evolved in Chile over these years remains a subject of controversy, in large part because there is no consistent household information available at the national level for the adjustment period. However, wide fluctuations in aggregate consumption and deterioration in the distribution of goods suggest an increase in the incidence of

TABLE 12.9. Estimates of Poverty in Chile, 1969–1996 (percentage of total population)

Year	Cowan & De Gregorio[1] Poverty	Indigence	Raczynski[2] Poverty	Indigence	MIDEPLAN Rural Poverty	PREALC[3] Poverty	Indigence
1969			17.0	6.0		28.5	8.4
1970					27.7		
1980						40.3	14.4
1983				30.0			
1987	44.6	16.8	38.0	13.0	52.5	48.6	22.6
1990	40.1	13.8	34.0	12.0	42.8	29.9	8.8
1992	32.7	8.9			34.3		
1994	28.5	8.0					
1995	26.0	7.0					
1996	24.0	6.0					

Sources: Cowan and De Gregorio 1996. Raczynski 1995. Estimates from MIDEPLAN appear in World Bank 1995. PREALC's estimates are referred to in Raczynski and Romaguera 1995.

[1] In the Cowan and De Gregorio study, the indigent were defined as households whose income level was below the monetary value of a pre-specified minimum consumption basket that satisfied basic nutritional needs. The poverty line was twice the value of the line of indigence for urban households and 1.75 times for rural households.

[2] Raczynski defined poverty and indigence in a way similar to the definition used by Cowan and De Gregorio, but the measurement of family income included the value of monetary subsidies received by households.

[3] PREALC's estimates are for the Greater Santiago area.

poverty. Estimates by the Regional Employment Program for Latin America and the Caribbean (PREALC) for the Greater Santiago area support such a hypothesis. The incidence of poverty in Santiago increased from 28.5 percent of the population in 1969 to 40.3 percent in 1980 and to 48.6 percent in 1987, while extreme poverty increased from 8.4 to 14.4 to 22.6 percent, respectively, in these same years (see table 12.9). Information from Chile's Ministry of Planning (MIDEPLAN) indicates that poverty in the countryside increased from 27.7 percent of the rural population in 1970 to 52.5 percent in 1987. Similarly, Raczynski (1995) found that the percentage of indigent households rose from 6.0 percent in 1969 to 13.0 percent in 1987, and during the 1982–1983 crisis, the percentage reached 30.0 percent. The percentage of poor households rose from 17.0 percent in 1969 to 38.0 percent in 1987 (table 12.9).[17]

Part of the controversy regarding poverty measurement relates to the definition of poverty itself. The figures presented above correspond to measures of poverty based on family income or expenditures. Often, however, poverty has been measured as a composite index of four variables—housing, crowding, sewage disposal, and ownership of durable goods. According to this latter methodology, extreme poverty in Chile decreased from 21 percent of the population in 1970 to 12 percent in 1990; increased ownership of television sets accounted for 80 percent of this reduction (Raczynski and Romaguera 1995: 288).[18] Yet despite methodological differences in the various estimations of poverty, there is widespread agreement about the high social cost of Chile's economic adjustment process, including high and persistent unemployment, deterioration of household expenditures, decreasing real wages, and increasing inequality.

In the late 1980s, poverty began to decrease as a result of Chile's dynamic economic growth. MIDEPLAN estimated a decline in rural poverty from 52.5 percent in 1987 to 42.8 percent in 1990, and to 34.3 percent in 1992 (table 12.9). The United Nations Economic Commission for Latin America and the Caribbean estimated a decline in the incidence of poverty for the country as a whole from 38.2 percent in 1987 to

---

[17] Indigence is defined in relation to the cost of a basic food basket. Families with incomes less than or equal to the value of the food basket were classified as indigent. Poor families were those with incomes less than or equal to two times the value of the food basket in urban areas. The factor of expansion was 1.75 for rural households (Raczynski 1995: 212).

[18] One explanation for the increasing ownership of durable goods, even among the poorest households, focuses on the large changes in relative prices that occurred in Chile following trade liberalization.

34.5 percent in 1990 (Raczynski and Romaguera 1995: table 8-7), although this was still twice as high as the parallel measure in 1970.

The democratic government that took office in Chile in March 1990 gave high priority to eradicating poverty and reducing income inequality, consistent with long-term export-oriented economic growth. In fact, strong economic growth and the implementation of comprehensive poverty-alleviation programs produced a substantial reduction in the incidence of poverty in Chile. The number of people below the poverty line fell from 44.6 percent in 1987 to 28.5 percent in 1994, and to 24.0 percent in 1996. There was a corresponding decline in the proportion of indigent households from 16.8 percent in 1987 to 8.0 percent in 1994, and to an estimated 6.0 percent in 1996 (see Cowan and De Gregorio in table 12.9).

Where substantial economic growth has been achieved, poverty has been reduced. On this point there is little controversy. What is most relevant for the present discussion is the character of growth—namely, whether growth translates into increasing income and well-being for the poor.

Economic Growth and Poverty Reduction

In order for growth to reduce poverty substantially, it should be broad based. Three factors are especially important in this regard. First, the sectoral composition of growth directly affects resource distribution throughout the economy. Sectors where the poor are concentrated need to grow—either through their own dynamics or through linkages with more rapidly expanding economic sectors. The distribution of resources between rural and urban areas is particularly important because, in most developing countries, poverty is concentrated in rural areas. Thus, laying the conditions for growth in rural production is typically a crucial component of a poverty eradication strategy.

By the 1990s, Costa Rica had succeeded in changing the composition of its output in favor of sectors that had a beneficial impact on the poor. Rapid growth in nontraditional agricultural exports helped to decrease rural poverty. The rapid growth of tourism and manufactured exports also contributed to expanded urban employment, especially for low-skilled workers.

In Chile, economic growth in the late 1980s and 1990s was based on relatively labor-intensive activities that expanded employment, particularly in manufacturing. Policies to promote growth in exporting sectors placed special emphasis on the creation of backward and forward linkages to amplify exports' multiplier effects. This was particularly true in the case of agribusiness, where government policies were designed to promote research and development applicable to the production and commercialization of agricultural exports, the construction of infrastructure to facilitate access to export markets, the expansion of foreign markets, and so on.

An important issue highlighted by these countries' experiences is that export-oriented growth benefits the poor when it stimulates employment creation and income in sectors where the poor earn their livelihood or in sectors with which their livelihood is connected. Macroeconomic policies (exchange-rate policy, for example) that promote a stronger export orientation are likely to increase the income of the poor when export crops are produced in small-scale units, as the Costa Rican case illustrates; when manufactured exports are relatively labor intensive, as in the Chilean case; and, more generally, when exporting sectors are closely linked to the rest of the economy and thus become a source of demand and employment creation elsewhere. Among the three countries considered in this chapter, only Chile adopted specific policies to foster linkages with exporting sectors that could produce notable employment multiplier effects. In Mexico, by contrast, trade liberalization has had minimal effects—or even negative effects—on poverty reduction because exporting sectors are concentrated in relatively capital-intensive activities with few strong links to the rest of the economy.

A second requisite condition for economic growth to contribute effectively to poverty reduction is an enabling environment that enhances the economic opportunities of the poor, in the form of paid employment or self-employment. The greater the employment intensity of growth, the more likely it is to benefit the poor. But more beneficial still is the expansion of the kinds of jobs that the poor are most likely to fill. In Chile, poverty reduction was aided by the adoption of policies to promote the growth of labor-intensive sectors. However, the expansion of economic opportunities for the poor should encompass more than employment; it should also include increased access to productive assets and an expansion of support services for the poor who are self-employed. In Costa Rica, investment in infrastructure and the promotion of external market access for traditional and nontraditional crops produced in small agricultural units were important factors in reducing rural poverty.

Yet promoting access to productive assets is only part of the enabling environment. The other major component involves helping to increase the economic returns of those assets. This, in turn, entails accompanying investments in physical infrastructure (such as rural roads and irrigation works), ready access to credit, and extensive technical assistance to raise productivity levels in agriculture and other economic activities that are relevant to the poor.

The third element that contributes to poverty reduction is developing the basic human capabilities of the poor—through public health, education, nutrition, and family-planning services. These public services enable the poor to take advantage of expanding economic opportunities. These enhanced capabilities, in turn, create options for further development by stimulating new economic activities that can employ the productive capabilities of the poor—in much the same way that the public provision of physical infrastructure opens up new investment opportunities for business by making transport, communications, or utilities cheaper and more readily available.

Countries that have successfully reduced poverty have allocated substantial resources to primary education and preventive health services. The improvement in overall human development in Chile and Costa Rica was based on long traditions of universal coverage of basic social services—dating back to the 1920s in Chile and to the democratic revolution of 1948 in Costa Rica. During the period of structural economic reform, total spending on health care and education declined in both countries, but the provision of basic services was maintained through the reallocation of resources to primary education and health care. Costa Rica has achieved virtually universal coverage, particularly in the health area, with a fairly progressive distribution of expenditures to the poorest sectors.

One of the paradoxes of economic reform in Chile was the continuous improvement in human development indicators during the military regime despite a contraction of public spending. This improvement was attributable in part to the adoption of health care and nutrition programs targeted specifically to the extremely poor. However, the success of such targeted social programs was also due in part to preexisting universal coverage of basic services programs.

Although health and education spending has increased in Mexico in recent years, it remains a relatively small share of GDP. Moreover, health care and education resources remain fairly concentrated in urban areas, and coverage is still skewed toward middle- and higher-income groups.

Income Distribution and Poverty

Latin American countries traditionally have been characterized by a highly unequal distribution of income and wealth, and in 1990 income distribution in the region was the most unequal anywhere (Londoño and Székely 1997b). In the three countries considered in this chapter, this trend became even more notable during the period of economic adjustment.[19] Even where adjustment led to reductions in poverty, income distribution worsened, indicating that even though the poor in those countries may have benefited from growth, the wealthy gained more.[20] Had income distribution been more equal, economic growth would have translated into a more substantial reduction in poverty. Efforts to reduce poverty in Latin America highlight the importance of adopting both objectives simultaneously—decreasing poverty and improving income distribution. Not only does increased inequality reduce the efficiency of economic growth as a means of reducing poverty (resulting in a low output elasticity of poverty reduction),[21] but it also may threaten the sociopolitical sustainability of development by precipitating social conflict.

Poverty Reduction Programs

The Costa Rican government has implemented several poverty reduction programs targeted at specific groups, such as female heads of household, low-income schoolchildren, and producers of traditional crops. However, social policy has generally emphasized the provision of broad-based programs of universal coverage, particularly through comprehensive health and education policies. Poverty reduction in Costa Rica has occurred primarily through the express promotion of economic activities that benefit the poor and through large investments in broad-based human development programs.

Poverty reduction programs in Chile have differed depending upon whether they were implemented during or after the period of military rule. During most of the military regime, strictly targeted programs to restore minimum levels of employment, health, and nutrition among the extremely poor proved effective in counteracting the most deleterious impacts of recession. However, there was a substantial increase in moderate poverty, and access to basic services deteriorated for large

---

[19] Although data restrictions do not allow for proper measurement of family income in Costa Rica, available estimates show no improvement and perhaps a slight deterioration in income distribution.

[20] Increasing inequality in income distribution in countries where poverty declined—such as Chile and Costa Rica—suggests that the two phenomena can move in opposite directions. It is possible for poverty to decline while income distribution worsens if economic growth is dynamic enough to compensate, or if the regressive distribution of income is occurring somewhere other than in the lower deciles, where the poor are located.

[21] The proportion by which poverty decreases when the economy grows is small.

segments of the population. Social spending increased with the return of democratic governments in the 1990s. The country's new poverty reduction strategy was based on increasing the complementarities between economic growth and poverty reduction; promoting further decentralization in social services delivery, mainly by increasing the participation of civil society organizations; and increasing the productivity of the poor by investing in human capital, thereby generating productive projects for the poor and improving their level of organization and participation in society. Targeted programs helped further reduce poverty by effectively incorporating the poor into expanding economic sectors.

International experience shows, then, that poverty reduction programs have been most successful when they have been able to enhance economic opportunities for the poor within the context of a growing economy. Such programs are rarely successful on their own, as illustrated by the Mexican case. The experiences of Chile and Costa Rica show that even during economic recession, the bases for future growth and poverty reduction can be protected through investments in human capital, rural infrastructure, and increased productivity in economic activities that constitute the livelihood of the poor.

Targeting

Any discussion of the effectiveness of poverty alleviation programs must address the pros and cons of targeted programs versus programs providing universal coverage. In countries that have succeeded in reducing poverty, poverty programs (whether or not they are identified as such) start with a reallocation of resources to provide universal coverage of basic social services. Universal coverage can promote growth by expanding people's human capital, and it is guaranteed, by definition, to reach the poor. Even during Chile's military dictatorship, the effectiveness of targeted programs for the poor was based in significant degree on the preexisting network of broad-based social services. Thus the Chilean experience indicates that social policy is most effective when it is implemented in three stages: universal coverage of basic health and education, followed by programs targeted to the remaining pockets of poverty, followed, in turn, by an emphasis on boosting the quality of – and equity of access to – basic services.

Whether government programs have an enduring impact on poverty often depends upon whether they are designed to increase the economic opportunities of the poor or merely to transfer resources to them. Programs of the latter type may alleviate poverty temporarily, but they are not likely to lead to a more permanent reduction in poverty and they certainly cannot compensate for the lack of pro-poor growth. Even in periods of economic expansion, income transfers cannot be regarded as a mechanism that enables the poor to participate in the growth process and to benefit from it. Policies that are more likely to achieve these objectives would be similar to those that invested in the poor's human development in Costa Rica and Chile, expanded urban employment in Chile, or expanded the rural poor's access to productive assets in Costa Rica.

CONCLUSION

So far, economic reform in Mexico has not been able to restore the conditions for stable growth. Greater integration with North American markets and incentives to exporters stimulated rapid growth of manufactured exports, but these factors have not generated an equivalent expansion of manufacturing employment. Contrary to predictions, the reorientation of production toward exports has stimulated new investments in relatively capital-intensive technologies and increased imports of intermediate goods as inputs in production. The most dramatic example is the maquiladora sector, whose dependence upon imported inputs limits its multiplier effects on employment in other sectors of the economy.

The contraction of employment in the most dynamic sectors of the Mexican economy has been countered by the rapid expansion of jobs in micro and small enterprises. However, these firms still lack the level of organization that could turn them into a dynamic source of productive employment. Production in rural areas, where a large proportion of the poor resides, has declined during the economic adjustment period.

Unstable economic growth, low rates of employment creation in the most dynamic sectors, and declining production in rural areas all help explain the prevalence of poverty in Mexico. The failure of programs like PRONASOL and PROGRESA to reduce poverty points to the importance of establishing a degree of coherence between poverty alleviation programs and macroeconomic reform. No poverty alleviation program can substitute for development policies that effectively incorporate the poor into growth-oriented sectors of the economy. Nor can poverty alleviation programs compensate for loss of productive employment, drastic reductions in real wages, or lack of investment in productive and human assets. Not even large-scale poverty reduction programs can counteract the adverse impact of economic instability and the contraction of sectors from which the poor obtain their income.

Obviously, the effectiveness of targeted programs designed to reach the poor depends upon various factors. These include: the definition of clear criteria to identify the targeted population; a clear and transparent mechanism to allocate resources for the specific purpose of reducing poverty; establishing a certain degree of independence from conjunctural political concerns at the stage of program implementation and resource allocation; and the cost-effectiveness of the mechanisms for targeting and delivering services to program beneficiaries.

Beyond the issue of targeting as a mechanism for the delivery of social services, the Latin American experience indicates that an optimal program of poverty reduction should benefit from complementarities between targeted programs for poverty reduction and programs of universal coverage of basic services. Emphasizing the universal provision of basic services—health care, education, and so on—creates a solid foundation upon which to overlay more specific targeting to particular regions or sectors of the poor.

The experiences of countries that have succeeded in reducing poverty indicate that the only way to make poverty alleviation sustainable over time is by adopting macroeconomic policies that expand employment for large fractions of the population; strengthen the productive capacity of micro, small, and midsize enterprises; and help reestablish the growth potential of small agricultural producers. Similarly, social policies that contribute to broad-based expansion of popular education and health care access raise labor force productivity and thereby contribute to a country's economic growth potential.

Judged by their welfare implications, good macroeconomic policies are those that expand income opportunities for large segments of the population. Similarly, good social policies are those that expand productive potential. In the most general sense, the only poverty alleviation policies that are sustainable in the long run are those that promote the productive incorporation of the poor into the dynamics of the rest of the economy. And in a market economy, the only way to incorporate the poor into the dynamics of the market is by placing productive assets into their hands and increasing returns on those assets.

REFERENCES

Alarcón, Diana. 1993. "Evaluación del impacto de Solidaridad sobre el nivel de vida de la población objetivo en Coahuila, Tamaulipas y Durango." In *Evaluación del Programa Nacional de Solidaridad en tres estados del norte de México: Tamaulipas, Coahuila y Durango*, edited by Oscar Contreras. Tijuana: El Colegio de la Frontera Norte.

———. 1994. *Changes in the Distribution of Income in Mexico and Trade Liberalization.* Tijuana, Mexico: El Colegio de la Frontera Norte.

————. 1997a. "National Poverty Reduction Strategies: Case Study of Costa Rica." Paper prepared for the project "Evaluation of Poverty Alleviation Programmes, Poverty Reduction, Lessons Learned," sponsored by Social Development and Poverty Elimination Division/Bureau for Programme and Policy Services (SEPED/BPPS), United Nations Development Programme.

————. 1997b. "National Poverty Reduction Strategies: Case Study of Chile." Paper prepared for the project "Evaluation of Poverty Alleviation Programmes, Poverty Reduction, Lessons Learned," sponsored by SEPED/BPPS, United Nations Development Programme.

————. 1997c. "National Poverty Reduction Strategies: Case Study of Mexico." Paper prepared for the project "Evaluation of Poverty Alleviation Programmes, Poverty Reduction, Lessons Learned," sponsored by SEPED/BPPS, United Nations Development Programme.

Alarcón, Diana, and Terry McKinley. 1994. "Gender Differences in Wages and Human Capital: Case Study of Female and Male Urban Workers in Mexico from 1984 to 1992," *Frontera Norte* 6 (12): 41–50.

————. 1997a. "The Paradox of Narrowing Wage Differentials and Widening Wage Inequality in Mexico," *Development and Change* 28 (3): 505–30.

————. 1997b. "The Rising Contribution of Labor Income to Inequality in Mexico," *North American Journal of Economics and Finance* 8 (2): 201–12.

Alarcón, Diana, and Eduardo Zepeda. 1998. "Employment Trends in the Mexican Manufacturing Sector," *North American Journal of Economics and Finance* 9: 125–45.

Bailey, John, and Jennifer Boone. 1994. "National Solidarity: A Summary of Program Elements." In *Transforming State-Society Relations in Mexico: The National Solidarity Strategy*, edited by Wayne A. Cornelius, Ann L. Craig, and Jonathan Fox. La Jolla: Center for U.S.-Mexican Studies, University of California, San Diego.

Barrón, Luis, and Guillermo Trejo. 1995. "La pobreza en México: la paradoja de la política social." Paper presented to the "Reunión de Consulta sobre las Formas y Métodos de Medición de la Pobreza," SEDESOL, Mexico City, March 24.

Cárdenas, Enrique. 1996. *La política económica en México, 1950-1994*. Mexico City: Fondo de Cultura Económica/El Colegio de México.

CEPAL-INEGI (Comisión Económica para América Latina y el Caribe–Instituto Nacional de Estadística, Geografía e Informática). 1993. *Magnitud y evolución de la pobreza en México, 1984-1992*. Mexico: CEPAL and INEGI.

Cornelius, Wayne A., Ann L. Craig, and Jonathan Fox, eds. 1994. *Transforming State-Society Relations in Mexico: The National Solidarity Strategy*. U.S.-Mexico Contemporary Perspectives Series, no. 6. La Jolla: Center for U.S.-Mexican Studies, University of California, San Diego.

Cowan, Kevin, and José De Gregorio. 1996. "Distribución y pobreza en Chile: ¿Estamos mal? ¿Ha habido progreso? ¿Hemos retrocedido?" Santiago de Chile. Manuscript.

Feenstra, Robert, and George Hanson. 1994. "Foreign Investment, Outsourcing, and Relative Wages." Paper prepared for the conference "Political Economy of Trade Policy."

Gershberg, Alec. 1994. "Distributing Resources in the Education Sector: Solidarity's Escuela Digna Program." In *Transforming State-Society Relations in Mexico: The National Solidarity Strategy*, edited by Wayne A. Cornelius, Ann L. Craig, and Jonathan Fox. La Jolla: Center for U.S.–Mexican Studies, University of California, San Diego.

Gómez de León, José. 1998. "Correlative Dimensions of Poverty in Mexico: Elements for Targeting Social Programs." Paper presented at the first meeting of the Latin American and Caribbean Economics Association/IADB/World Bank Network on Inequality and Poverty, Buenos Aires, Argentina, October.

González Tiburcio, Enrique, and Aurelio de Alba. 1992. *Ajuste económico y política social en México*. Mexico City: El Nacional.

Graham, Carol. 1994. "Mexico's Solidarity Program in Comparative Context: Demand-based Poverty Alleviation Programs in Latin America, Africa, and Eastern Europe." In *Transforming State-Society Relations in Mexico: The National Solidarity Strategy*, edited by Wayne A. Cornelius, Ann L. Craig, and Jonathan Fox. La Jolla: Center for U.S.–Mexican Studies, University of California, San Diego.

ILO (International Labour Office). 1998. *1998 Labour Overview: Latin America and the Caribbean*. Geneva: ILO.

INEGI (Instituto Nacional de Estadística, Geografía e Informática). 1984. Encuesta Nacional de Ingreso-Gasto de los Hogares (ENIGH). Micro Data. Mexico: INEGI.

———. 1985. *Estadísticas históricas de México*. 2 vols. Mexico City: Secretaría de Programmación y Presupuesto.

———. 1989. Encuesta Nacional de Ingreso–Gasto de los Hogares. Mexico: INEGI.

———. 1992. Encuesta Nacional de Ingreso–Gasto de los Hogares. Mexico: INEGI.

———. 1994. Encuesta Nacional de Ingreso–Gasto de los Hogares. Mexico: INEGI.

INEGI–STPS (Instituto Nacional de Estadística, Geografía e Informática–Secretaría del Trabajo y Prevención Social). 1992. Encuesta Nacional de Micronegocios. Mexico: INEGI–STPS.

———. 1994. Encuesta Nacional de Micronegocios. Mexico: INEGI–STPS.

Laurell, Cristina. 1994. "La cuestión social mexicana y el viraje en la política social," *Coyuntura* 44/45.

Londoño, Juan Luis, and Miguel Székely. 1997a. "Persistent Poverty and Excess Inequality: Latin America, 1970–1995." Working Paper Series, no. 357. Washington, D.C.: Office of the Chief Economist, Inter-American Development Bank.

———. 1997b. "Sorpresas distributivas después de una década de reformas: América Latina en la década de 1990." Paper presented at the seminar

"Latin America after a Decade of Reform: What are the Next Steps?" Inter-American Development Bank, March.

Lustig, Nora. 1994. "Solidarity as a Strategy of Poverty Alleviation." In *Transforming State-Society Relations in Mexico: The National Solidarity Strategy*, edited by Wayne A. Cornelius, Ann L. Craig, and Jonathan Fox. La Jolla: Center for U.S.–Mexican Studies, University of California, San Diego.

Lustig, Nora, and Miguel Székely. 1998. "México: evolución económica, pobreza y desigualdad." In *Política macroeconómica y pobreza en América Latina y el Caribe*, edited by Enrique Ganuza, Lance Taylor, and Samuel Morley. Washington, D.C.: UNDP/ECLAC/IADB.

McKinley, Terry, and Diana Alarcón. 1995. "The Prevalence of Rural Poverty in Mexico," *World Development* 23 (9): 1575–85.

Mejía, José Antonio, and Rob Vos. 1997. "Poverty in Latin America and the Caribbean: An Inventory, 1980–95." Working Paper Series, no. I-4. Inter-American Institute for Social Development. Washington, D.C.: Inter-American Development Bank.

Molinar Horcasitas, Juan, and Jeffrey Weldon. 1994. "Electoral Determinants and Consequences of National Solidarity." In *Transforming State-Society Relations in Mexico: The National Solidarity Strategy*, edited by Wayne A. Cornelius, Ann L. Craig, and Jonathan Fox. La Jolla: Center for U.S.–Mexican Studies, University of California, San Diego.

Morley, Samuel, and Carola Álvarez. 1992. "Poverty and Adjustment in Costa Rica." Working Paper Series, no. 123. Washington, D.C.: Inter-American Development Bank.

Pánuco-Laguette, Humberto, and Miguel Székely. 1996. "Income Distribution and Poverty in Mexico." In *The New Economic Model in Latin America and Its Impact on Income Distribution and Poverty*, edited by Victor Bulmer-Thomas. New York: St. Martin's.

Poder Ejecutivo Federal. 2001. *Primer informe de gobierno*. Mexico City: Presidencia de la República.

———. n.d. *Progresa, Programa de Educación, Salud y Alimentación*. Mexico City.

Raczynski, Dagmar. 1995. "Programs, Institutions, and Resources: Chile." In *Strategies to Combat Poverty in Latin America*, edited by Dagmar Raczynski. Washington, D.C.: Inter-American Development Bank.

Raczynski, Dagmar, and Pilar Romaguera. 1995. "Chile: Poverty, Adjustment, and Social Policies in the 1980's." In *Coping with Austerity: Poverty and Inequality in Latin America*, edited by Nora Lustig. Washington, D.C.: Brookings Institution.

Skoufias, Emmanuel, Benjamin Davis, and Jere R. Behrman. 1999. "An Evaluation of the Selection of Beneficiary Households in the Education, Health, and Nutrition Program (PROGRESA) of Mexico." Washington, D.C.: International Food Policy Research Institute.

Skoufias, Emmanuel, Benjamin Davis, and Sergio de la Vega. 1999. "Targeting the Poor in Mexico: An Evaluation of the Selection of Households into PROGRESA." Washington, D.C.: International Food Policy Research Institute.

Trejos, Juan Diego, and Pablo Sauma. n.d. "Pobreza y distribución del ingreso en la era del ajuste: Costa Rica, 1980–1992." Mimeo.

UNDP (United Nations Development Programme). 2001. *Human Development Report.* New York: UNDP.

World Bank. 1990. *Costa Rica Public Sector Social Spending.* Report No. 8519-CR. Population and Human Resources Division. Washington, D.C.: World Bank.

———. 1995. "Chile: estrategia para elevar la competitividad agrícola y aliviar la pobreza rural." World Bank Countries Studies Series. Washington, D.C.: World Bank.

Zepeda, Eduardo. 1994. "El gasto social en México: de la estabilización ortodoxa al neoliberalismo social," *Frontera Norte* 1, Special issue.

Zepeda, Eduardo, and David Castro. 1996. "Solidaridad: combatiendo la pobreza extrema." Presented at the Congreso Nacional de Ciencia Política, Mexico City, September 25–28.

Zepeda, Eduardo, and Ranjeeta Ghiara. 1996. "Returns to Education and Economic Liberalization." Mexico: Centro de Estudios Socioeconómicos, Universidad Autónoma de Coahuila. Mimeo.

13

The Dialectics of Urban and Regional Disparities in Mexico

Gustavo Garza

Mexico's strong economic growth from 1940 to 1980 brought about rapid urbanization characterized by increasing regional disparities and by Mexico City's predominance in terms of economic and demographic concentration. This situation marginalized large sectors of the population, depleted natural resources, and hindered economic growth. Moreover, by virtue of its size, Mexico City required increasing investments and ultimately threatened the sustainability of its ecosystem. In response, the Mexican government has, since the 1940s, implemented a series of policies to slow the concentration process.

In the 1940s, the population of central Mexico was "numerically much greater than that in any other region, . . . and the central region accounted for . . . 44.7 per cent [of population growth since 1930]. The increase in the Distrito Federal alone amounted to more than half a million inhabitants, owing almost entirely to the phenomenal growth of the population of Mexico City" (Whetten 1948: 34). Ten years later, scholars predicted that the population explosion in the central region would slow because of diminishing returns to growth (Zamora Millán 1959). And to remedy Mexico City's concentration of industrial activity, analysts recommended a policy of deconcentration (López Malo 1960).

As the Mexican government implemented a series of deconcentration measures, scholars began to focus on the dynamics of territorial concentration. In the 1970s, they analyzed the relative failure of large projects to reduce regional disparities (see, for example, Barkin 1972, 1978). Others identified Mexico City's industrial structure as the most highly developed and diversified in the country (Garza 1980: 105). A systematic study of economic and social variables found that the states that were the most developed in 1960 were the same ones that had been the most developed in 1900. Moreover, the gap separating the more developed states from the less developed ones had widened (Appendini et al. 1972). In terms of per capita income, the most developed regions achieved a higher rate of growth between 1940 and 1970 than did the most backward states, further increasing the disparities between them (Unikel, Ruiz, and Garza 1976: 328). And regarding industrial concentration, Mexico City's share of national industry rose from 27.2 percent in 1930 to 48.6 percent in 1970. That is, by 1970 almost half of national manufacturing production took place in this single urban center (Garza 1985: 154).

Regardless of the indicators or spatial units used for analysis, there is broad consensus that regional disparities in Mexico increased significantly between 1940 and 1970. Yet interpretations differ regarding what happened in the 1970–1980 decade. Some studies indicate that regional disparities decreased in terms of per capita gross domestic product (GDP) (see Hernández Laos 1984: 161; Gómez and Cortés 1987: 50; Osuna 1990: 26). Others suggest that disparities increased during these years (Ramírez 1986: 368; Palacios 1988: 23).[1] There are few studies on the dynamics of inequalities from 1980 to 1999, the last year for which statistical data are available.

In the context of the current state of knowledge regarding regional disparities in Mexico, this chapter first analyzes the dynamics of regional disparities in GDP between 1970 and 1999 in an attempt to detect changes in the prevailing pattern during the last decade of this period, the years of Mexico's liberalization strategy. Second, it examines the growth of the urban population by region, as well as its distribution by city size, between 1970 and 2000. City size is particularly important given that Mexico today is essentially an urban nation, and it is in the urban world that spatial disparities are increasingly apparent. Third, this chapter reviews the urban and regional policies of Mexico's federal government in the 1990s in an effort to identify their characteristics and determine their impact on the organization of the national landscape.

It is important to note that the extended economic crisis of the 1980s had a significant influence on the territorial distribution of economic activities. This makes it difficult to determine whether contemporary regional disparities are the result of the government's deconcentration policies, a product of an inflection in the concentration process in favor of midsize cities or backward regions, or a consequence of the crisis itself. The problem becomes more complex if one adds the possible ter-

---

[1] The differences in interpretation stem from conceptual difficulties concerning the units of analysis (states, regions, or cities) in the different studies, as well as problems with the variables (total versus per capita GDP, industrial sector versus all sectors, and so on). For a discussion of these differences, see Garza and Rivera 1995: 49–50.

ritorial impact of economic liberalization that has occurred since the 1980s, particularly since the implementation of the North American Free Trade Agreement (NAFTA) in 1994.

In order to tease out these various influences on the regional distribution of GDP and population, along with others embedded in the dynamics of the system of cities, this chapter examines three periods in Mexico's recent economic evolution: (1) the "decade of prosperity" (1970–1980), when GDP rose in real terms at an annual rate of 6.8 percent;[2] (2) the "lost decade" (1980–1990), when GDP increased only 1.9 percent per annum on average and actually declined (at an annual rate of 0.4 percent) between 1982 and 1988; and (3) the "recovery" (1990 to 2000), when the Mexican economy recouped somewhat, with GDP rising 3.6 percent annually in real terms between 1990 and 1994 and 3.4 percent per year between 1994 and 2000. This last period included the crisis of 1995, when GDP plummeted by 6.2 percent, bringing the overall average annual growth rate for 1990–1995 to 1.5 percent (Garza 1999: 270–71; www.inegi.gob.mx).

THE DYNAMICS OF REGIONAL INEQUALITIES

Since early in the twentieth century, Mexico has been characterized by an increasing economic and demographic concentration in the country's central region, with Mexico City as the nucleus. Estimates suggest that the Federal District and the State of México together accounted for 15.7 percent of GDP in 1900 but 33.0 percent by 1999, with growth rates far outpacing broad areas of the country, at least until 1970 (Garza and Rivera 1995: 49).

In terms of GDP by region and by state between 1970 and 1999 (see table 13.1), region V (Center-East, including Mexico City) increased its share slightly during the period of rapid economic growth between 1970 and 1980 (from 43.0 to 43.3 percent), but it then declined significantly (to 40.7 percent) in 1988, a time of severe economic crisis.[3] Between 1980 and 1988, the Federal District and the State of México's combined share of GDP fell from 36.1 to 32.8 percent, with other states in region V (with the exception of Puebla) increasing their shares corre-

---

[2] In fact, the boom extended through 1981, when GDP grew at 7.8 percent. The exchange-rate crisis occurred in 1982. However, because demographic data refer to ten-year periods, population distribution analysis places the end of the boom in 1980.

[3] Most of the loss registered in 1988 was attributable to the Federal District, and this loss was not offset by the expansion of the Mexico City metropolitan area into the surrounding municipalities of the State of México.

TABLE 13.1. Mexico's Gross Domestic Product by Region and State, 1970–1999 (percentages)[1]

Regions and States	1970	1980	1988	1993	1994	1995	1999
I. NORTHWEST	9.5	8.1	8.7	8.9	9.0	9.2	9.0
Baja California	2.6	2.3	2.5	2.8	2.9	2.9	3.1
Baja California Sur	0.4	0.4	0.5	0.5	0.5	0.6	0.5
Nayarit	0.9	0.8	0.7	0.7	0.7	0.6	0.6
Sinaloa	2.5	2.1	2.2	2.3	2.2	2.3	2.0
Sonora	3.2	2.5	2.8	2.6	2.7	2.8	2.8
II. NORTH	10.2	9.0	10.4	10.7	10.8	11.0	11.4
Chihuahua	3.4	2.8	3.2	3.9	4.0	4.0	4.4
Coahuila	2.8	2.7	3.0	2.9	2.9	3.1	3.2
Durango	1.4	1.3	1.3	1.3	1.3	1.3	1.3
San Luis Potosí	1.6	1.4	1.8	1.8	1.8	1.7	1.7
Zacatecas	1.0	0.8	1.0	0.8	0.8	0.9	0.8
III. NORTHEAST	9.1	8.9	9.1	9.2	9.4	9.4	9.8
Nuevo León	5.9	5.9	6.3	6.4	6.5	6.5	6.8
Tamaulipas	3.2	3.0	2.7	2.8	2.9	2.9	3.0
IV. CENTER-WEST	14.0	13.0	13.9	13.8	13.8	13.9	14.0
Aguascalientes	0.6	0.6	0.7	1.0	1.0	1.0	1.1
Colima	0.4	0.5	0.5	0.6	0.6	0.6	0.6
Guanajuato	3.4	2.9	3.3	3.4	3.3	3.4	3.3
Jalisco	7.1	6.6	6.8	6.6	6.5	6.4	6.5
Michoacán	2.5	2.4	2.5	2.3	2.4	2.5	2.5
V. CENTER-EAST	43.0	43.3	40.7	42.4	42.2	41.2	41.7
Federal District	27.6	25.2	21.4	23.9	23.8	23.1	22.5

Hidalgo	1.3	1.5	1.7	1.5	1.5	1.4	1.5
México	8.6	10.9	11.4	10.3	10.3	10.1	10.6
Morelos	1.1	1.1	1.3	1.5	1.4	1.4	1.4
Puebla	3.2	3.2	3.1	3.2	3.2	3.2	3.5
Querétaro	0.8	1.0	1.3	1.4	1.4	1.5	1.7
Tlaxcala	0.4	0.5	0.6	0.5	0.5	0.5	0.5
VI. SOUTH	4.8	5.8	5.5	5.3	5.3	5.5	4.9
Chiapas	1.6	2.7	1.9	1.8	1.8	1.9	1.7
Guerrero	1.7	1.7	1.9	1.9	1.9	1.9	1.7
Oaxaca	1.5	1.4	1.7	1.7	1.6	1.7	1.5
VII. EAST	7.6	9.8	7.5	5.8	5.9	6.2	5.5
Tabasco	1.2	4.0	1.9	1.3	1.3	1.4	1.2
Veracruz	6.5	5.8	5.7	4.6	4.6	4.8	4.3
VIII. PENINSULA	1.8	2.1	4.1	3.8	3.8	3.8	3.7
Campeche	0.4	0.5	2.2	1.2	1.2	1.2	1.1
Quintana Roo	0.2	0.4	0.7	1.3	1.3	1.3	1.3
Yucatán	1.1	1.2	1.2	1.3	1.3	1.3	1.3
Statistical Measures[2]							
Standard deviation	4.9	4.6	4.0	4.3	4.3	4.2	4.1
Mean	3.1	3.1	3.1	3.1	3.1	3.1	3.1
Coefficient of variation	1.57	1.47	1.28	1.39	1.80	1.34	1.32

Sources: For 1970–1988, INEGI 1996: 4; for 1993–1996, INEGI 1999: 30; for 1999, www.inegi.gob.mx.

Note: Percentages may not add to 100.0 because of rounding.

[1] The original data for 1970 and 1980 give 0.02 percent and 0.34 percent, respectively, as gross domestic product in territorial waters. The figure for 1970 was added to Baja California and Baja California Sur; the figure for 1980 was added to the seventeen states with coastal borders.

[2] Calculated for the thirty-two federal entities. The coefficient of variation is the standard deviation divided by the mean.

spondingly. During the period of post-crisis recovery (1988–1993), region V increased its share of GDP to 42.4 percent, but it declined once again (to 41.2 percent) with the economic downturn of 1995—but then rose again marginally to 41.7 percent in 1999. These figures suggest that GDP concentration in Mexico City does not so much reflect a trend toward decentralization as the economic ups and downs of the country as a whole, particularly given that economic crises hit highly industrialized Mexico City especially hard. Nevertheless, despite having lost relative importance in terms of GDP between 1970 and 1999, the Federal District and the State of México still accounted for over a third of Mexico's industrial production at the end of the period under study.

The dynamics of Mexico's other regions and states can be summarized using a variation coefficient that measures the degree of GDP distribution among states.[4] This coefficient was 1.57 in 1970 and 1.28 in 1988, indicating a lessening of GDP disparities among the states over these years. During the economic recovery, the coefficient increased to 1.39 in 1993 and remained basically unchanged through 1999 (table 13.1).[5] Yet despite this indication of a slight decrease in Mexico's territorial disparities since 1970, 41.7 percent of national production remained in the Center-East region.

It is important to determine which states gained economic prominence in Mexico, especially between 1988 and 1999, in order to test the following hypotheses regarding economic liberalization: (1) that regions I, II, and III will reap substantial benefits from the growth of the *maquiladora* (in-bond processing) sector; (2) that region V, especially Mexico City, will face significant difficulties in restructuring its industrial base because some firms are relocating to neighboring states; and (3) that region VI, the South, will continue to be excluded from the North American economic integration process, except for a few tourist spots (Hiernaux 1995: 119–20).

During 1970–1999, region VIII (Peninsula) increased its share of national GDP by 114 percent. This dynamic growth reflected both the region's low baseline (1.8 percent in 1970) and the explosive development

---

[4] This coefficient is obtained by dividing the standard deviation by the mean, neutralizing the influence of the size of the mean in the different measures (Sen 1997: 22). The higher the coefficient, the greater the regional and state disparities.

[5] It should be noted that the two data series on GDP by state are not fully comparable. The 1970–1988 series comes from a 1996 INEGI publication, and the series for 1993–1996 comes from a 1999 INEGI publication (see source note on table 13.1). The 1999 publication notes that in 1993–1996 it was possible to estimate indexes of the increase in the physical volume of production, something not calculated in the first series. To avoid difficulties in comparing the series, the present study uses only national GDP percentages for the states.

of Cancún, which pushed growth to 3.7 percent of national GDP in 1999. Second in relative GDP growth was region II, the North, which raised its share of national GDP from 10.2 percent to 11.4 percent, followed by regions III and VI. The four regions that increased their share in GDP between 1970 and 1999—regions VIII, III, II, and VI—concentrated 29.8 percent of national GDP in 1999, still well below the 41.7 percent concentration in the Center-East. Quintana Roo led among individual states, with a 644 percent increase in its share of national GDP over the 1970–1999 period, followed by Campeche, Querétaro, Aguascalientes, and Baja California Sur.[6]

Two important features emerge when reviewing the states' participation in national GDP during this period. First, Querétaro, Tlaxcala, Morelos, and México were among the top ten states in relative increases in GDP, and all were within the area surrounding the Mexico City metropolitan area (MCMA). Second, the states along the Mexico–U.S. border ranked in positions 8, 11, 13, 14, 24, and 27. This suggests that the reduction in disparities in GDP share from 1970 to 1999 largely favored the states bordering the MCMA, making way for a new megacity concentration. Other states that benefited include Quintana Roo and Campeche, which were economically depressed at the beginning of the period but were able to improve their situation over time through tourism (Cancún) and petroleum extraction (Campeche). Although states in the north did not exhibit significant growth throughout the entire 1970–1999 span, the years 1993 to 1999—when liberalization would have begun to have a strong impact—are probably a more appropriate subject for analysis.

From 1993 to 1999, the five most economically dynamic states were Querétaro, Aguascalientes, Baja California, Chihuahua, and Coahuila, only three of which are on the Mexico–U.S. border.[7] Taken in combination, the six northern border states' share of national GDP decreased from 21.1 to 20.6 percent between 1970 and 1988 but then rose from 21.4 to 23.3 percent between 1993 and 1999.[8] The border states that registered the greatest relative increases during this six-year period were Chihuahua, Baja California, and Coahuila. Although Nuevo León experienced the lowest growth, its share of national GDP remained the highest of the northern border states.

The impact that changes in economic structure have on the territorial distribution of production and population will become clearer over

---

[6] Author's calculations based on data in table 13.1.

[7] Author's calculations from data in table 13.1. Tamaulipas, Sonora, Puebla, Michoacán, and Nuevo León were the next five most economically dynamic states.

[8] Author's calculations from data in table 13.1.

the longer term. A protracted urbanization process governs such a distribution, and it would be premature at this point to assess the territorial impact of Mexico's economic liberalization and increasing integration into the North American bloc. Nevertheless, the analysis of GDP by regions and states between 1970 and 1999 uncovered no significant impact.[9] An in-depth analysis that could help explain this fact might best focus on cities as the most refined unit of territorial analysis in a hegemonically urban country.

METROPOLITAN CONCENTRATION IN URBAN MEXICO, 1970–2000

This section analyzes population dynamics at the regional and the city levels for three subperiods. It seeks to determine whether changes have occurred in the territorial concentration of total population and urban population. The discussion gives special attention to the position of large cities in the national landscape.

The Uneven Distribution of Population by Region

In view of the strong links that exist between population movements and differential economic dynamics among regions, areas that register an increased share of total population also show high rates of economic growth. Between 1970 and 1995, there were no substantial changes in the distribution of total or urban population in the eight regions that appear in table 13.1. Mexico's most populous region in 1970 was the Center-East (region V), with 15.9 million persons, of whom 10.9 million were urban inhabitants (33.0 and 45.7 percent, respectively, of the country's total and urban populations; see table 13.2). The Center-West (region IV) followed, with 8.5 million total and 3.5 million urban inhabitants (17.5 and 14.7 percent, respectively, of the corresponding national values). Thus these two regions together contained 50.5 and 60.4 percent, respectively, of Mexico's total population and total urban population. The North (region II) was third, with 12.2 percent and 11.0 percent, respectively, for these values. The remaining regions ranged from 2.3 percent (region VIII, the Peninsula) to 10.9 percent (region VI, the South) of Mexico's total population.

Baja California increased its share of total and urban population significantly — from 1.8 and 2.7 percent, respectively, in 1970 to 2.3 and 3.1 percent in 1995.[10] Sonora remained steady at 2.3 percent of the total

_____

[9] The six border states did make a 1.9 percent gain in their share of national GDP over the 1993-1999 period.
[10] Author's calculations from data in table 13.2.

population, though its share of the urban population fell slightly, from 2.7 to 2.6 percent. Coahuila rose from 2.3 percent of total population in 1970 to 2.4 percent in 1995, remaining virtually unchanged in its share of both total and total urban population. Chihuahua dropped from 3.3 to 3.1 percent in its share of total national population during the period, while its share of urban population increased from 3.8 to 3.9 percent, indicating that the growth of the maquiladora industry in Ciudad Juárez was not sufficient to increase the state's relative importance in terms of population. Tamaulipas, which contains the border cities of Nuevo Laredo, Reynosa, and Matamoros, lost national demographic importance, dropping from 3.0 to 2.8 percent of total national population between 1970 and 1995. And Nuevo León, with no real border city, increased its demographic share from 3.5 to 3.9 percent of total population and from 5.1 to 5.5 percent of urban population between 1970 and 1995.

Overall, between 1970 and 1990 the six border states held their combined share of total national population steady at 16.3 percent, but they registered a decrease in urban population share from 22.1 to 21.1 percent. Then from 1990 to 1995, they increased their share of total national population to 16.7 percent and their share of urban population to 22.1 percent, the same level as twenty-five years earlier.[11]

In summary, no significant changes were observed in the distribution of total national population between 1970 and 1995. The Center-East increased its share only slightly, while the six border states held steady between 1970 and 1990 and then rose moderately by 1995. Thus the predicted change in population distribution in favor of northern Mexico — at the cost of the Center — was not yet visible in 1995. This has important implications for the distribution of GDP, as noted previously. But the spatial distribution of population changes very slowly, and the pattern that emerges in Mexico during the first decades of the twenty-first century is likely to be strongly influenced by the evolution of the Mexican economy and its integration with the United States.

Polycentric Concentration in the Urban System

By the 1980s, Mexico had become essentially an urban country, and the organization of its national space depends increasingly upon the demographic and economic dynamics of its cities. Consequently, the evolution of the urban national hierarchy adds another dimension to the portrait of territorial disparities.

---

[11] Author's estimates based on data in table 13.2.

TABLE 13.2. Characteristics of Mexico's Urbanization by Region and State, 1970–1995

Regions and States	1970			
	Total Population (000s)	Urban Population (000s)	Cities with 15,000+ Inhabitants	Level of Urbanization[1]
National total	48,315	23,828	166	49.3
I. NORTHWEST	3,908	1,886	24	48.3
Baja California	870	643	4	73.9
Baja California Sur	128	47	1	36.7
Nayarit	544	127	3	23.3
Sinaloa	1,267	424	6	33.5
Sonora	1,099	645	10	58.7
II. NORTH	5,900	2,612	27	44.3
Chihuahua	1,613	900	8	55.8
Coahuila	1,115	797	10	71.5
Durango	939	342	1	36.4
San Luis Potosí	1,282	415	5	32.4
Zacatecas	951	158	3	16.6
III. NORTHEAST	3,152	2,271	12	72.0
Nuevo León	1,695	1,334	4	78.7
Tamaulipas	1,457	937	8	64.3
IV. CENTER-WEST	8,470	3,505	43	41.4
Aguascalientes	338	185	1	54.7
Colima	241	139	3	57.7
Guanajuato	2,270	989	14	43.6
Jalisco	3,297	1,575	12	47.8
Michoacán	2,324	617	13	26.5
V. CENTER-EAST	15,922	10,899	20	68.5
Federal District	6,874	6,874	1	100.0
Hidalgo	1,194	121	2	10.1
México	3,823	2,557	2	66.9
Morelos	616	288	3	46.8
Puebla	2,508	835	7	33.3
Querétaro	486	132	2	27.2
Tlaxcala	421	92	3	21.9
VI. SOUTH	5,281	732	16	13.9
Chiapas	1,569	215	6	13.7
Guerrero	1,597	289	4	18.1
Oaxaca	2,115	228	6	10.8
VII. EAST	4,584	1,489	19	32.5
Tabasco	768	133	3	17.3
Veracruz	3,816	1,356	16	35.5
VIII. PENINSULA	1,098	434	5	39.5
Campeche	252	107	2	42.5
Quintana Roo	88	24	1	27.3
Yucatán	758	303	2	40.0

TABLE 13.2 continued

Regions and States	1980			
	Total Population (000s)	Urban Population (000s)	Cities with 15,000+ Inhabitants	Level of Urban-ization[1]
National total	66,847	37,578	229	56.2
I. NORTHWEST	5,483	2,979	32	54.3
Baja California	1,178	917	4	77.8
Baja California Sur	215	116	2	54.0
Nayarit	726	220	5	30.3
Sinaloa	1,850	777	9	42.0
Sonora	1,514	949	12	62.7
II. NORTH	7,556	3,816	31	50.5
Chihuahua	2,006	1,244	9	62.0
Coahuila	1,557	1,174	11	75.4
Durango	1,182	512	1	43.3
San Luis Potosí	1,674	644	6	38.5
Zacatecas	1,137	242	4	21.3
III. NORTHEAST	4,437	3,432	13	77.3
Nuevo León	2,513	2,113	5	84.1
Tamaulipas	1,924	1,319	8	68.6
IV. CENTER-WEST	11,112	5,776	55	52.0
Aguascalientes	519	294	1	56.6
Colima	346	206	3	59.5
Guanajuato	3,006	1,524	17	50.7
Jalisco	4,372	2,755	18	63.0
Michoacán	2,869	997	16	34.8
V. CENTER-EAST	23,534	17,038	33	72.4
Federal District	8,831	8,831	1	100.0
Hidalgo	1,547	252	7	16.3
México	7,564	5,690	5	75.2
Morelos	947	489	6	51.6
Puebla	3,348	1,317	7	39.3
Querétaro	740	260	3	35.1
Tlaxcala	557	199	4	35.7
VI. SOUTH	6,564	1,227	22	18.7
Chiapas	2,085	367	8	17.6
Guerrero	2,110	489	5	23.2
Oaxaca	2,369	371	9	15.7
VII. EAST	6,450	2,438	32	37.8
Tabasco	1,063	250	5	23.5
Veracruz	5,387	2,188	27	40.6
VIII. PENINSULA	1,711	872	11	51.0
Campeche	421	202	2	48.0
Quintana Roo	226	109	3	48.2
Yucatán	1,064	561	6	52.7

TABLE 13.2 continued

Regions and States	1990 Total Population (000s)	1990 Urban Population (000s)	1990 Cities with 15,000+ Inhabitants	1990 Level of Urbanization[1]
National total	81,250	49,435	309	60.8
I. NORTHWEST	6,832	4,204	37	61.5
Baja California	1,661	1,370	4	82.5
Baja California Sur	318	188	3	59.1
Nayarit	825	317	7	38.4
Sinaloa	2,204	1,053	10	47.8
Sonora	1,824	1,276	13	70.0
II. NORTH	9,042	5,308	38	58.7
Chihuahua	2,442	1,694	9	69.4
Coahuila	1,972	1,638	13	83.1
Durango	1,349	691	2	51.2
San Luis Potosí	2,003	911	7	45.5
Zacatecas	1,276	374	7	29.3
III. NORTHEAST	5,349	4,444	17	83.1
Nuevo León	3,099	2,758	7	89.0
Tamaulipas	2,250	1,686	10	74.9
IV. CENTER-WEST	13,983	8,776	79	62.8
Aguascalientes	720	492	4	68.3
Colima	428	298	4	69.6
Guanajuato	3,983	2,742	25	68.8
Jalisco	5,303	3,764	25	71.0
Michoacán	3,549	1,480	21	41.7
V. CENTER-EAST	27,073	19,872	44	73.4
Federal District	8,236	8,236	1	100.0
Hidalgo	1,888	486	12	25.7
México	9,816	7,691	7	78.4
Morelos	1,195	691	5	57.8
Puebla	4,126	1,973	11	47.8
Querétaro	1,051	490	4	46.6
Tlaxcala	761	305	4	40.1
VI. SOUTH	8,850	2,294	38	25.9
Chiapas	3,210	753	13	23.5
Guerrero	2,620	934	14	35.6
Oaxaca	3,020	607	11	20.1
VII. EAST	7,730	3,208	39	41.5
Tabasco	1,502	476	9	31.7
Veracruz	6,228	2,732	30	43.9
VIII. PENINSULA	2,391	1,329	17	55.6
Campeche	535	273	4	51.0
Quintana Roo	493	296	3	60.0
Yucatán ·	1,363	760	10	55.8

TABLE 13.2 continued

Regions and States	1995			
	Total Population (000s)	Urban Population (000s)	Cities with 15,000+ Inhabitants	Level of Urban-ization[1]
National total	91,120	58,319	348	64.0
I. NORTHWEST	7,888	5,194	42	65.8
Baja California	2,108	1,799	5	85.3
Baja California Sur	375	240	4	64.0
Nayarit	896	387	8	43.2
Sinaloa	2,425	1,246	11	51.4
Sonora	2,084	1,522	14	73.0
II. NORTH	9,924	6,323	44	63.7
Chihuahua	2,793	2,293	12	82.1
Coahuila	2,172	2,069	13	95.3
Durango	1,431	435	3	30.4
San Luis Potosí	2,192	1,057	7	48.2
Zacatecas	1,336	469	9	35.1
III. NORTHEAST	6,075	5,212	18	85.8
Nuevo León	3,549	3,215	8	90.6
Tamaulipas	2,526	1,998	10	79.1
IV. CENTER-WEST	15,601	10,297	84	66.0
Aguascalientes	862	698	4	81.0
Colima	487	352	4	72.2
Guanajuato	4,393	3,138	27	71.4
Jalisco	5,990	4,388	27	73.3
Michoacán	3,869	1,722	22	44.5
V. CENTER-EAST	30,501	22,921	56	75.1
Federal District	8,484	8,484	1	100.0
Hidalgo	2,112	602	13	28.5
México	11,705	9,436	14	80.6
Morelos	1,443	970	10	67.2
Puebla	4,624	2,287	12	49.5
Querétaro	1,249	788	3	63.1
Tlaxcala	884	354	3	40.0
VI. SOUTH	9,746	2,852	41	29.3
Chiapas	3,607	975	15	27.0
Guerrero	2,915	1,129	16	38.7
Oaxaca	3,224	748	10	23.2
VII. EAST	8,484	3,718	45	43.8
Tabasco	1,749	600	12	34.3
Veracruz	6,735	3,118	33	46.3
VIII. PENINSULA	2,901	1,801	18	62.1
Campeche	642	340	4	52.9
Quintana Roo	703	494	5	70.3
Yucatán	1,556	967	9	62.2

Sources: For 1970–1990, Garza and Rivera 1995: 29; for 1995, Consejo Nacional de Población.
[1] Urban population as percentage of total population.

Metropolitan Concentration and the Preeminence of Mexico City, 1970–1980 Mexico's urban population in 1970 numbered 23.8 million, distributed in 166 cities (localities with 15,000 or more inhabitants), and these individuals accounted for 49.4 percent of the country's total population. In order to analyze the level of concentration in the urban system, the total number of cities has been divided here into small cities (15,000 to 49,999 inhabitants), midsize cities (50,000 to 499,999), and large cities (500,000 or more inhabitants). Mexico's urban system in 1970 was characterized by a high concentration of population in four large cities (Mexico City, Guadalajara, Monterrey, and Puebla), which together accounted for 52.0 percent of the total urban population (see table 13.3). This system was dominated by Mexico City, which accounted for 38.1 percent of the national urban population. With 9.1 million inhabitants, it was six times larger than the second-largest city.

In 1980, at the end of Mexico's economic boom, 37.6 million people (56.2 percent of the nation's population) lived in a system of 229 cities. Puebla had joined the ranks of cities with a million or more inhabitants, and four others had reached the 500,000 mark. Metropoles thus increased their share of the country's urban population to 58.1 percent, and cities with a million or more inhabitants accounted for 51.3 percent (see table 13.3).

Mexico's rapid economic growth between 1970 and 1980 was, then, accompanied by a significant concentration of population in a few metropoles—primarily Mexico City, which in 1980 reached 13 million inhabitants. Future growth in the total urban population could produce various outcomes: a more balanced urban hierarchy, a change in concentration from one metropolis to a few metropoles, or the emergence of a new megalopolitan conglomeration or polycentric urban region.

Territorial Impacts of Economic Crisis, 1980–1990 In 1990 Mexico's total urban population numbered 49.6 million, urban areas contained 60.8 percent of the total national population, and the number of cities had increased to 309. That is, economic crisis or no crisis, Mexico's urbanization process had continued unabated. Nevertheless, the crisis did have two notable spatial impacts: the rate of urbanization in 1990 was only 0.8 percent, the lowest in all of the twentieth century;[12] and the proportion of the total national population living in cities with a million or more inhabitants fell to 45.0 percent. As a result, small cities

---

[12] The urbanization rate (the mean annual increase in the level of urbanization) was 1.4 percent in 1900–1910, 2.4 percent in 1910–1921, 2.7 percent in 1921–1930, 1.8 percent in 1930–1940, 3.7 percent in 1940–1950, and 2.9 percent in 1950–1960 (Unikel, Ruiz, and Garza 1976: 34).

increased their share slightly, from 10.4 to 10.8 percent. The number of large cities (500,000–999,999 inhabitants) rose from four to twelve, and their share of total population increased to 16.3 percent (table 13.3).

These numbers explain why some specialists have concluded that the 1980s marked a point of inflection, a reversal in the previous trend toward concentration and the beginning of a process of more uniform urban growth, in which midsize and small cities acquire greater importance.[13] Yet this conclusion may be premature (Garza 1999: 154). Rather than a somewhat spontaneous process of decentralization, what has occurred is a change in the scope of concentration toward megacity conglomerations and polycentric urban regions. By the 1980s, the Mexico City metropolitan area and Toluca had merged, creating a megalopolis. Between 1980 and 1990, Toluca and the MCMA increased their combined population from 13.6 million to 16.1 million. Once Cuernavaca, Puebla, Cuautla, Pachuca, and Querétaro are "annexed" toward the middle of the twenty-first century, this megacity will concentrate approximately 36.7 million people, or about 30 percent of Mexico's urban population (Garza 2000: 9).

The fact that metropoles with 500,000 or more inhabitants raised their share of the total urban population to 61.3 percent in 1990 demonstrates a trend in concentration from a single metropolitan area to several. Of the sixteen cities that ranked in this category in 1990, some fall within the Mexico City megalopolis (Puebla, Toluca, and Querétaro), two are on the border with the United States (Tijuana and Ciudad Juárez), and four are in northern border states (Monterrey, Torreón, Chihuahua, and Tampico). These urban centers could provide a counterweight to megacity conglomeration in the long term. However, Tijuana and Ciudad Juárez are isolated from the national urban system, and they are subordinated, respectively, to San Diego, California, and El Paso, Texas. The remaining conglomerations of note are Monterrey and Guadalajara. Evidently, the trend favors the continued, undisputed hegemony of the Mexico City megalopolis, balanced somewhat by the central Bajío region (with Guadalajara just to the west) and the Monterrey urban subsystem, as well as a number of isolated border and tourist cities. An analysis of the 1990–2000 period confirms this tendency.

Polycentric Concentration and Trade Liberalization, 1990–2000   In 1995, after the relative economic recovery experienced over the 1989–1994 period, Mexico's cities increased in number to 348, with a total

---

[13] See, for example, Aguilar, Graizbord, and Sánchez 1996; Aguilar and Rodríguez Hernández 1995; Arroyo 1993; CONAPO 1994; Graizbord 1988; Lemus Gas 1994; Navarrete and Vera Bolaños 1994; Ruiz Chiapetto 1994.

TABLE 13.3. Distribution of Mexico's Urban Population by City Size, 1970–2000

	Urban Total	Small			Medium			Large[1]		
		15,000–19,999	20,000–49,999	Subtotal	50,000–99,999	100,000–499,999	Subtotal	500,000–999,999	1,000,000 or More	Subtotal
1970										
Population (000s)	23,828	707	1,950	2,657	1,510	7,284	8,794	732	11,645	12,377
Percentage	100.0	3.0	8.2	11.2	6.3	30.5	36.8	3.1	48.9	52.0
Cities[2]	166	41	65	106	21	35	56	1	3	4
Degree[3]	49.4									
Rate[4]	1.8									
1980										
Population (000s)	37,584	1,010	2,876	3,886	1,633	10,230	11,863	2,553	19,282	21,835
Percentage	100.0	2.7	7.7	10.4	4.3	27.2	31.5	6.8	51.3	58.1
Cities[2]	229	59	94	153	24	44	68	4	4	8
Degree[3]	56.2									
Rate[4]	1.3									

1990										
Population (000s)	49,604	1,386	3,937	5,323	2,800	11,070	13,870	8,076	22,335	30,411
Percentage	100.0	2.8	8.0	10.8	5.6	22.3	27.9	16.3	45.0	61.3
Cities[2]	309	78	132	210	39	44	83	12	4	16
Degree[3]	60.8									
Rate[4]	0.8									
1995										
Population (000s)	58,643	1,494	4,482	5,976	3,034	9,884	12,918	12,042	27,707	39,749
Percentage	100.0	2.5	7.6	10.1	5.2	16.9	22.0	20.5	47.2	67.8
Cities[2]	348	87	152	239	42	43	85	18	6	24
Degree[3]	64.3									
Rate[4]	1.2									
2000										
Population (000s)	64,673	1,265	4,877	6,142	3,342	11,044	14,386	11,069	33,076	44,145
Percentage	100.0	2.0	7.5	9.5	5.2	17.1	22.2	17.1	51.1	68.3
Cities[2]	362	74	167	241	48	47	95	17	9	26
Degree[3]	66.3									
Rate[4]	1.0									

TABLE 13.3. continued

Sources: For 1970–1990, Garza and Rivera 1995:5; for 1995, Consejo Nacional de Población; for 2000, XII Censo General de Población y Vivienda, INEGI. Garza and Rivera give the number of cities in 1990 as 309, although only 305 are reported here. In the present work, four metropolitan areas were adjusted: El Pueblito was added to Querétaro; Ramos Arizpe to Saltillo; Santa Cruz Xoxocotlán to Oaxaca; and Tizayuca, Hidalgo, to Mexico City.

[1] Of the twenty-four large cities in 1995, six with more than 500,000 inhabitants are not conventionally considered to be metropolitan zones because they are located in one municipality. They are: Ciudad Juárez, Chihuahua (995,770 inhabitants); Acapulco, Guerrero (592,528); Mexicali, Baja California (505,016); Morelia, Michoacán (505,518); Culiacán, Sinaloa (512,169); and Hermosillo, Sonora (504,909).

[2] Localities with more than 15,000 inhabitants.

[3] Urban population as a percentage of total population.

[4] Average yearly increase in the degree of urbanization. The 1970 rate is for 1960–1970, and so on.

population of 58.6 million people. The country's degree of urbanization rose to 64.3 percent, and the annual rate of growth in urbanization increased to 1.2 percent (see table 13.3). Over the same period, Mexico's total population rose from 81.2 million to 91.2 million. Of the 10 million new inhabitants, 9.1 million lived in cities. In other words, 91 percent of the demographic expansion occurred in urban Mexico.

The number of small cities rose to 239 in 1995, and they added 0.8 million inhabitants. Midsize cities increased to 85 in number, but their population decreased by 0.7 million. And large cities, which now numbered 24, increased their total population by 8.3 million inhabitants. By 1995, megacities accounted for 67.8 percent of the national urban population, whereas midsize cities' share dropped to 22.0 percent and that of small cities decreased slightly to 10.1 percent. Thus, between 1990 and 1995, Mexico's urban development occurred basically in the 24 existing metropoles, consolidating the pattern of polycentric concentration.

Polycentric concentration advanced in 1995 by increasing to six the number of cities with a million or more inhabitants. It merits noting that the Mexico City metropolitan area (Mexico City and Toluca) raised its annual growth rate to 1.9 percent in 1995, reaching 17.9 million inhabitants and consolidating its position as a megacity center.

The dynamic characteristic of Mexico's 24 large cities repeated the scenario noted in the preceding decade. Tijuana and Ciudad Juárez presented the highest growth rates, due primarily to their position as in-bond assembly enclaves linked with the U.S. economy. However, they remained isolated in terms of Mexico's national urban system.[14] Cuernavaca, Querétaro, and Toluca ranked third, fourth, and sixth, respectively, in rate of growth. Toluca was already integrated into the MCMA, and the other two were in the process of being so integrated. León, which forms part of the polycentric Center-West region anchored by Guadalajara, also displayed accelerated growth. Saltillo grew by 3.3 percent, while Monterrey (with which Saltillo is articulated) grew at an annual rate of 2.7 percent in 1990–1995.

By the year 2000, Mexico's urban population reached 64.7 million, distributed in an urban hierarchy of 362 cities. The national population expanded by 6.3 million people over the 1995-2000 period, and the urban population grew by 6.0 million. This signified that 95 percent of the

---

[14] This analysis of Mexico's urbanization process is limited to the national territory. The situation of border cities like Tijuana and Ciudad Juárez argues for a binational approach that would include U.S. border cities. Such a focus exceeds the scope of this chapter, but many excellent works are available that adopt this approach. See, for example, Alegría 1992; Gondard and Revel-Mournoz 1995; Herzog 1991; Rubin-Kurtzman 1996.

country's total demographic growth occurred in the urban sector. The cities of Torreón, Toluca, and Ciudad Juárez joined the ranks of metropolises with a million or more inhabitants, and large cities' share of the total urban population rose to 66.3 percent (see table 13.3).

Mexico's insertion into the global economy in the late 1980s and throughout the 1990s produced rapid changes in the structure of the national economy, in the centralization of capital, and in the ownership of companies, with foreign investors moving quickly to acquire majority control in many areas. However, this economic metamorphosis did not change the polycentric concentration pattern. A dialectic of regional inequalities persisted, and Mexico's spatial organization was still dominated by three hegemonic, polycentric regions—the megalopolis of Mexico City; the Center-West, anchored by Guadalajara; and the Northeast, with Monterrey as its principal hub.

Given the close relationship that exists between economic development and urbanization, one can expect that this process of population concentration in three urban polycentric regions would be accompanied by a similar agglomeration of production. The following section examines GDP distribution by city in order to add another key variable to the analysis of spatial disparities.

Services Concentration in Major Cities, 1985–1993

Most research on territorial disparities in Mexico has focused on regions and states. However, given the growing economic and demographic hegemony of the urban sector, the city offers a better unit of analysis for understanding the evolution of such inequalities. The only study known to have adopted this focus for Mexico concluded that, between 1970 and 1990, urban disparities decreased in the manufacturing sector and increased in the commerce and services sectors. The result was greater overall concentration of GDP in the system of 125 cities studied (Garza and Rivera 1995: 56–57). Pursuing this same line of investigation, this section compares the evolution of GDP in the manufacturing, commerce, and services sectors in 112 cities between 1985 and 1993 (see table 13.4).

In these cities, GDP in these three sectors accounted for 91.3 percent of the national value of the sectors, which, in turn, represented 76.6 percent of total GDP and approximately 70 percent of the national economy. In 1985 Mexico City concentrated 39.2 percent of national GDP for the three sectors under consideration: 30.9 percent of manufacturing GDP, 36.4 percent of commerce GDP, and 46.2 percent of services GDP. Adding the percentages for the four cities that followed in importance (Monterrey, Guadalajara, Toluca, and Puebla), the concentrations rose to 56.8 percent of total national GDP and 50.0, 51.2, and 60.1 percent, respectively, for the three sectors.[15] And adding the ten cities with a GDP between 1 and 2 percent of national GDP, the share of total national GDP reached 67.5 percent. In other words, these fifteen cities were the main focal points within the national economy; Mexico's other 97 cities had very limited economic bases.[16]

In 1993, Mexico City's share of national GDP dropped to 36.9 percent (manufacturing GDP fell to 32.2 percent; commerce and services GDP rose, respectively, to 36.7 and 47.1 percent). Because of an overconcentration in the services sector, Mexico City accounted for almost half of the activity nationwide in that sector.

A similar picture emerged for Mexico's five major cities, whose total GDP dropped to 55.1 percent of the nation's total, while the share for the commerce sector increased to 53.6 percent and that for services rose to 62.1 percent.[17] Furthermore, if the ten cities with a GDP share between 1 and 2 percent are added, the fifteen cities together increased their share of GDP to 68.2 percent, 0.7 points above the 1985 level. It merits noting that the share of manufacturing GDP accounted for by this group of cities fell from 73.2 percent in 1985 to 68.7 percent in 1993, whereas their share of commerce GDP increased from 57.7 to 64.3 percent and their share in services rose from 65.4 to 71.4 percent.[18]

Taken as a group, the 112 cities exhibited a variance coefficient of 4.56 in 1985 and 4.25 in 1993, which indicates a trend toward a reduction of economic disparities among cities during that period. However, this decrease was due solely to the decentralization of manufacturing, given that the commerce coefficient increased from 4.21 to 4.23 and the services coefficient increased from 5.0 to 5.13 between 1985 and 1993 (see table 13.2).

Thus some sectors experienced a decline in economic inequality across the national urban system at the same time that others saw an increase in inequality. Nevertheless, in 1993 economic overconcentration still dominated in Mexico's five major metropoles, which together concentrated 55.1 percent of national GDP in commerce and services (Mexico City alone concentrated 41.2 percent). To the extent that Mexico replicates the "services-sector revolution" that characterized industrialized countries during the second half of the twentieth century, the trend in its national

---

[15] Author's estimates from data in table 13.4.

[16] Nuevo Laredo, Durango, and Oaxaca represented only 0.3, 0.3, and 0.2 percent, respectively, of total output in the three sectors.

[17] Author's estimates from data in table 13.4.

[18] Author's estimates from data in table 13.4.

TABLE 13.4. Mexico's Gross Domestic Product by Main Cities and Sectors, 1985 and 1993 (millions of 1993 pesos)

Cities	Gross Domestic Product, 1985[1]				Gross Domestic Product, 1993			
	Total	Manufacturing	Commerce	Services	Total	Manufacturing	Commerce	Services
National total	258,244.8	145,435.8	76,585.1	36,223.9	378,707.6	185,191.8	107,997.9	85,517.9
Cities total	231,559.7	128,878.2	68,676.4	34,005.1	345,674.4	167,385.4	98,051.0	80,238.0
Mexico City[2]	101,275.6	56,681.6	27,873.8	16,720.2	139,594.2	59,714.2	39,612.0	40,267.8
Monterrey[2]	20,353.6	13,837.8	4,089.4	2,426.4	28,461.3	15,017.2	7,007.8	6,436.4
Guadalajara[2]	14,389.0	7,701.7	4,829.3	1,858.1	24,417.6	12,484.1	7,815.0	4,118.6
Puebla[2]	6,797.2	4,576.0	1,628.4	592.8	7,802.2	3,973.5	2,288.4	1,540.3
Minatitlán[2]	4,071.7	3,898.6	126.0	47.1	2,964.4	2,747.6	140.5	76.3
Toluca[2]	3,871.6	2,934.6	763.6	173.3	8,251.4	6,349.3	1,185.4	716.7
Saltillo[2]	3,174.8	2,688.9	321.7	164.3	4,536.7	3,400.7	602.3	533.8
Querétaro[2]	3,147.9	2,388.9	570.9	188.1	4,390.1	2,588.7	1,036.4	765.1
Monclova[2]	3,077.6	2,641.5	360.0	76.1	1,418.9	854.7	266.6	297.5
Ciudad Juárez	2,970.6	1,757.9	791.7	421.0	5,748.9	3,572.4	1,033.8	1,142.7
San Luis Potosí[2]	2,852.5	1,970.8	705.0	176.7	4,941.9	3,228.7	1,099.6	613.6
Veracruz[2]	2,828.3	1,565.0	952.8	310.6	2,911.9	824.7	1,128.6	958.5
Coatzacoalcos[2]	2,776.2	2,162.0	441.1	173.1	4,780.7	4,075.8	422.6	282.3
Tampico[2]	2,666.7	1,541.9	775.0	349.9	3,552.9	1,989.8	873.3	689.8
Torreón[2]	2,556.3	1,194.5	1,020.6	341.2	5,111.8	2,795.9	1,438.3	877.5

Hermosillo	2,480.9	503.1	1,346.2	631.7	3,600.5	1,813.0	1,170.4	617.1
Tijuana	2,475.2	747.7	1,031.4	696.1	5,527.1	2,312.9	1,730.7	1,483.5
Cuernavaca[2]	2,464.4	1,640.5	493.1	330.7	5,397.5	3,879.0	866.3	652.2
León[2]	2,284.5	908.9	1,075.4	300.3	5,119.5	2,226.6	1,964.3	928.6
Mérida[2]	2,066.3	632.2	1,059.4	374.7	3,697.6	1,370.9	1,475.3	851.4
Mexicali	2,042.0	790.6	909.4	342.0	3,000.8	1,203.9	1,115.9	681.0
Chihuahua[2]	2,036.7	717.9	1,063.1	255.7	3,976.8	1,832.1	1,407.8	736.9
Matamoros	1,778.7	1,160.0	505.5	113.2	2,277.2	1,514.4	455.0	307.8
Culiacán	1,665.8	398.8	1,069.4	197.6	2,161.2	444.8	1,088.7	627.8
Salamanca	1,651.6	1,491.1	117.4	43.1	1,895.2	1,594.4	183.5	117.3
Celaya[2]	1,553.9	858.9	585.9	109.1	2,406.1	1,395.2	597.9	413.0
Acapulco	1,516.0	93.6	545.8	876.7	2,037.0	306.1	924.1	806.8
Reynosa[2]	1,335.6	702.2	498.7	134.6	1,828.4	986.9	486.2	355.3
Aguascalientes[2]	1,325.8	668.6	446.0	211.2	3,331.3	1,882.9	872.3	576.1
Ciudad Obregón	1,091.8	312.2	604.8	174.9	1,469.8	513.4	640.1	316.2
Mazatlán	1,006.7	272.6	417.6	316.5	1,312.2	410.6	465.9	435.8
Ensenada	927.4	502.0	282.9	142.5	1,320.0	494.9	484.0	341.1
Villahermosa	897.7	258.9	503.1	135.7	2,156.1	807.3	891.3	457.5
Orizaba[2]	882.2	637.8	169.9	74.6	1,759.7	1,437.5	210.6	111.5
Los Mochis[2]	830.0	341.4	384.7	103.8	1,214.5	421.4	574.4	218.7
Durango	812.7	238.3	479.0	95.4	1,178.2	374.1	496.3	307.7

TABLE 13.4 continued

Cancún	778.7	33.3	221.7	523.6	2,217.5	150.6	661.2	1,405.6
Irapuato	693.8	254.5	324.5	114.9	1,132.1	502.5	430.9	198.7
Morelia[2]	672.3	162.0	359.1	151.1	1,825.4	631.8	795.0	398.5
Salina Cruz	668.0	576.2	71.4	20.5	2,982.1	2,883.2	52.8	46.1
Nuevo Laredo	660.0	84.0	291.1	284.9	1,415.3	619.7	274.1	521.5
San Juan del Río	657.6	546.8	82.2	28.6	1,301.4	961.4	120.3	219.7
Tepic[2]	599.6	189.8	309.4	100.4	969.2	421.9	362.8	184.4
Tuxtla Gutiérrez	517.9	31.7	398.5	87.6	891.0	91.2	671.3	128.6
Xalapa[2]	497.1	82.7	322.2	92.1	1,361.9	473.8	446.0	442.0
Oaxaca[2]	489.8	67.8	330.4	91.6	987.5	194.9	457.3	335.2
Pachuca[2]	326.2	126.4	155.8	44.0	777.9	235.2	341.5	201.2
Tehuacán	278.5	145.5	100.3	32.6	846.6	439.1	304.1	103.4
Poza Rica[2]	245.6	15.3	176.3	54.0	806.7	428.2	277.9	100.6
Lázaro Cárdenas	99.8	112.0[3]	77.9	48.0	1,399.3	1,159.8	106.7	132.7
Remaining 62 main cities[4]	14,439.4	5,169.4	6,617.5	2,652.4	21,209.0	7,352.5	8,697.1	5,159.4
Statistical measures								
Mean	2,120.1	1,183.6	629.4	316.5	3,153.5	1,523.1	897.1	741.7
Standard deviation	9,679.6	5,482.0	2,648.7	1,579.7	13,402.5	5,861.6	3,794.5	3,806.2
Coefficient of variation	4.56	4.63	4.21	5.00	4.25	3.85	4.23	5.13

Sources: Industrial, commercial, and service-sector censuses, 1986 and 1994.

Note: The table contains data for 50 cities from a sample of 112 urban areas. Data for the remaining 62 cities are reported in combined form at the bottom of the table.

[1] The gross domestic product implicit deflator for 1985 values is 0.04956.

[2] Metropolitan area; that is, cities located in more than one municipality.

[3] Food and drinks production and "other manufacturing activities" are excluded from this calculation; including them would have yielded a negative aggregate value of -26.1.

[4] Mean, standard deviation, and coefficient of variation were calculated taking into account the individual values for each of the 62 cities.

city system toward a pattern of economic concentration in a few metropoles will be reinforced.[19]

THE END OF DECENTRALIZATION POLICIES

Urban and regional planning in Mexico evolved through five phases
during the twentieth century: (1) the emergence of pioneering planning
actions, 1915–1940; (2) policies with isolated territorial impact, 1940–
1970; (3) regional policies coordinated with a national economic strategy, 1970–1976; (4) institutionalization of spatial planning, 1977–1988;
and (5) abdication of authority and devolution of urban and regional
policy making, beginning in 1989.[20] The present study focuses on the
last of these periods, with the analysis covering the years up to 1994.[21]

This period began with the administration of President Carlos
Salinas de Gortari (1988–1994), when the Mexican government adopted
neoliberal policies that included privatization of the banking system, a
massive sell-off of state-owned enterprises, and the implementation of
the North American Free Trade Agreement. As part of the reduction in
the federal government's sphere of action, some urban and regional
planning authority was devolved to state and municipal governments.
Mexico's federal planning law still requires the preparation of plans
and programs, although these have tended to be more rhetorical or
"virtual" than real.

National-level urban planning was "virtual" in preceding periods as
well, in the sense that policies were ineffectual in influencing the layout
and development of the nation's cities.[22] But the real phase of virtual
urban and regional policies began with the dissolution of the Ministry

---

[19] Foreign direct investment (FDI) in Mexico between 1994 and 1997 totaled US$28.2
billion; 62.0 percent went to the Federal District, 4.0 percent to the State of México,
and 12.6 percent to Nuevo León, for a total for these three states of 78.6 percent of
FDI (*Reforma*, January 12, 1998). Furthermore, of the 273 Japanese firms in Mexico,
52.7 percent are located in the Federal District and 8.1 percent in the State of
México; that is, the MCMA contains 60.6 percent of Japanese investment in Mexico (*El Financiero*, February, 25, 1999). This strong tendency toward high investment concentration in central Mexico will continue into the foreseeable future.

[20] This section was adapted from Garza 1999: 156–65.

[21] For an evaluation of the first four stages, see Garza 1986, 1992, 1999; Garza and
Puente 1992.

[22] Nevertheless, some urban plans were partially implemented and enjoyed important financial and institutional support. One example was the construction of more
than a hundred industrial parks, although that project fell short of its original
goal.

of Urban Development and Ecology (SEDUE) in May 1992. This period continued throughout the presidency of Ernesto Zedillo (1994–2000), which carried forward the policies of the Salinas government.

The Salinas administration published its 1989–1994 National Development Plan on May 31, 1989, the last day allowed by law. The plan's stated goals were economic growth through price stability and an improved living standard for the population (Poder Ejecutivo Federal 1989: 16). Its final chapter specified the need to design twenty-one sectoral programs (twenty-three were ultimately published; see Garza 1999: 162), all of which had clear implications for cities and regions. The following discussion focuses on two of these programs: the National Urban Development Program, 1990–1994 (PNDU), and the 100 Cities Program, which derived from the former. It is important to note that governmental initiatives with territorial impact were implemented through the National Solidarity Program (PRONASOL), the signature instrument of the Salinas administration.

The National Solidarity Program, 1988

President Salinas outlined the National Solidarity Program on his first day in office; it was published in December 1988, six months before the National Development Plan. PRONASOL was designed to mitigate the deleterious impacts of the post–1982 economic crisis and of the new liberalization strategy, which was deepening social inequalities through growing unemployment and underemployment and a precipitous contraction in real wages.[23] In its attack on poverty, PRONASOL aimed to: improve health, nutrition, education, housing, basic services, and access to land; create employment by supporting agricultural, agro-industrial, microindustrial, and fishery activities; and implement regional infrastructure development programs (SHCP 1992: 463).[24]

Under PRONASOL the federal government promoted sixteen regional programs[25] to be implemented at the state and municipal levels. It is not possible to describe, much less evaluate, each one. However, it can be noted in general terms that each of these programs specified a series of priority actions — a certain infrastructure or policy objective to

---

[23] One innovation was PRONASOL's incorporation of citizen participation in order to guarantee openness in the use of resources.

[24] Important infrastructure projects supported by PRONASOL included the paving of streets and sidewalks, the installation of street lighting, the rehabilitation of public squares, self-built housing, the regularization of land tenure, and road construction and maintenance (SHCP 1992: 475–77).

[25] For more on these programs, see Garza 1999: 162

be established, modernized, supported, or strengthened (SHCP 1995). Because the orientation of regional-level social actions came from the center, the programs were not in fact "regional," and territorial disparities remained almost the same despite the PRONASOL initiative.[26]

The National Urban Development Program, 1990–1994

The Salinas administration presented the National Urban Development Program (PNDU) in August 1990, the third instrument of its kind in Mexican history. It included diagnoses, objectives, strategies, targets, and instruments that pertained to altering the country's system of cities and urban services (SEDUE 1990: 3–4). Objectives were subdivided into those relating to territorial patterns and those dealing with improvements in public services.

These objectives, which accorded with Mexico's earlier urban development plans, were: to promote a less concentrated distribution of cities; to channel economic activity toward optimal locations while discouraging areas of overpopulation; to consolidate urban-regional systems as an alternative to Mexico City; to build up midsize cities; and to regulate the growth of metropolitan areas. The PNDU specified that the urban population should have necessary services and infrastructure, provided by the coordinated efforts of social and private actors working in a manner consistent with the purposes of urban reorganization (SEDUE 1990: 32–33).[27]

The strategy for territorial reorganization set forth three lines of action: development of high-potential urban subsystems, consolidation of linkages, and distribution of services by rank order. To achieve these ends, cities were ranked as follows: cities to be regulated (Mexico City, Guadalajara, Monterrey); those to be consolidated (Puebla); midsize cities to be consolidated (León, Irapuato, Guanajuato, Toluca, Cuernavaca, Pachuca, Jalapa, Querétaro, Ciudad Juárez, Acapulco); and midsize cities in the process of industrialization (almost all Mexico–U.S. border cities and the major cities of most states not included in one of the preceding categories). Strengthening linkages referred to improved communications among the city groups listed above. The delivery of services involved ranking cities in four categories: 17 regional centers; 32 state centers; 44 subregional centers; and 111 urban-rural integration centers (SEDUE 1990: 44–51). Regardless of the strategy's overall valid-

---

[26] For more on PRONASOL's financing and its achievements, see Garza 1999: 161.

[27] A comparison of the objectives of the urban development programs for 1978, 1984, and 1990 appears in Aguilar, Graizbord, and Sánchez 1996: 114–21.

ity, its implementation depended upon setting specific targets and the instruments available.

Targets cannot be set without detailed measurements and forecasts of urban development. In this regard, the 1990–1994 PNDU proved sorely lacking. It predicted that Mexico's urban population would increase by 14.7 million over the course of the 1990s (SEDUE 1990: 65). Yet, based on the results of the 1995 population census, the urban population actually increased by about 17.4 million. Any future urban development plan should include different projections concerning the urban structure of each city, and it should identify the factors that determine the location of economic activities that must be controlled if territorial organization is to be modified. In the absence of such forecasts, targets can only be general recommendations.[28]

In sum, the 1990–1994 PNDU contained serious technical and methodological limitations, which explains why its directives did not extend beyond the Ministry of Urban Development and Ecology. Unlike PRONASOL, the PNDU received no special financing, primarily because it was overshadowed by the former program. This situation was reinforced by two events. One was the 100 Cities Program; the second was the disappearance of SEDUE and its replacement in May 1992 by the Ministry of Social Development (SEDESOL). SEDESOL formalized the federal government's social welfare assistance to mitigate poverty, and it ended the brief and fruitless stage of institutionalizing urban planning that had been initiated in 1976 with the creation of the Ministry of Human Settlements and Public Works (SAHOP).

Given a total lack of financial and political support, the PNDU could not reduce regional inequalities. Since the early 1990s, then, the location of economic activities has been governed primarily by market forces, which have tended toward a concentration of services in Mexico City and a relative decentralization of manufacturing activities.

The 100 Cities Program, 1992

The general pattern of disregard for the PNDU in government circles was broken when Luis Donaldo Colosio, then minister of social development and a leading contender for the governing Institutional Revolutionary Party's (PRI) presidential nomination in the 1994 election, resurrected and implemented a program focused on Mexico's midsize cities.

Like the PNDU, the 100 Cities Program (P-100-1992) recommended that Mexico's decentralization effort should focus on the nation's 116

---

[28] See, for example, SEDUE 1990: 67–68, 71–73.

midsize cities.[29] The 100 Cities Program claimed as its principal achievement the empowerment of local governments to regulate urban development, with technical assistance from SEDESOL (SEDESOL 1994: 15).[30] Despite the theoretical advantages of decentralization in adjusting the supply of public services to demand, more than ten years after municipal governments were granted this authority there had been no planning, even at the metropolitan level.[31] The goal of P–100–1992 was to resolve this problem.

One specific function of the 100 Cities Program was to help local governments modernize their property registers for taxation purposes. The Property Registry Modernization Program was established in August 1992 under SEDESOL auspices. Between 1993 and 1996, thirty-two property registers were updated. In almost a third of these cases, the areas were mapped using geographic information system technology (SEDESOL 1997: 23).

In 1993 and 1994, a total of 4,584 hectares were set aside for future urbanization in the midsize cities targeted by the 100 Cities Program, along with an additional 468 hectares in other localities (SEDESOL 1994: appendix). From 1990 to 1995, Mexico's urban population increased by 1.8 million annually, adding 3.6 million inhabitants in the two years when the future urbanization areas were set aside. Assuming an average of seventy inhabitants per hectare, these land reserves could meet the needs of only 9.7 percent of the individuals added to the urban population over a two-year period.

The Zedillo administration continued the 100 Cities Program, updating plans for 24 urban development projects, 16 historical centers, and 465 infrastructure projects. However, the true magnitude of the program can best be judged by the federal funds allocated to it. The 100 Cities Program received 192 million pesos in 1995, 361 million in 1996, and 385 million in 1997 (in constant 1995 pesos). In contrast, PRONASOL received 7.4 billion pesos, on average, during each of its first five years in operation. In the 1997 federal budget, the allocation for the 100 Cities Program equaled only 5.2 percent of the PRONASOL allocation, possibly reflecting the Zedillo administration's focus on sectoral and economic adjustment programs at the expense of urban and regional instruments.

---

[29] A total of 309 cities comprised the national urban system in 1990.

[30] For a detailed description of the 100 Cities Program, see SEDESOL 1994; Comité Preparatorio de México 1996: 65–69.

[31] The inefficiency of local bureaucracies has been a major obstacle to the allocation of federal funds among Mexico's municipalities (see Prud'homme 1994).

CONCLUSION

In principle, macroeconomic adjustment and insertion into the global economy may have significant impacts on regions and cities, not all of which are equally well positioned to become internationally competitive (Harris 1996: 2–3). The ability to become competitive depends upon the speed of modernization and diversification of economic activity, geographic location, the evolutionary stage of the business community and labor market, research and development capacity, and the flexibility and efficiency of governmental institutions, among other factors. Combining these considerations with the present analysis of inequalities in urban Mexico from 1970 to 1999 allows us to anticipate some likely trends.

The dynamics of regional disparities result from a complex historical interweaving of the determinants of the spatial location of economic activities and population. Most salient among them are the distribution of natural resources, technological developments in the production and distribution of goods, existing urban and regional policies, the distribution of public investment, trends and fluctuations in national economic activity, the strategies of multinational firms, and, in general, trends in international financial markets and the global processes in which Mexico is inserted. This reality more than justifies the use of the term *dialectic* when referring to the territorial restructuring process. However, in attempting to understand this process, we should also take note of the methodological difficulties involved in selecting units for analysis and the challenge of differentiating the impacts of the various factors that influence the process.

Although there was a slight easing of regional disparities in Mexico between 1970 and 1999, a high concentration of economic activity still prevailed at the end of the period, with 41.7 percent of national production taking place in the Center-East region, where Mexico City is the major metropolis. An examination of the states' relative shares of national GDP over this same period reveals that the slight reduction in inequalities that occurred does not reflect the elimination of Mexico's typical pattern of urban concentration so much as its extension into the states surrounding the Mexico City metropolitan area, giving birth to a new megalopolitan concentration.

Although the six Mexican states that border the United States decreased their share of national GDP between 1970 and 1988, they registered an increase between 1993 and 1999, indicating a pattern of rapid growth. However, as the maquiladora industry's tax advantages fade and ultimately disappear under the NAFTA's provisions, these border states will have to develop new strategies to exploit their favorable location vis-à-vis the United States and Canada.

For these reasons, it is still too early to assess the territorial impact of Mexico's economic liberalization strategy and increasing integration into the North American bloc. But an analysis of GDP distribution among regions and states from 1970 to 1999 shows that, at least until the end of the twentieth century, no significant impact could be observed.

Adopting cities as units for spatial disparities analysis revealed that between 1970 and 2000 an urban system based on the primacy of Mexico City evolved toward a polycentric concentration in four other metropolitan areas, all closely linked in an emerging cluster around Mexico City. This pattern will likely become consolidated in upcoming decades. The only cities able to compete with the Mexico City metropolitan area are Guadalajara and Monterrey. The latter is also the most important city in the "NAFTA corridor" connecting Mexico City with U.S. Interstate 35, the highway that runs north from Laredo, Texas. Thus Monterrey—together with its subsystem of Saltillo, Nuevo Laredo, Reynosa, and Matamoros—can be expected to become a very dynamic pole of economic growth.

The analysis of GDP in 112 cities between 1985 and 1993 seems to confirm the tendency toward metropolitan concentration. It revealed a decline in economic differences among cities in terms of their manufacturing activities but increasing disparities with respect to commerce and services. Nevertheless, economic overconcentration persists in Mexico's five major cities (particularly in Mexico City), which together concentrated 55.1 percent of national GDP in manufacturing, commerce, and services. As Mexico marches toward a services revolution, the concentration in major urban centers will tend to consolidate. This process will be shaped primarily by policies adopted at the level of state governments, as well as by the federal government's ability to design a functioning territorial paradigm to support enterprises with the potential to compete in the global marketplace.

Under the neoliberal model, however, the trend toward an urban system dominated by a few large cities has deepened, and it may gain speed with the spread of laissez-faire urban policies. Thus, despite dozens of urban and regional plans, programs, and individual actions taken by the federal government since the 1970s, a recent study by the Organisation for Economic Co-operation and Development (OECD) concludes, "Mexico does not, strictly speaking, have a regional policy but *national policies with strong territorial implications*, such as social, training or R&D policies" (OECD 1997: 9). In fact, in the 1990s the federal government renounced its leadership in urban development planning in the belief that the market could control land use and build basic infrastructure. At the same time, the central government gave state and local governments authority over urban planning in their respective jurisdictions.

However, this strategy is flawed. It will lead to a dysfunctional urban system, and it will increase regional inequalities. These inequalities, in turn, will hinder sustained economic development, for the following reasons. First, the spatial organization of economic activity and population settlements cannot be regulated through market mechanisms because of significant externalities that do not show up in the price system. Second, it will be a long time before state governments are able and willing to undertake urban and regional planning responsibilities. And third, the notable failure of privately financed highways during the 1990s clearly demonstrates the limitations encountered when trying to marry public works to a private business approach (Garza 1999: 168).

Laissez-faire urban policies, combined with economic globalization, will intensify the concentration of population and economic activity in two or three polycentric regions dominated by the Mexico City metropolitan area. Mexico's federal government should not abdicate its planning functions with respect to the national landscape. Such a move would exacerbate urban and regional inequalities, jeopardize the country's long-term economic well-being, and deepen social inequities.

REFERENCES

Aguilar, Adrián Guillermo, Boris Graizbord, and Álvaro Sánchez. 1996. *Las ciudades intermedias y el desarrollo regional en México*. Mexico City: Consejo Nacional para la Cultura y las Artes/El Colegio de México/Instituto de Geografía, Universidad Nacional Autónoma de México.

Aguilar, Adrián Guillermo, and Francisco Rodríguez Hernández. 1995. "Tendencias de desconcentración urbana en México, 1970–1990." In *El desarrollo urbano de México a fines del siglo XX*, edited by Adrián Guillermo Aguilar et al. Mexico: Instituto de Estudios Urbanos de Nuevo León/ Sociedad Mexicana de Demografía.

Alegría, Tito. 1992. *Desarrollo urbano en la frontera México–Estados Unidos: una interpretación y algunos resultados*. Mexico City: Consejo Nacional para la Cultura y las Artes.

Appendini, Kirsten Albrechtsen, et al. 1972. "Desarrollo desigual en México," *Demografía y economía* 6 (1): 1–39.

Arroyo, Jesús. 1993. "Migración hacia los Estados Unidos, desarrollo de ciudades medias y la política de liberalización económica: el caso de Jalisco." In *Impactos regionales de la apertura comercial, perspectivas del Tratado de Libre Comercio en Jalisco*, edited by Jesús Arroyo. Mexico: Universidad de Guadalajara.

Barkin, David. 1972. *Los beneficiarios del desarrollo regional*. Mexico City: Secretaría de Educación Pública.

———. 1978. *Desarrollo regional y reorganización campesina: la Chontalpa como reflejo del problema agropecuario mexicano*. Mexico: Centro de Ecodesarrollo.

Comité Preparatorio de México (for the United Nations Summit on Cities, Habitat II). 1996. *Informe nacional*. Mexico City: Secretaría de Desarrollo Social.

CONAPO (Consejo Nacional de Población). 1994. *Evolución de las ciudades en México, 1990*. Mexico City: CONAPO.

Garza, Gustavo. 1980. *Industrialización de las principales ciudades de México*. Mexico City: El Colegio de México.

———. 1985. *El proceso de industrialización en la ciudad de México, 1821–1970*. Mexico City: El Colegio de México.

———. 1986. "Planeación urbana en México en período de crisis (1983–1984)," *Estudios Demográficos y Urbanos* 1 (1): 73–96.

———. 1999. "Global Economy, Metropolitan Dynamics, and Urban Policies in Mexico," *Cities* 16 (3): 149–70.

———. 2000. "La megalópolis de la Ciudad de México, año 2050," *El Mercado de Valores* 60 (5): 3-9.

Garza, Gustavo, ed. 1992. *Una década de planeación urbano-regional en México, 1978–1988*. Mexico City: El Colegio de México.

Garza, Gustavo, and Sergio Puente. 1992. "Racionalidad e irracionalidad de la política urbana en México: el Plan Nacional de Desarrollo Urbano, 1978." In *Una década de planeación urbano-regional en México, 1978*–1988, edited by Gustavo Garza. Mexico City: El Colegio de México.

Garza, Gustavo, and Salvador Rivera. 1995. *Dinámica macroeconómica de las ciudades en México*. Mexico City: INEGI/El Colegio de México/Instituto de Investigaciones Sociales, Universidad Nacional Autónoma de México.

Gómez, Pablo, and Armando Cortés. 1987. *Experiencia histórica y promoción del desarrollo regional en México*. Mexico City: Nacional Financiera.

Gondard, Pierre, and Jean Revel-Mournoz, eds. 1995. *La frontière Méxique– Etats-Unis: mutations économiques, sociales et territoriales*. Paris: Institut des Hautes Etudes de l'Amérique Latine.

Graizbord, Boris. 1988. "Las necesidades de urbanización en el largo plazo." In *México: el desafío de largo plazo*, edited by Gerardo Bueno. Mexico City: Libreros Mexicanos Unidos, S.A.

Harris, Nigel. 1996. "Introduction." In *Cities and Structural Adjustment*, edited by Nigel Harris and Ida Fabricius. London: University College London Press.

Hernández Laos, Enrique. 1984. "La desigualdad regional en México (1900– 1980)." In *La desigualdad en México*, edited by Rolando Cordera Campos and Carlos Tello. Mexico City: Siglo Veintiuno.

Herzog, Lawrence A. 1991. "Cross-National Urban Structure in the Era of Global Cities: The U.S.–Mexico Transfrontier Metropolis," *Urban Studies* 28: 519–33.

Hiernaux, Daniel. 1995. "Globalizing Economies and Cities: A View from Mexico." In *North American Cities and the Global Economy*, edited by Peter Karl Kresl and Gary Gappert. Thousand Oaks, Calif.: Sage.

INEGI (Instituto Nacional de Estadística, Geografía e Informática). 1996. *Sistema de Cuentas Nacionales de México: producto interno bruto por entidad federativa*. Aguascalientes: INEGI.

———. 1999. *Sistema de Cuentas Nacionales de México: producto interno bruto por entidad federativa, 1993–1996*. Aguascalientes: INEGI.

Lemus Gas, Marino, ed. 1994. *Ciudades mexicanas*. Mexico City: Fundación Mexicana Cambio XXI, Luis Donaldo Colosio.

López Malo, Ernesto. 1960. *Ensayo sobre localización de la industria en México*. Mexico City: Universidad Nacional Autónoma de México.

Navarrete, Emma Liliana, and Marta G. Vera Bolaños, eds. 1994. *Población y sociedad*. Mexico: El Colegio Mexiquense/Consejo Estatal de Población del Estado de México.

OECD (Organisation for Economic Co-operation and Development). 1997. *Regional Development and Structural Policy in Mexico*. Paris: OECD.

Osuna, Germán. 1990. "Dinámica de la desigualdad regional en México, 1970–1980," *Estudios Demográficos y Urbanos* 5 (1): 5–35.

Palacios, Juan José. 1988. "Las inconsistencias de la política regional en México, 1970–1982: el caso de la asignación de la inversión pública federal," *Estudios Demográficos y Urbanos* 3 (1): 7–37.

Poder Ejecutivo Federal. 1989. *Plan Nacional de Desarrollo, 1989–1994*. Mexico City.

Prud'homme, Remy. 1994. "On the Dangers of Decentralization." Policy Research Working Paper, no. 1252. Washington, D.C.: World Bank.

Ramírez, Delfina. 1986. "Las desigualdades interregionales en México, 1970–1980," *Estudios Demográficos y Urbanos* 1 (3): 351–76.

Rubin-Kurtzman, Jane. 1996. "Population in Transborder Regions: The Southern California–Baja California Urban System," *International Migration Review* 4: 1020–45.

Ruiz Chiapetto, Crescencio. 1994. "Hacia un país urbano." In *La población en el desarrollo contemporáneo de México*, edited by Francisco Alba and Gustavo Cabrera. Mexico City: El Colegio de México.

SEDESOL (Secretaría de Desarrollo Social). 1994. *Programa de 100 ciudades: una estrategia de desarrollo urbano regional sustentable y concertado*. Mexico City: Dirección General de Desarrollo Urbano, SEDESOL.

———. 1997. "La modernización catastral en el programa de 100 ciudades," *Federalismo y Desarrollo* [Banobras] 10 (58): 21–28.

SEDUE (Secretaría de Desarrollo Urbano y Ecología). 1990. *Programa nacional de desarrollo urbano, 1990–1994*. Mexico City: SEDUE.

Sen, Amartya. 1997. *On Economic Inequality*. Oxford: Clarendon/Oxford University Press.

SHCP (Secretaría de Hacienda y Crédito Público). 1992. *Antología de la planeación en México. 22. La planeación del desarrollo en la década de los noventa*. Mexico City: SHCP/Fondo de Cultura Económica.

———. 1995. *Antología de la planeación en México. 25. Programación para el desarrollo regional en los noventa*. Mexico City: SHCP/Fondo de Cultura Económica.

Unikel, Luis, Crescencio Ruiz, and Gustavo Garza. 1976. *El desarrollo urbano de México: diagnóstico e implicaciones futuras*. Mexico City: El Colegio de México.

Whetten, Nathan, L. 1948. *Rural Mexico*. Chicago: University of Chicago Press.

Zamora Millán, F. 1959. *Diagnóstico económico regional*. Mexico City: Secretaría de Industria y Comercio.

14

Employment and Wages: Enduring the Costs of Liberalization and Economic Reform

Carlos Salas and Eduardo Zepeda

INTRODUCTION

As Mexico enters the twenty-first century, it continues to face a major, long-standing challenge: the need to create more jobs. The import-substitution industrialization model followed during the 1960s and 1970s did not favor labor-intensive activities, and the number of Mexicans working in the informal sector mushroomed as a result. The stabilization and structural adjustment policies adopted in the early 1980s had a deep impact on labor, but they did not improve Mexico's ability to create employment. And the trade liberalization and economic reform policies adopted in the late 1980s and early 1990s failed to deliver on one of economic opening's promised benefits—more and better-paying jobs.

This chapter reviews the evolution of urban employment and wages in Mexico from the mid–1980s through the 1990s. We contend that, on the whole, workers lost ground during this period—despite the fact that a growing number of workers were using improved technologies, were employed in globally competitive businesses, and had links to the international economy. The discussion begins with a brief review of Mexico's employment challenge. It then examines the following topics: overall trends in urban employment; wage work, job creation, and the skill mix in large, domestic-market–oriented manufacturing plants and *maquiladoras* (in-bond processing plants); sectoral responsiveness to economic reform; and regional changes in employment and wages.

The authors thank Diana Alarcón, Enrique Hernández Laos, and Kevin J. Middlebrook for their comments on an earlier draft of this chapter, and Rodrigo Milán for his research assistance.

THE EMPLOYMENT CREATION CHALLENGE

Despite recent declines in Mexico's population growth rate, high rates in past decades had by the late 1990s created a huge potential labor supply (people between the ages of 15 and 64). From 1970 to 1997, the potential labor supply climbed from 49 percent to 61 percent of the total population, rapidly changing Mexico's labor landscape (CONAPO 1998). Between 1991 and 2000, the population aged 12 years and older increased by an annual average of 1.4 million, and the economically active population (EAP) grew by an average of 934,000 people each year during this period. Such strong growth means that labor force participation rates soared. Among the working population, prime age rates (20 to 44 years) displayed the largest increases, with most of the overall growth explained by women's rising participation in economic activities.

Women's involvement in economic activities outside the home, which had been increasing since the 1940s, accelerated markedly after 1982 (CONAPO 1998).[1] In fact, young workers—both men and women—displaced older men from the labor force as discrimination against mature male workers hardened, especially in wage-earning occupations. In urban areas of at least 100,000 inhabitants, the entry of women aged 12 to 39 into the labor force increased the EAP's share in the total population from 53 to 56 percent between 1991 and 2000. Dependency ratios simultaneously declined as Mexico moved toward a more mature labor structure. Indeed, for large urban areas, the ratio of minors and others outside the labor force to the total labor force fell from 1.5 to 1.3 between 1991 and 2000. Although a reduction in dependency ratios presents a great opportunity for Mexico to increase income per capita, the challenge of creating sufficient jobs for the burgeoning potential labor force continues to be a major challenge.

Feminization of the labor force resulted from interrelated economic, social, and demographic forces. Women delayed marriage, birth rates dropped, and women's educational levels rose. Technological changes facilitated women's entry into the workplace by reducing the time required for household tasks and the physical strength needed for many production activities. At the same time, worsening employment conditions and falling incomes have operated as push factors, forcing women to seek employment outside the home.

---

[1] In contrast, men's labor participation rates have declined, especially in the 40- to 45-year-old age group, as young men and women have replaced male workers in the 40- to 45-year-old cohort in highly urbanized areas (CONAPO 1998; Rendón 1999).

Such rapid growth in labor supply would seem to have a parallel in the impressive growth in employment. Between 1991 and 1998, the average number of employed workers in Mexico increased by slightly less than 1.3 million per year, while unemployment remained relatively low, varying only with short-term fluctuations in economic activity. Mexico's unemployment rate countrywide was 2.2 percent in 1991 and 2.6 percent in 1997, and unemployment in urban areas measured between 2 and 3 percent from 1987 to 1999. Even among young people, unemployment rates remained low by international standards, rarely exceeding 8 percent. The highest unemployment rates corresponded to the 1994–1995 economic crisis, when overall rates exceeded 6 percent and rates for teens approached 14 percent.

It would be misleading, however, to conclude from these unemployment figures that Mexico was able to escape the employment creation problems common to most market economies. Following the standard set by the International Labour Office, Mexico considers someone to be employed if he or she worked at least one hour during the week preceding the survey. Under this definition a person is counted as employed whether working half time in a family business for no pay, or full time in a modern manufacturing plant. Yet Mexico's low rate of open unemployment is less a reflection of definitional categories than of its particular labor structure.[2] Because a large proportion of the population has no savings capacity and because there is no unemployment insurance, to be openly unemployed in Mexico is — to borrow a phrase from Gunnar Myrdal — a luxury few can afford.

The Mexican economy's inability to create good jobs is best demonstrated by the large and growing number of people holding low-productivity, low-paying jobs in urban areas. In Mexico's major cities, the proportion of workers who were self-employed or employed in businesses with fewer than five workers (the "informal sector") rose throughout the 1990s (see figure 14.1).

In sum, fed by the high population growth of previous decades and by changes in women's labor force participation, Mexico faced a critical need in the 1980s and 1990s to create jobs for a rapidly expanding labor force. The country's response was weak, and labor conditions worsened; the result was not open unemployment but an expansion of the informal sector.

---

[2] Open unemployment refers in part to frictional unemployment — that is, to people who feel certain they will be hired in the near future (Rendón and Salas 1993). For further discussion of measures of unemployment in Mexico, see Fleck and Sorrentino 1994.

FIGURE 14.1. Informal Sector Employment as a Proportion of Total
Employment in Mexico, 1987–1998

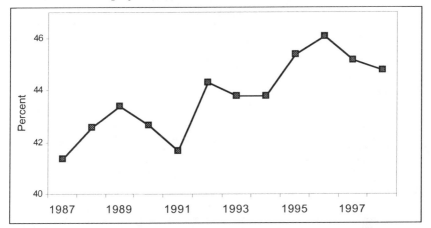

Source: Authors' calculations based on data from the Instituto Nacional de
Estadística, Geografía e Informática's employment survey, 1987–1997.

Note: The informal sector is defined as the self-employed and those working
in businesses with fewer than six workers in services and fewer than sixteen
workers in manufacturing. Data correspond to the April–June quarter of
each year.

THE URBAN LABOR FORCE

The primary trend in Mexico's urban employment during the 1990s
was the growth of the tertiary sector. Two key factors suggest that the
growing prominence of trade and service industries in Mexico's total
employment (and production) are cause for concern. First, unlike the
situation in industrialized economies, the expansion of nonindustrial
activities as a proportion of total urban employment did not include a
strong and dynamic sector of high-value-added services.[3] Instead, Mexico's tertiary sector is characterized by extreme heterogeneity—from
street peddlers to stock brokers. Second, unlike some other newly industrializing economies, Mexico's adoption of a development strategy
based on manufactured exports (primarily for the nearby U.S. market)
did not increase manufacturing's share of national employment.

---

[3] Even for financial services—an activity closely linked to privatization and new
investment—growth could be attributed largely to continued protection and a
lack of regulation, rather than to the development of highly competitive, world-
class services.

TABLE 14.1. Structure of Employment in Mexico's Urban Areas, 1991–2000 (percentages)

	1991	1998	2000
Owners	4.8	4.0	5.0
Self-employed	16.6	22.8	17.1
Wage earners	73.9	61.2	74.3
Unpaid	4.6	12.0	3.6
Other	0.1	0.1	0.0
Total	100.0	100.1	100.0

Source: Authors' calculations based on data from the Instituto Nacional de Estadística, Geografía e Informática's National Employment Survey, 1991 and 1998.

Note: Totals may not add to 100.0 because of rounding.

Mexico's urban labor landscape apparently remained unchanged over the course of the 1990s. This is the picture one obtains from comparing different occupations' share of total employment in 1991 and 2000 (see table 14.1). However, the 1994-1995 economic crisis had a profound impact upon labor markets. Indeed, the effects were still visible as late as 1998, mainly in the decline of the wage-earning proportion of the total employed population (from 73.9 to 61.2 percent) that occurred between 1991 and 1998. The proportion of self-employed workers rose by 37.3 percent, and the proportion of workers listing unpaid employment as their first occupation grew by 160.9 percent (table 14.1). The drop in the number of wage earners was particularly dramatic for women; the 1994–1995 crisis exerted strong downward pressure on the demand for female wage labor.

Patterns in wage employment shifted as well, with changes especially working against men above a certain age. The proportion of wage earners in total employment fell steadily after age 24 (see figure 14.2). In the 15- to 29-year-old cohort, women were more likely than men to hold wage-earning jobs.[4] Reductions in the proportion of wage earners affected all age groups, men and women alike, but persons younger than 20 and older than 50 were hardest hit. Changes in the age profile of different occupations suggest that older wage earners switched to self-employment while younger workers moved into unpaid positions or open unemployment.

---

[4] Most of this difference is explained by the fact that wage-earning employment creation is strongest in services, a sector that employs substantial numbers of women.

FIGURE 14.2. Type of Ocupation by Age Group in Mexico, 1998

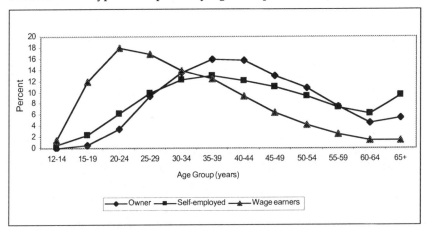

Source: Authors' calculations based on data from the Instituto Nacional de Estadística, Geografía e Informática's National Employment Survey, 1987–1997.

TABLE 14.2. Distribution of Urban Employment in Mexico by Selected Occupation and Age Group, 1991 and 1998 (percentages)

	1991	1998	Percent change, 1991–1998
Owner			
Up to 19 years of age	0.2	0.1	-0.1
50 years and older	9.7	7.5	-2.3
Wage earner			
Up to 19 years of age	78.9	63.0	-15.9
50 years and older	52.0	36.2	-15.8
Self-employed			
Up to 19 years of age	5.2	4.2	-1.0
50 years and older	34.7	49.2	14.6
Unpaid			
Up to 19 years of age	15.8	32.7	16.9
50 years and older	3.4	7.1	3.7

Source: Authors' calculations based on data from the Instituto Nacional de Estadística, Geografía e Informática's National Employment Survey, 1991 and 1998.

TABLE 14.3. Proportion of Wage-Earning, Self-Employed, and Unpaid Workers among Mexico's Employed Urban Population, by Economic Activity, 1991 and 1998 (percentages)

	Wage Earners		Self-Employed		Unpaid	
	1991	1998	1991	1998	1991	1998
Agriculture	46.2	29.2	27.3	38.8	10.2	30.0
Oil and gas	99.8	100.0	0.0	0.0	0.0	0.0
Other extractive activities	84.5	87.9	1.6	7.9	0.7	2.2
Food products	81.5	65.4	7.7	18.3	5.6	11.3
Textiles	93.8	75.7	3.9	16.7	0.8	5.7
Apparel	80.6	65.6	15.6	25.9	0.6	7.1
Leather	89.6	84.3	3.3	5.7	2.9	4.1
Wood	80.4	72.8	10.4	16.6	3.5	4.5
Basic chemicals	93.4	85.8	2.2	6.3	2.0	5.0
Petrochemicals	99.6	100.0	0.0	0.0	0.0	0.0
Basic metals	97.2	99.0	0.6	0.4	0.5	0.1
Machinery and equipment	90.0	88.8	4.5	5.9	1.3	2.0
Construction	77.9	72.6	13.0	15.2	1.0	1.2
Electrical power generation	99.9	99.8	0.0	0.2	0.0	0.0
Trade	51.2	45.5	31.0	33.1	11.5	16.2
Hotels and restaurants	56.9	53.6	20.7	23.6	15.7	15.4
Transportation	72.8	73.5	22.8	18.6	1.2	1.2
Communications	98.0	91.6	0.0	3.8	1.8	3.4
Finance	79.8	77.8	11.1	13.4	0.8	1.2
Education	92.7	90.2	4.6	7.0	0.9	1.0
Government	99.9	99.7	0.0	0.0	0.1	1.0
Embassies	90.6	92.0	6.0	5.2	0.4	0.3
Other	59.8	59.6	32.1	32.8	2.7	2.2
Nonclassified	60.8	79.2	1.3	3.6	0.0	0.0
Total employed urban population	73.9	60.8	16.6	23.8	4.6	11.2

Source: Authors' calculations based on data from the Instituto Nacional de Estadística, Geografía e Informática's National Employment Survey, 1991 and 1998.

Note: The percentages in each row do not necessarily add to 100.0 percent because total employment includes—in addition to the three categories listed in the table—owners, piece-rate workers, and undefined categories.

A comparison of the weights of different occupations within age groups between 1991 and 1998 indicates that the proportion of wage earners decreased by 9 to 15 percentage points in all age groups. However, reductions for workers under age 20 and above age 50 were consistently at the extreme (a 16 percent reduction). In the case of workers under 20 years of age, such declines were offset by a proportional increase (16.9 percent) in the share of unpaid occupations, while the proportion of those working as owners or as self-employed remained practically constant. As for workers 50 years of age and older, the offsetting change was a 14.6 percent increase in the share of those working as self-employed and an increase of 3.7 percent in those working in unpaid jobs (table 14.2).

Most industries experienced a decrease in wage employment during the 1990s, but there were important differences by activity. Table 14.3 displays data on wage employment as a proportion of total employment by industry for 1991 and 1998, along with corresponding figures for self-employment and unpaid employment (family and non-family). A high proportion of wage jobs reflects a modern production structure; a large proportion of self-employed and unpaid workers might be interpreted as an indication of a backward production process. For example, two categories—commerce, and hotels and restaurants—ranked very high in terms of the proportion of their workforce that was self-employed or unpaid, but transportation and other services also had large numbers of self-employed workers. The strong presence of non-wage employment was due to the prevalence of micro enterprises in these sectors, as well as to the fact that jobs in these sectors generally entail very easy tasks.

Comparing total employment for 1991 and 1998 reveals that the loss of wage-earning positions closely paralleled increases in the proportions of self-employed and unpaid workers. The sharpest relative reduction in wage jobs occurred in traditional manufacturing, followed by modern manufacturing (domestic appliances, chemicals, machinery and equipment), construction, commerce, and communications. These changes are explained in part by the impact of the 1994–1995 economic crisis on non-modern activities, but they also reflect the long-term segmentation of labor markets.

The growing number of self-employed workers means that people moved into poorer work situations, not only because of the inherent insecurity attached to this type of occupation but also because their relative incomes deteriorated. While the overall real hourly income from labor decreased 40.0 percent between 1991 and 1998 and wages fell 26.6 percent, labor income for the self-employed was cut in half (by

TABLE 14.4. Mean Hourly Income from Labor in Mexico, 1991 and 1998 (constant 1993 pesos)

	Real Wages		Percent change,
	1991	1998	1991–1998
Owners	20.53	10.71	-47.8
Subcontractors	12.47	NA	—
Self-employed	7.71	3.89	-49.6
Co-operatives	4.22	7.01	66.2
Wage earners	6.57	4.83	-26.6
Wage earners by piecework or percent	8.31	4.40	-47.0
Other	6.12	NA	—
Total employed population	7.04	4.22	-40.0

Source: Authors' calculations based on data from the Instituto Nacional de Estadística, Geografía e Informática's National Employment Survey, 1991 and 1998.
NA = Not available

(49.6 percent; see table 14.4). The relative income position of the self-employed shifted from 17.4 percent above to 19.5 percent below that of wage earners. In reality, the relative well-being of the self-employed did not deteriorate as much as income comparisons would suggest, but this is not the whole story. During the same period and for every type of fringe benefit (health insurance, paid holidays, and so forth), the proportion of wage earners receiving such benefits decreased (see table 14.5).[5]

Given that incomes for the self-employed are typically highly volatile, one could argue that these shifts in relative incomes for wage earners and self-employed workers mainly represent the short-term effects of the 1994–1995 crisis. However, monthly employment surveys for sixteen major Mexican cities provide a better sense of the temporal evolution of these two groups' relative earnings, and they suggest that more fundamental forces might explain these changes. Relative incomes for the self-employed improved during the early years of the economic reform process, deteriorated at the height of the reform pro-

---

[5] The only improvement was in the proportion of workers receiving housing credits. However, even this change should be viewed with caution. The 1994–1995 crisis had the effect of extending the maturity date for many loans because rising interest rates meant that a smaller proportion of monthly payments was applied to principal.

TABLE 14.5. Proportion of Urban Wage Earners in Mexico Receiving
Different Kinds of Fringe Benefits, 1991 and 1998
(percentages)

Benefit	1991	1998
End-of-year bonus	62.7	54.5
Participation in profits	19.2	15.4
Paid holidays	59.3	50.4
Credit for housing	13.3	21.8
Health insurance (IMSS)[1]	45.5	42.7
Health insurance (ISSSTE)[2]	7.0	4.6
Private health insurance	12.5	9.3

Source: Authors' calculations based on data from the Instituto Nacional de Estadística,
Geografía e Informática's National Employment Survey, 1991 and 1998.

[1] Instituto Mexicano del Seguro Social.

[2] Instituto de Seguridad y Servicios Sociales de los Trabajadores del Estado, the principal
health care agency for public employees.

cess, and stabilized once the impacts of the 1994–1995 crisis had eased.[6]
These findings indicate that earlier comparisons of wage earnings in
the formal and informal sectors are not definitive.[7]

During the 1990s, then, the deterioration in urban labor markets was
characterized by four processes: tertiarization, with little employment
in high-value-added services; a relative reduction in wage labor and an
increase in self-employment, particularly in traditional services and
manufacturing; falling incomes for the self-employed relative to wage
earners during the economic reform process; and a negative net change
in wage earners' income and employee benefits in the 1990s.

Employment Growth in Small Businesses

Micro enterprises of five or fewer workers account for a sizable proportion of total employment in Mexico. In 1991 these units accounted
for 30.5 percent of the total urban labor force. In the aftermath of the
1994-1995 economic crisis, however, micro enterprises became a refuge

---

[6] The mean income of the self-employed increased relative to that of wage earners
between 1987 (0.94) and 1991 (1.04), decreased between 1991 and 1994 (0.87), and
remained steady through 1998 (0.86).

[7] These studies include Maloney's finding (1999) that a significant number of informal-sector workers in Mexico have productive and income-rewarding working
lives. Marcouiller, Ruiz de Castilla, and Woodruff (1997) contend that the income
gap between informal- and formal-sector workers in Mexico is very small compared to other developing countries.

TABLE 14.6. Structure of Urban Employment in Mexico by Industry and Size of Economic Unit, 1991–2000 (percentages)

Sector and year	1–5 persons	6–100 persons	101 and more persons
Agriculture			
1991	57.1	35.5	7.4
1996	76.6	16.3	7.2
2000	61.9	24.4	13.7
Manufacturing			
1991	15.2	25.2	59.6
1996	24.0	23.6	52.4
2000	20.2	20.0	59.9
Retail trade			
1991	59.8	19.8	20.4
1996	73.2	12.7	14.1
2000	66.9	15.2	17.9
Total urban employment			
1991	30.5	20.7	48.8
1996	44.5	16.9	38.7
2000	40.4	17.3	42.2

Source: Authors' calculations based on data from the Instituto Nacional de Estadística, Geografía e Informática's National Employment Survey, 1991, 1996, and 2000.

Note: Percentages in rows may not add to 100.0 because of rounding.

for those who lost their jobs in massive layoffs. As a consequence, in 1996 a total of 44.5 percent of the urban labor force worked in such enterprises, while companies with 101 or more workers accounted for 38.7 percent of total employment (see table 14.6). The importance of micro enterprises in this regard varied by sector; they accounted for the highest proportions of employment in agriculture (76.6 percent) and retail trade (73.2 percent) and a lower though still significant share in manufacturing (24.0 percent).[8]

Despite the intense concentration of assets that occurred during these years, small businesses became an increasingly important source of new jobs. Between 1988 and 1993, micro and small businesses accounted for 94.7 percent of the jobs added in businesses with fixed locations (table 14.7). Here, too, there were some significant differences across sectors. For example, job growth during this period was strong in commerce and manufacturing, and it was even stronger in these sectors' micro and small enterprises.[9] In the service sector, the rate of employment growth was similar across micro, small, midsize, and large businesses. The weight of micro and small businesses in total manufacturing employment had been consistently on the rise for years; their proportion (that is, those with fifteen or fewer workers) of manufacturing-sector employment in all fixed establishments increased from 15.8 in 1985 to 18.0, 21.4, and 22.7 percent in 1988, 1993, and 1998, respectively.[10]

The increased importance of small firms is also apparent in the number of establishments and in the source of value added in manufacturing, commerce, and services. However, this does not mean that small businesses have emerged as an engine of growth and development; rather, their proliferation reflects the overall deterioration of labor conditions in Mexico. Indeed, data from the early 1990s indicate that small manufacturing firms were weak performers. They had lower wages and productivity, and poorer access to technology and training, than large companies. They also lagged in technology and productive improvements, thus widening the gap between small and large enter-

---

[8] Authors' calculations based on data from the Instituto Nacional de Estadística, Geografía e Informática's (INEGI) National Employment Survey (1991, 1996, 2000).

[9] The only exception was commercial establishments employing between 101 and 250 workers. In these cases, the workforce grew at a rate similar to that in micro enterprises. This exception may be attributed to the notable expansion of commercial chains in several Mexican cities.

[10] Zepeda, Alarcón, and Félix 1999: 26, for 1985–1993 data; INEGI economic census data for 1998. Excluded here are service workers in small businesses with and without a fixed location, and manufacturing workers in small businesses without a fixed location.

TABLE 14.7. Changes in the Number of Fixed Business Establishments and Employees in Manufacturing, Commerce, and Services in Mexico, 1988–1993

	Number of Establishments			Number of Employees		
	Absolute Increase, 1988–1993	Percent of Increase by Category		Absolute Increase, 1988–1993	Percent of Increase by Category	Employment Growth Rate (annual average, in percent)
Manufacturing	126,592	100.0		605,570	100.0	4.3
Micro and small	122,360	96.7		312,243	51.6	12.8
Medium and large	4,232	3.3		293,327	48.4	2.0
Commerce	455,336	100.0		1,043,523	100.0	8.1
Micro and small	437,969	96.2		730,285	70.0	10.1
Medium and large	17,367	3.8		313,238	30.0	5.4
Services	296,376	100.0		1,079,354	100.0	10.2
Micro and small	271,212	91.5		479,644	44.4	11.0
Medium and large	25,164	8.5		599,710	55.6	9.7
Total	878,304	100.0		2,728,447	100.0	6.8
Micro and small	831,541	94.7		1,522,172	55.8	9.4
Medium and large	46,763	5.3		1,206,275	44.2	5.3

Source: Authors' calculations based on the Instituto Nacional de Estadística, Geografía e Informática's economic censuses, 1989 and 1994.

Note: Size groups are defined as follows: micro and small, 1 to 100 employees; medium and large, 101 and more employees.

prises (see Zepeda, Alarcón, and Félix 1999). In fact, in 1991, value added per worker was 2.3 times higher in large companies than in small companies; by 1994 it was 2.6 times higher. Wages in large companies were nearly two and a half times higher than those in small companies.[11]

The other side of the story was falling employment in large manufacturing firms, whose workforce as a proportion of total manufacturing employment fell from 50.6 percent in 1985 to 47.1 percent in 1988 and to 43.0 percent in 1993. Large plants increased their share of total fixed-establishment employment in manufacturing from 43.0 to 46.5 percent between 1993 and 1998, mainly as a result of the implementation of the North American Free Trade Agreement (NAFTA) in January 1994 and a deep peso devaluation in 1994–1995. However, these changes appear to have been a short-lived phenomenon. Data from Mexico's monthly industrial survey indicate that employment growth in these enterprises slowed significantly in 1998 and 1999 (see Alarcón and Zepeda 2000).[12]

EMPLOYMENT IN LARGE MANUFACTURING FIRMS AND EXPORT-ORIENTED COMPANIES

Large manufacturing firms played a key role throughout Mexico's import-substitution industrialization phase, and they continued to do so under economic liberalization. Despite their importance, however, large manufacturing firms failed to create the jobs needed to transform the work landscape for modern production. In the 1980s and 1990s, new jobs came from export-related activities, but the added employment did not equal the growth of new entrants into the labor force. Moreover, the new positions that appeared did not come in well-integrated manufacturing plants, but in the export-platform plants typical of Mexico's maquiladora program.[13]

---

[11] These estimates are based on data from Zepeda, Alarcón, and Félix 1999: tables 7 and 8. In contrast to the definition used elsewhere in this chapter, these data come from census tabulations that define size by the number of employees and the value of production. For details, see Zepeda, Alarcón, and Félix 1999.

[12] Because micro firms also increased their share in total fixed-establishment employment between 1993 and 1998 (from 21.4 to 22.7 percent), it turns out that the 1994–1995 crisis affected employment most severely in manufacturing plants with more than 15 but less than 250 employees.

[13] The Mexican government established the maquiladora program in 1965 in order to permit duty-free imports to be processed in Mexico for re-export. Maquiladoras were exempted from restrictions on foreign ownership, but they were prohibited

Large Manufacturing Firms

Employment in large manufacturing firms decreased by an average of 2.0 percent per year between 1987 and 1994, for a net loss of 139,000 jobs.[14] Employment decreased in 100 of the 129 manufacturing subsectors for which information is available. In the subsectors that experienced job growth, 37,000 jobs were added across a broad range of production activities; nevertheless, the bulk of new jobs came from only a few subsectors. Indeed, half of the added jobs were in just two areas — automobile assembly and nonalcoholic beverages, the first oriented toward exports and the second toward the domestic economy. Other manufacturing subsectors where employment increased included automobile bodies, flat glass, and milled corn.

Subsectors with declining employment accounted for about three-quarters of all manufacturing jobs in 1988. They encompassed a wide range of activities, but the steepest reductions occurred in areas that had formerly enjoyed strong trade protection: metal products, electrical power generation, and goods that faced strong international competition, such as toys and cotton and other natural-fiber textiles. Surprisingly, some export-oriented subsectors had relatively large job losses, including cement and automobile and truck engines. Thus, on a first approximation, it is difficult to link employment performance with export orientation in manufacturing (4–digit) subsectors.[15]

Mexico's 1994–1995 economic crisis further exacerbated large manufacturing plants' shortcomings in employment creation. Total employment in large plants fell by 148,000 between August 1994 and August 1995, a pattern common across most subsectors. Most interesting is the fact that the number of jobs increased rapidly over the longer term. For 1994–1998 as a whole, large manufacturing firms added nearly 44,000 jobs, equivalent to an annual average increase of 0.8 percent.[16] Export

---

from selling their products in the domestic market. On the evolution of the maquiladora program, see, for example, Carrillo 1989 and Mendiola 1999.

[14] These figures are based on INEGI's monthly industrial survey (EIM), which collects information on the business establishments that account for about 80 percent of total production in the 6–digit industrial classification. The EIM excludes plants affiliated with the maquiladora program. During the period considered in this chapter, INEGI expanded its sample twice, first in 1990 and then in 1994–1995. Data are fully comparable from 1987 to 1994 and from 1994 to 1998, but not across the two periods.

[15] Other studies have also failed to identify a link between employment creation and exports. See, for example, Unger 1993 and Dutrenit and Capdevielle 1993.

[16] Data before and after 1994–1995 are not fully comparable due to sampling changes in INEGI's monthly employment survey.

markets were the major engine driving employment creation in these years. In contrast, the economic activities that suffered longest and hardest during these years were industries heavily dependent upon the domestic market, such as alcoholic and nonalcoholic beverages and those linked to construction (cement, metal products).

Employment performance during and following the 1994–1995 crisis varied sharply across productive activities. Just over half of the manufacturing subsectors examined (108 of 205) experienced a net employment increase between 1994 and 1998, and approximately 30 experienced average annual growth rates of 5 percent or more. The most vigorous employment growth occurred in export-oriented subsectors of the automotive industry (engines, electrical parts, and so on), computers, some textiles, pharmaceuticals, and food products, among others. Several exporting subsectors of the textile industry experienced very strong employment growth rates, although their contribution in absolute terms was not large. Foreign markets' importance in sustaining manufacturing employment during these years can hardly be exaggerated. Employment in non-exporting sectors, meanwhile, declined on a par with the general downturn in domestic economic activity.

The subsectoral pattern during the 1994–1995 crisis and post-crisis recovery period suggests that exports compensated for the lack of employment growth in large manufacturing firms, although this trend had reached its limit by the late 1990s. Without new policy initiatives to cushion the impacts of macroeconomic instability, Mexico's working population was left vulnerable to the negative effects of sharp employment reduction in domestic-oriented manufacturing activities.

Maquiladora Plants

The maquiladora sector's employment performance contrasts significantly with that of Mexico's large manufacturing plants. The maquiladora sector initially consisted of in-bond processing plants in Mexico's northern border cities that employed an industrially inexperienced labor force to perform simple assembly tasks in traditional manufacturing. Although maquiladoras evolved over time, they remained largely isolated from the rest of the Mexican economy. Maquiladora employment grew rapidly, from 60,000 workers in 1975 to 120,000 in 1980, and (after a brief net reduction in 1982) to 210,000 in 1985 and 420,000 in 1990. The pace of job creation slowed somewhat in the early 1990s, but it accelerated again after the 1994–1995 peso devaluation. In 1999, maquiladora employment totaled 1,130,000, concentrated in electrical and electronic products and accessories, auto parts, and apparel and textiles.

Maquiladoras made an important contribution toward offsetting weak job creation in domestic manufacturing.[17] Maquiladora workers accounted for about 5 percent of total manufacturing employment in fixed establishments in 1980 and about 15 percent from 1988 to 1993, and they approached 30 percent in the year 2000. Maquiladora plants contributed half of all new manufacturing employment between 1980 and 1988 and one-fourth between 1988 and 1993. Most of the remaining jobs created during these periods were in small non-maquiladora plants (Alarcón and Zepeda 1997, 1998, 2000).

The 1995 recession's impact on maquiladora plants was relatively mild, which is not surprising given their almost complete specialization in export markets.[18] Maquiladora job growth actually accelerated between 1995 and 1997, adding 150,000 positions each year of this three-year period. This sum far exceeds the 40,000 jobs that maquiladora plants created annually between 1992 and 1994 or the 60,000 jobs added each year between 1987 and 1989. Employment in apparel maquiladoras rose rapidly from 1995 to 1997, a fact closely linked to the relaxation of Multi-Fiber Arrangement quotas after the implementation of the NAFTA (O'Day 1997). Maquiladora employment in the electronics and auto parts sectors expanded as well, in line with those industries' global strategies (Carrillo and González 1999).

During the 1980s and 1990s there was significant change in the composition of maquiladora-sector employment. In the early 1980s, auto parts, chemicals, electronics, machinery, and metal products accounted for about 70 percent of maquiladora employment; by the second half of the 1990s, these activities' share had dropped to around 60 percent. There were also important regional changes as maquiladora plants were established in cities far from the Mexico–U.S. border. Between 1994 and 1999, the proportion of maquiladora workers in non-border locations increased from 16 to 22 percent as maquiladora production began shifting southward to sites such as Jalisco, the State of México, Mexico City, Puebla, and Yucatán. Apparel maquiladora plants, in turn, moved to areas (such as the states of Puebla and Morelos) where compliance with labor laws was low (Mortimore 1999).

Although economic liberalization stimulated exports by prompting many manufacturing plants to reorient production to foreign markets,

---

[17] Prior to the 1994–1995 economic crisis, domestic-oriented and export-oriented manufacturing plants were approximately even in terms of employment creation. However, the 1994–1995 devaluation of the peso gave exporters a boost, and maquiladora employment rose.

[18] In fact, short-term economic or political events appear to have little effect on maquiladora activities.

critics argue that Mexico's economic reform strategy was shortsighted and ultimately de-industrializing. Little was to be gained if rising exports came at the cost of reduced production for the domestic market. In contrast, other observers argue that maquiladoras have evolved and no longer fit the sweatshop pattern. In fact, maquiladora plants producing auto parts and electronic products have proliferated, and the average size of maquiladora plants has grown. Average plant size in 1980 was about 200 workers; by 1997, it was 320. This shift has been especially evident in the sector's most modern manufacturing activities. For example, in 1997 average plant size in the automobile sector was 870 workers, and the electrical products and electronics sector averaged 585 workers per plant.[19]

Other critics have observed that maquiladora plants have few linkages with other economic sectors. In this regard, it is interesting to note that by the late 1990s the differences between export-oriented and domestic-market-oriented manufacturing firms were beginning to blur. Traditional manufacturing plants were increasing their imported inputs, and maquiladora plants were developing into more than mere assembly operations. As these two types of plants converged, what emerged looked not totally unlike a maquiladora.[20]

SKILL COMPOSITION IN MANUFACTURING EMPLOYMENT

Reorienting Mexico's manufacturing industry toward export markets did not produce the expected increase in aggregate employment, but it did increase overall productivity. Thus one could hypothesize that economic reform improved the *quality* of jobs at the cost of the *quantity* of jobs. One way to test this hypothesis is to look at the skill dimension of employment (approximated by the mix of production and nonproduction workers) in large manufacturing establishments and in maquiladora plants.

Focusing on the mix of employment is admittedly a crude measure of job quality. Adding managers, chauffeurs, and messengers to the payroll would not represent the use of enhanced technology. However, to the extent to which production is subject to competitive pressures, hiring practices should eliminate unnecessary workers. To the extent to which this is the case, the addition of non-production workers to the payroll over the medium term could be taken as an

---

[19] These are the authors' calculations based on data available in INEGI's "Banco de información económica" (www.inegi.gob.mx).

[20] About 97 to 98 percent of the total inputs used in maquiladora operations are imported. This pattern has not varied over time.

indication that these employees are indeed necessary, and that the production system requires more people in such areas as design, research, and services.

Along the same lines, one could well argue that flexible production methods break the link between skill levels and the mix of production and nonproduction workers. The reason is that flexible manufacturing implies that production workers carry out some tasks formerly assigned to nonproduction workers. In other words, production processes can increase in skill level without a change in the mix of employees. Thus a better indicator of skill upgrading might be a description of workers' tasks and responsibilities, along with their level of education and training.

Nonetheless, the use of flexible labor strategies in Mexico does not appear to be extensive enough to provide a very accurate gauge of skill level and thus invalidate the employee-mix indicator. For example, survey data indicate that a significant 15 percent of a sample of manufacturing plants introduced work teams and/or quality circles into their production processes between 1989–1991 and 1994–1995. Yet it is unlikely that such changes were spread uniformly through the plants surveyed. Data from the same survey suggest that there was little differentiation across subsectors in terms of workers' formal education; workers in all activities displayed an increase in average years of schooling and training. Differences did appear, however, in the frequency with which workers received in-house training and in the proportion of workers whose professional and semi-professional skills were utilized in production (see Alarcón and Zepeda 1998; Alarcón, Zepeda, and Félix 1999: 40).

Large Manufacturing Plants

Mexico's import-substitution/petroleum-export development strategy during the 1970s and early 1980s left its mark on the composition of the labor force. Overvaluation of the exchange rate and trade protection of sectors producing consumer durable goods shifted employment toward capital-intensive sectors and reinforced the use of skilled labor. Throughout this period, employment clustered in modern, capital-intensive sectors, and the skill mix improved. Economic liberalization beginning in the mid–1980s affected both total employment and the skill mix in many manufacturing plants. Yet no significant change was apparent in the aggregate skill level, as measured by the mix of employment. Looking at large non-maquiladora manufacturing plants, one finds little change in the employment mix between 1987 and 2000. Production workers as a proportion of total employees hovered around 70 percent, increasing slightly between 1987 and 1990, falling from 1990 to 1994, rising again through 1998, and then stabilizing thereafter.[21]

Small aggregate changes in the skill composition of the workforce actually conceal offsetting trends across sectors. In terms of sectoral changes in these three subperiods (1987–1990, 1990–1994, and 1994–1998), there was a highly uneven process at work that resists simple explanation. First, the period of skill upgrading also included the biggest differences in skill-mix change across sectors. Broad differences appeared again after the 1994–1995 devaluation crisis. The period with least variation in trans-sector changes in skill composition was the initial phase of trade liberalization, predating the economic reforms of the 1990s.[22] Second, skill upgrading between 1990 and 1994 was driven by medium-skill manufacturing activities and by the rising proportion of nonproduction workers in leading subsectors. Third, rather than pushing all subsectors to a lower share of nonproduction workers, the 1994–1995 crisis had the effect of accelerating skill reductions in sectors where skill downgrading was already occurring. Fourth, on the whole, there was neither clear convergence nor clear polarization of skill levels across manufacturing subsectors.

As expected, individual subsectors did not all change their skill mix in the same direction, or at the same rate, over the 1987–1998 period. If one compares the 1987–1990 and 1990–1994 periods, one finds some regularities. Somewhat less than a fourth of all manufacturing subsectors (twenty-seven) changed their skill mix very little (less than two percent in either direction in both periods).[23] Half of the remaining subsectors showed consistent changes in both periods, mostly in the direction of skill downgrading. Again as expected, most subsectors that changed their skill level significantly did so consistently. Among those activities that most increased their skill level were the textile, electronics, automobile, and food products subsectors. Those in which skill levels fell significantly included auto parts, machine tools, and glass and other nonmetal products. Given this broad range of subsectors, it is dif-

---

[21] There were three different directions of movement. First, the share of production workers increased between 1987 and early 1990 from 69.5 to 70.5 percent. This proportion then decreased to 69.0 percent in 1994. Finally, the 1994–1995 crisis and its aftermath reversed the downward trend, and the proportion of production workers reached 71.0 percent in 1998. Authors' calculations based on data in the INEGI's monthly industrial survey.

[22] Dispersion, as measured by the inter-quartile range, was 3.30, 5.03, and 4.42 for 1987–1990, 1990–1994, and 1994–1998, respectively.

[23] Due to sampling and reporting changes, the authors cannot easily identify and compare subsectors before and after 1995.

ficult to establish a connection between shifts in skill levels and export, technological, or production trends.

On theoretical grounds as well, there are difficulties in attempting to identify a relationship between changes in skill mix, on the one hand, and export, technological, and production conditions, on the other. To the extent that economic reform improved efficiency and enhanced technology, one would expect increases in the share of nonproduction workers — assuming technology and skill are complements, particularly in activities where international competition is strongest (that is, in export-oriented and import-competing sectors).

However, if one takes price correction and adequate factor utilization as the dominant effects of liberalization, then one should expect a *decrease* in the skill mix of manufacturing jobs (Krueger 1990). The actual effects of these forces depend upon the pattern of sectoral protections that existed prior to liberalization. If, for example, trade policy favored skilled over unskilled workers, then one might see corrections reducing the relative employment of skilled workers — and vice versa.[24]

Given the complex and sometimes contradictory set of quotas, tariffs, and price regulations that characterized industrial promotion in Mexico prior to the 1980s, it is difficult empirically to disentangle these types of effects in order to predict either aggregate skill changes or skill modifications by subsector.[25] In addition, Katz (2000) has suggested that major changes occurred in manufacturing before the economic reforms of the late 1980s and early 1990s. Nevertheless, a preliminary analysis of skill changes between 1990 and 1994 suggests that skill upgrading was directly related to modernization. It correlated positively with organizational changes, rendering labor more flexible. It also varied directly with subsector increases in value added and labor productivity (value added per worker). However, skill upgrading correlated negatively with exports as a share of total sales in 1989, and it was unrelated to changes in exports as a proportion of sales.[26]

Job Quality in Maquiladora Plants

Maquiladora plants initially employed mostly young women to perform simple tasks, often under questionable labor and environmental

---

[24] For a detailed discussion of these issues, see Robertson 1999.

[25] A careful analysis of the "law of one price" (which specifies that an item sell for the same price across borders — adjusted, of course, to local currencies) between Mexico and the United States, carried out shortly after the beginning of trade liberalization, was unable to identify any correction in the irrational structure of international relative prices. See Ten Kate and De Mateo 1989.

[26] These issues are discussed in detail in Zepeda 2000.

conditions. During the 1980s, when electronics and auto parts manufacturers joined the maquiladora sector, women workers as a proportion of total maquiladora employment began to fall, and labor conditions improved.[27]

Maquiladora plants have indeed changed with regard to the composition of their labor force and the organization of their productive
processes, but these changes were not definitive. The number of women
employed in routine tasks decreased in importance, workers' education
levels increased, and there was some improvement during the 1980s
and 1990s in maquiladora workers' skill mix. Production workers as a
proportion of the total workforce decreased from 85.3 percent in 1980–
1983 to 81.5 percent in 1996–1998 and 80.5 percent in 1998–2001. The
proportion of technicians in the workforce increased from 9.0 percent in
1980–1983 to 11.4 percent in 1996–1998 and 12.2 percent in 1998–2001.
However, even after these changes, the maquiladora industry compared
poorly with non-maquiladora manufacturing, where the proportion of
nonproduction workers averaged around 30 percent.[28]

In sum, the quality mix of employment improved in some manufacturing subsectors over the course of the 1980s and 1990s. The ratio of
nonproduction to production workers rose in maquiladora plants, but
it did not reach the level found in non-maquiladora manufacturing facilities, where the skill mix improved consistently in many subsectors
from 1987 onward. Plants that increased their proportion of nonproduction workers tended to be in activities benefiting from investment
and new technologies. However, there was no apparent connection
between export orientation and improved skill mix in employment.

WAGES IN THE STABLE LABOR FORCE

Mexico's economic reform process has negatively affected wages and
living conditions for a sizable proportion of the working population.
During the 1980s, average real wages decreased dramatically in a two-
fold process of reduced income per capita and a more concentrated
distribution of income. Wages as a proportion of national income collapsed as the per capita net wage fell and the number of people in wage-

---

[27] The issue of labor conditions in maquiladora plants was revisited during the
NAFTA negotiations, when these plants began to be viewed as fully developed
manufacturing plants.

[28] This is a substantial difference even if one takes into account the fact that maquiladora plants tend to operate three production shifts rather than two. These are
the authors' calculations based on data available in the INEGI's "Banco de información económica" (www.inegi.gob.mx).

earning positions decreased. The recovery of a growth trajectory in the early 1990s presented an opportunity to reverse these deteriorating trends, and real wage levels did improve. However, wage gains were not equal for all workers, and most of what was gained was lost again in the 1994–1995 crisis.

The following discussion of wage changes over time focuses on the stable segment of the labor force: year-round, full-time wage earners, a category that accounted for approximately 75 percent of total employment between 1987 and 1994. Full-time wage earners with year-round jobs increased from 74.6 percent of total employment in 1987 to 77.2 percent in 1994; their share fell to 73.7 percent with the 1994–1995 crisis, but it recovered to 75.5 percent in 1998. In other words, stable wage jobs represented about the same proportion of total employment in 1998 as they had in 1987.[29] By focusing on this segment and leaving aside the informal sector, one can assess economic liberalization's impact on wages.

Wage Increases: 1987–1994

Between 1987 and 1994, wages recovered some of the purchasing power they had lost during the post–1982 economic stabilization process. The year-around, full-time wage segment of the labor force increased its average real hourly wage by about 30 percent over this period. However, averaging wage changes does more than conceal normal wage differentials. In the Mexican case, averaging obscures sharp contrasts between different segments of the labor force, differences that feed into the income inequality that has characterized Mexico since the 1980s.[30]

Inflation-adjusted wages increased by 23.7 percent and 19.7 percent in traditional manufacturing and services, respectively, over the 1987–1994 period, but they rose by 32.8 percent and 31.0 percent in modern manufacturing and services, respectively (table 14.8). Disaggregated sectoral data reveal that wages rose modestly (5 to 25 percent over the 1987–1994 period) in firms producing machinery and equipment, traditional services, and (publicly owned) electrical power. Other sectors—leather goods, chemicals, metal products, construction, and retail and wholesale trade—realized wage increases of between 25 and 40 percent. Sectors with larger increases (above 40 percent) included education (presumably in private schools), government, finance, and petro-

---

[29] These are the authors' calculations based on INEGI's National Urban Employment Survey.

[30] For a recent study of income distribution in Mexico, see Boltvinik and Hernández Laos 1999.

chemicals.[31] Similarly, wage gains differed by firm size. Between 1987 and 1994, average wages increased by 20.0 to 25.8 percent in businesses with fewer than 100 workers, and by 35.5 to 39.4 percent in firms with more than 100 workers (table 14.8).[32]

These growing wage gaps reflect workers' demographic and occupational characteristics (men versus women, high- versus low-ranking occupations, and skilled versus unskilled workers). The wage ratio between more educated and less educated workers increased from 2.0 (both men and women) to 2.7 for women and 3.0 for men over the 1987–1994 period. Wages by occupation followed a similar path. The wage ratio of managers to laborers increased from 1.8 to 2.6 for men and from 1.6 to 2.3 for women (Zepeda 1997).

Increasing returns to education provide one explanation for this wage pattern. Earning equations like those pioneered by Mincer (1974) and estimated changes in relative wages for various segments of the working population all show increases in returns to skill (measured as a function of education). The fact that relative wages rose primarily in occupations where employment expanded suggests that the shift in demand toward educated labor explains wage increases. Mexican companies presumably needed increasing numbers of skilled workers in order to adopt skill-based technologies and compete in global markets (Robbins 1995; Cragg and Epelbaum 1996; Tan and Batra 1997; Wood 1997).

By the present authors' estimates, education premiums within the stable labor force grew rapidly. In 1987, the wages of university-educated workers were between 1.6 and 2.4 times those of other workers. By 1994 the gap had widened to between 2.4 and 3.7 times the wages of less educated workers. Most of the increase in education premiums derived from the divergent wage trends for high-skill and low-skill workers. Workers with less than twelve years of schooling increased their real wages by up to 13.6 percent between 1987 and 1994; the wages of workers with university education increased by 63.1 percent (see table 14.9).

Estimating earning equations for labor markets in Mexico yields results comparable to those for other developing countries. Neverthe-

---

[31] Somewhat surprisingly, the traditional wood products manufacturing sector also fell within this group. For petrochemicals, increasing exports and modernization could account, at least in part, for such strong wage increases.

[32] This cursory inspection of highly aggregated data does not reveal a close relationship between wages and manufacturing modernization or export performance. However, it does suggest that economic activities linked to the public sector did tend to experience wage increases.

TABLE 14.8. Real Wage Trends in the Stable Labor Force[1] in Sixteen Major Mexican Cities, 1987–1998

	Hourly Wages (1993 pesos)				Percent Change		
	1987	1994	1995	1998	1987–1994	1994–1995	1995–1998
By size of business establishment[2]							
Micro	3.25	4.09	3.38	2.90	25.8	-17.4	-14.1
Micro-small	4.65	5.58	5.05	4.27	20.0	-9.5	-15.3
Small	5.35	6.59	5.83	4.97	23.0	-11.5	-14.8
Medium	5.76	8.03	6.39	5.53	39.4	-20.5	-13.3
Large	6.50	8.81	7.42	6.93	35.5	-15.7	-6.6
By sector[3]							
Traditional manufacturing	4.73	5.85	4.61	4.24	23.7	-21.2	-8.0
Modern manufacturing	6.32	8.40	7.07	7.19	32.8	-15.8	1.7
Traditional services	4.67	5.59	4.18	4.07	19.7	-25.2	-2.8
Modern services[4]	6.03	7.90	6.91	5.82	31.0	-12.5	-15.8
Primary	6.40	9.36	7.00	9.08	46.2	-25.3	29.8
Total stable labor force	5.38	6.93	5.86	5.30	28.8	-15.3	-9.6

Source: Alarcón and Zepeda 2000, based on authors' calculations from the Instituto Nacional de Estadística, Geografía e Informática's National Employment Survey data.

[1] The stable labor force is defined as those working for a wage more than 35 hours per week all year round.

[2] Means. Size groups are defined as follows: micro, between 1 and 5 employees; micro-small, between 6 and 15 employees; small, between 16 and 100 employees; medium, between 101 and 250 employees; large, 251 or more employees.

[3] Unweighted averages from sector mean wages. Sectors include the following subsectors: traditional manufacturing (food, textiles, apparel, wood); modern manufacturing (chemicals, basic metals, nonmetallic minerals, machinery and equipment); traditional services (construction, trade, transportation, other services); modern services (electricity, communications, finance, education, government).

[4] Includes personnel in embassies, consulates, and the like.

less, at its best this methodology explains only about 40 percent of the wage variance, leaving considerable room for competing or complementary explanations. Indeed, even after accounting for sociodemographic factors, wage differentials increased steadily between 1987 and 1993 (Ghiara and Zepeda 1996). That is, there were growing unexplained disparities in wage determination even after education is taken into account.

Scattered observations support the view that factors other than technological and organizational changes affected relative wages. For example, the technological intensity of Mexico's manufacturing sector was strongly influenced by maquiladora-type activities and their extensive use of cheap labor.[33] There were also institutional factors that may have constrained wage increases for unskilled workers, including the Mexican government's broad leeway to control wages as part of its economic stabilization efforts (Aspe Armella 1993). Zepeda and Ghiara (1999) suggest, for example, that the time pattern of education premiums for workers who received a university education between 1987 and 1993 was significantly influenced not only by long-term structural changes, but also by wage-freeze policies associated with short-term stabilization packages.

Government control over organized labor and union bargaining mechanisms translated into tight wage controls in key industries. These controls — together with the government's restrictive wage policy — were a powerful mechanism for restraining wage increases for large sectors of the wage-earning population. Alarcón and McKinley (1997a, 1997b) and Fairris (2001) found that Mexican unions were not as strong a factor in wage differentiation in the 1990s as they had been in the past, a fact that surely contributed to the downward homogenization of wages for unskilled and semi-skilled workers. Such constraints would not apply, however, to employees in managerial, administrative, and high-level production positions, whose wages are generally not subject to union bargaining.

Wage Collapse: 1995

The 1994–1995 economic crisis and the Mexican government's policies to address it more than eliminated the wage gains achieved between 1987 and 1994. Beginning with the first quarter of 1995, real wages for the stable labor force began a prolonged decline that lasted until the third quarter of 1997. Average real wages increased modestly thereafter,

---

[33] See Dutrenit and Capdevielle 1993 and Unger 1993, among others.

TABLE 14.9. Hourly Wages in Mexico's Stable Labor Force by Educational Level, 1987–1998

Educational Level	Hourly Wage (1993 pesos)				Percent Change				
	1987	1994	1995	1998	1987-1994	1994-1995	1994-1998	1995-1998	1987-1998
6 years	4.09	4.64	3.73	3.32	13.6	-19.7	-28.4	-10.8	-18.6
6–9 years	4.97	5.47	4.64	4.10	10.0	-15.2	-25.0	-11.6	-17.4
10–12 years	6.19	6.88	5.98	5.43	11.1	-13.1	-21.0	-9.2	-12.2
12+ years	9.97	16.27	13.60	12.04	63.1	-16.4	-26.0	-11.5	20.7
Total stable labor force	5.38	6.93	5.86	5.30	28.8	-15.3	-23.5	-9.6	-1.5

Source: Alarcón and Zepeda 2000, based on authors' calculations from the Instituto Nacional de Estadística, Geografía e Informática's national employment survey data.

Note: The stable labor force is defined as those working for a wage more than 35 hours per week all year round.

but in the second quarter of 1998 they were still 23.5 percent below their 1994 level and 1.5 percent below their 1987 level (table 14.9).

Wage losses varied by company size and by sector. Employees in firms with 250 or fewer workers suffered the largest wage cuts. Although real average wages declined by 21.3 percent in large companies between 1994 and 1998, the loss was closer to 30 percent in businesses with between 100 and 250 workers or fewer than 6 employees (table 14.8). However, wage declines displayed little differentiation by market orientation (domestic or foreign) or sector type (modern or traditional). Among export sectors, for example, wage cuts were modest in the metal products branch but deep in the chemical products branch. Wages behaved differently in traditional sectors (such as food and wood products) than in the textile, apparel, and leather sectors, with the latter experiencing much sharper wage reductions than the former. Services also displayed a varied wage pattern across subsectors. For instance, wages fell most precipitously in the financial sector, the same sector that had secured the biggest gains in the 1987–1994 period.

Nor was there a clear association between wage reductions and education levels. Between 1994 and 1998, workers with only a basic education suffered the deepest wage cuts (28.4 percent), but university-educated employees were a close second, at 26.0 percent. Workers with six to nine years of formal education lost 25.0 percent, and those with ten to twelve years of formal schooling lost 21.0 percent. These aggregated data confirm that the 1994–1995 crisis and its aftermath worsened wage distribution for some segments of the stable labor force (table 14.9).

In summary, average real wages for the formal, stable labor force increased between 1987 and 1994, but they then fell with the onset of the 1994–1995 crisis. The period of rising wages was also one of widening wage gaps; wages of managers and educated workers increased, while wages for workers in low-skill jobs and those with minimal education stagnated. Skilled workers' wage gains reflected the rising education premium driven by technological change, trade, and a rapidly changing economic environment. But wage inequality also increased as a result of stabilization policies that froze wages for low-skill workers. Wages collapsed after the 1994–1995 crisis, driving unskilled workers' wages below their 1987 levels. Skilled workers' wages also fell, but not so far as to represent a setback to 1987 levels.

TABLE 14.10. Hourly Wages of the Stable Labor Force in Sixteen Major Mexican Cities, 1987–1988 and 1993–1994[1]

	1987–1988 (average)				1993–1994 (average)			
	All 16 cities	Border	Monterrey	Mexico City	All 16 cities	Border	Monterrey	Mexico City
Educational level								
Up to 3 years	3.79	4.79	3.70	3.73	4.16	5.09	4.30	4.14
4–6 years	4.37	5.30	4.40	4.22	4.71	5.39	4.89	4.62
7–9 years	4.84	5.59	4.75	4.84	5.65	6.15	5.79	5.58
More than 9 years	7.85	8.68	8.14	8.10	12.05	11.91	13.90	13.32
Occupation								
Laborers	4.26	4.78	4.18	4.22	4.82	4.76	5.01	4.77
Technicians	6.60	7.75	7.37	6.32	9.16	8.40	10.19	9.47
Managers	7.13	7.57	7.98	7.28	11.77	10.87	13.81	12.30
Other	4.30	5.20	4.60	4.29	5.10	5.85	5.79	5.00
Total	5.44	6.28	5.49	5.46	7.35	7.72	8.04	7.70

Source: Alarcón and Zepeda 2000, based on authors' calculations from the Instituto Nacional de Estadística, Geografía e Informática's national employment survey data.

[1] Wages are in 1993 constant pesos and were calculated using city-specific consumer price indexes. Border cities include Ciudad Juárez, Matamoros, Nuevo Laredo, and Tijuana. The remaining cities are Chihuahua, Guadalajara, León, Mérida, Orizaba, Puebla, San Luis Potosí, Tampico, Torreón, and Veracruz.

REGIONAL TRENDS

The restructuring of production and employment in Mexico since the 1980s has been closely associated with regional reorganization. Perhaps the most important change in this regard was Mexico's rising prominence in manufacturing, largely as a result of the growing maquiladora sector that was first established along the country's northern border.[34] As noted earlier, maquiladora plants are now found in cities further removed from the border (Hermosillo, Chihuahua, Saltillo, Monclova, Torreón, Monterrey, and San Luis Potosí), where they produce auto parts, electronic goods, and textiles. Hiernaux (1995) has described the rising importance of these new maquiladora zones as the "second border"; others have viewed them as manufacturing and service corridors (see Zepeda, Castro, and Félix 1996).

The northward shift in manufacturing under the impetus of the maquiladora sector transcends simple explanation. In many instances, industrial production has boomed in cities that had no experienced industrial labor force or sophisticated industrial infrastructure, or in areas with relatively high wages. Geographic proximity to the U.S. market appears to have strongly influenced the maquiladora industry's siting decisions, although econometric exercises reveal that northern Mexico's advantages in this regard (lower transportation costs for inputs and exports, and ease of communication) are not conclusive explanatory variables (see Mendoza and Martínez 1999).

Although academic analysts, government officials, and business associations alike describe northern Mexico as a leader in technology and modernization, the available evidence does not fully support this view. The maquiladora sector's increasing proportion of nonproduction workers suggests that these plants' skill requirements have risen, but overall skill levels in maquiladora plants remain below those in the manufacturing sector as a whole.[35] Furthermore, not all maquiladora plants generate a stream of high-value-added products and services.[36] Indeed, with the exception of Monterrey, during the 1990s skill premi-

---

[34] The regional distribution of agricultural employment has also changed significantly. For example, non-wage agricultural jobs proliferated in most regions between 1970 and 1990. For a discussion of regional changes, see Garza 1992 and this volume; Graizbord 1995; Krugman and Livas 1992; Mendoza and Martínez 1999; Zepeda and Félix 1995; Zepeda, Castro, and Félix 1996.

[35] See Zepeda 1997 and Ghiara and Zepeda 2000. For an alternative view, see Feenstra and Hanson 1994, 1997.

[36] See Zepeda, Castro, and Félix 1996; Zepeda and Castro 1999. Consistent with this view, Katz (2000) argues that manufacturing changes in Latin America's largest countries have reduced the demand for engineering services.

TABLE 14.11. Relative Wages by Region in Mexico, 1987–1988 and 1993–1994

	Ratio of Hourly Wages: High to Basic Education		Percent Change in Relative Wages,	Ratio of Hourly Wages: Technicians to Laborers		Percent Change in Relative Wages,
	1987–1988	1993–1994	1987–88 to 1993–94	1987–1988	1993–1994	1987–88 to 1993–94
All 16 cities	1.84	2.73	48.4	1.55	1.90	22.6
Border	1.69	2.34	38.5	1.62	1.76	8.6
North-central Mexico	1.83	2.35	28.4	1.59	1.80	13.2
Monterrey	1.86	2.78	49.5	1.76	2.04	15.9
Mexico City	1.92	2.94	53.1	1.50	1.98	32.0

Source: Authors' calculations based on data from the Instituto Nacional de Estadística, Geografía e Informática's national surveys of urban employment.

ums continued to rise more rapidly in Mexico City and in nonborder cities generally than in the northern border region. The fact that regional differences in the availability of skilled workers seem not to have played a major role in this regard (Ghiara and Zepeda 2000) suggests that technological and modernization pressures on wages may be stronger at a distance from the Mexico–U.S. border.

Average real wages increased in all large cities in Mexico in the late 1980s and early 1990s, though they did not do so uniformly. Border cities lost some of their wage advantage, while Monterrey and Mexico City emerged as high-wage regions (table 14.10). This situation suggests that economic recovery in core industrial cities (and corresponding increases in the stable labor force) pushed wages up. One can attribute a substantial portion of the wage increase in Mexico City and Monterrey to strong increases in skill premiums; the wage ratio between highly educated and less-educated workers increased faster in these two cities than elsewhere in Mexico (table 14.11). The wage ratio of technicians to laborers also rose fastest in Mexico City, suggesting that demand shifts for skilled labor were strongest there and in Monterrey.

CONCLUSION

In the late 1980s government policy makers based their decision to liberalize Mexico's economy on the premise that a market-driven economy geared toward exports would drive growth, enhance productivity and competitiveness, increase well-being, and boost employment. However, the record of economic reform has been ambiguous in general and outright disappointing in terms of job creation and wage recovery. Although unemployment rates remained low on the whole, the dominant note was deteriorating employment conditions—a characteristic that is evident if one looks at the sectoral distribution and nature of newly added jobs. As demonstrated above, the occupational structure was skewed toward low-paid and low-value-added services, as well as toward employment in small businesses and self-employment in services and manufacturing. New jobs overwhelmingly originated in small businesses (in many instances, self-employed individuals) that increasingly lagged behind in productivity and wages relative to leading sectors and activities.

The dominant employment trend can also be expressed in terms of the progressive relative decline in wage-earning occupations, a process that in itself should not be considered either positive or negative. The real problem has been that shifting people out of wage-earning occupations has not meant an improvement in labor conditions for either those moving into other types of employment or those remaining in wage-earning positions. Most people leaving wage occupations became self-employed, some managed to acquire a micro business, and others — less fortunate — ended up in unpaid positions. Far from the illusion of freedom, entrepreneurship, and high income sometimes attached to such occupations, these informal workers did not improve their income relative to those in wage-earning occupations during years of economic growth. They did, however, suffer more harshly during periods of economic crisis. Having a wage-earning occupation certainly offered some stability, but nothing close to comfort; during the 1987–1998 period, access to fringe benefits continuously declined among wage earners.

The insufficient availability of wage-earning positions was not an "unavoidable adjustment cost" of the early phases of economic reform. Nor was it exclusively the result of the 1994–1995 economic crisis. During the crisis, many businesses did cut jobs, and unemployment rates increased sharply. However, Mexico's employment problems are endemic. The inability to create jobs has persisted through years of macroeconomic stabilization and years of economic growth, through years of institutional change and government deregulation and years of consolidation. Mexico's adopted export-promotion model and the tightening of domestic consumption have proved to be a poisonous mixture. A worsening distribution of income, wage stagnation for the majority of workers, and expanding informal labor markets do not provide much basis for domestically driven economic activity. Thus Mexico's export success story has not translated into new employment opportunities in any proportion close to the challenge posed by demographic trends. Exports from capital-intensive industries like automobiles and electronics with an increasingly high content of imported inputs may swell export statistics, but they can hardly provide the many jobs that Mexico so desperately needs.

The much-touted recovery in real wage levels that occurred during the first half of the 1990s meant little to the majority of low-skilled wage earners. Even among workers who have benefited from Mexico's new economic orientation, gains have been unequally distributed. Moreover, average incomes for the sizable proportion of the population employed in informal occupations did not improve as much as those of wage earners. Additional research is needed on the question of changes in the income of low-paid wage earners relative to low-income informal-sector workers. Although the 1994–1995 crisis might not have meant an across-the-board worsening of income inequality, low-skilled workers and informal workers did suffer the sharpest income setbacks.

Household living standards should not have deteriorated as much as the income and labor conditions of individuals did during the long years of economic stabilization and reform. Dependency ratios have been decreasing as the feminization of the labor force proceeds and as the age profile of the population shifts, expanding the proportion of people older than sixteen and thus able to work. However, under the harsh employment situation that has prevailed in Mexico, these changes do not come without costs. The fact that more young people are looking for jobs has not necessarily meant more stable income earners in the household. Many young workers are filling unpaid positions, and unemployment is higher among the young. Moreover, when young men and women entrants to the labor force do place themselves in stable wage-earning jobs, they drive adult male workers out and into informality — if not into unemployment or economic inactivity. Not surprisingly, social tensions have been scaling up even during periods of economic recovery, productivity growth, and export success — not to mention at times of recession and crisis. It is, therefore, urgently important to design and implement active policies that help shape an economic strategy capable of generating better-paid, higher-skill jobs.

REFERENCES

Alarcón, Diana, and Terry McKinley. 1997a. "The Paradox of Narrowing Wage Differentials and Widening Wage Inequality in Mexico," *Development and Change* 28 (3): 505–30.

———. 1997b. "The Rising Contribution of Labor Income to Inequality in Mexico," *North American Journal of Economics and Finance* 8 (2): 201–12.

Alarcón, Diana, and Eduardo Zepeda. 1997. "Stabilization, Structural Adjustment, and Labour Market Performance." In *Innovation, Productivity, and Competitiveness in North America*, edited by Robert Anderson et al. Montreal: McGill-Queen's University Press.

———. 1998. "Employment Trends in the Mexican Manufacturing Sector," *North American Journal of Economics and Finance* 9: 125–45.

———. 2000. "Liberalización, empleo y salarios." Paper presented at the Asociación Latinoamericana de Sociología del Trabajo, Buenos Aires, May.

Aspe Armella, Pedro. 1993. *El camino mexicano de la transformación económica.* Mexico City: Fondo de Cultura Económica.

Boltvinik, Julio, and Enrique Hernández Laos. 1999. *Distribución del ingreso en México.* Mexico City: El Colegio de México/Siglo Veintiuno Editores.

Carrillo, Jorge. 1989. "Transformaciones en la industria maquiladora de exportación: ¿una nueva fase?" In *Las maquiladoras: ajuste estructural y desarrollo regional*, edited by Bernardo González-Aréchiga and Rocío Barajas.

Tijuana, Mexico: El Colegio de la Frontera Norte/Fundación Friedrich Ebert.

Carrillo, Jorge, and Sergio González. 1999. "Empresas automotores alemanas en México: relaciones cliente-proveedor." Cuadernos del Trabajo, no. 17. Mexico City: Secretaría del Trabajo y Previsión Social.

CONAPO (Consejo Nacional de Población). 1998. *La situación demográfica de México*. Mexico City: CONAPO.

Cragg, Michael Ian, and Mario Epelbaum. 1996. "Why Has Wage Dispersion Grown in Mexico? Is It the Incidence of Reforms or the Growing Demand for Skills?" *Journal of Development Economics* 51 (1): 99–116.

Dutrenit, Gabriela, and Mario Capdevielle. 1993. "El perfil tecnológico de la industria mexicana y su dinámica innovadora en la década de los ochenta," *Trimestre Económico* 60 (239): 643–74.

Fairris, David. 2001. "Unions and Wage Inequality in Mexico." Working Papers in Economics No. 2001-05. University of California, Riverside.

Feenstra, Robert C., and Gordon Hanson. 1994. "Foreign Investment Outsourcing and Relative Wages." In *Political Economy of Trade Policy: Essays in Honor of Jagdish Bhagwati*, edited by Robert C. Feenstra, Gene M. Grossman, and Douglas A. Irwin. Cambridge, Mass.: MIT Press.

———. 1997. "Foreign Direct Investment and Relative Wages: Evidence from Mexico's Maquiladoras," *Journal of International Economics* 42: 371–93.

Fleck, Susan, and Constance Sorrentino. 1994. "Employment and Unemployment in Mexico's Labor Force," *Monthly Labor Review*, November, pp. 1–31.

Garza, Gustavo. 1992. *Desconcentración tecnológica y localización industrial en México*. Mexico City: El Colegio de México.

Ghiara, Ranjeeta, and Eduardo Zepeda. 1996. "Returns to Education and Economic Liberalization." Documentos de Investigación 4. Mexico: Instituto de Economía Regional, Universidad Autónoma de Coahuila.

———. 2000. "Relative Wages and Education Premium in Tijuana, 1987–1996." Working Papers Series. La Jolla, Calif.: San Diego Dialogue.

Graizbord, Guillermo. 1995. "La reestructuración regional en México: cambios de la actividad económica urbana," *Comercio Exterior* 45 (2).

Hiernaux, Daniel. 1995. "Restructuración económica y cambios territoriales en México: un balance, 1982–1995," *Estudios Regionales* 43: 151–76.

Hussmanns, Ralf, Farhad Mehran, and Vijay Verma. 1990. *Surveys of Economically Active Population, Employment, Unemployment, and Underemployment: An ILO Manual on Concepts and Methods*. Geneva: International Labour Office.

INEGI (Instituto Nacional de Estadística, Geografía e Informática). 1987–1998. *Encuesta Nacional de Empleo Urbano (ENEU)*. Mexico City: INEGI.

———. 1991. *Encuesta Nacional de Empleo (ENE)*. Mexico City: INEGI

———. 1998. *Encuesta Nacional de Empleo (ENE)*. Mexico City: INEGI.

Katz, Jorge. 2000. "Pasado y presente del comportamiento tecnológico de América Latina." Serie Desarrollo Productivo, no. 75. Santiago: Comisión Económica para América Latina y el Caribe.

Krueger, Anne O. 1990. "The Relationship between Trade, Employment, and Development." In *The State of Development Economics: Progress and Perspectives*, edited by Gustav Ranis and T. Paul Schultz. Oxford: Basil Blackwell.

Krugman, Paul, and Raul Livas. 1992. "Trade Policy and Third World Metropolies." Working Paper 4238. Cambridge, Mass.: National Bureau of Economic Research.

Maloney, William F. 1999. "Does Informality Imply Segmentation in Urban Labor Markets? Evidence from Sectoral Transitions in Mexico," *World Bank Economic Review* 13 (2): 275–302.

Marcouiller, Douglas, Verónica Ruiz de Castilla, and Christopher Woodruff. 1997. "Formal Measures of the Informal-Sector Wage Gap in Mexico, El Salvador, and Peru," *Economic Development and Cultural Change* 45 (2): 367–92.

Mendiola, Gerardo. 1999. "Las empresas maquiladoras de exportación, 1980–1995." In *Pensar globalmente y actuar regionalmente: hacia un nuevo paradigma industrial para el Siglo Veintiuno*, edited by Enrique Dussel, Michael Piore, and Clemente Ruiz Durán. Mexico City: Universidad Nacional Autónoma de México/Fundación Friedrich Ebert/Editorial Jus.

Mendoza, Eduardo, and Gerardo Martínez. 1999. "Globalización y dinámica industrial en la frontera norte de México." Centro de Investigaciones Socioeconómicas, Universidad Autónoma de Coahuila. Mimeo.

Mincer, Jacob. 1974. *Schooling, Experience, and Earnings*. New York: Columbia University Press.

Mortimore, Michael. 1999. "La industria de las confecciones en la cuenca del Caribe: ¿un tejido raído?" *Revista de la CEPAL* 67: 113–32.

O'Day, Paul. 1997. "ATC Phase Out: A Few Big Winners, Long List of Losers," *International Fiber Journal* 12 (February).

Rendón, Teresa. 1999. "Tendencias del empleo en México," *Comercio Exterior* 49 (3): 251–59.

Rendón, Teresa, and Carlos Salas. 1993. "El empleo en México en los ochenta: tendencias y cambios," *Comercio Exterior* 43 (8): 717–30.

Robbins, Donald. 1995. "Trade, Trade Liberalization, and Inequality in Latin America and East Asia." Cambridge, Mass.: Harvard University. Mimeo.

Robertson, Raymond. 1999. "Trade Liberalization and Wage Inequality." Department of Economics, Macalester College. Mimeo.

Tan, Hong, and Geeta Batra. 1997. "Technology and Firm Size–Wage Differentials in Colombia, Mexico, and Taiwan (China)," *World Bank Economic Review* 11 (1): 59–83.

Ten Kate, Adrian, and Fernando de Mateo. 1989. "Apertura comercial y estructura de la protección en México," *Comercio Exterior* 39 (4): 312–29.

Unger, Kurt. 1993. "Productividad, desarrollo tecnológico y competitividad exportadora en la industria mexicana," *Economía Mexicana* 2 (1): 183–237.

Wood, Adrian. 1997. "Openness and Wage Inequality in Developing Countries: The Latin American Challenge to East Asian Conventional Wisdom," *World Bank Economic Review* 11 (1): 33–57.

Zepeda, Eduardo. 1997. "Salarios relativos y region, 1987–1993: el caso de la frontera norte de México," *Estudios Sociales* 7 (14): 123–52.

———. 2000. "Exportación, tecnología y salarios: la manufactura mexicana, 1987–1998." Universidad Autónoma Metropolitana–Azcapotzalco. Mimeo.

Zepeda, Eduardo, Diana Alarcón, and Gustavo Félix. 1999. "Empleo, competitividad y apertura económica: la pequeña y mediana empresa en la manufactura mexicana, 1985–1993." In *Reestructuración económica y empleo en México*, edited by Eduardo Zepeda and David Castro. Mexico: Universidad Autónoma de Coahuila/Fundación Friedrich Ebert.

Zepeda, Eduardo, and David Castro. 1999. "Servicios al productor y manufactura en el corredor de Saltillo, Monterrey, Nuevo Laredo." In *Reestructuración económica y empleo en México*, edited by Eduardo Zepeda and David Castro. Mexico: Universidad Autónoma de Coahuila/Fundación Friedrich Ebert.

Zepeda, Eduardo, David Castro, and Gustavo Félix. 1996. "Empleo y desarrollo y servicios al productor en los corredores del norte de México." In *El sector servicios: desarrollo regional y empleo*, edited by Fernando Chávez and Eduardo Zepeda. Mexico: Universidad Autónoma de Coahuila/Fundación Friedrich Ebert.

Zepeda, Eduardo, and Gustavo Félix. 1995. *El empleo y los servicios en la frontera norte*. Mexico City: Fundación Friedrich Ebert.

Zepeda, Eduardo, and Ranjeeta Ghiara. 1999. "Determinación del salario y capital humano en México, 1987–1993," *Economía, Sociedad y Territorio* 2 (5): 67–116.

Part VI

Historical and Comparative Perspectives on Mexican Development

15

Mexico's Development Challenges

Víctor L. Urquidi

Although favorable reports in the media and from official and international sources might suggest the contrary, Mexico has been in a state of economic and social stagnation over the last two decades. This sluggishness followed a thirty-year period of expansion during which economic and social development had advanced at an impressive pace. This chapter examines Mexico's economic and social policy experience across both periods, with an emphasis on the last twenty years, in hope of drawing some lessons for future sustainable development. The chapter is divided into five sections covering, respectively, the 1951–1980 expansion, the period of stagnation, policy inconsistencies in the 1990s, near-term prospects, and the outlook for sustainable development.

THIRTY YEARS OF EXPANSION

In the aftermath of World War II, wartime inflation and pent-up demand for imports introduced a degree of instability into the Mexican economy. After a period of currency flotation in 1947–1948, the government, with the support of the International Monetary Fund (IMF), tentatively stabilized the peso at 8.65 to the U.S. dollar. However, successive administrations were unable to regain investor confidence, and foreign earnings were depressed by the drop in export prices for basic products at the end of the Korean War. By April 1954, Mexico's currency reserves were depleted. At that point, the government, again with the consent of the IMF, made a bold move, adopting an undervalued peso parity at 12.5 to the dollar.

The author benefited from comments from Kevin J. Middlebrook and Eduardo Zepeda Miramontes on an earlier draft of this chapter.

TABLE 15.1. Average Annual Economic and Population Growth Rates in Mexico, 1951–2000[1]

Period	Gross Domestic Product (GDP)	Population	GDP Per Capita
1951–1960	6.1	2.9	3.1
1951–1970	6.3	3.0	3.1
1951–1980	6.4	3.0	3.3
1981–1990	1.7	2.2	–0.5
1981–2000	2.4	2.1	0.4
1991–1994	2.8	2.0	0.8
1991–2000	3.2	1.9	1.3

Source: Table 15.2 (population and GDP in constant 1980 pesos).

[1] Percent change. For each period, the base year is the immediately preceding year.

During this period, Mexico was also embarking on a new course of growth and development to stimulate investment, exports, and tax revenues. From 1951 through 1970—Mexico's period of "stabilizing development"—gross domestic product (GDP) increased an average of 6.3 percent annually in constant terms, and per capita GDP rose 3.1 percent on average (see table 15.1). Although structural problems deepened toward the end of the 1960s[1] with an anticipated decline in crude oil production and a creeping overvaluation of the peso, annual inflation during this period never exceeded 4 percent.

In the 1970s Mexico's economic policies diverged sharply from those of preceding years, veering toward deficit spending, public-sector investment, and credit expansion—all supported by the discovery and exploitation of new oil and gas deposits and by heavy external borrowing. Mexico's petroleum exports made the country a player in the global economy, and vast new industrial projects were launched under import-substitution policies (Urquidi 1997; Maddison and Associates 1992). By 1980, GDP growth over three decades measured 6.4 percent annually in constant terms, and per capita growth, 3.3 percent.

Although these rates were not the highest among developing countries, they were the peak rates in Latin America and they identified Mexico as a fast-growing economy. Living standards were on the rise, and the country was urbanizing rapidly. The industrial structure had

---

[1] Structural problems were already in evidence at the end of the 1950s (Vernon 1963).

undergone a shift toward iron and steel, metal working, pulp and paper, chemicals, motor vehicles, and household appliances, and the *maquiladora* (in-bond processing) sector was beginning to make an important contribution in several of these sectors. By 1980, the petroleum boom had added its impact to aggregate figures: GDP increased by 9.2 percent that year, followed by 8.8 percent in 1981. Social expenditures had risen throughout the period, although income inequality remained considerable.

Nevertheless, this thirty-year expansion had taken place under serious constraints, and not even the petroleum boom at the end of the period could fully compensate. These constraints included: (1) a lagging peasant agricultural sector; (2) high tariff and nontariff protection for manufacturing industry, which led to inefficient production; (3) limited domestic savings and limited access to external credit and foreign direct investment (FDI) — at least until the mid–1970s, when loans became plentiful; (4) low tax revenues; (5) high population growth, averaging 3.0 percent annually, with a resulting increase in the labor force; (6) an inadequate educational structure; and (7) periods of currency overvaluation, which usually ended in capital flight and abrupt devaluations, as in 1976.

Were it not for the 1973 international oil shock, which raised the value of Mexican petroleum and enabled the country to borrow in the global commercial banking system under fairly liberal terms for petroleum development[2] and large industrial schemes, Mexico would have had to liberalize its economy much earlier. Without rising petroleum prices, Mexico would have been obliged to attract larger inflows of FDI and to support costly research and development efforts in order to promote its manufactured exports. Increased petroleum export revenues also allowed Mexico to maintain its overvalued currency, which raised the price of national exports, even though a floating exchange rate would have been more appropriate to the inflationary conditions of the 1970s. In effect, the oil boom, with its bounty in foreign exchange receipts, allowed the Mexican government to postpone many needed policy reforms. The discovery of Mexico's vast petroleum deposits was not so much a blessing, then, as a threat to the nation's development.[3]

---

[2] Mexico does not allow private foreign investment in petroleum exploration and development, and practically no external loan funds were directly available at that time for the petroleum sector other than supplier credits and limited bond issues.

[3] Mexico's incorporation into the world petroleum market has been analyzed by many authors. This author's modest contributions include Urquidi 1982a, 1982b, and 1997.

TABLE 15.2. Mexico's Population and Gross Domestic Product, 1950–2000

Year	Population (millions)	Gross Domestic Product (GDP) — Constant 1980 Pesos (billions)	Percent Change	GDP per Capita in Pesos — Constant 1980 Pesos	Percent Change	GDP per Capita in U.S. Dollars — Constant 1980 Dollars	Percent Change
1950	27.8	693.0		2,495.2		545.6	
1960	37.0	1,252.0		3,388.8		908.0	
1970	50.6	2,340.0		4,624.9		1,573.8	
1980	67.0	4,470.0		6,666.9		2,903.6	
1981	68.5	4,862.2	8.8	7,094.3	6.4	3,342.9	15.1
1982	70.1	4,831.7	-0.6	6,896.7	-2.8	2,153.4	-35.6
1983	71.6	4,628.9	-4.2	6,463.8	-6.3	1,438.9	-33.2
1984	73.2	4,796.1	3.6	6,551.8	1.4	1,844.8	28.2
1985	74.8	4,920.4	2.6	6,575.6	0.4	1,716.0	-7.0
1986	76.5	4,735.7	-3.8	6,191.3	-5.8	1,390.5	-19.0
1987	78.2	4,823.6	1.9	6,169.3	-0.4	1,570.1	12.9
1988	79.9	4,883.7	1.2	6,110.5	-1.0	1,854.5	18.1
1989	81.7	5,047.2	3.3	6,177.9	1.1	2,095.6	13.0
1990	83.5	5,271.5	4.4	6,313.5	2.2	2,302.9	9.9
1991	85.2	5,462.7	3.6	6,414.0	1.6	2,673.9	16.1
1992	86.9	5,616.0	2.8	6,465.5	0.8	2,993.0	11.9
1993	88.6	5,649.7	0.6	6,376.0	-1.4	3,213.2	7.4
1994	90.4	5,899.1	4.4	6,527.7	2.4	3,266.7	1.7

Year	Population (millions)	Gross Domestic Product (GDP) Constant 1980 Pesos (billions)	Percent Change	GDP per Capita in Pesos Constant 1980 Pesos	Percent Change	GDP per Capita in U.S. Dollars Constant 1980 Dollars	Percent Change
1995	92.2	5,535.3	-6.2	6,003.4	-8.0	2,136.6	-34.6
1996	94.1	5,820.6	5.2	6,189.0	3.1	2,370.3	10.9
1997	95.7	6,214.7	6.8	6,491.2	4.9	2,795.9	18.0
1998	97.5	6,522.1	4.9	6,691.8	3.1	2,907.1	4.0
1999	99.1	6,760.2	3.6	6,820.2	1.9	3,201.4	10.1
2000	100.8	7,228.0	6.9	7,170.3	5.1	4,006.6	25.2

Sources: Data for correcting underreporting in population censuses during the 1950–1990 period and a population estimate for 1995 are from Gustavo Cabrera Acevedo, "Cambios en el tamaño y crecimiento de la población total," *Demos: carta demográfica sobre México* (1997): 4-5; the author interpolated population figures for non-census years and for the 1996–2000 period. Gross domestic product data at constant 1980 pesos are from CIEMEX-WEFA (Eddystone, Penn.), *Perspectivas económicas de México*, various issues (Section 10, Historical Data), based on data from the Instituto Nacional de Estadística, Geografía e Informática; the author converted the base year from 1993 to 1980 prices. The data on GDP per capita in 1980 U.S. dollars were obtained by converting gross domestic product data at current prices into U.S. dollars at the average annual rate of exchange, divided by population and corrected by the purchasing power index of the U.S. dollar reported in U.S. Department of Commerce, *Statistical Abstract of the United States: 2000* (table 767, p. 485), and *Survey of Current Business* 81 (12): table C.1.

The second oil shock, in 1979, brought domestic constraints and policy inconsistencies to the fore, revealing petroleum's paradoxical impact on the economy. Despite annual crude oil exports of over US$15 billion in 1979–1980, real GDP declined by 0.6 percent in 1982 and by 4.2 percent in 1983 (table 15.2). By 1982, Mexico's foreign debt had soared to over twenty times its level just twelve years earlier, and in September 1982, the fact that Mexico could not service its debt became public knowledge. At 16 percent of GDP, the public-sector deficit also was out of control. Capital flight ensued, driving down the value of the peso; years of virtual insolvency and slow, sometimes negative, GDP growth followed.

TWO DECADES OF STAGNATION

The 1980s were a period of adjustment. From 1981 to 1990, annual GDP grew by only 1.7 percent on average in real terms, and GDP per capita *declined* by 0.5 percent annually. In 1983 the Mexican government undertook efforts to achieve some recovery by holding the exchange rate steady while also meeting Mexico's external debt obligations. However, uncertainty and financial turbulence made this extremely difficult in the absence of new sources of foreign funding. The domestic economy had become inelastic in terms of tax revenue. International petroleum prices, which had remained fairly high through 1985, dropped precipitously in early 1986. Mexican authorities were unprepared for such a loss in foreign exchange receipts and the resulting reduction in tax revenue derived from petroleum exports. Inflation resurfaced with a vengeance: from 1981 through 1986, the consumer price index experienced a twentyfold increase, and in 1986 inflation-adjusted GDP fell 3.7 percent. An artificial boom in the stock exchange in 1987, which helped drive consumer prices up another 132 percent, further contributed to the country's economic distress.

The approach of the 1988 elections forced the adoption of a novel stabilization program in December 1987. It hinged on an agreement with business and labor on price and wage policy, and it included an unprecedented budget surplus target of 8 percent of GDP (excluding the financial sector) and a fixed buying rate of exchange. This "economic pact" brought inflation to manageable levels within eighteen months— from 114 percent in 1988 to 20 percent in 1989. However, it failed to stimulate GDP growth, which measured a mere 1.2 percent in 1988 and 3.3 percent in 1989 in real terms. The only practical course for meeting the fiscal target was to curtail spending—a recessionary (demand-depressing) adjustment. In addition, this approach depended on a non-declining currency value, deceptively announced as a sliding rate for imports of goods and services while the buying rate remained unchanged — that is, an expanding, officially managed, preannounced exchange-rate spread. At the same time, Mexico was moving toward trade opening. It joined the General Agreement on Tariffs and Trade (GATT) in 1986, which brought a sharp drop in tariffs and the elimination of nontariff barriers. A rise in imports was unavoidable.

These policy decisions were intended to set Mexico on a path toward macroeconomic stabilization, in the hope of restructuring the country's external debt and stimulating an increase in foreign direct investment and short-term capital inflows. To halt capital outflows, the government set interest rates for foreign deposits at a high level, eventually rising to about 14 percent in dollar terms. This strange combination of policy elements functioned well for a while and helped to restore confidence and slow inflation. Unfortunately, the new rates set to attract foreign capital inhibited Mexican domestic investment. Although the extremely high real cost of money to domestic enterprises (which bordered on 20 to 25 percent per year) did not seem to concern policy makers,[4] it marked the beginning of the steady destruction of midsize and small businesses in Mexico.

At the end of the oil boom in early 1986, Mexico was determined to expand manufactured exports by inviting foreign direct investment — in automobile and auto parts production and in electronics, for example — under more liberal terms, as well as by encouraging large Mexican enterprises to form alliances with transnational corporations in order to gain a foothold in external markets. Simultaneously, the declining value of the peso lowered the cost of Mexican labor, stimulating rapid growth of the maquiladora industry and leading to some immediate job creation in that sector. During these years the Mexican economy was essentially just "bumping along."

The U.S.–Mexican debt negotiations in 1989 helped relieve some of the pressure of Mexico's external debt. But little space remained in which to achieve a full economic recovery, and there was even less leeway for avoiding cuts in social spending, infrastructure maintenance and development, and intangibles of development policy such as the need for initiatives to protect the environment. Social policy began to suffer severely, and the only approximation to a social safety net was the government's policy of allowing the expansion of informal economic activities such as street vending.

---

[4] It is customary for Mexican commercial banks to operate with large interest spreads and to require borrowers to pay high commissions and special charges.

By 1990, the Mexican government had no integrated medium- to long-term development strategy.[5] The oil boom had pushed Mexico into global markets in the mid-1970s, but manufacturing policies and government investment plans remained closely constrained by the preexisting tendency to rely too much on the public sector and too little on the private sector. The "economic opening" of 1985–1986 did not increase nonpetroleum exports significantly, and by 1990 manufactured exports still measured a paltry US$14.9 billion (excluding gross maquiladora exports). Net maquiladora operations (the value added by cheap Mexican labor) yielded between US$3 and $4 billion. The administration of President Salinas de Gortari (1988–1994) entered office determined to take a giant step toward globalization and modernization, in which the negotiation of the North American Free Trade Agreement (NAFTA) would be a primary instrument.

POLICY INCONSISTENCIES IN THE 1990s

The 1990s was, however, a decade of economic fluctuations and serious external and domestic constraints. From 1991 to 1994, after a series of economic reforms—including the reprivatization of Mexico's banks and some state-owned companies, and a more liberal policy toward investment by transnational corporations, especially in the automobile industry—real GDP increased by a mere 2.9 percent per year on average. This was higher than the figure for 1981–1990 but still only about 44 percent of GDP growth during the 1951–1980 "golden years." Per capita GDP rose by only 0.8 percent per year in 1991–1994. Growth was particularly slow in 1993 (0.6 percent), followed by a mild recovery in 1994 to 4.4 percent (table 15.2), the same year in which the NAFTA was implemented.

The main goal of Mexico's macroeconomic policy at this point was to bring inflation down to single digits, a goal first achieved in 1993, at 9.9 percent, followed by 7 percent in 1994. However, 1994—an election year—was a year of undoing.[6] A major policy inconsistency had led, beginning in 1988, to a six-year gradual overvaluation of the peso. Expansion and recovery had taken place with a fixed buying rate (parity) set at 3.06 pesos to the dollar, while the peso's selling rate was allowed to slide. This gave a false impression of stability, especially as the spread widened. The current account deficit escalated from US$7.4 billion in 1990 to $14.9 billion in 1991, $23.4 billion in 1993, and an alarming $29.2 billion in

---

[5] Constitutional amendments adopted in 1984 setting up a national planning system would remain largely a rhetorical return to past planning ideas. See Urquidi 1999.

[6] Compounding the uncertainty in 1994 were the actions of the Zapatista Army of National Liberation (EZLN) and a series of high-profile political assassinations.

1994 (table 15.3). Banco de México authorities continued to assert that the peso was not overvalued, and the overvaluation was masked by huge short-term inflows of foreign capital attracted by very high rates of return. By midyear, peso-denominated treasury bonds (*tesobonos*) had been converted into dollar-denominated liabilities. By the end of 1994, the reverse flow of short-term capital (including outflows of Mexican liquid assets) had depleted the Mexican central bank's foreign reserves. Government authorities' sudden announcement in December of a further widening of the exchange rate spread led to the immediate collapse of the peso's value.

A US$57 billion rescue package developed by the U.S. Department of the Treasury and the IMF enabled the Mexican government to stitch together a new stabilization program in early 1995, which perforce had to be deeply recessionary. GDP declined by 6.2 percent in real terms in 1995, and GDP per capita fell by 8.0 percent. At the same time, inflation soared to 35 percent per year, mainly due to currency depreciation. A slow recovery followed, with real GDP rising 6.8 percent in 1997. However, because the baseline for this figure was so low, it disguises the fact that total growth over the whole 1995–1997 period was only 5.3 percent (an annual compound rate of only 1.8 percent). GDP per capita *declined* at an average annual rate of 0.2 percent, and in 1997 it was actually 0.6 percent *lower* than in 1994.

The overall result for the two decades from 1981 through the year 2000 was that the mean annual growth rate in GDP per capita remained virtually at zero (0.4 percent) (see table 15.1). Adding the year 2001 (when, according to official reports, GDP declined by 0.3 percent) would yield an even lower 21–year average of 0.3 percent.[7] Is this growth? Or is this lingering stagnation?

Economic adjustments and export policies since the mid–1990s have produced uneven results. Mexico's post–1995 economic recovery is confined to certain regions, branches of activity, and social sectors. There has been some recovery in the luxury goods and services market. The automobile and electronics industries have emerged as sources of growth and of exports, but again, their impacts are limited to specific regions. Many industrial subsectors have been moving out of the Mexico City metropolitan area since the late 1980s, and this process seems to have acceler-

---

[7] A calculation in U.S. dollars of constant purchasing power (1980 = 100) yields substantially the same result: an average annual GDP per capita growth rate of 0.5 percent for the 1981–1999 period, with an improvement to 1.6 percent through the year 2000 (partly the result of the overvaluation of the peso).

TABLE 15.3. Mexico's Balance of Payments, 1990–2000 (billions of current U.S. dollars)

Year	Exports Totals (1)	Exports Totals (2)	Exports Manufactured Goods (2)	Imports Totals (1)	Imports Totals (2)	Value Added by Maquiladoras
1990	45.1	26.8	14.0	41.6	31.3	3.6
1991	42.7	27.1	15.8	50.0	38.2	4.1
1992	46.2	27.5	16.7	62.1	48.2	4.8
1993	51.9	30.0	19.8	65.4	49.0	5.5
1994	60.9	34.6	24.1	79.3	58.8	5.8
1995	79.5	48.4	35.5	72.4	46.2	4.9
1996	96.0	59.1	43.4	89.5	59.0	6.4
1997	110.4	65.3	49.6	109.8	73.5	8.9
1998	117.5	64.4	53.0	125.4	82.9	10.6
1999	136.4	72.5	58.2	142.0	91.6	13.5
2000	166.4	87.0	65.8	174.5	112.8	17.8

Year	Trade Balance Excluding Maquiladora Production[1]	Current Account Balance
1990	–4.5	–7.4
1991	–11.1	–14.9
1992	–20.7	–24.4
1993	–19.0	–23.4
1994	–24.2	–29.7
1995	2.2	–1.6
1996	0.1	–2.3
1997	–8.2	–7.4
1998	–18.5	–16.0
1999	–19.1	–14.3
2000	–25.8	–17.7

Sources: CIEMEX–WEFA, *Perspectivas económicas de México* (Eddystone, Penn.: CIEMEX–WEFA, 1998); Banco de México, annual reports and *Indicadores económicos*, several editions.

Note: Column 1 includes gross-valued maquiladora exports and imports; column 2 excludes maquiladora exports and imports.

[1] This is the difference between non-maquiladora exports and non-maquiladora imports (columns 2 in the top portion of the table).

ated, with major industries and service units moving to center-west and northern Mexico.

The maquiladora sector has expanded rapidly, both in the number of plants and in employment. There has been a slight change in the origin of maquiladora inputs. Although the bulk of sales are exports based almost exclusively on duty-free imports, more locally made intermediate products are being incorporated into these firms' operations. The gross declared export value of maquiladora manufactures in 2000 was US$79 billion—21 percent more than exports of non-maquiladora products. On the other hand, the imported content of non-maquiladora exports has risen, particularly in the automobile industry. Beginning in 2001, the distinction between maquiladora and non-maquiladora exports all but disappeared under the terms of the NAFTA, which means that non-maquiladora manufactures will henceforth be able to compete more fully in the U.S. market.[8] It may be assumed that technological innovation, brought by transnational firms and through licensing agreements, will continue to make Mexican manufactured exports competitive in world markets, provided the currency does not become overvalued. It should be remembered, however, that such manufactures have a limited impact on domestic employment.

THE NEAR-TERM OUTLOOK

Mexico will likely face some serious problems in the near future.[9] One is a slowing in export growth. In 1999, the trade deficit returned—even when one includes gross maquiladora trade, which in past years yielded a surplus. Agricultural and petroleum exports may be less dynamic in the future. Falling world oil prices reduced the value of Mexico's petroleum exports by more than 30 percent in 1997, a trend that was reversed in late 1999 but which reappeared in 2001. Meanwhile, imports of petroleum products—mainly high-octane gasoline—are rising and will continue to do so. Grain imports have surged, augmented by the NAFTA's adverse impacts on Mexican traditional agriculture.

A second problem is the markedly rising deficit in the current account, which during the deepest moments of the 1995 recession had shown a small surplus. The current account ran a deficit of US$17.7 bil-

---

[8] Until that happens, however, it will remain useful for analytic purposes to distinguish between maquila and non-maquila manufactured exports, instead of including all maquila operations (both inputs and gross output) in aggregate trade figures, as some analysts and government officials are prone to do.

[9] For a more optimistic perspective, see OECD 1998.

lion in 2000 and was expected to remain at that level in future years, mainly due to debt service owed by both the public and private sectors.

This means that, barring an unexpected rise in exports, net tourism receipts, and migrant workers' remittances, Mexico may have to impose some restrictions on imports in order to protect its balance of payments. It is clear that Mexico's borrowing capacity has reached a limit; new issues in international capital markets can only be made to replace old issues and to restructure existing medium- and short-term debt, at annual interest rates of up to 10 or 11 percent. Given this situation, gaps will persist in the current account and, consequently, in the foreign exchange market.

It is important to emphasize that the years of stagnation brought a serious decline in real terms in expenditures on education, health care, community and rural development, low-cost housing, and so on. According to official figures, over 60 million Mexicans (out of a population of 102.4 million in 2001) now live below the poverty line, 25 million of them in extreme poverty.[10] Given the increased polarization brought about by the growth patterns of recent years, this means that income inequality has increased. The last few years have seen an impoverishment of the lower middle class, whose purchasing power was undermined by high interest rates and the limits on wage increases that formed part of Mexico's stabilization policy.

A PATH TO THE FUTURE

It will not be an easy task to move a stagnant Mexico toward a steady and cumulative expansion, with rising incomes, reduced inequality, and a lowering of extreme poverty rates. It is not a matter of selecting a desired rate of GDP growth and then calculating the investment needed; too many structural problems remain unresolved. It is not a matter of assuming that domestic savings can be increased with ease and in sufficient amounts to dispense with more net external borrowing; in fact, net borrowing may be constrained by the existing external debt structure. Nor is it a matter of supposing that foreign direct investment will be adequate to achieve a high and sustained growth rate. FDI may not flow to the sectors that could help develop the domestic market, which has been repressed as a matter of policy. It is much more likely that FDI will continue to go mainly to sectors that have proved to be successful exporters to global markets, especially the United States and Canada. How to encourage midsize and small enterprises to supply the domes-

---

[10] Most of Mexico's poor are concentrated in rural areas and in unregulated settlements in marginal urban areas.

tic market efficiently, simultaneously creating employment and local purchasing power, remains an unanswered question.

If there is no clear policy for industry, the situation is even worse for agriculture. The government has no coherent project to help peasants become market-oriented producers of cash crops. In effect, there is no acceptable long-range policy in any sector, because the government has embraced market-oriented policies without any planning or specific objectives. Such shortsighted policies, first formulated in the mid–1980s, proliferated throughout the 1990s. Although the social consequences of these policies—unemployment and underemployment, extreme poverty, inadequate educational and health care programs, and a deficit in basic services—have been recognized, partially and belatedly, this does not mean they can be reversed in the short run.

After more than twenty years of stagnation broken by occasional bursts of uneven economic activity, it is time for a serious reassessment of the Mexican political system and its impact on socioeconomic development policy. Mexico lives too much in its past, with a focus on the postrevolutionary period and the "golden years" of stabilizing growth in the 1960s and 1970s. Yet the policies that underpinned stabilizing growth, though generally positive, lacked three essential elements: a long-term energy policy, an ability to organize small-scale agriculture, and a comprehensive tax reform. In the current context of petroleum boom followed by post-boom crises, a heavy debt burden, half-baked policies to promote modernization, and Mexico's asymmetrical position within the NAFTA, it is extremely doubtful that the policies of the 1960s and 1970s have any relevance. Today the Mexican economy is open, exposed to external shocks and trade competition as never before. The real challenge is to harvest benefits from this process, including diversification in manufactured exports and in external markets, and to formulate a new industrial policy that can begin to rebuild a semi-abandoned domestic economy at the same time that it reconstructs markets based on the low-income population (De Maria y Campos 1998).

Such a challenge cannot be met without serious political reform including, especially, a fully developed participatory democracy and the constitutional changes that attend it. One such change involves defining and guaranteeing the right to own property as a prerequisite for developing domestic enterprise. The Mexican Constitution is not clear on this point; it gives the president and government officials undue leeway, even though the federal government no longer has the resources to promote development on its own. Full compliance with the rule of law—not only administrative ethics and functionality, but also full recourse to the justice system—is indispensable.

To ensure such conditions, the protections now in place to guarantee free and fair elections must be carried all the way to the legislature, to make lawmakers accountable and responsible to the electorate. Reforms should include overturning the single-term rule to give members of Congress, governors, and mayors the right to reelection (with term limitations, if necessary). The single-term rule does not encourage elected officials to be responsive to their electorates or to abide by democratic processes.[11]

Without comprehensive political reform, any development strategy — including sustainable development — is subject to the whim of the government in power, as well as to the excesses of free-market mechanisms in which interest groups make decisions and create power systems that override the will of the electorate, the views of civil society, and even the perceived needs of the nation. Of what use is an "IMF–approved" macroeconomic and fiscal policy if there is no regard for social problems that require enhanced and efficient spending programs? How can public officials be given free rein on monetary policy, interest rates, and currency valuation without legislative and civil society oversight or without full disclosure? How can a country function without a banking system that reports responsibly to the legislature, to civil society, and to public opinion, and which demonstrates that it can perform its core function — lending money to qualified borrowers? This list can easily be expanded to include a truly long-term sustainable development strategy that combines growth with equity and a strong environmental policy.[12]

Another area in need of reform is Mexico's educational system, which still operates under the hand of corporatist forces. Mexico has gained a reputation for enlightened educational policies, but the system lacks structure and is deficient in many areas. Basic education has improved, but it still lags behind other developing nations. Education at the high-school level is the weak link, with very negative implications for higher education. The human and financial resources that Mexico allocates to education fall far short of international standards, and the country's growing labor force continues to be made up primarily of uneducated and unskilled workers. Training as a supplement to formal education is notoriously insufficient, although some strides are being made in so-called distance learning.

---

[11] Presidential reelection might best be left for the future unless the president's term is reduced to four years, as in other countries.

[12] In a report issued by the Mexican Association for the Club of Rome in 1996, several working groups reviewed the prospects for many of these issues in light of world trends and long-range problems arising as part of the globalization process (see Urquidi 1996).

As regards the environment, the inadequacies of Mexican policies on water, forestry, land use, fisheries, alternative energy sources, public transportation, urban growth, regional development, and—not least important—population growth are becoming acute as these problems overwhelm the government's ability to address them. Environmental policies have enjoyed widening support since 1995, but nothing indicates that sustainable and equitable development will be achieved over the next generation. Despite legislative changes and improved program design that incorporate the concerns of business and civil society, environmental deterioration has not slowed. Air and water pollution, encroaching urbanization, and inadequate disposal of industrial and household waste continue unabated. Mexico is a growing contributor of the greenhouse gases responsible for global climate change, and the country is losing its rich biodiversity. Environmental policy is not yet a sufficiently high priority for the government or for society at large.

Increasing social and income inequality, along with the persistent undermining of social cohesion over the last decade, have been recognized, diagnosed, and measured.[13] But these problems have yet to be addressed with well-conceived, well-funded programs that incorporate civil society. The recent resurgence and reorganization of social programs have come more as an afterthought than as a targeted effort to address the fundamentals of social equity. Poverty-alleviation efforts are based on short-term compensation rather than on programs designed to establish the conditions under which poverty could be eradicated. Conditions are particularly deficient in the areas where Mexico's indigenous population is concentrated, but there is a nationwide need for sanitation systems, potable water, low-cost housing, urban infrastructure for small towns, preventive health care, and all the other services that urban families need, including schooling, day-care centers, and a reduction in crime and street violence.

As Mexico's political system now operates—on outdated social and economic premises—it is unlikely to unleash the nation's potential for sustainable development under globalization. Mexico's future will depend upon core reforms of the country's political institutions and of all related constitutional and legal provisions.

---

[13] A report prepared in 2001 by the Mexican Association for the Club of Rome draws attention to these issues for the first time; see De Maria y Campos and Sánchez 2001.

REFERENCES

De Maria y Campos, Mauricio. 1998. *Necesidad de una nueva política industrial para el México del Siglo XXI.* Mexico: Centro Lindavista.

De Maria y Campos, Mauricio, and Georgina Sánchez, eds. 2001. *¿Estamos Unidos Mexicanos? Los límites de la cohesión social.* Informe de la Sección Mexicana del Club de Roma. Mexico City: Planeta Mexicana.

Maddison, Angus, and Associates. 1992. *The Political Economy of Poverty, Equity and Growth: Brazil and Mexico.* Oxford: Oxford University Press, for the World Bank.

OECD (Organisation for Economic Co-operation and Development). 1998. *OECD Economic Surveys–Mexico.* Paris: OECD.

Urquidi, Víctor L. 1982a. "Not by Oil Alone: The Outlook for Mexico," *Current History* 81 (472): 78–81, 90.

———. 1982b. "Perspectivas de la economía mexicana ante el auge petrolero," *Revista de Occidente* [Madrid] 11 (June–July): 45–64.

———. 1997. "México en la globalización: avances y retrocesos," *Revista de Occidente* [Madrid] 198 (November): 35–46.

———. 1999. "Mexico's Development and Environmental Strategies: Looking Backward and Forward." Paper presented at the conference "The Environment of Greater Mexico—History, Culture, Economy, and Politics," Center for U.S.–Mexican Studies, University of California, San Diego, March 5–6.

Urquidi, Víctor L., ed. 1996. *México en la globalización: condiciones y requisitos de un desarrollo sustentable.* Informe de la Sección Mexicana del Club de Roma. Mexico City: Fondo de Cultura Económica.

Vernon, Raymond. 1963. *The Dilemma of Mexico's Development: The Roles of the Private and Public Sectors.* Cambridge, Mass.: Harvard University Press.

16

Confronting Human Development in Mexico

Keith Griffin and Amy Ickowitz ·

A radically new development strategy has been evolving in Mexico for roughly the last two decades. A rise in petroleum prices in 1973 and again in 1979—on both occasions engineered by the Organization of Petroleum Exporting Countries (OPEC)—enticed Mexico to modify its import-substitution industrialization strategy, first, by giving higher priority to petroleum exports, and second, by relying on foreign capital rather than domestic savings to finance its ambitious expansion program. These initial steps in global commodity and capital markets were followed by other measures—some virtually imposed on Mexico by external creditors after the 1982 debt crisis—which cumulatively produced a new development strategy based on market liberalization and openness to the international economy. This strategy promised to increase prosperity, reduce poverty, and create a more equitable society. Let us compare the promise with the reality and consider whether the new strategy has succeeded.

SLOW AND UNSTABLE GROWTH

The trend rate of growth in per capita output since 1980 has been very low. Indeed, when measured in constant pesos, gross domestic product (GDP) per capita was virtually the same in 1998 as in 1980 (Urquidi, this volume, table 15.2). Given the age structure of the population, this implies that the great majority of people in Mexico, those born after 1980, have experienced stagnation of real income throughout their entire lifetime. The new development strategy has failed to deliver prosperity.

·The authors are grateful to Diana Alarcón and Steven Helfand for comments on an early draft of this chapter.

On two occasions severe depressions have punctuated economic growth. The first was the 1982 debt crisis, when Mexico was caught between a sharp fall in the price of oil (a major export) and a sharp rise in real interest rates on the foreign borrowing used in part to finance expansion of the petroleum sector. The second was the 1994–1995 currency crisis in which Mexico was subjected to a severe speculative attack on the peso when it became clear that the exchange rate was overvalued and devaluation was inevitable. Both of these episodes produced a painful decline in real incomes, followed by a slow recovery after 1982 and a rapid recovery after 1995.

Whatever the long-term benefits of economic openness, experience has shown that managing an open economy can be difficult and that policy mistakes are harshly punished. The record in Mexico so far is that the new development strategy has been associated with a reduction in the average rate of growth and an increase in the volatility of growth rates.

There is always a temptation to attribute poor performance to "bad luck" or external "shocks" rather than to misguided policies. A deterioration in the external terms of trade caused by a decline in world petroleum prices, or repatriation of short-term capital by foreign investors, or a rise in global interest rates that increases the cost of servicing the foreign debt, or capital flight by domestic savers and investors—all are relevant examples for Mexico. Analysts looking for excuses can usually find plausible examples of negative shocks and bad luck to explain away disappointing economic performance. But it is equally easy to find examples of good luck, such as the sustained rapid growth of the U.S. economy in the 1990s, which provided a huge, near-by, and expanding market for exports.

Indeed, in an open economy one should anticipate periodic external shocks (both positive and negative) and incorporate appropriate policies into the overall development strategy to cope with them. Particularly important are policies toward foreign borrowing, exchange rates, and international reserves. For example, in 1997 Mexico's foreign exchange reserves per capita were only 70 percent the size of South Korea's and Thailand's reserves, and this helps explain why it takes Mexico somewhat longer to recover from external shocks compared to the relatively fast recovery in South Korea and Thailand after their 1997 external financial shocks. In other words, countries can make their own luck to some extent. In the specific case of Mexico, we believe that slow growth has less to do with external shocks than with domestic policy.

EXPORT-LED GROWTH

Such growth as has occurred has been export-led, and this tendency accelerated in the 1990s. Closer integration into the world economy began before the 1982 debt crisis and was reflected in increased reliance on foreign capital to finance development and increased petroleum production for export. More general market liberalization began in earnest after the 1982 debt crisis, and it was carried further after the 1994–1995 currency crisis. Tariff rates in the late 1990s, for example, averaged between 2 and 6 percent, and because of changes in the structure of incentives favoring international trade, export expansion accounted for half or more of GDP growth (Vega and De la Mora, this volume). Exports in 1980 represented only 11 percent of GDP; in 1997 they were nearly three times higher, at 30 percent of GDP.

The volume of exports increased nearly 5 percent a year between 1980 and 1996; exports grew two and a half times faster during the 1990–1996 period than during 1980–1990. Because of Mexico's deteriorating terms of trade, however, the value of exports increased much less rapidly than their volume. Over the entire 1980–1996 period, the value of exports grew by only 2.2 percent a year, and average annual growth was much slower in the years between 1980 and 1990 (1.2 percent) than between 1990 and 1996 (4.0 percent).

In per capita terms, export earnings increased only 0.2 percent a year. Thus, although foreign trade undoubtedly was the engine of growth, it was a rather feeble engine. This does not imply that it was a mistake for Mexico to seek greater integration with the global economy, but it does suggest that market liberalization and openness do not suffice to produce a successful development strategy.

INCREASED DISARTICULATION OF THE ECONOMY

The structure of the Mexican economy has become increasingly disarticulated. One would anticipate that as development proceeds, changes in the composition of output and the allocation of labor would result in a narrowing of differences in factor productivity among sectors and greater uniformity within sectors. This has not happened in Mexico.

The share of total output originating in agriculture has been falling for decades, and agriculture now accounts for only 5 percent of GDP.[1] Similarly, the share of the labor force employed in agriculture has been falling steadily, although agriculture still absorbs 28 percent of the la-

---

[1] World Bank 1999a: table 4.2. Other figures in this paragraph are the authors' calculations based on World Bank data.

bor force. The productivity of labor in agriculture has been falling, compared with some increase in per capita production in industry and virtually no change in services. In 1997 the productivity of agricultural labor was only 13.5 percent of average productivity in the rest of the economy, whereas in 1970 it measured 17.3 percent. In other words, agriculture is falling behind, the allocation of labor is increasingly inefficient, and the disarticulation of the economy is rising over time.

The same is true of the rest of the economy. One symptom of this is the growing "informalization" of the economy — that is, an increase in the proportion of the urban labor force that is self-employed or working in very small enterprises (Salas and Zepeda, this volume). Another symptom is the relative success of large enterprises — domestic and foreign — producing for the export market, as compared to the relative failure of small and midsize local enterprises producing for the domestic market. Nonagricultural enterprises in Mexico are becoming increasingly polarized, and the degree of concentration appears to be rising (see Zepeda and Castro 1999). Yet another symptom is the great contrast between the strong growth of manufactured exports and the weak growth of manufacturing-sector employment, especially in large enterprises apart from *maquiladora* firms (Alarcón and Zepeda 1998).

Something similar seems to be occurring within agriculture. Although the sector as a whole is depressed, large agricultural corporations producing export products have done well, whereas small farmers producing for family consumption or the domestic market have become impoverished. These patterns of structural disarticulation are, of course, related to changes in the distribution of income and wealth, discussed below.

THE SOFT STATE

The federal government's revenue and expenditure policies have contributed to neither growth nor equity. The state has abdicated responsibility for ensuring rapid economic growth, improving the distribution of income and wealth, and promoting human development. In this sense, Mexico has suffered from a soft state,[2] and its new development strategy seems to be based on an assumption — rhetoric notwithstanding — that a change in the structure of incentives and the privatization of state enterprises are the core reforms. The implication is that, with

---

[2] The concept of the "soft state" was introduced by Gunnar Myrdal (1968: 895–900). We use the term in a restricted sense to describe a state that has not created a structure of incentives, or used its tax and expenditure policies or its power to regulate the private sector, to promote equitable and sustainable development.

minimal support from the state, the private sector can achieve the country's development objectives. Evidence to date suggests that this assumption is wildly optimistic.

Resources available to the government for development and other purposes are limited. Central government revenue in 1996 was only 15.4 percent of Mexico's GDP.[3] This is below the average for countries classified by the World Bank as middle income (17.4 percent), and it is well below the revenues available to governments in more successful developing countries in East and Southeast Asia. For example, in 1996 government revenue accounted for 21.3 percent of GDP in South Korea, 24.9 percent in Malaysia, and 29.0 percent in Singapore (World Bank 1999a: table 4.13). That is, government revenues in these three countries, relative to GDP, are between 38 and 88 percent higher than in Mexico. This is one indication of the Mexican state's inability to mobilize resources for development. Tax reform should be high on the agenda of a revised development strategy. This is especially important because resources available from state-owned enterprises have diminished as a result of privatization (Dussel Peters, this volume).

Turning to the expenditure side of government accounts, the proportion of central government expenditure allocated to capital formation in Mexico has fallen dramatically, from 32 percent in 1980 to 12 percent in 1996. The state no longer assumes responsibility for promoting growth through government investment. Again, there is a stark contrast with the more successful developing economies in East and Southeast Asia. In 1996, capital expenditure accounted for 23 percent of all government spending in South Korea, 19 percent in Malaysia, and 29 percent in Singapore (World Bank 1999a: table 4.14). In other words, the Mexican state devotes a much lower proportion of its resources to financing investment than do several other "open economy" countries.

The state's withdrawal from investment does not mean that it has given higher priority to direct transfer payments and other programs intended to reduce poverty and improve income distribution. Although anti-poverty programs have been much publicized, the fact remains that "general government consumption" in Mexico—the category that includes expenditures on anti-poverty programs—has fallen from 10 per-

---

[3] Central government revenue in 1980 was about the same proportion of GDP as in 1996. The difference was in the role of state-owned enterprises. The share of GDP accounted for by state enterprises declined sharply, as did investment in state enterprises as a percentage of total investment. Between 1985–1990 and 1990–1996, for example, state enterprises' share of GDP fell by nearly 27 percent, and the share of state enterprise investment in total investment fell by 28 percent. Privatization of state-owned enterprises greatly reduced the resources under the government's direct control.

cent of GDP in 1980 to 8 percent in 1997. Given that per capita GDP was stagnant or falling during this period, it is clear that real government expenditure fell substantially—indeed, by about 20 percent. Liberalization has been accompanied by a shrinking state. Something similar, but on a larger scale, has occurred in many "transition economies," with devastating effects (see UNDP 1997).

HIGH AND INCREASED INEQUALITY

Mexico, like much of Latin America, has a very unequal income distribution. This is not new. Indeed, one of the unfortunate consequences of the import-substitution industrialization strategy that was followed until the 1980s was a high degree of inequality.[4] The new strategy was expected to reduce inequality; instead, it has increased it.

According to World Bank estimates, in 1984 the poorest 20 percent of Mexico's population received 4.1 percent of total income, and the richest 20 percent received 55.9 percent, giving a quintile ratio of 13.6. By 1995, the bottom quintile's share had fallen to 3.6 percent of total income, and that of the top quintile had risen to 58.2 percent. The quintile ratio in that year was 16.2, or 19.1 percent higher than in 1984.[5] Moreover, the degree of inequality is much higher in Mexico than in East and Southeast Asia. The Gini coefficient in Mexico in 1995 was about 53.7; it was 48.4 in Malaysia, 36.5 in Indonesia, and 36 in South Korea (in 1982).

The conclusion is inescapable: Mexico's new development strategy has failed to raise average incomes over a period of nearly two decades, and it has failed to reduce inequality in income distribution. A highly unequal distribution of income among persons and households can be analyzed from other perspectives. Rural-urban inequalities are very great, largely because the poor are disproportionately located in the countryside while the rich are concentrated in the cities. Similarly, regional inequality is high, although possibly diminishing somewhat (Garza, this volume). There are sharp inequalities among ethnic groups, and the indigenous population in particular is a victim of persistent discrimination.

Finally, there is gender inequality. One overall measure that is increasingly used is the "gender-related development index" (GDI) developed by the United Nations Development Programme (UNDP). Ac-

---

[4] For a general analysis of the import-substitution industrialization strategy, see Griffin 1999a: chap. 5.

[5] The data for 1984 were taken from World Bank 1993: table 30. Data for 1995 came from World Bank 1999a: table 2.8.

cording to this measure, discrimination against women in Mexico is less than in the median Latin American country, but Mexico's record is poorer than those of Argentina and Chile (though better than that of Brazil). Perhaps more illuminating is the fact that the GDI in Malaysia, South Korea, and Singapore is higher than in Mexico; indeed, in the case of Singapore it is 9.6 percent higher (see UNDP 1998: tables 2 and 4).

Moreover, the available evidence suggests that the economic position of women in Mexico deteriorated, relative to men, during the 1984–1994 period (Alarcón and McKinley 1999). In urban areas, the ratio of female-to-male wages declined from 77.1 percent in 1984 to 72.8 percent in 1994. Women became more concentrated in low-wage sectors of the economy and in low-wage jobs within sectors. This occurred, furthermore, at a time when women had more technical training than men and the gap in general education favoring women actually increased. In rural areas, female wage differentials were narrow and declined only modestly, but earnings differentials declined sharply, from 85.1 percent in 1984 to 62.4 percent in 1994. The new development strategy has been a disaster for women.

SEVERE AND INCREASED POVERTY

Slow growth, greater inequality in the distribution of income and wealth, informalization of the economy in a context of stagnation, rising wage inequality in nonagricultural activities (Salas and Zepeda, this volume), and a decline in per capital agricultural output have combined to produce a high incidence of poverty, as well as an increase in the absolute number of people and the proportion of the population living in poverty. Whatever the precise figures may be, Mexico's new development strategy has failed to keep its promise to the poor.

There are numerous studies of poverty in Mexico. They differ in details but are in agreement on broad conclusions. In summarizing, we shall rely on data from the national income and expenditure surveys of 1984, 1989, 1992, and 1994, although the figures reported will be limited to 1984 and 1994 to simplify presentation. The concept of poverty used here is the conventional one of income poverty, and the nutritionally based threshold is equivalent to an expenditure in September 1989 prices of US$25 per person per month. Those living below this threshold are said to be in "extreme poverty."[6]

The number of people living in extreme poverty in Mexico increased from 13.1 million in 1984 to 18.2 million in 1994, or by nearly 39 percent.

---

[6] The data presented here are from Kelly 1999.

TABLE 16.1. Mexican Population Living in Extreme Poverty,
                1984–1994 (millions)

	Rural	Urban	Total
1984	9.1	4.0	13.1
1994	14.4	3.9	18.2
Change, 1984–1994	5.3	−0.1	5.1

Source: Kelly 1999: table 4.5.

TABLE 16.2. Proportion of Mexico's Population Living in Extreme
                Poverty, 1984–1994 (percentages)

	Rural	Urban	Total
1984	34.5	9.0	18.3
1994	38.4	7.3	20.3
Percent change 1984–1994	11.3	−18.9	10.9

Source: Kelly 1999: table 4.1.

Most of the poor (79 percent in 1994) live in rural areas.[7] Moreover, the
number of extremely poor rural people increased by 58 percent in just
one decade, 1984 to 1994. In urban areas, there was a slight decline in
the number of poor over the same period (see table 16.1). As a result,
poverty in Mexico has increasingly become a rural phenomenon, in
contrast to other parts of Latin America. For example, rural poverty
accounts for only 9 percent of the total number of poor people in Venezuela, 17 percent in Chile, 35 percent in Peru, and 46 percent in Colombia (Griffin 1999b: table 1). The data for Mexico almost certainly understate the extent to which extreme poverty has increased, given that
poverty in the year of the baseline study (1984) had already increased
over 1980 or 1982 (the year the debt crisis erupted) levels. Furthermore,
data for 1994 cannot have captured the increase in poverty that occurred after the 1994–1995 currency crisis.

Of course, some of the increase in poverty can be attributed to
demographic expansion, but there was also an increase in the incidence
of poverty. Between 1984 and 1994, the proportion of Mexico's population living in extreme poverty rose from 18.3 percent to 20.3 percent.
This represents an increase of 10.9 percent in the incidence of poverty.
Once again, the heart of the problem is located in the countryside. In
rural areas, the incidence of extreme poverty rose from 34.5 to 38.4 per-

---

[7] For a detailed analysis of the structure of rural poverty in 1989, see McKinley and
Alarcón 1995.

cent, an increase of 11.3 percent in one decade. In urban areas, in contrast, the incidence of extreme poverty declined from 9.0 percent in 1984 to 7.3 percent in 1994 (see table 16.2). This is an aspect of the increased disarticulation of the economy mentioned earlier.

Once again, the data understate the severity of the problem because the incidence of poverty in the base year (1984) already was higher than in the years immediately preceding the change in economic strategy. Although the depth of poverty (as measured by the proportional poverty gap) declined in urban areas between 1984 and 1994 (from 2.3 to 1.8 percent), it increased both in the country as a whole (from 5.7 to 6.2 percent) and in rural areas (from 11.5 to 12.3 percent) (Kelly 1999: table 4.1). In general, not only were the poor more numerous, absolutely and relatively, but they also were poorer at the end of the period than at the beginning.

THE POLICY POSTURE

The increases in inequality and poverty that occurred in Mexico during the 1980s and during the 1990s were not inevitable; they were the result of policy choices made in the context of the liberalization strategy. Although it could be argued that there was a need to reduce public expenditures in the immediate aftermath of the 1982 debt crisis, the cuts that occurred were extreme. The reduction in investment expenditure not only lowered the overall rate of growth, but it also made structural adjustment much more difficult because resources needed to exploit opportunities in newly profitable activities were not available in sufficient volume. The change in the structure of incentives thus led to adjustment through contraction rather than adjustment through growth. Adding insult to injury, the government reduced the level of social expenditure, although social expenditure as a percentage of a contracting GDP actually increased during the 1989–1996 period. What matters most, however, is that the level of expenditure and its decline meant that those harmed by adjustment through contraction had the social safety net removed from beneath them.

Even if one argues that the government was unable to increase substantially expenditures on social protection, it would have been possible to reallocate public expenditure so as to accommodate a greater concern for reducing poverty and inequality. For example, in 1996 expenditures per primary school student were the equivalent of 11.9 percent of the average income (per capita gross national product, GNP), whereas expenditures per tertiary school student were equivalent to 46.9 percent of the average income. Compare this with South Korea, where expenditures per primary school student were equivalent to 18.8 percent of GNP per capita, and expenditures per tertiary school student were equivalent to 6 percent of the average income (World Bank 1999a). In other words, South Korea's public expenditures on primary school students were three times more than public expenditures on tertiary school students, whereas in Mexico public expenditures on each primary school student were roughly a quarter of public expenditures on each tertiary school student. Not only did Mexico's pattern of spending worsen inequality, but it was also inefficient because there is strong evidence that the returns on expenditures on primary and secondary education are higher than the returns on tertiary education (see, for example, Psacharopoulos 1994).

The "economic pacts" that the Mexican government first negotiated with organized labor in 1987–1988 effectively acted to repress wages — and hence the real incomes of low-skilled workers in the manufacturing sector. Rather than constituting a short-term emergency measure designed to control inflation at a particularly vulnerable time, the pacts appear to have become a semi-permanent incomes policy designed to lower the level—and then the rate of increase—of real wages. Indeed, one study estimates that blue-collar workers' real wages fell by 30 percent between 1980 and 1994 (Alarcón, this volume). The real minimum wage fell by 65 percent between 1980 and 1995, at a time when wages for skilled workers rose slightly (Wilkie 1997). Thus wage inequality increased. Over time, as workers' economic situation failed to improve, the labor movement became increasingly reluctant to tolerate the unequal distribution of the structural adjustment burden. In 1995, organized labor refused to endorse another "economic pact."[8]

At the same time that these pacts increased inequality by reducing the income of those at the bottom of the pyramid, the massive privatization of state-owned enterprises increased inequality by raising the income of those at the top. The number of state-owned enterprises decreased from 1,155 in the mid–1980s to 200 in 1994. In this same period, the number of Mexican billionaires increased from one to twenty-four (Summa 1994: 24). The privatization process was hastily implemented and poorly regulated, and the result was an "undesirable concentration of wealth and ownership in some of the privileged areas" (Lustig 1998: 153).

The liberalization of Mexico's financial markets in 1989–1990 probably increased inequality both directly and indirectly through the crisis that ensued. The ostensible justification for opening financial markets was to gain greater access to foreign capital in order to supplement

---

[8] The 1994 currency crisis was, of course, the precipitating cause of labor's refusal.

domestic savings and to increase investment. Increased investment was supposed to accelerate growth and bring prosperity for all. In practice, however, most of the capital inflow appears to have supplemented consumption rather than investment. In fact, "commercial bank lending for consumption grew in real terms by 457.7 percent over the period 1987–1994. . . . By contrast, lending for the manufacturing industry grew by 130.6 percent" (Ramírez de la O 1996: 13) This change in the pattern of bank lending made the financial system — and hence the economy as a whole — vulnerable to shocks.

The desire to attract foreign capital generally puts pressure on a country to adopt anti-inflationary policies and maintain high interest rates. High interest rates, in turn, tend to discourage productive investment in plant and equipment and to encourage speculative activities (Grabel 1995). This is precisely what has occurred in Mexico. In such an environment, it is the small and midsize enterprises that encounter the most difficulties in obtaining credit. This not only results in greater inequality, but it also reduces efficiency in resource allocation.

The 1994–1995 currency crisis was the result of financial liberalization. While the benefits of financial liberalization appear to have accrued to members of the Mexican elite who participated in the stock market boom, the costs of liberalization were socialized. Analysts estimate that the Mexican government spent 20 percent of the country's 1999 GDP on rescue programs for financial institutions (Dussel Peters, this volume).

One consequence of the currency crisis was the near collapse of the Mexican financial system. Although the system survived, credit to the private sector as a whole fell by 25 percent in real terms between the second quarter of 1995 and the first quarter of 1999 (Trigueros 1999). Even in the pre-crisis years, lending to small and midsize enterprises was low; since the crisis, the problem has become even more serious. That is, Mexico's already underfinanced small and midsize enterprises have seen a further reduction in the availability of credit.

The reform of the *ejido* sector that began in 1992, combined with other institutional changes in the rural economy, is yet another example of a policy posture that has increased inequality. Although there were many things wrong with the state's policies toward the ejido sector in the past, the solution adopted is not one that will reduce extreme poverty or inequality. It is true that the relationship between the state and ejidos has been complex and not always unequivocally beneficial for the latter. However, the state at least provided some institutional support through the National Rural Credit Bank (BANRURAL) and through its agricultural pricing policies. But from the 1980s onward, institutional support has declined, and ejidos have effectively been abandoned. Agricultural reforms have reduced the availability and increased the cost of credit, insurance, and essential inputs. By the late 1990s, "only commercial farmers [were] obtaining loans in amounts sufficient to induce experimentation with productivity-enhancing technologies. The vast majority of basic grains producers have been abandoned by the Mexican rural financial system" (Myhre 1998: 61–62). These changes are increasing social differentiation in the countryside, with a small group of producers able to take advantage of market reforms while the great majority of *ejidatarios* lag behind. "The successful entrepreneurs tend to be those who either have more land or more access to credit and irrigation, that is, the relatively better off. On the other end of the spectrum are the small farmers and indigenous community members who find it difficult to modernize and diversify because of the limited access to investable funds and institutional services" (Lustig 1998: 207–8).

It is unclear whether the reforms are leading to a further concentration of land ownership, but they certainly will not reduce the concentration of ownership. The land reform that occurred after the Mexican Revolution and that was codified in Article 27 of the Constitution improved land distribution, but it fell short of ensuring an equitable distribution of land. The Gini coefficient for land distribution declined from 0.78 in 1923 to 0.58 in 1970, demonstrating a significant improvement (Jazairy, Alamgir, and Panuccio 1992: app. 10). A Gini coefficient of 0.58, however, is still indicative of substantial inequality. Moreover, several recent studies have found a negative relationship between asset inequality and growth (see, for example, Birdsall, Ross, and Sabot 1995; Griffin and Ickowitz 2000). And many analysts claim that part of the explanation for the exemplary performance of the South Korean and Taiwanese economies is their high degree of equity in the distribution of productive assets. The implications for Mexico are obvious. While Mexico's Gini coefficient for land distribution was 0.58, the Gini coefficient for South Korea (in 1980) was 0.33. Instead of taking steps to remedy existing land ownership inequalities, the Mexican government unfortunately has adopted policies that are likely to exacerbate them.

If the reforms begun in 1992 had been accompanied by measures enabling ejidatarios and small farmers to make their existing assets more productive, then perhaps the overall impact would not be detrimental to income inequality even if the reforms were to worsen asset inequality. One main justification for the reforms was that they would enable ejidatarios to use their land as collateral and thereby improve their access to credit which, in turn, would facilitate the purchase of essential inputs and the adoption of better technologies. This has not occurred, however. The state has withdrawn from providing institutional support such as loans to small farmers, and the private sector has not moved in to fill the vacuum. This is not surprising given that the agricultural sector in Mexico, as in most developing countries, is riddled with market imperfections, and in such circumstances a laissez-faire policy posture is unlikely to be efficient.

COMPARATIVE POVERTY

It is instructive to compare poverty in Mexico and in other broadly similar countries. To do this, we have selected, somewhat arbitrarily, nine countries for which comparable data are available. Five of these countries are in Latin America (Brazil, Chile, Colombia, Costa Rica, and Venezuela) and four in Asia (Indonesia, Malaysia, Philippines, and Sri Lanka). This comparison employs two rather different notions of poverty. The first is income poverty, the indicator for which is the World Bank's standard of one U.S. dollar per day (in purchasing power parity terms). In the Mexican context, this is a very low poverty threshold, only slightly more generous than the "extreme poverty" threshold used in the previous section. Hence one should be careful in interpreting the results produced by using this measure.

Measures of income poverty are sensitive to the poverty line adopted and to the distribution of income in the neighborhood of the poverty line. They are also sensitive to the unit of observation (household, household income per capita, income per adult equivalent, and so on) and to the concept of "income" used (total expenditures, income net of subsidies and taxes, income including the imputed value of self-provided goods, and so on). In addition, international or cross-country comparisons of the incidence of poverty must confront the problem of selecting an international poverty line that is universally applicable and that makes sense in countries that differ greatly in terms of average income per capita. This universal poverty line then has to be expressed in a common currency (the U.S. dollar, for example) by using either market exchange rates or, as in the World Bank's standard, purchasing-power-parity prices. There are numerous points at which estimates of income poverty can be challenged, and poverty estimates should be used only for making broad comparisons in changes over time and across countries. And there is a further problem: alternative definitions of poverty may not be highly correlated with one another.

The second concept of poverty used here is "human poverty" as measured in the UNDP's Human Poverty Index (HPI), a simple average age of three components: (1) the proportion of the population not expected to live to age 40; (2) the adult illiteracy rate; and (3) the percent-

TABLE 16.3. Comparisons of Income and Human Poverty among Ten Countries, 1990s

	Gross National Product per Capita (US$)	Population Receiving Less Than US$1 per Day		Human Poverty Index Rank
		Percent	*Rank*	
Chile	5,020	15.0	7	2
Brazil	4,720	23.6	9	7
Malaysia	4,680	5.6	2	6
Mexico	3,680	14.9	6	4
Venezuela	3,450	11.8	=4	5
Costa Rica	2,640	18.9	8	1
Colombia	2,280	7.4	3	3
Philippines	1,220	28.6	10	8
Indonesia	1,110	11.8	=4	10
Sri Lanka	800	4.0	1	9

Sources: Gross national product per capita and income poverty, World Bank 1999b; human poverty, UNDP 1999.

age of the population that does not enjoy a decent standard of living. This last component, again, is a simple average of the percentage of people without access to safe water, the percentage without access to health services, and the percentage of underweight children under age five.[9] Note that the HPI attempts to measure deprivation directly and does not rely on a money metric.

The countries included in this comparison are ranked in table 16.3 in descending order of GNP per capita. The range is between US$5,020 per capita in Chile and $800 per capita in Sri Lanka in the late 1990s. Mexico ranks fourth, at $3,680. With regard to income poverty, using the World Bank's standard, the range is between 4.0 percent of the population in poverty (in Sri Lanka) and 28.6 percent (in the Philippines). Mexico ranks sixth, at 14.9 percent. The rank ordering of countries under the Human Poverty Index differs considerably from the ordering under income poverty. According to the HPI, Costa Rica has the lowest incidence of poverty and Indonesia the highest; Mexico ranks fourth, after Costa Rica, Chile, and Colombia.

---

[9] For details of the calculations, see UNDP 1999: 163.

It is evident that income poverty and human poverty are not as closely correlated as one might imagine. Sri Lanka, which ranks tenth in per capita income and ninth in human poverty, ranks first in income poverty. Chile, which ranks first in per capita income and second in human poverty, ranks only seventh in income poverty. A country (like Sri Lanka) may have a low average income and be unsuccessful in eliminating the most serious forms of deprivation and yet succeed in ensuring that almost everyone has an income of at least US$365 a year. Another country (such as Costa Rica) may have a relatively low income by Latin American standards and a high incidence of income poverty, and yet succeed in minimizing the extent of human poverty. This suggests that differences in policies account for differences in outcomes.

Although Mexico ranks fourth in terms of average income, it has a higher percentage of the population suffering from income poverty than four of the six countries (Venezuela, Colombia, Indonesia, and Sri Lanka) that are poorer on average. On the other hand, Mexico has done much better than Brazil. Turning to human poverty, Mexico's relative performance improves. It ranks fourth in terms of average income and human poverty. Even so, Mexico has done less well than Costa Rica and Colombia, both of which have lower average incomes than Mexico.

Hence one is forced to conclude that Mexico's performance is not particularly good when viewed in international perspective. Indeed, market liberalization and openness to the international economy have yet to fulfill the promise of less poverty and greater prosperity for all. Moreover, the findings here have a clear policy implication—namely, that if government is concerned about reducing human poverty, it would be wrong to assume that a reduction in income poverty would suffice, and vice versa. One should address all forms of poverty directly.

CONCLUSION

Over a period of two decades, Mexico has adopted and gradually implemented a new development strategy based on market liberalization and openness to the international economy. This strategy has been a failure whether viewed in international comparative perspective or from the perspective of Mexico's past achievements. Mexico's growth rate since 1980 has been well below that of the rest of Latin America and the Caribbean—or, for that matter, the 156 other low- and middle-income countries taken as a whole (World Bank 1999a: table 4.1). The growth rate is also lower and more volatile than it was in the pre-reform period. Indeed, the average Mexican has experienced no increase in real income since the new strategy was adopted.

Mexico is a relatively rich country, however. The UNDP estimates that in real per capita GDP (measured in purchasing power parity terms), Mexico ranks 47th out of the 174 countries for which data are available. One should not take such estimates too seriously, but the fact remains that Mexico is a member of the Organisation for Economic Co-operation and Development (OECD, sometimes referred to as the "Rich Countries' Club") and could reasonably aspire to become a high-income country. Unfortunately, human development has lagged behind material progress. According to the UNDP's Human Development Index, Mexico ranks 50th out of 174 countries. In other words, in relative terms Mexico has been somewhat more successful in generating income for its people than in achieving human development.

One reason for this has to do with the high degree of inequality in Mexico. The World Bank publishes data on income distribution in ninety-six countries (World Bank 1999a: table 2.8). Using the Gini coefficient as an indicator of overall inequality, it appears that only twelve countries have an income distribution more unequal than Mexico's. Most of these countries are in Latin America, and the rest are in sub-Saharan Africa—two regions with disappointing development records. Mexico thus finds itself in unsavory company. Moreover, since the introduction of the new development strategy, inequality in Mexico has increased.

So, too, has poverty, as we have seen in some detail. Sadly, Mexico has been even less successful in reducing human poverty than in increasing human development. The UNDP has compiled a human poverty index for ninety-seven developing countries (UNDP 1999: table 4). Among these countries, Mexico ranks tenth on the HDI but only thirteenth on the Human Poverty Index. Thus, Mexico has been most successful in achieving a high average real income, somewhat less successful in pursuing human development, and least successful in reducing human poverty.

Among all the problems Mexico faces, it would be relatively easy to eliminate income poverty, particularly extreme poverty. All that is needed is some combination of faster growth in average income and a modest redistribution of income in favor of the poor. Consider the growth rate. During the 1990–1997 period, per capita GDP in Mexico increased only 0.2 percent per annum; in developing countries as a whole, the growth rate was six times faster, at 1.2 percent per annum. If Mexico could achieve and sustain even such a meager growth rate, poverty would decline slowly but steadily. Next, consider income distribution. If Mexico could raise the poorest 20 percent of the population from its current share of about 3.6 percent of total income to the share enjoyed by the bottom quintile in Tunisia, for example (namely, 5.9

percent), the average income of the poor would rise 63.8 percent. This alone would suffice to eliminate poverty. Neither of these objectives is terribly ambitious; both are perfectly feasible. The obstacles to achievement are political, not economic.

We have emphasized Mexico's slow and unstable growth, the feebleness of its export-led strategy, the increased disarticulation of its economy, the state's withdrawal from responsibilities to promote investment and social equity, high and rising inequality, and the increase in severe poverty. These are economic manifestations of a society in distress, operating well below its potential. Of course, there are many other symptoms of disarray, including deeply imbedded corruption that extends from the police to the highest levels of government, massive illegal drug trafficking, widespread crime and general lawlessness, rural unrest and even rebellion in Chiapas, disrespect for human rights, and weakness of democratic institutions.

Not all of these problems can be blamed on the new development strategy; some antedate it, and others are only loosely connected to it. However, the new economic policies have made many problems worse, and they have failed to deliver on their promises. The fundamental error, we believe, was an error of omission rather than of commission. That is, it surely was correct to liberalize many markets and place greater reliance on the price mechanism in allocating resources. Similarly, it was sensible to reduce the degree of autarky and take advantage of opportunities arising from closer integration into the world economy. These things were necessary, but they were not sufficient, and the government's minimalist approach resulted in a development strategy that was full of holes.

If liberalization and openness are to succeed in Mexico, they will have to be complemented by the following:

- credible interest-rate and exchange-rate policies that reduce the economy's vulnerability to macroeconomic disturbances;
- a structure of incentives for both the private and public sectors that encourages a high level of savings and an efficient allocation of investment among physical, human, and natural capital;
- a more prudent approach to foreign borrowing;
- better arrangements for supervising and regulating the banking system;
- mechanisms for controlling large movements of short-term capital;
- a stronger and more competent state committed to remedying the disarticulation of the economy; and
- redistributive policies that seriously address problems of poverty and inequality.

This list is neither exhaustive nor sufficiently detailed to provide practical help to policy makers, but it does indicate which areas of economic policy merit priority attention. A minimalist approach of market liberalism and an open economy is never likely to produce satisfactory results. Mexico's own experience and that of many other countries provide abundant evidence of this. If Mexico is to confront human development, it must have an activist but focused state.

REFERENCES

Alarcón, Diana, and Terry McKinley. 1999. "The Adverse Effects of Structural Adjustment on Working Women in Mexico," *Latin American Perspectives* 26 (3): 103–17.

Alarcón, Diana, and Eduardo Zepeda. 1998. "Employment Trends in the Mexican Manufacturing Sector," *North American Journal of Economics and Finance* 9: 125–45.

Birdsall, Nancy, David Ross, and Richard Sabot. 1995. "Inequality and Growth Reconsidered: Lessons for East Asia," *World Bank Economic Review* 9 (3): 477–508.

Grabel, Ilene. 1995. "Speculation-led Economic Development: A Post-Keynesian Interpretation of Financial Liberalization Programmes in the Third World," *International Review of Applied Economics* 9 (2): 127–49.

Griffin, Keith. 1999a. *Alternative Strategies for Economic Development.* 2d ed. New York: St. Martin's.

———. 1999b. "Rural Poverty in Latin America." INDES Working Papers. Washington, D.C.: Inter-American Development Bank, April.

Griffin, Keith, and Amy Ickowitz. 2000. "The Distribution of Wealth and the Pace of Development." In *Studies in Development Strategy and Systemic Transformation,* edited by Keith Griffin. New York: St. Martin's.

Jazairy, Idriss, Mohiuddin Alamgir, and Theresa Panuccio. 1992. *The State of World Rural Poverty: An Inquiry into Its Causes and Consequences.* New York: New York University Press, for the International Fund for Agricultural Development.

Kelly, Thomas. 1999. *The Effects of Economic Adjustment on Poverty in Mexico.* Aldershot: Ashgate.

Lustig, Nora. 1998. *Mexico: The Remaking of an Economy.* Washington, D.C.: Brookings Institution Press.

McKinley, Terry, and Diana Alarcón. 1995. "The Prevalence of Rural Poverty in Mexico," *World Development* 23 (9): 1575-85.

Myhre, David. 1998. "The Achilles' Heel of the Reforms: The Rural Finance System." In *The Transformation of Rural Mexico,* edited by Wayne A. Cornelius and David Myhre. La Jolla: Center for U.S.-Mexican Studies, University of California, San Diego.

Myrdal, Gunnar. 1968. *Asian Drama: An Inquiry into the Poverty of Nations.* New York: Pantheon.

Psacharopoulos, George. 1994. "Returns to Investment in Education: A Global Update," *World Development* 22 (9): 1325–43.

Ramírez de la O, Rogelio. 1996. "The Mexico Peso Crisis and Recession of 1994–95: Preventable Then, Avoidable in the Future?" In *The Mexican Peso Crisis,* edited by Riordan Roett. Boulder, Colo.: Lynne Rienner.

Summa, John. 1994. "Mexico's New Super-Billionaires," *Multinational Monitor* 15 (10).

Trigueros, Ignacio. 1999. "Mexico's Recent Economic Performance and Policy Challenges." Paper presented at the conference "Confronting Development: Assessing Mexico's Economic and Social Policy Challenges," Center for U.S.–Mexican Studies, University of California, San Diego, June 4–5.

UNDP (United Nations Development Programme). 1997. *The Shrinking State: Governance and Sustainable Human Development.* New York: Regional Bureau for Europe and the CIS, July.

———. 1998. *Human Development Report 1998.* New York: Oxford University Press.

———. 1999. *Human Development Report 1999.* New York: Oxford University Press.

Wilkie, James W., ed. 1997. *Statistical Abstract of Latin America,* vol. 27. Los Angeles: Latin American Center, University of California, Los Angeles.

World Bank. 1993. *World Development Report 1993.* New York: Oxford University Press.

———. 1999a. *World Development Indicators 1999.* Washington, D.C.: World Bank.

———. 1999b. *World Development Report 1998/99.* New York: Oxford University Press.

Zepeda, Eduardo, and David Castro, eds. 1999. *Reestructuración económica y empleo en México.* Mexico: Universidad Autónoma de Coahuila/Fundación Friedrich Ebert.

17

A Comparative Perspective on Mexico's Development Challenges

Clark W. Reynolds

Several essays in this volume present a major indictment of Mexico's "no growth" economy since 1981.[1] During the formative stages of post–World War II economic development, the country's decision makers used its raw material and primary product resources to build a diversified urban industrial economy that, subject to selective institutional and policy measures, prospered for a time. Mexico was part of an international system that, from Bretton Woods through the 1970s, experimented with audacious institutional innovations in an attempt to avoid the pitfalls of the interwar period. The problems experienced by Mexico and other developing countries at the beginning of the twenty-first century demand as experimental and daring a spirit as the measures

---

[1] The views of Víctor Urquidi, for example, take on particular importance given his role in helping shape Mexico's early economic development policies. His reflections cover the birth of the Bretton Woods institutions, in which he played an important role (Urquidi 1996). Urquidi speaks about the need for "learning by doing" in the formulation of Mexico's post–World War II monetary and financial policies and the need at the time to develop "as clear a vision for the future of *developing countries* as, for instance, John McCloy held of European reconstruction when he left the Bank [World Bank] to become U.S. High Commissioner for Germany."

In other writings, Urquidi correctly insists on the need for both domestic policy reform and a proper global institutional response to the challenge of interdependence between regions at different levels of development. The forced march of globalization has taken Mexico far beyond its post–World War II economic "miracle," and it has widened the gap between rich and poor. Urquidi notes that, although developing countries cannot stop globalization, neither are they fully benefiting from the process. In many countries, domestic markets are unable to reconcile the gains from trade expansion with domestic productivity growth and employment, while financial policies fail to bring interest rates below 20 percent per year and the public sector faces severe fiscal and monetary policy constraints (Urquidi 1999).

taken in the 1940s as the world emerged from a great depression and global war. However, the current pattern of globalization constitutes a very different international environment. Mexico now faces greater flexibility in trade and finance, more constraints on domestic policy (given the limitations imposed by openness and increased transparency in decision making), a burden of inherited debt, and the mixed blessing of abundant petroleum reserves. One can only hope that Mexico's pragmatic good sense will triumph over obstacles that include the lack of a clear alternative model of development, one in which market completion and social access are combined with the inexorable openness of the information age.

For many observers, the North American Free Trade Agreement (NAFTA) has been more successful at promoting trade among the three member countries than serving as an engine of growth for Mexico. The principal reason is that, despite Mexico's considerable trade gains under the NAFTA, over half the country's economy (both rural and urban) remains mired in stagnation. As a number of the chapters in this volume note, the problem is that the domestic economy has languished, unable to offset losses from the failure of old import-substituting industries (now stripped of their subsidies, favoritism, and protection) with gains from newly productive export activities. The surviving national firms that do prosper appear unable to serve a liberalizing market in terms of quality and price sufficient to raise output per capita and diffuse productivity and income gains throughout the country. Foreign investment is somewhat limited by prior indebtedness, exchange-rate uncertainty, and the Mexican government's retention of discretionary decision-making authority, while domestic investment is discouraged by a lack of adequate demand growth and the pervasive high cost (in real terms) of money—in an inadequately developed capital market that is overly dependent upon the international ebb and flow of funds. Uncertain peso investments must compete with the attractiveness of a "sure" return on domestic and foreign government debt and the perception of somewhat less risky overseas security markets. In the face of such daunting challenges, many analysts call for a new perspective on Mexico's development options.

AN ASIAN PERSPECTIVE ON MEXICO'S DEVELOPMENT PROBLEMS

The experiences of China and the newly industrializing countries of the Pacific Rim provide valuable comparative perspectives on Mexico's development challenges. Although very different in many of its characteristics, this is also a region that is attempting to deal with the exigencies of international opening and domestic unevenness. Asia's development record—beginning with post–World War II Japan, followed by South Korea, Taiwan, Thailand, and Singapore—suggests that openness to the "global" market works when a country has a special window for exports. China's current window is through Hong Kong to Taiwan, Japan, South Korea, its Southeast Asian partners, and the United States. It has even signed a treaty with the European Union, all of whose members supported its entry into the World Trade Organization (WTO). China's trading partners are likely to tolerate its slow, step-by-step liberalization of the capital account, as well as the very gradual reorganization and strengthening of a state-controlled banking and financial system that complements the country's de facto exchange controls and pegged currency. Yet despite the still-heavy hand of the state, the results of China's liberalization model are unbalanced.

Like Mexico, China has a very uneven pattern of economic development. But China is still growing rapidly, while Mexico has scarcely regained the gross domestic product per capita it achieved before the debt crisis of the early 1980s. In both cases, most of the gains from growth are concentrated in the about one-fifth of the population that has benefited from opening the economy to trade and investment and export-led industrialization and commercialization of agriculture. The difference is that one-fifth of China's population is over twice as large as Mexico's total population; it is a market large enough to promote economies of scale and to generate growth and capital accumulation even without the diffusion of development. Even so, Chinese decision makers have begun to recognize that a strategy of "grow now, distribute later" is inconsistent with the adequate expansion of productivity-based domestic markets, and as a consequence, they have already begun to modify key policies.

Until recently, the Chinese model emphasized selected export-led growth points. Established as "special export zones" in the 1980s, eastern entrepôts such as those in the Pearl River Delta around Hong Kong, Xiamen, Shanghai, and elsewhere received preference in trade liberalization. These areas all had traditional ties to foreign markets and access to finance and transportation on favorable terms. As a consequence, these areas have constituted China's most important success stories. But the remainder of China has followed slowly and haltingly, especially in the 1990s during a period when growth slowed (though it did not stop, despite the Asian financial crisis, nonperforming public investments in state-owned enterprises, and deflationary monetary policy). In particular, many parts of China have been hurt by policies that have encouraged the transfer of real resources to the urban East, leaving the lagging regions to suffer from drought, soil erosion, depletion of underground aquifers, and periodic flooding. The sustainability of

China's impressive economic growth is even threatened by the pollution of eastern cities, which are darkened by smog produced by burning fossil fuels and periodic sandstorms from a desertifying West.[2]

But Chinese decision makers are adopting a new approach to the development of the country's backward regions, and even the problems of agriculture are being given new consideration by administrators in Beijing. Pervasively high savings rates by the private sector and the absence of a vibrant banking and financial system willing and able to translate those savings into private investment have forced the government to consider a dual strategy: (1) continued trade opening in goods and services to the globalizing market economy (through WTO membership and bilateral trade agreements with the European Union, the United States, and other countries), and (2) state support for infrastructure, education, and investment in order to develop further the eastern and central urban areas as well as to rehabilitate rural areas and accelerate development in the lagging regions of western China.

Some aspects of the Chinese experience may be especially relevant to the definition of a new development model for Mexico. Like China, Mexico has pursued an economic opening and liberalization policy regime. Mexico's main export window is to the United States, as it seeks expanded markets in Europe, Asia, and the Americas. Yet the country has been unable to diffuse its growth experience widely enough. Even though some of Mexico's subregions (like Guadalajara, capital of the central-western state of Jalisco) have prospered, large parts of Jalisco and other states are being left behind, just as major areas of rural and western China are not being pulled forward by the engine of exports.

Both the Chinese and the Mexican economies might be considered (non-optimal) "currency areas" because they are regional economies linked ("integrated") by a single currency, the renminbi (RMB) and the peso. This makes their domestic trade subject to absolute rather than comparative advantage, given the fact that they engage in exchange through financial transactions rather than barter. As a consequence,

---

[2] For a fascinating account of the successful but uneven growth performance of China's many regions, see Wang and Hu 1999. This study was prepared by a top government research team and it was initially designed for incorporation into the country's 1996–2000 development plan. However, the policies it advocated were postponed until recently because of opposition from eastern export-led regions, which did not want to lose their privileges (and which provided the lion's share of public revenues).

For an assessment of the Chinese government's attempt to formulate a "western development program" and open up the financial system so as to reduce the drain on very high rates of private savings (used by the state-controlled banking system to support nonperforming loans to public enterprises), see Lardy 1998.

backward regions in these countries cannot gain from comparative advantage if their productivities are lower in traded activities because they are unable to devalue vis-à-vis the rest of the country.[3] Instead, both capital and labor migrate from the backward regions to those that lead the export-led growth process. In Mexico, migrant remittances (estimated to be as large as income from major exports) help spread the benefits of growth, but they are insufficient. As a result, Mexico needs conscious policies favoring diffusion, market completion, and social access to the gains from the engine of growth.

Since the 1980s, Mexico has in essence been flying on only one engine: exports. Its domestic market languishes, and small and midsize firms are caught between a tightly squeezed capital market (limiting the source of funds) and inadequate domestic demand (a consequence of unequal income distribution), as well as facing competition from the flood of imports released by trade liberalization. Lowering import barriers has helped control prices, but it has also reduced incentives for further investment in the domestic economy at a time when the national market is not broad enough (with the exception of emerging industries like telecommunications) to accommodate much widening of competition.

In contrast, China is flying on two engines: exports and that portion of society that participates in the modern economy. A numerically huge one-fifth of the population is driven by the new industrial stimuli provided by the opening to international trade and domestic liberalization. The lowering of import barriers has reduced the cost of inputs for those firms that process goods not only for export but also for the large (though still limited) domestic urban market, much of which is located in eastern cities. These companies are engaged in vicious competition with one another, keeping prices low and even causing price deflation as they expand. And China has many more engines that could potentially be started but which, because of uneven growth, are not working

---

[3] The idea of "optimal currency areas" was conceived by Robert Mundell and developed by Ronald McKinnon, among others. It has been applied to contiguous regions with a single currency (the United States, for example) and to integrating economies such as the European Union which, despite reservations, adopted a single currency. Where a single currency has been adopted, it is often argued that backward regions within the area should receive assistance to bring them up to productivity levels competitive with the rest of the currency area. In the European case, this was accomplished through regional development funds that targeted needy subregions (and even nations, such as Greece). In the United States, fiscal federalism–type transfers have provided support for backward regions even while support for direct regional development programs (such as the Tennessee Valley Authority and the Appalachia project) has declined.

at present. Although the economic costs and benefits of the Western Development Program remain to be analyzed in detail, this initiative seeks to start growth engines in backward regions by diffusing productivity gains, cost-benefit analysis, and the principles of financial soundness and sustainability.

Although the Mexican economy is in no danger of crashing, its one engine is not sufficient to lift the entire country onto a long-term trajectory of growth with development. The twenty percent of the Mexican population that comprises the modern market amounts to less than twenty million people, compared to an absolute number in China that is ten times larger. Even in Asia's smaller "emerging market" economies, countries such as Taiwan and South Korea have not neglected their own markets. As a result, they have experienced the diffusion of productivity gains among sectors, regions, and social groups that has permitted them to move up the value-added ladder. Indeed, they have quite openly protected their markets from undue foreign competition (though not at the ridiculously high rates of protection that in Latin America built pyramids of privilege for an already established elite).

The newly industrializing countries of Asia have also pursued financial policies that offer both savings potential and lending capability to emerging enterprises and households in rural as well as urban areas. These policies have certainly not been optimal, as the region's financial crisis in the late 1990s emphasized in revealing the extent of insider trading, cronyism, and unbalanced bank lending for powerful interest groups in countries such as South Korea, Indonesia, and Thailand. But the Asian record is more positive than negative in terms of the use of financial policy to mobilize and diffuse resources to increase both savings and investment.

In contrast, Mexico, after adopting admirable financial policies from the 1940s through the mid–1960s that induced rising rates of saving and investment from domestic sources, eventually fell prey to the lure of foreign loans. This turn came especially in the 1970s when increased liquidity from high international petroleum prices caused real interest rates to plummet. But since then, foreign loans have become both costly and sensitive to adverse exchange-rate expectations. One serious consequence is that domestic financial policy reforms have been left by the wayside.

THE ROLE OF THE STATE AND THE "GROWTH VERSUS DISTRIBUTION" DILEMMA

The role of the state in starting the "second, third, and fourth engines of growth" is heavily debated. Some analysts believe strongly in the government's need to address externalities and the social costs involved in generating increasing returns from market expansion and regional development, while others emphasize the clearly evident inducement such policies provide for rent-seeking, corruption, and inefficiency. In fact, a World Bank study conducted in the early 1990s found that state intervention was central to the success of virtually all the Asian "tigers."[4] Taiwan was a particularly important case in point.

In Mexico, the state initially made important contributions to rapid growth in gross domestic product per capita and the country's post–World War II economic success. Although Mexico eventually bogged down in a morass of rent-seeking and excessive protectionism, and although the domestic market failed to grow to a size capable of increasing productivity and the quality of production in many import-substituting industries, for several decades the "Mexican miracle" was there for all to see.[5] During those years, Mexico also gradually opened its financial market, freeing real interest rates while favoring with selective reserve requirements the private sector's use of funds for investment in growth-related activities. Through such policies (similar to those adopted in postwar Taiwan), the state and the private sector cooperated to promote the capture of voluntary savings and direct them to investments in both industry and export agriculture, rather than into the middle-class consumption loans and residential construction that banks tend to favor. As a result, economic growth continued.

The Mexican model ran out of steam by the mid–1970s, a victim of its own success in drawing voluntary savings into import-substituting industries through measures such as a fixed exchange rate (from 1954 to 1976) and foreign borrowing. The peso became seriously overvalued, and productivity growth was extensive rather than intensive. Were it not for the *deus ex machina* of new petroleum discoveries in the mid-1970s, the liberalization and economic openness model that prevails today would have been adopted even earlier than it was. Had this been the case, it is arguably possible that the model would have been more

---

[4] See World Bank 1993. The principal exception was Hong Kong, which had the particular advantage of being an entrepôt with the immense Chinese economy. Paul Krugman (1999) cites this study to underscore his argument that Asian countries tended to use extensive increases in savings and investment (rather than intensive improvements in the productivity of capital, or "capital deepening") to generate growth.

[5] See Reynolds 1970 for a discussion of how Mexico used its export potential—especially state support for land policies and infrastructure development that favored the development of commercial agriculture—to finance urbanization and the growth of industry.

reasonable in its content and less devastating in its impact on existing investment.

Instead, the crisis of the early 1980s induced a collapse of the entire production structure, not just of inefficient firms. Petroleum revenues not only delayed inevitable reforms, but they also made the policy shifts more extreme and uncertain than was desirable. And, of course, the peso crisis of 1982 also provided an excuse for the government to nationalize the banking system. The desire to cover a large and rising public deficit with "voluntary" savings led the government to draw on the resources of its nationalized banks, raiding the savings that had been painfully accumulated to fund the growing public deficit and thus crowding out private investors (especially small and midsize enterprises) from financial markets. Petroleum also permitted policy makers to saddle the country with debt by borrowing against future oil rents rather than dealing with domestic deficits at an earlier time (before 1982).

Petroleum thus proved to be a curse rather than a blessing. It allowed policy makers to postpone necessary reforms, and it created a false impression that Mexico was rich when it was not. Administrations that came to power after 1982 really did not have a chance. They could scarcely run fast enough to stay in place, much less move forward.

Mexico's policies of the 1980s and 1990s notwithstanding, that myth still holds. With it was implanted the policy of "growth first and distribution (even of productivity gains) later," a policy that is still in effect and that is supported by the macroeconomic straitjacket of globalization and capital mobility in the age of the Internet. Mexico's policies of the 1980s and 1990s, despite the best efforts of brilliant foreign-trained practitioners, lacked the imaginativeness and resourcefulness of the post–World War II years—when the country had charge of its own destiny. In that earlier period, the United States and foreign investors were not adverse to statist measures, and they went along with the Mexican model because it worked, bringing benefits to firms that operated behind protectionist barriers. There were real resources to be mobilized, resources that sustained a social development program driven by migration from less developed to more developed regions (in essence, an "extensive" development model involving "shifts" in productivity through labor movement rather than improvements in the productivity of capital itself).

Yet by the 1980s, the old Mexican model was dead, and there was nothing new to replace it except to open the economy, increase competitiveness, and force the "factor price equalization area" to extend south of the Mexico–U.S. border (whether or not North America is an optimal currency area). Robert Mundell's "optimal currency area" model became the tacit model of North American integrationists, going well beyond the facts of growing economic interdependence. Their view might be summarized as, "If you have major commercial and financial flows, and if labor is in fact moving across the border, then make the most of it."

The problem, however, is that growth in an interdependent system is uneven and asymmetrical. There is no place in the world—from Asia's newly industrializing countries, to the European Union, to the Americas—where this rule does not hold. Some areas and industries (and those employed in them, whether they are workers or managers) thrive as a result of liberalization processes, but others advance more slowly—and some go backward. The lagging regions take time to catch up, a process in which the state can play an important role.

Indeed, in the context of the United States' own economic development, the state has played just such a role. In the late 1950s, economists such as Paul Rosenstein-Rodan argued in favor of a "big push" to bring the South up to the development level of the North, and one consequence of such compensatory public policies was the emergence of the "new South." And well before that, government infrastructure projects (such as the Hoover Dam and the California Water Project) and combined public and private commitments to education in California and other western states promoted rapid growth along the country's western frontier. Similarly, the "new frontier" of technology is now taking that growth process beyond the closing of the physical frontier.

Two aspects of technology-driven growth in the United States are particularly relevant to this discussion of Mexico's development challenges. First, the new information technology itself began with state support for military and strategic purposes. Second, even in the contemporary United States, growth has not spread evenly across sectors, regions, or income groups. And the waiting period is a long one for those who are discouraged or prevented from migrating away from lagging regions and sectors. It is clear, then, that it will take Mexico a long time to catch up with the more developed United States, and much of Mexico is not yet even in the game.

The Asian model suggests that it is necessary for Mexican policy makers to jump-start growth and foster the formation of infrastructure, education, and capital necessary to serve not only foreign but also local markets. Hong Kong, for example, has its own burgeoning market, with its population spending its rising real income on locally provided services and low-cost imported goods. As its once vibrant industrial base has been increasingly priced out of competition by mainland industries, imports have swamped local manufacturers, which have either closed or shifted to regions with lower-cost labor such as China's

Pearl River Basin. Yet Hong Kong is marching up the value-added ladder as an entrepôt for the "new" China, and it has prospered in the process by intermediating in both commercial and financial markets. Similarly, Taiwan has advanced through the product cycle and added value to exports, thereby keeping its broadly educated and increasingly prosperous population both employed and in the development game. And despite political pressures from China, capital and trade between the island and the mainland are growing as never before.

Mexico, however, has benefited from trade-induced growth only in particular localities and for a small share of its total population. Its vast potential market languishes. Its labor force, which once migrated extensively among its own regions, now moves increasingly across the Mexico–U.S. border in response to a growing real wage and income gap with its northern neighbors. There is scope for major improvement, yet the legal and institutional basis for protection of investor rights and labor rights has yet to be confirmed. The incentives for productive investment and the opportunities for education and broad-based participation for individuals, regions, and embattled rural and urban productive activities are missing, notwithstanding the best efforts of simplistic liberalization. These are among the most pressing challenges facing Mexico at the dawn of a new century.

REFERENCES

Krugman, Paul. 1999. *The Return of Depression Economics*. New York: W.W. Norton.

Lardy, Nicholas R. 1998. *China's Unfinished Economic Revolution*. Washington, D.C.: Brookings Institution.

Reynolds, Clark W. 1970. *The Mexican Economy: Twentieth Century Structure and Growth*. New Haven, Conn: Yale University Press.

Urquidi, Víctor. 1996. "Reconstruction vs. Development: The IMF and the World Bank." In *The Bretton Woods–GATT System: Retrospect and Prospect after Fifty Years*, edited by Orin Kirshner. New York: M.E. Sharpe.

———. 1999. "La globalización de la economía: oportunidades e inconvenientes." Presented at the Fondo de Cultura Económica seminar on "La globalización y las opciones nacionales," July.

Wang Shoguang and Hu Angang. 1999. *The Political Economy of Uneven Development: The Case of China*. New York: M.E. Sharpe.

World Bank. 1993. *The East Asian Miracle: Economic Growth and Public Policy*. New York: Oxford University Press.

Index

Additional Benefits for Mortgage Holders Program, 114
Aegon, 328
Agricultural and livestock sector: credit crisis in, 31, 76n24, 361, 364-65, 588; and economic liberalization, 63n8, 65n9, 182, 351ff, 356, 377, 573; employment in, 28-29, 65n9, 357, 365-69 *passim*, 373, 376f, 579-80; exports by, 28, 181f, 356, 360, 455; importance of, 28, 35, 350, 373; imports by, 356-57; and migration, 369, 371, 377f; and the NAFTA, 27-28, 173, 181-82, 356-57, 571; segmentation in, 35, 182n30, 354, 360-61, 376-77, 580, 588; stagnation in, 27, 350-56 *passim*, 361, 365, 373, 454-55, 467-68, 580. *See also* Article 27 reforms
Anheuser-Busch Companies, 135n12
Apparel and textile industry, 227, 229, 233, 235; commodity chains in, 19, 222-28 *passim*, 234-35; employment in, 180, 191; exports by, 19, 147, 178, 180, 219, 225-26; investment in, 19, 179, 234; and the NAFTA, 19, 178n22, 179, 209, 219f, 224, 229, 233f; North American integration of, 179, 228, 235-36; restructuring and upgrading in, 19, 210-11, 220-24 *passim*, 228-29, 233-36 *passim*. *See also the names of individual apparel and textile firms*
Argentina, 131, 187, 281, 583; development experience in, 6, 134, 151, 203
Article 27 reforms, 12, 31, 322, 352, 587ff
Aspe Armella, Pedro, 119
Austria, 187
Automobile industry, 175, 177n20, 190-91, 212, 263, 266n24; employment in,

19n41, 175, 214, 262-63; exports by, 19n41, 20, 147, 151, 175f, 178, 205, 213ff, 263, 569; investment in, 18, 134, 141, 145, 147, 176-77, 568; and the NAFTA, 19f, 175f, 177n19, 178, 214-15; North American integration of, 175ff, 212; restructuring and upgrading in, 18, 175, 209, 211-15 *passim*, 219. *See also the names of individual automobile firms*

Baker, James A., III, 9n13
Baker plan, 9
Banamex, 80n34, 118, 119n27
Banca Serfin, 115-18 *passim*
Banco CREMI, 365
Banco de México: autonomy of, 9n14, 22; policies of, 61, 103, 109-12 *passim*, 189
Bancomer, 118
Banco Santander Central Hispano, 116, 328
Bancrecer, 115f, 116n23
Banking system: bailouts of, 29f, 42, 75-81, 97, 106, 111-17, 587; investment in, 76, 80n34, 151n29; legislation on, 99, 113, 115, 118; nationalization of, 14, 97n4, 99, 105f, 603; privatization of, 14-15, 15n31, 75-76, 92, 99, 108, 111n11, 116, 244, 568; regulation of, 99, 105-21 *passim*. *See also* Bank Savings Protection Fund; Bank Savings Protection Institute; *and the names of individual banks*
Bank of International Settlements, 119
Bank Savings Protection Fund (FOBAPROA), 76-81 *passim*, 111-21 *passim*
Bank Savings Protection Institute (IPAB), 30n63, 77-80 *passim*, 115-18 *passim*
Banorte, 116n23

Belgium, 187
BMW Group, 19n41, 176n18, 177, 214f
Bolivia, 24n52, 180, 183
Brady, Nicholas F., 9n13, 108
Brady plan, 9, 108
Brazil: development experience in, 6, 45n91, 134, 151, 203, 583; foreign investment in, 18, 133f, 199, 214nn. 3, 4; poverty in, 589, 591
Bretton Woods institutions, 596, 596n1
British American Tobacco, 135n12
Burlington Industries, 179n25, 209, 229

Cabal Peniche, Carlos, 365
Canada, 24, 24n51, 135; trade with Mexico, 28, 146, 172-73, 180; trade with the United States, 4, 180, 215, 220
Canada-U.S. Free Trade Agreement, 171
Capital formation: and economic growth, 45, 125-30, 137-43 *passim*, 155, 157, 467; public sector role in, 18, 26, 128, 130, 156, 581; rate of, 126-30 *passim*, 155-56; sectoral focus of, 18, 128ff, 138, 140-41, 144-45, 156; and uncertainty, 141-44. *See also* Foreign direct investment
Cárdenas, Cuauhtémoc, 12n23
Cardoso, Fernando Henrique, 196
Caribbean Basin Initiative, 224, 227, 233
Chile: development experience in, 45n91, 131, 134, 151, 281, 469, 478, 583; poverty in, 34f, 473-76 *passim*, 584, 589ff; social policy in, 39, 329, 473-80 *passim*; trade with Mexico, 24n52, 180, 183f
China, 179, 188; development experience in, 27n57, 597-601, 605; exports by, 147, 178, 220-24 *passim*, 233, 247
Chrysler Corporation, 177. *See also* DaimlerChrysler Corporation
Cigarrera La Moderna, 135n12
Cigarrera La Tabacalera Mexicana, 135n12
Citibank, 328
Citicorp, 80n34
Coca-Cola Company, 151
Colombia, 24n52, 180, 183f, 584, 589ff
Colosio, Luis Donaldo, 515
Commerce sector, 506-7
Commodity chains, 46-47, 197, 202-4, 266-67
Common Market of the South (MERCOSUR), 134

Compañía Industrial de Parras, 179, 179n26
Cone Mills Corporation, 179n25, 229
Confederation of Mexican Workers (CTM), 14, 14n29, 23
Constitution of 1917, 10
Consumption, 85-86, 400
Costa Rica: development experience in, 39, 45n91, 469, 473-79 *passim*; poverty in 34f, 469-73, 589ff; trade with Mexico, 24n52, 180, 183f
Cuba, 185
Cummins Engine Company, 177n18
Currency areas, 599, 600n3, 603-4
Currency devaluation, 14, 104, 108, 138, 561, 563, 566
——— in 1982, 56n1, 97n4
——— in 1994-1995, 4n2, 9, 59, 110f, 128f, 166, 189, 234, 237, 569, 578
Current account balance, 57, 72ff, 82, 166, 246, 568-69, 571-72

DaimlerChrysler Corporation, 18, 175n15, 176n18, 177, 212, 214f. *See also* Chrysler Corporation
Dana Corporation, 213
Dan River, Inc., 179n25
Davon Corporation, 235n10
Debt. *See under* Private-sector debt; Public-sector debt
Decentralization, 47, 63
De la Madrid Hurtado, Miguel, 8, 12, 23, 198, 351, 413n24
Del Monte Corporation, 365
Del Monte Fresh Fruit, 365n17
Delphi Corporation, 213
Democratization. *See under* Political democratization
Denmark, 187
Denso Corporation, 213
Dependency theory, 195-96
Devaluation. *See under* Currency devaluation
Development policy, 45-48, 567f, 572-75, 593-94; the private sector's role in, 573, 581; the state's role in, 320-21, 344, 388-89, 459, 580-81, 589, 593-94, 601-4 *passim*
Dina, 176n18
Domestic savings, 45, 75, 85-89 *passim*, 192, 332-33, 563, 601f
Dupont, 179n25

Economic Commission for Latin America and the Caribbean, 388

Economic crisis:
—— in 1982, 8, 578; as catalyst for economic liberalization, 3, 6, 40, 56, 577, 579; causes of, 56, 105, 242, 246, 447; general effects of, 4, 12n22, 22, 26, 29, 105, 155, 500, 504, 603; and poverty, 31, 435, 578, 584f
—— in 1994-1995: and the banking system, 30, 76, 111, 587; causes of, 82, 89, 166, 270, 569, 587; employment and income effects of, 237, 526, 530, 535n12, 536ff, 548-49, 578; general effects of, 59, 120, 163, 175, 215, 314, 323, 341, 538n17, 569, 579; and investment, 29, 133, 140; political impact of, 9, 13n26, 23; and poverty, 414, 584

Economic growth, 57, 447, 591f; constraints upon, 26f, 29f, 41, 82-83, 120-21, 128, 191-92, 563, 572-73, 578, 597, 600, 605; and investment, 126, 130, 140, 143, 155, 158, 332-33, 388n4, 572, 597, 600; and regional disparities, 21-22, 572, 582

Economic liberalization: and the agricultural and livestock sector, 351-53, 377; catalysts of, 8-9, 40, 577, 579; and economic and regional disparities, 22, 32, 156, 266-70, 495, 506, 518, 583, 585; and economic growth, 124-25, 156-57, 578; and employment and wages, 31n65, 536, 540, 543, 553; general effects of, 3-4, 16-28 *passim*, 56, 121, 156, 271, 582, 593; goals of, 4, 40, 55, 75-76, 123-24, 246, 437, 450-53 *passim*, 567, 577, 582, 586-87; and industrial policy, 244-48 *passim*; and investment, 3-4, 141, 143n21, 145, 155-57; limits to, 14-16, 244n5; and social policy, 320-23; political bases for, 10-14, 16, 124; political impact of, 13, 22-25 *passim*; policies of, 3f, 8f, 124, 156, 164-65, 167n4, 242-44, 278, 450, 567f, 580, 593; reasons for, 3, 40, 164, 242, 447; sustainability of, 24, 84, 241, 270; timing of, 7, 563, 602f

"Economic solidarity" pacts, 102, 128, 243n2; and control of inflation, 56n1, 59, 108, 164, 566, 586; and wages, 243f, 586

Economically active population, 31, 192, 523-24, 544, 555, 558

Ecuador, 185

Education: and Article 3 reforms, 277, 310-11, 322-23; and economic development, 36-37, 281-85, 574; equality in, 400-401; and income, 282, 546; level of, 36, 281, 399-400, 459; public spending on, 34n73, 417, 585-86; reform of, 43, 289, 574. *See also* Higher education; Primary education; Secondary education

Ejidos, 12, 587-88

Electronics industry, 18f, 141, 147, 180-81, 191, 569. *See also the names of individual electronics firms*

El Salvador, 24n52, 184

Employment, 30, 189n36, 192, 237, 252n19, 524; distribution of, 525-26, 529, 531, 533; in the manufacturing sector, 30-31, 252n19, 261ff, 270, 453-54, 535-37

Environmental policy, 574f

Eurodollar market, 101

European Free Trade Area, 186

European Union, 25n52, 135, 173, 185ff, 598f, 600n3, 604

Evans, Peter B., 196

Exchange rate, 83-84, 97n4, 146, 156f, 561, 568, 569n7; government policy on, 58-62 *passim*, 82-85 *passim*, 109f, 120, 124, 166, 244f, 562-71 *passim*, 578, 602

Exchange-Rate Risk Hedge Fund (FICORCA), 107

Export-processing zones, 225

Exports: composition of, 17, 137, 146, 149, 153, 155, 165n2, 199, 205, 227; and economic development, 21, 27, 46, 153, 157, 164, 190, 247, 270, 477, 554, 597, 600; and economic growth, 4, 106, 163, 166, 169, 189, 251, 579; firms engaged in, 17, 190, 199, 253; growth of, 4, 16-17, 129, 146, 167, 199, 251, 578; and investment, 18, 137, 140, 153, 155; and job creation, 21n46, 189, 261f, 269-70, 453f, 467, 481, 535-38 *passim*, 554, 571, 580; of manufactured goods, 4, 17, 19f, 165n2, 169, 205, 213, 261, 263, 563, 568, 571; value of, 17, 58n2, 169, 199, 571, 579; and wages, 189, 263

Federalism, 47

Federal-Mogul Corporation, 213

Federal Roads and Bridges (CAPUFE), 111n10

Federation of Mexican Private Institutions of Higher Education (FIMPES), 313
Financial crisis. *See under* Economic crisis; financial-economic cycles
Financial-economic cycles, 42, 90-91, 99, 101-11, 117
Financial-industrial conglomerates, 90-93, 104-12 *passim*, 117-18
Financial Strengthening Program (PFF), 84-85
Financial system. *See under* Banking system
Financial system regulation, 90, 93, 99, 107, 110
Finland, 187
Fiscal deficit, 62, 166, 242
Fiscal policy, 26, 58, 62
Fiscal reform, 43-44, 121
Flexible production, 266f
FOBAPROA. *See under* Bank Savings Protection Fund
Ford Motor Company, 18, 175n15, 176n18, 177, 212-15 *passim*, 219
Foreign direct investment, 135n10, 137, 512n19; flows of, 17-18, 83, 129-35 *passim*, 188, 199, 512n19, 563, 569; government policy on, 8, 46, 62, 92, 101, 118, 128, 131, 165n1, 198, 246, 563n2; sectoral focus of, 17ff, 133-37 *passim*, 141, 143, 151, 176-81 *passim*, 567, 572; sources of, 135, 137, 188
Foreign exchange reserves, 41, 82, 569, 578
Fox Quesada, Vicente, 25, 41-44, 47, 80
France, 187
Frank, André Gunder, 195
Free-trade agreements, 24n52, 170, 171n9, 183-87. *See also* North American Free Trade Agreement; Trade liberalization
Free Trade Area of the Americas, 185
Fruit of the Loom, Inc., 229
Fund for Educational Modernization (FOMES), 310

Gender inequalities, 582-83
General Agreement on Tariffs and Trade: and Mexico, 3, 8, 56n1, 65n9, 164, 170, 183, 198, 243n2, 351, 567; and Uruguay Round, 65n9, 170f, 182n29

General Coordination of the National Plan for Depressed Areas and Marginalized Groups (COPLAMAR), 438n41, 440
General Law on Education, 277, 310f
General Motors Corporation, 18, 175n15, 176n18, 177, 212, 214f
Germany, 176f, 187
Globalization, 195, 280, 285, 575; and financial markets, 87, 101, 119f, 597, 603; and trade and investment, 197, 202, 236, 266, 519, 596n1, 597
Gold standard, 101
Greece, 187, 600n3
Gross domestic product, 451n1; aggregate growth rate of, 6, 7n7, 25-26, 56-57, 82, 124ff, 139, 157, 163-67 *passim*, 198, 251, 281-82, 448, 450f, 489, 562f, 566, 568f, 591; per capita growth rate of, 6, 26, 57, 125f, 448, 451, 562, 566, 568f, 577, 582, 592; sectoral structure of, 6, 251, 373n25, 455, 563, 579; territorial distribution of, 489, 492-94, 506-7, 515
Grupo Coppel, 179
Grupo Industrial Zaga, 179n25
Guatemala, 24n52, 183
Guilford Mills, Inc., 179n25

Haiti, 185, 425
Health care, 34n73, 39, 43, 333-38, 345
Helms-Burton Law, 185
Hewlett-Packard Company, 191
Higher education, 306, 314-15; enrollments in, 300ff, 305; modalities of, 300-301, 305; problems affecting, 36, 281, 292, 302, 313, 323; public spending on, 279, 291-92, 310-11; reform of, 37, 306-16
Honda Motor Company, 19n41, 176n18, 177, 214f
Honduras, 25n52, 183
Hong Kong: development experience in, 196, 210-11, 598, 602n4, 604-5; exports by, 221, 224, 233
Human Poverty Index, 589-90, 592

Iceland, 25n52
Immediate Support Program for Debtors (ADE), 114f
Import licenses, 8

Import-substitution industrialization, 196, 203, 577; contributions of, 6, 20, 212, 448, 562; "exhaustion" of, 3, 56, 104f, 124, 138, 164, 242, 435; policies of, 6f, 13n27, 198, 245, 322, 540; problems with, 7, 137, 198, 245-46, 448-53 *passim*, 522, 582, 602; the state's role in, 10n19, 123, 245, 459; and transnational firms, 203, 212, 245

Import tariffs: increases in, 167, 168n5, 351; level of, 8, 164-65, 170, 180, 246, 579

India, 247

Indonesia, 582, 589, 591, 601

Industrial clusters, 249

Industrial policy, 27, 45-46, 47n99, 157n34, 244-50, 271, 573

Industrial upgrading, 17, 197, 204, 209, 211

Industrialized Milk CONASUPO (LICONSA), 388n5

Inequality: degree of, 31-32, 563, 582, 592-93; and economic liberalization, 32, 582, 585ff; measures of, 393, 403, 582-83; trends in, 31-32, 34n72, 400-404, 455-56, 572, 575, 582

Inflation: control of, 14, 26, 56n1, 58f, 61n5, 62, 83, 164, 243-44, 467, 567f, 586, 600; rate of, 82, 165, 242, 562, 569; trends in, 168, 189, 563, 566

Informal sector, 453, 524, 554, 567; employment growth in, 170, 454, 481, 522, 524, 529, 531, 580

Institutional Revolutionary Party (PRI), 11, 11n20, 14, 42, 198, 515; declining support for, 12, 13n26, 23f, 41, 339

Instituto Tecnológico de Estudios Superiores de Monterrey, 315

Integral Program for the Development of Higher Education, 307

Integrated poverty measurement method, 418, 441-43

Intel Corporation, 204

Inter-American Development Bank, 84, 112n13

Interest rates: and control of inflation, 26, 58, 62, 567; domestic, 58f, 69, 73-74, 83n36, 166, 168, 189, 567; and economic growth, 4, 58, 157, 567, 587; and foreign investment, 26, 45, 83-84, 109, 567; international, 450, 596n1

International Business Machines Corporation (IBM), 181, 191, 267

International Conference on Financing for Development, 40-41

International financial shocks, 4, 29, 84, 270, 573, 578, 587

International Food Policy Research Institute, 466

International Monetary Fund, 40, 101f, 119f; and economic and social reform in Mexico, 3, 9, 196, 322; and financial stabilization in Mexico, 84, 164, 323, 561, 569

Investment. *See under* Foreign direct investment; Portfolio investment

Investment agreements, 187

Investment units, 77n27, 114

Investment Fund for Agriculture (FIRA), 364-65

Israel, 25n52, 187

Italy, 187

J.C. Penney Company, Inc., 202

Jamaica, 235n10

Japan, 135, 187, 425; development experience in, 196, 221, 233, 598; trade with Mexico, 173, 177; trade with the United States, 172, 180, 211

Johnson Controls, Inc., 213

Kahn-Keynes multiplier, 61n5

Kenworth Truck Company, 176n18

Knowledge society, 279-80

Labor force participation, 30n64, 523-24

Latin American Integration Association (ALADI), 131n8, 133, 183

Lawson, Nigel, 70n15

Lázaro Cárdenas Federal Preparatory School, 286

Lean production, 267

Lear Corporation, 213

Levi Strauss & Co., 209, 229

Liechtenstein, 25n52

Limited Brands, Inc., 202

Liquidation Fund for Credit Institutions and Supplementary Credit Organizations (FIDELIQ), 111n10

Liz Claiborne, Inc., 202

López Portillo, José, 438n41

Lucent Technologies, 191

Luxembourg, 187

McKinnon, Ronald, 600n3

Malaysia, 581ff, 589

Manufacturing sector: characteristics of, 252f, 261-66 *passim*, 488, 506-7, 515, 539, 551, 563; employment in, 170, 252n19, 253, 261f, 453-54, 529, 535-43 *passim*; exports by, 137, 146, 165n2, 169, 205, 261, 263; growth of, 137ff, 145-46, 247, 261f, 448; investment in, 134-45 *passim*, 156; wages in, 263, 455, 544-45, 549

Maquiladora industry: characteristics of, 190, 200-201, 225n8, 535n13, 539; and economic development, 21n45, 153, 190f, 201, 453-54, 537, 539, 563, 568; employment in, 20, 180f, 190f, 199, 201, 225n8, 261, 453-54, 467, 535-38 *passim*, 542-43; exports by, 20f, 146, 153, 190, 199, 214, 225n8, 253, 571; growth of, 20, 129, 135n11, 191n38, 500, 538f, 551, 567, 571; investment in, 18, 21, 135, 201; wages in, 189-90, 201

Masa, 176n18

Mercedes-Benz AG, 177, 214f

MERCOSUR. *See under* Common Market of the South

Metropolitan Autonomous University (UAM), 302n15

"Mexdollar" accounts, 97n4, 106

Mexican Food System (SAM), 438n41

Mexican Petroleum Company (PEMEX), 128-29, 168n5, 268

Mexican Revolution, 10, 13

Mexican Social Security Institute (IMSS), 37, 38n80, 323f, 438n41; coverage of, 33n70, 324ff, 415; funding shortfall for, 325-26, 334ff

Mexico-European Union Free Trade Agreement, 185-86

Microsoft Corporation, 204

Migration, 35n75, 369, 377, 603, 605; remittances from, 28n59, 369, 371, 378, 572, 600

Ministry of Agriculture and Livestock (SAG), 351

Ministry of Commerce and Industrial Development (SECOFI), 249f

Ministry of Finance and Public Credit (SHCP), 110, 112, 115n20

Ministry of Human Settlements and Public Works (SAHOP), 515

Ministry of Programming and Budget (SPP), 308

Ministry of Public Education (SEP), 285-86, 307-15 *passim*

Ministry of Social Development (SEDESOL), 341n16, 515f

Ministry of Urban Development and Ecology (SEDUE), 512-15 *passim*

Modernization theory, 195

Monetary base, 58, 62n6

Monetary policy, 26, 58f, 81, 109, 120, 189, 243

Moral hazard, 90, 93, 97, 114, 120

Mortality rates, 387, 426-29, 432-34, 435-39 *passim*

Multi-Fiber Arrangement, 221, 233

Mundell, Robert, 600n3, 603

Myrdal, Gunnar, 524

NAFTA. *See under* North American Free Trade Agreement

National Action Party (PAN), 12, 14, 41f

National Association of Universities and Institutions of Higher Education (ANUIES), 287, 307-13 *passim*

National Autonomous University of Mexico (UNAM), 287, 302n15

National Basic Foods Company (CONASUPO), 438n41

National Center for the Evaluation of Higher Education (CENEVAL), 309

National College of Professional-Technical Education (CONALEP), 286, 297n10

National Commission for Higher Educational Planning (CONPES), 308f

National Commission for Higher Middle Education (CONAEMS), 288n5

National Commission for Planning and Programming of Higher Middle Education (CONPPEMS), 288

National Commission on Retirement Savings (CONSAR), 328

National Committee for Productivity and Technological Innovation (COMPITE), 250

National Council of Science and Technology (CONACYT), 308

National Credit Bank (NAFIN), 108, 249f

National Development Plan, 307, 513

National Foreign Investment Commission (CNIE), 165n1

National Foreign Investment Registry, 135n10

National Foreign Trade Bank (BAN-COMEXT), 115n20, 249

National High-Technology Maize Program, 357n9

National Institute of Anthropology and History (INAH), 301

National Institute of Fine Arts (INBA), 286, 301

National Polytechnic Institute (IPN), 287, 301n13

National Preparatory School, 287

National Program for the Economic Modernization of the Countryside, 352

National Rural Credit Bank (BANRURAL), 364, 587

National Solidarity Program (PRONASOL), 35, 308, 322, 339, 459-60, 513-14; funding for, 339, 460-61; impact of, 339, 461-64, 468; politicization of, 13n26, 339, 341, 463; targeting in, 461, 463. *See also* Poverty alleviation policies

National System of Researchers (SNI), 309

National Union of Workers (UNT), 23

National Urban Development Program (PNDU), 513ff

Navistar, 176n18

Nestlé, 151

Netherlands. *See under* The Netherlands

Nicaragua, 25n52, 183f

Nike, Inc., 202

Nissan Motor Company, 176n18, 191, 214f

Normative basket of essential satisfiers, 439-41

North American economic integration, 18, 183, 200, 495, 604; political implications of, 24n51, 25; and regional disparities, 21f, 518

North American Free Trade Agreement, 125, 172f, 573; implementation of, 20n44, 25, 27, 147, 172n11, 175n14, 182, 200, 571; Mexico's accession to, 3, 171, 199, 352, 568; and Mexico's domestic policies, 14f, 19-20, 46, 65n9, 247, 356-57; and rules of origin, 177n19, 178, 200, 214; trade expansion under, 147, 172, 200, 237, 247, 597

Norway, 25n52

Omnibuses Integrales, 177n18

100 Cities Program, 513-16 *passim*

Open-economy model, 59, 84

Organisation for Economic Co-operation and Development, 24, 242, 313, 592

Organization of Petroleum Exporting Countries, 577

Organized labor, 13-16 *passim*, 23-24, 244, 586

Original brand-name manufacturing, 204, 210f, 222, 233f

Original design manufacturing, 204

Original equipment manufacturing, 204, 210-11, 222, 233-34

Ortiz, Guillermo, 114n16

Oshmex, 177n18

Panama, 185

Party of the Mexican Revolution (PRM), 11n20

PEMEX. *See under* Mexican Petroleum Company

Pension reform, 38, 327-33, 345

PepsiCo, 151

Perkins Engines Company, 177n18

Peru, 185, 584

Petroleum, 74n21, 168, 571, 597; and economic growth, 7, 450, 562f; international price of, 7, 9, 67, 104, 124, 164, 168, 242, 450, 563, 566, 571, 577f, 601; revenues from, 67, 74n21, 90, 104, 168, 205, 450, 566, 571

Philip Morris, 135n12

Philippines, 589f

Political democratization, 23-24, 41-44 *passim*, 573-74

Political technocrats, 11, 23

Population growth, 30, 326, 376, 523, 563, 572, 584

Portfolio investment, 59, 62, 83, 109, 133, 165n1

Portfolio Purchase Program, 113

Portugal, 187

Poverty: causes of, 59, 389, 459, 481, 583, 585; incidence of, 386, 418-24, 456-57, 572, 583ff, 591; intensity of, 419-20; measures of, 386, 405nn18,19, 418, 420-21, 439-43, 457, 458n6, 475, 583, 589-90; and mortality rates, 425-35 *passim*; and public policies, 34, 36, 39; in rural areas, 35, 43, 373, 450, 458-59, 572n10,

582-85 *passim*; trends in, 32-33, 404-7, 411, 413-15, 438; in urban areas, 458-59, 572n10, 584f

Poverty alleviation policies, 336, 337, 341, 343-44, 378; efficacy of, 35-36, 343, 575; and macroeconomic policy, 34-35, 345, 468-69, 476-82 *passim*; public spending on, 341n16, 343, 585; rationale for, 338, 388-89, 459; targeting in, 35-36, 338, 343, 388, 480ff. *See also* National Solidarity Program; Program for Education, Health, and Nutrition

Preventive Support Fund for Multiple Banking Institutions, 112n14

Primary education, 36, 281, 291-92

Private-sector debt, 68-71 *passim*

Privatization. *See under* State-owned firms, privatization of

Productivity growth, 17, 263, 579

Program for Education, Health, and Nutrition (PROGRESA), 35, 341-44, 464ff. *See also* Poverty alleviation policies

Program for Industrial and Foreign Trade Policy (PROPICE), 247

Program for Subcontractor Development, 250

Program for the Improvement of Academic Personnel (SUPERA), 310

Program for the Improvement of the Professoriate (PROMEP), 314

Program of Educational Development (PDE), 312, 314

Program of Educational Modernization (PME), 277-78, 288, 307, 310

Program of Incentives for Performance of Career Teaching Personnel, 314

Program of Temporary Imports to Produce Export Goods (PITEX), 249

Program to Promote Industrial Clusters, 249

PROGRESA. *See under* Program for Education, Health, and Nutrition

PRONASOL. *See under* National Solidarity Program

Property Registry Modernization Program, 516

Public investment. *See under* Capital formation

Public-private partnerships, 46, 47n99, 602

Public-sector debt:

—— domestic: amount of, 62n6, 74-75; and bank bailouts, 75, 79, 97, 99, 107, 115n20, 120; burden of, 30, 63, 65, 74f, 80-81, 108, 121

—— foreign: amount and maturity structure of, 66-74 *passim*, 104, 566; burden of, 63-74 *passim*, 106, 198, 437, 566, 572; rescheduling of, 30, 67, 69, 106, 567

Puebla-Panama Project, 43

Reagan, Ronald, 171n9

Reebok International, Ltd., 202

Regional Centers for Business Competitiveness (CRECE), 250

Regional development policies, 43, 599, 604

Regional disparities, 47, 267-69, 487-94 *passim*, 517-18

Renault, 177n18

Research and development spending, 284

Retirement Fund Administrator (AFORE), 38, 327-31 *passim*

Retirement Savings System (SAR), 323

Revolutionary National Party (PNR), 11

Robert Bosch Corporation, 213

Rosenstein-Rodan, Paul, 604

Royal University of Mexico, 287

Russia, 102, 168. *See also* Soviet Union

Salinas de Gortari, Carlos, 11, 12n23; and economic liberalization, 8, 11-16 *passim*, 23, 198-99, 243, 246, 278, 352, 512; and educational reform, 277f, 290, 307-11; policies of, 15, 16n32, 23, 25, 67, 352, 512ff, 568; and PRONASOL, 13n26, 35, 339, 341, 460, 513

Samsung Electronics Company, 181

San Ildefonso College, 287

Sara Lee Corporation, 209, 229

Scania, 176n18

Sears, Roebuck and Co., 202

Secondary education, 36, 281, 285-89 *passim*, 295, 298; enrollments in, 290-95 *passim*; goals of, 43, 289, 296, 298f; modalities of, 286f, 289-90, 295; problems affecting, 37, 281, 290ff, 296-97; public spending on, 279, 291-92; reform of, 290, 297n10, 298ff, 316

Serra Puche, Jaime José, 387n3

Services sector, 506-7, 544, 549

Singapore, 180, 187; development expe-

rience in, 196, 210-11, 581, 583, 598
Social progress index, 391, 399n14
Social reform of the state, 320-23
Social Security Health Fund, 335
Social Security Institute for State Workers (ISSSTE), 37, 38n80, 323-26 *passim*
Social Security Law, 323-30 *passim*
Social welfare: measures of, 391-99 *passim*; opportunities for, 391-92, 435, 437-38; and public spending, 34, 386f, 413-17 *passim*, 435, 437-38, 478, 572, 581-82, 585; sources of, 387-92 *passim*; trends in, 399-402
Social welfare system: coverage of 38, 324ff; principles of, 320-27 *passim*, 337-38, 345; public spending on, 37-38, 62-63, 325, 341, 344n19, 345f, 585-86
Sony Corporation, 181
South Korea, 137, 180, 187, 583; development experience in, 196, 210-11, 578, 581f, 585-86, 588, 598, 601; exports by, 221, 224, 233
Soviet Union, 186. *See also* Russia
Spain, 45, 187
Specialized Investment Retirement Fund (SIEFORE), 327-28, 331
Sri Lanka, 221 589ff
"Stabilizing development" period, 198, 562, 573
State Commission for Planning and Programming of Higher Middle Education (CEPPEMS), 288-89
State-owned firms, 93, 104-5, 581n3; privatization of, 3f, 8, 14, 15n30, 92n3, 124, 128-29, 145n23, 198, 244, 246, 352, 568, 580f, 586
Stock market, 44, 107ff, 111n10
Stock Market Rescue Program, 111n10
Structural adjustment policies, 3, 8, 23
Structural-change index, 145
Sweden, 187
Switzerland, 25n52, 187

Taiwan: development experience in, 196, 210-11, 588, 598, 601f, 605; exports by, 180, 221, 233
Tarrant Apparel Group, 179n25
Tax reform, 44-45, 121, 581
Tax revenues, 45, 62, 65, 67, 563, 566, 581
Technocrats. *See under* Political technocrats
Technological specialization index, 151

Teléfonos de México (TELMEX), 8n11, 151n29
Temporary Capitalization Program (PROCAPTE), 112
Tesobonos, 102, 106n6, 118, 119n27; and public-sector foreign debt, 69, 74n22, 110, 119, 189, 569
Textile industry. *See under* Apparel and textile industry
Thailand, 133, 168, 578, 598, 601
The Netherlands, 187
Torricelli Act, 185
Tourism, 572
Toyota Motor Corporation, 212
Trade balance, 59, 72-73, 82, 357, 571; persistent deficit in, 29, 246, 261-62, 266, 270
Trade liberalization, 8, 124, 164-71 *passim*, 188-89. *See also* Free-trade agreements; North American Free Trade Agreement
Transnational firms, 196f, 213
Tunisia, 592

Unemployment, 189n36, 341, 524, 555
United Kingdom, 187
United Nations Development Programme, 582
United Nations Industrial Development Organization, 145
United States, 45, 135, 220, 237; trade with Canada, 4, 205, 215, 225n7, 237; trade with Mexico, 4, 28, 73n21, 146, 172, 178-82 *passim*, 191, 205, 215, 224, 237. *See also individual U.S. government agencies*
Universal Scientific Industrial Company, 181
Universidad Iberoamericana, 314-15
Universidad La Salle, 315
Urban disparities, 494f, 500f, 505ff, 512, 518
Urbanization, 487, 500, 505, 514-19 *passim*, 563
Uruguay 184n31, 187
U.S. Department of the Treasury, 119, 569
U.S. EXIMBANK, 85
U.S. Federal Reserve System, 99, 101n5, 106n6, 119, 166
U.S. Reciprocal Trade Agreement Program, 171n9

Value-added tax, 44, 67
Venezuela, 25n52, 131, 134, 180-84 *passim*, 584, 589, 591
Vocational education, 574
Volkswagen, 16n32, 18, 176n18, 177, 178n21, 214f, 219
Volvo Group, 176n18

Wages: determinants of, 37, 282, 546-49
passim, 553; and exports, 4, 15, 263; and fringe benefits, 31, 530; government policy on, 14f, 33f, 56, 59, 435, 437, 467, 547, 572, 586; level of, 15, 26, 166, 189-90, 263, 325n2, 586; trends in, 33, 263, 437, 455, 529f, 544-49 *passim*, 553, 583
Wal-Mart Stores, Inc., 202
Warnaco Group, Inc., 229
Washington Consensus, 3, 41, 387
World Bank, 40, 84, 102, 112n13; and economic and social reform in Mexico,
3, 9, 196, 322f, 387
World Trade Organization, 598f; and Mexico, 24, 40, 46, 170, 182n29, 183

Xerox Corporation, 191

Yang Tse River United Development Corporation, 179

Zapatista Army of National Liberation (EZLN), 10n18, 568n6
Zedillo Ponce de León, Ernesto: and economic liberalization, 124, 167, 243, 278; and educational reform, 277f, 290, 306, 312-15; and post-1995 bank bailout, 42, 75, 117; policies of, 25, 39, 157n34, 513, 516; and PROGRESA, 35, 341, 464
Zurich Insurance, 328